Italy and its Monarchy

Italy and its Monarchy

DENIS MACK SMITH

Yale University Press
New Haven and London

Set in Linotron Bembo by Best-set Typesetter Ltd, Hong Kong
Printed and bound in Great Britain at The Bath Press, Avon

Library of Congress Catalog Number: 89-51311
ISBN 0 300 04661 8

Contents

Illustrations

All photos, except for those otherwise credited, are courtesy of RCS Rizzoli Libri, Milan.

Introduction

Italy became a united kingdom in 1861. Four kings succeeded each other in the next eighty-five years until a republican regime was chosen in 1946 by popular referendum. Each of these royal heads of state exercised considerable influence on the course of Italian history. But usually the extent of that influence is not easily calculated because the documentation is slanted or otherwise inadequate. Documents were sometimes withdrawn from the archives or destroyed to conceal views expressed and actions taken by successive sovereigns. There exists nothing comparable to Queen Victoria's diary, nor to her political correspondence with ministers, nor anything as illuminating as the marginal notes made on state papers by Kaiser Wilhelm of Germany, and certainly nothing at all like the presidential archives in the United States. What makes this deficiency more serious is that some important Italian politicians had their diaries and letters tactfully pruned before publication, because they or their heirs could risk criminal prosecution if they blamed a king or held him responsible for acts of government. For the same reason, and because they were employed by the state, historians had to be reticent and sometimes submitted to an imposed or self-imposed censorship.

More importantly, the private archives of the royal family were taken away by the last two kings when they went into exile. A few people were privileged to see some of these papers and reported that one day they would clarify some central questions of national history, but how much remains in existence is a matter for speculation. None of the four monarchs liked writing letters. They were not easy in conversation, and court protocol prescribed that no topic of discussion could be initiated except by themselves. Any correspondence from them was usually returned to them on the death of its recipient and so disappeared, or else royal officials might intervene to confiscate whatever they wished from private and public collections. Moreover, cabinet ministers habitually and illegally carried off official papers when they left office, so that other important documents never reached the national record office.

The last two kings, more literate than their predecessors, said that they intended to use the material in their possession for writing their own version of events, and more than one person at court claimed to have been allowed to read memoirs that were said to be voluminous, illuminating, and polemical. But what these were or what they said remains a mystery, and their existence has sometimes been officially denied. Whether by destruction, casual loss, or deliberate concealment, it can be assumed that many relevant documents may never enter the public domain, and at the very least we must wait for more information from the executors of the last king who died in 1983.

This lack of documentation has discouraged scholarly attempts to study the institution of monarchy as an active force in Italian political history; and admittedly much of that influence must remain hypothetical for the even more important reason that it was often exercised in unrecorded conversations or through back-stairs pressure. This proviso has to be kept in mind when treating such a controversial subject. Inevitably judgements must sometimes depend on probability and inference rather than on irrefutable knowledge. But the monarchy had a central role in the story of how Italy developed into a modern nation state. Even when the evidence is partial or lacks corroboration, even if successive sovereigns were often economical with the truth or tried to cover their tracks, this is a topic that cannot be ignored by anyone interested in the history of liberal and fascist Italy.

The four kings differed in personality and made their own different contribution to national history. None of them had exceptional personal qualities that in other careers might have raised them above the ordinary; nor were their private lives particularly interesting or noteworthy; and yet all of them confronted political problems that would have severely tested people of greater intelligence and force of character. When trying to appreciate their achievement in resolving these problems, allowance must be made for partisan and often prejudiced criticism by republicans and clericals in opposition; also for an excessive adulation by loyal monarchist historians. These extreme attitudes of praise and criticism must be assessed in the light of what evidence is available in print or can be pieced together from the archives. Particularly useful are the comments of foreign ambassadors who, although sometimes misinformed, were relatively impartial as well as trained to report accurately, and with whom a sovereign could talk on something like level terms.

One prior assumption is that heads of state in Italy were involved actively or passively in almost all the major policy decisions taken by governments. Of course they cannot always bear responsibility when events turned out badly, any more than when things went right. Occasionally they were irritated by what was done in their name. Often, especially in domestic policy, they were almost indifferent and expressed no views at all. Nevertheless, although they frequently talked of abdicating if ministers acted against their wishes, none did in fact abdicate until 1946. Their approval for the most part, whether active or qualified and unenthusiastic, can therefore be taken as a fact of history. Equally interesting is that they sometimes overrode ministers and parliaments by imposing a decision of their own.

Vittorio Emanuele III, who reigned for more than half of these eighty-five years, took a number of personal decisions that affected all his subjects; despite which he remains a somewhat shadowy and inscrutable figure in retrospect. This same king was fascinated by history and especially by events in which his family took part. In January 1934 he told one of his aides that historians had an absolute duty to be frank in their judgement, without fear or favour, so as to help his people to understand their own past. Of course, he was well aware that the truths about national history are very much more than those that involve its head of state.

> How small, of all that human hearts endure,
> That part which laws or kings can cause or cure.

Only a small part it may be, but decisions of peace and war can change the lives of everyone, and some enigmas of Italian history can be explained only by an investigation of events at the summit.

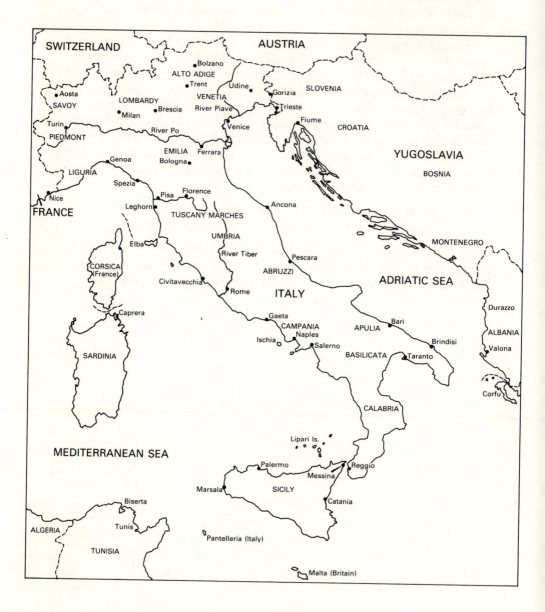

SWITZERLAND

AUSTRIA

Bolzano

ALTO ADIGE
Trent

Udine

Gorizia
SLOVENIA

Aosta

SAVOY

LOMBARDY
Brescia

Milan

VENETIA
River Piave

Trieste

Turin

PIEDMONT

River Po

Venice

Fiume

CROATIA

YUGOSLAVIA

Genoa

LIGURIA

EMILIA
Bologna

Ferrara

BOSNIA

Spezia

Pisa
Florence

Nice

FRANCE

Leghorn

TUSCANY MARCHES

Ancona

Elba

CORSICA
(France)

UMBRIA

River Tiber

MONTENEGRO

Pescara

ABRUZZI

Civitavecchia

Rome

ITALY

ADRIATIC SEA

Caprera

Gaeta

CAMPANIA

Durazzo

Bari

SARDINIA

Ischia

Naples

Salerno

APULIA

ALBANIA

Valona

BASILICATA

Brindisi

Taranto

Corfu

CALABRIA

MEDITERRANEAN SEA

Lipari Is.

Palermo

Reggio

Marsala

Messina

SICILY

Catania

Biserta

ALGERIA

Tunis

Pantelleria (Italy)

TUNISIA

Malta (Britain)

1
Vittorio Emanuele II

1   The king and the constitution, 1861

In March 1861 Vittorio Emanuele II, at the age of 41, was proclaimed the first sovereign of a united Italy. He had been a king since 1849, but only of a small region comprising Piedmont, Savoy, and Sardinia. His new kingdom in 1861 included most of the Italian peninsula, though lacking Rome, Venice, Trieste, and the area round Trent south of the Alps. He had successfully deposed and replaced his relatives who ruled in Tuscany, Naples, and Sicily. He had conquered much of central Italy from the pope. By ceding Savoy to the French he had won their support in taking Lombardy from the Habsburg empire. Plebiscites had then been held in the various regions to justify their annexation and the creation of a united kingdom with the Piedmontese city of Turin as its capital.

Not everyone was pleased by the triumph of this second Italian renaissance or *risorgimento*. The papacy was an aggrieved party and refused to recognise the existence of a united Italy. Successive popes, together with die-hard adherents of the deposed dynasties, continued to believe or hope that the clock could be put back. Nor was a monarchist victory welcome to all Italian patriots, especially as the dynasty of Savoy had a history that was as much French as Italian and had been slow to accept the idea of unifying the peninsula. The greatest patriot of all, Giuseppe Mazzini, would have much preferred the establishment of a democratic republic.

The republicans had been the first to formulate the concept of a unified Italy and fight for it at a time when Piedmont and the House of Savoy had shown either hostility to or at best a very moderate interest in what seemed a utopian dream. Mazzini accepted, if with reservations, that a monarchical Italy was better than no Italy at all. One of his early disciples, General Giuseppe Garibaldi, had even been responsible for the final triumph of the monarchy when in 1860 he led a private army of volunteers to conquer Naples and Sicily from the Bourbons. The victorious Garibaldi was the first to issue in Sicily a proclamation acclaiming Vittorio Emanuele as King of Italy. But the contribution to national unification of Garibaldi and Mazzini was depreciated and sometimes denied by the conservative monarchists who thereafter monopolised government in Turin. The two wings of the patriotic movement, conservative monarchists on the one hand, radicals in the so-called Action Party on the other, continued to co-exist in an uneasy and often hostile relationship.

3

Italy in 1861 was governed under a written constitution taken unchanged from a *statuto* that in 1848 had been reluctantly conceded by Vittorio Emanuele's father to his small kingdom of Piedmont-Sardinia. King Charles Albert had in that year given way to pressure and surrendered his absolutist powers. His *statuto* was drawn up in French, the language of the royal court. It was modelled on constitutions granted earlier in France and Belgium, and was devised in a hurry, which explains why it turned out to be insufficiently precise. Nor was there any provision for a constitutional court that could resolve its ambiguities and make adjustments to meet changing circumstances.

By this *statuto* the king agreed to permit the election of a parliament and guarantee civil rights and equality before the law, but he insisted that the constitution should keep 'as much power for the monarchy as possible'.[1] Vittorio Emanuele had the composite title of sovereign 'by grace of God' as well as – to the dismay of other crowned heads – 'by will of the people'. His person was 'sacred and inviolable'. The executive power belonged to him alone, which in theory meant that he was both head of government and head of state. Ministers were appointed and dismissed by him at will. Nor could he be called to account by anyone for his actions; indeed, to hint at his responsibility became a criminal offence. Legislative powers were shared between him and two houses of parliament, these being a senate whose members were chosen by himself, and a chamber of deputies elected on a very restricted suffrage. As well as appointing to all public offices, he kept a theoretical right to veto legislation approved by parliament. He could authorise expenditure and then come later to parliament to confirm the necessary taxation.

In addition, he was personally commander-in-chief of the armed forces. He had authority on his own to declare war, make peace, and arrange treaties. He did not even need to inform parliament about a treaty so long as he could claim that it imposed no financial burden on taxpayers, and he was permitted complete concealment if he thought that secrecy was in the interests of the state. As a result of these constitutional provisions the most important national treaties were kept secret, and wars could be begun without parliamentary consultation or agreement. One further but indefinite residual power allowed him to issue royal decrees where he thought this necessary for effective implementation of any law.

Vittorio Emanuele was proud to belong to the oldest ruling dynasty in Europe. He had grown up in the autocratic traditions of his father's court and did not easily adapt to the restrictions imposed on royalty by the novel provisions of constitutional government. Nevertheless, in his coronation oath he swore to accept and enforce the eighty-four articles of the *statuto*, and though he sometimes expressed a dislike of parliament, he avoided taking antagonism too far. He had the right to dissolve the chamber of deputies whenever he wished, though he was obliged to call another within four months, and one very important limitation on his power was that by law he needed parliamentary consent for new taxes. Another limitation was that no legislation was valid without the signature of a minister alongside his own, and ministers were, unlike himself, 'responsible', which meant that they could be called to account in parliament. Though the constitution made no mention of a prime minister or cabinet of ministers, he adjusted to the fact that by 1861 these had emerged as necessary institutions without which the system would not work – with the result that parliament gradually acquired more importance than Charles Albert had intended.

Two remarkable ministers in Piedmont, Marquis Massimo d'Azeglio until 1852 and then Count Camille de Cavour, had gradually been able to shift the balance of power in their own favour, so changing 'constitutional' into an approximation of 'parliamentary' government; and they did this because they feared the blunders that might otherwise be made by such a wilful and often unstatesmanlike sovereign. They could not always prevent his acting on his own, and sometimes had to humour him by tacit collusion in stretching to the limit the royalist element in the constitution. Whenever possible they loyally tried to cover up his excesses and indiscretions because, notwithstanding any danger or embarrassment that this might cause, the outward prestige of the monarchy had to be protected as a vital symbol of the fatherland. The Italian version of constitutional monarchy thus came into existence because a small group of enlightened politicians needed it: first of all to preserve national unity; secondly as a check on irresponsible monarchist action; thirdly as a barrier against republicanism and the minority of radical democrats in parliament.

Vittorio Emanuele had nine prime ministers between becoming King of Italy in 1861 and his death in 1878. Usually he treated them with a restrained cordiality, but had political disagreements with nearly all of them, because he was determined so far as possible to govern as well as reign. He told Queen Victoria that his own political judgement invariably surpassed that of any minister, and he was writing a book to prove it.[2] This typical boastfulness reflected a fear that other people were not taking him seriously. In fact, he was incapable of writing a single page of literate prose, and though he tried to impress visitors by telling them that Cavour and the other ministers were puppets in his hand, this was far from the truth.

Certainly he enjoyed authority and the prestige derived from having presided over the national risorgimento. His occasional talk of abdication and of disliking power was not very serious. And yet, as his court chaplain Monsignor Anzino recalled, he lacked the application and dedication to assert himself for more than a few weeks in the year.[3] Monarchy, as the king well knew, was rendered less sacrosanct by the fact that he had himself deposed other dynasties in the peninsula. Indeed, he was king by virtue of popular plebiscites as well as 'by grace of God', and to that extent a hereditary throne was also in one sense elective. Usually he had sufficient practical sense to be pleased that ministers could take an unwelcome load off his shoulders, and despite his farouche language and bragging he lacked the drive and imagination, or even perhaps the wish to act as a tyrant. Though at first he liked to preside over cabinet meetings, he quickly lost interest in the day-to-day trivialities of ordinary administration.

The tragic and unexpected death of Cavour in June 1861 removed one important restraint on royal authority. Several months earlier, not for the first time, the king had tried to get rid of his prime minister so that he could choose a weaker and more malleable replacement. But he had failed because everyone else admired Cavour as the architect of Italian unification and as possessing a unique competence as a parliamentary leader. After June 1861, however, with the appointment of the much less able and less experienced Baron Ricasoli, active political intervention by the royal court became easier.

Ricasoli was leader of the Tuscans in parliament, one of a number of groups in the chamber of deputies – groups that often had a strong regional loyalty which weakened the coherence and effectiveness of the elected representatives. Though a strong believer in monarchy, Ricasoli, like both Azeglio and Cavour, had reservations about this particular monarch whose political intrigues made government difficult and whose notorious sexual peccadillos were thought to be undermining respect for the throne: the new prime minister once told a foreign ambassador that the king was 'unworthy of Bettino Ricasoli'.[4] Among other objections he criticised the title 'Vittorio Emanuele II'; he would have preferred 'Vittorio Emanuele I' so as to confirm that Italy was a new nation created by popular plebiscites and not merely a continuation of the former legitimist state in Piedmont. But the king refused to give way, so causing considerable offence to Italians from Tuscany and other regions.

Ricasoli was an admirable man and an innovative agriculturalist with a strong sense of patriotism and social obligation, but he was too proud and unyielding to be an effective politician and had no experience before 1861 of the operation of constitutional government. Like Cavour he sometimes treated his own cabinet high-handedly, but with none of Cavour's finesse. To the king he spoke with respect but occasionally with an untactful air of moral superiority. Nor did he try to placate the royal favourite, Urbano Rattazzi, or the other Piedmontese at court who resented their momentary loss of power and influence after Cavour's death. Ricasoli was generally able to rely on support from parliament and in December 1861 won an impressive vote of confidence. But this did not stop the king looking for an excuse to replace him by Rattazzi. Nor did it stop Rattazzi, despite holding the office of Speaker in the chamber of deputies, from helping to reassert the powers of the crown as a means of depreciating parliament and securing his own accession to power.

2   An abortive march on Rome, 1862

Underlying this political division between the king and his chief minister were disagreements over foreign policy, and it was to prove a test case, since foreign affairs came particularly into the orbit of the royal prerogative. For instance, although there was general agreement that Italy should one day take the city of Rome from the pope and make it into the Italian capital, people differed over how this should be done. Ricasoli was a deeply religious man who believed that the Church needed to be radically reformed and purged from worldliness by voluntary surrender of its corrupting temporal authority. Over-optimistically he hoped that, if only the population of Rome would give some public indication of wanting to join the rest of Italy, its annexation to the other provinces might be achieved in a matter of months.[1]

The king had a less straightforward attitude. He had already been excommunicated more than once by Pope Pius IX, most recently for annexing the papal provinces of Romagna, Umbria, and the Marches; in addition to which his government confiscated throughout Italy a vast amount of property and revenues belonging to the Church. He himself had not the least interest in theology and sometimes talked of wanting to shoot all priests, yet he still hoped for papal absolution and combined anti-clericalism with an almost superstitious attitude to religion – along with an affectionate regard for 'that poor devil of a holy father'. When visiting Naples he wanted people to know that he had gone to the chapel of St Januarius to kiss the holy relic with the dried blood of the saint and obtain the regular miracle of its liquefaction. Regrettably, and unusually, the miracle failed to work. Nevertheless, he was eager to believe and make others believe that, whatever the Vatican might say, he himself was an instrument of divine providence and king by God's special grace. As such he hoped to persuade the pope to yield over Rome and allow the monarchy to take credit for what would be the greatest of all triumphs in the process of national unification.[2]

One minor obstacle was his disorderly private life. His queen died young after numerous pregnancies, but he had fathered many illegitimate children by various mothers, such behaviour being customary among even the most devout representatives of the House of Savoy. The Church called him to particular account for his attachment to the daughter of a non-commissioned officer in the army. Rosina Vercellana was someone to whom he was genuinely devoted and whom he ennobled as Countess of Mirafiori. But the pope repeatedly called on his fellow sovereign to set a better example by giving up the 'public scandal' of living with this 'trivial and dishonest' woman. Vittorio Emanuele had no intention of taking such advice, nor of giving back confiscated Church property, nor, indeed, of introducing penalties against non-Catholic religions as the Vatican requested.[3]

Failing to find a solution to the 'Roman problem', he turned to another matter and urged his ministers to prepare for the conquest of Venice from Austria. His education and upbringing had been almost exclusively military, and his constant day-dream was that of charging at the head of his soldiers to a glorious victory in battle. He had once been self-confident enough to offer his services as commander of the British and French armies in the Crimean war, and his genuine surprise at the rejection of this offer was very much in character. As the Prussian ambassador complained, audiences with the king rarely moved away from the topic of fighting. Another foreigner reported that he liked to speak of battles and slaughter 'in a somewhat coarse and butcherly way as if he rather enjoyed the idea of a field of carnage'. Not cruel by nature, he perhaps thought that this kind of talk would create an impression of soldierlike courage. In the same vein, he told Queen Victoria that he had no sentimental feeling about casualties in battle; he informed her that he lived for nothing else except the prospect of war, so much so that he would gladly 'exterminate' the Austrians if only he could find a plausible excuse.[4]

Similar fantasies about provoking war against Austria were in his mind when, late in 1861, without telling ministers, he sent personal envoys to various parts of Europe armed with plenty of money and secret ciphers for direct communication with himself, thus bypassing the Italian foreign office. The existence of this royal secret service was common knowledge in other European capitals where it was deplored because it confused the transaction of foreign affairs.

Some of its members were picturesque buccaneers in search of excitement. Others were obscure mercenary characters not far removed from the criminal underworld, as befitted what the British ambassador described as the king's 'strong predilection for blackguards of the spy genus, male and female'.[5]

Among his more trustworthy agents was Count Ottaviano Vimercati, who, after a dissolute youth and service in the French Foreign Legion, was strategically planted on the staff of the Italian embassy in Paris. Another was General Paolo Solaroli who made a fortune in the Far East by marrying an Indian princess, before returning to service at the palace. A third was General Stefano Türr, a Hungarian refugee who had fought with distinction under Garibaldi and later did well for himself by marrying a discarded mistress of the king's who was a relative of Napoleon III, the French emperor. Another, less reputable, was the Cavaliere Enrico Bensa, whose wife was also notoriously intimate with the monarch, and who created a great deal of trouble for the Italian government until he blackmailed it into pensioning him off as a consul in North Africa. This was the main disadvantage of such secret diplomacy, that the king's preference was for clumsy amateurs whose clandestine missions rarely remained secret, and who confused the direction of Italian policy as well as damaging the prestige of their employer. When one of them was captured by the Austrians in possession of compromising and belligerent documents it made nonsense of Ricasoli's attempt to win for Italy a peaceful reputation in the rest of Europe.

Another more respectable but equally unsuccessful emissary was Rattazzi, whom the king sent to Paris in October 1861 to persuade Napoleon that their two countries should immediately attack Austria. Should this request be turned down, Rattazzi was instructed to ask whether, if Italy attacked the Austrians single-handedly and lost, France would guarantee that Italy would not forfeit any territory when peace returned. The prime minister was not informed about this astonishing mission, which was in direct contradiction to government policy. In retrospect it is hard to credit that anyone could have believed that Napoleon would respond affirmatively to something so much against French national interests, and the emperor reacted by secretly warning Vienna, with a promise to support Austria against any attack.[6]

Unaware of this betrayal of his plans, Vittorio Emanuele in January 1862 sent Türr to tell the French that other royal agents were preparing a vast insurrectionary movement stretching through Greece, Serbia, Montenegro, and Albania. He added that the Hungarian revolutionary, Lajos Kossuth, had promised to initiate a simultaneous revolt inside the Austrian empire, and that Garibaldi had orders to

start the revolution by landing with a military expedition on the
Dalmatian coast. The king confessed to Napoleon that the cabinet
had not been informed of this project but explained that since
ministers were obstinately refusing to accept his demand for their
resignation they would shortly be dismissed.

Ricasoli knew what was afoot and for that very reason was determined not to resign so long as he could help to avoid such folly. He
feared that the whole continent would unite against an aggressive
Italy, and grave damage would incidentally be done to the credit of
the Italian monarchy. Any such damage would be a domestic disaster
because loyalty to the crown helped to preserve national unity.
Ministers, and indeed most politicians except the king, knew that the
Austrians and Turks had easily enough strength to put down any
insurrection. The various revolutionary groups in the Balkans were
merely milking the royal privy purse for reasons of their own, and
were in any case far too suspicious and jealous of each other to join
the kind of concerted revolution that the king had in mind.

Such a reckless scheme as soon as it became known was bound to
antagonise England and France, the two countries whose support
was most necessary to the king and without whose help a unified
Italian state would not yet have come into existence. He tried to
repair any damage by giving London 'the most positive assurances'
that he had no intention of promoting war or revolution. But
although the British were more than ready to help him peacefully
win Venice, they had learnt from earlier experience to disbelieve any
promise he made. Instead it was feared that what they called his
'crusade' against parliament meant that he was returning to the
illiberal traditions of his dynasty. That, in turn, would destabilise
Italy and endanger his throne, while his warlike obsessions made
him a permanent nuisance to everyone. So the British joined the
French in sending word to Vienna that they must all combine to
prevent Italy from breaching the peace of Europe.

There is little indication that this consequence of his behaviour was
understood by the king. On the contrary, he proceeded on Rattazzi's
advice to contrive the downfall of his own government on the
pretext that it was obstructing his plans for war. As he told the
British ambassador James Hudson, Ricasoli mistakenly thought that
a king should 'reign but not govern', an interpretation of the *statuto*
that 'would have deprived me even of the shadow of royalty'. More
welcome was the view of Rattazzi who reminded him that ministers
in Italy were crown appointments, and though dismissing them
would be safer if they first lost a vote in parliament, this was not a
prerequisite.[7]

Early in 1862 a newspaper campaign was accordingly launched, with funds provided from the palace, designed to undermine his prime minister's authority.[8] Here was another grave and dangerous scandal. Ministers admitted that the powers of parliament could legitimately be curtailed whenever national interests were at stake, but the present royal policy would lead to almost certain military defeat and could not possibly be in the national interest. Ricasoli privately complained that he was doing his best to educate the king in the duties of a constitutional monarch, only to be met with persistent disloyalty and 'crazy' backstairs intrigue, with the result that homage to and affection for the monarchy were diminishing even among conservative politicians.[9]

The deputies in parliament, though aware that a constitutional conflict was developing, continued to support Ricasoli through February. The prime minister then received a peremptory letter from the royal palace to say that his policies were wrong and parliamentary votes were irrelevant. A copy of this letter was carefully preserved in the royal archives and in subsequent years was produced as a model of how such delicate situations should be handled. At the time, however, some conservatives labelled it as a virtual *coup d'état*, and Hudson called it a 'piece of vulgar buffoonery' that showed how the crown was bent on its own and the country's destruction.[10]

Ricasoli at this point resigned in order to avoid a damaging constitutional crisis, and Rattazzi was then told to form a government, only to find that few people would join a minority administration led by a royal favourite. Some politicians thought that the correct procedure would be to satisfy the accepted proprieties by holding a general election, but the king refused because he had good reason to fear that elections would go the wrong way and intrude a further obstacle to his warlike plans. He was relying on the fact that many Piedmontese deputies were not sorry to see a Tuscan replaced by one of their own number; yet Giovanni Lanza, himself a conservative ex-minister from Piedmont, while not overtly criticising the king, opened a debate by expressing alarm that a prime minister could be appointed in direct defiance of parliamentary wishes, something that had never happened before.

This was a dangerous moment for crown and parliament, but a solution was providentially found when Ricasoli, who inwardly was indignant and in private wrote of the sovereign in highly disrespectful, even contemptuous terms, made a public statement in parliament on 7 March that took the blame on himself and persuaded his friends to vote for Rattazzi. His tactful and magnanimous intervention was applauded by many deputies who feared a constitutional clash. Rattazzi, an able lawyer with considerable experience in managing parliament, then cobbled together a disparate cabinet containing representatives of Right and Left, some of whom were imposed on him by the king against his wishes. Their formal installation in office took place at a house belonging to the royal *maîtresse en titre* where the king happened to be spending the night.[11]

Already before the new ministers were appointed, Garibaldi on his island home in Caprera was summoned to the palace for discussion of a plan to raise an army of volunteers with the aim of triggering a grandiose series of revolutions throughout eastern Europe. Rattazzi, on the same day that he took office, saw Garibaldi and reported that this plan was agreed. To conceal what was happening, another message was sent to London pretending that no recruitment of volunteers would be permitted and everything would be done to prevent revolution anywhere. But in London it was known that Bensa was hard at work at the king's command stirring up trouble in Serbia and the Danubian principalities where several shiploads of arms had arrived from Italy. In Greece the intention was to organise a palace revolution to depose King Otto and replace him by Vittorio Emanuele's younger son Amedeo. Switzerland was another possible field of action and a provocative hint was dropped about Italy's annexing the Italian-speaking Canton Ticino if only the Swiss could be found compensation at Austria's expense.[12] By 22 April all was said to be ready since, according to the king, Garibaldi was about to carry fire and sword through the Balkans, while a strong Italian army was poised to invade Austria.

But in truth nothing was ready, not even a clear agreement over objectives. The army was in no state to fight. Garibaldi took Rattazzi's money but aimed at a different revolution of his own in the Austrian Trentino, until government troops intervened to stop him. In June Garibaldi therefore sailed instead to Sicily where he started recruiting volunteers after letting it be known that, far from planning an invasion of the Balkans, he intended to cross the Straits of Messina and march on Rome. Yet the police made no attempt to arrest him and a rumour circulated that the palace was a secret party to this alternative strategy.

All through the tragic confusion of these summer months, one certain fact is that Garibaldi had plenty of money and arms, presumably from official sources. No doubt he went too far when he issued incendiary proclamations from Sicily in Vittorio Emanuele's name, but he claimed to have been given a private assurance that the conquest of Rome was part of official policy, and other people were told much the same by both king and prime minister.[13] Similar encouragment had been given to Garibaldi in 1860 when his volunteers conquered Naples; and now again, in 1862, he was once more ready to be disowned if his march went wrong but confident of approval from the palace if he succeeded.

Throughout July the army of volunteers grew in strength and, with the unambiguous war-cry of 'Rome or death', slowly moved toward the eastern seaboard of Sicily. Meantime, the government looked increasingly impotent and ridiculous as it took no serious action either to help or hinder while it waited to see how other countries would react. On 10 August the king made the cryptic admission to Hudson that Garibaldi 'had my orders to a certain extent but he adds something of his own to them and makes a mess of everything'. Hudson commented that the king was 'drifting helpless on the tide of events which he created and cannot control save by the loss of his own agent [Rattazzi] and at the risk of his own popularity'.[14]

Rattazzi by this point would have liked to halt an operation that was dangerously alarming the rest of Europe. But though he made a few half-hearted attempts to regain control of events, he was afraid of public opinion if he used the army against a national hero and had reason to fear that the monarchy was secretly colluding with the rebels more than ministers were allowed to know. Any orders issued by the government were therefore so hesitant and ambiguous that no one took them seriously, and the military authorities in Sicily, who were present in strength and could easily have arrested the movement, understood that they were expected to let it proceed. Many soldiers deserted to join the revolution after being led to believe that, as in 1860, this was official policy and they would not be punished. Naval vessels stationed in the part of Catania turned a blind eye as Garibaldi requisitioned ships to embark for the mainland, and their commander later excused himself on the grounds that this was in conformity with 'superior orders'.

The most likely explanation of so much muddle and irresolution was that the authorities hoped for a re-run of what had happened in similar circumstances two years earlier. Napoleon, in September 1860, had reluctantly allowed Cavour to occupy the papal provinces of central Italy on the pretext that this would prevent Garibaldi from marching on Rome. The supposition in 1862 was that, if only the French would withdraw the garrison that they had kept in Rome since 1849, Italian soldiers would win enormous prestige for the king by themselves occupying the Holy City, and once again they could claim to be merely protecting the pope against an invasion by radical revolutionaries. Such an expectation or hope betrayed a strange lack of realism, especially as Napoleon had in any case been a reluctant supporter of Italian unification; his own preference was for a smaller state of northern Italy in which French patronage replaced that of Austria. Above all, he did not want the Italians to have Rome, and his Catholic subjects were insistently demanding that the French garrison continue to defend what remained of the pope's temporal power.

Whatever the reason, an almost farcical situation was allowed by default to sink into tragedy when on 28 August a royal privy council of senior politicians accepted the need for a quick change of direction in order to regain some credibility for the crown. A few hours later the Italian army opened fire on two thousand volunteer compatriots at Aspromonte in Calabria, badly wounding their leader. Some regular soldiers who had joined Garibaldi were executed at once without trial. Several radical members of parliament were imprisoned for suspected collusion, at the same time as scores of medals for bravery were given to the regular army for a sad and minor engagement which in desperation was hailed as a glorious success for the monarchy.

How to treat the wounded Garibaldi was a serious problem because it revived acutely the latent conflict between conservatives and the Action Party. To 'cover' the crown, Garibaldi would have had to be treated as a rebel acting against royal authority, yet, since he was the most popular person in Italy, a jury would almost certainly acquit him. A second royal council therefore decided that it was safer to bring him to trial in either the senate or a military tribunal – until it was realised that witnesses might produce evidence of royal involvement. So a month later, on a pretext provided by the marriage of the king's young daughter Maria Pia to the King of Portugal, a general amnesty was issued to all except soldiers who had deserted, so more or less resolving an embarrassing predicament.

3   *From Turin to Florence*

At the end of 1862, to divert attention from this disaster, the king revived his plan to start a war in the Balkans. Ministers were told to prepare troops for an invasion of Greece to support the royal aspirations of his son. Austria was the main enemy he had in mind, though in moments of excitement he could also use unprintable language against the French who, by keeping troops in Rome, stopped his scoring a coveted political success. If necessary, he said, Italians would accept war against Napoleon III – in other words, against the greatest benefactor of the Italian nation. If really necessary, he would fight against the British as well.[1]

This senseless bravado impressed no one and was totally without public support. Rattazzi held grimly to office though he was said to have the reliable backing of no more than twenty out of five hundred deputies. Politicians from other regions were hostile to his government for being too Piedmontese in composition. Other critics spoke of its resort to corruption and jobbery on an unprecedented scale. The king's favourite, the royal 'doll' as Hudson called Rattazzi, was variously denounced for censoring the press and violating the constitutional freedoms of speech and assembly, as well as for exposing the crown to criticism by the tragic events in Calabria. Garibaldi went further and publicly attacked the monarch as a would-be despot who had broken his promise to aid a revolution which at Aspromonte he had then cynically put down in blood.

This was another dangerous moment when the survival of constitutional monarchy seemed in danger. In some parts of the country the king's portrait disappeared from shop windows and public buildings. Mazzini wrote from exile in London to hope that Rattazzi would remain in power because his continued presence was sure to aid the republican cause. Other politicans would have liked to impeach the prime minister for the catastrophe of Aspromonte and were deterred only by the taboo against bringing the crown into political controversy; all they could do was ask that the king should dismiss those officials who had given him bad advice.[2]

At last, on 1 December the prime minister resigned. He did not wait to confront parliament, because a hostile vote would not only have excluded himself from the succession, but would have limited the king's choice by indicating which other politician enjoyed the most popular backing. Rattazzi was rash enough to tell the chamber that he was still supported at court and evidently had reason to believe that he would be asked to form a new administration; except that few politicians were ready to risk their reputation by joining him.

In some despair the king threatened to dissolve parliament if it continued to oppose what he presumed to call the national interest, until he was reminded that the critics would almost certainly emerge strengthened from an election. Leading politicians tried to dissuade him from appointing another government that lacked parliamentary support, and a perhaps decisive as well as ominous intervention came from Enrico Cialdini, one of the senior generals, who reported that the army could not be relied on if Rattazzi were reappointed.[3] Several group-leaders in the chamber were then invited to join what was said to be a non-political or non-partisan administration, yet all refused when they understood that they would be expected to carry out an adventurous foreign policy in defiance of public opinion. Their refusal, instead of serving as another lesson in political realism, was accepted at court with reluctance, even with anger. Rattazzi's colleagues finally handed back their seals of office at a glacial ceremony during which the king addressed not a single word to anyone.

They must have been astounded to discover who was to be the new premier. When the first choice, General Ponza di San Martino, made the unacceptable condition that there should be economies at court and in the army, the king turned instead to someone whom he had recently called a complete imbecile and who was notoriously afflicted by a recurrent and disabling mental illness. Dr Luigi Carlo Farini became prime minister and remained in office for four long months, but even at the moment of his appointment his mind was wandering, his speech indistinct, and foreign ambassadors found him 'unfit for even the very mildest business'. Nor was such a choice accidental. The true intention was revealed in an announcement that policy would henceforward be conducted from the royal palace. Hudson's comment was that the king must himself be 'half-mad': conceivably he was a good soldier, but 'no power living, no circumstances ever will make him a politician'.[4]

Three governments had fallen in two years without parliament's being allowed to register any clear pointer for a succession. In the infancy of the parliamentary system this was not entirely surprising, but it had the disadvantage of giving the king an exaggerated view of his own competence. At a private meeting with a group of deputies on 1 January 1863 he took issue with them for failing to support the forceful foreign policy that Italy needed, and then asked Rattazzi to find out how they reacted to this sermon.[5] After a few weeks, however, he realised that personal rule by the palace was too burdensome and time-consuming. A forceful policy would require strong ministers. Not without trouble, he persuaded the now perilously deranged Farini to resign in favour of the minister of finance, Marco Minghetti.

On taking office in March, Minghetti was hardly surprised at receiving instructions from the king to start making preparations for winning the glory in war that is 'the great dream of my life'. The new minister was the most cultured and intellectual premier of the reign. At once he caused some offence by trying to tone down a warlike speech that his sovereign had spent several days drafting. Reports were soon circulating that a court camarilla was acting behind the scenes as the secret government of the country and was waiting for the approval of the annual budget before finding more complaisant ministers who would lead the country into war.[6]

To various foreign ambassadors the king continued to talk of his urge for heroic deeds in order to establish Italy among the great powers of Europe. He used to send personal messages to Italian ambassadors, whose diplomacy was tested as they had to reconcile warlike communications from the palace with peaceful despatches from the foreign office. Minghetti, too, realising that he was in power on sufferance under a monarch who claimed a dominant role in foreign policy, had to go carefully and provide the money for undercover royal agents who continued to tour through Albania, Serbia, and Romania in search of real or imaginary revolutions.

A yet more serious problem was the pacification of southern Italy. Cavour had warned that this might prove harder than fighting against Austria, and it would hardly become easier so long as available resources were pre-empted for war preparations. Rebellion in the south was fuelled by those whose interests had been damaged in the patriotic revolution, by families edged out of their former monopoly of local government, and by loyal partisans of the deposed Bourbon dynasty for whom the new king was a revolutionary usurper. At the opposite political extreme there was some resentment from those who nostalgically recalled Garibaldi's brief but glamorous and highly popular regime in the south in 1860.

Opposition came also from those, especially in Sicily, who wanted a greater devolution of power to the regions than the government was ready to concede; also from southerners whose consciences rejected the anti-clericalism that prevailed in Turin with its wholesale secularisation of schools, its dissolution of monasteries, and its confiscation of ecclesiastical charities. Alarmist information reaching Turin showed that, despite a huge majority in the obviously rigged plebiscites, almost no one in the south wanted a united nation state and the king was occasionally described as a new Attila more despotic than the autocratic regime before 1860. Rumours were even spreading that the Bourbons would soon be back on the throne of Naples, and in Sicily there was mention of seceding from the union, as the southern states were attempting in North America.

All this came as an enormous shock to northern Italians who believed the conventional patriotic myths and expected to be greeted in the south as liberators. Few in the north had any idea of southern social conditions. Few had any idea how to meet the challenge of southern disaffection and separatism except by armed repression. The king's glib talk of marching on Vienna looked increasingly at odds with reality as half the effectives in the Italian army were sent south to fight what by 1863 became a major civil war, and another rumour suggested that he would not be sorry to get rid of these troublesome southern provinces.[7]

Other northerners gave colour to this rumour by referring to their southern compatriots as uncivilised barbarians. More and more people began to understand what Cavour and Azeglio meant when they sometimes wondered if the unification between north and south might have been premature. No doubt some fault was on both sides. Twice when the king spent a few days in central and southern Italy he perplexed his new subjects by behaving with discourteous impatience, absenting himself at the last minute from formal receptions, or not saying a single word to anyone, or refusing to eat anything at public banquets held in his honour. He 'hates speaking Italian', reported one foreigner who knew him well,[8] and anyway the southern dialects were incomprehensible to a Piedmontese sovereign whose preferred language was French. His son, Prince Umberto, equally tactless, talked with embarrassing distaste of Naples and Neapolitans.[9]

Naturally the educated classes in the south resented this and took it as evidence that their region was being treated as a conquered colony. Northern laws were imposed universally, some of which, for instance the laws on administrative centralisation, the jury system, and free trade, seemed directly at odds with conditions in the south. Piedmontese civil servants were appointed to almost all the provincial prefectures. Southerners who had enjoyed power and prestige under the Bourbons found themselves excluded from posts at court. Nor did southern deputies like the expense of having to travel north and live in Turin during parliamentary sessions; especially as members of parliament received no salary.

Many years passed before anyone could attempt a structured solution to this festering 'southern problem', and it was never something that Vittorio Emanuele even began to understand. Much more to his taste was a different problem: how to win the support of Mazzini's republican associates whose patriotic and revolutionary beliefs might possibly be harnessed to the project for starting insurrections inside the Austrian empire.

Some of these republicans were elected to parliament but refused to take the oath of allegiance and so had their elections annulled. Among them was Alberto Mario who provocatively contended that the House of Savoy was disregarding a promise made in 1848 to summon a constituent assembly for the discussion of a new constitution to replace the Piedmontese *statuto*.[10] Some republicans, however, swore allegiance with tacit mental reservations. Other ex-republicans, notably Agostino Depretis and Francesco Crispi, took the oath without qualms and accepted that the monarchy would unite most people in the nation, whereas republicanism could only divide them further; and Crispi was another politican who realised that what he called the 'premature' annexation of the south[11] had created a division that would need emergency treatment. A tentative attempt was made by ministers in 1862 to allow Mazzini, the great republican ideologue of Italian nationality, to return home from exile in England, but the proposal was quashed and the chamber voted more than once to overrule his election and exclude him from parliament.

All the more extraordinary was the fact that early in 1863 the king was personally in touch with this greatly feared outlaw, using a trusted if not very trustworthy intermediary whose salary and expenses the government had to pay. Vittorio Emanuele was sensibly anxious to demonstrate that the two wings of the national movement could profitably work together. He even hoped to make Mazzini believe the improbable story that he intended to win Rome without foreign help, particularly without French help, knowing that any association with the Emperor Napoleon was anathema to all radical democrats. The republican leader was ready to give the conservatives a chance to show whether they were serious patriots worthy of support, or whether on the contrary they saw united Italy as merely 'the expansion of Piedmont' – to use Cavour's phrase. For over a year there was occasional but indirect contact between the monarch and this dedicated revolutionary, even mention of arranging a personal meeting between them, and they seem to have exchanged photographs.[12] Neither of them, however, trusted the other, and there was evidently some deceit or pretence on each side. But the fact of their contact at least reveals the king as being more open-minded and uninhibited, if perhaps less honest and scrupulous, than some of his ministers.

Equally tense was his relationship with Garibaldi who, after having been wounded by royal troops, was crippled and utterly disillusioned with official policy. At the end of 1863 Garibaldi clamorously resigned from his parliamentary seat in protest against application of martial law in Sicily and failure to treat southerners with due respect. In April 1864 he accepted an invitation to visit England where, to the king's immense indignation, this rebellious subject was given a quite extraordinary and rapturous welcome. Half a million Londoners spontaneously lined the streets to greet him; he received the rare and prestigious honour of being made a freeman of the City of London; the Prince of Wales broke protocol by coming to visit him; the British prime minister and foreign minister each invited him to lunch – something that could never have been done by their counterparts in Italy. Vittorio Emanuele greatly resented the adulation given to a simple subject, and what he chiefly disliked was the obvious implication that Garibaldi, not the sovereign, was the true liberator of Italy. But there was little that could be done in protest except to send a petty instruction that the Italian ambassador should refuse to attend celebrations in Garibaldi's honour.

At the same time another under-cover messenger from the royal palace arrived in London with the suggestion that Garibaldi should cut short these celebrations. As an inducement for him to return home, the message said that the radical leader was needed as commander of another revolutionary expedition to eastern Europe. Some of his friends in the Action Party interpreted this improbable scheme as a transparent attempt to lure an unwelcome rival well out of the way to where he was bound to be defeated and perhaps killed; so they published news of the invitation, thus creating a public scandal and bringing the project to a full stop. They may well have been correct in their supposition. The British ambassador in Turin thought that 'nothing would give the king greater pleasure than to know that Garibaldi was knocked on the head'.[13]

Early in 1864 Bensa secretly visited Vienna on an equally unlikely mission to discover if Austria would consider selling Venice to Italy. Another agent from the king with a similar message was Laura Bon, one of his pensioned ex-mistresses and mother to two of his children, who had other intimate contacts at the very top of the Austrian army.[14] When both missions failed, the king said he would declare war by the beginning of March. He assured the incredulous British that on his own he could defeat the great Austro-Hungarian empire and 'it is by the sword alone that the final constitution of Italy must be accomplished'. If necessary, he added, his army would fight against Austria and France simultaneously; or, alternatively, with French help his soldiers would be a match for the whole of Europe.[15] Which enemy to choose was evidently a secondary matter.

Once more he sounded Napoleon about the possibility of a joint war against Austria, or, failing that, of permission from the French to fight on his own.[16] Napoleon was discouraging, but the British informed him that, while eager to avoid war, they would not actively intervene to stop him fighting. The private view of politicians in London was that they still wished Italy well. If she fought and lost, they would regret the fact but at least try to ensure that the Austrians did not regain Lombardy or receive anything more than a financial indemnity.[17]

The king notoriously jumped quickly from one bright idea to another, and his interest soon switched from one possible war to something quite different. When the pope became seriously ill he suddenly realised that, should Pius die, the Italian army might have an opportunity to invade the Papal State. Any parallel revolutionary movement by the Action Party would in that case have to be repressed. If Garibaldi and his volunteers were to carry out a separate invasion, the monarchy would at the very least suffer a grave loss of face. Urgent negotiations were therefore opened in Paris, since, even if the French could not connive actively at letting Vittorio Emanuele take Rome, they might be persuaded to withdraw their garrison in time to let him proceed while avoiding the actual appearance of collusion.

The answer given to this crucial request was that the French garrison in Rome would be withdrawn only if French public opinion could first be satisfied with a plausible pretext, perhaps by making the world think that the king was not intending to exploit its departure. If, for example, he moved his capital from Turin to Florence or Naples, that might be taken as indicating that Rome was off the agenda; in other words, a French withdrawal would not be construed as abetting an Italian attack against the pope. Of course the Piedmontese would not like losing the capital to another region. Nor would the king be particularly pleased, because Turin was his home and Piedmont very close to his heart. But Minghetti guessed that Vittorio Emanuele willed the result without being ready to take the blame for it, so ministers gave the French the assurance they wanted and informed the palace only when all was settled.

For ministers to take such an initiative on their own was unprecedented and they would hardly have proceeded without tacit encouragement from above. The king claimed to be gravely shocked; he sent General Menabrea to Paris to reassure himself that there was no alternative and then accepted the inevitable. He consulted the senior generals who, although most of them came from Piedmont, agreed that there were good military reasons for choosing a new capital far from the northern frontier. A majority in the cabinet preferred transferring it to Naples. But the generals, after considering Pisa as a possibility, decided on Florence as more central and better protected than Naples or Pisa from attack by sea. Florence had in its favour that it was a city with great cultural traditions and the one provincial capital where the commonly spoken language was Italian, not some incomprehensible dialect.

In the middle of September 1864 a convention was therefore signed with France promising that the capital would move to Florence, and in return it was understood that the French garrison would leave Rome in two years' time. The Italians additionally undertook that they would never attack Rome or the Papal State, and, indeed, would protect the pope from any invasion. This satisfied Napoleon. He did not know, or pretended not to know, that Minghetti secretly intended this Convention of September to be one more step on the road to Rome by freeing that city of its French defenders. In fact, a

revolutionary committee in Rome was already being secretly subsidised by the Italian government to lay the groundwork for an
insurrection that before long, it was hoped, would permit annexation of the Holy City.[18]

The immediate result of the convention was a popular demonstration of protest in Turin against the prospect of losing the status and
privileges of a capital city. This became a serious riot after soldiers
began shooting on an unarmed crowd and, by a tragic mistake, firing
on each other. For three days the tumult lasted, and the king was
sufficiently frightened to refuse his ministers' urgent request for him
to return from his country estate to help them pacify people by his
presence. He even feared briefly that the violent popular reaction in
Piedmont might raise the question of abdication. Instead of supporting Minghetti in this difficult crisis he preferred to placate the
Piedmontese loyalists by blaming his own government and asking
for its resignation.

The ministers could still count on a clear majority in the chamber
and felt that resignation would associate themselves with a violation
of parliamentary government; instead they requested that the king
use his prerogative and issue a written instruction dismissing them,
which thereupon he did. Minghetti accepted dismissal and in mitiga-
tion explained that Vittorio Emanuele was no ordinary sovereign: he
was the *Re Galantuomo*, the gallant gentleman king, the liberator, for
whom the ordinary norms of parliamentary government did not
apply, and his whims had to be indulged because his authority and
prestige were necessary for the nation's survival.[19]

Nevertheless, the next weeks were full of danger, and some of the
king's closest advisers were not easily reconciled to the fact that he
had allowed events to get out of hand. According to Rattazzi he
ought to have intervened more strongly and repudiated a convention that his ministers had wrongly persuaded him to sign. Count
Sclopis, in protest at the abandonment of Turin, resigned as president of the senate and feared that the reputation of the monarchy
was lost for ever, There was even talk of Piedmont seceding from
Italy on the grounds of being a French-speaking province that was
not integrally part of an Italian nation. Prominent citizens in Turin
spoke with contempt of Florence. They referred to Tuscany as being
the least warlike, the most bourgeois, the least truly monarchist and
aristocratic region in Italy.[20]

Henry Elliot, the new British ambassador, was appalled to observe
what he called this intense 'hatred between the Piedmontese and the
foreigners as they call the other Italians', a hatred that was especially
noticeable close to the royal court. Elliot took note that 'a large
majority of the Piedmontese would prefer the disruption of the

kingdom to the change of capital, and they do not scruple to tell you so'.[21]

This represented a strong undercurrent of opinion in one province of the country, but the king was fortunate to find some responsible Piedmontese politicians who, even if far from keen on moving to Florence, were prepared to enter a new cabinet to stop the country falling into further disorder. Rattazzi prudently refused the succession, but another prime minister was found in the person of the senior general in the army, Alfonso Lamarmora. Others from Piedmont who joined him were the physician Giovanni Lanza at the interior ministry, an industrialist Quintino Sella at finance, and General Agostino Petitti at the war office. With their support, parliament gave its appoval to the controversial convention with France.

In January 1865 further ugly scenes took place in the streets of Turin when ordinary citizens were heard shouting 'long live Garibaldi', 'long live the republic', 'death to the king'. Carriages arriving for a ball at the palace were pelted with rotten eggs and ink bottles. Failure to prevent this insulting and frightening incident turned the court against Lamarmora and seriously undermined confidence in the new government's ability to defend social order. Elliot reported of the new premier that 'the king does not like him, for without Ricasoli's want of courtliness, he is equally straightforward and unbending on anything he considers a question of principle. The king's dislike of an honest minister is, I am afraid, past cure.'[22]

4   *The war for Venice*

Lamarmora was a bad general, an indifferent and unpractised politician, but an honest man and devoted servant of the monarch. As an army officer he had sworn an oath to obey the crown and this may have been one reason for his new appointment, in the same way as other generals had become prime minister during crises before 1860 when the king needed unquestioning obedience. Nevertheless, it must have tried Lamarmora's loyalty almost at once to find, like his predecessor, a secret court camarilla working against him. He had no party supporting his cabinet but had to rely on a balance of power between various political groups, and knew that Rattazzi was preferred by both the king and the Countess of Mirafiori.

Particularly in the field of foreign policy the new prime minister was allowed little autonomous initiative and could at most act as a brake. He had to watch from the side-lines when another royal messenger was sent to negotiate with Austria about Venice. He was entirely sceptical about the king's belief that stirring up insurrections inside the Austrian empire would one day help an Italian army to march on Vienna. Many millions had been spent over six years in subsidising revolutionary movements in eastern Europe, but there was no audit over this expenditure and Lamarmora was sure that the money had disappeared into private pockets without a single shot being available for use against the Austrian authorities.

One fundamental and insufficiently discussed question was whether the effort to become a great power was costing more than Italian resources warranted. Some of the finer liberal minds, for instance Carlo Cattaneo, were sure that such ambition would damage the development of liberal institutions,[1] and damage to the economy was immediately obvious. Cavour used to warn people that if they wanted a strong Italian nation they must find the money, but it took time for parliament to learn the extent of Italy's indebtedness, and those who talked of wanting great power status were often the most expert at tax avoidance. Costs were regularly running at a third above revenue, and united Italy was spending almost twice as much as had been expended before 1861 by all the former Italian states put together.

This imbalance produced other problems. Successive governments followed Cavour's example by sometimes spending money before requesting parliamentary consent, which was a breach of constitutional convention. Taxes continued to fall preponderantly on the great majority of citizens who had no vote in parliamentary elections, and this, while not unconstitutional, was unfair and short-sighted. Although many rich people were getting richer as a result of the unified national market produced by the risorgimento, parliament was informed that many of the poor were becoming poorer; and yet the capacity of ordinary disfranchised citizens for paying taxes was assumed to be increasing.[2]

Quintino Sella, an able financier as well as successful industrialist, was brave enough to propose more taxes and reduced expenditure. He persuaded the king to set a good example by renouncing three million lire, or one fifth of his income from parliament. No publicity was given to the fact that a much larger amount of royal debt was quietly settled by the government as part of the bargain.[3] The civil list granted by parliament was very large, almost the largest made to any sovereign in Europe, because Cavour had realised that this would help to reconcile the monarch to the practice of parliamentary government. Though the stories were no doubt exaggerated that spoke of bribery and financial corruption at court, no accounts were ever presented, and suspicions of extravagance were easily aroused when the civil list was so disproportionate to other economic realities. A great deal of this grant went towards essential upkeep in the vast number of 343 royal palaces and hunting establishments which had mostly been inherited from the deposed dynasties in Lombardy, Tuscany, Naples, and Lucca. But his own prime minister condemned the king in January 1866 for a degree of dissipation and dishonesty that made him very difficult to work with. Vittorio Emanuele also spent 'fabulous sums' on horses. He spent much less on women, despite popular belief, and was mean towards most of his female conquests.[4]

The greatest burden on the nation was the cost of military preparations for the war against Austria that he was determined to provoke. He continued to pretend to the Austrians that he was their friend, reminding them that his mother and wife were both Habsburgs from the imperial family.[5] However, the Austrian emperor was reluctant to recognise the existence of a united Italian kingdom, and his own empire still included the 'unredeemed provinces' of Venice, Trent and Alto Adige. Irredentist ambitions to conquer these regions explain why the Italian army and navy continued to absorb nearly half the disposable revenue of the state. Moreover, parliament had almost no say over how the military budget was spent. Discussions on this subject were notoriously uninformed and superficial, especially since this was another area of policy pertaining to the royal prerogative.

Sella was so frightened of national bankruptcy that he succeeded in making some reductions in military expenditure. The king continued to assume that the army was strong enough to win a major war, though in truth it was under strength, under-trained and under-equipped. General Petitti was the seventh minister of war in five years, all of them designated by the king personally; but none remained long enough in office to develop co-ordinated plans and keep abreast of technical developments. None paid sufficient attention to warnings that Italy was nowhere near strong enough to fight Austria, or that the country might split up into its component regional states if the army suffered a major military defeat. Nor were any of them anxious to risk their careers by making a public issue of any alleged deficiencies.[6]

The navy was also far less powerful than public opinion was allowed to know. Parliament in 1863 set up a committee to find out how the naval budget was being spent, but could not extract the necessary information and gave up the task. The minister in charge of the navy, and there were nine in five years, was usually an army general who had no idea of what was required except to build more tonnage than the Austrians. Despite the fact that a war against Austria was assumed in royal and military circles to be inevitable, the strategy and tactics of such a war were largely left to chance: there were no adequate charts of the Adriatic, and the training at sea of crews and commanders was considered unimportant. Perhaps worst of all was that the senior ranking admiral, Carlo di Persano, was an incompetent who had reached his position through blatant self-promotion and contacts at court. Twice he had run his flagship aground, on one occasion with the whole royal family aboard. The fact that Persano was disliked and despised by his subordinates, as well as being not on speaking terms with the prime minister, did not help.

Though the armed forces were defective, war was the aim, and Vittorio Emanuele continued to speak of Italy's being able to defeat Austria unassisted. Fortunately he could rely on the fact that Bismarck was planning a parallel war against Vienna to establish Prussian domination in central Europe. Equally encouraging were occasional hints dropped by Napoleon III who realised that a European war, if well prepared and well timed, might be exploited to push the frontier of France into Belgium and the Rhineland.

Towards the end of 1865 the king took an active part in discussions with Prussia about a joint war against Austria. In these negotiations he sometimes acted behind the back of his prime minister who he feared might be indecisive and unenthusiastic. He advised his brother sovereign in Prussia to disregard parliament and aim at establishing a unified German nation on the pattern set by Piedmont in Italy.[7] With this in mind a treaty was eventually signed at Berlin in April 1866, and only then was Lamarmora able to inform the rest of his cabinet that the king had decided upon war: because making treaties and declaring war were for the sovereign alone, and the palace had feared that ministers might try to prevent it had they been consulted in advance.

According to one officer, the king when talking to his staff always spoke of his civilian ministers with disparagement: they were fools who would ruin everything if he failed to keep his eyes open and unless he worked day and night directing their work.[8] Never can he have suspected that most people assumed the opposite. Nor did he ever admit that he himself carried any share of responsibility for the disastrous conduct of the war that was about to begin. One last chance was given him to avoid fighting when, early in May, in return for nothing more than Italian neutrality, the Austrians offered to cede Venice to France who would then give it to Italy. But he decided, and Lamarmora agreed, that after having signed a formal alliance with Prussia this generous offer would be too dishonourable for Italy to accept. More importantly, he had no doubt at all that a war would be won, and victory would not only win prestige for himself but would result in the annexation of the Trentino as well as Venice.

One reason for his obsession with war was that, since he was constitutionally commander-in-chief, the glory of what he took to be certain victory would be his. He would therefore capture for himself some of the military renown that, to his dismay, had been won previously by the irregular forces under Garibaldi. Another reason was that while war lasted he would wield emergency powers and be free from interfering civilian ministers. But a few soldiers and politicians knew from the war in 1859 that he had not the remotest idea about how to command an army, and in the intervening years he had sometimes not even bothered to turn up at the annual military manoeuvres. Unfortunately his deficiencies had been concealed after 1859 when the official history of that war was carefully suppressed, and monarchist propaganda instead manufactured mythical stories of how he had been responsibile for strategy and had in person led the charges that took his troops to victory.[9] Some of his own remarks indicate that he accepted such flattering tales as true, or half true.

In April 1866 he told his ministers that he needed the prestige of being in command and of being seen to command. Their reply was to warn that in the event of defeat he would be blamed and might have to abdicate. In their opinion he would be wiser to act as his father in 1849 and appoint a professional soldier with full authority to direct operations. Lamarmora and Cialdini, the two senior officers, agreed on this fundamental point, if on little else. A draft decree was therefore prepared naming Lamarmora as effective commander. But the king refused to sign this ministerial recommendation, thereby taking on himself a grave responsibility. All he would do was to appoint Lamarmora as chief of staff, with power to advise and then transmit orders from the supreme commander, but no more.

A civilian minister might have resigned if his advice were rejected, but Lamarmora as a soldier was obliged to accept this decision. The truth was that the king wanted others to take the blame for any failure while he himself took the credit for success. Unlike the King of Prussia or the Emperor of Austria, he had been brought up to think that he should be seen personally leading his army into battle and never stopped to think that this might be anachronistic. Once war began, the chief of staff would have to obey orders like everyone else.[10]

Unfortunately those orders were never forthcoming, and without them neither Cialdini nor Lamarmora felt fully free to act, which meant in practice that there was no clearly defined responsibility of command. Cialdini knew that the king would not countenance any doubts about his ability as a soldier, and thought it best to be tactful lest the monarch be driven to spurn the advice of his generals and turn instead to Garibaldi. Cialdini would have agreed to accept the job of supreme commander with full powers, and that would have been the best solution since he had the best qualifications, but he was too proud to act effectively in a subordinate position where he would have to obey someone he knew to be incompetent.

This led to the very unfortunate decision of Cialdini being given an independent command far away from the supervision of either the chief of staff or the commander-in-chief. Personal jealousies were involved, and also the fact that Cialdini, who came from Modena, resented what he called the excessive *piemontesismo* in the higher command. He also had his own distinct ideas about strategy. Whereas the other commanders preferred to concentrate against the Austrian 'quadrilateral' of fortresses in central Lombardy, he was allowed to follow an independent plan of attack further to the east, and for this purpose the army was divided into two quite separate forces.

Looking back it is hard to understand how the royal commander-in-chief can have left such important questions of command and strategy to the last moment. Indeed they were solved, very unsatis-factorily, only a few days before war broke out, despite the fact that this was a war that for years had been anticipated. Lamarmora, because he already held the two positions of prime minister and foreign minister, had little time to spend on war preparations in his third capacity as chief of staff. Only at the eleventh hour was the king persuaded to appoint Ricasoli as prime minister, and the change-over took place on 20 June, just three days before war began. Ricasoli therefore had no time to discover major flaws in the struc-ture of command.

Nor did Lamarmora have any time at all to organise a proper headquarters' staff. He met Cialdini at Bologna for a few hours on 17 June in an attempt to co-ordinate strategy, but no other staff officer was present and we can only guess that the two generals completely misunderstood each other. Not only did they distrust each other's plan of campaign, but each returned from this meeting under the impression that the other would be making a diversion to draw enemy forces away from what both disagreed in thinking was the main area of attack; and this disagreement was to prove fatal.

Their common ground was to discourage any popular insurrec-tions in Venetia and so to allow Garibaldi as small a part as possible in the war. They as well as the king were jealous of Garibaldi and feared the volunteer movement as not merely a threat to the army but a danger to the conservative organisation of society. Garibaldi had already proved himself to be by far the most successful general and admiral in Italy, and the quite different plan of attack that he favoured had the full support of the Prussian army. But the Italian general staff, if they agreed on nothing else, were determined to win without him and ignore his suggestions. Not daring to defy public opinion and leave him out altogether, they were at least anxious to keep him away from the main field of operations and to leave him short of arms and men. Here was another costly mistake.

Prussia declared war on 16 June; Italy, not until a week later, much to the annoyance of Bismarck who felt sure that his ally was waiting for Prussia to take the main brunt of the fighting. However, the king was full of confidence when on the 21st he at last left Florence for the field of battle. The Austrians, having to fight on two different fronts, were heavily outnumbered by the Italian army, but at least they had a carefully considered plan of war, as well as better maps, better information services, and an excellent field telegraph which was surprisingly lacking on the Italian side. They also had a single effective commander, whereas Vittorio Emanuele issued his own orders, and so did Lamarmora and Cialdini, all three with separate headquarters and without adequate machinery to co-ordinate plans and avoid cross purposes.

Within a few hours of hostilities beginning, Lamarmora ran into an Austrian force whose existence, because the telegraphic system was overloaded with congratulatory messages, he had not even suspected. By the end of the first day of the war the battle of Custoza was decisively lost and the king ordered a general retreat. Not one Italian commander emerged with credit from this disastrous day; certainly not Lamarmora who seemed completely bewildered by what was going on; nor Cialdini who disobeyed a royal order to cross the Po and draw off the enemy forces. Nor did the king who, despite great courage and fighting spirit, had made the mistake of overruling the specific advice of his ministers by retaining and yet not exercising his powers as commander-in-chief. He either could have allowed others to command or could have imposed his own authority, and did neither.

Custoza was a major reverse but need not have been the calamity that it became. A bigger misfortune was that a very large Italian army remained inactive for the next fifteen days while the king recovered his self-confidence and dithered about how to proceed. The Austrians were as surprised as delighted by this pause in the fighting because it let them concentrate their forces against Prussia. Lamarmora would now have been ready to resign as chief of staff in favour of Cialdini, but neither general wanted the responsibility of this post so long as their royal superior would neither take decisions nor let others do so.

The king nevertheless categorically refused to leave the front, because preserving the prestige of the monarchy was as important for him as an Italian victory. No one, so he told a Prussian officer, could teach him how to make war, and returning unsuccessfully to Florence would be an insufferable humiliation.[11] Only after two more weeks was a rough compromise reached by which Cialdini was given unhindered authority, but the king as commander-in-chief would remain close at hand for the sake of appearances. However, this did not end the matter, and Cialdini three times tried to resign during July because of continued interference with his strategic plans.

At the beginning of this month several dramatic events altered the military and political situation. First the Prussian army, despite Vittorio Emanuele's confidently pessimistic prediction, won a decisive battle at Sadowa. Then the next day, on 4 July, the Austrians tried to divide their two enemies by renewing the offer to cede Venice, not directly to Italy whom they had so soundly beaten, but once again through the medium of France. The French strongly backed this offer: after Sadowa they feared the emergence of Prussia as a major military power and therefore pressed the Italians to make peace.

Napoleon was pleased to see the king defeated and was heavily sarcastic over the latter's delusions about being a military commander. The emperor pointed out that Italy might get nothing at all if she refused such generous terms. Ricasoli on the other hand thought that a military victory was absolutely necessary to restore national morale and judged that the humiliation of receiving Venice as a gift through France might lead to the final collapse of the Italian monarchy. Bismarck, too, demanded that the Italian army should immediately end the suspicious inactivity that had allowed the Austrians to bring their troops back to the Prussian front. Ironic comments were made in Berlin about the king's being so sure of obtaining Venice that he was no longer fighting seriously.[12]

In mid-July the king's son-in-law found him in a desperate state, at odds with Ricasoli and his ministers as well as with his two chief generals, pressed by the French to make peace and by the Prussians to make more serious war. And yet while he brashly continued to talk of his intention to capture Trieste and advance on Vienna, he still failed to co-ordinate policy or launch a serious attack, or even formulate a possible strategy.[13] Too late he realised that had he given enough arms to Garibaldi, Trent would probably have been captured and Italy would have scored at least one victory.

Too late he also discovered that the navy still had no plan what-soever for operations in the Adriatic. On 14 July he sent a per-emptory order threatening to dismiss Admiral Persano if the naval commanders did not use their superior strength and attack. The inept and fearful Persano was thus forced into an action for which he was unprepared and for which his crews had not been trained. The result was a battle off the island of Lissa where Italy suffered her biggest naval defeat of the century. The government at first tried to suppress the news and informed the outside world that Persano had scored a brilliant victory,[14] but the truth was soon known and the admiral, after being brought to trial before the senate, was dismissed for incompetence.

Bismarck had by his point won all he wanted from the war and, realising that little further help would be forthcoming from Italy, agreed to an armistice, inviting the king to send plenipotentiaries to settle terms of peace. One difficulty was that Vittorio Emanuele, because he insisted on remaining with the army, was out of touch with his government at Florence, and hence there were further delays as messages went to and fro considering how to reply. He was angry to imagine that the Prussians were leaving him in the lurch just when he was boasting about an attack on the Austrian capital. His first reaction was to say that he was ready to continue the war alone and overrun Trent and Trieste.

But when the armistice with Bismarck brought Austrian troops pouring back into Italy, his remarks could be seen as empty boasting, especially when Cialdini once more tried to resign his command on the grounds that the king's indecision and interference were hinder-ing operations.[15] As late as 7 August the ministers in Florence continued to hope that a battle could yet be won, even though the basic problem of who was in command had still not been settled, and despite the fact that the Austrians were massing in strength on Italy's northern frontier.[16]

Lamarmora was almost alone in keeping his head, realising that Italy had no chance at all if she continued the war single-handed. Her only choice was submission to an Austrian ultimatum. He therefore persuaded the king that the reputation of the crown would be preserved only if ministers were allowed to take upon themselves the responsibility and the blame for making peace. Here was another useful lesson in the advantages of constitutional government, and it enabled Vittorio Emanuele, when speaking to foreign ambassadors, to blame all that had gone wrong on the incompetence of his mini-sters and generals. Ricasoli, had he known of this, would have re-sented such an imputation. Saying such things to foreigners was ill-bred, unpatriotic, and above all was a travesty of the truth. The king had been more anxious to save his personal prestige than to win the war. By his own mistakes he was left with the humiliation of having to accept Venice as a present from Napoleon. Simple diplomacy could have obtained the same result three months earlier without loss of life and without the fatal words Custoza and Lissa that weighed so heavily on national consciousness for the rest of the century.[17]

5   Court politics, 1866–7

The small political class in Italy was, like the king himself, out of touch with the views of ordinary citizens who had other priorities than war and military victory; so out of touch indeed that the deputies applauded Crispi's pretentious statement that the country was eager for a 'baptism of blood'. What passed for public opinion was in fact a purely artifical construct produced by time-serving placemen and journalists who depended for their livelihood on justifying every twist of royal or governmental policy.[1] That policy had sometimes been based on the absurdly unrealistic assumption that Italy possessed a stronger army that either Prussia or Austria,[2] and defeat in 1866 suddenly exposed the extent to which rhetoric had created a dangerous self-delusion about national strength and internal cohesion.

Another grave shock was registered in September 1866 when a revolt broke out in Sicily and had to be put down by the army. Patriotic rhetoric found difficulty in accounting for the continued existence of Sicilian separatism. Almost as hard to explain was that the acquisition of Venice caused much less excitement than had been expected. Garibaldi was surprised that so few Italians had volunteered to fight in the war of 1866, and at Naples the prefect confirmed that out of a population of nearly a million, only 230 volunteers were forthcoming. When a plebiscite in the Veneto gave the usual vote of approval for joining Italy, there was a suspicious 0.01 per cent of contrary votes, but officials on the spot nevertheless noted a strange lack of enthusiasm, and the king must have contributed to this by his ungracious and indeed uncivil behaviour when he arrived in Venice for a celebratory reception.[3]

In October he at last left command headquarters and returned to join his ministers in Florence. He was feeling ill, and what may have been a slight stroke temporarily paralysed one arm. Once again he spoke, not very seriously to be sure, of abdicating.[4] He disliked

Florence where he thought the air did not suit him, but most of all he disliked the prospect of having to surrender his wartime powers and return to unheroic civilian government. He talked of his intention to spend most of the time hunting until the chance arose for a further grand initiative on the world stage. Meanwhile, he urged his government to enforce martial law in Sicily and liquidate without pity what he called the vulgar *canaille* who dared to want Sicilian autonomy.[5]

His chief interest in politics remained foreign affairs. He complained to the French that his ministers were trying to interfere in foreign policy, and asked that Napoleon should therefore disregard the Italian foreign office by communicating directly with the royal court, by-passing their respective embassies. He brazenly suggested that France and Italy might now combine against Prussia, the country whose victories had just won Venice for Italy; and with a strangely perverted logic threatened that otherwise he might change sides to join Berlin against France. This was too much for the French emperor, who replied that the king would be advised to keep quiet and concentrate on more important matters, for example restoring national finances and making peace with the Church.[6]

The prestige of the head of state undoubtedly suffered as a result of the war because, as ministers warned, his insistence on refusing their advice involved him in personal responsibility for a national humiliation. Apart from his failure as a soldier, he was further criticised for failing in his duties and responsibilities as a constitutional sovereign, by sometimes overriding his cabinet and by being often away on his hunting estates unless private interests needed his attention.[7] As far as possible, this kind of criticism was not made public, and no explanation was given of how the universal expectation of military victory in June 1866 had been so incomprehensibly dashed on the first day of hostilities.

This was to become a familiar story and the need to protect the royal reputation contributed to prevent the nation from acquiring a proper self-awareness of its strengths and weaknesses. The official history of the 1866 war, like those of 1848–9 and 1859, was not published until many years later and only after being tactfully 'corrected' by the authorities. Crispi proposed holding a public enquiry, but this was refused. The second volume of Lamarmora's elaborate self-defence was suppressed altogether, one good reason being the need to protect the reputation of the royal commander-in-chief.[8] The historian Luigi Chiala was even arrested for an inadvertent indiscretion.[9] Popular histories eventually tried to conceal the fact of defeat, claiming that Custoza and Lissa were actually victories under inspired royal leadership, and in this way the same patriotic myths were perpetuated that had been an important contributory cause of a national disaster. Alternatively the blame was conveniently placed on ordinary soldiers who were said to have run away from fighting.[10]

Some politicians, among them Minghetti as well as Napoleon and cabinet ministers in London, again appealed to the king for a reduction in the military budget as a prerequisite for Italy's becoming economically strong and respected. But in January 1867 he replied that military economies would be 'fatal'. His plans for foreign policy required even more to be spent.[11] As well as offering to sign a military alliance with Napoleon against Bismarck, he told Bismarck that he would ally with Prussia 'against everyone' and that their two countries ought to be on particular guard against Napoleon. Still more absurd, when speaking to representatives of Austria he declared that he would gladly join Vienna against both Bismarck and Napoleon, neither of whom could be trusted; whereas he himself was a man of honour whose word was his bond. 'The one thing that truly gives me pleasure', he explained to them, 'is fighting wars; I do not like governing, and prefer to leave that to my ministers'. He offered to put the Italian army at the service of Austria, his recent enemy, and he added that any objection from parliament in Florence would be treated as irrelevant.[12]

Despite the fact that foreign politicians had become familiar with such remarks and had learnt to overlook them, he expected his offers to be taken seriously; otherwise he would not have gone on speaking in such a boastful and inconsequential manner. Already before the end of 1866 he was once more at odds with his ministers, whose lack of respect for him and whose 'exaggerated pretensions' to political power he called a danger to the state. Elliot confirmed that he was still surrounded by a court camarilla of favourites, all of them from Piedmont and 'for the most part inspiring the very reverse of respect': 'the king and the royal family were at no pains to conceal their predilection for Piedmont and their comparative indifference for the other parts of the kingdom'. Ricasoli was sufficiently upset about the entourage of courtiers to consult the now-retired Hudson about the practice in Britain; and Hudson, from personal experience as private secretary to King William IV, advised that officials of the royal household in England were accountable to parliament and could be dismissed if they interfered in politics.[13]

The prime minister did not immediately feel strong enough to take a stand on this issue. He was already, like Cavour before him, out of favour at court for criticising scandals that were becoming public knowledge. Not only the king's illegitimate children, but his stinginess on public occasions, his notorious debts and payments to ladies of uncertain repute were again said to be losing him public respect, and there had been unpleasant rumours about blackmail.

Ricasoli lacked Cavour's cleverness in dealing with either parliament or king, and this deprived him of the main weapon that his predecessor had used to curb the power of the throne. Impatient with opposition, the chief minister offended the liberals, who accused him of failing to prevent the sovereign from curtailing the basic individual liberties guaranteed by the constitution. In February 1867, after losing a vote of confidence, he offered to resign, but the king encouraged him to ignore the vote and stay, explaining that the elected representatives of the people showed themselves by their opposition to be irresponsible and 'demented'. Further rumours began to circulate that Vittorio Emanuele was secretly bent on a coup backed by the army.[14] But he already had enough troubles without risking further provocation of popular feeling. Instead he punished the deputies by dissolving parliament and convening a general election.

The new legislature still supported Ricasoli and for one month after the election his government survived, but he pushed his luck too far when he proposed more taxes and an increase in the constitutional powers of the premier. He ran into even more opposition when he invited Sella to become minister of finance. Sella insisted on a programme to reduce the crown's civil list and make royal household officials publicly accountable. The king therefore vetoed his appointment and made the surprising suggestion that one of his own private secretaries should instead become minister of finance. Ricasoli refused and on 4 April the palace, without waiting for any consultation of parliament, accepted the prime minister's resignation 'for reasons that parliament does not need to know'.[15]

The head of state, who also called himself head of government, was determined to implement his own personal policy, and all his premiers were sooner or later forced to resign because of this. He was equally determined to have his way in choosing the next cabinet. While he no doubt consulted members of his personal military household, few politicians were summoned to give their views, and this seems to have been the first constitutional crisis in which he did not ask advice from the principal army commanders.[16] His plan was to appoint a predominantly Piedmontese or Savoyard administration. Using the faithful Rattazzi as messenger, he sent an invitation to the venerable Count Sclopis who had held office in 1848 and would have been a convenient figurehead. Sclopis said he was too old, and another refusal came from the next choice, the ultra-conservative General Menabrea who had been born in what was now French Savoy. Rattazzi then accepted the premiership. The fact that he lacked any strong backing in the lower house of parliament was not thought important.

Of Rattazzi's eight ministerial colleagues, after Crispi and others on the Left refused the invitation to join his cabinet, two were army generals and two came from the senate. This caused alarm because, apart from being an unimpressive cabinet, it seemed to confirm that the balance of the constitution was being deliberately shifted against the chamber of deputies. General Di Revel at first refused to join any cabinet under Rattazzi, but the king commanded him to accept and explained that the new prime minister had agreed to obey orders from the palace. The same was said to the Austrian ambassador, who was in addition told that Ricasoli was an imbecile and Sella a lunatic; also that the previous government had been dismissed for trying to usurp royal authority, whereas Rattazzi had loyally promised to co-operate in preparing for another war.[17]

Urbano Rattazzi was an experienced Piedmontese parliamentarian whose political views were usually those of the Centre-Left, but it was generally known that he was in power on sufferance because of protection at court. One problem was his wife, the daughter of a British cabinet minister and cousin of the French emperor, who was also thought to have been the mistress of both Napoleon and Vittorio Emanuele. Unfortunately she had made herself socially unacceptable by publishing a novel lampooning Italian politicians. Rattazzi tried to withdraw copies of this book, but too late. When challenged to a duel by an offended party he replied that as premier he could not accept, though he had himself challenged and fought a duel with Minghetti while the latter was prime minister.

In the royal palace, where the pretensions of politicians were not taken very seriously, the reverberations of this indiscreet novel caused much hilarity. The king was grateful to Ricasoli who once again, as in 1862, protected his sovereign by refusing a request in parliament to explain why he had left office. In private, much like Cavour earlier, Ricasoli said he would prefer never again to have personal dealings with a monarch whose behaviour had been dishonest, nauseating, even corrupt, and who had appointed Rattazzi so as to have fewer obstacles to his personal authority.[18]

Ricasoli was a moralist whose standards were too high for the harsh world of politics, but he was far from alone in thinking that the reputation of the crown had suffered another blow. Other loyal conservatives came close to agreeing with George Marsh, the representative of the United States, who opined that the institution of monarchy had little support from public opinion and might not continue much longer. Once again, abdication was mentioned as a possible outcome, but this could hardly appeal to the political élite in the Centre and on the Right who knew that the monarchy was their best defence against republicanism and red revolution.[19]

1. *Vittorio Emanuele II.*

2. M. Gordigiani, *Count Camille de Cavour.*

3. *The Royal Family*. Engraving showing, from left to right: Don Luigi I, King of Portugal and his wife, Maria Pia (seated); Prince Gerolamo Bonaparte and his wife, Maria Clotilde; Prince Umberto, his wife, Princess Margherita, and their son, Vittorio Emanuele; Vittorio Emanuele II; Amedeo I, King of Spain and his wife, Maria Vittoria; Emanuele Filiberto, Duke of Puglie; Prince Tommaso and his wife, Maria Elisabetta; Eugenio of Savoy, Prince of Carignano.

4. *The Liberators of Italy*. Engraving showing, from left to right, top row: Gen. Della Rocca; Admiral Persano; Vittorio Emanuele II; Gen. Giuseppe Garibaldi; Menotti Garibaldi; Gen. Milbitz; middle row: Gen. Cavalli; Rattazzi; Nigra; Ricasoli; Gen. Bixio; Bertani; Gen. Cosenz; bottom row: Gen. Dessonaz; Gen. Menabrea; Gen. Orsini; Gen. Sacchi; Gen. Medici; Gen. Türr; Gen. Sirtori.

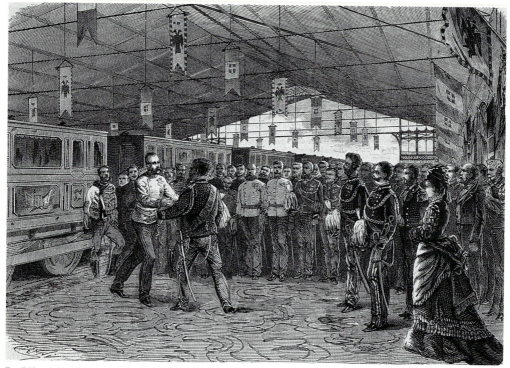

5. Vittorio Emanuele II and Emperor Franz Joseph meeting at the railway station in Venice, 5 April 1875.

6. G. Induno, *Garibaldi visits Vittorio Emanuele II (30 January 1875)*.

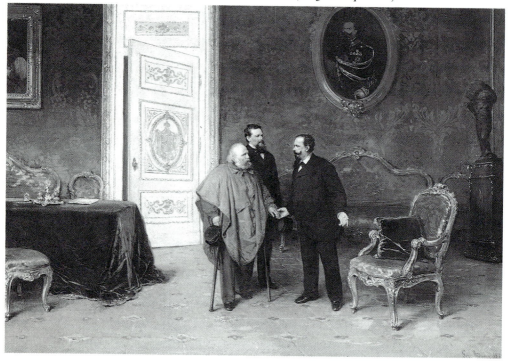

A more immediate problem was the danger of national bankruptcy as the regular annual deficit alarmed foreign banks and investors. The king bravely tried to convince a group of incredulous deputies in April that for months he had personally been working night and day to calculate how they could balance the budget. Four successive ministers of finance in less than two years had failed to clarify the accounts, which were obviously in a hopeless muddle and quite beyond any possibility of parliamentary comprehension or control. Sella's proposed remedies had received a royal veto when they included bringing court expenditure under public supervision. The king's annual income from parliament had been again increased after the acquisition of Venice to over sixteen million lire, in other words about two per cent of the total national budget. People noted that this was in absolute terms almost twice what was given to the British monarchy and ten times that enjoyed by the American president; yet the monarch had also run up further debts of six millions on the civil list, apart from other loans chargeable to his personal estate. To prevent the threat of outside supervision he again agreed to give up a quarter of his income, but only in return for the government quietly paying his creditors.

6   *A failed revolution, 1867*

Elsewhere in Europe it was remembered with alarm that Rattazzi's previous administration in 1862 had seen royal encouragement of Garibaldi's revolution and the disaster of Aspromonte. Foreign ambassadors reported from Florence in May 1867 that there was danger of a repeat performance since the king once again had the bit between his teeth and was pursuing an independent policy with little reference to his ministers. As he was frequently away in his Alpine hunting grounds, perhaps deliberately away in order to avoid meeting ambassadors who might have expressed their alarm, the ordinary contacts of diplomacy were difficult. One British representative had to report that the new ministers were without exception 'nonentities': other ambassadors agreed that

> the feeblest among them is Count Campello, the minister of foreign affairs. His intelligence is very limited and he appears to be so entirely ignorant of all matters belonging to his own department as to make it a mere waste of time to attempt to hold any conversations with him.[1]

What chiefly worried the rest of Europe was that the king might have deliberately appointed such a feeble government so as to have no ministerial opposition to another attack on Rome. The French garrison had been withdrawn from this city in accordance with the convention of September 1864, but there were strong suspicions that Italy did not intend to keep her part of the bargain – which was to defend what remained of the Papal State from invasion by anyone. Official policy in Florence maintained that Rome must at some point in the future become the national capital, and it now seemed to Vittorio Emanuele that this would have to be achieved by force. He still suffered the indignity of having been excommunicated by the Church, though without letting it bother his conscience excessively. As he teasingly repeated to his saintly daughter Clotilde, the success of Italy's risorgimento proved that God must have willed a united nation to exist; and that meant that the king would be the instrument of providence if he punished the papacy for betraying its divine mission and for stooping to deeds of 'infamous turpitude'.[2]

Already before the new ministers took office in April, he was again in touch with a revolutionary committee in Rome that continued to receive a regular monthly subsidy from Florence, and this provocative fact was known in Paris.[3] His chief preoccupation was that a French expeditionary force was waiting near Toulon to return to Italy in order to defend the pope at the first sign of any trouble, and his immediate problem was how to persuade Napoleon to keep these troops at home. Rattazzi therefore repeated 'a thousand times' the improbable claim that the pope's defence was completely safe in the king's hands.[4]

A second problem was how to stir up a 'spontaneous' insurrection by the Roman population that would give Italy the excuse to 'restore order' and occupy the city before the French could intervene. This would not be easy, partly because the Romans, even those who wanted annexation by Italy, preferred to wait to see that happened; partly because Garibaldi would be needed to trigger the insurrection, despite the fact that the king had promised to stop volunteers crossing the papal frontier. An even greater difficulty was that Garibaldi, though he would have to be secretly encouraged to start a revolution, could not be allowed to carry that revolution to success. The capture of Rome had to be a victory for the monarchy, not for the Action Party, and indeed the king's intention was to deceive two opponents by simultaneously destroying the temporal power of the pope and the forces of democratic radicalism.

Garibaldi had a much more straightforward policy, which was to force the government into action by raising another volunteer army and marching on Rome. When the French learnt of this and protested, they were given another positive assurance from Florence that such a march would never be permitted, and were fobbed off by stories of these volunteers being recruited for some unspecified action in South America. But by the middle of September there was no disguising that an army of irregulars was assembling on the papal frontier. The news came as a shock even to cabinet ministers in Florence who could only assume that, just as in 1862, Rattazzi, in obedience to higher orders, was providing arms and money for a revolution.

The prime minister was not a man to let this happen unless with royal approval. The government had quietly given two or possibly three million lire to Garibaldi's agent, the deputy Francesco Crispi, and some of the money had already been sent to Rome to finance the revolution and bribe officers in the papal militia. Foreign representatives in Florence were informed by Rattazzi that a 'spontaneous' insurrection would break out in Rome at any moment, and he pretended that this would come as a great embarrassment to him.

The real embarrassment, however, was that, despite what newspapers in Florence tried to pretend, Rome remained tranquil and her leading citizens seemed to be actively supporting not the hoped-for revolution but the papal police. The king prudently remained well out of the way at one of his mountain hunting lodges, though closely in touch through three or four telegrams each day. It can hardly have been against his wishes that a regular army officer was sent to Rome to help co-ordinate the insurrection. His plan was the same as in 1860 and 1862, for Garibaldi to start the ball rolling but no more, because the final capture of Rome must without question be left for the royal army.[5]

On 24 September a momentary halt was called to this remarkable project. Garibaldi's indiscreet talk of invading Rome was compromising the government, and some members of the cabinet had threatened to resign. Ministers not only feared that the palace was more closely involved than they were allowed to know, they also feared the indignity of Garibaldi and the Action Party succeeding too well and gaining credit for presenting Rome to the king. Even worse might be if Garibaldi was defeated by the papalists and if the blame for his defeat fell on the monarchy. Worst of all would be if he won too quickly and called for a constituent assembly in Rome, because that would lead to revision of the *statuto* and the terrifying prospect of its replacement by a more democratic constitution.

Garibaldi was therefore arrested. But it was a half-hearted gesture because he was simply sent to his home on the island of Caprera from which escape would be easy. He was still needed for the original plan which the king and Rattazzi tried to keep to themselves.

On very little evidence, indeed against the evidence, they went on assuming that a general insurrection was on the point of breaking out in Rome. Once the revolt began, the plan was that the volunteers would reappear and cross the frontier in its support, at which point the regular army would invade the Papal State on the pretext of protecting the pope.

Another dubious assumption was the king's belief or hope that the French, just as in 1860, would issue threats but take no practical steps to halt what was proposed. He therefore gave them warning of his intentions and explained that the survival of his dynasty depended on reaching Rome before Garibaldi could anticipate him. The French in reply repeated that such a cynical project would constitute an entirely unacceptable violation of the 1864 convention; and with equal frankness they warned that the Catholics in France would insist on Italy's being prevented from destroying the last vestiges of the pope's temporal power. Rattazzi would have been ready to call their bluff even if it meant war; but the king rejected this advice from his prime minister, as a result of which rejection on 19 October the cabinet resigned. They agreed to remain in office only until General Cialdini could form an emergency administration.

On the same day Garibaldi reappeared in Florence after escaping from Caprera. For the next forty-eight hours he remained undisturbed in the city and made no secret of his presence or of his intention to attack Rome. He had a cordial meeting with General Cialdini the premier-elect, and apparently another meeting at the royal palace. Volunteers meanwhile continued to arrive from other Italian towns, sometimes travelling free of charge on special trains organised by the authorities and given weapons from the royal armouries. One of the resigning ministers was assured that the king knew perfectly well what he was about,[6] but this assurance looked increasingly improbable as time went by. Either the king did not dare to arrest Garibaldi, or more likely he wanted to keep the volunteer army as a threat with which to persuade the French to let him send his army to 'protect the pope'; or possibly he had no idea at all about what to do except to wait for the Romans to revolt. If only he had arrested Garibaldi again, or even if he had given the volunteers a formal order to desist, another tragedy could almost certainly have been avoided. Instead he refused to issue any public pronouncement, so giving credence to the growing impression in France and elsewhere that he was secretly abetting the revolutionaries.

General Cialdini, a former royal aide-de-camp, was meanwhile trying to form a government but found no one ready to join him in underwriting a palace policy that threatened war against France. On 22 October Garibaldi crossed the papal frontier unhindered. At the last minute an order was sent to arrest him, but it arrived too late, hardly by accident. Information was given to the newspapers that revolution had already broken out in Rome. But the news was untrue. Even after Garibaldi scored a minor victory and reached the outskirts of Rome, the city remained tranquil and the American consul reported that everyone without exception was loyal to the pope. Patriotic sentiment was evidently not strong in this remnant of the papal domain, whereas fear of revolution was widespread, and possibly the money sent by Rattazzi had disappeared before it reached the papal officials who were to be bribed.[7]

Five times in succession Napoleon ordered his expeditionary force to embark at Toulon, and each time the order was countermanded after the king begged for a short reprieve. But when Cialdini still failed to form a government, these royal requests looked like deliberate tactics to evade responsibility, and on 26 October the French expedition set sail. Both Cialdini and Rattazzi, when asked their views, assumed that Garibaldi was on the point of victory and recommended that the time had come for the regular army to invade, even at the risk of a clash with the French.[8] Yet the king could not make up his mind to so positive an action. To cover himself he summoned a special council of senior generals and politicians who agreed that the Italian army should cross into papal territory, not to help the revolution, but only on the pretext of assisting the French in restoring order, which would inevitably put them in conflict with Garibaldi.

At this council the king had, very unusually, to listen to indirect hints that duplicity on his part had landed the country in another perilous predicament. At one point in the discussion he asked General Durando to take the place of General Cialdini and form a cabinet, but Durando could not find enough support. Another suggested appointment, General Lamarmora, ruled himself out by making the unthinkable suggestion what Vittorio Emanuele should first abdicate in favour of the crown prince, Umberto.[9] The choice then fell on yet another general, the senior royal aide-de-camp Menabrea, who, after being given the positive instruction to form a government, succeeded immediately.

While French troops proceeded to re-occupy Rome, the Italian army crossed the frontier supposedly to help them to 'restore order', but almost at once withdrew after an ultimatum from Paris. Garibaldi had no hope of winning against a French army, so a royal proclamation repudiated him just before the volunteers were defeated by the French at Mentana. The defeat was a substantial reverse for the patriotic cause; and yet conservative politicians were not altogether sorry to see the revolutionaries given a salutary lesson.[10]

Neither was the king. As he confirmed to a number of people, his private plan had been to use Garibaldi's invasion of Rome as an excuse to march at the head of his soldiers and defend the pope, incidentally 'exterminating' the volunteers in what he pleased to call a 'bloodbath'.[11]

Whether or not this brutal excuse can be believed, the king had played a devious and unheroic role in another national disaster. Politicians did their best to conceal his part in these events,[12] but there was murmuring against him in parliament and more loose talk of possible abdication, while in Turin and Milan there were republican demonstrations.[13] In self-defence he became increasingly wild in his remarks, throwing the blame on others, even trying to convince the British ambassador that the pope was gratuitously provoking conflict by preparing to invade Italy.[14] To Pius IX he sent a message denying any responsibility for what had occurred and promising that he would always respect the territorial possessions of the Church; on hearing which the pope sorrowfully commented on the king's 'inveterate mendacity'. An angry Napoleon even talked once more of punishing Italy by allowing it to split up into three independent states.[15]

7   *Personal rule*

In December 1867 the British foreign secretary, Lord Clarendon, was in Florence talking to Italian politicians about what had happened, and heard the kind of criticism that was reserved for private conversation. He discovered general agreement 'that the king was the great obstacle, that he was ignorant and false, and an intriguer whom no honest man could serve without damage to his own reputation';

> There is universal agreement that Vittorio Emanuele is an imbecile; he is a dishonest man who tells lies to everyone; at this rate he will end by losing his crown and ruining both Italy and his dynasty.

On the one hand he was said to have no talent for the consensus politics of parliamentary government; yet he also lacked the energy to impose his will forcefully. Nor, reported Clarendon, was he likely to find any reputable ministers who would trust his leadership if he ever tried to govern on his own.[1]

Not that he needed to get rid of parliament, because neither chamber nor senate made things particularly difficult for him. He regarded them less as co-partners in government than as an alibi, in other words they were to take the blame whenever his own policies went wrong. He told Clarendon that 'he had been infamously betrayed by Rattazzi' and at one point had even ordered the prime minister's arrest. Ministers were in general adept at taking responsibility for his mistakes even when they admitted his faults in private. He pretended when talking to the Austrian ambassador that the existence of parliament made governing Italy difficult, but he also said that he knew how to manage those 'mauvais drôles' in the lower house, because even deputies who in public criticised the monarchy were glad to ask him in secret for grants of money. He used to mention his private files which contained their begging letters, and this enabled him in any emergency to silence their criticisms or make them vote the way he wanted. To Paget, 'the king spoke with the utmost scorn of Italian politicians…"There were only two ways", His Majesty said, "of governing Italians, by bayonets and bribery; they did not understand and were quite unfit for the constitutional regime"'.[2]

Such remarks may have been casual and designed merely to sound impressive, but the fact that he made them did not help his reputation among foreigners. Among Italians, apart from senior politicians who expressed criticisms to Clarendon, Mazzini was again in full opposition and Garibaldi was more hostile than ever. The events leading up to Mentana led Garibaldi to call the king a liar whose word could never be trusted and who was a major cause of Italy's being undervalued by other nations. If many local critics nevertheless remained basically loyal, in the sense of rejecting republicanism, that was because the sovereign continued to be the most effective symbol of national unity. Yet symbolism was a shallow basis for allegiance. Ricasoli and Lamarmora both said that they would prefer to have no personal dealings with him again, and his position was hardly unassailable if foreigners could think that only French support now kept him on his throne.[3]

Vittorio Emanuele naturally resented the fact that he and his country were thought to be dependent on French patronage. He was particularly resentful of Napoleon, as well he might be at the French government's threat to punish any future backsliding by dividing Italy into component regions and returning the Bourbons to the throne of Naples.[4] Bismarck as well as Napoleon continued to wonder whether Italy would survive as a united state and whether the monarchy before long might have to make way for a republic.[5] In recognition of the country's inherent weakness, the traditional policy of the Italian foreign office was to manoeuvre between France and Prussia and play off each against the other. But the king had little notion of the subtle diplomacy this required. Crude hints were dropped in Berlin that he might be ready to join Prussia in a war to prevent the hegemony of France in Europe,[6] while to the French he again said the opposite, that he detested the Prussians and would join Napoleon in helping to curb their pride.[7]

What he was still waiting for was another major European conflict in which, irrespective of its nature, he could tip the scales by joining the winning side, because successful war in whatever cause would restore his own prestige and consolidate national unity after the setbacks of 1866–7. Paget, after another meeting, described how 'his head is always full of battles gone by and of imaginary battles to come with himself at the head of his army'.[8] These were and would remain among the constant themes of his private conversation.

From many quarters there arrived renewed advice that, after acquiring Venice, Italy should reduce the crippling annual expenditure on her armed forces; but the new prime minister, General Menabrea, replied with the familiar argument that a strong army, as well as helping to bring together the various regions of the country, was needed to supply deficiencies in the police and the criminal courts. 'The Italian kingdom can hardly yet be said to be properly constituted', so Menabrea told Paget; 'the army was the instrument by which order had to be maintained and society and prosperity maintained'. This opinion was shared by the king who was confident he could use his influence to persuade parliament to vote against reducing the military budget, and was equally confident that an aggressive foreign policy would eventually fulfil his personal destiny and win for the nation the glory it deserved.[9]

Forgetting the lessons of Sadowa, he decided to act on the assumption that France would defeat Prussia in any future war, and during the years 1868 and 1869 he therefore worked to conclude a defensive and offensive treaty between Italy, France, and Austria. By the terms of the constitution he could make treaties on his own initiative, so once again he negotiated not through ambassadors, not through the Italian foreign office, but through his private agents Vimercati and Türr. Until the end of 1868 he did not even inform the prime minister that these negotiations were in course, and for a further six months the other ministers were told nothing at all.[10]

What he suggested to Paris and Vienna was that Italy would provide 200,000 soldiers to help Napoleon win part of Belgium and the Rhineland, at the same time as Austria would extend her authority in eastern Europe and recover the dominant position in Germany which in 1866 she had lost to Prussia. In return he sought territorial rectifications for Italy on her northern and north-eastern frontier; he also asked for Nice, but Napoleon was willing to cede only one small Alpine valley and suggested that Italy take part of Tunisia instead. If Switzerland became involved on the other side, Italy might also annex Canton Ticino. But the king's main stipulation was that French troops withdraw once more from Rome, and in return he would again promise (not very sincerely) to defend the pope from invasion or insurrection.

On this last requirement the negotiations ran into difficulties. Napoleon knew that war between France and Prussia was possible and would therefore have liked to bring back his garrison troops from Rome, even though he feared to antagonise the pope or French Catholics by putting this withdrawal into a formal document. But in June 1869, when Vittorio Emanuele at last informed his ministers of the general plan, their reaction was that only if the French left Rome would Italian opinion accept an alliance with the victor of Mentana against the Prussians, who had so recently won Venice for Italy.

This delicate point had to be left without any formal resolution in a treaty. The only commitment was by the king personally, who pledged his word to help France fight against Prussia, in return for which the French garrison would be removed from Rome in the not too distant future. On the basis of a purely personal promise the French emperor stated that he considered a triple alliance between France, Austria, and Italy as 'morally signed'. Franz Joseph in Vienna and Vittorio Emanuele in Florence concurred in calling it a binding engagement, and the king undertook that when the time came to fight he would dismiss any minister who objected.[11] This was court politics of an extreme and dangerous kind. Cavour's practice of parliamentary government seemed to be past history, effectively superseded.

These negotiations for war would hardly have been possible had the submissive Menabrea not remained prime minister for over two years. He was a loyal, upright soldier who, very unusually, was a senator and not an elected representative, and was far from at home in the practice of parliamentary debate. His colleagues in office were hand-picked by the crown and some were household officials taken from the royal court. The same disorganised parliament that had first backed Ricasoli, and then turned indiscriminately to Rattazzi, now switched with little difficulty to support the much less 'parliamentary' administration of this general from Savoy.

What eventually saved the country from reverting to absolutism was that some conservative politicians became worried by the prospect of national bankruptcy and worried above all by a possible default of interest payments on government stock, because such a default would have undermined the loyalty of the whole political and

rentier class. Giovanni Lanza and Quintino Sella, both from Piedmont, were among the first to be frightened after hearing rumours
that the king was secretly bent on war. Sella would have been more
than ready to cut the size of the navy by half and he also renewed
Ricasoli's complaint that the palace was setting a bad example of
extravagance and immorality. Since his resignation as a minister in
1865, Sella's strong feelings over financial irregularities at court had
kept him distant from the centre of national politics, but in the years
1868–9 he began to fear that, if parliament did not assert its control
of taxation and expenditure, the economy would run into grave
difficulties that might threaten the established order of society. Under
pressure, Menabrea in 1868 agreed to impose a tax on cereals, which
was in effect an additional imposition on the very poor and as such
caused serious popular rioting which the army had to put down by
force. But he held out against proposals for an income tax on the rich
or any serious reduction in military strength. As a result the annual
deficit remained quite out of control.

One ill-considered financial reform was to surrender management
of the tobacco monopoly to a private consortium, which enriched a
few speculators at the expense of the general public. Lanza, who was
Speaker of the chamber, resigned over this issue in August 1868
because such a private monopoly was not only bad finance but
a glaring example of corruption. Probably the king was one of
those who stood to profit financially from it, just as he was sometimes assumed to have profited from deals in railway contracts and
the sale of nationalised ecclesiastical land. Newspapers were seized
and editors sent to prison as royal complicity in these transactions
became a matter for public comment, and judges were punished
for resisting government pressure to find verdicts of guilty against
the journalists involved. Garibaldi was encouraged once more to
denounce the king as no longer worthy of respect by honest folk.
Failure to investigate these alleged irregularities led to further popular demonstrations and appeals for abdication.[12]

The tobacco monopoly and the king's financial extravagance were
two ingredients in a political crisis that developed in the autumn of
1869 and threatened to thwart the sovereign's preparations for pre-
cipitating a European war. Before the crisis could be resolved he fell
seriously ill, perhaps with one of his recurrent malarial fevers. Fearing he might die, a message was sent to beg the pope to release him
from excommunication. The reply from Rome was that he must first
make amends to the Church and regularise the scandal of his private
life by marrying Rosina Vercellana. A religious marriage hurriedly
took place on his sick-bed, although ministers succeeded in persuading him to omit the civil marriage ceremony that would have
made this plebeian lady into a regnant queen.

On the other point at issue the king explained to his confessor that, although he had not personally wanted to act against the Church, a constitutional sovereign was obliged to accept the advice of his ministers. For this same reason he could not sign a retraction as the pope wished. When the illness became critical he was given absolution and the last rites, upon which he made a verbal apology for his earlier anti–clericalism and promised that if he lived he would try to repair the damage.[13]

He recovered and did not keep his promise. When a new session of parliament opened in November he was still too ill to attend and the inaugural speech from the throne had to be read for him, which was as well since it spoke of Italians being unanimous in their desire to avoid war. Immediately afterwards Menabrea suffered a political reverse when his candidate for Speaker failed to secure election and Lanza was chosen again. The government thereupon resigned at this sign that the deputies were once again threatening to demand retrenchment and a greater share in government.

The king momentarily considered reappointing Rattazzi as prime minister, but a veto arrived from Paris against the man held responsible for Garibaldi's attempts to march on Rome in 1862 and 1867.[14] One possible alternative was to reappoint Menabrea with a different cabinet, which would certainly have brought about a clash with parliament. When Menabrea failed to find sufficiently submissive colleagues, Lanza was invited to take up office, but in ten days of discussion did not succeed in locating potential ministers who could agree about how to reduce military expenditure. Here was a crucial issue for the king, because any such reduction not only would threaten his private plans for war but was opposed to his conviction that a strong army was a necessary support for the institution of monarchy.[15] Another cause for alarm at court was Lanza's intention to demand the dismissal of those officials of the royal household held responsible for the extravagant foreign policy and life-style of the palace.

To avoid such unwelcome demands, General Cialdini once again spent several days trying to patch together an administration that would leave the army and the royal prerogative intact; but without success. On 14 December it was Lanza who at last succeeded in becoming prime minister and was supported by Sella as his minister of finance. This was a triumph for civilian and parliamentary government over an attempt at personal rule by the palace. Lanza was first asked by the king to include among his ministers some of Menabrea's colleagues, presumably because they alone would have known about the secret alliance with France; but the request was refused. Another refusal came when the new cabinet was asked to make no reduction in the army grant. Lanza's clearly expressed view was that a monarch had the constitutional right to choose ministers, but must then allow them freedom to act or else appoint others. Lanza also insisted on the principle that court officials must never again work against cabinet policy.[16]

The king's reluctant but good-humoured acceptance of these conditions was praised by Paget, especially as 'he don't like Lanza and can't bear Sella who, when he was last minister, showed a certain determination to curtail the royal expenditure and a disposition to reform the royal morals'.[17] The monarch, without enthusiasm, had to accept that there was no alternative. Lacking the energy and experience required for the day-to-day business of personal rule, lacking also the subtlety and sophistication needed for international diplomacy, he was forced to find civilian ministers who knew how to manage parliament and tranquillise public opinion. Nevertheless, unknown to his new ministers, he privately intended them to serve as a cover while he continued secretly to plan for war.

8   *The conquest of Rome*

The appointment of Lanza was subsequently seen as an important factor in the development of parliamentary government. But the king's intention was to surrender no more than the outward trappings of power. Quite deliberately, and it must be said unwisely, he omitted to tell his new ministers that he had secretly pledged Italy to join another European war. Instead he continued with his private diplomacy behind the back of the foreign minister, Marquis Visconti-Venosta, having become accustomed to using private diplomatic agents backed up by a network of informers paid either by the government or out of his own pocket. Four days after the new administration took office, he reassured the Austrians that he looked forward eagerly to war in the fairly near future, but begged them not to mention such a delicate matter to the Italian foreign office.

What he hoped to gain from that war was the credit and glory of military victory, as well as finally destroying the temporal power of the papacy. Visconti-Venosta, according to the king, was too much of a lightweight for such serious matters, and a change in ministers would certainly not be allowed to mean a change in Italy's foreign policy. The monarch was expecting the French garrison to be withdrawn from Rome in a few months' time, and that would be the right moment for the signature of a formal offensive treaty between Italy, Austria, and France. He also mentioned to the Austrians a much less welcome possibility, that Napoleon might be deposed by a republican revolution in Paris; in which case he thought that a joint Italian and Austrian army ought to march at once into France to crush the revolution and restore the emperor to his throne. This, too, was something to be discussed between sovereigns without informing Lanza and Visconti-Venosta. He further explained that he intended to dismiss his cabinet and recall the more reliable Menabrea when the time came for military action, because a minister's signature would be needed for wartime legislation.[1]

Since he was commander-in-chief of the armed forces he should have known, as his senior generals knew, that the army was barely strong enough to defend the Italian frontier, let alone fight against Prussia; but all realistic considerations were set aside when he saw a chance to promote the dynastic ambitions of the House of Savoy. One daughter, Clotilde, was already married to Prince Jerome Napoleon who was second in line to the throne of France; another daughter, Maria Pia, was Queen of Portugal; and in 1869 he tried to persuade Amedeo of Aosta, his second son, to accept the throne of Spain after the deposition of Queen Isabella. Amedeo had already been thrust forward as a possible king in Greece and then in Romania, but was too sensible or too timid to be enthusiastic about any of these proposals. Failing Amedeo, Vittorio Emanuele suggested to Spanish politicians the candidature of his nephew, Tommaso Duke of Genoa, who was a boy of 15 at school in England. But Lanza's cabinet was unanimous in opposing any involvement in the mysterious politics of the Iberian peninsula.

The suggestion that Amedeo should become King of Spain was nevertheless kept in reserve and revived in July 1870 as an alternative to the candidature of the German prince, Leopold of Hohenzollern, which precipitated the events that launched the Franco-Prussian war. The first rumour of imminent hostilities caught the king by surprise when hunting in the Alps. His reaction on 3 July, still without consulting the cabinet, was that he would be committed in honour to fight alongside Napoleon in what he assumed would be a victorious war. Unfortunately he had failed to keep any record of his promises to France and the foreign office knew nothing about them, so he urgently had to ask Menabrea to remind him of what precisely had been agreed. Even when Visconti-Venosta warned him that war was about to begin he refused to return to Florence, but preferred to resume secret negotiations with the French, once again through the medium of Vimercati who held the office of Master of the Royal Hunting Grounds.

Only on 9 July did he at last inform ministers of his 'promise' to enter such a war. His orders were for them to stay out of any discussions and not make trouble. Kept in ignorance they could say nothing when the French ambassador, to the king's annoyance, approached them directly to know their views. Lanza and Visconti-Venosta could neither encourage nor dissuade the ambassador because they knew only that the king was personally, and to them mysteriously, pledged to fight in what they feared would be an expensive and probably unwinnable war. But Napoleon was encouraged by their non-committal reply to take steps making war more likely and informed the Italians that he did so on the assumption that they were bound by the king's promise to join him. For the next week Vittorio Emanuele remained in the mountains, during which time there was an abortive attempt by royalists in Florence, no doubt on his personal instructions, to make the government resign in favour of more belligerent ministers. When finally he returned to the capital it was too late for Lanza to use his influence to secure peace, and the French declared war before there was any chance to dissuade them.

Thanks largely to Lanza and Sella, two devoted monarchists who were also realists and responsible politicians, Italy by the slenderest margin remained neutral in the Franco-Prussian war and so avoided a defeat that not only might have endangered national unity but would certainly have threatened the dynasty. The king himself, insensible of public opinion or of prudent military calculations, tried until the last moment to join France: he 'is no joke under these circumstances', was Paget's comment.[2] Two opposed policies thus continued to run concurrently: his own, dead-set on war, and that of his ministers who were playing for time and for postponing any commitment. Lanza loyally avoided an open confrontation because exposure of this dual policy would have forced the government's resignation, which in turn would almost certainly have led to war and dangerously 'uncovered' the responsibility of the palace. At the very least the ministers had to hold office until the king's assumption of a French victory was proved correct or false.

Though the sovereign was shaken by their reaction, he told a representative of the Austrian government on 31 July that he would look ridiculous if he failed to fight after spending two years encouraging Napoleon to make war. He explained his delay in joining the war by protesting that he had relied on being given more notice by the French; they had unfortunately left him insufficient time to prepare for the dismissal of that 'imbecile' Lanza and his colleagues, whom he now called incompetent nonentities. In the meantime he was putting pressure on Italian newspapers to work up enthusiasm for fighting and was confident that the country would follow his lead; he would be ready to declare war in two weeks' time.[3]

Without telling his ministers he sent Vimercati on one more missions to France and Austria to settle the necessary details. Meanwhile in Florence on 3 August the matter was raised in the senate when General Cialdini, no doubt instigated by the court, demanded that the government resign and make way for new ministers who would declare war on Prussia. Sella replied to this attack by warning senators against what seemed like a military *pronunciamento*. Some of the generals, so Sella suggested, had selfish and perhaps corrupt reasons for wanting an excuse to spend more money on the armed forces. Cialdini had argued in the senate that a strong army was needed to defend the propertied classes in Italy against threatening social disorders. But the truth, according to Sella, was almost the opposite: a stronger army would mean higher taxation on the poor and hence a greater threat of social disorder, whereas Italy needed peace and lower taxation so as to make the country more prosperous and diminish social disaffection.

Sella was an enlightened politician and financier whose pacific opinions were shared by many moderate conservatives in northern Italy. His argument for not fighting was strengthened when the French suffered a military reverse early in August, because the Austrians at once became neutralist and lukewarm about what seemed a losing cause. Until this moment his ministers in Florence were wavering, moved by an anxiety to conceal that the king had been conducting a personal policy unknown to parliament or cabinet. But Sella, after encouraging his colleagues to remain in power and cling to neutrality, was finally bold enough to confront Vittorio Emanuele in a personal encounter. Accused by the latter of lacking the sense of national honour needed at such a moment of destiny, Sella explained that secret diplomacy by the palace was leading the country as well as the dynasty to dishonour and ruin. The king's reply was an insulting remark about how a mere cloth merchant could not help being a coward.

On 5 August Vittorio Emanuele was still hoping to join the war, but at least he knew by now that there were arguments on the other side and that the French might not win. Evidently he had not bothered to consult some of the army commanders who had thought all along that the French would lose, and he was now astonished to be told by General Lamamora that his armed forces would never have been strong enough to give serious help to Napoleon. He was also surprised to be told that discontent in Italy would compel him to keep a large part of the army at home. Despite everything, however, as late as 10 August he again tried to reassure the French that he would soon be at war.[4]

One new development was the arrival of a message from Garibaldi who suggested that another army of volunteers could easily march on Rome now that the French garrison was being repatriated. This gave Lanza the opportunity to point out that the threat of a republican revolution in Rome was another reason against aiding France. The army should instead be concentrated on the papal frontier because the dynasty might be overthrown if Garibaldi or, worse still, Mazzini reached Rome first.[5] Using a false passport in the name of John Brown, Mazzini had secretly returned from England to Italy in the hope of starting just such a revolution; but his presence at Naples was betrayed by a government agent among his followers, and on 13 August before any damage could be done, he was arrested.

Napoleon, after another lost battle, made one final attempt to bring Vittorio Emanuele into the war and sent a message to say that the Italians could name their own terms. The king then seems to have agreed to replace his ministers if they refused to co-operate.[6] But he was foiled on 20 August when Rattazzi, Crispi, and other leading deputies on the Left threatened to boycott parliament and even raised the prospect of civil war. They were persuaded to hold their hand, only by a promise made to them by Sella that he would resign and expose the king's secret diplomacy if the army was used against Prussia instead of against the pope.[7]

At the beginning of September, when Napoleon was taken prisoner at Sedan and France became a republic, an astonished Vittorio Emanuele was keenly embarrassed at realising how nearly he had brought his own country to share in such a crushing defeat. 'With a malicious smile' he told Sella that ministers were at fault for not warning him earlier that the Prussians might win, as though he himself should not have suspected this possibility and listened to General Lamarmora's advice after the Prussian victories in 1866.[8]

On 7 September he provoked one last clash with the cabinet by demanding their acceptance of his own personal nominee as minister of war. But Lanza and Sella now felt strong enough to threaten resignation. They told him they could not remain as ministers so long as in cabinet meetings he regularly objected to the policy of his own government.[9] Prudently he at last gave way and adopted their alternative policy to invade the Papal State. He acknowledged that he had formally undertaken in an international treaty to prevent any such invasion, but accepted as an excuse that the national interest forced him to break his promise. He also produced the hypocritical argument that as a loyal Catholic he was obliged to safeguard the Holy See and prevent a republican revolution in Rome.[10]

Mazzini had looked forward all his life to winning Rome from the pope, but success came while he was imprisoned in the fortress of Gaeta, an outcast from Italian society. This final achievement of the risorgimento was coming about not as a result of the popular initiative he had hoped for, but, just like the acquistion of Venice, as the by-product of the military victory of an autocratic Prussian regime that he detested. The Italian monarchists had finally been driven into accepting Mazzini's policy of annexing Rome, but without acknowledgement or gratitude. On the contrary they had to pretend, just as Cavour in 1860, that their main motive in completing the unification of the peninsula was rather to prevent any popular initiative, in other words to defeat Mazzini and the Action Party. Already the repeated election to parliament of this greatest of Italian patriots had been disallowed as though he were the nation's principal enemy. When he died in 1872 he was living obscurely at Pisa under an assumed name. Not until March 1890, when republicanism no longer seemed a danger, did Right and Left combine unanimously in parliament to make ostentatious public reparation to the man who had taught most ministers of the crown that Italy should be and could be a united nation.

On 10 September 1870 Vittorio Emanuele sent a disingenuous message to the pope in which he hoped that an invasion by Italian troops would not be seen by the Vatican as a hostile act. He told his daughter that he had again prayed for divine guidance and was more convinced than ever that he was an instrument of divine retribution against the papacy.[11] He still hoped that violence would not be necessary and that Pius would not resist. But to be on the safe side the government sent more money to bribe influential clerics and to organise a rising Rome which could be used as proof that the invaders were advancing at popular request – or, alternatively and inconsistently, were coming to put down popular disorder.[12]

Unfortunately Rome remained quiet and probably, as on previous occasions, the money disappeared along the way. Evidently the inhabitants of Rome preferred to wait upon events before committing themselves. The king was therefore disgruntled to find himself left with an unheroic role to play. If he could not defeat the Prussians, he might at least have soundly defeated Garibaldi. Ideally, or so he maintained, if only thirty thousand of Garibaldi's volunteers had occupied Rome, he would have had an excellent excuse to kill every one of them and 'purge the country of such vermin'.[13]

The papal government put up no more than a token resistance and, after artillery opened a breach in the city walls on 20 September, the Italian army occupied Rome with only a few score of casualties. A plebiscite was held that gave the usual 99 per cent majority in favour of union with the rest of Italy, which allowed Rome to replace Florence as the national capital. The pope told Catholics not to vote, and after calling the king a bully and a hypocrite, issued another major excommunication against those responsible. Lanza confiscated any newspapers in Florence that printed this papal condemnation, and Vittorio Emanuele's conscience was once again only moderately disturbed. He repeated the convenient excuse that, being a constitutional sovereign, not himself but his ministers carried the entire responsibility for acts of government and they alone could be blamed.

He was reluctant to go in person to Rome, fearing that he might not be well received by the local population, and it was thought wise not to organise a triumphal entry such as he had made in Milan, Florence, Naples, Palermo, and Venice. The problem was solved at the end of December when heavy rains resulted in the River Tiber's overflowing, and he accompanied his ministers in a furtive appearance for a few hours to show his sympathy with the victims. At the same time he sent a note to the pope protesting his deep respect for the Holy See, but received no answer.

9   The Left in power

Garibaldi shared with Mazzini a sense of tragedy and disillusionment with the way the risorgimento had turned out, and in particular criticised the king for subordinating patriotism to selfish dynastic objectives.[1] Both of these radical leaders had been vainly hoping for a patriotic insurrection in Rome to prove that Italian nationality was a product of democratic self-determination, not of foreign patronage or imposition from above, nor of a succession of bitter civil wars between contending Italian factions.

Another of their hopes had been that, after reaching Rome, a national assembly would discuss and agree to radical changes in the constitution. Many people, not only on the Left, accepted the need for constitutional change because they were unhappy with the way that parliamentary government had been functioning.[2] Some politicians remembered that the concession of the original *statuto* in 1848 had been accompanied soon afterwards by a promise that a constituent assembly would eventually meet to discuss possible changes – a promise that had then been discreetly forgotten. The *statuto* had been imposed on Piedmont during a time of emergency when a strong monarchy seemed particularly desirable as a directing and moderating element in the national constitution. Since then, circumstances had radically changed, for instance by the incorporation of other regions with quite different traditions, and by a series of plebiscites which introduced a new element of popular election into what had been a hereditary monarchy.

The acquisition of Rome might have provided the occasion to carry out the promise of 1848 and recognise that some modification or reconsideration of the *statuto* was advisable. On the other hand, too many vested interests had become embedded in the political structure and had good reason to fear any drastic change. There was a legitimate anxiety among conservatives that political radicalism or even regional separatism might emerge very strongly if there was any discussion of fundamentals. Worse still, it would give a free public platform to the republicans, because Mazzini had continued to assert that without a constituent assembly the nation would not properly exist and the voice of the people would not have been adequately heard.[3] Though the issue was raised once again in parliament, the government quickly let it drop.

If the practice of parliamentary government seemed defective, some politicians blamed not so much the constitutional provisions of the *statuto* as the fact that other parliaments functioned most effectively with an alternation between parties in government; and such an alternation was lacking in Italy. There was no clear demarcation between political groups, almost no sense at all of party organisation and loyalty. Two prominent political thinkers Stefano Jacini and Sidney Sonnino, argued that there was no point in attempting to mimic English constitutional practice with its broad alternation between Tory and Whig. The Italian parliament was developing a different model, being divided into many small groups that were held together not so much by policy as by personal loyalty to an individual leader, or else by a purely regional allegiance. When cabinets continued to succeed each other at the rate of one a year, one reason was that every government had to be a coalition, with the disadvantage of lacking collective discipline or fully agreed policies.[4] Why organised parties were lacking was still not entirely easy to determine, but the fact made government difficult as well as making the example of Westminster irrelevant.

Among practical politicians, Lanza was one of those who sought a system of political alignments closer to the English model. He was himself on the right of centre, but he believed that for parliament to work well there was a need for a better-organised party on the left. Such a party might form a coherent opposition to the liberal conservatives who in different combinations were repeatedly returned to power by reason of the restricted suffrage. Ideally it would present a different policy on major issues and one day might provide the alternation in power that, by encouraging a greater mobility in politics, would stop corrupt vested interests taking root.[5]

Sella was another politician who talked of the need for a 'transformation of parties', and some people briefly hoped that he might support the Left so as to break the mould and give more of a choice to the electorate.[6] But Sella was a natural cross-bencher who felt uncomfortable in the role of a party man and was in any case far more conservative than radical in most of his views. Disillusioned by the uselessness of an 'opposition' in Italian political practice, he, like Lanza and Rattazzi, often preferred to stay away from parliament when not in office. Like Ricasoli and Lamarmora, indeed like Cavour and Azeglio earlier, he had acquired a distaste for working in close proximity to Vittorio Emanuele. He especially resented having to provide a cover in parliament for whimsical and wilful intrusion by the court in politics.[7]

The most prominent member of the moderate Centre-Left in parliament, until his death in 1873, was Rattazzi. This man had once been a compliant instrument of the royal court but had learnt from experience. In 1871 he refused to join Lanza's government, and one reason was his fear that the king was extending too far the competence of the royal prerogative.[8] Other critics on the Left objected to the practice of dealing with the growing national debt through taxes raised by royal decree, because such decrees, even if subsequently presented for retrospective validation by parliament, were an infringement of good constitutional practice. Rattazzi complained that budgets were customarily voted *en bloc* and hurriedly, sometimes with little discussion, and always without providing sufficient statistical information. In his view, now that the peninsula was effectively unified, there was less need for emergency legislation by royal decree, and the time had arrived for governments to be more directly answerable to parliament, less to the head of state.[9]

But in the absence of organised parties, a multiplicity of group loyalties gave continued scope for the assertion of royal influence. In the king's view, as he told Lanza, parliaments had no business to discuss 'matters of high policy'.[10] Rattazzi's death further weakened the Left, while on the right of centre there were strong personal differences that permitted Minghetti to break ranks and vote against Lanza. His contrary vote caused a government crisis in the summer of 1873. The king, who liked to spend the summer months in his Alpine hunting grounds, hastily chose the moderately conservative Minghetti as prime minister and suggested his own list of appointments to the cabinet. Mindful of Cavour's successful *connubio* or marriage with the more radical Rattazzi in 1852, Minghetti hoped to include in his list the most prominent group-leader of the Left,

Agostino Depretis. But Depretis made excessive demands for social and political reform, so instead a government was constituted with another strongly conservative bias.

Minghetti, supported by Visconti-Venosta who remained foreign minister, believed that Italy needed an unadventurous foreign policy and priority should be given to solving the many financial and administrative problems of the united kingdom. Without wanting to adopt a neutralist stance like Switzerland and Belgium, there were good prudential and economic reasons for fearing the king's notorious desire to cut a figure on the world stage. Once again ministers had to exert themselves in trying to tone down the royal speech at the opening of parliament. They much preferred to earn for Italy the reputation of a satisfied power that would hencefor-ward be an element of order and peace in Europe.[11]

Vittorio Emanuele usually had the good sense to give way to advice on the rare occasions when ministers were courageous enough to stand up to him. In 1871, when the French republic asked for military assistance in the last stages of the Franco-Prussian war, he was at first flattered and pleased to be offered another chance to show his military prowess – forgetting that a few months earlier he had been equally eager to march on Paris and crush the republicans. But after a lively discussion with leading generals and politicians he prudently refused.[12] He went even further and tried to stop Garibaldi winning yet more prestige by fighting for the French republic against Prussia. Many Italian volunteers were accordingly arrested at the French frontier and Garibaldi was threatened with loss of Italian citizenship, but this inspired leader of guerrillas nevertheless reached the battlefields of southern France and again won military laurels that mysteriously eluded the sovereign and his army.

To the king's delight after the war was concluded, his son Amedeo at last agreed to accept the still-vacant throne of Spain. Amedeo knew not a word of Spanish and immediately felt bewildered by the disorderly internal politics of his new kingdom. He was also obliged to depend on continual financial subsidies from his father. Vittorio Emanuele advised his son to assume dictatorial powers in Madrid as the only way to impose royal authority over such a turbulent society.[13] But two years of confusion and turmoil ended in Amedeo's humiliating abdication. After returning to Italy he claimed that he had gone to Spain unwillingly and begged the pope's absolution for having sinfully sworn to enforce the liberal Spanish constitution.[14] If the aim had been to win prestige for the House of Savoy, it failed.

Here was another lesson in the advantages of listening to mini-sterial advice about playing a more cautious and unambitious role in Europe. In the search for new allies, Lanza joined Minghetti in suggesting a state visit to Vienna and Berlin. The king was reluctant. He had fought against Austria in 1866. He had even wanted to fight against Prussia in 1870, as Bismarck well knew. But Napoleon's defeat showed that the centre of gravity in the continent was moving away from the Atlantic towards central Europe, and there were obvious reasons why the three conservative monarchies, Italy, Austria, and the new German empire, might find common ground against republicanism in France and popular revolutions everywhere. Vittorio Emanuele was particularly pleased with his reception when he travelled to Berlin in 1873. No formal treaty was proposed, but he was delighted to find that Italy was welcomed as a necessary factor in the concert of Europe. His warlike instincts were especially gratified by Bismarck's calculated hint that Italy might rely on German help in any future war against republican France.[15]

Back home he found domestic politics more unstable. If Sella could have been induced to join Minghetti, together they might have formed an effective coalition to the right of centre, but unfortunately they disliked each other, and the animus at court against Sella prevented the monarchy's using its influence to bring the two together. Sella was inclined to think that the Right might have run out of ideas and it was time for Depretis and the Left to try their hand at government. Minghetti on the other hand feared or pretended that the arrival of the Left in power would be a disaster which might even threaten the break-up of the united kingdom. Ricasoli likewise argued that, while an alternation of parties might be possible in the 'more compact and homogeneous' environment of England, this was not yet possible in Italy where regional and personal rivalries ran too deep and cut across political loyalties.[16]

In March 1876 Minghetti suffered an unexpected defeat in parliament when dissident groups among the conservatives, especially those representing commercial interests in Lombardy and Tuscany, joined the Left against his proposal to nationalise the railways. Confronted by such divisions on the Right, the king made the courageous decision that Depretis, who called himself leader of the 'constitutional opposition', should become prime minister.

This was the nearest Italy had come to an alternation of parties in power and was seen at the time as an attempt to discover if a truly representative parliamentary regime could be made to work effectively in a 'Latin nation'.[17] Many deputies who supported Depretis had in the distant past been republicans, but the 'constitutional opposition' had come to accept in the 1860s that the monarchy was a uniting force, whereas republicanism would be divisive. In practice, despite their programme of substantial reforms, they proved in office to be as docile as the conservatives and indeed less critical of the monarchy than Sella or Ricasoli or even General Lamarmora had been.

By his appointment of Depretis it seems that Vittorio Emanuele was in fact expecting less difficulty in conducting a personal foreign policy of his own. Aristocrats such as Ricasoli and Cavour had combined loyalty to the crown with a certain disrespect for the king's person, whereas the new ministers from the Left were more easily impressed by the aura of majesty and more ready to enjoy his occasional bounty. He liked to explain that if ever they 'showed symptoms of being troublesome' he would call them to a personal meeting and 'always found he could do what he liked with them'. Hence he was able to reassure the conservatives that there was no need to be alarmed, because he remained personally in charge and would know when to 'apply the brake'.[18]

Depretis was an experienced parliamentarian and presided skilfully over eight governments in the ten years after 1876. Cavour had thought him too indecisive and too frightened of unpopularity to be a successful politician. Rattazzi criticised him for lacking sincerity. But he was a good administrator, an effective debater, and a loyal servant of the crown. The reforms he now proposed included abolition of the death penalty, a fairer distribution of taxes, compulsory education, more local autonomy, and less use of government pressure on the judiciary or in parliamentary elections. He also wanted a wider suffrage so as to lessen the dangerous gap between the 'real country' of the electorate and the 'legal country' represented in parliament.[19] The king was fully aware of this reformist programme when he appointed the new government, which confirms that in domestic politics he was far from being a dyed-in-the-wool reactionary. Had the programme been fully carried out, the country would have been fundamentally changed, no doubt for the better.

Elections were held later in 1876 and for the first time resulted in a big swing to the left. The vote also confirmed a dangerous imbalance between north and south that he already been observed in the previous election: the impoverished south of Italy voting overwhelmingly for the Left, while the more industrialised north tended to support the conservatives. The interior minister, Giovanni Nicotera, shamelessly violated the government's proclaimed policy by using extraordinary pressure through the prefects to secure an electoral victory. He could argue that Cavour and Minghetti in the past had behaved similarly, and so did all future governments. Reforms were evidently more easily preached than practised, and only superficially was victory for the Left in 1876 the political watershed that some people hoped for or feared.

10   Death, and retrospect

Already before Depretis was installed in office the irrepressibly bellicose Vittorio Emanuele was looking for another excuse to make
war, and was heard to regret that after taking Venice and Rome there
was no obvious territory left for him to conquer. In a private conversation he told Paget that he had asked the emperors of Austria and
Germany to give him a free hand in solving the 'Eastern Question'.
His simple solution to this complex and baffling problem would be

> to remove the Sultan from Turkey and put him somewhere in
> Central Asia; after which I would tell other powers to help them-
> selves to whatever they wanted of the Turkish empire, and would
> myself take *quelque petite chose* for Italy. England, too, could have
> anything she wanted.

When reporting this conversation the ambassador commented that
such a crude attitude towards international problems was not uncharacteristic and should not be taken too seriously.[1]

Later in 1876 Paget became less sure that ministers would be able
to restrain the belligerent policy of the royal court. Once more the
king sent to inform London that he would like a more active role in
eastern Europe because 'he could not remain passive, it was contrary
to his nature not to be doing something'. He thought that England
might like to annex Egypt when the Turkish empire disintegrated,
and a partition of the spoils might then form the basis for a closer
understanding between their two countries. He was sure that 'with
200,000 soldiers I could solve the Balkan question'.[2]

In November 1876 Lord Salisbury on a visit to Rome was alarmed
to discover that, while cabinet ministers were 'very peaceful', the
king and his son Umberto 'are for war'. In particular, to the dismay
of the British for whom this was a very sensitive point, the court was
strongly in sympathy with Tsarist Russia and its expansionist policy;
and officials informed Salisbury that the personal opinions of the
sovereign had a preponderant influence in foreign affairs.[3] What
made this the more alarming, as ambassadors in Rome reported, was
that the new foreign minister, Luigi Melegari, was a very sick man
'without the slightest influence or authority with his colleagues or
over the direction of foreign policy', and like some of his predecessors had so little grasp of affairs that there was not much point even
talking to him.[4] Inevitably this led to the suspicion that a nonentity
had been chosen with the intention of masking the fact that foreign
policy was devised in the palace.

Political circles in Rome were of course aware that Vittorio

Emanuele continued to work on his own with a private secretariat which kept in touch with its own secret agents in the various European capitals.[5] In addition, he again encouraged Italian ambassadors to keep up a private correspondence with him, and sometimes instructed them to make communications to foreign governments without so much as keeping the foreign minister informed. Not by accident almost all the senior ambassadors were Piedmontese, and most were army generals who had sworn a personal oath of obedience to the crown. Lanza was heard to say that 'unfortunately' and 'unconstitutionally' the king was in practice his own foreign minister, and this was something that Right and Left, however much they might disapprove, had to accept as a fact.[6]

Outside Italy the existence of a distinct and separate foreign policy conducted from the Quirinal was regretted as a hindrance to normal diplomacy, and it explains why disparaging remarks were made about Italy's claims to contribute usefully in European affairs. Bismarck sometimes treated Italy as of no account at all or as a negative force. When asked to bypass the Italian foreign office and keep in touch privately with the palace, he refused to countenance such parallel diplomacy because he had seen its results in 1870 and knew that it was unreliable, confusing and dangerous.[7]

Bismarck nevertheless felt that German national interests would be served by closer relations with Italy, and Vittorio Emanuele responded eagerly in the hope that a German alliance might be a preliminary step towards the more forceful policy he wanted.[8] The advice he received from his senior military officers was that Italy would carry too little weight in Europe unless her intervention could tip the balance of power; and since she could hardly side with radical and republican France, the obvious alternative was a triple alliance with the Austrian and German emperors.[9] The king himself would have preferred a dual alliance with Germany, directed against Austria, because in that way he could keep alive Italy's claims to annex the still 'unredeemed' territories of Trentino and Trieste. He was not being completely truthful when he repeatedly told the Austrians that he had no outstanding claims against their empire, nor when he said that he despised those Italians who continued to nourish irredentist ambitions.[10]

In August 1877 he sent the Speaker of the chamber, Francesco Crispi, on a private mission to persuade Bismarck that their two countries should make a defensive and offensive alliance against Austria and France. The Italian ambassador in Berlin was told nothing of this project. London and Paris were even given a firm assurance that it was a purely private visit with no political overtones. But Crispi in fact carried a cipher for direct communication not with the foreign office but with the royal palace. His secret instructions, though in public he denied it, were to prepare the ground for a war that 'would crown the reign by a military victory and give the Italian army the force and prestige that it still lacks'.[11]

Crispi was a devious, bellicose, and greatly ambitious person whose conspiratorial nature revelled in the performance of such a delicate task; but he was without the necessary experience, tact, and judgement. In order to put people off the scent he went first to Paris where he told an incredulous French foreign minister that their two Latin nations should make common ground against the 'German race' which had no love for Italy.[12] Moving to Germany he had two long meetings with Bismarck, to whom he communicated his master's wish (almost certainly against his instructions from Depretis) for an alliance directed against Austria and France. Unfortunately, when he suggested that German unification would not be complete without annexing part of Austria, Bismarck made the disappointing reply that Germany was already quite large enough, and while they might possibly find common ground in opposition against France, no help would be forthcoming for Italy in fighting Austria.[13]

After this partial rebuff, Crispi left for Vienna and Budapest where he found that unwelcome rumours were rife and there existed what he called an inexplicable distrust about Italian intentions. He did his best to sound convincing when he insisted that Italy was a trustworthy friend of Austria; and he explained that Italians desired a further consolidation of the Austrian empire as a bastion of civilisation against Slavs and Turks.[14] He also visited London where he complicated matters by suggesting yet another alliance, this time between Vittorio Emanuele and Britain, and incidentally undertook that Italy was striving her hardest to maintain the peace of Europe.[15]

Crispi was naïve enough to feel sure that this strange mission had been a great success, whereas in fact he had created annoyance or suspicion in all four capital cities by leaving an impression of duplicity that did a great deal of harm and suggested the opposite of everything he tried to say.[16] His one positive achievement was in Berlin where he reminded Bismarck that Italy might be an ally in the event of hostilities against France. Back home he was immediately invited to stay in one of the royal palaces to be minutely questioned about every detail of his tour, especially about whether there was any hope of starting a 'general war'. He was then requested to use his influence as Speaker in parliament to hasten the process of rearmament, something that he himself believed was necessary, 'whatever the cost might be'.[17] Six weeks later, no doubt at royal suggestion, he joined the government as minister of the interior.

A bold but clumsy initiative in foreign policy was abruptly curtailed when in January 1878 the king became ill with another bout of malaria which proved fatal. His last public statement was to a group of senators and deputies in which he spoke of great events that he hoped were imminent in Europe. According to the London *Times*, his actual words were too strong to be allowed through the telegraph office, but one ominous phrase leaked out about Italians' needing to make the outside world afraid of them, since mere esteem was not enough. To be respected was insufficient; they must be feared. This strange message was held by some monarchists to be his chief legacy for the future.[18]

Vittorio Emanuele II had earned a secure place in history by presiding over the great achievement of national unification. Perhaps his popularity had been waning in the last few years,[19] but there was widespread grief at his death, even among some who still clung to a residual republicanism. Catholic newspapers had serious reservations. The pope could not excuse the imposition on Rome of Piedmontese anti-clerical legislation and naturally resented both the suppression of monasteries and the compulsory secularisation of schools and universities. Nevertheless, Pius relented sufficiently to lift the interdict in the Quirinal palace so that absolution could be given to the dying king. A bishop arrived from the Vatican in one final attempt to obtain a humble apology and retraction, and a statement was issued that this mission had succeeded; but in fact the bishop was refused admission. The sacrament was administered by a court chaplain who received a death-bed expression of sorrow for any offence inadvertently given to the Church.[20]

Vittorio Emanuele was 57 years old at his death. No doubt it was fortunate that he had no time to risk his own and Italy's reputation in the new European war that he had in mind. Another defeat would have meant disaster, and Bismarck as well as Napoleon thought that Italy would split into its pre–1860 divisions in the event of any major military reverse. Regional loyalties were still as strong as patriotism, and sometimes were stronger. The king himself, although properly proud to be the sovereign of a united Italy, remained very much a Piedmontese and caused some offence by continuing to prefer speaking either French or the dialect of his native region. He was unhappy living in Florence or Rome and provoked protests by spending so little time in the capital. As he once told Rattazzi, he had no particular love for the population of Rome nor for that of southern Italy, and was able to admit that he had not particularly wanted union with the south; only the need to defeat Garibaldi and Mazzini had compelled him to annex Naples and Sicily in 1860.[21] Sincere patriot though he became, his original desire for national independence had been as a means of 'destroying liberalism'.[22] Eventually he had

accepted Cavour's liberalism, at least in part, but this too was more
an expedient than a principle.

One reason for his disliking Rome was the continued presence of
the pope after 1870 and the fact that ceremonies at court were
boycotted by the 'black' aristocracy who remained loyal to the
Vatican. He disliked the receptions and dances that his presence in
the Quirinal required, while the lack of a queen put a damper on the
festive court occasions which might have helped to ingratiate the
wealthier citizens of Rome. At official state banquets he continued
his practice of not eating, but would sit glumly and mute until he
could escape to a private supper at the villa he had bought for Rosina
Mirafiori outside the city walls. His uncouth rusticity and habitual
vulgarity of speech, as well as his manifest contempt for women, put
him slightly at odds with fashionable society. He instructed his own
children that wives should stay at home and confine themselves to
domestic matters: 'divine laws and human laws make women subject
to their husbands', and their role in life was to obey and keep quiet
about it.[23]

Ill at ease in high society, the king felt at home on his various
country estates, and here he found the male and female companion-
ship that he preferred. The numerous palaces and villas inherited
from the various dynasties he had deposed were a constant expense,
though most of them he never visited. In addition, he bought or built
other hunting lodges for himself. His friend Castelli estimated that
one third of his life must have been spent in the hunting field: chasing
wild boar at San Rossore in Tuscany, or bears in the Abruzzi, ibex
and chamois in the Alps, and birds of every kind everywhere. He
kept a vast stable of horses, and dogs of many breeds, and on each
estate there was an army of keepers to drive game to within twenty
metres of his shooting box.[24] Hundreds and sometimes over a thousand animals could be killed in a single day. To attract him more
often to Rome, Lanza agreed that the government should buy him a
30,000-acre estate nearby which was well stocked with game, and it
was hoped that some of the unused residences could in return be
converted for use as hospitals and barracks.

Apart from his private income, which possibly may not have been
very substantial, the king continued to enjoy a large civil list voted
by parliament. Twice he accepted reductions in return for the government's paying his debts. But Depretis in 1877 raised the civil list
once again to over 14 million lire, which was more than the government spent on national education. Almost no other sovereign in
Europe was paid so much,[25] and parliament was given no information
on how such an extravagant grant was spent.

In addition, he repeatedly asked his governments to provide extra money for special purposes, whether for paying off mistresses or furnishing palaces. Ministers sometimes argued about this but usually agreed to help him, and preferred to do so without informing parliament so as to avoid invidious debate.[26] Sometimes they made a counter-request that he should gain credit for the monarchy by spending more in largesse and on encouraging science and the arts, but he had absolutely no interest in culture of any kind. He hardly ever seems to have opened a book and was usually both embarrassed and contemptuous if he had to meet artists and scholars.

One reason why he favoured Depretis was that the Left responded more generously to his financial demands than the more economically minded Lanza and Sella. He was further helped by the fact that Crispi and Nicotera represented a new class of politician on the Left who accepted and indeed angled for private grants of money from the crown – which may have influenced their readiness to accommodate him in return. But his insatiable extravagence led him into contracting more debts, which at his death were thought to be over thirty-five million lire. He seems to have borrowed extensively abroad, and also from the notorious Bernardo Tanlongo, a Roman banker who later suffered imprisonment for fraud and political blackmail.[27]

Even after his death, strong political reasons existed for protecting the reputation of such a fallible monarch from public criticism. The legendary *Re Galantuomo* was given almost universal posthumous praise, to the point of being called the greatest sovereign in the whole history of Christian Europe.[28] The monarch who said that Italians could be ruled only by bayonets or bribery was extolled for his impeccable deference to parliament. The incompetent commander-in-chief was hailed as a brilliant soldier and strategist. Giuseppe Massari wrote a highly readable and semi-official panegyric in his honour, while privately confessing that a good deal of tactful concealment had been necessary, and any less tactful writers could risk prosecution. Ricasoli encouraged Massari to be superlative in praise, but acknowledged in private that the most essential qualities in a ruler were brains, heart, and education, of which Vittorio Emanuele lacked all three.[29]

Admittedly the king possessed the common touch and, like Garibaldi, conferred a great advantage on Italy by appealing to ordinary people who knew nothing about national politics. He was good natured and possessed a more attractive and forthright personality than his two successors on the throne. He could be charming and amiable whenever he chose. Like most of his dynasty he was courageous, and occasionally showed more practical common sense than some of the professional politicians in parliament. But although circumstances gave him a great role in history, it was far less heroic and noble than that played by Garibaldi, Mazzini, or Cavour, and his military and political incompetence more than once brought the country close to ruin.

Unlike his father, Vittorio Emanuele lacked all refinement and elegance. Indeed his uncouth habits and lack of physical and moral resemblance to Charles Albert fuelled the rumour that his true father was someone else;[30] but such gossipy stories were not unfamiliar in the annals of the House of Savoy. Though flatterers accorded him the title of 'the gallant gentleman king', the Austrian emperor complained that in his personal behaviour he sometimes forgot to act like a gentleman. Though hailed officially as the architect of national unification, there were critics nearer home, for example the loyalist Alfredo Oriani, who saw him as too egoistic, too vulgar, too small a man for the great risorgimento to which he lent his name.[31]

According to a flattering commemorative oration by Minghetti, in his last years the king spoke once again of abdication and retirement to a peaceful life in his beloved Alps. He had no inordinate love of power, said Minghetti, but was a model constitutional sovereign worthy of imitation elsewhere, someone who could easily have made himself a dictator but loyally chose to work within the bounds of the *statuto*.[32] The letter of the constitution allowed royalist politicians to argue that a king was within his rights if he ignored parliament and public opinion.[33] No law was broken when he dismissed Minghetti in 1864 or when he appointed Menabrea in 1867. No constitutional law prevented his presiding personally over cabinet meetings, and he sometimes used such occasions to lecture ministers in unparliamentary, even unquotable, language.[34] Cabinets, he used to say, did only what he told them to do. That is why he could refer to himself as 'head of government', while his prime minister was no more than 'president of the council'.[35]

Most outside observers, however, thought that he deluded himself and in practice had far less power than he liked to imagine or pretend. Usually he was too misinformed to be able to overrule expert opinion and too lazy to try, except on occasions when the royal prerogative was directly in question. Ministers regularly arrived two or three times a week for his signature to laws, but increasingly in later years he signed without taking the trouble to read what was put before him.[36] If he often made attempts to assert himself, and if at various times he actively undermined the authority of every one of his prime ministers, it is also true that he usually had the sense to stop short of imposing his own views whenever he met firm opposition.[37] No doubt he liked the reputation of being seen to command. But experience taught him the value of constitutional government where ministers took responsibility for any political mistakes and inadequacies, even mistakes attributable to himself. Parliament as an institution was not particularly healthy in 1878, and was indeed less vigorous than under Cavour in 1861, but at least it had survived some difficult moments and was strong enough to remain in existence for another fifty years until Vittorio Emanuele's grandson accepted its abolition.

2
Umberto I

1 The new reign

The new king lacked his father's strength of personality and self-assurance. Nor did he inherit the homespun manners or the panache that attracted the masses. Umberto was a comparatively pallid character who, for want of a better label, was given by loyalist historians the appellation of 'Umberto the good' – though he was hardly a very good king, nor a particularly good man. His most admirable quality was physical courage, as he showed in the war of 1866 and when confronting a number of assassination attempts. Queen Victoria noted on meeting him that he was shy and somewhat nondescript, 'shorter than his father but is like him in features and rolls his eyes just in the same way; he has also the same gruff, abrupt manner of speaking', but without his predecessor's 'rough speech and manners'.[1] Like his father he was poorly educated, without intellectual or artistic interests of any kind, and averse from reading books. He found the act of writing so tiresome and awkward that he seldom sent letters and did not like to sign his name if anyone was watching.[2]

Umberto was unprepared for the job of reigning, because the Savoy dynasty was traditionally so distrustful of each new generation that the heir to the throne was given no training in government and allowed no serious experience of public life. Politics seem to have been rarely a subject of discussion inside the royal family, and princes were allowed to fill no public position except as army officers. To a quite extraordinary extent they were kept austerely in a state of personal subjection where in private and public they had to kiss their father's hand and stand to attention in his presence. Often they were shown little affection, with results that can be imagined. They were taught obedience not decision-making, and given no encouragement to exercise personal initiative or understand the subtleties of constitutional government.[3]

Not unnaturally there was a temptation for each sovereign to react against his parents on becoming king. Umberto dismissed his father's closest cronies, selling off a thousand horses from the royal stables and refusing any contact with his step-mother Rosina or her illegitimate children. He intended to be less spendthrift as a monarch and to countenance fewer spongers and hangers-on at court. Without much difficulty he paid his father's enormous debts, which shows

71

that the crown's income from parliament was well in excess of ordinary expenditure.

The new king was thought to resemble in appearance members of the Habsburg dynasty of Vienna. During many generations no royal heir had married an Italian, and Umberto was the son and grandson of Austrian princesses. He himself nearly married yet another Habsburg, but his intended bride tragically burnt to death when her dress caught fire from a furtively smoked cigarette. The wife then chosen for him was Margherita, the daughter of his father's brother, for which consanguineous union a papal dispensation was requisite. Marriage between close relatives was another unfortunate tradition of the family because suitable and willing princesses were not easily found. Dynastic considerations again took precedence over eugenics when the king's brother Amedeo subsequently married his own niece.

Umberto's enforced marriage, despite what the official claque sometimes pretended, was a cold and distant relationship. He was far more attached to two of his many mistresses, especially Eugenia, the wife of Duke Litta Visconti-Arese. This lady remained a constant companion until his death and bore what appears to have been his favourite child. In execrable taste he kept her at court by making his wife choose her as a lady-in-waiting attached to the royal household.

Margherita was a far more interesting personality than her consort. Her elegance was legendary and Queen Victoria found her fascinating as well as pretty.[4] Italian was not her first language, but she became a proud champion of Italian patriotism; and, despite inheriting fair hair and blue eyes from her Saxon mother, she reproved flattering courtiers who, in an attempt to please her, argued that Italians were racially inferior to the fair-skinned peoples of northern Europe.[5] One of her achievements was to create a fashionable salon where writers and intellectuals were beguiled by her civility and affable compliments, in return for which they helped to develop myths that reinforced the august mystique of royalty. They praised her knowledge of Latin; they spread improbable stories about her knowing half of Dante's *Divine Comedy* by heart, and admired the musicianship that equipped her to play simple piano duets with the German ambassador. No serious poet could have been greatly inspired by Umberto or his father, but Giosuè Carducci deserted republicanism to write odes in honour of Queen Margherita, and it was important that politicians on the Left could applaud him for doing so.

Some of the conservatives were surprised and even shocked when the queen danced with deputies from the extreme Left at court receptions, but such modest acts of gracious condescension created much good will. Umberto was sensible enough to encourage this. He knew that Europe contained a growing number of princes exiled for inability to adapt to a more egalitarian and middle-class world. In November 1878, when touring the former republican stronghold of the Romagna, he was heard to say that 'the dynasty must become democratic or it will fall', though he himself did little to turn this aspiration into practice.[6]

In the same month he barely escaped death when his carriage was attacked in a Neapolitan street, and this generated a helpful wave of monarchist sympathy: even Aurelio Saffi and Alberto Mario, the best-known among surviving republicans, were moved to denounce regicide as an insane crime. When describing the incident, Umberto confessed that he was 'more or less of a fatalist in these matters' and had even derived from the occasion 'an agreeable little excitement', but was sorry he had not drawn his sabre to 'inflict summary punishment on his assailant'; in future he would carry a revolver for better safety.[7]

During the first months of his reign he confirmed the impression of being 'a soldier to the heart' but also a constitutional monarch with no autocratic ambitions.[8] By his own choice he presided less often than his father at cabinet meetings and was less eager to correspond secretly with Italian ambassadors. The liberal-conservative Milanese newspaper *Corriere della Sera*, while welcoming this change in behaviour, warned that it should not go too far. The paper praised the Italian version of constitutional monarchy as the most perfectly balanced system of government in the world, yet hoped or pretended that Umberto, while remaining irresponsible in the sense that ministers would take responsibility for any political mistakes, was nevertheless ready to intervene actively and every day in the direction of affairs.[9]

Such a balancing act was far from easy and some would say impossible. There was an obvious danger that the monarch might intervene too actively and inadvertently draw upon himself the blame that ministers ought to take. Or he might be blamed for intervening too little, because he personally signed every law and so was almost inevitably associated at second hand with any ministerial misbehaviour. Already in the early 1880s leading conservative politicians, including Visconti-Venosta, Di Robilant, and Silvio Spaventa, were worried by Umberto's lack of self-confidence in asserting his own views and influence.[10] The Neapolitan writer, Pasquale Turiello, complained that he went too far in allowing his statutory duty of appointing senators to be usurped by ministers; and Lamarmora maintained that the king could and should use his constitutional right to appoint ministers even if they lacked parliamentary approval. Other conservatives agreed that Italy was too young a country and possessed too many authoritarian traditions of government to follow English practice and 'degrade' the monarchy into an inoperative symbol; the crown had to recover and increase its powers if it was to survive.[11]

The politician who most assiduously developed this argument was a future prime minister, Sidney Sonnino, who launched an attack in 1878 on 'parliamentarism', by which he meant the growing authority of parliament at the expense of the king and the executive. The monarch, in Sonnino's view, ought to represent the general interest of the nation. He should therefore possesses a right to overrule sectional parties and decide the major direction of national policy in the light of what he took to be the interests of the whole Italian people. In one sense a king could even be more representative than parliament, since parliaments represented a minority interest so long as there was a very restricted parliamentary franchise. *Parlamentarismo* ought therefore to be checked by a strong regal executive, which on the one hand would be an extra barrier against social revolution, and on the other could encourage social reforms that rich people in parliament might otherwise have opposed. Moreover, only a strong monarchy, by transcending party squabbles, could, according to Sonnino, make Italy a military power to be reckoned with in the outside world.[12]

Some of these views on the conservative wing of politics were accepted for different reasons by a few politicians on the Left. Francesco Crispi, another future prime minister, had been a democratic republican conspirator in his youth, but while exiled in England in the 1850s had learnt that civil liberties could co-exist with an enlightened monarchy,[13] and in the years after 1861 became more respectable and also more authoritarian as he moved closer to the inner circles of the governing class. Already before becoming a minister in 1877, Crispi was trying to ingratiate himself with the authorities by advocating the right of a sovereign to override an unrepresentative parliament and appeal to the 'true will of the people'.[14]

Crispi had not always been greatly liked or trusted by Vittorio Emanuele and sometimes annoyed Umberto by the abrupt imperiousness of his behaviour.[15] After a brief period in office, in March 1878 he was forced back into the political wilderness when, responding to an accusation of bigamy, he had to admit deceiving one woman into an invalid marriage and then deserting her to legitimise his child by another. Only much later did he return to become the favourite politician at court.

2   *The Triple Alliance*

Had Crispi remained in office a few weeks longer he might have changed the direction of foreign policy by replacing the far less assertive Senator Corti as Italian representative at the important international Congress of Berlin. Luigi Corti was a professional diplomat who approved of what Minghetti and Sella had done before 1876 to restrict military expenditure and curb belligerent ambitions at court. Whereas Crispi demanded that Italy be feared abroad, Corti and Sella felt that she would not deserve even respect if foreign policy outran her economic capacity or if extravagant views were advanced about the need for national prestige and military victory. Some Italians, as one foreign observer in Rome reported, 'do not feel particularly proud of the manner in which their kingdom had been formed' and sought self-respect by picking another fight against Austria to capture Trieste, so seeking to win supremacy in the Adriatic.[1] Others were possessed by imaginary fears about the British wanting to annex Sicily, and occasionally there was irresponsible talk of the need to defeat not only Austria but also Britain so as to turn the Mediterranean into an 'Italian lake'.[2]

Such exaggerated expectations made the Berlin congress, from which Austria won a protectorate over Bosnia and Herzegovina, seem a diplomatic defeat when Italians obtained nothing in compensation. Umberto realistically had expected little from this congress.[3] Fully aware of the damage done to Italy's good name in diplomatic circles by his father's belligerent talk against Austria, he gave instructions that the aim in Berlin must be to avoid antagonising Vienna.[4] He and Corti knew in advance about Austria's intention to take Bosnia, but were backed by Minghetti, Jacini, and Visconti-Venosta in deciding that Italy would win more respect if she emerged 'with clean hands' from her first major international conference.[5] This meant that she ought not to risk a rebuff by pressing for territorial compensation in what were already being called the 'unredeemed lands' in the extreme north and north-east of the Italian peninsula. The government was sufficiently disinterested to reject an offer from Britain for preliminary talks in order to present a common front at Berlin, because joining any European alliance might force Italy into some future war, and even a victorious war might in Corti's opinion have 'fatal results' for the economy.[6]

Corti returned from Berlin hoping that he had achieved moderate success: Italy had acquired no new territory, but emerged with honour, dignity, and the esteem of other countries. Umberto and

the new prime minister, Benedetto Cairoli, agreed at first, perhaps reluctantly, that no more could have been done.[7] This was
also the initial view of the Italian ambassador in Berlin, Count De
Launay, and the ambassador in Vienna, General Di Robilant, two
strong monarchists who saw international problems at first hand
and thought that Corti's 'immense service to the country' would
be recognised by every serious Italian politician.[8]

But the government in Rome was unable or unwilling to restrain
the press from a frenzied outburst of irredentist feeling against
Austria, so destroying any good that had been done and causing the
king to change his mind over what soon became the main issue
in foreign policy. Some of the extreme patriots argued that if the
Trentino was not on offer, Corti could at least have used the occasion to annex somewhere else, perhaps Albania. Such a view was in
strident opposition to Garibaldi's belief that the Italian risorgimento,
being based on the principle of national self-determination, would
lose some of its justification if Italy attempted to annex other countries. But Garibaldi's opinion was drowned by the self-serving
rhetoric of politicians on the make. Realistic considerations told
equally against an expansionist policy. 'Italian politicians', said Corti,
'argue as if we were a rich, powerful, and prosperous country, when
they are but too well aware that we are weak, poor, and barely
constituted'.[9]

Such an accusation might have been directed against the king
himself whose opinions were often based on bad advice, inadequate
information, and a greatly over-simplified view of political questions.
Instead of proportioning foreign policy to available revenue and
resources, he assumed that taxes could without much difficulty be
raised to meet the requirements imposed by 'great-power status'.
Umberto spelt out in detail that he hoped to double the size of the
army by increasing military expenditure each year until he had an
effective front-line army of 500,000 men; he even mentioned a figure
of 750,000 as possible, adding in explanation that 'only the strong
were respected'.[10]

This objective was not shared by the realists who pointed out that
Italy was one of the few countries with no external danger to fear.[11]
But at court there was an alternative conviction that the army would
be required for its offensive and not merely defensive capacity, and
in any case would be needed to repress or discourage disorders at
home.[12] On the Left, too, Depretis accepted the force of this latter
point, and Crispi went much further in advocating that Italy must
somehow find the money to prepare for war.[13] Expenditure on the
army, which had decreased under the Right in the years immediately
before 1876, significantly increased after the Left came to power, and

this was another reason why Umberto was glad to support its continuance in office.[14]

Crispi was among those who believed that Italy, now that she claimed to be a great power, ought to join the scramble for colonies and reactivate in Tunisia and Libya the imperial traditions of ancient Rome. Vittorio Emanuele had toyed with the idea of a colony in Sumatra or New Guinea and had personally contributed funds to a geographical expedition for exploring East Africa.[15] The first practical move was made in 1869–70 when a private company at government expense set up a coaling station at Assab in the Red Sea. In public this was officially called a purely private venture by a commercial firm in what was technically Egyptian territory, but in fact from the very beginning the government prepared to assert Italian rights of territorial sovereignty.[16]

A more promising field of action was Tunisia where there existed a large and flourishing community of Italian settlers, and public opinion was allowed to believe that Italy's pre-emptive right to the annexation of Tunis was generally admitted. The Emperor Napoleon III had earlier been ready to support this claim at least in part, though he warned that it would cost more than the place was worth.[17] But the republican government in Paris after 1870 had a less generous policy and made clear that, while they did not intend to annex Tunisia, this North-African region must be an exclusively French sphere of interest, and Italians should rather look to Libya or Albania if they wanted a colony.[18] Only when Umberto and Cairoli took action to support a rival Italian claim did the French react by occupying Tunis in 1881.[19]

Such a setback created a dangerous mood of despondency in Rome and led to further questioning of current illusions about Italy's strength and internal cohesion. In retrospect the risorgimento was beginning to seem less glamorous and less successful than patriotic propaganda tried to claim. National unification could be seen as having succeeded mainly because of military victories by France and Prussia. There had been too little sacrifice on the part of Italians, and indeed the bulk of the population could be said to have looked on it with indifference if not hostility.[20]

This realisation was disillusioning and helped to harden some political attitudes. Perhaps a more authoritarian style of government would be needed so as to impose a clearer sense of national unity, quite apart from the need to withstand possible domestic disaffection from those who found little advantage or excitement in the national movement. Perhaps the monarchy, in order to survive, needed much greater prestige, and possibly Umberto lacked the gifts and strength of character that were required. To some people Italian self-esteem demanded that the country become more important in Europe and not be satisfied with neutrality like Belgium. Perhaps only a militarist or militarised nation would justify the entitlement to be numbered among the major powers in Europe.[21]

Failure to annex Tunisia was a blow to morale for those who had been led to expect much more than politicians could conceivably have delivered and who had been deceived about the realities of international politics. Parliament was as usual ill-informed about what was possible or desirable in foreign policy, in particular because such matters were held to be mainly the concern of the king and the executive. A further disappointment came in the following year when the government first offered to help the British in Egypt, and then refused an invitation from London to share in a military occupation aimed at defending the Suez canal. The king was advised to refuse this invitation by a specially convened crown council of senior politicians who argued that the possible gains would have been dubious and the expense enormous. But Crispi and Minghetti created an artificial sense of disappointment by calling the refusal a disastrous error. Pasquale Mancini, the foreign minister, tried to repair the damage and suggested entering into a formal alliance with England for joint action in the Middle East, until an outburst of anti-British feeling in the Italian press showed that there was too much mutual distrust.[22]

Queen Margherita, a stronger character than her husband and more tactless and outspoken, agreed with Vittorio Emanuele and Crispi that Italians would never be adequately respected until they could create a sense of alarm and trepidation in Europe.[23] Among her admirers were militant patriots who demanded another war to recover the self-confidence forfeited in the battles of Custoza and Lissa. Turiello bemoaned that not since the battle of Legnano in 1176 had Italians won a war without outside help; in his opinion only military victory would earn necessary prestige for the dynasty, and his personal wish was to make Italy not merely feared but actually hated. The populist deputy, Rocco De Zerbi, repeated Crispi's demand that Italians must strengthen their sense of nationality in a 'bath of blood'.[24]

Such demands were connected with the well-founded expectation that another war would one day be provoked by France to revenge her defeat by Germany in 1870. Crispi had come away from meeting Bismarck in 1877 convinced that Italy would in that case be welcomed as an ally on the German side. He had no idea of the impression he made in Berlin as an irresponsible and dangerous warmonger. Nor did he know that the Germans had reacted by telling Paris of his tactless suggestion about Italy's annexing French territory in Savoy.[25]

Umberto had other dynastic reasons for wanting an alliance with the German empire against France, especially as the republican government in Paris was believed to be subsidising an anti-monarchist movement inside Italy.[26] It was also known that Bismarck, despite his not very high opinion of Umberto or of Italy as a possible ally,[27] had good conservative reasons for wanting to help the Italian monarchy against republicanism, and was particularly anxious to prevent Italy from pursuing alternative irredentist ambitions against Germany's Austrian ally.[28]

Cairoli sympathised up to a point with irredentist aspirations to annex the Austrian provinces of Trentino and Trieste, and this was one reason why Umberto preferred the more amenable Depretis as prime minister. The king's instincts were rather to side with conservative and monarchist Austria against republican France, especially since he knew that irredentism was backed by anti-monarchist elements in Italy. His, moreover, was a decisive voice on such a matter, despite the fact that some deputies, not only on the Left, were once again agitating for parliament to be given more say in foreign affairs.[29] He believed that most Italians would want their representatives to present a united front with a single foreign policy well removed from party political differences, and such a policy would best be decided by the sovereign and his chief ministers with as little parliamentary intervention as possible.[30]

In 1882 his wishes prevailed when he signed with Germany and Austria a formal alliance that remained in force for the next thirty-three years. He used to claim that the main initiative for this Triple Alliance came from himself, and it seems that he overrode the objections or at least the reluctance of his prime minister.[31] In its unpublished preamble it stated that the defence of monarchy and social order was a principal objective which the three signatories shared in common. Another even more secret intention was to encourage Austria to move into the Balkans, because that would give Italy a claim to future territorial compensation nearer home.[32]

The Germans had some doubt whether any king of Italy was strong enough constitutionally to be a reliable ally, because parliaments were mutable and might one day disown his signature on a treaty. But Bismarck was assured that Umberto alone had the right to make treaties and was not obliged to consult or even inform parliament. In any case, so Berlin was told somewhat enigmatically, the king as commander of the armed forces could in the last resort rely on the army if his decisions over foreign policy were ever challenged.[33] In practice, the text of the Triple Alliance was kept secret for as long as it remained in force and was never thought to need parliamentary validation. Any public debate on such a fundamental fact of foreign policy would have called in question this central dogma of the royal prerogative and upset the balance of the constitution.

3 Depretis and the transformation of parties

Though the strength of republican sentiment was much exaggerated, the arch-republican Mazzini was widely revered after his death and enjoyed a reputation of being the chief ideologue and champion of Italian patriotism. Occasional cries of 'death to the king' and 'long live the republic' could sometimes be heard in the streets, and murmurs against the dynasty reached even the chamber of deputies itself.[1] A small radical group existed on the extreme left of parliament where Agostino Bertani and Felice Cavallotti continued to remind deputies of the fundamental contribution made by republicans to the risorgimento. These two radical politicians, while they continued to believe in a republic as ideally the best kind of government, nonetheless realistically accepted the monarchy as an established fact without which the preservation of a united Italian nation might be in doubt.[2]

This was a divisive issue inside groups on the extreme Left and therefore made the task of government easier. One prominent radical, Alberto Mario, never entered parliament because, although elected, he still conscientiously refused to take an oath of loyalty to the crown. Mario continued to resent the royalist and Piedmontese takeover of the risorgimento; he objected to the fact that most regiments in the army continued to have Piedmontese colonels and use the Piedmontese vernacular as the army's basic language of communication. His anti-monarchist journalism led to frequent sequestration of articles and even landed him in prison because his opinions singled him out as a possibly dangerous personality in politics.[3]

The less intransigent Cavallotti took the oath, albeit with mental reservations, and so obtained for his radical views a legal platform in parliament that was relatively free from censorship. Even when his poetry and theatrical writing led to prosecution for sedition, Cavallotti nearly always found juries to acquit him, and in practice discovered that he acquired notoriety without penalty if he hinted at the king's indecorous private life or compared the Savoy dynasty unfavourably with the authoritarian Neapolitan Bourbon king who had been deposed in 1860.[4] Moreover, in practical politics neither he nor Mario was the dangerous revolutionary that some of the ultra-monarchists pretended to think.

Garibaldi was another critic who won immunity from prosecution both by his membership of parliament and as a national hero whose enthusiastic support from public opinion made him hard to attack. Garibaldi accepted the monarchy and split away from Mazzini's 'pure republicans', but before his death in 1882 had begun to campaign once more for a constituent assembly to devise a truly democratic constitution. He was able to repeat quite openly that, if Italians were despised abroad and if many seemed more impoverished than they had been under absolutist governments before 1860, the dynasty must be largely to blame. Umberto was accused by this prominent radical of hiding behind the deceptive façade of 'ministerial responsibility' and of governing through flatterers and 'court lackeys' who depended on the army to keep popular disaffection in check. Garibaldi added the warning that monarchies were not eternal and might be toppled if they acted in defiance of public opinion.[5]

Garibaldi's was a prominent but lonely voice in politics. His former friend Depretis, who was prime minister for most of the decade after 1878, had reneged on much of his early radicalism and like nearly all prominent parliamentarians was by now a dedicated monarchist. Although Umberto once made an ineffectual attempt to ignore parliament and bring back an administration of the Right under Sella, the palace was generally content with a succession of short governments under Depretis and Cairoli on the Left. If cabinets continued to change each year – five under Depretis and three under Cairoli between 1876 and 1883 – that was because of an inherent instability caused by the fact that Left and Right were both divided into many small personal factions, all of them ready to barter their support so as to secure the perquisites of office or to prevent a return of their opponents to power.

The existence of small political groups was encouraged by the fact that Catholics were instructed by their bishops not to vote, with the result that the largest of all potential parties was excluded from national politics, which also meant that the liberals lacked an incentive to combine against clerical influence. Another relevant fact was that political groups continued to be sometimes regional rather than nationwide, and also were personalised round an individual group-leader rather than based on any clear political principle. Elections to parliament were regulated by a system of *ballottaggio* which required repeated votes until one candidate had an absolute majority, and this practice gave an extra representation to minority parties by allowing them to combine or to bargain their support at a second or third vote.[6] As these groups achieved most influence if they periodically shifted their allegiance, it was hard for any government to find a settled parliamentary majority, and the consequent formation of transient coalitions contributed to the apparent instability that characterised Italian politics under both Right and Left.

Many politicians continued to deprecate coalition governments as short-lived, unreliable, and contrasting with the practice in some other countries of an alternation between large parties with more or less distinct policies.[7] Depretis theoretically shared this nostalgic regret for a two-party system. So, again in theory, did the conservatives Minghetti and Spaventa; and so did Crispi and Giovanni Giolitti, the two most prominent politicians of the future.[8] But the practice of quick-changing and heterogeneous coalitions, which by 1883 had earned the derogatory name of 'transformism', had deep roots in conservative administrations before 1876 and was indeed recognised as deriving from Cavour himself.[9] Depretis realistically accepted transformism as a fact of life and perfected the art of shifting his coalition to right or left so as to propitiate as many groups as possible, thereby winning for himself a paramount position in parliament for the ten years until his death in 1887.[10]

Critics of this process were able to hint that transformism might bring the monarchy into discredit by associating Umberto with an unprincipled and sometimes corrupt form of politics, but he saw things differently. After at first complaining that Depretis was failing to use the prefects to prevent election of radicals from the extreme Left, he came round to accept the explanation that 'these men were better in parliament than out of it' and would there acquire 'more reasonable principles'. Learning from experience he eventually expressed 'unbounded confidence' in Depretis's practice of including in his cabinet men of differing views.[11] Since a rough consensus in the centre might help to keep the royal prerogative out of political controversy, it could only be welcome that Minghetti and Sonnino of the Right should give more or less active support to governments that were predominantly from the Left; and even more welcome when the Church let it be known that, notwithstanding papal condemnation of the 'usurper' who had seized Rome, critics of royal authority might also be enemies of the authoritarian Vatican.[12]

A broad consensus between many politicians on Right and Left was revealed in the widespread support for Depretis's programme of suffrage reform and compulsory education. The pope objected to compulsory state education as a 'disaster' that would damage Church schools, and another substantial objection was that a better-educated electorate might challenge the *notabili* who had hitherto enjoyed a monopoly of political power in local government;[13] but many people backed educational reform for these same reasons and it passed into law by an overwhelming majority.

Other objections were raised to a widening of the parliamentary suffrage, because anti-clericals argued that it would enfranchise the strongly Catholic peasantry. On the other hand, even the conservative Sonnino felt obliged to criticise as inequitable and dangerous the existing practice by which only one citizen out of every ninety voted in elections. Poor people had to pay taxes and serve in the army, but deprived of representation in parliament they had a legitimate grievance; they might therefore possess insufficient affection for the monarchy or for parliamentary institutions; and hence many conservatives supported a law of 1882 that widened the franchise from 600,000 to about two million electors out of a population of some thirty millions.[14]

Depretis was twelve times a minister as well as prime minister in eight cabinets, and this gave him the opportunity to introduce necessary reforms. But because of his versatile management of multiform coalitions he went down in history as the great corrupter of politics. Though honest in private life, he frankly admitted that as a practical politician he was obliged to exploit the avarice and careerism of others,[15] and the kind of persons elected to parliament were often ready to accept minor bribes and favours.[16] One ministerial colleague criticised him for 'an abasement of moral and political principle, a tendency always to follow the line which for the moment appeared more likely to conduce to obtaining power and to holding it'.[17] But it was hard to envisage how else, given the necessary practice of coalition government, he could have carried out his programme of reform.

Ruggero Bonghi, a conservative ex-minister who sometimes supported Depretis, wrote in 1884 of the 'decadence of the parliamentary regime',[18] and this same theme became a general topic of discourse in the writings of other commentators on the Right, notably Jacini, Mosca, Spaventa, and Turiello. Too many deputies were beneficiaries of the system of transformism and, in expectation of favours to come, tended to switch support to every successive government of whatever complexion. Deputies needed official support for their candidature at the next election and were often ready to trade their vote accordingly. But their allegiance was superficial and would very generally change when the king chose a new prime minister, because matters of principle and policy took second place or were not always clearly identified between one government and the next. Many deputies spoke infrequently in parliament, some never, and some leading politicians attended debates rarely when out of office. Ministers therefore could afford to treat the chamber without much respect. Criticism of official policy was neither encouraged nor valued, and if any deputy accused a minister of disregarding the rights of the legislature he could be silenced by an over-zealous Speaker on the trumped-up pretext of violating parliamentary regulations.[19]

One area where the government acted on its own with only minimal parliamentary consultation was Africa, in particular when Assab was claimed as Italy's first colony in what later became Eritrea. This was a bold claim, because Assab in 1882 was under nominal Turkish and actual Egyptian sovereignty, as well as being claimed by the Abyssinians. The Italian government tried to tranquillise the outside world by undertaking 'in the most categoric and peremptory manner' that Assab would always remain a commercial station with no Italian sovereignty and no military garrison.[20] In addition, a legend was invented that the British had invited or even forced Italy to create this colony;[21] whereas in fact they had warned that it might prove to be a mistaken adventure, and were pacified only after being promised that Turkish suzerainty would remain intact.[22]

Some Italians agreed that this colony might be a mistake and others rejected all colonisation on principle.[23] Nevertheless, Crispi insisted that Italy needed a colony to justify her new status in the world; nor was he alone in pretending, against all appearances, that public opinion 'almost unanimously' supported this view. Some isolated voices went further by demanding 'methods of terror' to subjugate the populations of East Africa.[24] In December 1884 a cabinet meeting, presided over by Umberto, decided to send a military expedition to Beilul and Massawa further along the East-African coast. The king's attitude was once again thought to be a determining factor in this decision, and certainly he was much keener than Depretis.[25]

Apart from these two, only the foreign minister Mancini and the minister of war had much idea of what Italian troops were meant to do at Massawa,[26] and perhaps not even they were completely sure. The fact that the commanding officer was left in doubt about their intentions suggests that very little thought had gone into the matter.[27] Parliament was given a promise that no unbudgeted expenditure or further military operations were intended and the soldiers were needed only for garrison duties.[28] But Mancini's private papers show that his secret but vague plan was to move either into the Sudan or towards Abyssinia with the hope of establishing a much more substantial military presence over a large area of East Africa.[29]

In view of Crispi's colonial aspirations and future behaviour, it is strange to recall his immediate reaction that this open-ended and expensive decision was misguided, and also his strong criticism that it was made without parliamentary approval. His argument now, quite unlike what he would say later, was that, whatever the letter of the constitution said about the king's personal prerogative to declare war, it must be wrong for a government to start an offensive military campaign in violation of Turkish sovereignty without consulting parliament and without asking for the necessary funds.[30]

Millions of lire in fact were soon being spent arbitrarily without the parliamentary consent that the constitution prescribed.[31] Mancini admitted as much. He also repeated the claim that colonisation was supported by a unanimous public opinion,[32] though others believed that this was almost the opposite of the truth and that the serious impulse came 'from higher quarters', in other words from the palace.[33] Unfortunately, once troops had landed, there was little chance of backing down with dignity, so that members of parliament, not for the last time, had to give retrospective consent to an ill-considered commitment about which they were still told almost nothing.

The same search for national prestige soon led successive governments to assume that, after meeting local resistance, honour demanded further 'punitive expeditions' into the highlands of the Eritrean interior. The king's speech to parliament in June 1886 called for more taxation to enlarge the army and defend the flag, after which the new foreign minister, General Di Robilant, caused amused commiseration in parliament when he disparaged by comparison the unwarlike failure of Britain to revenge the death of General Gordon in Khartoum.[34] Di Robilant was close to Umberto and as an army officer had a special obligation of obedience to the crown. He had opposed the occupation of Massawa on grounds of military prudence and at first tried to make his appointment as foreign minister conditional on a withdrawal, only accepting office when Umberto gave him a positive order. He was therefore very much a representative of the court. In his opinion the king, not parliament or the cabinet or 'so-called public opinion', should decide foreign and colonial policy, and this was a doctrine with which Mancini entirely agreed.[35]

To Di Robilant in 1887 fell the task of renewing the Triple Alliance with Germany and Austria, and he negotiated with success, increasing the obligations of these two countries to Italy without extending Italy's corresponding commitments. The two houses of parliament were still left completely ignorant of what promises were made in this treaty, to uphold which they would be expected to find the funds; and one deputy remarked that only in Italy was such arbitrary behaviour possible.[36] Nevertheless a comforting if inaccurate assumption was allowed to circulate that her two powerful allies must have underwritten Italian expansion along the Red Sea coast.

Allied support appeared all the more necessary when, early in 1887, a column of Italian troops moving inland from Massawa ran into a much larger Abyssinian force at Dogali and was destroyed. So little was known in Rome about what was happening that Di Robilant, speaking a few hours before hearing of this defeat, was able to tell the chamber that the 'rebels' would be easily defeated and punished. Mancini tried to blame Abyssinia for what he called 'an iniquitous and treacherous piece of aggression of a kind that ought to be impossible between truly civilised peoples'.[37] The queen joined those who demanded a war of revenge,[38] and Crispi, to loud applause, insisted that 'our national flag must be respected even by savages'.[39] When other deputies protested that Italian soldiers were being sent to die for an unknown cause without parliamentary consent and in defiance of Egyptian and Turkish sovereignty, they were reproved by the Speaker for lack of patriotism.[40]

Opinions were of course divided. Some politicians perversely put the blame for military defeat on those deputies who criticised and weakened the hand of the executive.[41] Others more persuasively blamed the king and the executive for irresponsibly acting in defiance of public opinion. A particular target of criticism was what was becoming known as 'the court party', with its evident disdain for the niceties of parliamentary government,[42] and some deputies began to talk of a deliberate attempt by the ultra-royalists to change the balance of the constitution.[43] On the conservative benches there were responsible politicians nevertheless who advanced military reasons against the folly of challenging the large Abyssinian army, because it was hardly possible that this fierce people would ever voluntarily submit to having its main outlet to the coast cut off by an invading Italian army.[44]

In February 1887, faced by mounting opposition, an ailing Depretis offered to resign, and Di Robilant left office very indignant at receiving no support from the palace. For the next month Umberto tried to construct another coalition that would take responsibility for carrying out his wishes, and there was apprehension that he might be using this crisis to impose a more authoritarian kind of government.[45] In particular he tried to persuade Crispi to join the same government as Depretis – despite the fact that these two politicians regularly voted against each other in parliament. Crispi at first held out on the pretence that he was dogmatically against coalitions between politicians of differing views, but in April accepted, only after making clear that he intended to have a deciding voice in policy. Three months later, when the elderly Depretis died, Crispi became prime minister for the first time, just short of his sixty-eighth birthday.

4   Crispi, 1887–91

The new premier was a remarkable personality who dominated Italian politics for the next ten years. He had moved a long way from his early republicanism, though he continued to maintain that the republican Mazzini was the greatest Italian of the century. He also moved away from his belief in parliamentary supremacy. One reason for becoming a loyal servant of the crown was his hope that the monarchy stood for strong government at home and an expansionist policy abroad. Not that he shared Turiello's mystical and autocratic idea of kingship. Although Crispi lacked a personal following in parliament and was himself very much a royal appointment, he was reluctant to share power even with a king. Certainly he aimed to increase Umberto's popularity, but his ideal form of government was a limited monarchy where the king would be obliged to follow the advice of a strong minister, and sometimes he was ready to say that without such a minister the dynasty might not survive.[1]

Crispi was soon being called a dictator, indeed a reactionary dictator, who imposed policy and bothered little about consent. Yet whatever his behaviour, he never entirely renounced some of the radical principles of his youth, and the king appointed him in full knowledge of this fact. As prime minister he still believed, or rather claimed to believe, in free speech, minimal use of police action, radical social reform, abolishing capital punishment, and enlarging the powers of local elected authorities at the expense of central government. At first he also claimed to believe in an omnipotent parliament and to have no wish to play the dictator. In practice, however, his authoritarian temperament and immense self-confidence belied his liberal theories, and the contradiction became clearer when he found the king strongly behind him.

As well as being prime minister, Crispi took the posts of minister of the interior and foreign minister, despite objections against a concentration of power that had not been seen since the time of Cavour. In addition to boasting that he had already done more for Italy than anyone else, he justified these multiple appointments by insisting that he alone was competent to run foreign and domestic policy, all the more so since he found that the foreign office took up very little of a minister's time.[2] Not everyone at court liked having to deal with such a self-confident and unsubmissive person, and offence was taken when he demanded that the queen should invite his much-disliked wife to receptions at the palace. But in the course of time it became clear that the king not only lacked the strength of will to stand up to him, but was positively grateful to have a chief minister who, as well as simplifying or over-simplifying problems, knew his own mind and was ready to act forcefully.[3]

The office of prime minister had already been given greater pre-eminence over other ministers by a royal decree of August 1876, and it is noteworthy that this change in the constitution, which became the basis of Crispi's 'parliamentary dictatorship', had not needed submission to the legislature for approval. A new style of prime-ministerial government, as some people soon recognised, threatened to reduce the authority of the king as well as of parliament.[4] 'Characteristically', quoted the British minister in Rome, Crispi said 'I am Italian policy and Italian policy is myself'.[5] With such a degree of self-assurance he frequently treated the chamber with condescension or even contempt and publicly asserted his readiness to overrule its decisions and legislate by royal decree. At least on one occasion he abused the Speaker with such vehemence that the parliamentary record had to be altered to conceal his words.[6]

Crispi explained that the practice of politics must change to take account of the fact that the categories of Right and Left carried less and less meaning. Constitutional government, according to his eccentric view, implied 'substituting the despotism of a minister for the despotism of a king'; though he added, not very plausibly, that he hoped for the eventual reappearance of better organised conservative and radical parties which one day would make parliamentary government more of a reality.[7]

Crispi 'has no personal following', reported one detached observer; 'his majority is made up of a variety of groups', and what kept him in power is that 'there is practically no serious constitutional opposition in the sense of a party capable or willing to take office in the event of the defeat of the ministry'.[8] This lack of organised parties enabled or perhaps compelled him to adopt the tactics of transformism and, notwithstanding his earlier criticism of Depretis for doing the same, to continue the practice of periodically changing his coalition to include politicians of widely differing opinions.

Umberto could admit in private that he was not always happy with Crispi's arbitrary methods of government, but there was no obvious alternative and 'we had better have him with us than against us'.[9] Individual voices vainly protested that the prime minister was becoming drunk with power. He often showed little respect for the constitutional rights of public assembly and press freedom. He circumvented parliamentary control over expenditure when he needed money for Africa. If he foresaw any danger of a hostile vote in parliament he would resign before it took place, which permitted the king to reappoint him with a new coalition to include some opponents as a way of disarming the critics; and on one such occasion he even had the effrontery to tell the deputies that a hostile vote would have been unpatriotic and against the national interest.[10]

King and minister found common ground over foreign affairs when Crispi denounced the policy of 'clean hands' that Umberto now regretted having initially supported at the Congress of Berlin. Italy in Crispi's view should not be satisfied with political unity but must aim at military victories and 'grandeur'; she was not a second-rank power, nor like the Belgium or Switzerland that he despised as unwarlike, but rather had the capacity for conquering an empire. The ancient Romans had pointed the way, and he thought it tragic that, after discovering America in the fifteenth century, Italians had failed to create their own empire in the New World.[11] They must not fail to create one in Africa, and he had no patience with those who argued that Italy lacked the resources to support an imperial policy: such a pacifist argument he took to be merely a pretext of rich people who disliked the higher taxation it would involve.[12]

One of Crispi's first acts in government was to visit Germany. He was anxious to show his admiration for Bismarck and for the German practice that allowed parliament only a minor role in government;[13] but this visit had an additional and practical purpose. Earlier, when still in opposition, he had criticised as shameful the Triple Alliance with Germany;[14] now, as a minister, he preferred to seek Bismarck's backing against France and took with him to Berlin a proposal about how they might provoke France into starting a European war. He copied Umberto in boasting that in six months' time he would double the Italian army, and somewhat frivolously promised to send five army corps to Germany when war broke out. The German chancellor agreed to sign a military convention to this effect, but in fact distrusted such belligerent talk and insisted that there must be no war until Germany saw it to be in her own interests. Although Crispi of course consulted Umberto and obtained agreement on a policy of gradual mobilisation for war, there seems to have been some lack of enthusiasm in court circles for the unsubtle and undiplomatic manner in which this delicate mission to Berlin was conducted.[15]

On returning home, Crispi set himself the task of trying to isolate France and increase international tension. He took steps to intensify a tariff war with the French which he said would greatly benefit the Italian economy – despite the fact that Italian exports to France were proportionally far larger than French exports to Italy. The country suffered severely from this brave but miscalculated and provocative policy. As he informed the German ambassador, war would sooner or later be necessary to create a more genuine or more useful balance of power in Europe. To the British he spoke contemptuously of France and talked of a plan for 'bringing her to her knees', which provoked the pungent comment that 'Crispi is unfitted for the position of minister for foreign affairs in which he delights'.[16]

Misgivings in London were heightened when the British in 1888 were asked to send urgently part of their fleet to foil what Crispi said was an imminent French naval bombardment in the gulf of Genoa: warships were sent at considerable expense, only to discover that the scare had no other basis than an unconfirmed rumour heard inside the Vatican. This unfortunate episode caused surprise and embarrassment to the king and his ministers when much too late the matter was mentioned to the cabinet.[17]

Italian foreign policy suffered by thus acquiring in London a reputation for both gullibility and adventurousness. Hitherto, the friendship of Britain had been taken for granted by every Italian government in turn. Umberto said that England of all countries 'had his greatest esteem and admiration'.[18] Depretis, too, had earlier admitted that, despite allying with Germany and Austria, he regarded England as Italy's 'best friend' and believed, or at least was reported as saying, that the Mediterranean 'must always be an English lake'.[19] In the same spirit, Italy's partners in the Triple Alliance had already been warned that Italians would never fight against Britain, and hints were sometimes dropped in London that a formal treaty with the British would be welcomed.[20]

Crispi on becoming prime minister made overtures in this sense. But the reply came that, while England had more friendly feelings for Italy than for any other country, and while she was likely to help if Italy suffered aggression, she 'never promised material assistance in view of an uncertain war of which the object and cause were unknown'. This reply did not stop Crispi from pretending to Berlin and Vienna that he had a promise of active support from the British navy. He told Umberto that a written promise to this effect had arrived from London: in his opinion the Italian and British fleets would work together to dominate the whole Mediterranean.[21]

The king apparently believed him, but few other people can have done so. The British already distrusted him as 'the greatest firebrand in all Italy, which is not saying a little', and although his accession to power had at first been welcomed as that of an anglophile, his conspiratorial temperament quickly confirmed the impression that he was a bombastic, dangerous, and unserious statesman.[22] Lord Salisbury continued to trust Umberto as a restraining influence on Crispi's desire for war, and by the end of 1888 the British were hoping that this headstrong minister would be removed before permanent damage was done.[23] Italy had no natural enemies, wrote Gladstone, and yet gratuitously abandoned this immense advantage, with the result that no one could any longer accept Cavour's argument about a united Italy becoming a force for peace; instead, 'the demon of ambition and of grasping at other peoples' soil has entered the hearts of Italian leaders since 1876', so that they must be treated with suspicion and perhaps hostility.[24]

This change in attitude was regrettable and may help to explain why Umberto spent several weeks in March 1889 looking unsuccessfully for a new prime minister. If Crispi nevertheless remained in office, that was because despite all his defects he was a sincere patriot, a man of great drive, who had the gift of inspiring many members of parliament and cowing others into general acquiescence. He was hopeful that the breach with the British did not run too deep, and in this expectation he had the great advantage of intercepting secret reports sent to London from the British embassy in Rome.[25]

He enjoyed the further advantage that ties with Germany became stronger in 1888 when a new and more belligerent emperor succeeded to the throne in Berlin. The young Wilhelm on a visit to Italy in October signed a photograph for Crispi with the ominous words 'au gentilhomme, gentilhomme; au corsaire, corsaire et demi'.[26] Wilhelm talked scornfully to the Italians about his British grandmother, that 'fat dumpling' Queen Victoria, and spoke with positive hatred against France. Representative institutions, the emperor told them, should be recognised as worse than useless: one day he and Umberto would enter Paris as conquerors, and he hoped that the victorious Italian army would then be used in Rome to put parliament in its place.[27]

Umberto was somewhat scandalised by this characteristic outburst, but was inclined to agree that the Italian parliament was not working well and made governing the country difficult. He accepted the need to consolidate support for the monarchic principle in Europe by holding fast to the Triple Alliance, and promised that he would never permit ministers to renege on what was an essentially dynastic partnership.[28] Crispi needed little persuading and went again to see Bismarck in May 1889. Once more he raised the question of Italian claims to Nice, Tunis, and Corsica in the event of a major war,[29] but found Bismarck still unwilling to underwrite such an acquisitive and aggressive policy. One deputy in Rome, who criticised this visit as an act of servility to a foreign power, was silenced for using what was once again called 'unparliamentary language'.[30]

Confidence in the German alliance suffered a setback in 1890 when Bismarck quite unexpectedly fell from power, and Crispi may have feared that he himself was similarly vulnerable. But Umberto in fact criticised Wilhelm for not supporting his chief minister.[31] Crispi now tried to convince the French that he had no hostile intentions, evidently unaware that his secret belligerent plans were known in Paris.[32] But simultaneously he again attacked those Italians who wanted a more neutral position in Europe, and in private continued to assume that war against France was not far off. He relied on active intervention by the palace in preparing for this war, and told an incredulous Umberto that an attack by the French was imminent. He also used the not very persuasive argument that, so long as France remained a republic, the survival of the Italian monarchy was in doubt.[33]

Opposition inside Italy to the Triple Alliance came principally from radicals and republicans who still hoped to win Trent and Trieste from Austria. In great secrecy Crispi subsidised these irredentists so as to keep their anti-Austrian policy as a possible option for the future,[34] but officially he repudiated them. He knew that Germany stood behind Austria, and also feared that any premature break-up of the Austrian empire would leave Italy's north-eastern frontier exposed to a new and perhaps greater danger from the Slavs.

On this issue he was characteristically two-faced, if not contradictory. Although he knew that the alliance with Vienna was hardly popular in Italy, he promised the Austrians that they could count on immediate help from the Italian army in any war against Russia and Turkey.[35] He believed that one day the Austrian empire would disintegrate of its own accord, but until then, with the king's full support, he was ready to suppress any public irredentist demonstrations in Italy. Without waiting to consult his colleagues he even persuaded Umberto to issue a royal decree dismissing a ministerial colleague who presumed to question this policy.[36]

Another official dismissed by Umberto from a senior position in the army was General Mattei, a member of parliament who had been rash enough to tell journalists that the army was costing more than the country could afford.[37] Military expenditure had almost doubled since the Triple Alliance was signed in 1882, and though Crispi denied that the two facts were linked, his denial seemed inherently improbable. The British chargé d'affaires took note that some of this expenditure lacked parliamentary approval; and the same diplomat reported that the minister in charge of the navy, Admiral Brin, agreed in private that military expenses were kept unnecessarily high by the exigencies of the German alliance. 'The great ambition of Signor Crispi and perhaps the mainspring of his actions is to obtain a military success for Italy, no matter where or how'; but by this policy he had 'systematically sacrificed the true interests of Italy to his personal ambition'. He was a 'windbag' and 'humbug' who was leading the country to ruin by attempting to emulate Bismarck in a 'restless anxiety for self-glorification'.[38]

While critics talked of Crispi as a megalomaniac, he was greatly admired by others as a man of vision who accepted a 'mission' of conquest in Africa and eastern Europe. He told people that Italy must not only be ready to stake her territorial claims when the inevitable clash came with France, but one day the succession to Constantinople would be open when the collapse of the Turkish empire permitted a new dispensation in the Balkans from which Italy could profit. Crispi despised Depretis and Giolitti who doubted whether the country was rich enough to manage such a policy. He himself on the contrary preferred to consider Italy as possessing 'an immense economic potential': one day she would be among the richest countries in the world and indeed should aim at being second to none; she must have a large army and a large navy to make herself feared 'by everyone'.[39]

His first colonial venture was in East Africa where another military expedition arrived at the end of 1887 to revenge the defeat of Dogali. The admitted motive for this costly operation was to punish the 'barbarians' who had been guilty of 'unjust aggression' against Italian soldiers.[40] He was warned that it might turn out to be a dangerous move from which he could never retreat without further loss of face,[41] but he reassured any doubters that the risks had been precisely calculated: he promised that he had no intention of trying to conquer Abyssinia, which indeed would be 'madness', nor would the expeditionary force remain in Eritrea once honour had been vindicated.[42]

This assurance was almost certainly insincere and merely designed to thwart criticism in parliament, and a year later the deputies were still asking when or whether these troops would ever be withdrawn. Gradually it emerged that Crispi had altogether renounced his earlier doubts about colonialism and already had other projects in mind. In 1889 he claimed an Italian protectorate over part of Somalia and was with difficulty restrained from ordering a naval bombardment of Zanzibar. He also allocated funds to assert an Italian presence in Morocco and Tripoli, two countries that no other colonialist power had yet occupied.

His true objectives were known to few people apart from the king, yet they reflected the wishes of the 'court party' and a small group of politicians who advocated ignoring the methods of diplomacy and using armed force to impose Italian sovereignty in Africa. De Zerbi in May 1888 repeated his earlier demand for a purging bath of blood, arguing that failure to expand would amount to national suicide, and insisting that only colonial conquests would win sufficient prestige for the crown. Crispi even advanced the implausible claim that the growing tide of Italian emigrants, instead of going to America, would find ample room to settle and prosper in what soon became known as Eritrea. Colonial expansion, he said, was also a necessary prerequisite for 'social pacification' at home. Others used the equally far-fetched argument that Eritrea, as well as becoming economically self-sufficient, would provide Italy with a native army for use in a future European war.[43]

Regrettably these improbable claims could not be fully discussed and tested in parliamentary debate. Crispi in opposition had formerly maintained that any military action in Africa needed prior discussion and consent by parliament,[44] but once in office preferred to seek approval only retrospectively or when it was too late for anyone to protest. Nor did he dare to admit in public that he was bent on further territorial conquest. He preferred to rely on the convention that the king's right to declare and conduct war was absolute and could not be challenged in parliament without violating the constitution. Newspapers could sometimes take the risk of ascribing the loss of life in Africa to 'high personages who are said to be beyond criticism and whom we are not allowed to mention'; inside parliament, however, similar guarded references were out of order and could be struck from the record.[45]

Umberto was not much concerned with public opinion and in any case was largely insulated at court from critical voices. As he had little taste for reading, he possibly did not even follow the transcriptions of parliamentary debates, otherwise he might have suspected that there was only limited popular enthusiasm for African adventures. Some responsible politicians, including cabinet ministers, pointed out that Eritrea had far too inhospitable a climate to become a colony of settlement for even as few as one per cent of Italian emigrants; also that the treasury was much too poor to sustain an ambitious colonial policy, while another military reverse might have grave results on national morale and cause dangerous disaffection at home.[46]

Crispi knew of these criticisms but was either too cocksure or too fearful to heed them, and he repeatedly told deputies that they had no right to discuss matters that came under the royal prerogative.[47] He took pride in saying that he no longer bothered to read newspapers, though was careful to use his press office and the Stefani news agency to slant reports and censor information sent home from East Africa.[48] Cavallotti, the leader of the radical Left, was once again ruled out of order in parliament when he accused the prime minister of twisting news by corruptly subsidising the press, until it was shown that Crispi had not been silenced when making the same accusation against former prime ministers. The Milanese *Corriere della Sera* spoke for a growing number of establishment readers, especially among the rich burghers of Milan, who criticised the cost and the cost-effectiveness of the government's African policy. The radical *Secolo*, also of Milan, which claimed a million readers, kept its own correspondent in the British protectorate of Aden so as to bypass the censorship and was thus able to report that the military situation in Eritrea was far worse than the general public was allowed to know.[49]

In May 1889 the king signed the Treaty of Uccialli with Menelik who, with the aid of Italian money and weapons, had just won the imperial crown of Abyssinia. Umberto wrote to Menelik to say that another consignment of arms was being sent from Italy to confirm their alliance. Crispi claimed that there was no constitutional obligation to bring this treaty before parliament since no costs were involved that the deputies needed to know about. He merely informed them, inaccurately, that its terms bound Menelik to regard Abyssinia as an Italian protectorate and to 'assist Italy's plans for conquest in Africa', which made their position far more secure than that of other colonialist powers of Africa.[50] A novel doctrine, later challenged by the lawyers, claimed that Eritrea lay outside the provisions of the Italian constitution: so long as military operations continued, this colony could be governed directly and absolutely by the king as commander-in-chief, so that any detailed parliamentary discussion would be irrelevant as well as harmful to the national interest.[51]

The prime minister therefore refused outright to accept a motion that demanded that further expansion in Africa would need parliamentary sanction, and by threatening resignation won this highly dubious point. The minority who voted against him on the issue included the radical Cavallotti and the socialist Andrea Costa, but also leading conservatives such as Di Rudinì, Bonghi, Luzzatti, Prinetti, and Tittoni, all of them former or future ministers.

Without waiting for the vote, Crispi overrode objections from army leaders and his own minister of war by sending secret instructions to march on Asmara in the highlands of the interior.[52] Most of his colleagues opposed this at a cabinet meeting, arguing that it might invite another humiliating defeat, and were surprised to find that he proceeded to act against their opinion; when they protested that he almost never consulted them and took no account of their views, he confidently predicted that in ten months' time Abyssinia would have ceased to exist. An imperial Italy, he explained, 'needed more air for her lungs'.[53] Such enviable certainty appealed to Umberto who congratulated his prime minister on the treaty with

Menelik and the successful occupation of Asmara, only wondering if it would not be wise to take advantage of this success to move yet further inland.[54]

Menelik, however, the man whom Crispi now called his cordial friend but would before long be denouncing as another barbarian chieftain, indicated that his copy of the Treaty of Uccialli said nothing about Abyssinia being an Italian protectorate, and this at once raised doubts about whether either the Italian or the Amharic text had been deliberately falsified. Crispi could not admit the possibility of a mistake over so vital a point. He was not particularly keen to advance too far away from the coast, yet in January 1890 sent his congratulations when the army defied Menelik by temporarily occupying the Abyssinian village of Adowa. There were protests in parliament, because any more moves into unknown territory might gratuitously challenge not only Menelik but the dervishes in the Sudan, another of the more warlike peoples of Africa. Other colonial enthusiasts on the contrary were excited by the ease of this success and advocated further military action until a signal victory had fully revenged the defeat of Dogali.

Early in 1890 Crispi was rash enough to announce that the enlarged colony of Eritrea was unassailable. He would not need to come to parliament for more money since Eritrea would soon be paying for itself, and in any case its administration 'was entirely a matter for the king', not for parliament. He added that Italy's position was envied by the British who felt themselves far more vulnerable in Egypt. He assumed that Italy was in a position to dominate not only Abyssinia but the Sudan, and claimed that the British had forfeited their rights in that area, so that Italy was entitled to take their place.[55] Probably he never understood that British politicians were moved less by envy than by a growing fear that his 'suicidal African ambitions' would unsettle the whole area. Only his fall from power in January 1891 removed the risk of a serious collision between these two colonial powers.

5   Two interim governments

Crispi fell because he had taken parliamentary support too much for granted, failing to realise that once an election in November 1890 had given him an overwhelming majority, individual deputies no longer immediately needed his electoral support. He had alienated the Left by what he now referred to as his conservative domestic policies. Then on 31 January 1891 he proceeded to offend the Right when in a typically bad-tempered outburst he taunted them for damaging the country's reputation by servility to France and inadequate spending on the armed services. This remark may have been a momentary lapse, or possibly it was made deliberately as an excuse to form a new government with a differently balanced coalition. After a hostile vote he resigned, but at once tried to convince the king that he was the only conceivable candidate for the succession.[1]

Umberto, according to some politicians, was now more anxious to assert himself against his ministers in the same way as he had seen Wilhelm act against Bismarck. Lacking a clear parliamentary indication for a successor he was free to make up his own mind, and far from accepting Crispi's self-evaluation, let it be known that he blamed the outgoing ministers for mismanaging foreign policy, just as he had blamed Di Robilant four years earlier. They had damaged Italy's reputation by their aggressiveness. In addition, he had felt personally insulted when Crispi addressed him 'with an incredible violence of language prompted by an exaggerated and morbid conceit of his own abilities'.[2]

The Marquis Antonio Di Rudini, a liberal conservative from Sicily, was therefore chosen as prime minister, and many deputies who had recently been elected with Crispi's support quickly changed to applaud the next incumbent as a new fount of patronage. Crispi reacted with bitterness, referring to his sovereign as a 'simpleton' who not only lacked a proper sense of national grandeur and put the interests of monarchy above patriotism, but also let himself be guided 'by false scruples about parliamentary government that had no place in a new country such as Italy'. Writing to the king he protested that not parliament but the palace ought to decide foreign policy, and the country would expect the monarch to thwart Di Rudini's 'pernicious' attitude of friendliness to France.[3] Fortunately for Crispi's reputation, these injudicious remarks did not become public knowledge.

The new government was generally welcomed in Europe. To the Germans, Di Rudinì was someone who unlike Crispi accepted that the Triple Alliance was meant for mutual protection, not as an aggressive 'profit-making concern'. To the British he was 'a gentleman, preferable to his predecessor in every respect', who might even come round to see the German alliance as 'no better than a gigantic piece of political tomfoolery'.[4] But the Triple Alliance was renewed in 1891, and Umberto showed once again that he saw it as primarily a dynastic treaty for the defence of monarchy in Europe.[5] The renewal was not discussed in cabinet because it was again stated that foreign affairs were for the king rather than ministers to decide. Some of the deputies protested once more that they were being secretly committed to a completely unknown policy. Some called it evidence of 'servility' to Germany and were officially censured for using an 'unparliamentary' term.[6] The word 'servility' was permissible when Crispi used it of his political opponents; not when others seemed to be hinting at criticism of the crown.

Africa was a particular area where the king's reputation was immediately involved. Some politicians could admit that Eritrea was 'a blank cheque on the future that might cost untold money and blood'; nevertheless, to give it up would be damaging to Italian prestige and that of the palace.[7] Di Rudinì accepted that the colony offered no hope of an economic return, yet though he would have liked to surrender it or possibly sell it to the British, and although the military chiefs of staff would have preferred to hold only the coastal town of Massawa, sadly such choices would by now have meant an unacceptable loss of face.[8] He could therefore do little more than repair some of the damage by halting any further military action, temporarily at least. He was also courageous enough to set up an enquiry into accusations of torture and murder and corrupt financial practices that had been levelled against Crispi's colonial administration: the revelations were horrendous and came as a great shock to public opinion.[9]

Di Rudinì lasted fourteen months in office. His colleagues came mainly from the conservative wing of politics, but he had to include Baron Nicotera from the Left so as to obtain sufficient parliamentary support. He was warned from the first that such a coalition might spell impotence, because agreed policies would be hard to find and he would not be backed by a disciplined majority in parliament. In practice, like governments before and later, he was compelled by the lack of an organised majority to fudge his political commitments, even to circumvent the constitution and sometimes raise taxes by royal decree.[10] Effective parliamentary government in such circumstances was difficult. As he explained, the existence of organised parties, even parties composed of no more than twenty-five deputies, would have let him play off one against another with some hope of securing enough votes for legislation; but the extreme Left was 'almost the only united party in the house', and to get a reliable majority he would have 'to make a hundred concessions on one subject, a course which would render the passage of any measure impossible'.[11]

What particularly weakened him was the king's refusal to accept his proposal to reduce the military budget. To Di Rudinì and many others this was the one obvious area for economies so as to balance the annual accounts. But Umberto, by education and predilection a soldier, shared the belief prevalent in much of upper-class Italy that the army was the ultimate guarantee of social order as well as national security. Almost the only people he spoke to each day were the generals who took turns on duty as part of his military household. Their views were probably reflected in his remark that any reduction in the army would be 'an abject scandal, and we might as well give up politics altogether'. A reduction would also impugn his secret promise to send five army corps to Germany in the event of war – a promise that vitally affected national security yet was still unknown to the cabinet.[12]

Here was the issue on which Di Rudinì foundered. The king first tried and failed to persuade the prime minister to widen his coalition by including Giovanni Giolitti who was prepared to avoid this particular economy. Giolitti was then encouraged by a palace official, Urbanino Rattazzi, to lead a parliamentary revolt which brought the government down in May 1892. Accusations were, very unusually, made in parliament that the court was unconstitutionally acting to undermine the government, and some very strong words had again to be deleted before publication in the official parliamentary record. The accusations were accompanied by the veiled threat that, if economies could not be made in the army, then the king's civil list might have to be reduced to help make up the budget deficit.[13]

Like other prime ministers before him, Di Rudinì loyally avoided commenting on this dangerous constitutional issue in his resignation speech. With equal and less justifiable loyalty he left the monarch a free hand by not recommending a possible successor. Crispi was summoned to the palace for advice and, without actually suggesting himself as a candidate, was bold enough to say that the king's principal mistake was to have accepted the resignation of Crispi's government the previous year; if together they could not repair the damage, the result might put the risorgimento into reverse and Italy would split up again. In addition to this fanciful argument, Crispi pointed out that if the monarchy allowed itself to be criticised in parliament, the aura of majesty was bound to suffer. A strong minister was therefore required to save the throne and the country, someone who would treat petty questions of finance as unimportant, who would enlarge the army to over a million soldiers and fight to increase Italian prestige which had fallen lower even than that of Spain. Such a minister would 'if necessary govern without parliament or indeed against it'. As he spoke these words, Crispi was trembling with anger so that Umberto wondered if he might possibly be out of his mind; and though it must have been welcome to hear someone say that the army could and should be three or four times its present size, the king's immediate reaction was that the advice of such a man would in future be better disregarded.[14]

Several days later Giolitti was appointed prime minister, and this must have been a personal choice by the court because his name seems to have been suggested by no parliamentary leader. Crispi in a fury reminded the king that Giolitti had no experience of government and this was no time for new and untried men. In a further violent outburst he told another politician close to the palace that the king was 'a cynic, a liar and a traitor' who was ruining the country, a 'degenerate' who understood nothing of politics, an ingrate unmindful of the debt owed to Crispi who had risked his life in serving the crown.[15]

Umberto was able to select Giolitti because a multi-partite parliament composed of fluid personalistic groupings, while it might momentarily unite to dislodge a government, could seldom agree on indicating a successor. This characteristic of Italian politics was noted unfavourably in the British legislature as a dangerous symptom of constitutional malfunction.[16] Umberto probably knew little about Giolitti except that he was a prudent financial administrator who nevertheless promised to make no cuts in the army. However, another Piedmontese was welcome after two Sicilian prime ministers, and it may not be irrelevant that the Piedmontese dialect was still commonly used at court. Giolitti also accepted three royal nominees for the ministries in charge of foreign policy and the armed services. His other ministers came from left of centre, and Umberto welcomed this fact, explaining that so long as many conservative politicians wanted economies in the army he had no wish to see such men in power again.[17]

The king was delighted to find after a few weeks that he had chosen someone whose calmness and moderation was accompanied by an enviable sureness of touch in difficult circumstances. The new government was at once attacked from the Right and the extreme Left: the Right referred to Giolitti as another potential dictator; the extreme Left attacked him for being imposed by the royal court, and others called him another Cromwell come to subdue an unruly parliament. But although the crucial issue was raised of how far an intrusive monarchy was compatible with parliamentary government, this particular problem was allowed to drop and remained for future generations to confront.[18] After surviving for a few weeks with an uncertain majority, Giolitti persuaded the king to allow a dissolution of parliament which left him four months to govern unhindered while he carefully prepared for a new election.

Over the next thirty years Giolitti was five times prime minister. Seven times he was minister of the interior, and as such perfected his technique of managing elections to create a power-base more secure than anyone had enjoyed since the time of Cavour. In November 1892 this technique was still at an experimental stage. First of all he replaced two-thirds of the sixty-nine prefects in order to leave vacancies for loyal officials who were pledged to work for his electoral victory. Also, eighty new senators were appointed from among other supporters, in part so as to leave seats in the lower house for selected placemen. One senator-elect whose appointment the senate refused to accept was the banker Bernardo Tanlongo, who had used his bank to subsidise the candidature of government supporters. Revelations about this man were later employed to damage the political career of Giolitti who, evidently in return for favours rendered, failed to prosecute Tanlongo for secretly printing a series of false banknotes. But this damaging fact was not yet known and the election gave the prime minister what he prematurely imagined was 'a strong and unassailable majority'.[19]

Giolitti's promise not to reduce spending on the army was possibly a stratagem for self-advancement at court. He had once protested at how military expenditure was concealed from parliament, and had warned of how public opinion might react strongly against that item in the national budget if ever the full details became known.[20] As prime minister he succeeded in making a few useful economies in this field at the same time as he kept to his promise by pretending the opposite,[21] and was helped by the fact that parliament still found great difficulty in discovering the true facts during discussion of the annual financial review. There were occasional protests that previous military disasters in 1848 and 1866 had been due to the lack of public knowledge about this vital area of policy where the royal prerogative remained paramount,[22] but here was another controversial issue that he prudently left unresolved.

Some of the critics were nevertheless reinforced in their belief that 'militarism', especially by expenditure over Eritrea and the Triple Alliance, was a threat to Italy's social stability and one reason for the country's continuing poverty. Military expenditure was ten times as much as was being spent on education, and in the past fifteen years had doubled while the wealth of the country had not grown in proportion. Two leading military experts, General Marselli and General Ricotti, who spoke authoritatively as a minister of war in five previous governments, had come to believe that Italy would be stronger with a smaller but more efficient army if only the money were spent less wastefully under more critical public scrutiny.[23]

Italians could boast of having the third largest navy in the world, but were not allowed to know that the effectiveness of this fleet was flawed by a failure to plan or discuss what kind of navy was required, or how it could be used and against whom. The king knew that his much-praised battleships were less impressive than was claimed and, because of the quickening advances in technology, were outdated almost before they saw action.[24] Rich countries could afford an arms race; poor countries could not. Umberto was advised by his German and Austrian allies that the sensible policy would be to cut down on the armed services, but he said he would rather abdicate. Without a strong army he feared the possibility of insurrection at home, and abroad Italy would have to return to the regrettable policy of 'clean hands'.[25]

Giolitti was one among many politicians who learnt from experience that the regular succession of broad coalitions, for instance between Di Rudinì and Nicotera, deprived cabinets of an easily agreed policy and so weakened the effectiveness of parliamentary government. He was far from alone in regretting that Italy lacked a two-party alternation in which progressives and conservatives would succeed each other in turn, and ideally he hoped to avoid his predecessors' practice of transformist coalitions.[26] Once in government, however, he had to adapt to traditions that were so deeply entrenched that he preferred to exploit them and merely try to make them work better.

Another diagnosis of Italy's troubles was suggested in 1893 by the former conservative minister Ruggero Bonghi. As part of a campaign to defeat Giolitti, Bonghi advocated restoring some of the royal prerogatives that had been weakened ever since Cavour began to turn 'constitutional government' into 'parliamentary government'. The constitution of 1848 had originally allowed the monarch an unfettered power to appoint to the senate, but this prerogative had become attenuated as the king came to rely on ministerial recommendations. Moreover, ministers had sometimes tended to regard themselves as responsible to parliament as much as, or even more than, to the king, and this in Bonghi's opinion was quite wrong. Cavour, for what seemed good reasons at the time, had gone too far in trying to make the monarch more of a figurehead who reigned but did not govern and who was expected to act as his ministers chose. Hence the royal prerogatives had been partially usurped by cabinets and parliament. And yet it was generally admitted that cabinet government was working badly. Bonghi suggested that Italy needed a head of state with much greater powers to check the dangerous advance of democracy and the tyranny of cabinets; otherwise people might be tempted to suspect that the monarch's job could more suitably and economically be performed by the president of a republic.[27]

Umberto lacked the self-confidence and the energy to go far along this road so long as he had ministers who knew how to govern without opposing his wishes or exposing him to criticism. But in the course of 1893 he became alarmed when, despite Giolitti's electoral victory, an accumulation of grievances weakened the government to the point where the prime minister more than once offered his resignation. Umberto at first refused to accept these offers. Court circles were nevertheless worried by a mounting peasants' revolt in Sicily which Giolitti, despite a request by the king who knew that peasants made up the bulk of the army, did nothing to put down.[28] Further disaffection was caused by taxes being increased, sometimes surreptitiously by royal decree without parliamentary consent.

The king's civil list also came under renewed attack for its extravagance. Articles in the press pointed out that he continued to enjoy a tax-free income from parliament of over 14 million lire, more than either the Kaiser or Queen Victoria in countries that were far richer, much more than the French president who had only two million, or than the president of the United States who had even less. Another idea of its size is given by comparison with the salary of only 25,000 lire earned by the prime minister.[29]

Even more worrying was a growing public awareness of grave irregularities in the banking system, and it was these that finally brought Giolitti down. Their existence had been known for at least the past four years, but their seriousness had been concealed by politicians. The excuse subsequently given for secrecy was that a damaging run on the banks would have taken place if it were known that accounts had been falsified and vast numbers of duplicate banknotes had been printed in England; but a more urgent reason for concealment was that too many politicians were corruptly involved through bribes and interest-free 'loans', so that exposure of the truth would have brought a large section of the political class into disrepute or into prison. Three prime ministers, Crispi, Di Rudinì, and Giolitti, overcame their other differences and connived at concealing the facts, even improperly using parliamentary regulations to suppress public debate; and this was despite the alarming fact that irresponsible bank loans were fuelling speculation which by 1892 was in turn causing widespread bankruptcies.[30] Most reprehensible of all was that nothing was done by any of them to correct what was wrong, and the obvious explanation for this extraordinary state of affairs is that too many reputations would have suffered from publicity.

The man at the centre of the scandal was the director of the Banca Romana, Tanlongo, who claimed to have 'lent' money to many prominent Italian politicians back to and including Cavour, and who was thereby believed to 'dispose of the votes of a large number of deputies'. He had also helped both Umberto and Vittorio Emanuele with interest-free or low-interest loans and by raising large usurious borrowings in Germany.[31] These financial accommodations may help to explain why a royal decree nominated Tanlongo to the senate. They no doubt also explain why this foremost Italian banker threatened *The Times* of London with a lawsuit to stop rumours of malpractice from circulating abroad, and why he then tried to bribe the Roman correspondent of *The Times* to remain silent.[32] But when incriminating reports began to appear in the newspapers of Frankfurt and Paris, Italian credit suffered so badly that concealment was no longer possible.

In December 1892 Dr Napoleone Colajanni of the radical Left broke the tabu of silence after he discovered a secret official report that indicated that Crispi had received from Tanlongo a sum twenty times his salary. Crispi claimed that this allegation was untrue and supported Giolitti when the latter let people know that he would resign if parliament 'unpatriotically' decided to conduct an independent investigation. Colajanni lost a vote on this point by the remarkably large majority of 316 votes against 27, and ascribed such near unanimity to the fear that an unnamable but 'elevated personage', in other words the king himself, was involved.[33]

A month later as further details emerged, Giolitti was compelled to arrest Tanlongo, who defended himself by naming a score of ministers and ex-ministers who had accepted his money. Some of these payments must have been for the relatively innocuous purposes of fighting elections, subsidising newspapers, or supporting the value of the currency, but not all of them. De Zerbi, the champion of colonial war, committed suicide when it emerged that he had taken half a million lire for purposes that he was unwilling to explain. As many as a hundred deputies and fifty journalists seem to have been beneficiaries to a lesser extent, and one purpose of Tanlongo's duplicate series of banknotes was no doubt to purchase their support or their silence.[34]

Giolitti's personal involvement may not have gone beyond the serious and damaging fact of connivance at concealment. He was said to have personally borrowed the relatively small sum of 60,000 lire to help with the elections in 1892, though he denied this; nor would it have been either a novel practice or particularly scandalous. Nevertheless, his government had used the bank for short-term borrowing, as had at least three of his cabinet colleagues, despite the fact that they must have known from official reports that Tanlongo was involved in illegal activities; nor did the accounts always make clear if repayment was made, or indeed if it was expected.

Umberto, too, had to admit that he had borrowed from Tanlongo, and it seems that other members of the royal family had done the same for reasons that did not bear close scrutiny.[35] This may explain why the king continued after January 1893 to ask the government to conceal as much as possible and refuse a parliamentary enquiry.[36] But the scandal was by then too public, and parliament, as he told Queen Victoria, was becoming 'very troublesome',[37] An investigating commission was belatedly set up in March, though it dragged out its discussions and did not present a report until November, after which the government immediately resigned without waiting for a vote of confidence.

Giolitti's parting shot was to provoke the conservatives by asking for lower taxes on the poor and greater taxation of the rich. Though this represented a sincere conviction on his part, its timing suggested that he shared the hope or fear of those who thought that his resignation would force a general election and offer the chance of a more radical majority under his own leadership. But an election, coming so soon after the bank scandals, risked being too dangerous a challenge to the privileged classes, so the king instead spent ten wearisome days consulting leading politicians. Most of them agreed in backing the alternative candidature of Giolitti's friend, Giuseppe Zanardelli, a man who was disliked at court but who by general consent was untainted by corruption and the only person likely to command a sufficient parliamentary majority. The president of the senate, Domenico Farini, suggested to the king that another alternative might be to disregard parliament altogether, even to set up a dictatorship and use the army to arrest deputies who resisted;[38] but Umberto very properly refused to consider the suggestion.

After receiving an official invitation from the palace, Zanardelli drew up a provisional list of ministers on the basis of a policy that included economies in the army and the civil list. That was enough to make the king change his mind. But not wanting to use a royal veto he thought up an alternative strategem. Two ministers on Zanardelli's list were generals and one was an admiral; and messages were sent to all three from the palace that they should withdraw their names and so foil any attempt to form a cabinet.[39] However, the king went too far when he also informed Zanardelli that the Austrians would have objected to the choice as foreign minister of General Baratieri who was suspected of irredentist sympathies. Zanardelli responded that it would be too humiliating for the palace to let a foreign government influence the composition of an Italian cabinet; apart from which the king's intervention in such a matter might be considered a dangerous impropriety. A constitutional impasse was avoided only when Zanardelli followed previous practice and tactfully 'covered' the sovereign by agreeing to withdraw his candidature, but by that time the details of this unfortunate episode had become common kowledge.[40]

6   *Crispi and the politics of force*

The general expectation was that the palace would turn to either Di Rudinì again or else the venerable liberal, Giuseppe Saracco, but both ruled themselves out by refusing any increase in the army budget. Instead, to general surprise, the man chosen was once again Crispi, at the ripe age of 74, whose reputation as Umberto admitted had been 'shattered' by dark revelations of financial malpractice and whose huge personal debts were now being settled only through the king's private generosity. Documents held at the palace made quite clear that Crispi was also known to have been involved in selling titles and other 'sordid' operations.[1]

On the other hand, he was a man of energy who would accept increased expenditure on the army and who desperately needed power so that he could suppress the evidence of his own misdemeanours. Crispi could also be relied on to defend the prerogatives of the crown, especially because he knew that he would need Umberto's help to avoid prosecution. Although the king had not forgotten the difficulties of working with this over-mighty minister, he had some reason to fear for his throne and needed a government that would have no scruples in using armed force to crush alarming symptoms of social revolution in Sicily and Tuscany. Crispi additionally had in his favour the fact of wanting to reverse Giolitti's programme of progressive taxation and retrenchment in Africa.

These were difficult months for a king who was sometimes tempted to intervene too actively and so invite personal responsibility for acts of government. The Triple Alliance, the bank scandals, and the current economic depression could of course be called the responsibility of his ministers, but by refusing to remain aloof and impartial he inevitably attracted some unpopularity to himself. Newspapers again reported occasional catcalls and public demonstrations against him in the streets. According to one observer, some Italians in all classes were coming round to favouring republicanism, and others feared that the country was even in danger of breaking up because of 'the weakness and vacillation of their sovereign'.[2] Some of the radical members of parliament continued to demand that before too much harm was done he should at least be deprived of his constitutional right to make treaties and alliances on his own responsibility, and issue was taken with the appointments of Giolitti and Crispi as being due to 'unconstitutional influences emanating from the royal palace'. Three successive prime ministers had been chosen without any indication from parliament or from the main parliamentary leaders.[3]

On reappointment at the end of 1893, Crispi saw his chance of salvation in announcing that the country was in danger and in claiming that, since he belonged neither to Right nor Left, he was entitled to support from the whole of parliament as a patriotic duty irrespective of sectional allegiance. He even took the drastic step of offering cabinet posts to the radicals Cavallotti and Colajanni who understandably refused; and the ministers he finally chose were by his own confession nonentities who would do as they were told. He let it be known that the king had agreed to grant him dictatorial powers if necessary, and should parliament refuse to support him he would ignore it on the grounds that national security must take precedence over constitutional liberties.[4]

The new prime minister proceeded in the first months of 1894 to sequester opposition newspapers, prevent public meetings, even arrest deputies, and these technically unconstitutional acts were defended as necessary because of an emergency created by popular agitation in southern and central Italy. If the country was, as he repeatedly stated, almost in a state of civil war, he could claim justification in proclaiming martial law and setting up military tribunals. An army corps of 40,000 soldiers was drafted to Sicily, where he pretended or deluded himself into believing that a secessionist movement was supported by France and underwritten by a fictitious Treaty of Bisacquino between Sicilian rebels and Russia. This was pure fantasy and he was unable to produce the documents that he said would prove foreign involvement. But the scare enabled him to win the temporary support of Giolitti and Di Rudinì in the chamber where he won a substantial majority of 342 against 45, and this gave him the justification he needed for acting dictatorially.

The true reason for popular disorders was that many Italians lived close to starvation, and it should have been obvious that agricultural labourers, scores of whom died – the only casualties – in clashes with the army, were rather the victims of Crispi's tariff war with France and a tax system intolerably weighted against them. Governments since 1861 had done very little indeed to help the poorest classes of society, yet these deprived people were thought to produce most of the national wealth, and their lack of purchasing power was said to be a principal cause of the current economic crisis.[5] Umberto had been sufficiently alarmed to ask his ministers to study the question of social reforms, and Crispi promised to do so;[6] but instead, Sicilians, even when demonstrating with banners bearing portraits of the king and the Madonna, were punished and sometimes executed on the absurd pretext of being agents of some foreign power.

The sudden need to mobilise so many soldiers for what he called a civil war exposed weaknesses in the organisation of the army, and this at a time when many members of the ruling élite regarded the armed forces as the single most reliable public institution in the country.[7] Isolated voices continued to complain that Italy spent more on the army than the combined expenditure on the whole civil services of the state, and the words 'vainglory' and 'megalomania' were increasingly used by critics to describe a prime minister who ignored popular wishes and sacrificed other vital national interests to this one department of government.[8] But among nationalists at the opposite extreme there was a demand for Italy to find still more money to become nothing less than the strongest military power in Europe, and the king himself, while he never said anything so foolish, was determined at the very least to create a much bigger army.[9]

Here he found allies in ministers who hoped to turn the Triple Alliance into a more activist and even aggressive treaty. Crispi meant to run foreign policy himself, confident of support from the palace so long as he seemed to be successful. He appointed as foreign minister Senator Alberto Blanc, a Savoyard who had similar warlike instincts but who, as the king admitted, lacked initiative and would simply obey orders.[10] This permitted Crispi and the king to take important decisions by themselves, even bypassing the foreign office and Italian embassies abroad.[11]

There was almost bound to be some discomfort in working once again alongside such a headstrong, opinionated, but also simple-minded and credulous minister. Umberto knew this from past experience and occasionally revealed a scruple of disagreement against aiming at a more aggressive interpretation of the Triple Alliance than had been originally intended.[12] On one occasion he caused a minor scandal by contravening protocol and giving an interview to a French newspaper in which he seemed to contradict Crispi's bellicose posturing.[13] The minister complained at this, but basically their intentions were much the same: to line up with the central powers of Europe, even if it meant antagonising France and Russia. Umberto was incidentally hoping to involve Britain against France: if the British, he said, could be induced to occupy Tangier, that would usefully create friction with the French, and 'the stronger the British are in the Mediterranean, the better it will be for Italy'.[14]

His allies in Vienna and Berlin remained apprehensive that such a pugnacious policy might lead to war before it suited them. They were perhaps relieved to find that Crispi by January 1894 had become 'physically and mentally more feeble', while Umberto 'lacked initiative and energy'.[15] The king told the Austrians of his personal 'veneration and friendship' for their emperor and did his best to convince them that the Triple Alliance was popular in Italy.[16] But his chief enthusiasm was reserved for the magnificent discipline of the Prussian army which went far beyond anything he had imagined possible. He felt honoured when appointed colonel-in-chief of a German hussar regiment and took pride in personally leading these German troops over an assault course during their annual manoeuvres at Frankfurt. Once again, Kaiser Wilhelm's private advice was for him to prepare the Italian army against the day when it would be needed in Rome to turn the deputies out of parliament. Wilhelm 'is a strange type', was Umberto's comment.[17]

Another warning from Germany was against wasting military resources in Africa; but nor was this advice well received, especially after December 1893 when the Italians won their first important colonial victory at the battle of Agordat against the dervishes of the Sudan. The king was overjoyed at this success: he hoped it would make the British even more envious and was only bewildered when it aroused so little enthusiasm among Italians.[18] The independent *Secolo* repeated its warning that, just as defeats in Africa invariably led to demands for revenge, so victories were almost equally dangerous by generating a false optimism, and either way an extra momentum was given to the fatal and debilitating process of colonialism. True enough, the officially subsidised newspapers immediately demanded further military action to exploit the victory at Agordat.[19]

Blanc was hesitant because he had learnt the unwelcome fact that Italy's military potential nowhere near justified Umberto's confidence.[20] But Crispi was strangely optimistic that Italy could fight simultaneously on two quite different fronts against the dervishes and the Abyssinians. The prime minister persisted in his unrealistic claim that Abyssinia was an Italian protectorate by virtue of the dubious Treaty of Uccialli. Equally thoughtless was his continued assumption that Eritrea would soon produce enough tax revenue to take on itself the main financial burden of Italian colonisation.[21] Whether this was deliberate deceit of parliament or unintentional self-deception is an open question.

The existence of an alarming financial deficit in the national accounts is a constant theme of the diary written by one of the king's closest advisers, Senator Domenico Farini; and yet what chiefly frightened Farini was the demand from the extreme Right and the extreme Left for economies over the army. This president of the senate complained at money being 'wasted' on Italian railways and land reclamation instead of being used to develop a strong military state. Without a more powerful army 'everything will be lost' and Italy would continue to find her international reputation languishing below that of much-despised Spain or Switzerland. When it was proposed to allow army officers to marry, Farini feared that this was a plot to enervate the one sure support of the monarchy. He was nevertheless delighted with a law of July 1894 that turned denigration of the armed services into a criminal offence and so made public discussion more difficult than ever.[22]

In the spring of 1894 an unprecedentedly prolonged parliamentary debate took place over the military budget, because fears had once more been raised that the lack of accountability was leading to maladministration, perhaps also to corruption, and certainly to military weakness. Crispi tried to maintain in this debate that further military economies would not only undermine social order and discipline but would threaten 'the end of the Italian kingdom'. He eventually won a vote, but only by making concessions, and must have begun to fear that he had little chance of returning to the lavish expenditure of his previous premiership in 1889–90. In private he tried to persuade the king to placate the opposition and lessen the financial crisis by surrendering part of the crown's civil list, but met a firm refusal, and the king repeated that he would prefer to abdicate than reduce the army.[23]

On no other issue did Umberto show the strength of purpose that many loyal monarchists would have liked. Far from habitually imposing his own will in domestic politics, he was usually criticised by such people for lacking the determination and perhaps the brains to assert himself as his father had done and as the situation required. Some of his supporters, not only among the more extreme conservatives, would have liked him to fall back on the army and forget about parliament, but once again he sensibly replied that German traditions of authoritarian government would not suit Italy.[24]

Crispi was among those who privately accused the sovereign of infirmity of purpose and listening to irresponsible advice.[25] From the opposite standpoint of the extreme Left there were other critics who thought that the monarchy was now becoming a seriously divisive force in the nation.[26] Among the upper classes in Rome and Naples there was grumbling that Umberto lived too much apart, surrounded by northerners; while among the rich citizens of Milan there was some criticism of his extravagance, his mistresses, and the fact that he was rumoured to invest in London the huge savings made from the civil list.[27]

There also persisted a particular tension between himself and Crispi. The king was especially resentful when ministers demanded the exclusion from court of Urbanino Rattazzi who supervised the royal finances and was known to support Giolitti. Crispi despised such courtiers, yet equally resented the fact that his own unpopular wife was still cold-shouldered when attending the queen's receptions. After discussion with a medical specialist the king again wondered if his minister's rages and aggressiveness and delusions might indicate an incipient degree of mental alienation. Among other symptoms of nervous exhaustion were occasional fits of weeping and loss of memory, while a number of acquaintances confirmed that the ageing Crispi was strangely slow of speech and his mind could seem embarrassingly confused.[28]

But he survived, mainly because he had a splendid line in patriotic rhetoric and was a great fighter. As one of his friends explained, the minister delighted in confronting opposition from both Right and extreme Left: from the former because he had once been a democratic republican, from the latter because he was now part of the establishment.[29] He had to fight even some close collaborators who objected to his secrecy and obstinacy and unwillingness to listen to argument. Members of his cabinet were annoyed when he arrogantly interfered in their departments and unexpectedly proposed controversial laws without warning or consultation.[30] As a young man he had believed that breaches of the constitution by the king would justify an anti-monarchist revolution, but now made no concealment of his intention to defy parliament and continue raising taxes by royal decree.[31]

Even though he lacked the support of any organised party, his government was at first supported by a comfortable majority, for the familiar reason that most deputies automatically adjusted their allegiance to back any new prime minister until, as Pareto explained, he had exhausted his powers of patronage and they had more to gain from a change of ministry.[32] But Crispi knew that he could hardly survive without at least the tacit support of the king. Fortunately for him, both men shared certain convictions. Both were ready to suppress socialist manifestations by force. Both feared subversion and regional separatism. The social turbulence of the Sicilian *fasci* in January 1894 found them at one. Both resented that in the industrial north there existed minorities, conservative as well as radical, so scared of budget deficits and expensive imperialist ventures that there was renewed talk of breaking loose to form a separate Lombard republic.[33]

Both also agreed in wanting to suppress continued rumours about financial scandals in which their personal involvement was widely suspected. They used what influence they could, and were duly rewarded in July 1894 when a Roman court acquitted Tanlongo and the staff of the Banca Romana – whose legal defence was conducted by two former ministers of justice and a vice-president of the senate. The scandal over this verdict was enormous because the offences had been admitted: many millions of lire were still missing from the bank's accounts, millions of false notes were in circulation, and many politicians were publicly and continuously accused of peculation without daring to defend their reputations in an action for libel. At a time when many poor Sicilians were sent to penal settlements on implausible charges of sedition, Tanlongo was cheered in court as his acquittal was pronounced, and it was naturally assumed that not only had he been blackmailing powerful politicians, but magistrates and jurors must have been heavily bribed. One result was that Italian financial credit abroad and the reputation of Italian justice were both put in jeopardy. Newspapers called on the king to intervene quickly before corruption in high places brought the throne itself into question.[34]

Another cause for reproach was that the chamber of deputies after meeting on 11 July 1894 was not allowed to reassemble until 3 December, when the legislature met for ten days only and was again prorogued until 10 June 1895. Government during these eleven months had to be by means of royal decrees, which had the unfortunate effect of attracting to the king much of the responsibility and the odium that otherwise would have been carried by parliament and ministers. Taxes were imposed unconstitutionally; socialism, even moderate socialism, was outlawed; scores of Catholic associations and elected town councils were dissolved; newspapers were frequently sequestered; and many highly respectable dissenters were sent in chains to join criminals on the islands of Ponza and Ischia where the Bourbons had once incarcerated the 'martyrs' of the risorgimento.

When Crispi suddenly closed the legislature in December 1894, the immediate reason was his fear of public discussion about corrupt practices in the principal national banks. He was provoked into this when Giolitti in parliament produced further documents that proved beyond doubt the prime minister's improper behaviour. The latter had once admitted that any politican had an absolute duty to expose corrupt practices in government,[35] but in self-defence now accused the opposition of unpatriotic muck-raking. Caught by surprise, he announced that Giolitti's incriminating documents could be discussed by the chamber on the following day, which gave him time overnight to persuade the king to prorogue the legislature and thus 'save the dignity of parliament'. His private reaction was to explain that in a country such as Italy the existence of parliament might be incompatible with effective government. He wanted 'absolute power' in his own hands and explained that he hoped to stay in office for the rest of his life.[36]

Nearly two hundred protesting deputies, in other words over one third of the chamber, spontaneously assembled in a private meeting to deplore his suspension of parliament. The king, who sometimes used very violent language against his current ministers, briefly thought of intervening to appoint a new government,[37] but the renewed suggestion that he should restore a system of benevolent personal autocracy did not appeal to his timid and unadventurous nature.[38] Even though Crispi had become accustomed to treating his sovereign with a lack of courtly tact and sometimes in private continued to express positive dislike,[39] the king had to recognise that this spirited minister offered the best guarantee of intimidating politicians and judges into suppressing further revelations about the banks. Crispi therefore survived, because he and perhaps he alone could be relied on to fight strenuously against subversion at home and against the Abyssinians in Africa.

7   *Defeat in Africa*

No doubt it was not fully recognised at court that the prime minister's African policy was increasingly removed from realistic calculation or common sense. In the summer of 1894, with Umberto's support but against military advice, Crispi rashly agreed to what he called the 'defensive' occupation of Kassala in the remote Sudan, and had no idea why this was greeted with dismay.[1] He let it be thought that he had encouragement from England for a joint Italo-British occupation of the Sudan and possibly of Egypt, although no such encouragement had been given. He already had a front of 600 kilometres to defend in East Africa with only 8,000 soldiers, and further extending his commitments into the Sudan seemed to the British a provocative and gratuitous piece of folly.[2]

Since much of his African army was composed of Abyssinian mercenaries, it was the more strange to hear talk of deposing Menelik and crowning Umberto as emperor of Abyssinia (the mint, in preparation, struck coins with Umberto wearing the imperial crown[3]). In January 1895 reinforcements were sent with orders to move cautiously but to occupy the Abyssinian region of Tigre. The foreign minister and minister of war were both of them unenthusiastic, and the king dryly noted that 'Crispi wants to occupy everywhere, even China and Japan'.[4] Early in April General Baratieri set up his

command at Adowa, the Tigre capital, and the outside world was
then informed that 150,000 square kilometres of Abyssina had been
brought under Italian sovereignty.[5] After which an order was sent to
the army that yet another 'decisive step' was required, preferably
after bringing some soldiers back to Italy as an economy measure.
Baratieri was told to raise taxes locally and 'copy Napoleon who
made war with the money of those he had conquered'.[6] How such an
impoverished country could provide the funds was not specified, and
the order shows that Crispi was basing his policy on a complete
ignorance about the economic geography of East Africa.

When parliament reassembled after nearly a year in abeyance, he
won another large majority and was thereby encouraged to pursue
his private Napoleonic dreams. In a speech that disclaimed any wish
for further conquests, he nevertheless demanded the right to punish
African 'rebels and traitors' who had unwarrantably launched what
he still called an aggressive war against Italy. Just possibly he spoke
sincerely. Possibly he was merely exploiting patriotism to silence
the opposition. More likely he chiefly needed to divert attention from
growing domestic difficulties; and the British representative in Rome
was surprised to hear in explanation that the government 'was pessimistic about the future of united Italy'.[7]

Crispi's intention, according to Umberto, was to wait for the end
of another short parliamentary session so that he could then quietly
mobilise more soldiers without anyone's being able to protest. And
another incidental advantage of shutting parliament was that Giolitti
and other critics of his involvement in the bank scandals would lose
the immunity from arrest that deputies enjoyed by law. The less
cricitism there was, the freer he would be to organise the colonial
victory that would eventually give him the popular triumph he
required to defeat the opposition. Moreover, Africa was in his
opinion a military school where Italian soldiers would receive useful
training for future wars in Europe.[8]

Ordinary citizens were allowed little knowledge of the risks taken
in their name. Unknown to many of them, the existence of an
officially subsidised press created a completely fictitious 'public
opinion' that could be used as a pretended endorsement of government policy. Various procedures were adopted for slanting the news.
Journalists, who were poorly paid, were regularly bribed. Foreign
journalists could if necessary be expelled.[9] Crispi's personally owned
newspaper was secretly supported with taxpayers' money, whereas
opposition papers could have whole issues burnt and their editors
imprisoned.[10]

For much of 1895 the prime minister was permitted by the palace
to exercise what was openly called dictatorial authority, with little

acknowledgement of any responsibility to parliament or the public. He was the Tsar of Italy, wrote the socialist *Critica Sociale*. He acted like the boss of a central American republic, commented the *Secolo*.[11] Meanwhile, the courts and the official auditors of government expenditure, while they sometimes tentatively questioned his actions, feared to be thought unpatriotic and lacked the courage to call a halt to his extra-legal procedures. Nor did a single cabinet minister resign before the final catastrophe in 1896 – not Blanc, nor Sonnino, nor Giuseppe Saracco, despite the fact that all three sometimes disapproved strongly of Crispi's behaviour and policy.

The king alone could have stopped him and Umberto lacked either the wish or the spirit to do so. Instead he accorded almost full powers to someone known to be involved in major financial corruption. The parliamentary session of December 1894 had lasted only ten days and was followed by six months of personal rule during which the prefects could once again prepare to 'make the elections' under official direction. On one pretext or another a quarter of the voters had their names removed from national and local electoral rolls. Jobbery had already been taken to the point where government departments were said to have twice the number of employees required. The same man who in opposition criticised governments for using illicit pressure and secret service funds to influence elections, now used every means available, arresting opponents and resorting to intimidation and bribery on a scale that the king called quite incredible.[12]

As a result the election results in May 1895, despite a worrying rise in the small socialist vote, gave the government another large majority and showed a fall for the radicals and the followers of Giolitti and Di Rudinì. Umberto must have realised that, if Crispi had lost this election, the monarchy would have been in grave danger for backing someone under accusation of criminal misbehaviour. Nevertheless, as the king told one of his courtiers, 'Crispi is a pig, but a necessary pig', and despite his peccadillos must retain power 'in the national interest which is the only thing that matters'.[13]

Umberto's idea of the national interest was to bury the bank scandals and push ahead in Abyssinia, with or without parliamentary consent. He was not concerned that this might represent a minority view and alienate responsible politicians on both wings of the political spectrum. He had no qualms when Crispi later in May spoke of the 'absolute impossibility of continuing to govern through parliament'.[14] Even among conservatives it was now possible to question the usefulness of a sovereign who called parliamentary government 'a bad joke' and allowed it to lapse in a way that no truly liberal state would tolerate.[15]

One irony was that parliament posed no serious danger; it could have been a great help to the king if allowed to co-operate, and at worst was an occasional inconvenience. When the deputies at last reconvened in June 1895, by a two-to-one majority they retrospectively sanctioned the scores of royal decrees that over the previous year had replaced parliamentary legislation. But the hostile minority included the important names of Di Rudinì on the Right and Giuseppe Zanardelli in the Centre. The majority, wrote the radical Colajanni, apart from a small core of Crispi's personal following, was composed of servile placemen who by voting mindlessly for every successive government were damaging society far more than the socialists they claimed to oppose.[16] Not only was it possible for critics to say that there was less personal freedom in Crispi's Italy than in autocratic Austria, but government-subsidised newspapers were being allowed or encouraged to call parliament a useless institution that could be safely discarded. Crispi defended his imposition of martial law with the unconvincing argument that deputies could not discuss such a matter without violating the constitution, because this was another field where they would be trespassing on the royal prerogative.[17]

On 25 June took place a crucial debate in which Cavallotti asked for the appointment of a full parliamentary enquiry into the bank question, alleging new facts which if true must have brought the government down. Crispi simply refused to reply. He would not take part in what he called 'useless discussions' since 'after serving Italy for 53 years I have the right to consider myself invulnerable and above such defamatory accusations'; and the chamber supported him by the still substantial majority of 283 votes against 115. The king knew that at least some of Cavallotti's allegations were true and indeed fell short of the truth, but too much was at stake to let secrets of state become public knowledge. All that Cavallotti could thereafter do was to accuse Crispi repeatedly of being a 'common criminal' and defy the prime minister to sue; but the latter wisely refused to accept the challenge.[18]

After burying the bank question the government was free to concentrate on Africa. General Baratieri had vainly asked for a precise programme of military action with defined objectives. At the end of May he warned that his occupation of Tigre had produced an entirely unforeseen unity among the various Abyssinian chieftains, so much so that on this southern front alone he would soon face an army ten times the size of his own. Unless he was allowed to withdraw nearer to the coast he would need more soldiers. But from Rome came the unhelpful reply that he must do without more money or reinforcements, yet in no circumstances risk Italian pre-

7. *Umberto I.*

8. Umberto I and Queen Margherita returning to their apartments after the Carnival Ball at the Quirinal, 1 March 1885.

9. Umberto I, 1900.

10. Queen Margherita, 1900.

stige by withdrawing either from Kassala in the Sudan or Adowa in the Abyssinian Tigre.[19]

These two small towns were unfortunately named by Umberto in a public speech, no doubt written for him by Crispi, which claimed that their occupation was incontrovertible evidence of Italy's glorious victories against the 'barbarian' Abyssinians and Sudanese. After such a solemn claim it was impossible to investigate Di Rudinì's counter-argument that their occupation was a disastrous military error, nor could Crispi admit that a minor colonial enterprise had been gratuitously magnified into a major religious war against Copts and Moslems on two quite different fronts. The king confirmed to parliament that Eritrea would soon be financially independent of Italy, despite Baratieri's warning that this was quite impossible. Umberto added that, without wanting an adventurous policy, a further move into the Abyssinian interior might become necessary as a defensive measure.[20]

Inside the cabinet, Sonnino and Saracco were affronted by these symptoms of belligerence, and the leading Italian expert on Abyssinia, Count Antonelli, advised Crispi that the government was allowing itself to be persuaded by the 'military party' into an offensive war that was not only far too expensive but that for simple reasons of geography could not be won. This was an area of government where Umberto was known to possess views of his own, and presumably he was the 'very high personage' who intervened decisively in backing military action.[21] Unfortunately he did not take his duties as commander-in-chief sufficiently seriously to question the sending of untrained Italian conscripts, without a coherent strategy, without even adequate maps, against two much larger armies composed of the best soldiers in Africa.

Italian journalists on the spot, if they questioned what was happening, were at once sent home by Baratieri. But in November 1895 the news leaked back to Italy that, despite formal undertakings and without asking for the necessary funds, hostilities had surreptitiously recommenced. When challenged, Crispi promised once more that no extra money would be needed. Further statements confirmed his confidence that not only would Menelik soon be soundly defeated but the Abyssinians were already showing their delight at coming under Italian sovereignty.[22]

On 9 December a report reached Rome through foreign newspapers that the army had been defeated in a minor engagement when trying to occupy the outpost of Amba Alagi. Baratieri was responsible for this reverse, and officers under his command foretold an even bigger disaster unless he or his plan of war were changed at once; but 'mysterious influences' at the highest level intervened once again to prevent his dismissal. More money and troops were now sent, and parliament felt obliged to give retrospective sanction after Crispi repeated his undertaking that they would be used only for defence.[23] But Sonnino and Saracco at last threatened to resign in the realisation that Crispi was making fools of them by violating public promises and telling the cabinet nothing of his plans.[24] If only these two ministers had persisted in their resignation, the government would have fallen, which would have spared Italy one of the worst disasters in her national history; but in response to direct pressure from the palace they gave way and remained.

The king's responsibility was much greater than that of parliament or cabinet because he alone was in a position to known the relevant facts. He and not parliament had appointed Crispi, and he better than anyone should have been able to observe how his prime minister was losing touch with reality. Whereas Depretis had at once consulted other parliamentary leaders when faced with a military reverse in Africa, Crispi did not even consult his cabinet colleagues but only the king and the generals; which at least meant that responsibility for failure was on this occasion easier to locate. Already before the end of 1895 the opposition press was hinting that the dignity and authority of the crown had been damaged perhaps permanently by association with such a man. The time had come, said Cavallotti, for the elected representatives of the people to take back their supervisory powers which for too long had lain in abeyance; otherwise a yet greater military defeat might result from this 'cursed African dream'.[25]

Crispi, however, was too sure of himself and regarded such criticism as unpatriotic. With Umberto's support he was determined to recover his own and Italy's fortunes by a great military success. For a week after the engagement at Amba Alagi he did not appear in parliament to face his opponents and then came only to ask that discussion be put off until final victory had been won: everyone, he said, ought to agree that Italian casualties should first be avenged and Italian prestige restored before matters of general policy could be considered.

After these defiant words, the chamber gave him a vote of confidence by 255 to 148, and the senate by 87 to 5. He then persuaded the king to shut parliament for another ten weeks to silence the critics. To lessen his own responsibility he told Baratieri that the army leaders must decide on their own how revenge and prestige could best be won. But he made quite clear to them that an authentic victory was needed 'for the honour of Italy and the monarchy', a victory upon which their own reputation and future careers would depend.[26]

This message took irresponsibility to extraordinary lengths and

Crispi's state of dangerous excitement caused alarm at court. Quite apart from Africa, in these months of extra-parliamentary government he had talked of attacking France; also of a major European war about to break out at any moment; also of possibly sending troops to occupy Albania; of intervening in the Transvaal to arbitrate between Germany and Britain; even of some new military initiative in China; and five naval ships were sent to the Black Sea for possible action against the Turks. To avenge an entirely imaginary slight he broke off diplomatic relations with Portugal, after expressing the wish that this 'unimportant country' would get rid of its 'miniscule monarchy'.[27]

On such issues he treated advice from his foreign office as of little account, a fact that explains why many serious issues of foreign policy were allowed to drift almost by default as he gratuitously multiplied the number of Italy's enemies. It is astonishing to consider in retrospect that, if only he had agreed to make up his quarrel with the French, he could have used the Somalian port of Zeila and cut the cost of his Abyssinian war with far greater chances of success;[28] but humble pie was not to his taste, so the French had to be bullied into submission. This was why he wanted a radical change in the Triple Alliance: instead of this alliance being designed to preserve European peace, 'for Italy it must be the opposite; for us the Triple Alliance must mean war', and he meant war against France.[29]

Presumably the main documents on foreign and military policy were sent in copy to the Quirinal, and Crispi's frequent talks at the royal palace early in 1896 left him confident that he need fear no serious opposition at court so long as he was successful. The king said little to others, though privately seems to have had some further doubts about Africa, and once remarked with apprehension that Crispi was 'beside himself with anger' as they spoke together about the possibility of conquering the whole of Abyssinia.[30] But by allowing Crispi to govern without parliament, by failing to ensure that constitutional conventions were properly observed, Umberto had made himself into an obvious target for criticism. Newspapers ran the risk of crippling financial penalties if they pursued this theme, but enough was said in the press to make it clear that the future of the monarchy might depend on victory in Africa.

On 21 January, to the government's chagrin, a besieged Italian garrison at Makalle accepted generous terms of honourable surrender from Menelik, who used this success to send a letter to Umberto proposing a compromise peace. The king was advised by the prime minister not to reply as it would be humiliating to accept any compromise; indeed it would be humiliating even to write to such a barbarian chieftain. Stories nevertheless circulated suggesting that the king paid Menelik a large sum of money to obtain the garrison's release and prevent a much less honourable defeat.[31]

Crispi tried to keep secret that any peace offer had been received and repeatedly denied the news in cabinet, but at a stormy meeting on 8 February was forced to admit the truth. Pressed by his colleagues he then laid down impossible terms for any peace, namely that Baratieri's two recent defeats be first expunged by the surrender to Italy of Amba Alagi and Makalle; and Menelik must confirm publicly that the whole of Abyssinia was an Italian protectorate. Failing acceptance of these terms, Baratieri was ordered to continue fighting until he scored a decisive victory.

Such an attitude indicated a complete lack of realism or common sense. Count Antonelli had resigned earlier from the foreign office because twelve years spent in Abyssinia convinced him that the war was unwinnable, and now repeated this advice, especially as the rainy season would shortly make fighting impossible. When newspapers confirmed his warning with additional reports of how food and transport were lacking and even drinking water had to be shipped to the Red Sea from Naples, Crispi ordered the expulsion of more journalists from the colony. He also ordered the censoring of soldiers' private correspondence so as to maintain confidence at home in the 'glorious exploits of our army in Africa'.[32]

Two more expeditions were then sent to reinforce Baratieri – despite the latter's protest that he could not feed a larger army and they could be of no use whatsoever. Meanwhile, large numbers of native troops were reading the omens and deserting to join Menelik. In Italy itself, where Italians were enthusiastically volunteering to fight wars of liberation in Cuba and Crete, troop-carrying trains were sabotaged and hundreds of recruits were deserting across the Swiss and Austrian frontiers rather than take part in what was considered an unjust war in Africa.[33]

Since parliament was due to reconvene on 20 January before there was any victory to report, Crispi prorogued it once more, though deputies and senators met unofficially to express their alarm. Two ministers again wanted to resign over this closure of parliament, and a third, the foreign minister Blanc, registered a formal complaint that the cabinet was still being told none of the facts and nothing even about Crispi's objectives. Sonnino at the Treasury, the only minister who had visited Eritrea, knew that the cost of the war was wildly in excess of available resources. He was all the more angry when Umberto was mendaciously told by Crispi that no disagreement existed inside the cabinet. Sonnino's private reaction was to hope that the king would appoint new ministers with a more pacific policy: only the palace could now save the country, since the Abyssinians were proving to be far stronger and better organised than he and the other ministers had been allowed to suspect. But he and Saracco once more withdrew their resignation after Umberto appealed to their sense of patriotism.[34]

The whole country was seriously disturbed. Many towns witnessed public demonstrations of protest and there was talk of overwhelming popular opposition against a dishonourable war.[35] However, Crispi and the army leaders continued with plans for another major offensive under new military direction. On 22 February Umberto at last signed a decree dismissing General Baratieri, but ordered that he must not be told for the next ten days until a new commander had time to arrive in Eritrea; which makes it all the more incomprehensible that, on 25 February, a provocative telegram was sent by Crispi to Baratieri accusing him of incompetence and demanding some action 'at whatever cost to save the honour of the army and the prestige of the monarchy'.[36]

The result on 1 March was a crushing defeat near Adowa during which (it was estimated) more Italians were killed in one day than in all the wars of the risorgimento. Baratieri desperately tried to excuse himself by laying the blame for defeat on panic by his own soldiers. The same excuse had been made in 1866, and would be again in 1917 and 1943: in each case the senior general in command covered his own mistakes by creating the legend that his men refused to fight. A different opinion was expressed by the British military attaché in 1896 who reported from Eritrea that, while Italian soldiers were 'as good fighting material as is to be found in Europe', their commander was at fault on almost every count and during the battle had simply abandoned his men to their fate. The Italian minister of war confirmed this judgement, but when a deputy made the same accusation in the Italian parliament, the session was abruptly terminated by the Speaker.[37]

8   *Umberto reasserts his authority*

Crispi accepted no personal responsibility for this defeat at the hands of 'barbarians'. His first defiant reaction was to say that he intended to continue the war, keep parliament shut, and put down opposition by force.[1] Only when his colleagues objected did he agree at least to offer his resignation. By resigning he could avoid having to confront a parliamentary debate, and the head of state would then be left with the responsibility for any decision. Crispi was sufficiently insensitive to feel sure of being invited to form a new government and said so to a foreign journalist.[2]

The king realised the full gravity of his situation only when a hundred senators met of their own accord and demanded change. When parliament assembled, the government's fall was greeted with tremendous applause. A riot took place in the public galleries of parliament which had to be cleared by soldiers, something that was thought to be without precedent. The palace must have been further alarmed to hear more street demonstrations shouting 'death to the king' and 'long live the republic'. Even conservatives were learning to speak of republicanism with sympathy, especially as the monarchy seemed to be leading the united kingdom into a split between a generally anti-colonialist north and a more pro-colonialist south. Deputies as well as senators held private meetings where the king was personally blamed for supporting Crispi's misgovernment, and among those present were members of the royal household who held high positions at court. Never since 1860 had the crown been under such attack. Umberto briefly talked once again of possible abdication.[3]

Since Crispi resigned before parliament had an opportunity to vote and indicate a possible successor, the king's first preference for a new prime minister was Saracco, but as this man was a member of the outgoing cabinet his appointment failed to find support. Giolitti was ruled out of the succession, partly because the king had misguidedly broken off all contact with him, partly because his proposals for tax reform were too much feared by conservative opinion. Giolitti was not even summoned for consultation, despite the custom of asking the advice of former prime ministers at each change of government. The king then invited General Ricotti to form an administration, who in turn suggested a civilian from the parliamentary opposition.

Di Rudinì led the largest opposition group and was said to be indicated by public opinion, but was disliked by Umberto to such a degree that there was yet further talk of abdication if no one else could be found. When Di Rudinì was eventually chosen, this was only after his acceptance of two conditions that indicated the palace's order of priorities, namely to preserve the Triple Alliance and to make no more than a token reduction in the army.[4]

His appointment signalled a temporary return to a more parliamentary style of government, and the new prime minister hoped for a dissolution of parliament so that the country could indicate its views. But Umberto, though he had allowed an election to Crispi, feared the result and refused. Even without elections, however, Crispi's huge majority of deputies switched almost automatically to support his successor. Nor did observers familiar with parliamentary practice think this sudden transference of allegiance to be surprising. Though Di Rudinì was known to lack the king's full confidence, he was widely recognised to be an honest man, a loyal monarchist, and someone who unlike Crispi had taken money neither from the banks nor from the sale of titles. From Umberto's point of view he had the advantage of at least being more malleable and submissive than his predecessor.

The new government did its best to conceal any responsibility by the crown for military defeat and an empty treasury. Eight thousand men had been killed in Africa, fifteen hundred remained prisoners of Menelik, and vast sums of money had been spent fruitlessly; yet newspapers were impounded if they hinted at any royal responsibility, and a distinguished professor at Naples university lost his job for the same offence. Only in private letters or in publications abroad could Umberto be directly blamed. Domestic critics could do little more than refer disparagingly to what was euphemistically called the 'court party'. Or once again they could risk mentioning 'a person we all know' who was guilty of pursuing counter-productive fantasies of military glory; or a 'mysterious unnamable personage' who was reversing the liberal traditions of the risorgimento in an attempt to bring prestige to the dynasty and the army. One well-informed American journalist in Rome reported that 'the king is digging the grave of the monarchy more effectually than all the republicans in the kingdom'.[5]

Ministers had the embarrassment of having to tell parliament that many official files about recent events in Africa had mysteriously disappeared from the archives.[6] Some of the documents were later discovered in Malta where the telegraph office kept copies of messages in transit. Crispi could then be seen to have falsified some of the documentation that he had already published, and in addition he now tried to persuade Sonnino not to give the new administration a full statement of the treasury accounts which would reveal some of the unwelcome truth.[7] He had prudently prepared a bowdlerised official 'Green Book' to justify his African policy, and to prevent its authenticity being checked he took away four chests of official papers when he left office – which many years later had to be purchased from his heirs, though the abstraction of official documents was a criminal offence. Relying on this concealment he categorically denied in parliament that he had ever taunted Baratieri with inactivity – until a copy of his order demanding an 'authentic victory' was found in Malta.[8] Naturally he took offence when Di Rudinì put the record straight in a supplementary 'Green Book' to show how public opinion had been carefully hoodwinked over the previous two years.

The king, too, not very plausibly, claimed that he had been kept in the dark and had no idea how ignorant were his former ministers about the geography and economic conditions of East Africa. Crispi preferred to lay the blame on the 'treachery' of his colleagues Sonnino and Saracco. The disgraced minister kept a special file of documents to prove to posterity how he had also been betrayed by the palace when the king failed to reappoint him to continue the war after Adowa.[9] He even dared accuse Umberto to his face of failing to imitate Vittorio Emanuele's cavalier treatment of parliament. 'You are not responsible to parliament', he exclaimed, 'but you cannot escape being answerable before history', and history would condemn a ruler who failed to punish the 'barbarians' of Africa as had been done by even the 'little king of Belgium'.[10]

Another of the fallen minister's private grievances was Umberto's failure to halt a public enquiry into further accusations levelled at Crispi for embezzlement and misappropriation of charitable funds.[11] Although the ex-minister was one of the highest-paid lawyers in Italy, his lavish style of life always needed additional sources of income and he unobtrusively received large grants of money from the palace. He was also accused of raiding a public fund collected for the relief of victims of an earthquake in Calabria. After resigning he was involved in another financial scandal when Luigi Favilla, a defaulting director of the Bank of Naples, revealed in self-defence that Crispi had received substantial bribes in return for suspending several enquiries into millions missing from that bank's accounts.

Once again the accused man appealed to the king to save him from prosecution, and once again, as in the case of Tanlongo, the establishment rallied round to bury the scandal before more damage was done. As Domenico Farini noted, further publicity would impugn the king's reputation by the fact of his having trusted such a man, and other critics pertinently added that publicity would implicate many deputies and senators who had profited financially from *crispismo*.[12] The same parliament that had given Crispi huge votes of confidence now agreed to a formal motion of censure against him, something quite without precedent in Italian history, but refused permission for a criminal prosecution that would have brought the facts into the public domain. Farini, who still presided over the senate, had to admit Crispi's guilt, but to drag a former prime minister through the courts would tarnish the already none-too-savoury reputation of Italian politics. Revelations in the press were less to be feared because newspapers could be prosecuted or sequestered if they hinted at the king's responsibility for such a miscarriage of justice.

Most Italians, but not all, must have been relieved when in October 1896 a treaty of peace was signed with the Negus Menelik. Crispi was bitter about this treaty because, like Sonnino and Farini, he would have preferred the fighting to continue even if it meant condemning to execution the fifteen hundred Italian prisoners still in Abyssinia: barbarians should be treated like monkeys he said, or 'by fire and the sword', whereas ordinary Italian prisoners of war were expendable in the cause of defending national prestige.[13] When the prisoners were released, Umberto agreed to send a telegram of acknowledgement to Menelik but wanted this apparently humiliating fact kept secret. Unlike the German emperor, who sent warm congratulations to Di Rudinì on a realistic termination to a badly calculated war, Umberto was grudging and singularly ungracious about a peace that helped to rescue his own reputation.[14]

Di Rudinì would have preferred to go further and not merely make peace but withdraw altogether from Africa, or sell the colony if he could find a buyer. The new foreign minister, Prince Caetani, lamented that Italians were evidently lacking in patriotism, and expressed his continuing fear that another colonial defeat 'would seriously compromise the stability of the throne', but he equally feared to offend the king by suggesting withdrawal too positively.[15] In practice, however, the government agreed to surrender the Tigre and also persuaded a very unwilling Umberto to withdraw from the secondary front in the Sudan which had been a principal reason for military defeat. Italy officially recognised Abyssinia as being an independent sovereign state and no longer an Italian protectorate. But Eritrea had to be retained even if there was no expectation of its ever becoming economically profitable, because to abandon this colony after so much expenditure and effort would have dealt too great a blow to feelings of national honour.

Another issue on which the prime minister yielded to 'the court party' was finance for the army. Figures were produced to show that, since 1861, the armed services had taken almost half of what was left of spendable tax revenue after the payment of interest and salaries, and the war proved that much of this money had been badly spent or wasted since it escaped any parliamentary audit.[16] Di Rudinì accepted office only after obtaining the royal consent to some degree of retrenchment, but the details were not spelt out and Umberto was secretly determined to block any reduction.[17] When in July a parliamentary commission mysteriously reversed its views and decided to vote against the government's proposal for a reduction in the army, this strange occurrence was assumed to be in response to intervention from the palace.[18]

By undermining the authority and policy of his own ministers Umberto was once again playing a dangerous game. His allies in Vienna and Berlin were alarmed at his growing unpopularity and again made clear their view that the monarchy would be stronger with a smaller army, lower taxation, and no commitments in Africa.[19] But he could not agree, and within six weeks of the new government's taking office was secretly encouraging a rival politician to prepare a replacement administration with a more openly militarist policy. When the king refused to allow a general election, one motive was that a new parliament might ask for withdrawal from Africa and further investigation of the bank frauds; and any newspaper that hinted at a conflict between monarch and minister continued to risk a punitive censorship.[20]

The government survived the summer, but only by dropping General Ricotti, the minister of war, who advocated resistance to the king and reducing the army from twelve corps to eight. Naturally there was a suspicion that a palace intrigue lay behind Ricotti's resignation. The king's continued dislike of his prime minister was common knowledge.[21] Di Rudinì reacted by trying to bring Sonnino into his coalition, but the latter made the interesting objection that such a union of two conservative groups, his own and the prime minister's, would force the Left to combine in opposition, which would create a dangerous two-party system and run the risk of subsequently permitting a united Left to take office. The interests of true conservatism, in Sonnino's view, would best be met by transformist procedures that prevented a clear division between Right and Left.[22] Umberto agreed and told Sonnino to keep himself in reserve with an alternative policy of increasing the military budget by upwards of thirty millions a year. Sonnino was further instructed by the crown to oppose the government in parliamentary debates, but not oppose so strongly that he might make more enemies and hinder his eventual succession to power.[23]

When the Triple Alliance with Austria and Germany was renewed a third time, this was another point of policy where Di Rudinì was said to have given way to the palace.[24] The prime minister personally considered the Triple Alliance to be more a disadvantage than an advantage, since Italians would gain most from a neutral stance in Europe after restoring good relations with France. Crispi, for quite different reasons, would also have preferred to denounce the alliance unless it could be made of more practical use to Italy.[25] But treaties of alliance, as Sonnino pointed out again, were for the king to make without reference to parliamentary wishes. Some politicians continued to dislike this Triple Alliance for being dictated by dynastic rather than national interests,[26] while others defended it for the same reason, believing that an essentially dynastic policy had been needed to unite Italy, and also believing that the crown was still the only reliable cement binding the different regions together.[27] But this last was no longer as convincing and uncontroversial an argument as it had once been.

9   *Two turbulent years*

This division of opinion became more marked during the last tempestuous years of the century. A revived republican party was set up in 1895 which gained ground from the fact that Umberto was held responsible for failure in Africa and the heavy expense of 'militarism'. Small in numbers, the new generation of republicans won the reputation of being realistic patriots 'whose honesty and straightforwardness are above suspicion', unlike other more prominent politicians.[1] Some republicans continued to enter parliament and take an oath of loyalty to the king, whether or not with mental reservations. One of these, the Sicilian Colajanni, was censured by the Speaker for continuing, despite the oath, to call himself a republican, though usually this anomaly in nomenclature was tolerated. Colajanni challenged the orthodox idea that the dynasty was a necessary symbol of national unity: on the contrary, he believed that Italian patriotism derived far more from the anti-monarchist and revolutionary Mazzini, whereas the dynasty of Savoy had once opposed national unification, then accepted it – but only under pressure from Garibaldi – and finally had corrupted it into a means of defending conservative interests and social order. This, incidentally, was much the same view as Crispi himself had once propounded in the days before he accepted the premiership.[2]

Directly opposed to Colajanni were those conservatives who had always thought that a more authoritarian monarchist regime might one day be needed to defend their predominant position in politics.[3] Such people felt threatened by two potentially powerful forces that were beginning to appear in parliament, one being a group of Catholics who decided to ignore the pope's boycott of united Italy, the other a recently created socialist party. Both forces, by appealing to voters from outside the existing political élite, raised an altogether new and vital problem – whether mass parties could be accomodated inside the existing system, and how that system might consequently have to adapt.

The views of many on the Right were represented by Sonnino who in January 1897 wrote a polemical article reviving the argument that monarchy should resume the powers prescribed by the constitution of 1848. Sonnino was an enlightened social reformer who, more than most other conservatives, saw that the preservation of social order would be difficult without major concessions: for example, the introduction of rights to medical care, old age pensions, and possibly universal suffrage. Such reforms would not easily be granted by what he called a corrupt and oligarchic parliament. So he put up for discussion the challenging thesis that conservatism was best defended by reforms which required a much stronger monarchy, one with confirmation of its right to veto legislation, to dismiss ministers at will, and to override the clash of political factions that threatened to reduce the king to the status of a figurehead.[4] As Sonnino was close to the palace he can be assumed to have known that these suggestions would be acceptable at court.

Crispi's private comments show that he agreed, at least in part. He wanted parliament to confine itself to legislating, whereas the king, in addition to his constitutional rights as part of the legislature, ought to recover his prerogatives as sole head of the executive and untrammelled in practical application of the law. In the bitterness of enforced retirement, Crispi was now sorry to discover that the Italian monarchy had shallow roots. He himself had long since given up republicanism and rallied to the throne, but now confessed that this had been 'only for want of something better', and he criticised Umberto for not permitting a strong minister to rule effectively as Bismarck had ruled in Germany. While Sonnino wanted a stronger monarchy, Crispi believed, as did Mussolini later, that the Italian political system above all needed a more powerful prime minister who could govern as a chancellor with moral support from the palace.[5]

Quite different was the view of those who adhered to Cavour's doctrine that 'the king reigns but does not govern' and that ministers should be responsible to parliament quite as much as to the sovereign. This forty-year-old tradition had lately come under serious challenge from Sonnino and Bonghi: four times since 1891 a government had fallen without any parliamentary vote, and in the next four years as many extra-parliamentary governmental crises would take place without the chamber being consulted. This, to some people's surprise, was proving a recipe for ineffective government, because, while it made parliament seem almost superfluous, Umberto unfortunately lacked the capability and even the ambition to run government himself.

The various critics mostly agreed that Italy was continuing to fall between two stools, between the English model where dynastic interests were in practice almost wholly subordinated to those of the state, and the German tradition where a strong monarchy was firmly founded on two things that Italy lacked – an aristocratic *Junker* class and an army that enjoyed the prestige of great victories. The Italian middle way carried the danger that the true location of sovereignty was left vague and imprecise. And as the conservative *Corriere della Sera* commented, Sonnino's solution would have the disadvantage of leaving the monarch 'uncovered' by his ministers; if they were responsible to him and not to parliament, any further bank scandals or another Adowa would be blamed chiefly on himself and the monarchy would be destroyed by its own hand.[6]

Di Rudinì made much the same point. While accepting that the parliamentary system was not operating well, and though he knew that the 'court party' was privily seeking to replace him, he never questioned the need to 'cover' the king by the principle of ministerial responsibility. He knew that his task was far from easy, especially since dissatisfaction with the working of governmental institutions was now compounded by a severe economic recession. The years 1897–8 were a bad period for social unrest, and this gave many valid arguments to the political opposition. The extreme Left numbered about 75 deputies, of whom only 16 were socialists, but these critics of society included some of the best speakers and most intelligent members of parliament. They could be sure in future of attracting an increasing share of the popular vote unless more attention was given to problems of deprivation, malnutrition and illiteracy which underlay alarming symptoms of public disorder.

In May 1897 Umberto escaped an assassination attempt and was shocked to encounter fewer signs of the public sympathy than might have been expected. Once again he mentioned the possibility of giving up the throne if he truly lacked popular support,[7] but Di Rudinì saw such violence rather as a reflection of profound discontent by poorer people who blamed Italy's commitments in East Africa as a main cause of their poverty.[8] With this in mind the government spent several months hoping to persuade Belgium to buy or lease Eritrea,[9] until Umberto once again insisted that the colony must remain Italian. The king also made clear that Giolitti and the Centre-Left must never be allowed back into power with plans for economising over the army, because there could be no yielding on any point where national prestige was involved.[10]

This was a brave but provocative attitude to take at a time of economic recession, especially when he stood accused of using the army to support a dynastic policy abroad and as a strike-breaking force at home.[11] The danger was all the greater because the huge cost of the army continued to fall disproportionately on poorer, disfranchised people who were sometimes trying to keep their families alive on a wage of one lira a day. For such people the slightest rise in food taxes or the price of flour spelt catastrophe. While Crispi had boasted that the army was taking civilisation to Africa, deputies of the Left drew attention to the existence of villages just outside Rome where people lived in straw huts as in Abyssinia, equally condemned 'to a life of barbarism and slavery'. According to Sonnino's friend, the philanthropist Giustino Fortunato, poverty was the main danger to social order; not socialist agitation as some people supposed, but primitive living conditions that for some people made civilised existence or liberal government impossible.[12]

Economic recession was in fact driving more and more people to the edge of penury and providing the ingredients for a possible revolution. Nor could constitutional monarchy, preoccupied with other objectives, easily find a remedy, but was in Fortunato's words poised above a volcano. Leading ministers were accused of dishonesty as well as crass incompetence. Some politicians demanded a more authoritarian style of government that would stop strikes and food riots,[13] while others feared that 'colonels and generals, under pretence of defending military prestige, were ready for a *pronunciamento* against any government that asked for economies in the army budget'.[14] A different fear arose from the fact that policemen were few in number. Law enforcement was weakened by each government's dismissing senior police officers to make jobs available for its own friends.[15] Farini moreover wondered if a single general in the army could be relied on or would know how to act if revolution broke out.[16]

Umberto in May 1898 found a willing general in the person of Bava Beccaris who was given powers of martial law to put down what Farini called civil war in Milan. Elsewhere local authorities showed more sense, but in Milan, the richest Italian city, a tragic error led to hunger demonstrations being mistaken for an organised socialist revolution backed by French money. Numerous casualties were caused when Bava Beccaris used cannon against unarmed civilians, and cavalry charges cleared the principal streets; after which, savage prison sentences were imposed on many Catholic and socialist leaders who had mostly done their best to support law and order. Scores of newspapers were banned. Some foreign journalists were expelled. The radical *Secolo*, the Italian newspaper most read abroad, begged its readers in Milan to obey the military authorities, but was suspended for four months after daring to point out the damaging fact that none of those killed or arrested was in possession of arms. Its much-respected editor was sentenced to four years in gaol. Only later could it be admitted that a temporary lifting of the tax on flour would almost certainly have defused popular resentment, or even that 'a fire-engine or two would probably have ended the whole riot'.[17]

Not surprisingly the king, as commander-in-chief of the army, was saddled with responsibility for using soldiers in such a contro-

versial and unnecessary cause, especially when he ostentatiously rewarded Bava Beccaris for his services to monarchy and 'civilisation'
by gratefully appointing him to the senate and bestowing on him
one of the highest orders of chivalry. Conservative newspapers
applauded, but liberals in the centre of politics were appalled by this
'conflict between crown and people', because the monarchy was
bound to become unpopular if it could be seen as an essentially
military and reactionary institution.[18] Not even the discredited
Bourbons of Naples had condemned so many opponents for political
offences, and many respectable citizens now acquired first-hand
evidence that conditions in Italian prisons were little better than those
Gladstone had so dramatically and successfully denounced at Naples
in 1851.[19]

The government did not long survive the bloodshed of May 1898.
In a moment of panic, Di Rudinì suggested closing parliament and
passing the budget by royal decree, and Umberto momentarily
agreed until he realised that any suspicion of another palace coup
would leave the monarchy uncovered and vulnerable. He also refused a request by Di Rudinì to risk another appeal to the electorate.
The latter thereupon resigned without waiting for parliament to
register a hostile vote. Umberto could, and some constitutionalists
said should, have insisted on a vote, but he understandably feared
that the chamber might support Giolitti or might otherwise limit the
royal prerogative of choosing a more obedient successor.[20]

Further offence was caused when he again omitted the customary
consultation of other parliamentary leaders. He particularly hoped to
avoid having to meet either Giolitti or Zanardelli, and explained that
he would henceforth follow Sonnino's advice to pay less attention to
the views of parliamentary leaders. Another rumour spread that he
wanted a more despotic government based on military officers and
senators.[21] Eventually in June 1898 he chose another royal aide-de-
camp, General Pelloux, as the next prime minister, and he justified
this on the grounds that martial law was still required and parliamentary backing might be relatively unimportant.[22] Four times in
the previous reign Piedmontese or Savoyard generals had in similar
moments of crisis been appointed prime minister – and the fact that
yet another would be chosen to replace Mussolini in 1943 suggests
something of a pattern. Pelloux was a senator, not an elected member
of parliament, and his origins in what was now French Savoy were
indicated by the fact that he spoke Italian with a noticeably French
accent.

Pelloux at least had the advantage of being by reputation a moderate and as such won the initial backing of Giolitti's supporters.
But the king was hoping for much less conciliatory action against

what he called 'the corrupting influence of parliament and current tendencies of anti-patriotism'. He wanted new laws limiting press freedom and public meetings. He would have preferred a further restriction of the parliamentary suffrage.[23] Yet he lacked the determination to insist on such changes immediately, and when opening a new session of parliament renewed his promise to respect and enforce constitutional freedoms.[24]

Gradually Pelloux felt able to take a more forceful stance and was certainly under pressure from the palace to do so. He appointed new conservative senators and proclaimed a frankly 'conservative policy in defence of existing institutions and social order'.[25] Not wishing or daring to seek a popular mandate in a general election, in February 1899 he asked parliament for laws to punish strikes, forbid public assemblies, limit press freedom, and if necessary bring railway workers and postmen under military law. Giolitti still supported him, so one may assume that some increase in the powers of the executive was generally thought desirable. But tension rose when illiberal laws were enforced with undue harshness and newspapers were hounded out of existence. It was even said that in no other European country was there so little check on government action; and experience of the bank scandals and defeat in Africa showed how dangerous that might be.[26]

In the next few months a grave constitutional crisis built up and brought parliamentary government close to collapse. Some voices called for Crispi to return at the age of almost 80 with a more autocratic regime and a renewed policy of imperialism.[27] Despite the fact that local elections showed overwhelming opposition against the suppression of constitutional freedoms, in May the king allowed Pelloux to form a new cabinet more to the right than any other during his whole reign; and once again this was done without consulting other parliamentary leaders. Its programme included greater expenditure on the armed forces, as well as tax reforms intended to benefit the rich and further penalise the poor.

10   *The collapse of parliamentary government*

At this point the veteran Zanardelli resigned on a point of constitutional principle, because precedent decreed that he as Speaker of the lower house should have been consulted before a new government was appointed. His successor, the colourless Luigi Chinaglia, had no such scruples, and instead of trying to be conciliatory, ruled against allowing deputies to criticise the army or even so much as hint that the constitution was being violated, and such was the uproar against this ruling that on 27 May 1899 a parliamentary session had to be suspended in the middle of a speech by the prime minister. Another yet more drastic breach of precedent was an attempt to bring debate to a premature close by modifying parliamentary regulations; and when the opposition halted this move by using obstructionist tactics to postpone a vote, Pelloux obtained from Umberto a royal decree, the notorious *decretone*, which specified that further repressive measures could henceforward be introduced even if parliament objected.

This was a graver affront to the legislature than had been attempted in fifty years. Pelloux was acting with deliberation and felt sure he would succeed. He was confident that most deputies would back the government, and he failed to appreciate that many on Right and Left would resent losing part of their limited powers. Many members of parliament were shocked that the crown was thereby exposed to damaging criticism for being more revolutionary and 'unconstitutional' than the so-called revolutionaries. Sonnino supported the government; Di Rudinì was uncertain; but Giolitti and Zanardelli both denounced the *decretone* as illegal and provocative. On 30 June the socialists demanded the resignation of the new Speaker for failing to defend their freedom of speech, and three times another tumultuous session had to be suspended. After fighting broke out in the chamber there was an appeal for soldiers to restore order, and the socialists then brought proceedings to a close by carrying off two voting urns. Parliament had to be shut before the annual budget had been agreed, and was not allowed to reassemble until November.

One element in the growth of opposition was the fear that Umberto's arbitrary treatment of parliament reflected a determination to keep his hands free for the renewal of an expansionist and militarist foreign policy which would mean higher taxes on rich as well as poor. Foreign affairs, as he reiterated, were not a matter that the two houses could profitably discuss, and this view was still shared by enough people for any debate to be brief and inconclusive.[1] The more important Italian embassies, as in the old days of royal absolutism, were usually in the hands of Piedmontese generals chosen from among the aides-de-camp of the royal household. The prime minister in 1898–9 was another general, and the foreign minister was Admiral Felice Canevaro: neither had much experience or skill in parliamentary politics and both sat in the non-elected senate, something that had not happened for thirty years. In addition, the monarch used to preside at cabinet meetings when or if decisions on foreign policy were permitted to reach the agenda.[2]

Some courtiers close to the throne argued once again that another war might be needed to raise popular morale and strengthen the dynasty. Nor did the king forget that he was a soldier first and foremost. He was delighted to send Italian troops to join an international contingent in a civil war that broke out in Crete, employing money that had been voted for other purposes. He also had thoughts about seizing the island of Rhodes from the Turks.[3] Irritated by popular opposition to his African policy, he feared that Italians were lacking in patriotic fervour and might need the stimulus of outside adventures. Some politicians agreed and reacted against pacifism by adopting an aggressive and even racialist nationalism in place of the more liberal patriotism that had characterised the risorgimento.[4] Nor was Umberto immune from this new and dangerous infection.

Most people among the new breed of nationalists were enthusiastic supporters of the German alliance, for the good reason that it symbolised authoritarianism and offered the best chance of victory in a future European war. One reason for Pelloux's appointment was that Umberto disapproved of Di Rudinì's attempt to take a more neutral position between Germany and France.[5] Nevertheless, there was an increasing realisation that Crispi's tariff war against France had been a gratuitous act of folly which in ten years cost Italy some two thousand million lire in lost exports and the further expense of defences on her north-western frontier. Hostile as the king remained to the republican regime in France, he was also apprehensive that the Germans might involve him in war before the Italian army was up to strength. He had to accept that, while there were persuasive dynastic reasons for retaining the German alliance, Italy could only be further impoverished unless the trade war with France was ended or modified. A settlement with Paris was therefore arranged towards the end of 1898, but Canevaro explained that its motivation was purely economic and there would be no change in the general direction of foreign policy.[6]

Despite verbal promises, Umberto never received help from Germany in his colonial ambitions; but his sights were still set on Africa where he nurtured hopes of retrieving what had been lost in 1896. In South Africa he expressed support for the Boers in their fight for independence against the British.[7] In Somalia, to the annoyance of some strict constitutionalists, he profited from a parliamentary recess to issue a royal decree that took another step towards creating a new Italian colony.[8] Further north in Eritrea he acted to retain territory that by the treaty of 1896 should have been returned to the Abyssinians: against this former enemy, as he told the colonial governor Ferdinando Martini, 'I am what they call a warmonger, and my personal wish would be to strike back at Menelik and revenge our defeat'. Sensibly, however, he settled for a monetary transaction and offered several million lire of his own money to the Abyssinians in return for more favourable terms. The Negus agreed, though it seems that this indemnity fell eventually on the Italian exchequer.[9]

Much less sensible was the sudden decision to send an expedition to China early in 1899 to establish a naval base in the bay of San Mun. The Germans advised against this move as an expensive gesture of little utility, and Italian anti-militarists were mortified by what seemed another attempt to play the great power without the necessary resources. There was a division of opinion along familiar lines: on the one hand Crispi and his friends were delighted at further proof of national virility; on the other hand Giolitti saw it as 'one more example of that fatal law that makes every reactionary government seek a diversion abroad'.[10]

Once again in China, just as in Abyssinia, Italians found that considerations of national prestige obstructed any attempt to back down from a commitment that had been made hurriedly and secretly without calculating the cost or the possible gains. The prime minister confessed, astonishingly, that neither he nor the cabinet had been consulted ahead of time, and a number of people were sure that the initiative was taken by Admiral Canevaro at the instance of the king himself.[11] When asked whether he expected parliament to pay for a military expedition about which it had been told nothing, Canevaro replied that this was another of those great issues of state that were better kept well away from the embarrassment of public discussion.[12]

The Chinese government, presented with an unexpected request to allow Italy a naval station, sent a firm but polite note indicating that, while intending no offence, it must refuse. At which Canevaro demanded reparation for what he called an insult and ordered his representative in China to deliver a formal ultimatum threatening war. Four hours later a second order was sent countermanding the ultimatum, but unluckily the two telegrams arrived in the wrong order. Not knowing that his ultimatum had been presented, Canevaro publicly denied sending it, but only after its precise wording had appeared in the world press. In some confusion he broke off diplomatic relations with China and resigned.[13]

His successor as foreign minister was Senator Visconti-Venosta once again, who, although he was no belligerent imperialist, had to admit that Italian prestige would suffer too much from a withdrawal. Steps were taken to conceal a clumsy piece of amateurish diplomacy and prevent a parliamentary debate which might have brought 'dishonourable and undignified facts' to light,[14] but more troops were sent to China, and the king was pleased to nourish the illusion that a glorious military victory would soon expunge another moment of public shame.[15] Several years later the Chinese were forced to allow Italy a concession at Tien Tsin, which remained intact until 1947.

Umberto was here moved by illustions of national rank and status rather than by more realistic considerations or the wishes of ordinary citizens. Since he made little effort to hide his disdain for parliament,[16] he did not realise the danger of pushing Giolitti and Zanardelli into joining the extreme Left against a reactionary regime and an extravagantly jingoistic policy. Africa and China together had cost hundreds of millions of lire, with little to show in return except humiliation and a mounting national debt proportionately larger than that of any other country.[17] Meanwhile, General Pelloux was trying to evade parliamentary criticism by his *decretone* of June 1899, and continued throughout the next months to curtail the statutory right to personal freedoms. He also continued to use the army for suppressing popular unrest that he persisted in blaming on socialist agitators rather than on genuine hardship.

The obvious dangers of such a policy reinforced the political divisions in an increasingly polarised society. Pelloux was supported by what was said to be 'many younger conservatives', in particular by Sonnino who once again advised the king to hold firm and if necessary ignore parliament.[18] When Sonnino argued that this advice was in the true liberal tradition that derived from Cavour, Giolitti accused him of a gross falsification of history, since Sonnino's views were closer to those of the absolutist enemies of united Italy who had been defeated by Cavour in 1859–61.[19] Both sides in the debate appealed to divergent interpretations of history. The risorgimento could be viewed in retrospect as symbolising individual liberty and self-determination; or, alternatively, as an idealisation of the national state. It could apparently be interpreted as standing for either freedom, or authoritarianism; for either democratic self-government, or an imposed monarchist centralisation of government authority; for either the liberation of subject peoples everywhere, or an exaggerated patriotism that justified imperialist conquest.

Another group of conservatives was led by Luigi Luzzatti who as an expert economist had strongly criticised the tariff war with France as useless and damaging. He was also a professor of constitutional law who disliked the practice of government by royal decree because it evaded parliamentary control and encouraged the opposition to support extra-legal reaction. Luzzatti nevertheless had to hope that Right and Centre would join ranks in backing the king against the twin danger from socialists and clericals.[20] Di Rudinì sympathised with this view and criticised the obstructionist politics of the opposition, but also criticised Luzzatti and Pelloux for endangering the monarchy by bringing it into partisan politics on one side of a parliamentary controversy.[21]

When parliament re-opened in November 1899, the inaugural speech from the throne wisely made no mention of Eritrea or of the fiasco in China. The king pointedly spelt out the need for order and tranquillity but ignored the issue of constitutional liberties, and his main theme was an appeal for everyone to accept the 'religion of patriotism'. Some of the critics responded by lamenting that Italians, who during the risorgimento had been admired everywhere as champions of popular liberty, were now sometimes said to enjoy less domestic freedom than the inhabitants of autocratic Austria.[22]

One instance of this was the fact that distinguished academics such as Vilfredo Pareto and Maffeo Pantaleoni, like Cattaneo earlier, had to leave the country and teach in Switzerland. Another was that Italian newspapers every day continued to appear with blank spaces imposed by a censorship that was forbidden by the constitution and had no parliamentary sanction. Pelloux made no apology for these anomalies but rather proceeded with his plan for changing parliamentary regulations so as to strengthen the executive against the legislature. He was halted only when at a crucial moment the courts were emboldened to intervene and declare that his *decretone*, despite being signed by the king, was null and void because it violated the constitution.

This drastic and unexpected ruling greatly encouraged those members of the opposition who had repeatedly demanded a constituent assembly to discuss changes in the Italian system of government. The plebiscites of 1848–60 were said by these critics to have constituted a bilateral agreement between crown and people, and if Pelloux broke a solemnly accepted pact, ordinary citizens could claim to be released from it and demand a new one. In particular they recalled that the people of Lombardy, when voting in 1848 to join a larger Italy, made their vote conditional on the summoning of a constituent assembly, a proviso that was accepted by Charles Albert and again later by Vittorio Emanuele; yet this royal undertaking had ever since been carefully and deliberately ignored.[23]

In March 1900, when the government again demanded new regulations to curb parliamentary debate, radicals and socialists in the chamber caused another uproar by asking for this pledge of 1848 to be honoured so that a constitutional impasse could be resolved. Three days in succession the Speaker was forced to bring the session to a premature close. One deputy ominously compared Pelloux to the notorious Thomas Strafford whose attempt to shackle parliament in Britain had led to his own execution and that of King Charles I. Another member, the poet Gabriele d'Annunzio, vociferously crossed over from the Right to join the parliamentary Left in what he flamboyantly protested was 'a move towards life'.[24]

On 29 March, and again on 2 April, Pelloux used his majority in parliament to cut short debate despite opposition protests that such behaviour was revolutionary and illegal. Di Rudinì and Luzzatti at this point refused to vote for him. Zanardelli and Giolitti went further and, following an example already set by the conservatives a year earlier, led their supporters in walking out of parliament when refused permission to speak. On this dramatic occasion Di Rudinì was heard to cry 'long live liberty'; deputies on the Left shouted 'down with the king', 'long live the constituent assembly'; and those on the Right replied with 'long live the king'.[25] For the next six weeks parliament remained shut. When it reassembled on 15 May and Giolitti proposed a compromise, Pelloux still refused to give way, and again the legislature had to be closed after deputies of the Left started to sing the revolutionary 'hymn of Garibaldi'. The prime minister in desperation decided to appeal to the country in a general election.

Pelloux had in fact lost any taste for continuing the fight. With more energy and tact he could almost certainly have overcome the obstructionist tactics of the opposition,[26] but he failed to organise his own followers who frequently neglected to vote at crucial moments. What he also lacked in these last months was support from the palace, and this was probably decisive. In fact, he had at first advised against holding elections and the king rejected this advice, having clearly lost confidence that his prime minister would survive the mounting storm.

The elections in June were apparently held with less official pressure than usual,[27] yet the government nevertheless won a fairly comfortable majority. Nor was this surprising. Official figures were produced to show that the outgoing legislature included 165 deputies who held posts salaried by the government, apart from 74 more who enjoyed state pensions, and a further 109 in receipt of miscellaneous official payments: in other words, over half the deputies had a financial inducement to support Pelloux and seek his re-endorsement of their election.[28] This reflected one differentiation between political practice in Italy and that in some other countries. In Britain the usual tradition was for any party winning an election to form a new government; whereas in Italy the norm was for the king to appoint ministers of his own choice, after which the very fact of being in office provided them with sufficient authority and patronage to win a majority in the next election.

The precise results in June 1900 are as usual hard to quantify precisely, but nearly 300 of the new deputies were ready to back

Pelloux while about 210 constituted a variegated opposition. Sonnino's conservative group lost some seats, whereas the extreme Left won a larger representation of some 95, the socialists increasing their number from 16 to 33; and this indicated that the fight would continue unabated. Faced by that prospect, the government surprised its supporters and upset the king by resigning, but at least protected his freedom of choice by not giving parliament any chance to indicate a preference for the succession.

Once again the practice of consulting all former prime ministers was omitted when the 78-year-old Giuseppe Saracco was chosen as premier.[29] Saracco, like Pelloux, sat in the non-elected senate, and the king appointed another general to the senate so that he could enter parliament and take charge of the war office. But Saracco himself was someone of moderate views who, notwithstanding his friendship with Crispi and Sonnino, had once been on the left of centre, and this suggests that the king may have learnt that the demand for a greater monarchist bias in the constitution would have to be modified as impracticable or too dangerous.

Many members of parliament must have been apprehensive when they reassembled later in June. Deputies on the extreme Left again walked out during the opening ceremonies, and Umberto's hand was observed to shake as he read his inaugural speech promising once again to respect the country's constitutional liberties.[30] A few weeks later he died a sudden and violent death. Riding in an open carriage, having refused the guard of more than a single policeman, he was assassinated by an anarchist who thought to punish the symbol of an oppressive society. Italian anarchists had recently been responsible for killing President Carnot of France in 1894, the Spanish prime minister in 1897, and the Empress Elizabeth of Austria in 1898; the fact that the assassins were in each case Italians came as a special shock to patriots whose self-confidence was shaken by other recent events. Umberto was far from being one of the great tyrants of history, but he paid the price of occasionally adopting too active a role in politics and taking upon himself too much personal responsibility for what was seen as a repressive and unconstitutional policy.

11   Retrospect

Death came to Umberto at the age of only 56, a few months earlier than to his father. Hailed by loyalists as the 'martyr king' and 'Um-

berto the good', he had tried to do what he took to be his duty
but without much perceptiveness or talent for the job and without
much enthusiasm for liberal values or the subtleties of parliamentary
government.

In retrospect, penetrating behind the myths of official propaganda,
he seems curiously colourless in personality. One of his aides, the
Marquis Paulucci, had been surprised to find that he had very few
serious opinions of his own. Almost as surprising was that he made
no concealment of his contempt for everything pertaining to art and
literature. Others who knew him were ready to confirm that he
lacked either firmness of opinions or political judgement.[1] One
foreign and friendly ambassador had to admit that the legend of his
political acumen and great popularity was excessive. 'The poor king
was the best and kindest of men, but he was hardly fitted to grapple
with the enormous difficulties, financial and political, with which
the Italian government has to deal', and 'on several occasions he had
not given his ministers the support they had a right to expect in
carrying out measures which had been brought forward with his full
consent'.[2]

Another legend also tried to make out, again vainly, that his private life had been a model of domestic virtue and affection.[3] Queen
Margherita accepted with dignity the embarrassment of his ostentatious infidelities, and by her conduct under difficulties earned the
reputation of being the one indisputably regal presence in four generations of the House of Savoy. She alone had a sense of occasion
and liking for grand entertainment. Unlike all four kings she appreciated music, conversation, and intelligent company, so attracting
the loyal respect of far more than the ultra-conservative courtiers
whose attentions she personally much preferred. Without being an
intellectual, she was more intelligent than her husband. Though her
political influence was small, she was more of a political reactionary
than Umberto. Behind a façade of discretion, experience taught her
that parliament was a poisonous influence on society and she could
not understand why deputies were allowed so much freedom of
speech: opposition should in her view be tamed by 'the big stick', not
by reasoned argument.[4]

Umberto did not try very hard to keep up the outward appearances of a happy marriage, nor to support the myth of his poverty
that some conservative monarchists invented.[5] Few people can have
known that, apart from his inherited personal income, he could earn
several million lire a year from wines grown on estates belonging
to the crown,[6] and in addition his annual grant from parliament
remained much larger than that received by the royal house of
England – even a minor relative expected to receive a public grant

far higher than the salary of the head of state in the United States.[7] Pareto calculated that the average Italian contributed a hundred times as much to his sovereign's income as a much richer citizen of Switzerland paid to the Swiss president,[8] and it was reckoned that, after settling his father's very considerable debts, Umberto left an inheritance of nearly forty millions at his death. According to another estimate, savings on the civil list allowed him to invest a hundred millions in England.[9] This may refer to a large life policy that he took out with the Prudential Assurance Company, the proceeds of which were later providentially left in Hambro's bank in London by his successor.

Another difference of opinion was over how strong a monarchy he handed over to his son. Undoubtedly the trappings remained of the semi-divinity that hedged a feudal kingship. People sometimes knelt in the streets as he passed by. Ministers were expected to bow three times when admitted to the presence and leave the room walking backwards, a custom that was generally maintained by his son and grandson. More substantially he had succeeded under cover of ministerial responsibility in keeping considerable control over military and foreign policy. He also exercised an 'unlimited moral authority' over the choice of ministers and in general through the honours and sinecures in his gift.[10] Some critical observers thought that he acted as a virtual dictator behind the mere mask of parliamentary government. He was said to have imposed on his ministers a reactionary policy at home and an aggressive imperialism abroad, relying on the fact that no one was permitted to hint publicly at this damaging imputation.[11]

A quite different but equally exaggerated attempt was made to regard him as a model parliamentary monarch and the most 'modern' of sovereigns who never for a moment overstepped the boundaries of his prerogative; indeed, who by his tact and moderation saved the Italian parliament from certain ruin, whereas if only the two houses had co-operated fully with him they could together have made Italy as strong and glorious as Victorian England.[12] He himself claimed to believe that Pelloux might have given the country an altogether new status in the world if between them they had succeeded in taming the legislature, though he had to admit that the attempt failed and as a result the future looked bleak.[13] According to perceptive foreign as well as domestic observers, he had relied on 'the secret and unconstitutional influences of a court circle', or in other words on 'the court party, quite out of touch with the country, clinging desperately to its military policy'; and in so doing he was supported by rich people who in their fear of 'progressive forces' trusted him to assert royal authority in curbing the elected legislature.[14]

Despite posthumous eulogies it was possible to look back on his reign as a disappointment, even a disaster. After the bank scandals and Adowa the monarchy was discussed rather than revered. Sometimes it was accused of failing to justify its existence and its cost. Whether correctly or not it was given much of the blame for military defeat, financial collapse, and the inability to produce effective parliamentary government. On the Right as well as on the Left the admission could be made that, unlike his father, Umberto aroused no deep affection among the masses, so that the former enthusiasm for the crown was fading fast and might be moribund.[15] Though there was little active and practical disloyalty except among revolutionary anarchists, one result of his irregular private life was that 'even the conservatives had small respect for him'. Sometimes they blamed him for failing to protect their position in society against the gradual advance of the extreme Left.[16] Many of the liberals, on the other hand, would have preferred the British style of a less politically involved monarchy that did not back one party or one class; failing which there was almost inevitably a temptation to consider the comparative advantages of a republican regime.[17]

Here was a lesson that his son was already before 1900 beginning to learn. But Umberto did not have the temperament to reign without governing, while at the same time he lacked the qualities needed by the alternative and more interventionist German style of monarchy. He therefore failed to provide Italy with a powerful executive that was at once democratic and authoritative. One result was that, despite panegyrics by flattering courtiers, there was in practice almost a vacuum of power at the summit as he left uncorrected some of the weaknesses in the Italian style of parliamentary government.

Among independent contemporary commentators who had no reason to flatter him there was a sense of disillusion after his death. He was 'in many respects an unobjectionable monarch', but 'has not conferred any great and signal advantage to the kingdom over which he had been called to reign'.[18] One American living in Italy who personally liked and admired him came to see Umberto's reign 'as a long disaster to the kingdom' and himself as 'more than any other person the cause of the decline and anarchy in parliamentary government in Italy'. The king, so this observer remarked, had begun by inheriting the great prestige of his father; if he wished he could either have governed as a truly parliamentary sovereign, or else could have abolished the chamber, but instead 'allowed it to abolish him'.[19] Another American had a similar but slightly more charitable conclusion: the king 'saw parliament falling year by year into disrepute and uselessness, and socialism and republicanism menacing the throne itself; and yet kept neutral, passive, seemingly unconcerned. He tried to reign and yet not to rule, and, unhappily for Italy, he succeeded. The trend of the age is not against kings, but only against *fainéant* kings. King Umberto never realized this, and that is why, chivalrous, stout-hearted gentleman though he was, his reign must be written down a failure.'[20]

3
Vittorio Emanuele III

1   A new direction in politics

Vittorio Emanuele, Umberto's only legitimate child, became king in July 1900 at the age of 30, after which he ruled for 46 years. At the time of his accession he showed little natural inclination towards politics or government, and by his own account had half-convinced his father to let him renounce the throne in favour of his far more glamorous cousin the Duke of Aosta.[1] Caught unprepared by the tragedy at Monza he dutifully if without enthusiasm accepted his fate.

Before 1900 the royal prince had made little impact on the public outside the small circle of his brother officers in the army. He had been allowed no experience of public life and had been protected from forming easy friendships. Reticent and taciturn by nature, he evidently resented that neither parent showed him much affection,[2] and a solitary, introverted childhood was further embittered by physical disabilities: 'He is dreadfully short', wrote Queen Victoria.[3] As a boy, he had been forced to wear a variety of orthopaedic instruments to strengthen his legs, and his stunted growth no doubt explains much of his shyness and lack of self-assurance.

Although like all male children of the dynasty he had a strict military upbringing, he was unusual in possessing a less provincial and more intellectual bent than his forbears. He had an English nurse, followed by an Irish governess who was the widow of a colonel in the British army, and he remembered speaking more English than Italian until his fourteenth birthday.[4] Until the age of nineteen his education was then entrusted to Colonel Osio, a good soldier and exacting disciplinarian who had scholarly and artistic tastes. Osio taught his not very appreciative pupil to read some of Horace and Virgil in the original Latin, and succeeded in giving him an abiding interest in history and numismatics. By 1900 Vittorio Emanuele already possessed one of the finest coin collections in Europe. Though he modestly claimed to be a mere dilettante, his collection and personal annotations formed the basis of what became a considerable work of antiquarian scholarship, the *Corpus Nummorum Italicorum*.[5]

Courtiers were able to claim that he was the most intelligent and learned sovereign in Europe, but to his tutor's regret a prodigious memory for factual information was matched by a complete lack of imagination or artistic sensibility. A ritual visit to Bayreuth and the ability to play easy piano pieces by Schumann did not remedy a marked preference for military bands, and though he was genuinely

147

fascinated by archaeological excavations, Osio's conducted tours through the art galleries of Europe left him unmoved except for the antiquities. In literature and economics he admitted to an abject ignorance, and according to his mother he never progressed beyond the first pages of Manzoni's *I Promessi Sposi*. In history, however, especially military history, he became what one of his teachers called a walking encyclopedia, and he found time as king to read the *Cambridge Modern History* as each fat volume was published.[6]

Apart from his governess, Elizabeth Lee, Osio was the person from his early years for whom he retained a genuine affection, though he did not share all Osio's views: not for instance about using armed force against popular unrest.[7] At military college and then as a regimental commander he nevertheless followed his tutor's example and earned the reputation of a martinet. He was more apt for hard work than his father and possessed a much firmer character, though was less regal, less pompous and less outwardly self-assured. Inwardly, as his mother remarked, 'he had a tenacious will like all small men'.[8] Other descriptions referred to him as timid, unsociable, with a marked tendency to cynicism and in general a low opinion of human nature.

The initial impression given to Phillip Currie the British ambassador was that 'the new king is a sphinx. He is thought to have ideas but has never propounded them to anyone. The only thing about him that no one seems to doubt is his obstinacy'. On closer acquaintance Currie found him more confident in expressing very positive opinions on military matters. In particular, the king urged the British to adopt compulsory military service.

> His Majesty is quick of apprehension and his mind is stored with minute and accurate information on all subjects that interest him. He holds decided views, is able to see the humorous side of things, and he impresses one with a sense of his kindliness and simplicity.[9]

Americans were equally impressed with his lack of pretension and affectation. After meeting him for the first time William Thayer, the historian of Cavour, used the words affable, alert, frank, and interested,[10] while Cabot Lodge reported that 'he struck me as shrewd, clever, hard-headed and rather cynical'. Theodore Roosevelt was surprised to find him exceptionally intelligent, and thought that America would gain from having 'a few men like him in the senate at Washington'.[11]

The royal couple were totally uninterested in the glittering court functions that delighted the dowager Queen Margherita. They rarely entertained guests at home. This helped to earn him a reputation for aloofness and meanness. He pretended that his predecessors, after

11. Francesco Crispi (left) and Prince Otto von Bismarck (right) at Friedrichsruhe in 1887.

12. Vittorio Emanuele III, 1900.

13. Queen Elena, 1900.

14. Giovanni Giolitti and Count Carlo Sforza, 1920.

15. *The Meeting at Peschiera (8 November 1917).* Vittorio Emanuele III stands by the map on the table, explaining the defeat at Caporetto to the allied political leaders. Lloyd George is seated on the right.

16. Crown Prince Umberto with the Duke of York (shortly to be George VI of Great Britain) in 1935.

having been until the Napoleonic invasion of the 1790s 'the richest family in Europe', parted with everything except 'two small properties that brought in about 60,000 lire a year'. In practice, however, he found no difficulty in endowing an international agricultural institute with an annual income of six times this amount from a few of his many estates.[12] As well as personal property he enjoyed a usufruct of the inalienable *dotazione della corona* which made him perhaps the largest landowner in the country, though he refused a request to publish an inventory showing the income that this produced. In addition, apart from investments in London, he and members of the royal family continued to receive a very large official income, in his own case fifteen million lire a year, and when this was queried in parliament as excessive the discussion was cut short by an embarrassed government.[13]

He and his wife lived simply. His main extravagance was buying coins and breeding horses. His favourite pastimes of fishing, shooting, and photography cost little. Living in the Quirinal palace would have been too grand for his taste, so he bought a villa just outside the walls of Rome and visited the palace only for official business. Twenty-five miles from Rome on the coast lay another vast estate, Castelporziano, where he could shoot all the year. In spring he used to retire to another personal property, the lonely island of Monte Cristo which until recently had been owned by an Englishman. In summer he preferred to hunt Ibex and Chamois from various hunting lodges in the Piedmontese Alps. The autumn he spent largely at San Rossore, an estate confiscated from the last Grand Duke of Tuscany and that stretched for 25 miles along the Tuscan seaboard,[14] where it was not uncommon for a hundred wild boar to be killed in a single morning.

Vittorio Emanuele had initially worried his parents by his 'profound repugnance to matrimony',[15] but dutifully gave way after some badgering. During a visit to England he showed interest in a daughter of the Prince of Wales, but a Catholic wife was indispensable, and he was fortunate to find in Elena of Montenegro someone who would change her religion. Crispi was the first to suggest a Balkan princess, arguing that the House of Savoy was too in-bred by repeated marriage between cousins and needed the infusion of 'good blood'.[16] Elena had against her that she was the daughter of an unimportant and penniless princeling, but she possessed charm and good looks and good nature. Theirs was to be a truly happy marriage, and this was unique in four generations of the family.

The crown had lost greatly in reputation as a result of Adowa and the political repression of 1898–1900. No longer could it automatically rely on being the object of popular reverence as a divinely ordained institution above political controversy, but henceforward would have to justify itself by its practical utility, or otherwise its survival might possibly be in doubt. Nevertheless, the tragic manner of Umberto's death created a wave of sympathy that reinforced the dynasty and, as some observers believed, possibly saved it from collapse.[17]

Understandably his father's assassination made Vittorio Emanuele anxious about his personal security, and this accentuated a temperamental shyness about appearing in public,[18] which in turn helped to cut him off from society. While genuinely wanting to rule with popular support, in practice he relied mainly on his military entourage and a small circle of politicians to inform him about public opinion. At first he talked of instituting a privy council of personal advisers paid from his privy purse,[19] but on reconsideration decided instead to keep more aloof than his father from practical political involvement. There were distinct advantages in sheltering behind the convenient doctrine of ministerial responsibility.

Although Saracco continued as prime minister for a few months, at the age of 79 his could be only a temporary government and the new king told people that many things would soon have to change. Initially he preferred to study the situation so as not to act in haste, and made clear that he had little confidence in much of the advice that he received.[20] Without wanting to preside at cabinet meetings as his father had sometimes done, in these early months he intervened to appoint at least one minister of his own choice.[21] When advised to adopt forceful and reactionary measures, he sensibly replied that these had been counter-productive in the past.[22] As he told Queen Wilhelmina of Holland, he had learnt from his father's last years that crowned heads might find their greatest danger to lie in imposing their own views without seeking popular consensus.[23]

In obedience to the constitution he took a solemn oath before both houses of parliament calling God to witness that he would consecrate all his energies to defending liberal institutions against enemies from whatever quarter. Ten thousand prisoners, many of them victims of political repression, were released as a sign that a new and freer age had opened. Some of the conservatives were slightly alarmed. Sonnino still hankered after a more authoritarian style of government. Pelloux, another dedicated royalist, privately criticised the king in almost insulting terms for being 'ingenuous or worse' and feared that he might be too yielding, too democratic and unmartial for the sovereign that Italy required.[24] But the more liberal conservatives, among them Luigi Albertini, the editor of the *Corriere della Sera*, trusted that the crown would remain a moderating and beneficial influence above party squabbles. Albertini, while he admitted to being no dogmatic monarchist, accepted that kingship was needed as a unifying institution in a divided society, and welcomed the royal oath in parliament as showing that the monarch held the defence of personal freedoms to be a sacred duty.[25]

Another hope among constitutional loyalists was that the king would rescue parliamentary institutions from the discredit into which they had latterly fallen. Members of parliament were sometimes referred to collectively as 'the dregs of the country', and careful students of society reported that there was a striking alienation from politics among the general public; indeed 'an Italian today finds it difficult to believe that a politician can be disinterested'.[26] Although ministers habitually claimed to speak for the people, the historian Pasquale Villari guessed that public opinion meant ten thousand people at most, while Guiccioli said it was more like two thousand. According to the Neapolitan economist Arturo Labriola, only seven or eight hundred Italians had a serious interest in parliamentary politics, and Guglielmo Ferrero believed that liberal institutions were effectively manipulated by thirty individuals who held all the levers of power.[27]

This underscores the continued separation between 'real Italy' and the 'legal Italy' represented in parliament. When governments talked of popular wishes forcing them to fight in Africa, they were referring to the views of a very small minority. This minority, moreover, was largely dependent on government patronage and its opinions were artificially conditioned by an officially subsidised press.[28] Even some of the more serious newspapers would have collapsed without regular hand-outs from the secret service funds. King Umberto, following his father's example, had paid selected journalists from his own pocket,[29] though this was a practice that Vittorio Emanuele III was determined to avoid. An essentially private person, all his life the new king retained a suspicion or dislike of journalism.[30]

More than his predecessors he kept quiet about his personal political views, but these can in part be deduced from casual remarks as well as from his choice of ministers. For instance, he spoke with disapproval of anyone who advocated a strongly interventionist monarchy.[31] He is known to have been very doubtful about Crispi's African adventures and about Pelloux's attempt to curb free speech. He was heard to say, no doubt more sincerely than his father, that the monarchy would survive only if it frankly accepted and reflected the progressive democratisation of society. Another incidental remark referred to the need for governments to let private enterprise run railways, shipbuilding, and arms manufacture.[32] Ideally he believed in governing through parliament, despite its admitted imperfections, because he knew that the crown had been dangerously exposed by

appointing governments without reference to any parliamentary
vote. In February 1901 such views were put to the test when, most
unusually, a vote of no-confidence brought Saracco's stopgap administration to an end.

The king's immediate problem was that the conservatives were
divided on both sides of this vote and he was left with a difficult
choice: whether to select Sonnino who led the largest single group in
parliament, but who had backed the excesses of Crispi and Pelloux;
or else Zanardelli and Giolitti who were better placed to secure the
support of other minority groups, but who were to the left of centre
and had once joined the extreme Left in obstructionist tactics against
Pelloux. After consulting the main parliamentary leaders, with the
notable exception of Pelloux, he concluded that Sonnino aroused too
much suspicion and fear, yet there was no clear preference for anyone
else.

He therefore used his prerogative to choose the 75-year-old Zanardelli, and it was a courageous as well as revealing decision because
the latter formed a government with a quite unusual amount of
support from the Left. An attempt was even made to persuade two
radicals, Ettore Sacchi and Giuseppe Marcora, to accept office. When
they refused, another coalition cabinet was formed of which one
third represented moderate conservatism, and the king expressed
himself as delighted with this new manifestation of transformism.[33]
Some people on the Right nevertheless accused him of improperly
exercising his royal authority,[34] especially when Zanardelli issued
a programme that included progressive taxation, legalisation of divorce, and a more liberal attitude to strikes. The king replied to
the critics by asking 'what was I to do? The conservatives could
not agree among themselves.'[35] But some former ministers were
alarmed that this might indicate a dangerous penchant for democratic liberalism.[36]

The strong man of the new administration was the former prime
minister, Giolitti, who dominated Italian politics for the next twelve
years. Giolitti believed in parliament, partly because he better than
anyone since Cavour realised its potential value and discovered how
to make it work more or less as he wanted. He carried conviction
when he pointed out that recent misadventures in China and Africa
could hardly have taken place had parliament and people been allowed
to know what was happening, nor would national finances be in such
disarray if the chamber had not been regularly prevented from a full
and informed discussion of the annual budget.[37]

In particular, Giolitti was alarmed by a dangerous and widening
division in society, because he had watched the poor becoming
poorer over the past twenty-five years – at the same time as 'the

ruling classes were spending enormous sums of public money on their own exclusive interests' while using their over-representation in parliament to reduce their share of taxation. He saw little hope for the future if governments continued to side automatically with employers against employees, and he was even prepared to say that unenlightened conservatism now posed a greater danger to society than did socialists or republicans.[38] Only if governments were more impartial in the class war, only if greater attention were paid to elementary education and to convincing the working classes that government was not necessarily their enemy, would it be possible to minimise social disorder and win adequate respect in the hierarchy of nations.

Neither Zanardelli nor the king fully liked or trusted the other,[39] but the former's policy, despite fierce opposition from Crispi's friends who thought it too radical, aimed to strengthen the monarchy by giving it an altogether new association with external peace, domestic tolerance, and class co-operation.[40] A first priority was that taxes should become more equitable. The state, said Giolitti, still derived about 40 per cent of its revenue mostly from articles of everyday consumption, in other words mostly from the poor, whereas there was no single tax on wealth despite a precise article of the constitution about taxation having to be 'proportional'.[41]

Another constitutional violation made judges dependent on ministerial favours if they wanted a successful career, and on this point Zanardelli's proposed reforms found the king in full agreement.[42] The judicial system was badly in need of radical overhaul. Italy was said to have the highest crime rate in Europe; her prisons, according to those deputies who had first-hand experience of arbitrary arrest in 1898, were so insalubrious as to be likened to slaughter houses or the Black Hole of Calcutta; and Crispi's unconstitutional practice of house arrest, without judicial appeal, persuaded *The Times* of London that maladministration of justice was a graver threat than socialism to the Italian monarchy.[43]

Zanardelli was a good lawyer but an indifferent politician. Age and ill-health made it hard for him to carry through his ambitious programme of reform, and too many vested interests were opposed to it, some of them represented inside his own cabinet. The Catholics disapproved of divorce; the rich disliked progressive taxation; and law reform mobilised strong opposition from much of the legal profession. In protest at these barriers to change, the extreme Left withdrew its support, and the prime minister was succeeded at the end of 1903 by his more adept and subtle colleague Giolitti.

This so-called extreme Left had emerged from Pelloux's election in 1900 with almost one fifth of the deputies in the chamber, though it was divided into 33 socialists, 28 republicans, and 34 radicals. These three small groups were each internally divided in their attitude to the monarchy. Some leading socialists publicly condemned the assassination of Umberto, though all but a few of them decided not to attend his funeral and not to appear in parliament when Vittorio Emanuele took his coronation oath. Some remained intransigent republicans, but the 'reformist socialists', notably Filippo Turati and Leonida Bissolati, while theoretically opposed to kingship as 'necessarily authoritarian and illiberal', regarded this 'institutional question' as by now a relatively minor issue and even recognised that a more liberal monarchy might one day prove an ally against the conservatives.[44]

Despite its name, the republican party was often more opposed to socialism than to monarchy, and eleven republican deputies broke ranks after the assassination at Monza to sign an expression of sympathy with the royal family – though the party congress in 1901 deplored this attitude. Some republicans still believed in a total boycott of parliament.[45] Such fundamental and increasingly unrealistic divisions deprived this extremist group of a useful role in politics. No doubt there was some importance in the fact that many electors in the narrow electorate, though fewer as time went by, continued to vote for republican candidates, and in February 1903 there was a surprising demonstration in parliament with individual deputies crying 'Long live the republic'.[46] Increasingly, however, such antiquated intransigence came to seem an irrelevance when far more urgent issues were in debate. Giolitti was able to point out that, if the monarchy ever ceased to exist, those likely to gain would be not republicans but more dangerous factions on the extreme Right that so far had no representation in parliament.[47] This point was well taken by Menotti Garibaldi, grandson of the Liberator, who was heard to say that, while he remained republican at heart, 'if a republic were established, Vittorio Emanuele would be overwhelmingly chosen the first president'.[48]

The surviving republicans were sometimes a stimulus but no longer a danger to the institution of constitutional monarchy. Vittorio Emanuele even signed a decree in 1904 for the publication at state expense of a hundred volumes containing the complete writings of the once proscribed Mazzini, though this did not prevent Zanardelli and Giolitti punishing and confiscating newspapers that made political capital out of quoting Mazzini's republican manifestos.[49] One newspaper was banned for stating that 'we have the most rigidly feudal of all dynasties, less open than any others to the liberal spirit, the most foreign to our Italian genius'.[50] While the essential contribution made by republicans to the risorgimento could no longer be ignored or denied, the accepted version of history had to give Cavour and the monarchists pride of place.

The radicals, who were the third of these political groups, continued to sit on the extreme left of parliament, but their alignment was obviously changing when Marcora accepted election as Speaker of the chamber in 1904, and even more when two years later Sacchi joined the cabinet as a minister. Some radicals continued to complain that the authoritarian monarchy of Piedmont had perverted the liberal tradition of the risorgimento, and they were sure that policy was still largely decided in the royal palace.[51] Others gave the monarchy merely conditional backing and only so long as it continued to permit liberal reforms. This was the attitude of the *Secolo* which until 1905 claimed to be the most powerful of Italian papers with the biggest circulation at home and abroad.[52] But in general the radicals, as well as being internally divided, were losing support as the socialist challenge led to a greater political polarisation. By 1906 Albertini was able to claim that the more conservative *Corriere della Sera* had overtaken the *Secolo*[53] to reach a pre-eminence in journalism which it retained for the next eighty years.

2   *Foreign policy, 1900–4*

The *Secolo* suffered because under the direction of Teodoro Moneta it became increasingly pacifist – Moneta was awarded the Nobel peace prize in 1907 but his views met with little domestic recognition. The *Corriere* in general agreed with its rival that Italy's foreign policy should be less adventurous and more strictly proportioned to the country's limited financial resources. Both these leading papers opposed two current and contrasting opinions: they disliked the pessimism of those who had learnt from recent events to doubt Italy's capacity for a healthy political life,[1] while they also warred against those who were looking for another Crispi to make Italians feared abroad.[2] Both newspapers agreed with those who thought that Italy, until much richer, should not struggle to become the least of the great powers, but rather be content with first place in the second rank of nations; otherwise she would risk further military set-backs and a tax burden that would prove debilitating and socially divisive.[3]

The king's views on such a controversial matter were a topic of speculation. He spoke to Sonnino of how he envisaged a great future for their country, especially as France was in decline and this would leave a vacuum of power which Italy might fill; his main doubt was finance and how much Italy could afford.[4] The French ambassador, Camille Barrère, felt sure that Vittorio Emanuele wanted a foreign policy of his own, not that of his father, nor one that his ministers would decide, but which made Italy more independent of the Triple Alliance, because non-alignment would bring with it greater bargaining power in Europe.[5] The German and Austrian ambassadors both received the impression that the sovereign was likely to impose a new direction on policy: they found him ambitious and self-confident, but he 'does not wish to commit himself to any course until he can be supposed to have adopted it on his own initiative; he will not appear to follow blindly in his father's footsteps'. The British representative agreed and added that the king spoke of his predominant wish to avoid war, even to the point of abolishing regular armies and seeking an alternative system of international arbitration.[6]

Such pacific sentiments may have been encouraged by his surprise at finding that the army was quite unfit to fight even a defensive war. At once he drew up a plan to visit all major military units and asked for daily progress reports; yet the obvious remedy of much higher taxation was too dangerous to contemplate.[7] As a result of earlier wars and colonial adventures, interest payments accounted for nearly half of government revenue, yet the armed services continued to absorb half of what remained, and even conservative politicians such as Sonnino and Luzzatti were inclined to agree that no more could be spent without penal taxation that would endanger social peace.[8]

Others went further and claimed that a mistaken and unduly dynastic foreign policy not only had resulted in impoverishing the country but, by inviting military discomfiture, was actually defeating its object and diminishing Italy's reputation in the eyes of foreigners. These critics maintained that only if parliament could reassert itself and stop the bad habit of unauthorised expenditure on armaments, and only if the government were forced to withdraw from 'the useless and crazy expedition to China', would Italy recover her good name. Radicals, socialists, and republicans were joined on this issue by a group of 'Christian democrats' who were small in number but before long would become a major force in Italian politics.[9]

These opposition groups had some good arguments but insufficient representation in parliament to cause much trouble. A more serious worry for the king was that the diplomatic service, recruited from a very narrow social class, was producing unsuitable ambassadors who lacked the requisite experience and knowledge of foreign countries.[10] He himself had travelled extensively, far more than the new generation of cabinet ministers, and this single fact meant that 'the king's influence would be very great'.[11] Most of the political élite knew surprisingly little about the outside world. Not only did newspapers lack good foreign correspondents, but a narrowly inward-looking educational system had produced what Villari called a most unfortunate 'intellectual isolation'.[12] Even inside parliament a lack of interest and knowledge reinforced the acceptance of foreign policy as a matter for the king and the executive. Zanardelli confirmed that the foreign minister was 'a non-political appointment' normally made by the palace without reference to the political colour of other ministers.[13]

Vittorio Emanuele quickly let it be known that he was lukewarm about Eritrea and disliked Umberto's commitments in China. Unlike his ministers he had read books about China and Japan. Unimpressed by current propaganda, he knew that there was no conceivable economic gain to justify keeping two thousand soldiers at Tien-Tsin. On the contrary, he would have preferred to leave oriental trade to private enterprise and withdraw from territorial ambitions – though he thought that the Chinese should first be made to pay an indemnity to cover the cost of his father's military expedition.[14] But like his father he found difficulty in backing down without an unacceptable loss of face. A military presence was therefore retained in China, even though ten years later there were said to be only a dozen Italian civilians to be defended.[15]

Relations with Britain were at first clouded by the South-African war in which many Italians agreed with Umberto in favouring the Boers, but Vittorio Emanuele expressed the hope that the British would not give easy terms of peace to the Afrikaner rebels.[16] As one of his foreign ministers said, Britain had quietly given invaluable help to Italy in her African colonies, something that had often been gratefully acknowledged in private though sometimes was thought prudent to deny in public.[17] Italian diplomats took for granted that this help would continue; indeed, they sometimes spoke as though there existed an unwritten Anglo-Italian alliance. The king was therefore irritated at receiving no help from London in extricating himself honourably from China, and also protested when encouragement was given in Malta to the use of the English language instead of Italian.[18] As he told the British ambassador, 'sufficient account had not always been taken in England of the peculiarities of the Italian nature. It might be necessary at times to say "no" to a request, but Italians liked the "no" to be softened as much as possible'.[19]

His personal anglophile sympathies remained strong. All his children and grandchildren were given governesses from either England or Ireland who were accorded a prominent position in the royal household. He was particularly pleased when asked to mediate between Britain and Portugal over the frontier of Northern Rhodesia, and again over a frontier dispute between Brazil and British Guyana. On the latter question he was presented with five volumes of evidence and told an American that he read every word: 'the Brazilians published lots of maps which were absolutely false...I might have given the whole disputed territory to England, but I gave the Brazilians half, and then I heard that they abused me outrageously. Ugh!'[20]

Relations with Germany were less easy, especially as the two heads of state were never friendly. The king in private ridiculed the German emperor for his obsession with gaudy military decorations and for demanding five copies of the Italian China medal to wear on different uniforms;[21] also for an undue preoccupation with personal safety when he insisted that the Venetian bridges were cleared of onlookers before passing beneath them in his gondola.[22] Less easily forgiven was that Wilhelm was overheard making insulting remarks about Queen Elena and continued to treat his brother sovereign with patronising condescension.[23]

Italy remained tied to the Triple Alliance with Germany and Austria. To a Russian who attended Umberto's funeral the king casually spoke of this alliance as a stifling influence on Italy because it committed him to an anti-French policy,[24] yet he could hardly back down because to denounce it after twenty years would have been taken by his allies as a hostile act with grave consequences. Although plausible arguments were advanced for steering clear of any treaty that might one day involve the country in war,[25] the foreign office was hoping that the danger of hostilities could be minimised by artful diplomacy, and at least the Triple Alliance effectively eliminated one danger by removing Austria from the list of likely enemies.[26]

The precise obligations incurred by the alliance remained unknown to the Italian parliament and to nearly all ministers in successive cabinets. No one knew that those obligations were regarded by the king as less onerous than might have been assumed. Despite a strict reading of the original text, Germany and Austria had been unilaterally warned that Italy would in no circumstances join them in a war against Britain, and one foreign minister privately admitted that Italy from the very beginning secretly regarded the treaty as 'quite compatible with the pursuit of the most friendly relations with France'.[27]

Not a great deal of its original spirit seemed to remain when the Marquis Giulio Prinetti, foreign minister in 1901–3, was faced with the alternative of renewing the alliance once again or letting it expire when its full term was due. His own wish was to change its general tenor so as to win greater influence for Italy in the Balkans,[28] but he met objections in Berlin and the king told him to give way.[29] A somewhat ambiguous position was eventually formalised, if hardly clarified, when in June 1902 the alliance was renewed without change, but simultaneously a secret document was signed with Barrère promising that, despite the Triple Alliance, Italy would in no forseeable circumstances join in a war against France. Since both documents were secret, no one could point out that they might be mutually incompatible.

In long months of negotiations over the second agreement, Barrère found Vittorio Emanuele to be a more serious politician than his father and no less important in deciding Italian foreign policy.[30] But the Frenchman also knew that the king was embarrassed in case this Prinetti-Barrère agreement, if ever generally known, would seem a piece of deliberate deceit at the expense of Italy's central-European allies. Embarrassment was indicated when the king insisted on falsifying the date of the agreement with France to 1 November in the hope that the juxtaposition of dates in June might not be noticed by future historians.

To allay suspicion still further, the Germans were given a categorical undertaking that, despite rumours to the contrary, Italy would make no agreement with the French that diminished her obligations under the Triple Alliance. Moreover, the king tried to convince Berlin that he disliked Barrère as 'a liar and a nasty man' (he spoke to the Germans, as usual, in English). The French were simultaneously assured once again that the Italian government had no treaty or military convention with Germany that would conflict with this Prinetti-Barrère agreement.[31]

Without doubt he was being deceitful, and not only towards Germany and Austria: the Italian parliament was equally deceived. Article 5 of the constitution empowered the king to make treaties on his own, but only if they cost nothing. Any treaty that incurred expenditure 'was null and void until approved by parliament'; and expenditure was certainly involved in the secret convention of 1888 whereby half the Italian army would be sent to Germany if the Germans ever found themselves at war with France. This military convention was confirmed by Vittorio Emanuele, albeit with reluctance.[32] Yet by lacking parliamentary confirmation it was strictly invalid, and perhaps he purposely retained this ambiguity so as to be able to disregard it at some point in the future.

The Germans were also told that the king's initial reluctance in renewing the military convention was due to his fear that he might be unprotected against domestic revolution if so many Italian soldiers left the country in wartime.[33] By another strange ambiguity, Italian politicians were allowed to think that the secret military convention had been cancelled rather than renewed. And yet the king permitted his generals to reassure Berlin that he was planning to ignore Swiss neutrality and march through Switzerland to link up with the German army as soon as war began against France.[34]

These inconsistent undertakings were, of course, known only to perhaps half a dozen people, but considerable disquiet was expressed in the columns of the *Secolo* where the pertinent question was raised of why, especially if no expenditure was involved, the text of the Triple Alliance had never been published. Was it not true that, in defiance of the constitution, the alliance had in fact already cost tax-payers many hundreds of millions of lire in military expenditure? Was it not forcing them into an arms race beyond their means? Did the alliance, despite official denials, perhaps envisage an offensive as well as a defensive war?[35] Secrecy was bound to lead to this kind of justified speculation, which in turn forced even liberal governments to resort to censorship. Newspapers could be confiscated if they hinted at apparent discrepancies or suggested that the alliance with Germany might be another 'Holy Alliance' to defend the Savoy dynasty against domestic as well as foreign enemies.[36]

How far these speculative criticisms were widely shared is impossible to say, but the British minister in Rome, Rennell Rodd, thought that the alliance with Germany and Austria was opposed by 'a large number of politicians in Italy' who saw it as the handiwork of 'the same reactionary party which . . . is held by them responsible for plunging Italy into undertakings beyond her strength and fatal to her prestige'.[37] Similar opinions were expressed by German diplomats who were realistic enough to expect little military help from Italy and who backed the alliance mainly because it was in the interests of other European monarchies to keep Vittorio Emanuele on his throne and in charge of foreign affairs. In Vienna as well as Berlin, prominent politicians feared 'the slightness of the hold that monarchy in Italy has on the affection of the population' – except possibly on people in Piedmont.[38] The existence of such doubts and fears must have been well known in the Quirinal.

The king was careful to keep abreast of all the main issues of foreign policy, and he explained that this was the more necessary since the monarchy was a guarantee of continuity in foreign relations, as well as because this was an area where mistakes would be irremediable, whereas domestic policy could easily be changed if things went wrong. He was suspected of following his grandfather's example by receiving reports from his own private agents in foreign capitals, and he frankly admitted that he had learnt to disbelieve in official ambassadors for being 'rather a useless institution'.[39] His foreign ministers between 1901 and 1905, Marquis Prinetti, Admiral Morin, and Senator Tittoni, were a fairly undistinguished trio, a fact that reflected his intention to remain personally in charge. Morin, like some of his predecssors, was said to be so ignorant that ambassadors saw little point talking to him about foreign affairs, and the king complained that neither Prinetti or Tittoni spent enough time in their office to know enough of what was happening.[40]

His personal interest was above all in Balkan affairs where both the British and Germans found him to be secretly resisting the spread of Austrian influence. He was particularly sensitive over Montenegro, his wife's homeland, and let people know that if the Austrians pushed too hard he was ready to send troops to Albania as a sign that the far shore of the Adriatic was an essentially Italian sphere of interest. An Austrian occupation of Valona, he said, might mean the end of his dynasty and would never be tolerated.[41]

Another element in his resentment against Austria was the fact that Emperor Franz Joseph had never returned the visit by Umberto to Vienna, and Vittorio Emanuele wanted a Catholic sovereign to visit Rome so as to diminish any residual papal hopes for restoring the Church's temporal power. In 1902–3 he made State visits to Russia, Germany, France, and Britain, pointedly avoiding Vienna in reprisal for this omission. He also avoided Switzerland with whom diplomatic relations had been over-dramatically broken off after critical references to his father in the local Swiss press.

Personal contact between heads of state had a special importance in foreign policy, and in particular his appearance in Paris was a reminder to Berlin that the Triple Alliance might not be an exclusive contract. He had hoped to arrange matters so that his arrival in England would be in grand style on an Italian warship, but unfortunately none was available.[42] Nonetheless, the British gave him a truly royal reception, with the bonus of an honorary degree from Oxford University in recognition of his work as a numismatist. Tittoni, as foreign minister, published an unsigned article claiming provocatively that Italy's presumed 'alliance' with Britain had more domestic support than that with Germany or Austria, because the British alone had never tried to conquer Italy and had never so much as demanded gratitude for their help during and since the risorgimento.[43]

More important for the Italians were the return visits paid to Rome in 1903 by the rulers of Germany and the United Kingdom. King Edward was made particularly welcome, and his private secretary recorded their admiration at Vittorio Emanuele's 'extraordinary knowledge of almost any subject one might mention and by the wisdom of his comments': the sovereign was 'a remarkable and agreeable man' who 'certainly had all Italian politics at his fingers' ends'.[44] By comparison, Edward's uncle the Kaiser appealed more to Italian conservatives who were overwhelmed by his greater pomp and theatricality and ostentation of military power.[45] But even some Germans confessed embarrassment when they brought to Italy a troop of the imperial guard, all selected for their great height with the obvious intention of putting the diminutive king at a disadvantage. This gratuitous offensiveness was never forgotten by the Quirinal. Nor was the fact that, while Edward made a purely private call on the pope, Wilhelm paraded through the streets to the Vatican with a ceremonial escort of German soldiers, going out of his way to suggest that a papal audience was the chief aim of his visit and the Italian alliance was of secondary importance.

In private talks with the German emperor the king once again mentioned a determination to develop his own foreign policy without bothering too much about ministerial approval. This same intention was confirmed by the German ambassador in Rome who reported that Vittorio Emanuele kept control over foreign affairs and appointed only foreign ministers who would leave him effectively in command. The ambassador added that the king was hoping to win a much grander position in Europe than the weakness of his country warranted, and despite the Triple Alliance he evidently meant to steer a middle course between Germany and France.[46] Tittoni, who became foreign minister in November 1903, was appointed to find this middle way. As his colleagues confirmed, Tittoni was very much the personal choice of the king, and his appointment caused some astonishment because he was well to the right of the rest of the cabinet.[47] Both French and German ambassadors in Rome saw this minister as no more than an obedient instrument of court policy.[48]

Tittoni's first task was to organise a visit to Rome by Emile Loubet, the French president, an occasion for which lavish preparations were made on a scale that the king insisted should be much grander than the welcome given to other heads of state.[49] This prospect caused dismay in Berlin, and the Italians were at one point informed that the Triple Alliance might collapse unless the planned festivities were radically scaled down.[50] In case threats would not suffice, the German emperor decided to arrive simultaneously in Italy so that the reception might seem to be also for himself.[51] It was then the turn of the French to threaten that Loubet might not come at all unless the emperor's visit was unofficial and kept quite separate.[52]

Events reached the point of farce when president and emperor arrived simultaneously and had to be prevented from meeting each other; and both then tried to put pressure on Vittorio Emanuele to give them due recognition at rival banquets in their honour. The king kept his nerve in a difficult situation. Loubet's visit turned out to be a triumph. Wilhelm left in a bad temper and untruthfully pretended that he had come to Italy only on the assumption that the French visit had been cancelled. Tittoni was able to claim, with pardonable exaggeration, that a shift in alliances was in operation that would open a new chapter in world history and from which there could be no going back.[53]

3　*The beginning of* Giolittismo

Outside foreign policy and military matters the king allowed his ministers a fairly free hand. Not only were domestic problems too variegated and complex and too boring for his personal attention, but more than his father 'he found his wings clipped by the existence of political groups and cabinets'.[1] Everyone knew that the monarchy in the 1890s had put itself in peril by taking sides too obviously in political controversy – and on the losing side. Intervention in future had better be kept in reserve for emergencies. In November 1901 he signed a decree that, as well as extending the authority of the prime minister over other members of the cabinet, slightly attenuated the exercise of the royal prerogative and brought senior officials of the king's household under greater ministerial supervision. Although the changes were minor, this decree paved the way to what, already in 1904, was being called Giolitti's 'dictatorship'.

The crown was fortunate in having the guidance of this supremely skilful politician who, while never trying to upstage the monarch and never criticising him as Cavour, Ricasoli and Sella had criticised his grandfather, or never as both Crispi and Cavallotti from quite different positions had criticised his father, instead guaranteed as quiet a ride as possible through any political squalls. Giolitti replaced Zanardelli as prime minister in November 1903, and the choice suggests that the lesson had been learnt about first consulting the main politicians and deferring to parliamentary wishes if ever clearly expressed.

Giolitti formed a ministry of the Centre and Centre Right, but first opened yet another chapter of history by trying to persuade the socialist Turati to join the cabinet, and this cannot have been without the king's approval. Turati had in 1898 been sentenced to twelve years in prison as a dangerous revolutionary, but the political climate had changed and the offer, which Turati refused, caused remarkably little surprise or offence.[2] Giolitti had been hoping to tame or weaken the socialist party by bringing its more moderate wing into the orbit of the constitution, and, if successful, this would certainly have altered the course of Italian history. He tried the same with the radicals; and two radical leaders refused his offer for a second time, though with reluctance and only after long discussion.[3]

Already before taking office, Giolitti received favourable comment from the palace for the fact that he 'understood how to treat the masses'.[4] His urgent advice was for the crown to remain neutral in the class war because the appearance of always siding with the rich would sooner or later be disastrous for the dynasty; and he wanted to demonstrate that liberty and progress could be guaranteed under a monarchy as much as under a republic.[5] This intention was tested when in September 1904, coinciding with the birth of an heir to the throne, Italy had the novel experience of a general strike, and one that had anti-dynastic overtones. But the government reacted with none of the hysteria shown in 1898 and let the strike work itself out fairly peaceably. The king was delighted that a neutral stance seemed to work. It enabled him to visit what he called the 'red' areas of the country and encounter a positive welcome instead of the animosity he had feared.[6]

By red areas he was referring particularly to Emilia and Romagna where republican sympathies had always been strongest, but also to southern Italy and Sicily where hunger riots were a recurrent danger after every bad harvest and where local politics were highly personalised and idiosyncratic. As Giolitti well knew, whole districts in the south were policed and virtually controlled by underworld organisations, notably the mafia and camorra. Successive cabinets since 1861 had in those areas been forced to resort to a covert if unwilling alliance with known criminals, because without such connivance the south might have been ungovernable; nor without it would governments have succeeded in securing the election of enough supporters to give them a parliamentary majority.[7]

The king must have known about this because there were frequent public criticisms that the mafia and camorra depended for their existence on the fact that every government since 1861 had needed their help. Three visits to Sicily between 1898 and 1906 gave him first-hand information. He knew, for instance, that the mafia was not the single secret society that some people thought, but represented a much more disorganised lawlessness which was more dangerous and less easily controlled.[8] In May 1902, to his great indignation, stones were thrown in Palermo against the royal train.[9] As a prince he had also spent several years with his regiment in Naples and the experience gave him a keen interest in the excoriating investigation by Senator Saredo into Neapolitan misgovernment and corruption: Saredo, after a private audience in 1902, informed people that the king knew the terrible facts better than anyone.[10]

Southern poverty and backwardness, as Giolitti admitted, were perhaps Italy's most serious problem and were almost bound to keep her a second-class nation unless local conditions could be greatly improved; but the prime minister could not find the time or courage or inclination to go and investigate the facts for himself. One such fact was that two million agricultural labourers still suffered from malaria, mainly in the south and the islands. For political reasons his administration continued to tolerate the mafia and camorra because he needed their electoral support.[11] Though 70 per cent of southerners were illiterate – a percentage higher than anywhere in Europe except Portugal – he led his followers in voting against more schools for the south, because too many southern members of parliament feared to carry out the law of 1877 about compulsory education, or at least they preferred to spend any available money on other things than this indispensable step towards social improvement.[12] A realist, he needed the votes of southern deputies who, out of self-interest and misguided local patriotism, continued to deny the existence of the mafia and were against social change because they themselves represented the local ruling oligarchies who would suffer from change. When a cabinet minister from the south felt obliged for reasons of political advancement to deny the very existence of any 'southern problem', the safest response of each government was to let sleeping dogs lie.[13]

Keeping his composite parliamentary majority was absolutely necessary in order to carry out the limited degree of social reform that Giolitti believed was feasible. He had already in 1892 learnt how to 'make the elections', as the Italian phrase went. In 1904 the king allowed him to try again, this time with yet greater success, and the palace sent congratulations along with the information that all members of the royal household had been instructed to vote.[14] About 35 radicals were elected on this occasion, of whom half would sometimes vote for the government; the 30 socialist deputies were also divided and not all were unalterably opposed to reforms by a bourgeois government; while even the republicans, about 25 in number, included some who refused to adopt the uncompromising opposition to the crown demanded by their successive party congresses.

An interesting development in this general election was that Pius X, who became pope when Leo XIII died in July 1903, at last relaxed his advice against Catholics' voting. Many Catholics had of course voted in earlier elections despite the papal ban, but four avowedly Catholic deputies were elected to parliament in 1904, and their readiness to support the monarchy against the threat of socialism denoted a distinct softening of the *dissidio* between pope and king. Giolitti assisted this process by opportunely dropping from his programme the proposal to legalise divorce.

The House of Savoy was by tradition anti-clerical, if for no other reason than that the Vatican had been the one irreconcilable opponent of national unification. Vittorio Emanuele admitted that his father was a freemason and so was his grandfather, though he himself was not.[15] His grandfather had been repeatedly excommunicated, and his father had occasionally made highly offensive remarks, for instance about wanting all clergy to be castrated.[16] On the other side of the divide, Pope Leo had been adamant in refusing to recognise the existence of a united Italy and continued to expect its imminent dissolution by the operation of divine providence. He even continued secretly paying for the water supply to the Quirinal as a token of his continuing claim to possession of the royal palace.[17] Leo caused particular and unnecessary offence by the grudging manner in which Umberto was allowed a Christian burial.[18]

Vittorio Emanuele had mixed feelings about relations with the Church. He had to accept the *dissidio* as a fact. Despite the great piety of his mother, he sometimes spoke as though he was himself an atheist, and habitually blamed the papacy for most of Italy's historical disasters since the Middle Ages;[19] but in practice he kept up appearances and was prepared to turn up at mass on occasion. 'His Majesty hated the late pope and likes the present one', wrote the British ambassador after an audience in 1904. Despite their differences, the court realistically looked forward to help from the Church in the event of a fight against socialists and republicans on the extreme Left.[20]

In March 1905, after a severe bout of influenza, what Giolitti called 'nervous depression' left him unable to preside at cabinet meetings or attend parliament, and he resigned. As there was no obvious successor, Tommaso Tittoni took over for two weeks as an interim premier, and the king admitted using the royal prerogative to choose his own personal favourite since the advice received from politicans was so contradictory.[21] This gave time for further discussions, after which the choice fell on Alessandro Fortis, and the fact that Fortis many years earlier had been arrested for holding republican opinions is an indication that the institution of monarchy had successfully disarmed many of its critics. Fortis was a colourless personality of uncertain political complexion. After being marginally involved in the bank scandals, he had supported Crispi's adventures in Africa and took office with Pelloux before becoming an erratic supporter of Giolitti. He was prime minister for nearly a year in 1905–6, but his unimpressive success in legislation threw into relief the skill of Giolitti as a manipulator of parliament.

Some people thought that Giolitti dominated the legislature more than even Cavour or Crispi had done. By organising three successive general elections, in 1904, 1909, and 1913, he contrived to build up an almost guaranteed majority, at least so long as a sufficient number of subservient deputies needed the support of his electoral machine and of the government-appointed prefect in their constituencies. They would hardly change their allegiance to him unless or until the king let it be known that someone else, perhaps Fortis or Sonnino, would be allowed to 'make' the next general election. This possibility occurred to some people when in February 1906 Sonnino was invited to form a government, but the king was unwilling to allow another election so soon, and this was taken as indicating a slight bias against the conservatives.

Sonnino lasted in office for only a hundred days because he had no organised party as a political base and no ability in parliamentary management. His administration is noteworthy because, for the first time and perhaps surprisingly, two members of the radical Left accepted portfolios out of impatience with Giolitti's blatant election-eering. Nevertheless, it was in other respects a conservative cabinet, with the familiar result that an agreed policy was hard to find. The nationalists thought or hoped that the new premier would put the clock back and govern with little reference to parliament. The British minister commented that, when compared to Giolitti, Sonnino 'was utterly unable to gain the undecided votes which generally in the Italian parliament are attracted to the ministry; possibly this was the result of his scrupulous disregard of the usual methods of obtaining support for the government'.[22] Any election run by such an unso-phisticated politician would hardly produce any kind of majority, not even of placemen.

Neither Fortis nor Sonnino succeeded in building up an alternative coalition that could challenge Giolitti, and this marked a further attenuation of the sovereign's prerogatives by limiting his choice of a government. Some conservatives who opposed Giolitti looked to the palace for the change in political direction that they were unable to secure by parliamentary means. The *Corriere della Sera* on this occasion urged that a king need not be bound by parliament but in the national interest could 'appeal to the whole country'; or, more specifically, he could choose his own moment to dissolve the legislature and permit some other politician to produce a completely different chamber by the use of official patronage.[23] This was the doctrine of royal intervention which, again supported by the *Corriere* in 1922, eventually brought Mussolini to power, and on both occasions the newspaper was moved by a desire to keep Giolitti out of office because of what it called his excessive liberalism. But early in the century this doctrine was challenged by those who feared that royal intervention would dangerously divide the country. Worse still, it might risk the survival of the dynasty by again associating the crown with one side of a major political controversy.[24]

Vittorio Emanuele was aware of these differing opinions, but in the early years of his reign was, as Barrère described him, an enlightened liberal with 'very modern' ideas about the positive value of parliamentary institutions and his own need to appear as impartial as possible.[25] On a rare occasion when he spoke to the foreign press he was careful to avoid politics altogether, and he dogmatically refused to answer when a former minister tried to broach a political topic in conversation.[26] As well as being reluctant to preside at cabinet meetings, he never seems to have wanted to insert remarks of his own into the royal speech which the prime minister wrote for him to read at the opening of each new parliament.

In theory the royal prerogatives remained intact, and conservatives continued to assert that, unlike the British monarchy, in Italy the king actually governed as well as merely reigning.[27] Twice a week his ministers came for him to sign laws, often three hundred documents at a time, and he explained that he wanted to retain a discretionary right to refuse his signature because it 'might always be useful in order to compel resignations';[28] but it was a right best kept in reserve. Sometimes, as he confessed to the British military attaché, he used his personal influence to sway a vote in the senate. But in general he thought that the British monarchy 'is the example to follow'; whereas by comparison the German emperor, albeit 'a very clever and well-meaning man', had by tactless interventions 'reduced or jeopardised much of his own power for exercising real influence'.[29] Vittorio Emanuele mentioned that he disapproved of his father's tactics in 1898–1900 because 'in a modern parliamentary state it was impossible to work without parliament. If you used compulsion against parliament you set all people crying out that liberty was being trampled on'.[30]

Such views explain why Giolitti was allowed back into power for a third time in May 1906, to remain in office for the next three years. There was respect and loyalty on both sides in the personal relations between this politician and his sovereign, but little warmth. The king was glad to have ministers who were good administrators and knew how to manage parliament. He shared Giolitti's down-to-earth and simple tastes in private life; they had the same liking for books and history, the same reticence and dislike of rhetoric. Giolitti, like Cavour and Depretis before him, was also welcome for speaking the Piedmontese dialect which was still favoured at court. But the king showed no great friendliness and indeed showed little to any other of the two hundred ministers of his reign. It was appreciated that Giolitti told him no lies, unlike Zanardelli, Saracco, and Luzzatti who were criticised at court for their mendacity.[31] But Vittorio Emanuele in later life was more critical of Giolitti than of Mussolini: the Piedmontese minister was remembered as having been insincere, astute, crafty, and ignorant; also, perhaps strangely coming from such a monarch, as a cynic who denied altruism as a motive in others; as someone who, while uncorrupt himself, used minor methods of corruption in order to retain his parliamentary majority, and who kept a dossier on every single deputy so as to influence or blackmail them.[32] Similar dossiers are known to have been kept by Lanza and Depretis in the past, as later they were by Nitti and Mussolini; and no doubt were regularly used by successive Italian governments to keep their followers in line.[33]

Giolitti inherited a tradition of corrupt practices in politics, for which he was given most of the blame though he did little more than accept a pre-existing fact as incorrigible. Crispi had been formally censured by parliament for peculation and forced to resign his seat. Another minister in Zanardelli's administration had been convicted by the judiciary for financial irregularities, and the king not only welcomed this conviction as a good example, but encouraged the resignation of another accused (and probably innocent) minister, who committed suicide as a result of his public disgrace.[34] Outside observers in 1901 had found a degree of dishonesty 'in every branch of public life', whether in allocating government contracts, or appointments to lucrative jobs, or in using the mafia for winning elections.[35] Colajanni, reporting on his native Sicily during Pelloux's election of 1900, noted that a thousand mafiosi were released from prison on condition that they supported government candidates,[36] and on a smaller scale this was a not-uncommon procedure.

Giolitti in the general election of March 1909 claimed that he would not countenance the use of violence or bribery to win votes, but the testimony invalidating his claim is abundant. Possibly he behaved no worse than his predecessors, but it was an obvious scandal when one of his supporters could be elected with no dissenting votes at all, or when public auctions were regularly held to discover which candidate in a constituency offered electors the biggest payment for their votes. His reputation certainly suffered from the fact that the questionable methods employed in elections now became known to a growing newspaper-reading public.[37] Extra publicity was also given to these methods because of an increase in numbers of candidates on the extreme Left who found it convenient to blame official pressure for their defeat.

The election of 1909 registered another slight but significant switch to the Left, which was read by conservatives as proving the need for the use of even greater official pressure in future. The three parties of the extreme Left increased their strength to 110 out of 508 seats, and it was ominous that they won half the votes in important urban centres such as Rome, Milan, Turin, Venice, and Florence. The militant Catholics increased their representation to 16, and for some people this was almost as dangerous a sign of trouble to come. While many politicians on the Right welcomed Catholics in parliament as a probable reinforcement of social conservatism, others on Right as well as Left feared the influence of clericalism in a secular society where it would be one further divisive element inside the narrow political class. Already there were complaints that monasteries and convents, in defiance of laws which suppressed them during the risorgimento, were more numerous and richer than ever before.[38] To many anti-clericals it seemed as though Giolitti, by not enforcing the law, was playing for clerical support and selling out to Italy's enemy in the Vatican.

Despite the fact that his supporters retained a fairly comfortable majority, this slight reinforcement of the extreme Left and Right led people to suspect that he might prefer another temporary resignation so as to leave others to take the responsibility of government 'until the atmosphere is less electric'.[39] It was well known at the palace that at difficult moments he sometimes temporised or boggled over taking what he knew to be obligatory decisions, and 'when matters reach the point where problems cannot be resolved in tranquillity, almost always he would draw back until peace and quiet returned'.[40] He had to confront some ugly scenes in parliament, notably just before the summer recess when fighting broke out in the chamber and deputies threw ink wells at each other.[41] When parliament reassembled in the autumn, he therefore surprised his cabinet by once again, just as in 1893, putting forward a proposal for a progressive income tax which, as he must have calculated, would invite a hostile vote; he could then retire on a point of principle that would win support on the Left and prepare the way for a come-back in quieter times with a more secure majority.

One of Giolitti's problems had been the social discontent that accompanied growing national prosperity. He could rightly claim

that the Italian economy had profited from social reforms and
international peace to make gigantic strides in recent years, indeed
greater and faster than at any time in the past century.[42] But critics
could equally argue that, while the rich had become much richer, this
was partly because of high protective duties which damaged the
ordinary consumer, leaving the latter disadvantaged by a growing
disparity between profits and wages. Many rich property-owners,
said Fortunato, escaped taxation entirely, while poorer people
continued to carry the main burden of taxation and were often on the
verge of destitution. Even some conservatives could admit that in no
other European country had the political class done less to help
ordinary wage-earners.[43]

This was the background to Giolitti's proposals for progressive
taxation. But while these inevitably antagonised the rich, they were
disbelieved by others who had seen earlier promises of reform come
to little or nothing. The king had already signed laws regulating
night shifts for workers and the employment of women and children, and yet parliament had voted against setting up a system
of factory inspectors which alone could make such reforms a reality.
There was also said to be insufficient money to enforce other laws on
compulsory popular education and retirement pensions. But others
argued that the money could be found if there were a different
order of priorities, for example if economies were made in the army
budget or even if the king set an example by giving up some of
his income from the civil list – which he was unwilling to do.[44]
Such problems were perhaps too delicate to confront. Not daring to
disturb a nice political balance, Giolitti also chose to leave elementary
education in the hands of local authorities who lacked the resources
or indeed the wish to build schools.[45]

The Italian parliament was not well suited to the discussion and
resolution of such matters. Giolitti's remarkable personal ascendancy
helped to perpetuate the illusion of an effective parliamentary system, but the illusion became less credible when the tasks of government became more complex and new classes began to clamour for a
say in public affairs. Taking a phrase from the *Secolo*, Giolitti
explained his difficulties by saying that any tailor making a suit for a
hunchback must cut his cloth to suit the client.[46] He was tied by the
fact that every cabinet was still a mixture of Right and Left, since
otherwise there would be no majority for any legislation. He had to
accept that, lacking organised parties alternating in power, a single
'parliamentary dictator' was apparently needed to bind together and
win support from many small groups. Such a dominant personality
invariably won elections by use of official pressure, and that was by

itself a serious limitation to any system of representative government; but he still had to govern by a coalition that would inevitably
be unstable, changeable, and hence only partially effective. He had to
circumvent discussion by issuing 'royal decrees' in place of parliamentary laws; nor were such decrees always presented to parliament
for subsequent sanction as the constitution prescribed; or else they
could be presented so long after events as to make that sanction
illusory.[47]

Although Sonnino claimed to speak on behalf of a 'constitutional
opposition', in practice any opposition was diverse and disorganised,
which meant that criticism was blunted or voiced only by a few
extremists who carried little political weight. Sonnino rejected the
idea of progressives and conservatives alternating in office because he
thought that both should regard themselves as two wings of the
same liberal party fighting against the twin danger from socialism
and political Catholicism.[48] One result was that, when out of office,
he spoke rarely and for long periods did not see any need to appear in
parliament. The same was true of Giolitti when out of office, as it
had been true of Ricasoli, Lanza, and Sella. Crispi, too, had often
abandoned parliament when out of power, because there seemed
little point in criticism and much point in keeping sufficiently un-
committed to be able to join the next coalition government.[49] Some
prominent liberals thought it a matter for pride to call themselves
free-lancers with no group allegiance whatsoever.[50]

This was the political context in which the king had to operate,
where a strong premier could not help but encroach upon his constitutional powers as head of the executive, and an ineffective legislature encouraged the practice of government by decree. Inevitably
there had developed traditions of parliamentary practice which
differed from those elsewhere, but they were imperfectly successful
in producing an efficacious and credible system of their own.
Whether or not those theorists were correct who blamed technical
procedures in the method of election,[51] the result was an increasing
disillusion with a parliament that could not produce organised parties
or a workable alternative to 'parliamentary dictatorship'. Instead of
disciplined parties there was a continually shifting system of alliances
between small groups which all tried to keep a separate identity,
and it was hard for politicans while out of office to focus criticism
or present the electorate with an alternative leader and an alternative
set of policies.[52] Hence there was a tendency among some of Giolitti's opponents to depreciate parliament and give the king a more
active role in politics.

4   Great-power politics

Diffident and withdrawn by nature, Vittorio Emanuele became no more sure of himself as time went by. He was anxious not to appear as King Log, but, apart from appearances, was reluctant to challenge ministers by interfering too much in policy. Barrère in 1906 thought he was now becoming 'more inclined to follow than to lead', despite his continuing choice of mediocre foreign ministers who had no liking for the limelight or for taking responsibility.[1] The foreign office was housed immediately opposite the Quirinal in the Palazzo della Consulta. The selection of senior ambassadors still revealed a preference for Piedmontese courtiers. As late as 1916 thirty out of the fifty top posts at the Consulta were filled from the titled nobility, a class that was almost invisible in other prominent areas of national life.[2]

Count Anton Monts, the German ambassador in Rome, was scathing about the intelligence and effectiveness of such people. His personal belief was that the Quirinal rather than the Consulta remained 'the true arbiter of foreign policy', yet he also ascribed the confusion and uncertainty of policy to the king's 'lack of energy and will power'.[3] Foreign affairs were still rarely brought before the cabinet, and informative documents were seldom presented to parliament. Radicals and republicans continued to complain that ordinary citizens were called on to pay for commitments in the field of foreign policy, commitments about which they were told nothing,[4] and in December 1908, when there took place a debate about recent events in the Balkans, Giolitti claimed with some exaggeration that such a discussion was without precedent. On this occasion the conservatives in opposition objected to the debate on the grounds that foreign policy should be for the executive to decide, not for parliament to discuss.[5]

Monts was alarmed at signs that the king, instead of building up Italy's economic strength through public works and balancing the budget, secretly aimed at winning prestige by trying to copy Germany and play a greater role in world affairs than could be afforded. Italy still kept troops in China; also in Crete as part of an international peace-keeping force, despite a manifest lack of enthusiasm in parliament.[6] Vittorio Emanuele risked offending the Germans by his desire for closer relations with Russia, a country that he knew well from his travels and to whose ruling dynasty his queen was closely related. He was offended when the Tsar, after twice promising to visit Italy, changed his mind from fear of meeting the same fate as

Umberto, and this issue nearly caused a breach in relations because the king was sensitive on such matters of diplomatic protocol.[7]

Giolitti was reputed to have no great interest in other than domestic affairs, and though this was not entirely true, foreign policy for the best part of six years until 1909 was left in the hands of Tittoni who continued to be regarded as a spokesman of the royal court. This man belonged to what was still called the Right and in the past had usually voted against Giolitti. During all his time at the Consulta, Tittoni used to publish anonymous articles that hardly reflected the views of his cabinet colleagues. In these articles he confessed his admiration for Crispi as a 'political genius' whom he would like to emulate by making Italy a serious colonial power. He wanted a strong army and active intervention in all major international questions.[8] Under the cover of anonymity in these articles, he gave himself unstinted praise for clarity of vision and brilliant diplomacy, as well as for tact and modesty.[9]

In particular, Tittoni praised himself for being greatly liked and admired in London, and evidently had no idea that he had the reputation there of being deeply unsympathetic and untrustworthy.[10] Relations with Britain had been slightly soured while its embassy at Rome was held by Phillip Currie, whom the king resented as stupid and narrow-minded, and whose recall had been officially requested in 1903. Later the king found two officials at the British embassy whom he trusted and could talk to off the record: one was the military attaché, Colonel Delmé-Radcliffe; the other was Rennell Rodd, whose appointment was personally requested by the Quirinal[11] and who remained in Italy for nearly twenty years, eleven of them as ambassador.

With other diplomats in Rome the king was never familiar, and certainly not with the ambassadors of his two allies. He increasingly resented the arrogant and histrionic behaviour of the German emperor during annual holidays spent in Italy. He had more trust in the Austrian ruler Franz Joseph, but feared that 'the clerical and military parties in Austria' were preparing for war against Italy; or else that they might be intending to invade Macedonia and obtain an outlet on the Aegean sea at Salonica. Such an event would upset the balance of power in the Balkans. As he once declared, 'if Austrian moved, Serbia and Montenegro would not remain quiet. Italy had been caught napping when France took Tunis. She did not mean to have a repetition of the case in Macedonia by Austria'.[12]

The threatening attitude of Austria arose in part from the fact that the existence of Italy's non-aggression pact with France in 1902 had been discovered in Vienna and Berlin, and the knowledge put the Consulta in a dangerously false position. Sonnino and Di Rudinì deeply regretted the pact as immoral and inexpedient,[13] but it could not be denounced or even mentioned without 'uncovering' the king; nor of course could ministers afford to denounce the alliance with Germany, the precise implications of which were still unknown to most of them. This difficulty became acute when rival claims to Morocco were advanced by France and Germany, both of whom claimed a right to Italian support, and both of whom sent almost threatening notes on the subject to Rome.[14]

This left the king in a quandary, but he had privately promised to support the French over the issue and correctly decided to regard the German threat as bluff.[15] The Germans interpreted his attitude as unfriendliness and treated him accordingly. Monts even suggested that Berlin should terminate the alliance, and criticised the 'machia-vellianism' of a sovereign who would readily change sides if ever he thought it safe.[16] Wilhelm reacted by quoting the biblical precept about not serving two masters at once and talked of giving Italy a salutary lesson, if necessary by armed force. He privately referred to Vittorio Emanuele in extravagant terms as 'a *camorrista*', as 'a man of fixed ideas with whom no discussion is possible', as someone who was

> a socialist and prided himself on the fact that he was the only sovereign in Europe who could afford to be so. He had excessively ambitious views but no great authority in his own country, and his administration left much to be desired. As for the Italian ministers, it was impossible to believe a word they said.[17]

There was a degree of play-acting when the Italians in 1907 allowed the Triple Alliance to be renewed for the fifth time without changing the original commitment to join Germany in war against France. In public statements Tittoni continued to claim that the alliance with Germany and Austria was genuinely popular in Italy where the existence of a strong Austria was welcomed; and he even offended the irredentists by praising the Austrians for their excellent administration in Trentino and Trieste. Nevertheless, the French were quietly informed that Italy would never fight against them, not even if they felt obliged to launch a war against Germany, and the king confessed that he might lose his throne if he defied popular sympathy for France. Tittoni was sufficiently two-faced and irres-ponsible to let it be known in Paris that Italy might be ready in three years' time to fight against Austria.[18]

The French were under few illusions about such hypocritical talk, especially since from secret intelligence reports they knew more than the Italian cabinet about Italy's treaty obligations. To them as to the Germans this was 'the usual see-saw game', the traditional policy of the House of Savoy to change sides in order to join whoever was likely to win any European war.[19] The British remarked less unkindly that the king 'means to hang on to the Triple Alliance *pour se faire valoir* with the French government, and to be on good terms with France in order to be not towed along by Germany'.[20] Either way the ambiguity was not easily resolved. Tittoni disingenuously believed, or at least said, that he could at any moment desert his allies and join France 'on the best terms, with no loss of honour'.[21] Yet in parliament he thought it prudent to deny categorically that he would ever consider adopting the 'vulgar and puerile' policy of steering 'an oscillating zig-zag course' between the two rival groups in Europe.[22]

Another test of the Triple Alliance came towards the end of 1908 when Austria took a big stride into the Balkans by formally annexing her protectorates in Bosnia and Herzegovina. This was just what the king had been fearing. Franz Joseph wrote apologetically in the hope that his fellow sovereign in Rome would treat this move in a friendly spirit, and was gratified at receiving an 'unusually amicable' response.[23] To the French ambassador, however, Vittorio Emanuele expressed grave alarm at what he presumed to call a violation of 'international morality'.[24] To the ambassador of the United States, with whom he had no reason to conceal his inner feelings, he made an even more positive and revealing remark:

> I am more than ever convinced of the utter worthlessness of treaties or any agreements written on paper. They are worth the value of the paper. The only real strength lies in bayonets and canon.[25]

Evidently he accepted that the Triple Alliance had no more than a relative or contingent value, in other words that a see-saw or zig-zag policy might be a legitimate and desirable alternative if it could be practised without penalty.

The Austrian annexation of Bosnia provoked a mixed response among other Italians. Giolitti had difficulty in persuading parliament that no Italian interest was endangered and national honour not involved. But although he won his usual majority vote, there were prominent politicians of the Right and Centre, including Fortis, Luzzatti, Fortunato, and Sonnino, who disagreed and thought that the Triple Alliance would not last much longer if the Austrians could take such unilateral action without offering compensation. More people were now tempted to think that Italy's best position would be complete neutrality without the expense of military commitments. She could then judge each issue on its own merits and, as well as saving money, could reap maximum advantage from being able to bargain with both sides.[26]

Such views were held more strongly on the extreme Left. Radicals, republicans, and socialists immediately organised a big public demonstration to protest that the Triple Alliance was forcing Italy to connive at the suppression of Balkan nationalities in what was bound to seem a denial of risorgimento idealism and self-determination. At the very least, they argued, Italy should claim compensation by annexing the Italian-speaking areas of Trentino or Trieste. But preferably the alliance should be terminated: firstly, because it was disliked by most Italians; secondly, it seemed to be an essentially dynastic policy designed to support authoritarianism and the institution of paternalistic monarchy in Europe; thirdly, its existence positively encouraged Austrian aggression in eastern Europe, which might at any moment drag an unprepared Italy into a major war; and fourthly, the treaty had never been presented to parliament for approval and its precise commitments could only be conjectured.[27]

Vittorio Emanuele shared only the third of these objections. He felt sure that the militarist faction in Austria had further annexations in mind. He feared that Italy would thereby be pulled into a European war, especially as fighting might be triggered off at any moment by submerged nationalities in the Balkans rising against the Turkish sultan and against the threat of Austrian invasion. Or, more likely, 'the danger was that the Austrians might take advantage of the Serbian agitation as an excuse for military action'. More dangerous than the Serbs, in his opinion, were the Bulgarians, and he feared that they might act, because they 'were of a finer quality altogether than the other Balkan peoples': they were virile, ambitious, and already were sending many officers to be trained in the Italian military academies.[28]

The greatest worry of all was that he was tied to a German alliance at a time when a dangerous rivalry was developing between Berlin and London. He knew that the British had so far been glad for Italy to remain in the Triple Alliance – though he may not have guessed one reason, which was that 'the Italians will, owing to their inherent weakness, always be an excellent drag on the two Central European powers'.[29] The French occasionally took this argument even further, calculating that the alliance would weaken Italy and cause her to bankrupt herself by excessive expenditure on the army.[30]

But naval and colonial rivalry was by now producing a new and threatening degree of international tension which was bound to affect Italy. Vittorio Emanuele wanted a strong Britain as a check on German aggressiveness. In private communications to London he repeated his advice that Britain should introduce compulsory military service so as to have an expeditionary force ready to land on the continent and 'maintain her position in the world'. Conscription, he had found, 'always brought about a great improvement in the population'. Incidentally he also advised the British to modify their isolationism by adopting the metric scale and a decimal system of coinage. But chiefly he wanted them to rearm, especially now that long-range artillery might be able to strike Britain from across the Channel, and her glorious isolation would have to change as she became vulnerable to bombing aeroplanes.[31]

In a long talk with Ambassador Rodd in May 1909, he hoped that a European war could be avoided, yet if the British feared attack from Germany they 'ought to have anticipated the developments which are taking place and to have attacked yourselves while the advantage was all on your side'. This remarkable statement may have been prompted by his fear that Austrian naval rearmament was directed against Italy 'and means competition for naval supremacy in the Mediterranean', a competition that he intended to win 'at all costs'.[32] Somewhat surprisingly he thought that the Austrian army was 'first rate', while the German army was relatively weak. German strength 'was perhaps more apparent than real. Socialist ideas had penetrated much more deeply than was generally believed'. A few months later Rodd 'found His Majesty more than ever hostile to Germany and disposed to criticise the emperor'; from which it appeared that 'all his sympathies' were secretly with Britain and France; indeed, if only the two western countries were more resolute, Italy might change sides and join them against her present allies.[33]

Vittorio Emanuele told the Russians that it was important for monarchs in Europe, even constitutional monarchs, to keep not only foreign policy but the armed services under their direct personal control.[34] Of twenty-seven Italian ministers of war in over half a century, only one was a civilian; the rest were generals chosen by the king personally, men who by his own admission never carried or needed to carry much weight in parliament.[35] Responsible directly to himself as much as to the prime minister, they habitually remained in office from one cabinet to the next: General Ponza di San Martino continued under Pelloux, Saracco, and Zanardelli; General Pedotti under Giolitti, Tittoni and Fortis; General Spingardi under Giolitti, Sonnino, and Luzzatti.

The king confidently stated that his army was ready 'for any possible eventuality'. But he took his duties as commander-in-chief too lightly to be a reliable judge. He was even rash enough to say that 'on the twelfth day of mobilization they could put 800,000 men on either frontier without excessive effort, and another 800,000 within a month', complete with all their weapons and stores. He was pleased to note that the upper classes were now more ready to join the army, and a new generation of officers was a great improvement on the 'ignorant, uneducated, stupid' generals of the risorgimento.

> The moral improvement of the people of Italy was largely due to the army, which was an educating factor of inestimable value. Through the army a sense of responsibility to their country was engendered in the population, and the old hatred of conscription was just giving place to a satisfaction with and pride in the national army. The king said he remembered in the early days of the conscription how it was necessary to collect the recruits by force, surrounding villages by night to capture the men.[36]

This was cause for satisfaction even though some of his opinions betray a degree of ingenuousness and over-confidence. He knew that some serious problems remained. He qualified his earlier view when he told the British of his fear that

> the people have yet to be educated, to be taught habits of discipline, obedience and orderliness. The people in Italy have also yet to learn what patriotism, in the broad national sense, means. They are not yet a homogeneous people.

Service in the army was helping to correct this fault. But an even greater danger lay in

> the mischievous interference of ministers, who thought of their own popularity first and of the security of their countries afterwards. Nothing was more dangerous than politicians and parliamentary influence, which change with every breeze that blows.[37]

Critics in parliament, had they known of this remark, would have been appalled. They thought on the contrary that necessary reforms would be impossible without greater civilian supervision over the generals. They felt that parliamentary interference with the army was avoided deliberately, and it remained true that little of the requisite information was ever provided as a basis for informed debate. Deputies continued to complain that they had still been given no official explanation of mysterious military defeats as long ago as 1866 and even 1848, for which rumour held the crown directly responsible. There was little assurance for the future when so many millions of lire continued to be spent on the army without any vote in the chamber.[38]

Moreover, since ministers of war were sometimes not even consulted about foreign policy, military preparation could be based on quite unrealistic premises.[39] The chiefs of staff knew that they were pledged to send a large force to Germany in the event of war, yet apparently knew nothing of the Prinetti-Barrère agreement with France, nor of other undertakings made in the Triple Alliance.[40] The Germans were told by the Italian chief of staff that they could rely on active assistance by this expeditionary force, at the same time as the foreign minister pretended to the French that any military commitment to Germany had been cancelled.[41]

Since ministers and even prime ministers were allowed to know surprisingly little about details of military provision and preparation, the king alone could have properly co-ordinated military and foreign policy. He alone could have ensured that there was adequate supervision of training and equipment for the armed services, because the chief of staff remained answerable to him personally rather than to the minister of war or the cabinet. But he neither supervised nor encouraged others to do so, nor would he relinquish his nominal powers as supreme commander. One of the lessons from previous wars was that a king inevitably lacked the competence to command, yet in 1908 a clarification of this vital matter was again refused.[42]

Planning was also hindered by uncertainty over whether France or Austria was the more likely enemy in a future war. Moreover, resources were lacking for the simultaneous construction of adequate fortifications along both north-eastern and north-western frontiers. As the king frankly admitted, a top priority for Italy must be economic development, and he knew that the country could not simultaneously spend enough on arms, public works, and welfare.[43] Procurement and training were further hampered by the fact that the army was required for essential duties at home as an auxiliary police force, and indeed these were said in 1909 to take up most of its attention.[44] The generals found themselves with a restricted budget, without accurate directives about foreign policy, and without the assistance or criticism afforded by an expert parliamentary committee of civilians. Left to themselves they saw no overriding urgency to prepare for a major war whose nature or imminence they could hardly judge. Hence they failed to keep strategic plans properly revised and continued for years buying field artillery that was known to be out of date.[45]

The building of naval vessels was where rapid changes in technical development left Italy in most danger of falling behind. Great pressure came from the admiralty to spend more money and reject proposals for general disarmament that arrived from London in 1907.[46] The king was a keen sailor and particularly proud of a new class of Italian battleship that he told the British they ought to copy; whereas he thought that Italy had little use for the smaller ships which some experts preferred and which later proved to be far more

17. Vittorio Emanuele III, Mussolini and Umberto at a parade of troops during manoeuvres at Volturara, 1936.

18. Umberto II votes in the referendum, 1946.

19. Umberto II with his children in exile in Portugal, 1946.

effective.[47] In 1909 a further decision was taken to construct four even larger Dreadnoughts, and when Austria felt obliged to follow suit there was a demand to add to their number so as to meet the Austrians on at least equal terms.[48]

The king, by now very anxious about the mounting cost, received a direct appeal to call a halt to this extravagant arms race, and while fearing what people might say if he himself proposed a general disarmament, he made a fruitless attempt to persuade first the Germans and then the Americans to set an example which he could then follow.[49] But the momentum of rearmament was not easily arrested and had unforeseen results. The building of Dreadnoughts, simultaneously by Austria and her Italian ally, was interpreted in London as a direct and concerted threat to the British Mediterranean fleet. Its effect was therefore to accelerate the arms race still further, to alarm England as well as Austria, so increasing international tension while leaving Italy more isolated and insolvent.[50]

The socialists were among those who appealed for a fundamental change in policy, though their official newspaper was repeatedly confiscated for daring to do so. They agreed that Italy had a great mission in the world, but not a military one, nor had she any natural enemies, but was gratuitously creating distrust and hostility among her neighbours. Even some of the generals were ready to admit that by aiming too high they would end by further impoverishing and so weakening the country.[51] The *Corriere della Sera* spelt out the same message. Representing the views of financiers and industrialists in Milan, the *Corriere* pointed out that the building of Dreadnoughts had no parliamentary sanction, and meanwhile the legislature was being deceived by mendacious exaggerations of Italy's military capacity. Its editor Luigi Albertini furthermore suggested that secrecy was being misused to cover acts of blatant financial corruption, and secrecy was maintained because senior officials might find themselves in court if the true facts became known.[52]

The efficiency of the armed services and civilian bureaucracy was found wanting during an earthquake in 1905,[53] and a still greater test occurred when on 28 December 1908 another terrible earthquake and tidal wave struck Messina and the coast of Calabria. Russian and British ships arrived within hours to give immediate help, but the authorities in Catania and Palermo were much slower to react and two days went by before Italian naval vessels were able to leave Naples. The higher command of the navy showed up very badly, giving contradictory orders, failing to requisition stores, sometimes refusing to take responsibility for any action, and it was estimated that a quarter of the 80,000 deaths could have been avoided had it not been for inter-service rivalries and 'small-minded jealously'.[54]

Vittorio Emanuele went to Messina and helped to bring a measure of order and organisation into the relief work, for which he was applauded by even the republicans.[55] He was among the first to realise the unfortunate impression made on his allies and potential allies 'in estimating the value of Italy in the European equation'.[56]

5   *Victory in Libya*

Vittorio Emanuele was known by reputation to think poorly of his fellow men and was particularly cynical about politicians. Over half the ministers during his long reign were categorised by him as second-rate or worse, and many were 'absolute nullities'. One of the reasons he gave was that most of those who entered politics did so because of the opportunities for private gain. This was why he disliked Giolitti's proposal to pay a salary to members of parliament, because it would encourage the already existing temptation to look on public life as a means of personal enrichment.[1]

In the first ten years of his reign he had done a great deal to restore the prestige of the monarchy by showing greater tact and moderation than Umberto. He had kept aloof from too close an involvement with political factions, and unlike his father was not blamed for palace scandals or the existence of a court camarilla.[2] Ministers were to a large extent left to govern on their own and for long periods he used to stay out of Rome at Castelporziano, coming to the palace only to sign laws and decrees. Nevertheless, he kept a reputation among foreign diplomats of being 'the best informed man in the country', with a keen interest in all that was happening.[3] Sometimes he mentioned a longing to travel as he had done in his youth, to see more of the outside world, perhaps to visit England incognito so that he could study at leisure in the London museums. He had become almost deaf in his right ear, and said that if this became worse he might 'hand the government over to somebody and go away and enjoy myself'.[4]

Possibly bored by kingship, he had no desire to step outside the bounds of the constitution, and the Russian ambassador had to submit to a lecture about how the Tsar should adopt a parliamentary regime like that of Italy.[5] The king told Theodore Roosevelt that 'he wished his son to be so trained that if necessary he would be fit to be the first president of the Italian republic' – despite which, the prince was given the usual military education which was a poor apprenticeship for any constitutional sovereign. Roosevelt liked Vittorio Emanuele as a person, while criticising that he cut himself off socially from the 'really able men of the nation'. The American noted that the king lacked the driving force and energy and perhaps the wish to become more than 'a kind of sublimated American vice-president'.[6]

Another interesting judgement came from Rennell Rodd:

> In one special direction the crown has of late years exercised a potent influence in Italy. The most democratic of living monarchs had undoubtedly done much personally to mitigate the extreme views of the socialist party. His Majesty's dislike of all pomp and symbolism, which in the opinion of some critics is carried to an extreme length, his unpretentious demeanour and eminently domestic habits, his capacity for hard work and personal investigation of every public question, as well as his open-handed generosity, have disarmed the opponents of the monarchy, and to some extent upset them...The king has appropriately described his own conception of his duties as those of a permanent undersecretary to the ministry, holding in his hand the threads of tradition, and constantly ready to assist them with the counsels of his experience.[7]

The palace nevertheless retained considerable powers for use when necessary. After Giolitti resigned in December 1909 over a minor issue of subsidies for shipping, the king again chose Sonnino to succeed him as prime minister, followed soon afterwards in March 1910 by Luigi Luzzatti. On neither occasion was there a clear vote in the chamber to indicate a preference, so that Vittorio Emanuele, while he claimed that he would have preferred the assistance of such a vote and could easily have insisted on one, was able to use his personal discretion, and naturally some people disliked his choice.[8] He further offended the conservatives by once again denying Sonnino the right to hold a general election, which some people interpreted and strongly resented as favouritism towards Giolitti[9] – though more likely it indicates a characteristic preference for not taking sides over controversial issues. Not partisanship but an excessive desire to seem impartial and avoid embarrassment explains why he refused for the next few years to see Sonnino, despite the fact that this man was leader of the 'constitutional opposition'.[10] Other politicians when out of office were treated in exactly the same way.

When Luzzatti resigned in March 1911, Bissolati became the first socialist to be invited to give advice at the Quirinal: he purchased a pair of gloves for the occasion but shocked conventional opinion by refusing to wear the customary top hat and tails. When this patriotic and moderate socialist refused an invitation to join Giolitti's next cabinet the monarch was genuinely sorry, because 'such men are quickly sobered by office and become a moderating influence among their associates'.[11] Their meeting at the palace gave Bissolati the impression that the king was not only well to the left of centre in his political sympathies, but was reconciled to the likelihood that before long Italy might become a republic.[12]

This is one example of Vittorio Emanuele's being shrewd and diplomatic. He had no liking for the more extreme socialists, although fortunately 'the frothy nonsense they talked brought its own remedy by wearying the people, who in time come to realise how utterly impractical the socialists are'. For much the same reasons he disliked the practice in Spain and Russia of regularly using force against social agitation. Sometimes the Italian army had been employed in breaking strikes, but he thought that the use of armed force generally made things worse, and he himself preferred where possible to reduce penalties imposed on agitators or to use the royal prerogative of pardon. When agricultural workers went on strike he believed that often the fault lay with 'landowners who did not always do their duty to the people living on the land'. Speaking to someone who was no sympathiser with socialism he said, though he did not want it generally known, that his personal sympathies were mostly with those on strike, and 'he could not regret a movement that had for result to shorten the hours and ameliorate the conditions of labour'.[13]

One reason why social conditions in Italy were no worse was that hundreds of thousands of unemployed and under-employed were emigrating each year in rapidly increasing numbers. Most went to North and South America, or to France and French Tunisia. Two millions were by now in the United States, largely forgotten – in 1906 there were only twelve Italian consular officials in the United States, compared with thirty-seven in the Turkish empire. Virtually none of these emigrants went to Italy's colonies in Eritrea and Somalia, although irresponsible journalists continued to advise the king that ample room existed there for millions of settlers.[14] These East-African colonies had cost Italy a fortune with little return from it, and some of the continuing cost was being misappropriated by corrupt officials, while colonial commerce remained obstinately in the hands of foreigners. Emigrants to America, on the other hand, sent hundreds of millions of lire back to Italy each year in what was already a major factor in Italy's growing prosperity after 1900.

Vittorio Emanuele had learnt from Crispi's experience that investment in Africa was likely to be unproductive economically and counter-productive for national morale. He accepted that Eritrea for reasons of prestige could not be surrendered, and although he did not believe stories about its future profitability, wanted to 'get as much out of it as possible' and cut down the annual contribution from the Italian exchequer. He believed that colonial populations must be ruled autocratically, and it would be 'most unscrupulous and little short of criminal...to fill the minds of the natives with ideas that can only lead to serious trouble'. As well as keeping Eritrea, another possibility would be to capture Libya from Turkey, despite Italy's signature to an international treaty guaranteeing the integrity of the Turkish empire. He privately hoped that one day Libya would be acquired, preferably by peaceful means, and in full knowledge that neither Tripolitania or Cyreniaica were promising areas for commerce or settlement.[15]

The minister in charge of foreign and colonial policy in the years after 1910, the Marquis di San Giuliano, was like his predecessor Tittoni a senator, not an elected deputy. He accepted the foreign ministry with misgivings and only after strong pressure from the palace, but thereafter continued in office under three successive prime ministers, and this was by wish of the crown in order to preserve continuity in foreign policy.[16] Of all the ministers before fascism, San Giuliano alone received the king's unstinted praise, and the closeness of their relationship is confirmed by the eventual bequest to the monarch of this minister's personal papers.[17] He shared with Tittoni the fact of having been a follower of Crispi in his youth. Like Crispi he opposed irredentist agitation and claimed to want a strong Austria. Italy, he promised, would never defy international law or interfere in the internal affairs of other countries. In particular he said he believed in maintaining the integrity of the Turkish empire and preserving Libya as part of that empire so as to prevent it falling under the influence of any other European power.[18]

The king evidently accepted that this might be the most they could expect. In one public address he spoke of Italy's needing greater respect from the outside world but also of his 'devotion to the independence of all peoples'.[19] According to Barrère, neither the monarch nor San Giuliano wanted another war of colonial conquest. And yet other rhetorical speeches that accompanied the fiftieth anniversary of national unification revealed the existence of a new and belligerent mood in the country which he could hardly ignore.

A recently formed nationalist party, though at first ridiculed by San Giuliano as of little importance, proclaimed that Italy had urgent need of a war and called for the conquest of not only Libya but also Dalmatia, Malta, and Corsica. Patriotism, wrote one of its leaders, Enrico Corradini, was not enough: patriotism was altruistic, while nationalism was egotistic, imperialist, and therefore preferable.[20] Ever since 1903, Corradini had been writing articles condemning liberalism and calling for a new Italian 'primacy' in Europe. Italians had to learn that they were racially superior to the French; they would one day dominate the Mediterranean and must prepare for this by further rearmament; they must realise that only an aggressive and victorious war would win them due respect as a major power.[21]

The nationalists, in the same way as Mussolini later, threatened that the king would have to accept such ideas or face possible revolution. The monarch was ridiculed as too democratic and lacking in military panache.[22] Nationalism had wealthy backers who realised that colonies would enrich some individuals and refused to consider that Italy as a whole might thereby be impoverished. An organised press campaign propagated the mythical story that Libya was a country of immense mineral wealth, a 'garden of Eden' abundantly supplied with water for irrigation, where the local Arab population would welcome Italian help in liberation from Turkish rule.[23] Such improbable stories drowned the voices of those who warned against a repetition of the mistake made in Eritrea, since Arabs were unlikely to assist a Christian war against their Moslem Turkish overlords, and since Libya was no garden of Eden but 'an immense and valueless box of sand', indeed, one of the poorest countries in the world, which would cost a fortune to conquer and could give almost nothing in return. Far from making Italy one of the great powers, wrote Gaetano Salvemini, conquest of Libya could only postpone or permanently frustrate such an objective.[24]

As well as having guaranteed the integrity of the Ottoman empire, Italy was a signatory to the Hague Convention which bound her to seek the mediation of other friendly countries before resorting to war. But Corradini's friends saw positive merit in flouting international law. Until the autumn of 1911 the king was reluctant to authorise the conquest of Libya and resented that his hand might be forced to premature action.[25] Giolitti, too, by his own admission was unenthusiastic, yet he and previous governments had already prepared general plans to invade this Turkish province if ever it seemed necessary to forestall action by some other colonialist country.[26] In August 1911 Vittorio Emanuele informed one of his shooting companions that he was sure that the Germans had ambitions to occupy Tripoli, and this was something he could not permit. To the Germans he told a different story, of how he knew that the French were intending to invade Libya, and he would have to abdicate if they could not be stopped.[27] Almost certainly he must have known that his foreign office was already working through its diplomatic representative in Tripoli to purchase the support of local Arab leaders in case the government decided to take preventive action.[28]

On 3 September 80,000 troops were demobilised after the annual manoeuvres, which indicates that the minister of war and the chiefs of staff had still been told nothing. But on 17 September the king was asked to decide on an invasion, and ten days later an ultimatum was sent to Constantinople. By that time a group of Italian journalists had already been drafted to Tripoli to be on hand for the attack.[29] The plan, as San Giuliano informed the king, was for a quick and easy war before public opinion or other nations had time to register disapproval.[30] But for some reason the army leaders were given no prior notice to mobilise an invasion force,[31] with the unfortunate result that the first soldiers could not embark until a week after war was declared.

A declaration of war was by law a matter for the king alone, provided he had the counter-signature of one minister. Other cabinet ministers were told only a few hours before the ultimatum but were allowed no chance to discuss it and had to be dissuaded from resigning.[32] Nor did the king or Giolitti think it appropriate to inform parliament, which remained closed for seven months. The general public was given only rhetorical statements about an easy war that would last a few days with few casualties or none at all.[33]

A degree of secrecy was obviously needed. No publicity was therefore given to the fact that Turkey sent a prompt and conciliatory reply to the ultimatum and offered to discuss recognition of an Italian protectorate over Libya. Nor could ordinary citizens be allowed to know that this reply was strongly supported by other European countries. Italy's allies, Austria and Germany, had good reason to fear that the war would trigger off an insurrection in the Turkish-controlled Balkans and prove a threat to the peace of Europe.[34] Only in retrospect were patriotic Italians allowed to realise the existence of this threat. Nor did they know that they might have obtained effective control over Libya without a war that left their country impoverished and vulnerable.

Hostilities began haphazardly. Since no expeditionary force was ready, the navy bombarded Tripoli on 3 October and put 1,500 marines ashore, a fact that upset the army command who had to discard existing plans and embark their troops hastily without waiting for the full complement to be ready.[35] Over-confidence was generated by the knowledge that they had a five-to-one superiority over the defending Turkish garrisons and also by the quite untested assumption that the Arab population would be overjoyed at their arrival. The generals were therefore astonished at the end of October to suffer a minor reverse for which they were completely unprepared, and they then tried to disguise this mistake by inventing stories of Arab 'treachery'. During three days of panic a thousand 'rebel' prisoners were summarily executed for what was called treason, and although this could be concealed from the Italian public, gruesome details in the international press did great harm to Italy's good name,[36] as well as creating bitter animosities inside Libya that helped to make a quick victory impossible.

Another much-criticised decision at the beginning of November was a royal decree proclaiming the formal annexation of the whole of Libya, despite the fact that only a fraction of one per cent of the country was under Italian control. San Giuliano justified this on the surprising grounds that the war was already won. He even claimed that the proclamation of Italian sovereignty was dictated by the need to satisfy public opinion, without which the dynasty would have been in danger.[37] Outside observers, however, wondered whether a greater danger to the monarchy might not lie in risking a continuance of war once Italians could be seen as aggressors and not liberators.[38]

Evidently, there were some initial doubts at court about the wisdom of this decree of annexation, especially since it blocked the Turkish offer of a compromise peace. Talking of the war later in November the king admitted that 'he had not been enthusiastic about its initiation and the way it had come into being', though he was glad to find that the national emergency

> was drawing the country together and there was a genuine enthusiasm even in regions where it could not have been anticipated...
> The king also spoke with great frankness of the difficulties of his position as a constitutional sovereign in this country.[39]

Rodd was subsequently told by Luzzatti that the proclamation of Italian sovereignty had been an error, because Germany had been on the point of persuading the Turks to accept a formula that would have given Italy most of what she required.[40] Once annexation had been proclaimed, Giolitti was unable to back down with dignity, at the same time as he found himself condemned 'by public opinion in the whole outside world'.[41] Germany and Austria further criticised the Italians for contravening the Triple Alliance because they should have given advance warning before a delicate balance of power was upset. The decree of annexation, in the Kaiser's words, was tantamount to 'highway robbery'.[42] The Italians, he said, had also put themselves in the wrong by executing prisoners of war who were guilty of nothing more than courageously fighting for independence. He concluded that Italians were not a people who understood the proper conduct of hostilities. They would hardly be a reliable wartime ally.[43]

The Italian public was nevertheless encouraged to think that the war was being conducted brilliantly and exactly to plan.[44] No newspaper reader could have guessed that, already in November, Giolitti complained that the commander, General Caneva, was making Italy look foolish by his incompetence and would have been dismissed had he not been a protégé of the king. Some of the journalists attached to Caneva's command spoke of him derisively and their articles had to be censored.[45] Far from being a short campaign, for the next six months the war seemed almost at a stalemate as Turkish and Arab guerrilla tactics prevented any decisive success. Giolitti let it be thought that no war had ever been fought with fewer errors and Caneva had the government's full confidence. But privately he admitted that all the generals were 'nullities' and he had to falsify the news to conceal that they never risked an engagement without an overwhelming superiority in numbers.[46]

Such unwelcome facts had to be concealed when parliament was at last recalled in February 1912 to approve the declaration of war and to sanction months of taxation by royal decree. Giolitti told the deputies that colonisation, which he had once opposed, was the highest and most essential task of any civilised nation, but they must accept that military matters, like foreign policy, were part of the royal prerogative and not for them to question.[47] He was supported by a ten-to-one majority. Only a few deputies protested that the Turkish parliament was allowed a greater say in affairs than they were, and furthermore that the Italian government by its secretive behaviour was giving the impression that there was something to hide. Italy, said socialists and republicans in opposition, lacked the capital for investment in colonies, especially when vast areas of their own country were without schools, hospitals, and roads. Aiming to increase national prestige, the practical result was all too obviously the opposite, and it was said that a truly civilised nation would have behaved very differently.[48]

The king took little active share in the war despite his close interest in military matters. Each day he was sent lists of casualties and intelligence reports. He received copies of telegrams sent or received by the general staff and no doubt made comments in private, but he did not take part in conferences on strategy, and his views rarely appear in the documents.[49] In the last stages of the war he allowed Caneva to be unobtrusively replaced. At one point he hinted to the Germans that they might help him bring the war to an honourable conclusion, and this would enable him to return his army to Europe for what he suggested might soon be war against France. Failing that, he hoped that the Germans would at least exert their influence on Vienna to permit Italian naval action in the Aegean, because he wanted to attack Rhodes and the other Dodecanese islands whose possession would be a fine bargaining counter to use in the peace settlement.[50]

The Turks agreed to sign a peace at Lausanne in October 1912 when they needed their army to confront a major uprising throughout the Balkans. This was not an entirely satisfactory settlement for Italy because, apart from the fact that the Sultan was allowed to retain his religious authority in Libya, the local Arab population continued the war as fiercely as ever. Italy captured the Dodecanese but in Libya won effective control of only the coastal areas. She had spent, as the government admitted, far more than expected, and the expense continued for many years after 1912. Ministers tried to pretend that the immense hinterland would be effectively occupied in 'a few months time', and the expense would be reduced once the local population and a militia of Eritreans were able to provide the troops and officials needed to govern the country;[51] but in practice a metropolitan army had to remain there in strength and a bureaucracy had to be recruited in Italy. As a secret and damaging war continued, by 1915 only two garrison towns along 1,500 kilometres of coast were held securely, and fifteen more years passed before the enormous interior of Libya was more or less occupied.

Little idea of the difficulties was allowed to filter back home and the general public in Italy was heartened by what was called a great victory. The nationalists were satisfied that a notable lesson had been given to the world: they were proud that 'Italy in one gigantic step has smashed the restrictions of international law, has broken treaties, defied the rest of Europe, and revived the traditions of Caesar Borgia and Machiavelli'.[52] Others talked of Italy's great mission to civilise the barbarian peoples of North Africa and spoke of the magnificent achievements of the Italian army which were the admiration of the whole world. Maffeo Pantaleoni as an expert economist gave his highly questionable opinion that Libya could absorb an unlimited number of Italian emigrants.[53]

Self-confidence was a positive and welcome result of the war, but was not securely based. Emigration from Italy reached a peak of almost a million in 1913, but only a few score of these emigrants chose to go to Libya, and even fewer chose to stay. Some of the wiser and more responsible colonialists regretted in private that a legend had been created of the powerful and heroic qualities of the Italian army, because this was bound to be deceptive as a basis for future policy, and Giolitti was not the only minister who admitted that the legend was dangerous and untrue.[54] Rodd commented that an officially subsidised press had gone too far in its talk of brilliant achievements, 'and the impression now prevails that the net results of the peace are not quite commensurate with what the nation was persuaded it had accomplished. There is probably also a consciousness that things are not quite as they are represented to be.'[55] The young journalist Benito Mussolini said much the same even more forcibly, as he learnt from the surprising credulousness of the reading public what became the secret of his future success.[56]

6 *Giolitti in difficulties, 1912–14*

The power of the popular press was already well recognised by the government, though the king was inclined to disregard it except when journalists tried to pry into his private life.[1] Giolitti, who became prime minister for the fourth time in 1911–14, secretly tapped the telephone of the *Corriere della Sera*, a newspaper that criticised him and supported Luzzatti and Sonnino.[2] Nevertheless, Luigi Albertini, the distinguished editor of the *Corriere*, could sometimes be influenced to endorse official policy by making an appeal to his patriotism, and he dutifully championed the Libyan war even though he was privately worried that it might be a dangerous waste of money.[3]

At least thirty journalists enjoyed regular hand-outs from Giolitti's secret-service fund,[4] and presumably their lack of enthusiasm for Sonnino was not unaffected by the latter's discontinuance of this practice when in office.[5] Direct grants were paid by Giolitti to the not very reputable *Mattino* of Naples, to the *Popolo Romano*, and especially the more respectable *Tribuna*. Also the Stefani news agency, which had been secretly subsidised by Crispi in order to liberate it from French shareholders, was now working entirely under Giolitti's direction.[6]

As well as influencing people through the press, governments were anxious to ensure that the history syllabus in schools was given a more fitting patriotic and imperialist slant as befitted a great power.[7] Crispi and Tittoni had wanted people to believe that, unlike Germany, France, and Britain, the inhabitants of Italy had been unanimous in their patriotic struggles and made greater sacrifices for national unification.[8] It was the more strange, therefore, that the history of the risorgimento was so little taught in schools, and unfortunately Italians thereby developed an excessively pessimistic idea of their own past or had to depend on foreign historians who for some reason were assumed to be more objective.[9] One step towards greater historical awareness was taken when the government acquired the personal archives of Crispi and Mazzini, though some critics feared that this might rather be an attempt to muzzle the truth in the interests of political expediency.[10] Giolitti confirmed this suspicion when he refused to open the state archives for the years after 1830 for research. His reasons for concealment were too delicate to be explained in public, except that scholarly investigation, like a free press, might sometimes be 'inconvenient'. More positively he stated that popular morale depended on 'beautiful national legends' being protected from criticism.[11]

His anxieties were no doubt excessive, and his attempts at concealment were dangerous in that these beautiful legends, as he sometimes admitted, created exaggerated expectations of Italy's military capacity. He knew better than anyone about the army's failures in Libya, but indignantly denied them in parliament and allowed the illusion to persist that Italy might be as strong as Austria.[12] The nationalists, who in private he called 'a caricature of patriotism', were allowed to proclaim that Italy was entering a new phase of expansion and conquest at the expense of unnamed 'rich but decadent countries'.[13] San Giuliano was partly caught up in this mood of self-confidence and warned foreigners as well as parliament that Italy intended to exploit her new sensation of power. Speaking to an Austrian newspaper editor, he

> seemed like one intoxicated with the fumes of imperialism. He talked of Italian aspirations which seemed to know no limits, for his remarks embraced the Aegean islands, Albania, and even Tunis, and he gave vent to his irredentism by uttering the words 'Trentino' and 'Savoy'.[14]

Vittorio Emanuele could hardly be unaffected by this enthusiasm. He presided with dignity and modesty over celebrations for the fiftieth anniversary of Italian unification in 1911, and over the inauguration of the great monument dedicated to his grandfather on the Capitol hill. This vast and immensely costly mausoleum towering over the Roman skyline had taken thirty years to construct and was intended to celebrate the triumph of a monarchist and militarily powerful nation over the alternative concepts of Italy associated with Mazzini and the Vatican.[15] The building was, according to Giolitti at least, 'a magnificent work of art'.[16] But the king's personal tastes were less grandiose and more matter of fact. In the same year appeared two initial volumes of the history of Italian coinage prepared under his inspiration and nominal direction.

He was badly shaken when in March 1912 an attempt was made on his life by an anarchist. To congratulate him on his escape the deputies went *en masse* to the Quirinal palace, among them the moderate socialists Bissolati and Ivanoe Bonomi. For this act of obeisance, and for their support of the Libyan war, these two men were expelled from the rapidly growing socialist party. Other socialist leaders had radically different ideas and rather shared Mussolini's lack of sympathy with a monarch who was 'by definition a useless citizen'. Mussolini was a revolutionary socialist who had already suffered imprisonment for his violent opposition to the war in Libya when he had called the national flag 'a rag to place on a dunghill'. He could not condemn assassination outright. Indeed regicide was in his view justified against kings who acted tyrannically, and he praised those earlier politicians in France and Britain who had dared to execute their rulers.[17]

Giolitti was still hoping to enlarge his political base by attracting support from the moderate socialists and widening the gap between them and the 'maximalist socialists' further to the Left. His programme on returning to office in 1911 therefore included payment for deputies, the grant of workers' pensions, and setting up a government monopoly of life insurance. Believing that 'the working classes will one day command in Italy' and that their representatives would prove to be quite as intelligent as the lawyers who now predominated in parliament,[18] he also reduced the monetary qualifications for election and more than doubled the number of electors. Only six votes were cast against this fundamental reform in May 1912 since almost everyone hoped to gain from it.

The king was apprehensive about extending the suffrage, as he saw the old ruling class to be in danger of losing its monopoly of politics. It his view, those who gained would be the socialists, most of whom were republicans. Others to gain would be the Catholic masses and the Vatican which still refused to recognise the existence of monarchist Italy. Many familiar political landmarks were thus under threat, especially since over one third of the new electorate was classed as illiterate.[19] Although the king guessed that the liberals of the Centre might still keep a majority, they were bound to be weakened by a shift to what he called the reds and the blacks; and 'of the two he preferred the reds'. He also foresaw that these two extremes might one day combine to defeat the Centre. Unfortunately 'Italy was not yet ripe for government by two clearly defined parties', so that liberals and conservatives, who elsewhere might alternate in government, were insufficiently organised to act in such a role. Perhaps instead they ought to join forces against the extremists. If they failed to combine they were likely to be swamped by new mass parties that played by different rules.[20]

When the next election took place, in November 1913, the result partly confirmed this forecast. The socialists increased their representation to 78, the radicals, to 70. The Catholics won 29 seats and claimed that their support was also decisive in saving 228 liberals from defeat. Giolitti could count on a majority, but it would be partly conditional on Catholic support and had been won only by gerrymandering on a scale never known before.

Another shifting landmark was the contours of foreign policy. The Libyan war, as some outsiders wisely recognised from its commencement, upset the equilibrium of power in eastern Europe, as a result of which the Balkan peoples took the chance to assert their independence of the defeated Ottoman empire. Vittorio Emanuele knew the Balkans at first hand from his earlier travels and spoke more forcefully than his foreign minister on some of the problems that were beginning to emerge. He would have liked to extend the frontier of Montenegro which was governed by his father-in-law.[21] But San Giuliano was inclined to think that this small kingdom was an anachronism and better absorbed into Serbia. Giolitti, as well as being anxious to defend the independence of Serbia against Austrian encroachment, was equally determined to prevent the Serbs obtaining a major independent outlet on the Adriatic coastline, and also realised with alarm that a general war in the Balkans might drag Italians into fighting alongisde Austria.[22]

Vittorio Emanuele wanted to renew the Triple Alliance once more, not so much out of conviction as because he knew that without it the Austrians might well turn against Italy. This danger was known to exist by reason of information purchased from the Austrian secret agent, Colonel Redl, and was connected with the likelihood that the elderly Emperor Franz Joseph might soon be succeeded by his nephew, the strongly anti-Italian Franz Ferdinand whose forbears included the dispossessed Bourbon dynasty of Naples.[23] Fearing diplomatic isolation, the king did his best to reassure his allies that the Triple Alliance was widely popular in Italy, and he also confirmed that he was ready to support the Austrians 'to the last man' if war broke out.[24]

In December 1912 the alliance was therefore renewed. But it is fairly clear that the king had little or no intention of honouring its commitments if the war was against England or France[25] – which was increasingly probable. On the German side there was a similar lack of sincerity. The Kaiser's private comments about Italy, in particular about its king, were contemptuous, and tactless remarks were sometimes made in the hearing of Italians about the alliance being little more than a formality without substance.[26]

Vittorio Emanuele was no doubt speaking truthfully when he told the French how much he personally disliked the Kaiser.[27] He was even more disloyal to his ally when he informed the British of what was being planned against them in Berlin. 'The Germans are burning to fight somebody' and the enemy they most wished to destroy was England; so he told a British diplomat. They had many more submarines than was generally thought and had let him know that they planned to win a decisive naval battle lasting only fifteen minutes. They also had plans to defeat the French in a single week with a force of one and a half million men, after which they would turn to deal with Russia. They had informed him that they already knew from leaks in Paris about what had been said in recent talks between British and French staff officers. Furthermore, they intended to surprise the French by first invading Switzerland, and he illustrated their proposed plan of attack by drawing a detailed map for the British military attaché which showed his remarkable knowledge of the railway system of central Europe.[28]

The king had a reputation in foreign chancelleries for being a *Realpolitiker* and a convinced believer in secret diplomacy.[29] But the secrecy still surrounding the Triple Alliance continued to cause dismay among the parliamentary opposition in Italy who saw the alliance as no longer a force for peace but as making a major European war more likely. Italy would then find herself fighting alongside Austria to crush the subject peoples of the Balkans, and this could not be in the national interest. The alliance, wrote the republican Chiesa, was 'dynastic, militaristic...and a faithful reflection of the reactionary policy of the monarchist party in Italy'; otherwise its text would by now have been published.[30] Giolitti cut short a debate on this issue after deputies protested that, while public discussion was permitted in Vienna and Berlin, serious debates on foreign policy hardly ever took place in Rome, a fact that made parliamentary government a farce.[31]

One good reason for secrecy was that Italy had simultaneous commitments to France that would not bear close scrutiny. In response to Prinetti's promise of neutrality in 1902, the French had changed their defence system by removing troops from the Italian frontier, and Giolitti confirmed to Paris at the end of 1912 that there was no need for them to be afraid since he would carry out this promise 'with the most scrupulous loyalty'.[32] San Giuliano said the same, stressing 'the ethical value of loyalty, which he regarded as the strongest obligation in international relations'.[33]

Here the Italian foreign minister was trying to conceal his embarrassment about continuing in simultaneous and hardly compatible relations with both of the main rival alliances in Europe. Understandably he was fearful that publicity might alienate either side or even both sides at once.[34] Other countries in fact knew that he had landed himself with an insoluble political, if not ethical, problem. A leading official in the British foreign office commented that 'Italy wants to square the circle without exposing herself to a charge of breach of faith; she wants to remain in the Triple Alliance and yet not to go to war with France in accordance with its stipulations. No Anglo-Italian formula can solve this ethical problem'.[35]

Giolitti's promise of 'scrupulous loyalty' towards the French has to be reconciled with the information given simultaneously to Germany that Italians were planning to attack France along her Alpine frontier and destroy the French fleet.[36] Germany and Austria were even asked, with the king's permission, to specify what territorial compensations would be due to Italy in the event of a successful war.[37] Moreover, at Italy's request a naval convention was signed in June 1913 which undertook to place the Italian fleet under the wartime command of the Austrian Admiral Haus, and this too was authorised by the king. San Giuliano told the French on his honour that no such convention existed, but they knew about it through their possession of the Italian naval cipher.[38]

Giolitti and San Giuliano had no particular wish for a European war and were merely hedging their bets. They naturally wanted the maximum advantage from remaining in the Triple Alliance while at the same time minimising any possible damage to Italy. In July 1913 and again in October, with the king's approval, the Austrians were warned to go carefully and not rely on Italy's joining them in an aggressive war.[39] Yet the chief of staff, General Pollio, was allowed to say almost the opposite. Pollio, despite knowing that the Germans had in mind a *Vernichtungskrieg*, or war of annihilation,[40] reactivated plans to send 200,000 soldiers to Germany if war broke out. This he did after first consulting the minister of war who was responsible for keeping the army informed about foreign policy.[41] Presumably Pollio thought he was carrying out the king's wishes when he told the Austrians that they could rely on Italian help if they threw away 'false humanity' and started a pre-emptive war in the Balkans.[42]

This highly provocative remark was made in April 1914, a few weeks before the first world war began. Although San Giuliano cannot have wanted that war, such promises of support from Rome must have encouraged his two allies to start fighting, because with active Italian help they calculated on a quick victory.[43] In the same month San Giuliano met the Austrian foreign minister and confirmed that Italy needed a strong Austria to withstand a growing threat from Serbia. A communiqué was issued after this meeting about the 'perfect identity of views' between the two men and their entire confidence in each other's policy. Whether either party or both parties were intentionally deceiving each other is not easy to say.

7   Salandra, 1914

Giolitti, as the king noted, was ageing and his health was poor.[1] Though he could count on a majority in parliament, his doubling of the number of electors had produced a far less tractable legislature. Many socialists, scorning his advances, joined some of the republicans in boycotting the royal speech to parliament in November 1913, and shouts of 'Down with Savoy!', 'Long live the republic!' were once again heard in the chamber.[2] The prime minister must have been equally disturbed by other deputies who vociferously demanded a much more forceful policy in the Mediterranean, because he knew better than they did that it could not be afforded.[3] Fearing troubled times ahead at home and abroad, he preferred another period of what he may have hoped would be temporary retirement.

To replace him in March 1914 the king chose Antonio Salandra, a southern conservative who as a colleague of General Pelloux in 1899 had signed the famous *decretone* restricting free speech. Salandra was a strong champion of monarchy, even if he seems to have had no particular liking for Vittorio Emanuele.[4] His appointment was welcomed by former supporters of Crispi who wanted a firmer stance against socialism and now blamed the palace for permitting Giolitti's 'ultra-democratic policy' of enfranchising the 'plebs'.[5] Once again there seemed to be in prospect an approximation to a two-party alternation between Salandra's conservatives and Giolitti's liberals.

The king reacted to the elections of the previous year by welcoming what he saw as 'the almost complete disappearance of the republicans as a political factor' and was not particularly worried by the increased numbers of socialists because they were divided into rival groups.[6] But he was soon greatly alarmed by reports about the state of public feeling. These reports confirm that he had his own sources of information and was regularly told about gossip in cafés or in the corridors of parliament. He learnt in detail about the activities of anarchist and republican groups. Precise quotations were sent to him of anti-monarchist remarks made in private meetings. More publicly he must have seen a message chalked up on the palace walls which read 'Long live anarchism! Death to Vittorio Emanuele!'[7] Such minor acts of sedition suddenly came to look serious during 'Red Week' in June when would-be revolutionaries briefly took over entire towns in central Italy; railways were cut, bridges destroyed, and the red flag displaced the national flag on some public buildings. The army restored order but only after a rumour circulated that the royal family had gone into hiding.

A few weeks later, the Archduke Franz Ferdinand was assassinated by a Serbian terrorist at Sarajevo, and on 23 July the Austrians sent an ultimatum to Serbia which a week later detonated the first world war. Salandra's foreign minister was San Giuliano who the king had insisted be taken over from Giolitti's cabinet,[8] and San Giuliano knew as early as 17 July that Austria was determined to use force if the Serbs refused to surrender.[9] He nevertheless did not follow his own example of a year earlier when with Giolitti's support he had successfully advised the Austrians against a similar act of aggression. Instead he decided on a bolder policy of seeking to profit from their action, and since an attack on Serbia without prior discussion would violate a stipulation in the Triple Alliance, he suggested that Italy be offered territorial compensation in return for remaining benevolently neutral.[10] He said he would not create difficulties for Austria, and in fact hoped that the Serbs would surrender;[11] yet in the meantime his private intention was 'to leave everyone uncertain about what we decide to do, in the hope of eventually winning some tangible advantage'. An ominous hint was dropped that he might go further and assist the Austrians in fighting Serbia if only they would cede the Trentino to Italy.[12]

Unlike Giolitti in 1913, the new government was thus more concerned with obtaining compensations than preventing war; and the king raised no objection, perhaps because until the end of July he quite underestimated the danger.[13] He trusted San Giuliano more than any other foreign minister of his reign, and kept closely in touch. If their primary aim was to prevent war, they had good grounds for threatening to denounce the alliance, but they instead decided to exploit the clause in the alliance that specified that compensation could be claimed.

In taking this decision San Giuliano was influenced by his belief that Austria and Germany were invincible, whereas France and Britain were decadent nations who would lose if it came to a general European conflagration.[14] The king, too, encouraged the Germans by telling them that from private sources of information in England he understood that the British army was in no condition to fight.[15] Perhaps he would have acted differently had he known that the military leaders in Austria and Germany seriously feared that Italy might desert the alliance or even fight on the other side, in which case a major war would be too dangerous for them to contemplate.[16] In other words, a firmer reaction by Italy would have helped to avert a terrible catastrophe.

The king had recently shown signs of aggravated nervous depression. Rumours from the palace talked of quarrels with the queen, of possible abdication, even suicide. His chief aide-de-camp at one point wondered whether he was in full possession of his faculties.[17] Even more alarming was that San Giuliano was gravely ill and spent the following weeks away from Rome taking the radioactive waters at Fiuggi which the doctors prescribed for gout. Sometimes the foreign minister complained of an inability to sleep or eat, and ambassadors found him 'too ill to work'. He had to be regularly sedated with narcotics that must have affected his judgement, and before coming into Rome for meetings with Salandra had to take counter-injections that made him highly excitable.[18]

Another reason for Salandra's sympathetic attitude to Austria lay in domestic politics, because the strongest opponents of Austria were a dissident minority inclined to republicanism. Already at the end of July some militant republicans went to enlist in France out of opposition to the 'anti-national policy of the king'; and though a thousand of these volunteers were intercepted before they crossed the frontier, hundreds joined three of Garibaldi's grandsons who reached France. The young Giuseppe Garibaldi publicly denounced the monarchy for its 'culpable inertia' in refusing to side with Serbia and the western democracies against autocracy and imperialism.[19]

On the other hand the nationalist party, strong champions of the monarchy, demanded that honour and interest required an immediate declaration of war against republican and democratic France.[20] Sonnino was another politician who, along with many leading newspapers, favoured entering the war at once as an ally of Austria,[21] and the army leadership held the same opinion. The new chief of staff, General Cadorna, optimistically calculated that Italy would need only a month to defeat the French and annex Nice, Corsica, and Tunisia.[22]

Against these champions of the Triple Alliance, only a small minority apart from republicans and some socialists advocated joining France. A different view was held by Albertini: to consolidate the sense of Italian nationality by entering the war on whichever side, either with Austria, or preferably against her.[23] San Giuliano was more cautious. His instinctive preference would have been 'to march alongside his allies, but he was persuaded by political, military and above all naval arguments to prefer neutrality';[24] because he knew that, once the British entered the war on the other side, their navy could cut off Italy's sea-borne supplies at will, so that war was inadvisable unless the Germans were going to win very quickly indeed.

Salandra spoke on 1 August of his anguish at San Giuliano's failure either to prevent war or to win concessions from Vienna, yet also accepted that, once Austria found herself fighting against Britain as well as Serbia, the safe policy was to remain 'benevolently neutral'

towards his allies. The king agreed,[25] especially when further fears
were raised that joining Austria in an aggressive war might provoke
a revolution inside Italy and compel his abdication.[26] Salandra was
ready to concede that an Austrian victory might spell disaster for
Europe and he privately dared to hope for her defeat;[27] nevertheless,
he would not withdraw from the Triple Alliance until he saw how
the war developed. San Giuliano agreed in part but for different
reasons, because he continued to hope that the Austrians would soon
offer to surrender the Trentino, which would allow Italy to remain
their 'sincere friend' and help them to victory.[28] That, at all events,
was what he told them.

Inevitably there was some confusion in government policy during
these critical days, but it became more muddled than it need have
been, especially because of a surprising lack of co-ordination between king, ministers, and army. San Giuliano, incredibly and yet
presumably by deliberate choice, never told the prime minister that
in 1913 he and Giolitti had been successful in warning Austria not to
start a war. Equally incredibly, the prime minister had no knowledge
of repeated promises to the French that they could count on Italy's
neutrality. Nor did ministers consult General Cadorna and the army
leaders before deciding to remain neutral. Cadorna, quite against
government policy, moved troops to the French frontier. He also
wrote a memorandum to the king at the end of July about sending a
large expeditionary force to help the Germans invade France, and he
was ready to place his troops under German command. Salandra
never knew about this memorandum and was never told when for
some obscure reason, even after the government had decided to
remain neutral, the king on 2 August informed the army that their
preparations for war against France should proceed.[29]

Vittorio Emanuele was no doubt insuring against the possibility of
a quick victory by the Germans, in which case he might have to join
them. This was another compelling reason for not denouncing the
Triple Alliance – even though his allies had violated its terms by
not consulting Italy or offering her compensation as their treaty
prescribed. He was sure that the Austrians would sooner or later be
prepared to bargain for Italian support. On 2 August he therefore
sent a telegram to Vienna protesting 'his cordial friendship in conformity with Italy's treaty obligations', and this must have been with
his ministers' approval.[30]

He also sent his 'cordial good wishes' to the Germans in reply to
their request for military help. He told them, whether truthfully or
not, that he was still trying to persuade Salandra to join them. He
explained that although personally he was 'whole-heartedly' on the
German side, and though a few weeks earlier he would have had

no difficulty in declaring war on France, the Austrians made this difficult by refusing to offer compensation. He also repeated that he was afraid of domestic revolution if he declared war on France without first being promised some tangible inducement. He explained that his constitutional powers were limited, and although he could dismiss ministers, he could not easily find new ones who would agree to joining Austria without some such inducement. Wilhelm's reaction to this message was to call the king a liar and a scoundrel, but also to hope that an offer of territorial concessions would speedily be made to secure Italian support.[31]

Vittorio Emanuele in these crucial days used to preside at the more important cabinet meetings,[32] though ministers were still not informed in detail about foreign policy, let alone allowed much discussion. He did not thrust his own views on Salandra because he wanted ministers to take full responsibility for whatever was decided.[33] He agreed with their advice to keep on good terms for the moment with both sides in the war. Only when there was still no offer from Vienna by 9 August, were the British with his permission informed that Italy might conceivably desert her allies one day if the western powers helped her to win Trent and Trieste;[34] but his essential premise was to avoid any risk of being on the losing side, or indeed of joining either side unless in a very short war.[35] When towards the end of August the Germans seemed to be winning, San Giuliano told them once more that they could count on Italian benevolence; then in September, after France won the battle of the Marne, he veered back again. But he would not fight until he was 'ninety-nine per cent' sure of victory, and best of all would be if Austria and France both emerged so damaged as to leave Italy in a position of greater relative strength.[36]

The country's future depended on finding the correct policy in a complex and quickly changing situation. The king received further warning that the monarchy would fall if he entered the war and lost, but was also advised that the dynasty would lose reputation if he broke a binding treaty and deserted his allies.[37] The Italian ambassadors in Berlin and Vienna came to Italy to explain their strong conviction that Italy would be dishonoured if she deserted the Triple Alliance; they both offered to resign but the offer was refused, after which they returned to their posts in confusion because king and foreign minister appeared to disagree with each other at the same time as neither would state his views unambiguously.[38]

But by September two points were becoming clear. First, the fighting would not be short, and Italy could not afford to enter a long war. Second, the balance of patriotic sentiment made it unlikely that Italians would willingly fight on the same side as Austria so long as Trent and Trieste remained in the Austrian empire. Failing surrender of these two areas, the alternatives were narrowing down to either permanent neutrality, or else possibly joining France and England if ever they appeared close to victory.

The choice was not easy. To General Brusati the king expressed indignation at the way he had been forced into an impossible situation by the inconsiderate belligerence of his allies.[39] A few weeks after telling the Germans that he was whole-heartedly behind them, he sent several messages to the British sovereign asking for an exchange of views and explaining 'that Italy will do nothing that could hinder the just punishment that will overtake the cruel and unscrupulous aggressors in this war':

> it is splendid how England's sense of honour makes her defend her friends, and no other country would have done what England has done in a war which is not directed against her alone but against every law of justice and humanity, a war due to extravagant ambition.[40]

Salandra commented on 17 September that, without being sure, he thought the king now 'inclined towards war', and others received the same impression.[41]

At Paris, where information from Rome was perhaps reliable because the Italian ciphers were being read, it was reported on 19 September that

> His Majesty is suffering from over-fatigue and extreme nervous depression owing to the crisis. His Majesty intensely dislikes the idea of making war on his late allies and is also bitterly disappointed at learning that his army, which he had imagined was excellent, is in a very unfit state.[42]

Other reports confirm his dismay that people might regard him as 'the first member of the House of Savoy to break his pledged word to an ally', and it was especially humiliating to discover that the armed services were nowhere near ready for a serious war on either side.[43]

The army had not been mobilised. Nevertheless, on 12 September General Cadorna, who as chief of staff should have been in the best position to know, said he was now confident of victory if they could change sides and at once declare war against Austria; and it was the king who overruled him for being too hasty.[44] The full truth is hard to establish. Military unpreparedness was later given as an explanation or excuse for not fighting sooner. On the other hand, a number of other people subsequently agreed with Cadorna that the best moment for Italian intervention might have been September

1914, because the Austrians were unprepared on their southern frontier and were simultaneously heavily engaged on two other fronts against Russia and Serbia.[45]

Military decisions, however, had to be taken in the light of political realities which counselled caution. Public opinion was restless and on 13 September a number of citizens were arrested outside the Quirinal for crying 'Down with Austria!'[46] One fear voiced at court was that fighting might result in 'a serious spread of democracy' and of socialism.[47] This was balanced by the opinion of Giolitti, as well as Salandra and Sonnino, who all feared that a more serious danger for the survival of the monarchy was if by remaining neutral it failed to secure territorial rectifications from Austria by either negotiation or conquest.[48] Salandra wrote to the king on 30 September to say that either action or inaction, if not carefully considered, might be damaging, because failure to take the correct decision might encourage the extremists to combine and compel abdication; whatever else happened, Italy must not end up on the defeated side in a major European war.[49]

In October San Giuliano died after a protracted and incapacitating illness. A few days earlier he and Salandra had persuaded the king to take further soundings about possibly joining Britain and France.[50] But the prime minister, while agreeing that Italy might eventually be forced to fight against Austria, also agreed with San Giuliano and the nationalists that his war aims could not be the same as those of the western Entente. Italians had no quarrel with Germany, only with Austria. Italian soldiers should certainly not be called upon to die for abstract considerations of justice, humanity, democracy, let alone for the integrity of Belgium. This was the moment when Salandra made his famous pronouncement about 'sacred egoism' as the only correct determinant of policy.[51]

Shortly afterwards the foreign office was given to Sonnino. This former prime minister was unenthusiastic about what he took to be Salandra's premature readiness for intervention alongside France.[52] Indeed, two months earlier he himself had favoured fighting on the opposite side, but by now had changed his mind and backed neutrality. He was the strongest member of a succession of cabinets during the next five years, and the king was appreciative of having as foreign minister someone whose firm views and uncompromising character would leave little need for the palace to take responsibility over this crucial and difficult issue.

Sonnino agreed that, whichever decision was taken, the survival of the dynasty would depend on winning territory from Austria, preferably by agreement and not war.[53] Either way this would require delicate negotiation and precise timing. When not in office he had criticised governments for secretiveness about foreign policy and for refusing to consult parliament.[54] But as foreign minister he followed Salandra's lead in taking silence to the point of deceit. When at long last parliament met in December, its discussions were effectively gagged, and deputies were not permitted to raise questions about policy or about Italy's suspected military weakness, because these were once again stated to be matters for the royal prerogative.

Salandra simply announced, what he must have known to be untrue, that the army was perfectly ready for any eventuality; and he added that any deputy who doubted this was unpatriotic.[55] Such a statement was effective in winning him an unconditional vote of confidence; nor did he see any need to indicate how he intended to act, except to say that the war would end in the course of 1915 and only after Italy had acquired 'greatness and glory'. Only one senator dared to express dissent, arguing that Italy ought by now to have negotiated concessions from Austria; to which the prime minister brazenly replied, to huge applause, that even an attempt at such negotiation would be dishonourable.[56]

The king mentioned privately on 17 December that he thought public opinion was by now 'almost universally favourable' to France and Britain.[57] He must have known from Salandra and Sonnino of their hope that a favourable moment for entering the war would at some point arrive, despite their knowledge that few Italians wanted to abandon neutrality.[58] As an initial step, without informing other ministers, Sonnino decided to occupy part of Albania, and sent *agents provocateurs* to organise an 'incident' that gave him a pretext to land troops at Valona.[59] Vittorio Emanuele had always looked on Albania as a possible area for Italian expansion and was glad of the opportunity to help his relatives in adjacent Montenegro. He overruled the army commanders who had good reason to protest that such a dispersal of Italy's military resources might prove to be a costly mistake.[60]

While General Cadorna criticised privately and for military reasons, others condemned what they called a dynastic rather than a patriotic policy in Albania. One socialist deputy threatened that soldiers were likely to mutiny if called on to participate in aggression against a friendly Balkan county. When the republican volunteers Costante and Bruno Garibaldi were killed fighting for France, this helped to fuel a small but significant anti-monarchist movement on the Left which wanted a very different policy of 'clean hands' in support of national self-determination everywhere.[61]

On the extreme Right the small nationalist party wanted war for its own sake, at first on the Austrian side; but very quickly realised that their best chance of fighting was against Austria. They even began to talk of a possible coup to hasten this event by overthrowing the government and deposing the monarch. Mussolini, too, who had not yet completed his transition from socialism to nationalism, called for a revolution if the king failed to declare war against his allies.[62] Vittorio Emanuele was not popular, wrote the futurist Giovanni Papini (in an unusually offensive article that somehow escaped censorship), but was seen by rich and poor as merely the absurd dwarf of innumerable caricatures; he might be good and inoffensive as a person, but mistakenly surrounded himself with courtiers who gave him ridiculously bad advice, and had the further misfortune of governing a spineless population of Italians; if he failed to do his duty and march on Vienna he would certainly lose his crown.[63]

8 To fight or not to fight?

As the year 1915 opened, ministers unfortunately were still unable to make up their minds on the crucial question of who was likely to win the war. The king hoped it would be the Triple Entente – Britain, France, and Russia. He now helped in secret by giving the Russians reports about Austrian troop movements. He also sent a personal promise to King George that he would never fight against Britain. And his queen was yet more partisan when she said that the British should be less 'gentlemanly' and more punitive in treating the Germans.[1] But personal preference aside, Austria and Germany might still win, and to line up prematurely against them might forfeit the only chance to emerge from the war with advantage. Italy ought to aim at acquiring at least the Trentino, as well as part of Albania to ensure domination of the Adriatic; if possible she also ought to obtain Tunisia so as to displace French influence in the Mediterranean.[2] The question at issue was whether these territories could be won without war.

Sonnino, like his predecessor as foreign minister, hoped ideally that all the warring nations would exhaust themselves without any clear result, leaving Italy neutral until the very last moment when with minimum losses her intervention or mediation might be decisive. Preferably she would then favour the Entente, because he agreed with the king that a German victory would create a dangerous hegemony in Europe, whereas the Entente stood for a pluralist continent in which Italy would have some chance of swaying the balance of power. Certainly he had no intention of fighting against

Britain, and this reduced his favourite option of playing one side against the other.[3]

For the moment the most promising tactic was to discover how much Austria would pay for the continuance of Italy's benevolent neutrality. Over a period of two months he therefore discontinued negotiations with the Entente, while sending messages each day to Vienna and Berlin to find out what might be on offer. Nor did he hesitate to threaten his central-European allies that, since the Italian monarchy lacked a strong popular basis, the king would have to emerge with an undisputed acquisition of territory; otherwise he would be obliged to declare war against Austria or else face revolution at home.[4]

In pursuit of this objective, Sonnino informed the palace as a matter of urgency that the government needed to decide whether the Italian-speaking districts of the Trentino would suffice; if not, what else? He also asked the king how soon the army would if necessary be ready to fight. Vittorio Emanuele in reply produced maps from his family archives which suggested that there was a historical precedent for demanding the area round Cortina d'Ampezzo and Gradisca, but probably not Bolzano or Gorizia.[5] As for Trieste, Fiume, and the rest of the Alto Adige south of the Alps, these were less important, and in any case ministers, perhaps surprisingly, showed relatively little interest in them.[6]

When parliament reassembled in February after another two month gap, Salandra asked for a further vote of confidence, again refusing to permit a full discussion of policy because secrecy was vital. The conservatives knew and feared that Golitti, if he exerted himself in parliament, could command a majority and compel his own return to power.[7] But Giolitti had no wish for this until he knew enough of the relevant facts to find a clear policy. His own guess was that a more experienced and subtle negotiator than Sonnino could make Austria cede Trent, Trieste, and Istria in return for Italian neutrality. If that failed he was ready to enter the war, but only at the very last moment when the fighting was almost over.[8] To discuss these points, Salandra took the very unusual step of going to his predecessor's house, apparently at the request of the king who wanted these two parliamentary leaders to avoid a clash in public debate which would have brought many delicate matters into the open.[9] Giolitti at this meeting on 8 March, after hearing that Salandra was determined to consider war as only a last resort, agreed to persuade his followers to vote for the government.[10]

Salandra was being mendacious in an attempt to silence Giolitti and strengthen his own negotiating position by creating an illusion of near unanimity in parliament. He could not let a potential opponent know that, since the Austrians were proving intransigent, he once more had royal approval for reopening parallel negotiations to join the war on the side of the Entente. He had to move fast because the western allies seemed on the point of capturing Constantinople, and Italy by joining them might be in time to seize part of Turkey for herself.[11] But he also had a more important and more devious motive, because the prestige gained from a victorious war could be used to replace Giolitti's political system by a more authoritarian and less parliamentary style of politics in which the crown would recover some of the power it had enjoyed fifty years earlier.[12] Since the king still retained the right to declare war without consulting the legislature, this right could eventually be used to paralyse the neut-ralist majority in the existing parliament – which would be a great success for the conservatives.

After deceiving Giolitti into thinking the opposite, Salandra told Sonnino on 16 March that war was now likely and 'we two alone' would have to decide when 'to play this terrible card'. He explained that the king had not yet given his consent for actual fighting but would not make difficulties; and although parliament and the country at large would no doubt disapprove, their disapproval was irrele-vant. He had been told that the army would not be ready until the end of April, so they would be wise to continue talks with Vienna as a blind, 'pretending that we still hope for them to succeed'. Sonnino demurred, since he believed that Austria might still be persuaded to accept Italy's demands and make war unnecessary.[13] In his view they should continue negotiating with their central-European allies and simultaneously with the Triple Entente; either way Italy stood to gain, but there was a need to hurry before Turkey surrendered, because her surrender would reduce the price that the Entente might be prepared to pay.[14]

Since 'we two alone' would have to decide, the king was per-suaded to close parliament for another two months so that the government could work in secrecy without distractions. Nor even at this point was the cabinet consulted. In his first six months as foreign minister, Sonnino told his colleagues nothing at all about his objectives. Negotiations therefore proceeded for a month in London without the other ministers' knowing many vital facts. Only on 21 April were they informed that he was also negotiating with Austria, his demands from whom had grown to include Bolzano and Gorizia, as well as for Trieste to become an autonomous city but still inside the Austrian empire.[15]

Salandra was understandably anxious to disregard the many re-ports that showed only a small minority of Italians in favour of joining the war. In particular, the peasants and farm labourers, who constituted the vast bulk of the army and would inevitably suffer most casualties, were reported as strongly opposed to fighting.[16] Parliament could be kept in ignorance of policy decisions, but less easy to ignore was pacifist agitation in the country. Reported demonstrations for peace gave an extra argument to those conservatives who wanted war, because any disobedience and disaffection made it all the more necessary to find an excuse to increase the army's strength and prestige. Rich people had various ways of avoiding conscription for themselves and their families, but needed a strong army in order to assuage their fear of insubordination on the part of others who were less fortunate.[17]

Another fact of interest is that the Austrians almost certainly knew more than the Italian cabinet about Sonnino's intentions. Vienna seems to have had an informer inside the Consulta, another in Salandra's immediate entourage, many inside the Vatican, and also dispensed gratuities to a number of sympathetic Italian senators and deputies.[18] Sonnino was himself intercepting correspondence sent out of the Austrian embassy in Rome, though apparently without being able to decode passages in cipher.[19] One such report quoted the king saying that he was fairly sure of avoiding war and of being given the Trentino.[20] But a different account came from Rodd who reported that, although many Italians were 'scared to death by the fear of Germany', the king was ready to join the British if only the Entente would guarantee him control over the far shore of the Adriatic.[21]

Perhaps both these reports were close to the truth, but it is hard to know because the monarch kept aloof and secretive as he waited for his ministers to take the responsibility for action. One of those ministers, Ferdinando Martini, recorded in a diary that the king had too 'modern' an idea of his position:

> He does not believe in monarchy, or at least has no confidence in the future of monarchies in general. If he were not a king he would be a republican, perhaps even a socialist. He is intelligent and cultured, but by failing to believe in his own powers he is losing them. Today no one seems to bother about him or want to know his opinion about what our policy should be at this grave moment. If anyone thinks of him at all it is to be sorry that he does nothing and remains almost in hiding.[22]

Mussolini said much the same but more forcibly. What use was it to pay a salary of sixteen millions to someone who was almost invisible? Many monarchists, wrote Mussolini, were turning towards republicanism because with a republic they would get a more effective as well as cheaper head of state, and no one would shed a tear if a revolution made this possible. Other journalists wrote what, few people had ever quite dared to say, that the risorgimento was chiefly the handiwork of republicans, with the monarchy only a tardy and unwilling accomplice.[23]

Martini, as minister for the colonies, knew another important fact that he concealed from parliament, namely that an Arab insurrection almost chased the Italians out of North Africa in the first half of 1915. This colonial defeat at the hands of a scratch guerrilla force showed up serious weaknesses in the Italian army which if generally known would have been a compelling argument for remaining neutral in Europe. But Martini was so embarrassed by his failure, and so eager for war against Austria, that he censored the bad news from Africa and kept it out of the press. The enormity of this concealment is shown by Salandra's private admission that the defeat in Libya was almost as terrifying as that at Adowa, especially since the Italian army had a ten-to-one superiority over the rebels.[24] Martini improbably tried to blame this Arab victory on the 'bestial ferocity' of his own soldiers against the civilian population in Libya. He was equally irresponsible when he refused to listen to his military advisers over how to react to such an unforseen disaster, and only private intervention by the king prevented the consequent resignation of General Cadorna at a moment critical for the country's future.[25]

Despite this unnerving experience, and despite the fact that he knew parliament and the country were against fighting, Vittorio Emanuele on 26 April took the courageous decision of authorising the signature of a treaty in London which promised that he would declare war within a month against Austria and Germany. By now he knew that the Austrians would offer no more than a token cession of territory, whereas the Entente offered far more. But there was no consultation with the army leaders about this drastic change of front, and the omission was serious, because the Treaty of London awarded Italy a large stretch of the Dalmatian coast, and Cadorna could have explained that this territory would be not only indefensible but a dangerous military liability.

Here was an issue of quite fundamental importance and it was decided in secret by the king and Sonnino. Apart from military objections, two former foreign ministers, Tittoni and San Giuliano, had expressed strong reservations about war aims that included annexing large Slav-speaking and German-speaking areas.[26] But Sonnino wanted as much territory as possible. Dalmatia he sometimes referred to as the very minimum needed for Italy's security; at other times calling it a bargaining counter that he might surrender when the time came to haggle at the peace table.[27] He never bothered to reconcile these statements, nor to discover that military success against Austria would depend on joint military action with the Serbs who could only be bitterly affronted by such a treaty; and this was another omission that proved costly.

Such was the obsessive secretiveness of Salandra and Sonnino that the other ministers were given to understand on 1 May that no treaty with the Entente existed.[28] But its detailed provisions had already been leaked to journalists, by Salandra among others.[29] Naturally the Serbs protested in the strongest terms. Other critics, too, pointed out that the annexation of Dalmatia would be a violation of the very principle of self-determination to which Italy owed her own existence during the risorgimento. This leak made further concealment impossible, and on 4 May Sonnino agreed at long last to denounce the Triple Alliance with Austria.

Between 26 April and 4 May Italy found herself simultaneously allied to both sides in the war, a circumstance that caused much embarrassment when it became generally known, and that Sonnino attributed to the king's express wish.[30] Almost as embarrassing was that, when new proposals now arrived from Vienna, the king and Salandra thought they should be considered before carrying out the promises made in London,[31] and it was agreed to put these proposals to the cabinet. Especially disturbing was the fact that parliament was due to reassemble on 12 May and could be expected to show substantial majorities in both houses against fighting, which might well force a return to power of the greatly feared Giolitti. So the date for reassembly was put off until the 20th to give the government more freedom of manoeuvre before any irrevocable step was taken.

The king became more nervous as each day went by, because he feared that Salandra might leave him with the task of clarifying this confusion and exposing the clear evidence of bad faith with both his old and his new allies. He had given his word of honour to the Kaiser that he would never fight against Germany, but had promised the opposite in London. News reached Vienna that he privately spoke of fighting against Austria in the expectation that military victory would arouse patriotic enthusiasm and consolidate his dynasty.[32] When the pope sent a desperate personal appeal to save their common fatherland from the horrors of war, no reply was forthcoming.[33]

Another problem was that the Treaty of London, because it mentioned territorial changes, had by the terms of the constitution to be approved by parliament before taking effect, and its rejection would leave Italy with more enemies and without any allies for the first time since 1882. More than once in these days the king mentioned the word abdication. Very strangely, he added that in such a case the succession would go not to the crown prince but to his cousin the Duke of Aosta who had none of his own disinclination for the business of monarchy.[34]

Salandra at one point, whether sincerely or not, suggested the desperate course of arranging with Giolitti for a hostile vote in parliament to repudiate the Treaty of London, because that would relieve the crown of the responsibility for such an embarrassing decision; and the king accepted that this might possibly be one way out. But after he had unilaterally denounced one treaty with Austria, to denounce another so quickly with the Entente would, in his own words, make him look 'either perfidious or an imbecile'. He had allowed the politicians to manoeuvre him into a position from which it seemed that he could hardly emerge with credit. But of course, since 'the king can do no wrong', it would be their fault and not his own. As he ruefully commented, in fifteen years he had witnessed too much of the seamy side of Italian political life, and if forced into exile he might use his personal archives to write an account of what had happened for the benefit of posterity.[35]

At Salandra's request the king on 10 May met Giolitti, whom he had not seen for a year but who was known to command a majority in parliament. By that time the opposition leader had at last been told something of government policy – how much is not known – and was indignant to find that war was being imposed by a small minority on an unwilling country, whereas Austria had such need of Italian neutrality that in Giolitti's view a good negotiator could still win most of what Italy wanted. He was still ready to consider fighting as a last resort, but told the king of his complete lack of confidence in the country's being able to withstand a serious war, and now explained once again that he had been obliged to conceal the incompetence of the general staff by inventing imaginary victories in Libya during 1912. He agreed with Salandra in opposing abdication since that would damage the institution of monarchy. He could not become prime minister himself because his known support of neutrality deprived him of the necessary bargaining power with the Austrians, but he would support Salandra in arranging a parliamentary vote to release the king from his obligations to the Entente. Salandra and Sonnino, whether seriously or not, both expressed their readiness to resign if it would help such a solution.[36]

The sincerity of both Salandra and Giolitti was subsequently brought into question, and it is certain that the former, perhaps also the latter, was being disingenuous. Nevertheless, on 11 May, at least for a few hours, Salandra and Sonnino appear to have assumed that one way out of an impasse might be for parliament to reject the Treaty of London and accept a negotiated settlement with Austria.

Since the text of that treaty was secret and had not been ratified, another argument was advanced that it might morally bind the government but did not in practice bind the king or the state, in which case it could be discarded as easily as the Triple Alliance had just been denounced.[37]

Salandra realised that a decision either way would be necessary before parliament met on 20 May. On the 13th he therefore offered to resign, explaining that this would leave the king free to choose another government which could refuse to ratify the Treaty of London; and he must have been serious because he ordered the army to stop mobilising.[38] But Giolitti once again was adamant in refusing to resume office, since he now feared that the crown was pledged to fight. A refusal also came from two of Giolitti's friends who were in turn offered the succession but were afraid that the king was personally compromised and could hardly survive on his throne if a second treaty were broken so soon. Salandra's secret diplomacy left them with little choice, because he had not only 'uncovered' the king's personal responsibility, but Italy would be dangerously isolated if she changed tack and antagonised both sides in the war simultaneously.

Another reason for their refusal to become prime minister was fear of revolution, since widespread rioting broke out in two days during which Italy lacked a government. Both extremes denounced the king. The republicans, including Ricciotti Garibaldi, were actively preparing an insurrection. On 15 May a thousand students, apparently representing Left as well as Right, were led by some of their professors in trying to storm the parliament building, and Salandra did not object.[39] Many on the extreme Right were delighted by this attack on what they called the hated Italian Bastille; they, too, called for a civil war against the 'traitors' in parliament, and Pantaleoni demanded Giolitti's assassination. The nationalist party, believing that war would result in liquidating socialism as well as Giolitti, appealed for the king to join the war or abdicate. The distinguished philosopher Giovanni Gentile later recalled that he had not minded much whether war was alongside Austria or against her so long as it happened, because war promised glory and would 'cement the unity of the country in blood'.[40]

The violence of these days was deprecated by the editor of the *Corriere della Sera*, but he welcomed the motive behind it as 'profoundly noble and healthy', and later pointed to these riots as having been the main reason why the king finally declared war. Giolitti, wrote Albertini, was 'sabotaging the true interests of the country' by favouring neutrality, and the monarch's clear duty was to ignore parliament by entering the war without more ado.[41]

Another prominent editor, Mussolini, who in 1922 used this same doctrine to seize power for himself, wrote that these two days were the most terrible moment in the whole history of Italy. Mussolini still feared on 16 May that the government's resignation might put paid to his fervent hopes for war, and above all blamed the king, as indeed he now blamed the king for everything that was wrong in the country: 'The monarchy must be made to pay the price of failure: we must have war, or else a republic'. Looking back several years later, Mussolini confessed his mistake in not going one stage further and forcibly taking power during these critical days of 'radiant May'.[42]

Instead, Salandra was reappointed, and the king had little option because four other parliamentary leaders had been too frightened to take his place. Giolitti left Rome without even waiting for parliament to meet, and instructed his followers to save the honour of the country by putting up no opposition when the new government obtained a huge majority for joining the war. Ten days earlier most members of parliament had without doubt been behind Giolitti, but now only forty socialists and thirty others voted for his policy of remaining neutral, while the senate was unanimous for war. Some deputies and senators had changed their minds because they were simply afraid of being attacked by the mob. Others may have been moved by the familiar habit of voting for any successful government that had patronage to dispense. All of them must have feared that a contrary vote would seem a direct criticism of the monarchy. Salandra managed to prevent a full publication of Turati's speech in the chamber which lamented what was called the end of parliamentary government. Turati said that the decision for war was an unmitigated disaster and blamed Salandra for having sullied Italy's good name by putting her support up for auction between Germany and Germany's opponents.[43] But he was howled down, and the excited deputies after voting for war rose to their feet to join spectators in the galleries by singing the national anthem.

The king was delighted. He later recalled with complacency how, faced with many divergent opinions, he had taken personal responsibility for dragging an unwilling country into the war, and 'when a government is weak the crown must always assert itself'.[44] Victory in war would consolidate the dynasty, so he told the deputy Speaker of the chamber, whereas refusal to fight might have meant revolution and the collapse of the House of Savoy.[45]

German politicians, too, thought that the king was chiefly responsible for what had occurred.[46] The British ambassador, an interested party on the other side, wrote that 'the king managed the crisis admirably, and was of course criticised by those who did not know what he was doing'.[47] Vittorio Emanuele confessed to the ambassador that he had first calculated on only 94 deputies out of 508 being in favour of war and he knew that the great majority of Italians were for peace; he admitted that he 'had passed through one or two very bad days' and was fully aware that the 'ephemeral' pro-war vote of 20 May was due to politicians' being thoroughly scared; but dealing with 'a very mercurial and changeable' people he took credit for having played for high stakes and won.[48]

To King George of England he sent a special message admitting that it had been 'touch and go':

> He had been forced to play his last card, being determined that Italy should follow the policy which has now been adopted...Had his coup failed, he would certainly have to go at once; but in the face of very strong representations, he decided that he must make it known that he was determined to abdicate if the policy he knew to be the right one for Italy were not adopted. His success was immediate and complete.[49]

These remarks show his conviction that he had carried out a successful coup, and also that he had done so deliberately, against what he knew to be the wishes of parliament and people.

4
World War I, and the Rise of Fascism

1   Italy at war, 1915–17

Italy declared war on 23 May 1915 and Vittorio Emanuele moved to the frontier to assume titular command of his army. There he issued a proclamation announcing that the country would fight 'for the defence of civilisation and the liberation of oppressed peoples';[1] in other words, for something far removed from Salandra's sacred egoism or Sonnino's aim to occupy Albania and Dalmatia. But his true intention was concealed and different: to fight a separate war, not jointly with his new allies, not with their war aims or a common strategy, but a 'parallel war' against Austria alone and directed at securing Italian supremacy in the Adriatic.

In the Treaty of London the king had formally undertaken to fight against Germany as well as Austria, despite the fact that his negotiators had done their best to avoid any such commitment and had no intention of carrying it out.[2] Salandra knew that this major default would be resented by Britain and France, but was determined not to give way, not even when German troops were at once engaged against Italy and Italian ships were sunk by German submarines.[3] War was not declared against Germany for another fourteen months, not until after Salandra left office. Rodd warned from the beginning that the king had conscientious scruples of loyalty towards a fellow sovereign in Berlin with whom he had no quarrel.[4]

Since the monarch intended to stay near the frontier for what was hoped would be a short war, his uncle, the Duke of Genoa, was given authority to act in his stead in Rome. Some people thought that the head of state would have been more use back in the national capital where he could have helped the foreign minister and smoothed the always difficult relations between government and army; but he wanted to share the life of his soldiers, and appreciated the excuse to get away from civilian politicians with whom he was never on close terms.[5] A more valid criticism of his behaviour was that he neglected his military duties as commander-in-chief by not supervising the army's preparations. He was as surprised as anyone when mobilisation took weeks longer than expected, and equally surprised to find that his generals were expecting to fight a very different war from what the government had in mind, or at least were not at all sure what was expected of them.[6]

This damaging lack of co-ordination between ministers and generals was due to the fact that the former were reluctant to speak out over military matters, knowing that the army commanders were directly answerable to the palace and only secondarily to the minister of war. Here was a constitutional anomaly that meant that the king alone could co-ordinate policy, and this he failed to do. Salandra had reached his decision to fight only after being given to understand by the king that the generals were ready,[7] but apparently omitted prior discussion with the experts on strategy and military objectives. The prime minister either deluded himself or perhaps was only trying to delude others when he declared that nothing was lacking for success. He claimed, or rather guessed, that mobilisation had for some months been planned down to the last detail.[8] Probably he had no idea that Cadorna based his strategy on expectations that the Serbian army would draw off half the Austrian forces. Hence Sonnino was allowed to pursue quite contradictory political objectives which regarded the Serbs as more an enemy than a friend, with unfortunate results that might easily have been foreseen.

Vittorio Emanuele knew some of his own limitations and prided himself on never interfering with his chief of staff, so that in frequent talks with Cadorna he preferred silent acquiescence to discussion.[9] His own early manhood had been spent as a soldier and he always felt more at ease with soldiers than civilians. He had once made an academic study of Napoleon's campaigns and military history was always his favourite topic of conversation.[10] Military traditions were in his opinion the most vital of all factors in any country's history; as he said, echoing his grandfather, 'Italy was unified not by Dante but by bayonets'.[11] This helps to explain why, unlike the British and French, he discouraged civilian supervision over conduct of the war and protected the highly reputed but not very competent Cadorna from the slightest breath of criticism. Probably he shared Cadorna's ideas on strategy, which in fact were years out of date.[12]

So strong was the desire to fight a separate parallel war that there was no intention of forming a joint higher command with France and Britain – though Cadorna in July 1914 had agreed to merge his forces with those of Germany and Austria. Nor was anything done to consult allied military commanders in order to learn about the new methods of warfare that in the previous nine months had been experienced on the French and Serbian fronts. In May 1915, after months of preparation, Italy therefore lacked the new weapons, having only 300 effective machine guns and no hand grenades.[13] Though the king and Cadorna knew from the Libyan war about the importance of barbed wire, the lesson had been completely forgotten,[14] and the absence of wire-cutters brought Italy's first attack to an unexpected halt. Nor had any training been given in trench warfare. Cadorna excused himself by saying that the French refused to tell him about their experience in battle, though his own military attachés in France and Germany had warned him months earlier about revolutionary changes in arms and tactics; he himself had simply refused to admit that he had anything to learn about the conduct of war.[15]

Field artillery was another weakness. The king continued to tell people that Italian artillery was the best in the world and had no lack of shells, whereas in practice some 250 field guns were stretched out over 700 kilometres of frontier, and some of them were antiquated and unreliable.[16] The presumption must be that the king was being deceitful so as to keep up public confidence, because his chief aide-de-camp knew of this deficiency and was greatly alarmed by it.[17]

Such make-believe was all too easily protected from criticism in the absence of either parliamentary committees of control or effective royal supervision. Mystification and secrecy had regularly been employed to cover up inadequacies in previous wars, and no doubt deception was needed in order to persuade the various belligerent countries into paying a high price for an Italian alliance. Just as Giolitti's minister of war had knowingly deluded parliament into thinking that all was well with the army though he privately knew otherwise,[18] Giolitti himself likewise told parliament of his complete confidence in the generals, while warning Salandra that all of them in Libya had proved without exception to be thoroughly incompetent.[19] And the royal commander-in-chief did nothing to correct what was wrong.

Salandra and Cadorna were naturally anxious to conceal any deficiencies and doubtless thought that such facts did not matter since the war would be short. Subsequently they had to pretend that they had never expected anything but a long war,[20] but ample evidence testifies to their confidence that Italian intervention would decisively tip the scales and that the war was almost over. The king had been positive that Italy could otherwise never contemplate fighting.[21] The British were asked for a loan of only fifty million pounds, enough for what was known in advance to be a bare month of fighting. They were not initially asked for the coal and shipping that a longer war would require, and the reason was Cadorna's confidence that his greatly superior numbers would quickly penetrate into the Austrian heartland and move on Vienna.[22]

The king shared this confidence as he watched the first attack from his new home just outside Udine. According to a visitor invited to dinner on 4 June, he had never before looked so healthy and cheerful.[23] In recent weeks he had gone through a period of unpopularity when, more perhaps for reasons of illness than constitutional propriety, he had 'withdrawn too much from public life', but Rodd reported that by moving to the front line he 'has enormously strengthened his position, and is now the most popular man in Italy'.[24]

When successive Italian offensives ground to an immediate halt, he shared the surprise and despondency at headquarters. Evidently a failure of intelligence had also contributed to a mistake in choosing which sector to attack.[25] Two months into the war, and he was seriously worried if victory would be possible,[26] while Salandra was briefly tormented by the thought that the government was to blame for entering the fight too soon and might be forced to accept a premature peace.[27] Luckily the general public could always be protected from knowing too much. The number of casualties could be concealed and, to Cadorna's annoyance, non-existent victories were once again invented by the government to keep up public confidence.[28] Salandra in turn protested that Cadorna sent him exaggerated reports of successes and no other information except the daily war bulletins given to the press.[29]

Vittorio Emanuele was from the first moment aware of tension between the army command and Salandra, but instead of trying to reconcile the two parties, confessed to a British general that he was determined to support the military authorities 'with the whole weight of his authority should necessity arise'.[30] His confidence in them was not fully reciprocated. A staff officer was sent each evening to tell him the day's events, but Cadorna occasionally seems to have regarded the royal presence at the front as something of an embarrassment.[31] This chief of staff was a single-minded authoritarian who would take advice from no one, who despised parliament, and in the presence of a Frenchman tore up a message from the prime minister in order to show a foreigner what he thought of mere civilians. Neither would he listen to his own corps commanders, but used to talk of himself as a second Napoleon who had no need of a council of war or to hear the opinions of lesser men.[32]

By the end of 1915, after four successive battles had failed to push across the River Isonzo, ministers became nervous that the lack of success was undermining public confidence and leaving Italy with a weak hand to play when it came to what they still hoped would be an imminent peace conference. Since they were excluded from any say in the conduct of military operations, they asked the king to demand more action, but he put them off with a vague promise that success would not be delayed much longer.[33] His optimism was not widely shared. On the contrary, reports from the front indicated that the other generals were losing confidence in Cadorna, and also that the monarch was blamed for failing to take seriously his responsibilities as supreme commander.[34] Nor could he ever think of another candidate for the post of chief of staff, and this despite claiming to know the precise credentials of all the senior officers.

The relutance to devise a unified command structure in Rome was a serious disadvantage and compared unfavourably with the far from perfect practice of Germany or Britain. Such was the lack of mutual confidence that, since the army brooked no civilian interference at Udine, the government had its revenge by refusing to let Cadorna control other military operations in Libya and Albania. The chief of staff strongly opposed these parallel operations as a futile dispersion of limited resources, and a succession of defeats in Libya fully justified his realistic demand for a withdrawal. But the minister of colonies demanded more troops to support a losing campaign in Africa, while trying to conceal even from the rest of the cabinet what was happening there.[35]

Likewise in Albania, after insisting against military advice on occupying Valona, Sonnino sent a larger expedition to prevent Durazzo being occupied by the Austrians, or by Serbia, or by the Greeks. This was a purely political decision so as to be in occupation of as much territory as possible by the time peace was signed, and the troops soon had to be withdrawn in disarray. Vittorio Emanuele showed much greater realism by his doubts over the expedition to Durazzo and also by recognising the importance of co-operation with the Serbs,[36] whereas Sonnino's contrary determination to annex the Dalmatian coast continued to weaken the common front against Austria and certainly protracted the course of the war.[37]

The king's absence from Rome left him unable to influence such questionable decisions. The foreign minister was so determined to pursue a purely Italian interest in Albania that he opposed an alternative request by France and Britain, backed by Cadorna, to support a joint allied attack at Salonica.[38] Sonnino justified his refusal by citing 'the political situation in Italy', because he was afraid that a military setback might be exploited by Giolitti to overturn the government.[39] He did not want foreigners to know his real reason, which was that Albania remained 'the chief fulcrum' of his foreign policy, and indeed was more important to him than all the major theatres of war. A hundred thousand soldiers therefore remained tied up unprofitably in this area against strong military advice, and the king did nothing to stop it.[40]

From October 1915 onwards, ministers talked of asking the monarch for the dismissal of Cadorna, but without presuming to suggest an alternative name, and only at the end of January 1916 did Salandra call up sufficient courage to request the summoning of a council of war to devise a better and more co-ordinated fighting strategy.[41] Cadorna refused out of hand and the king automatically supported him against the prime minister.[42] When Durazzo had to be evacuated, Cadorna felt justified in insisting on one of his own nominees being appointed as minister of war. This replacement was then endorsed by the king against Salandra's wishes and without first consulting the cabinet. Though he was unable to beat the Austrians, Cadorna had carried out what one general called a successful *coup d'état* against the government without any objection from the palace.[43]

The Italian parliament, unlike the legislatures in France and Britain, was kept virtually in abeyance, especially since many deputies were perplexed by the unexpected stalemate on the Isonzo and might have used it as an excuse to bring back Giolitti.[44] Salandra was afraid of any public criticism, and even other ministers were given little chance to air their opinions. The king in one of his rare comments on constitutional propriety suggested that secrecy was being taken too far. In particular, he agreed with those who blamed his government for holding out against the appointment of permanent parliamentary committees that might assist official business.[45] No doubt Salandra had been hoping, just as during the Libyan war, that a quick victory would obviate any need for resort to parliamentary sanction. Only when hostilities dragged on was parliament allowed to meet in March 1916 to endorse a long series of earlier royal decrees, though discussion was still kept to a minimum.

In a short debate the familiar criticisms were made by socialist deputies that parliament had been given no information about what was happening, less than was given even in Germany. The text of the Treaty of London was not known even to the cabinet. Only from documents now published in Vienna was public opinion at last given positive confirmation that Italy had for thirty years been secretly committed in the Triple Alliance to a defence of the monarchic principle in Europe. One deputy pointed out that republican regimes in France and the United States permitted parliaments not merely much fuller information but a degree of initiative in foreign policy, whereas monarchist Italy was in this respect closer to the autocratic government of Tsarist Russia than to the western democracies. Another surprise was that the government's principal war aim appeared to be annexation of the Slav population in Dalmatia; in other words, Italian citizens had been called on to die for a secret, dangerous, immoral, and perhaps unrealisable cause. Until 1917 the censor tried to delete any public references to Dalmatia.[46]

Fortunately for the government, parliament was not sitting when in the middle of May the Austrians made a surprise attack on a different front in the Trentino, catching Cadorna unprepared. Once again he refused an urgent ministerial request to hold a council of war, but had to admit that he might be forced to withdraw from the Italian frontier to the River Piave. At this terrible news, Sonnino talked of treachery and called for the general's removal; and ministers agreed that either they or Cadorna ought to resign. When Salandra arrived at Udine to convey their opinion, the king at first gave the impression that he partly agreed, but he then let Cadorna know that no interference by politicians would be tolerated.[47]

A few days later the government carried out its threat and resigned. Salandra had proved completely ineffective as a war leader. He had chosen the wrong moment to fight by procrastinating until the Russians and Serbs were in retreat. His designs on Dalmatia had ruined his best chance of a quick victory. He had offended his new allies by ignoring a treaty obligation and fighting his own 'parallel war' against Austria alone. Moreover, he had entirely failed to galvanise the country or impose his own authority over the generals. Far from capturing Trieste at once, as had been expected, Libya was almost lost, Durazzo evacuated, and the war seemed about to end with the Austrian army a long way inside the Italian frontier.

Once again the king was reluctantly compelled by Salandra's departure into taking a political initiative and, without consulting Giolitti or other parliamentary leaders, appointed as premier the 77-year-old Paolo Boselli. This man was another signatory of Pelloux's *decretone*, a believer in monarchist paternalism, who had been a court favourite for thirty years but had nothing else to recommend him. Boselli was notorious for his empty patriotic rhetoric and was generally derided on Left and Right as a weak person of questionable views and no political ability. The king persuaded him to form a broad administration, including for the first time two reformist socialists, one of them Bonomi, the other Bissolati whose job would be to act as intermediary between government and the army command. Cadorna told people that the new government would not be permitted to interfere with the conduct of military operations, but said that he had no confidence in Boselli and even issued a statement banning Bissolati from visiting the war zone, until the king requested him to be more accommodating.[48]

Sonnino, after initial doubts, agreed to remain as foreign minister, and was soon at odds with Bissolati as well as Cadorna. He complained that the king remained uselessly at the front, neither assisting ministers to govern nor helping to compose the differences between politicians and army as all of them would now have liked; indeed, showing annoyance when asked to adjudicate between them.[49] Every day the head of state used to visit different fighting units where he indulged his passion for photography. Often, if not always,[50] his presence in the front line helped to raise morale, though he himself had no patience with the plethora of invented propaganda stories about his indomitable courage under fire.[51] Visitors to his personal headquarters received the impression that he neither wanted to exercise leadership nor had much grasp of military strategy.[52] In both Udine and Rome, as he must have known, there were renewed complaints that he might be better employed back in the capital,[53] but he categorically refused to return to the boring business and ceremonial of life at the Quirinal – which had now been converted into a hospital. Duty compelled him to be present where the laurels of war would be won.

Another welcome result was freedom from the importunity of foreign ambassadors in Rome. Barrère and Rodd continued to ask why Italy remained at peace with Germany; also, why hundreds of thousands of Italians were working in the German munitions industry, and why essential war material continued to be exported to what Britain and France saw as their main enemy.[54] These diplomatic representatives were perplexed to find little real enthusiasm in Rome for the war, and heard from Italian industrialists and generals that pro-German sentiment in government circles was one reason why military operations were being conducted half-heartedly.[55]

Vittorio Emanuele was sensitive on this point of helping Germany, especially as Italians were therefore left out of military conferences in Paris and London, and undeniably it was anomalous that there was no machinery for allied military and strategic co-operation such as Italians had previously accepted with Austria. He sent messages to Buckingham Palace in March 1916 to say that he personally was convinced that not Austria but Germany should be their main enemy and the Isonzo only a secondary front.[56] Cadorna and Sonnino would have been horrified to know this. War was in fact declared against Germany a few weeks later, and the king spoke of the need for a punitive peace as the only means by which Austria and Germany could be prevented from launching other wars in future.[57] 'Italy had really been at war with Germany all the time', he explained, but 'it had been for internal reasons inevitable to postpone the actual, formal declaration until an opportune moment'.[58]

After admitting the failure of his 'parallel war' it was at last possible to think of formulating a common allied strategy, and the British prime minister came to Rome in January 1917 with a proposal for their joint forces to concentrate in Italy and push the Austrians out of Trieste. The king, strongly backed by Bissolati, was enthusiastic, but Sonnino had his eye on the peace conference and still hoped to keep the allies at arm's length while the Italians won a separate war by their own effort. After a sharp altercation in cabinet, Bissolati and

Sonnino both offered to resign, but it was Sonnino who won the argument. Cadorna, too, although this was his best chance of a victorious battle, treated the proposal of allied concentration in Italy without much enthusiasm, possibly because it threatened his personal autonomy. A disillusioned Lloyd George went home empty handed; in London the British minister had been able to overrule the doubts of his own generals and assert a degree of civilian control over major strategy, but in Italy neither government nor monarch could act similarly.[59]

Several months later the news of revolution in Russia brought the king briefly to Rome. Cardinal Gasparri 'did not disguise his joy at the Russian revolution', because the Vatican not only wanted the war to end, but hoped that a Russian withdrawal would assist the triumph of Latin over Greek Christianity in eastern Europe.[60] Vittorio Emanuele said he was not surprised at the news from Russia and was already half resigned to the general collapse of monarchy in Europe. More serious was that the Austrians could now bring troops back from the Russian front to invade Italy. He complained that he was having difficulties with his new ministers, but was still hoping that the allies would renew their offer to send troops to the Isonzo, in which case he thought that Austria 'would topple down like a house of cards'.[61] But Sonnino was pessimistic. If the war lasted much longer, an exhausted Italy might in his view be obliged to stop fighting. This desperate possibility was communicated to the British by the Italian ambassador in London who added an unauthorised threat of his own that Italy might even change sides and join the enemy.[62]

Such irresponsible remarks only confirmed the anxious fear in London and Paris that most Italians were against continuing the war, and Cadorna contributed to the alarm by telling the British that his army was battle-weary and he was afraid of a domestic revolution like that in Russia.[63] In April an emissary from the Austrian emperor arrived in Paris with a not very probable story that Cadorna and Vittorio Emanuele were putting out unofficial peace feelers through Switzerland. When this messenger explained that the Austrians would give Italy the Trentino but nothing more, Lloyd George replied that after Cadorna's pessimistic remarks he would be glad to have both Austria and Italy out of the war, but could not ask the Italians to agree to a settlement unless Trieste was also surrendered to them.

When Sonnino was told about this exchange of views he insisted on claiming Dalmatia as well, which brought these very tentative talks to a stop. Although he must have suspected that most Italians had never so much as heard of Dalmatia, Sonnino pretended that the

people of Italy wanted so badly to annex this area that they would
rise in revolution to secure it and, if necessary, force the king's abdication. This assertion reflects his fear that the annexation of Trent
and Trieste might possibly have been won by negotiation in 1915, so
sparing the country two years of war. Such a hypothesis would
justify Giolitti's pacifism in May 1915, which in turn might force
the government's resignation. Other ministers were told nothing
about the Austrian peace proposal, though some of them subsequently criticised Sonnino's 'criminal refusal' to discuss this chance
of a peaceful settlement.[64]

The cabinet was astonished early in June to learn from the newspapers that their colleague at the foreign office had officially declared
Albania to be an Italian protectorate. This was another violation of
the Treaty of London, apparently decided without so much as
informing either king or prime minister.[65] Three ministers threatened
to resign in protest, until Vittorio Emanuele hurried back again to
Rome and begged them to avert a political crisis. Inevitably there
was great resentment in Serbia at Italy's acquisition of a protectorate
in the Balkans, and a week later a retaliatory proclamation was issued
by Serbs, Croats, and Slovenes pledging themselves to form a united
kingdom of Jugoslavia. This unexpected consequence of Sonnino's
foreign policy threatened to deprive Italy of Dalmatia and in his
opinion would make further fighting hardly worthwhile.[66] In
particular, the prospect embarrassed the king whose father-in-law
Nicholas, first and last king of Montenegro, was thereby threatened
with the loss of his throne. Nicholas was thought by some of his
subjects to be not only corrupt but pro-German, and the growth of
a revolutionary movement in Montenegro was one more problem
exacerbated by Sonnino's precipitate and unilateral action.[67]

2   *Defeat and triumph, 1917–18*

Vittorio Emanuele was unhappy that the foreign minister's clumsy
diplomatic initiatives generated distrust among Italy's allies and by
1917 had good reason to fear that the aim of annexing Dalmatia
might have been a futile and costly mistake. His own preference was
to send an Italian military expedition to the Middle East, either to
Syria or to help capture Jerusalem from the Turks.[1] But instinctively
he sought to avoid intervening in policy since he was so far away
from Rome. Talking to foreign visitors he defended his abstention
by repeating that a constitutional sovereign had very limited powers,

certainly less than an American president who derived an enviable strength from the fact of being popularly elected.[2]

Nor did he interfere in military matters where he could have spoken with more knowledge and authority. On this constitutional point there was still a surprising uncertainty. The minister of the interior, Vittorio Emanuele Orlando, argued that it was absurd for the army to be virtually free from any control by the civilians in government, whereas Sonnino chose to support Cadorna in thinking that the crown alone could overrule the chief of staff, to whom the king had only temporarily delegated his powers as commander-in-chief.[3] Profiting from this difference of opinion, the army continued to remain a law to itself and perilously free from outside supervision by either the sovereign or his ministers.

Cadorna's weaknesses as a leader and strategist were exposed in detail by a government commission when the war was over. The king was aware earlier of many criticisms, for instance of Cadorna's barbarous and sometimes random execution of soldiers – hoping that this would make their companions fight harder.[4] The king also knew of the summary dismissal of two hundred generals and thought perhaps that this number was too small.[5] Colonel Douhet, the most original strategic thinker in Italy, was sent to prison by Cadorna for daring to criticise military decisions, and the same fate befell Roberto Bencivenga who was Cadorna's assistant chief of staff. The king knew furthermore that army bulletins put out false news in order to cover mistakes and create an unjustified sense of confidence.[6] But his own, rarely voiced, criticisms were levelled not at Cadorna's generalship and strategy, but rather at the latter's lack of respect and deference to the monarchy.[7]

Another fact he knew about but preferred not to discuss was growing unrest in the country at large. Italy had begun hostilities in what some people called 'an atmosphere of civil war', and already before the serious anti-war riots of August 1917 there were fears inside the government and at court that Italians might not stand another winter of fighting.[8] There was resentment against the British, who at one point were accused of trying to bring the war to a premature conclusion, and were later thought to be obstructing a return to peace for selfish reasons of their own. The king received many anonymous letters protesting against a continuance of war,[9] and a general popular disaffection was reported in intercepted correspondence between the Vatican and its nuncios.[10] There was also an alarming increase in the number of soldiers deserting, and marauding bands of deserters were becoming a serious problem even in the hill country round Rome.[11]

Already before August there were clear signs that Boselli lacked support as prime minister, and politicians were urgently seeking a replacement.[12] By the beginning of October the cabinet was apparently doomed, yet since the king was absent at Udine, a paralysed and totally ineffective administration was allowed to continue in office at a critical moment when firm government was urgently needed.[13] Worse still was that the army was momentarily without its commander, because on 4 October, just before Italy's biggest defeat of the war, Cadorna left the front for two weeks' holiday: he was sure that the season was too late for an Austrian attack, and felt safe because he had superior numbers in what he called an impregnable position, which would leave him free to pass the winter writing up the history of his own contribution to the war.[14] The king was reading intelligence reports more attentively and warned that an Austrian attack might be imminent, but the implied criticism was not taken seriously at headquarters.[15]

Even after an enemy attack began in the Caporetto sector on 24 October, Cadorna spoke of his 'perfect serenity and complete confidence'.[16] Within hours, however, he discovered that he had lost control over his army and wrote in desperation to his wife that the monarchy might not survive a defeat, which was now increasingly likely.[17] Vittorio Emanuele soon found himself personally caught up in a chaotic mass retreat. 'What caused it all?' was the stark and bewildered question that, writing in English, he confided to his diary.[18] Foreign war correspondents reported that many Italians blamed him for such an incomprehensible catastrophe, and he confessed to Bissolati that he again thought of possible abdication so as to avoid the humiliation of surrender.[19]

Most humiliating of all was Cadorna's official communiqué which, without the least hint of self-criticism, identified a scapegoat by attributing defeat to the collective cowardice of soldiers who had made no attempt to fight. Vittorio Emanuele, in protest at what he called an entirely false accusation, backed the government in preventing publication of this bulletin in Italy.[20] But Cadorna had already sent it for publication to the foreign press so as to protect his own reputation, and unrepentently continued to insist that the communiqué was accurate and beneficial in its results.[21] Fortunately the retreat, what he grandiloquently called 'perhaps the greatest catastrophe in history', was more or less brought under control on the River Piave, but for the next few days the army could not be fully sure that this line would hold or whether Italy might have to sue for peace.[22]

At the end of October a new government was formed under Orlando to retrieve the situation. Sonnino remained at the foreign office and a minister of war was brought in from outside parliament. By that time Marshal Foch and the British chief of general staff arrived at the Italian front and confirmed the king's opinion that the line of the Piave would hold. They also told him that in their view the defeat was chiefly due to the shortcomings of Cadorna and his senior staff officers, all of whom should be replaced as a matter of urgency.[23]

On 5 November the chief political and military leaders of France and Britain met those of Italy at Rapallo, where it was at long last agreed to set up a supreme war council to co-ordinate inter-allied strategy. One person who had no time to come to Rapallo was Cadorna; and his second in command, General Porro, was unable to explain to the meeting what had happened or what could be done about it. Porro asked for the help of at least fifteen French and British divisions, far more than the railway system could carry. The figure was by consent reduced to eight, and fortunately the complex plans needed for such an expedition had already been prepared in London during the previous month in case they might be needed.[24]

Confidence was further sapped when, although there were known to be six or seven German divisions supporting the Austrian attack, the king and Porro spoke of three times as many,[25] and the estimated figure was later raised to twenty-nine and then thirty-five notional German divisions in at attempt to explain the defeat.[26] Foch and Lloyd George, deeply disturbed at Porro's incomprehension and lack of factual information, insisted again that he and Cadorna be replaced since this was further evidence that not the fighting soldiers but the general staff were mainly responsible; and when Orlando told them that only the royal commander-in-chief could take such a decision, the allied leaders requested a personal meeting with the sovereign.

This took place on 8 November at Peschiera. Evidently the meeting was thought unimportant , because no minutes were drafted by any Italian present, and the only written account was subsequently dictated by the South African, General Smuts. Vittorio Emanuele, deeply embarrassed and unhappy,[27] did not look a commanding figure, but put on an impressive demonstration of courage, confidence, and good humour as he had to admit that his country and throne had been in jeopardy. Speaking in excellent English (which Orlando did not understand), he said he was sorry that his ministers had turned down the offer of allied help the previous January, and had he been in Rome he would certainly have accepted. He would now gratefully accept any help that could be offered. He made no reference to the replacement of Cadorna and Porro until Lloyd George brought up the matter. He then admitted that their generalship had been at fault, even though he thought that the criticisms had been exaggerated.[28]

The meeting at Peschiera was in later years extolled by all loyalist

historians as the greatest personal triumph of his reign, since 'at
a critical moment he singlehandedly saved the country from destruction'.[29] But he himself modestly confessed that his role had
been exaggerated for reasons of propaganda and the meeting had
no purpose except to sanction what had been already decided at
Rapallo.[30] Cadorna, when confronted with the demand for resignation, at first tried to insist that public opinion would never allow
him to be dismissed in the same way that he had himself treated a
thousand other senior officers. The great disciplinarian had no sense
of discipline when applied to himself and rather blamed 'the notorious ingratitude of the House of Savoy' for his retirement.[31] He had
wanted to keep for himself the credit for success while leaving others
to take any discredit for defeat. He was not in fact dismissed but,
together with Porro, given another senior post.

In the weeks after Caporetto the monarch appeared outwardly
confident but tired and more than usually indecisive. 'Though not a
great personality', wrote George Trevelyan who was in charge of the
British ambulance service, he was widely admired for being brave,
democratic, and patriotic.[32] The French politician, Abel Ferry, found
him abstracted, inattentive, too much a mere spectator of events, and
his conversation inconsequential, never reaching to the heart of any
matter.[33] One of the new ministers, Francesco Nitti, was surprised
that such an obviously intelligent person exerted himself so little
and allowed so much to go wrong without trying to correct it. The
king now admitted failing to establish a close relationship with
Cadorna, Salandra, or Sonnino; nor had he been able to understand Boselli, whom he now criticised for being 'a very old man
who seemed quite ignorant of many things that it was his duty to
know'.[34] Others must have wondered if it was not rather the king's
responsibility if the wrong man was chosen.

Subsequently he claimed that he personally discovered the little-
known General Diaz who now took Cadorna's place as chief of
staff,[35] though a number of other people claimed credit for this for
themselves. The cabinet would have preferred the Duke of Aosta,
who was thought to have emerged better than other generals from
Caporetto, but the king vetoed the suggestion. Possibly his motive
was jealousy of a more outgoing and colourful personality; possibly
he feared another military defeat and abdication, in which case his
cousin's reputation ought to be preserved to be available for the
succession or for him to be regent to the young Prince Umberto.[36]

To replace Porro as Diaz's deputy the king chose General Pietro
Badoglio, presumably without knowing that Badoglio's careless-
ness or disobedience was thought by many people to be largely
responsible for the recent defeat. The later commission of enquiry

into the reverse at Caporetto devoted thirteen highly critical pages to Badoglio's conduct on 24 October, and to justify his appointment these pages had to be tactfully excised before the commission's report was published. General Caviglia's account of the battle was also, at the wish of both the king and Mussolini, partially censored.[37]

By mid-November there were hopeful signs of recovery. At last a broader government included some of Giolitti's friends, and this neutralised some potential opposition. At last a quarter of a million French and British troops arrived and by December were in place behind the Italian front line. At last there also took place regular meetings between army, ministers and the king, no longer all working at cross purposes. On the other hand, Sonnino was greatly depressed as growing dependence on allied help suggested that his 'parallel war' for supremacy in the Adriatic had merged into a larger war where Italian interests would receive less consideration. The senior permanent official in the foreign office advised him to establish contact with Vienna so as to be ready for a possible and radical change of policy.[38] The king, too, in mid-November, alarmed the British by again thinking that the Piave line might be broken, in which case there could be little hope of ultimate victory.[39]

Diaz succeeded in holding the line without need of active assistance from allied troops. Marshal Foch and the British commanders told the king of their admiration at the conduct of his soldiers at this critical moment,[40] though they were still not greatly impressed by some elements in the new higher command.[41] King George sent a tactful message from London in appreciation of 'the wisest of monarchs', and Vittorio Emanuele replied in suitable terms, though he expressed his fear that the British might be secretly negotiating for peace with Austria.[42] Presumably he knew that his own ministers were about to put out peace feelers of their own through the Vatican – in which, incidentally, they renounced a good deal of the hoped-for acquisitions that Sonnino in 1915 had claimed as an absolute minimum.[43]

Orlando and Diaz had to face the unpalatable fact that the shock of Caporetto, while it aroused noble feelings of patriotism among many Italians, convinced others that victory might be impossible or at least would be incommensurate with the sacrifices demanded.[44] Further instances were recorded of widespread desertion and of pacifist demonstrations preventing the movement of troops. The British military attaché was dismayed to find that the war had never been widely popular and was now 'absolutely unpopular',[45] while Rodd described the political atmosphere in Rome as continuing to be 'a witches cauldron of intrigue and conspiracy...distasteful and sordid'.[46]

Nor was allied military co-operation universally appreciated. When a joint allied command was set up in Paris under Foch, Orlando accepted in principle but not in practice, arguing that, while the British could afford to take orders from a French general, the Italian supreme commander was a monarch and could not be seen to take orders from anyone. Orlando in particular feared that Foch would order an attack on the Italian front which the government in Rome preferred not to risk.[47] Before the war the king had agreed to let an Austrian admiral command the joint Italo-Austrian fleets, but in 1918 the French and British were treated with far greater suspicion, and Sonnino especially objected to having his freedom of action restricted by the creation of a united naval command in the Mediterranean.[48]

One further embarrassment was that the Russian revolutionaries published the secret Treaty of London and everyone therefore knew that Sonnino in 1915 had entered the war for merely territorial gains with what Salvemini called 'the knife of Shylock rather than the liberating banner of Mazzini'. His chief war aim had been the annexation of Dalmatia. Sonnino was naturally upset by such a public revelation. The surprising excuse was advanced that this particular objective had been inserted into the treaty with every intention of surrendering Dalmatia when the time came to use it as a bargaining counter to trade-off against something else;[49] but now that the facts were public knowledge the nationalists seized on this acquisition as a minimum from which the government could not back down without renouncing the fruits of victory. The king, more realistic than Sonnino, was beginning to think that they would gain more by positively supporting Jugoslav independence, and claimed that he repeatedly urged this more sensible policy on his ministers.[50]

One result of Caporetto was that even Sonnino had to accept in theory the desirability of compromise with the Serbs, especially as it might encourage the defection of southern Slavs from the Austrian army. It would also please his allies, notably President Wilson of the United States who championed the principle of national self-determination. But although Sonnino in youth had backed self-determination in the Balkans, he categorically refused to give away his bargaining counter until 'the last minute',[51] nor would he consider any compromise that prevented Italian domination of the Adriatic. Otherwise, the war would have been fought in vain and Giolitti would gain enormously from saying that as much could have been won in 1915 without fighting. The need to keep Giolitti's liberals out of power was unfortunately a primary requisite.

In the summer of 1918 began the final push on the various allied fronts that eventually would bring this terrible war to an end. Urgent requests from Marshal Foch arrived in June and July for Diaz to launch a simultaneous attack, and Sonnino was ready to accept; but Diaz and Badoglio told the allied commanders that they preferred to remain on the defensive rather than risk what they called 'another Caporetto'.[52] A fine defensive battle was fought and won on the Piave in June, but when the king was once more asked to adjudicate about an offensive he backed Diaz so as to avoid unnecessary casualties until the war was quite clearly about to end.[53] The same view was taken by Nitti, and more tentatively by other ministers who suspected Foch of acting in mainly French interests, whereas it was vital for Italy to keep her own distinct war aims in mind and conserve as much as possible of her depleted resources for the future.[54]

This was an understandable decision, even if Foch strongly disagreed, but further procrastination became impossible when the German army in France began to collapse. At the beginning of October the war seemed on the point of ending when both Austria and Germany requested an armistice. Sonnino, greatly alarmed, besought his allies not to grant any armistice until Italy had a chance to organise a last-minute attack; which meant not until 24 October. Nitti, even then, feared that any action might be premature, but Orlando urged that even another defeat would be preferable to inaction. Diaz advanced, quickly reaching the old frontier, and at the beginning of November the battle of Vittorio Veneto brought Italy's war to a triumphant conclusion.

Vittorio Veneto was hailed by patriotic historians as being the greatest triumph in the whole of Italian history. Less plausibly it was magnified into the single decisive victory by any of the allies and was even described as the battle that forced Germany as well as Austria to surrender. By unnecessary exaggeration these writers generated extravagant hopes from the peace settlement which, when expectations were not fulfilled, turned a signal and well-deserved military victory into something that looked like political defeat.[55]

3 Post-war difficulties

Vittorio Emanuele was almost sorry that the armistice happened so soon. He would have liked time to invade Germany so as to win greater prestige and a stronger position at the peace table: the Germans, he thought, would be taught a salutary lesson if their country was occupied by the former ally that they affected to despise.[1] Germany was defenceless and its monarchy destroyed. Likewise the other great monarchies of Austria, Russia, and Turkey had collapsed. But by prudence, political tact, and some luck the Italian king had chosen the winning side and preserved his throne, one of the few monarchs to survive in a largely republican world. The wheel of fortune, to use his own phrase, was at last turning in Italy's favour and a great future was in prospect.[2]

Much would depend on President Wilson of the United States whose idealistic programme of national self-determination had been accepted by Austria and Germany as a basis for their surrender. In January 1919 Wilson received a tumultous reception in Rome, greeted as heralding a new age of international co-operation where secret diplomacy and imperialism would have no place. Entertained at the Quirinal palace, Wilson admired 'the plain, matter-of-fact manner of the king' who struck him as 'a simple, sincere and straight-forward little fellow'; though the latter was less impressed and found it hard to excuse the president's astonishing ignorance of Italian history.[3]

The American proposals for self-determination and 'peace without victory' had at first 'disgusted' Sonnino who had very different ideas, and who also knew from his reading of intercepted American correspondence that the State Department had debated asking for his own resignation.[4] Apprehensive that the Italian foreign office might make difficulties, Wilson asked and was given permission to explain his ideas at a mass meeting in the Piazza Venezia, but officials apparently arranged for the official motorcade to be diverted so that a disappointed American ambassador and other assembled dignitaries awaited his speech in vain.[5]

The existence of this latent controversy became public when the peace conference opened in Paris on 18 January, a conference that, largely because there was no prior resolution of this disagreement, lasted five times as long as Sonnino had expected.[6] The prime minister, Orlando, briefly considered gaining credit with Wilson by renouncing his two bargaining counters, Dalmatia and the Dodecanese islands. His foreign minister, however, successfully argued against this in the expectation that clever diplomacy might win most of what had been promised in the Treaty of London – or preferably even more than was promised.[7] While he would not risk openly repudiating Wilson's 'peace without victory', Sonnino intended to disregard it in practice. But unfortunately he and Orlando went to Paris without reconciling their divergent views; or rather they artfully agreed to retain two different policies, one for compromise, one for intransigence, which in order to confound the opposition they could produce alternately as occasion demanded. Almost as unfortunate, Sonnino chose to arrive in Paris with far less expert information than the other delegations, so that he was at a grave disadvantage in negotiation and the Italian case sometimes went by default.[8]

One quick and fortunate success for Sonnino was Wilson's decision to go against his own stated principles by letting Italy have not only Trieste but a northern frontier on the Alps, so annexing a large German-speaking population in the Trentino and Alto Adige. Wilson did this without consulting his own experts, who later convinced him that it was a major mistake; and it is interesting that Orlando had his own doubts about acquiring so much territory. Similar reservations were also expressed by Salandra, Giolitti, Nitti, and Bissolati who all feared the danger of German irredentism inside Italy.[9]

Even greater reservations were registered against Sonnino's determination to lay claim to as much as possible of Dalmatia. Bissolati resigned from the cabinet on this issue in December 1918, followed by Nitti the following month, and both Orlando and Diaz preferred to surrender any claim to Dalmatia in return for being permitted to annex Fiume. The frontier port of Fiume had a largely Italian-speaking population, and although Sonnino had omitted in 1915 to include it among Italy's war aims, undoubtedly it would be more economically profitable as well as more easily defensible than non-Italian-speaking Dalmatia futher south. Sonnino, however, refused to renounce prematurely what Nitti, as well as Salvemini, now called Shylock's pound of flesh.

The king must have considered the possibility of insisting on an agreed and practicable policy among the Italian delegates in Paris, but decided not to. Presumably he feared that a resolution of this point might mean the resignation of either Orlando or Sonnino and leave him with a political responsibility that he preferred to avoid. He was known to have doubts about the merits of annexing Dalmatia, the defence of which, according to both Cadorna and Diaz, would place an impossible burden on the army.[10] If there was a choice, he would have preferred Fiume as being more recognisably Italian, and also feared that this port might offer dangerous commercial competition to Italian Trieste if left in Jugoslav hands. In practice, he advised Orlando simply to demand as many as possible of the off-shore islands along the eastern shore of the Adriatic. But the prime minister's repeated appeal for the sovereign to intervene and mitigate Sonnino's intransigence over mainland Dalmatia met with no reply, except the unhelpful warning that the Italian people would expect the maximum satisfaction of their 'just aspirations'.[11]

To secure a compromise, the other national delegations at Paris were prepared to make what they called 'substantial concessions', for instance concessions in Africa.[12] But Sonnino had little interest in Africa. His attention was fixed on the contested region of the Adriatic, and although he continued to maintain that he was ready in general principle to offer 'minor concessions' in this area, he waited too long before showing his hand in detail. Wilson could not understand why Sonnino categorically refused to discuss this issue with what some Italian delegates persisted in calling the 'barbarian Slavs'. Nor was it clear to the American president why Sonnino, while showing almost no interest in the host of other questions in debate at Paris, concentrated on a settlement in the Balkans that would surely lead one day to war with Jugoslavia.

A quite different war, this time with Turkey and perhaps Greece, seemed about to break out when Italian troops were quite unexpectedly, and in defiance of an urgent request from London,[13] sent to set up an Italian colony in Asia Minor. An embarrassed Orlando, who was sure that most Italians had little interest in acquiring colonies, had to conceal that he had been given no advance warning of his colleague's provocative act.[14] Presumably the king had been first consulted, and he was known to like the idea of securing a foothold in Asiatic Turkey.[15]

Sonnino's notion of diplomacy was a simple mixture of obduracy and threats rather than a search for co-operation and compromise. He even subsidised a press campaign against his allies to demonstrate that Italian public opinion would accept nothing less than both Dalmatia and Fiume; and he was here being disingenuous because he had a manifest contempt for public opinion. He must also have known that a result of such propaganda would be to make Italians feel humiliated by any compromise solution, and no doubt he discounted this grave danger in the hope that an intransigent attitude would strengthen his hand in negotiation.[16] Samuel Hoare, head of British information services in Italy, reported that Italians seemed to hate the Slavs 'far worse than they ever hated the Germans'; moreover, they assumed that they had 'won the war not because of but almost in spite of allied help' and so could dictate their terms.[17]

Orlando was ready to accept much less, but gave way when Sonnino argued that Wilson was bound to yield if the Italian delegation threatened to leave Paris without signing the final treaty. The king was warned that this threat was being made and apparently did not dissent. Another even emptier threat was made that Italians would rise in revolt if their maximum claims were disregarded; to which Lloyd George replied that either Fiume or Dalmatia might be acceptable but hardly both, and the danger of an Italian revolution lay rather in the United States' losing patience and withdrawing the economic support upon which Italy depended. Orlando's bold rejoinder was that Italians would accept starvation but never dishonour; if necessary he was ready to back defiance by armed force – whatever that meant.[18]

On 24 April, just at the moment when Lloyd George thought that an agreed compromise was in sight, Orlando carried out part of his threat and returned home to secure a vote in parliament backing Italy's maximum demands. Clemenceau and Lloyd George begged him not to leave Paris, especially as popular demonstrations were being organised in Rome that would make it even harder for him to settle for anything less. But he went nevertheless. Back in Italy he waited for ten days in the miscalculated expectation that the allies would be frightened into giving way and would beg him to return. But on 4 May the king was alarmed to hear that the other delegations were about to sign the peace treaty in Italy's absence. Orlando hurried back but only after missing ten days of vital discussions during which his case had gone by default. He had been made to look foolish and antagonised potential friends at the conference. He had also aroused excessive expectations in Italy which were now bound to produce a dangerous sense of disillusionment.

Vittorio Emanuele fully shared his ministers' frustration. He sometimes sent them advice, but not insistently. In retrospect he thought that San Giuliano would have done far better than Sonnino.[19] He had convinced himself that his country had put more effort into the war than either France or Britain, and now tried to persuade Rodd's successor, George Buchanan, 'that Italy had come very badly out of the war' – since Fiume was an Italian town and Dalmatia had been promised to her in 1915. Nevertheless, speaking in private to Salandra, he agreed that it might have been a mistake to mention Fiume, especially as he had to accept that this port could flourish only as an outlet for its Jugoslav hinterland.[20] He grumbled that too much time had been wasted in Paris discussing a League of Nations which in his opinion was hardly an urgent or important matter.[21] He resented the general impression 'that now the allies had no longer any use for Italy they could afford to neglect or postpone the consideration of her interest'. He agreed that Sonnino had made the mistake of being too exigent, but the allies had misbehaved by giving Italy a series of 'ultimatums'. It was wrong 'that Italy was always put on one side, that Italian interests were always the last to be considered, that they were practically elbowed out of everything'.[22]

Evidently he was trying to foster the nationalist legend of a 'mutilated peace', that is to say a disadvantageous compromise settlement forced by selfish allies on an Italy that had saved them from defeat and then been chiefly responsible for their military success. In its extreme form this legend was developed into the belief that Italy was betrayed by her allies and even received no territory at all from the peace settlement.[23] But other Italians thought that Italy emerged quite as successfully as any belligerent country, with a frontier more secure than that of any other European state, with enormous gains of national territory in Trent, Alto Adige, Istria, and Trieste, and with her hereditary enemy in Vienna reduced to permanent impotence. If Italy felt diplomatically isolated in 1919, if she failed to obtain Fiume or Dalmatia or African colonies, if people had been led to expect too much, possibly Orlando, Sonnino, and the king were largely to blame for failing to agree over objectives and tactics; or possibly it was due to weaknesses in the Italian constitution, which allowed two politicians to act with little reference to parliament, or even to the king, or to genuine and not factitious public opinion.

During the first half of 1919 the prime minister was mostly away at the peace conference in Paris, leaving behind him a rudderless administration that almost ceased to function in his absence,[24] and this unfortunate fact was compounded by the king's decision to remain quite uselessly with his soldiers near the Austrian frontier. No doubt they both gambled on returning to Rome in triumph with a satisfactory settlement, whereas in practice, as leading newspapers warned, the government 'deliberately encouraged chauvinistic expectations to the point where almost any settlement was bound to seem a calamity'.[25] The penalty for this miscalculation was that parliament, which in April awarded Orlando an overwhelming vote of confidence, turned against him a few weeks later with another huge majority that forced his resignation.

Such a sudden and dramatic change highlighted the lack of party structure and the unreliability of parliament as an organ of government. Snubbed and disregarded in May 1915, neglected throughout the war, the legislature had become evidently more incoherent and less effective as a result of the wider suffrage introduced in 1912. Criticism of parliament continued to arrive from both Left and Right. Already towards the end of the war there had been an abortive conspiracy, supported by republicans as well as Mussolini, to replace the existing regime by a militarist dictatorship, and it appears that even Cadorna allowed himself to be briefly seduced by thoughts of rebellion.[26]

In June 1919 there were reports of another possible coup, this time involving a former war minister, General Giardino, with support not only from Mussolini and the nationalist Luigi Federzoni, but from the poet and war-hero, Gabriele D'Annunzio. Despite published denials, there was talk of seizing the parliament building, arresting Giolitti, even deposing the king if he resisted and replacing him by the Duke of Aosta. A principal objective was the assertion of Italian ambitions in the Adriatic. Money was collected for the purpose from wealthy people and commercial firms, some of whom were already employing groups of discharged veterans to curtail by force the spread of socialism among local authorities. Rodd noted the growth of 'an extra-parliamentary movement to take things out of the hands of the professional politicians' and did not envy the king's task in dealing with it.[27] An indignant Vittorio Emanuele reacted to rumours of a coup by saying that he was ready to take a gun and fight in the streets to defend law and order and the constitution.[28]

The next prime minister was Professor Francesco Nitti who boasted of belonging to no political party, who had voted against both Giolitti's liberals and Sonnino's conservatives, a man of great intelligence but 'whose main object is to be on the winning side' and 'to float with the changing currents of public opinion'.[29] Nitti succeeded in persuading the king to return to Rome and resume his constitutional duties which for three years had been in the nominal and irresolute hands of Tommaso Duke of Genoa. 'Nitti probably alone stands between us and something much worse', was the alarmist view of the British ambassador who feared either a military coup or popular revolution. But Nitti was optimistic to a fault, and reassured people that Italy had a much greater chance of internal quiet and stability than other countries. In his view there was absolutely no danger of revolution from either Left or Right.[30]

Nitti set great store on further widening the suffrage, as well as introducing proportional representation and replacing small constituencies by large electoral colleges. Part of his intention was to give greater representation to the socialists and also to the *popolari*, members of Don Sturzo's new party of Christian democracy. These two parties were much closer than others to the masses who, having borne the brunt of the war, had good claim to be given more say in affairs. By allowing them a more substantial participation in politics, Nitti particularly aimed to destroy the basis of Giolitti's political system which depended on small constituencies and the manipulation of middle-class electoral cliques.[31]

Since little time remained before the summer vacation, Nitti compelled deputies to cut short the debates on this vitally important electoral reform, and discussion sometimes took place in an almost empty chamber. Few politicians had time to consider whether proportional representation, by helping minority groups, would aggravate an existing defect and make stable majorities even harder to create. Aiming to destroy Giolitti, Nitti in practice destroyed much more when his reform bill was passed with only 63 negative votes. Henceforward the liberals in the centre would be less able to control events unless they could put aside their personal differences and form some approximation to a united political party, or unless some of them could ally with the moderate socialists and *popolari* to bring these mass parties actively into government; neither of which proved possible. But the king, perhaps surprisingly, thought that Nitti's extension of the suffrage might not go far enough. He told Rodd that he had for some time been urging successive prime ministers to change the electoral law. Despite his habitual anti-feminism he would have liked the vote given to women, because they would be 'an element of stability and rather a conservative force'; but the politicians thought this too revolutionary an idea.[32]

A number of people, including Salandra and the Swiss ambassador, had the impression that Vittorio Emanuele actively favoured the extreme Left and would not be sorry to see the socialists taking part in government. Without doubt, he wanted a fairer representative system, and can have been in no doubt that votes for women would have helped the Catholic *popolari* of whom he personally disapproved. He told one minister that Italy was sufficiently stable and mature to flourish under a government of either extreme Left or extreme Right. Nitti, while not so confident on this point, agreed in thinking that it was desirable to bring at least some socialists into the cabinet, while excluding the nationalists who constituted a greater danger. The king accepted this last point despite believing that ministers should be prepared if necessary for 'a brief period of repression'.[33]

Far removed as he was from the extreme nationalists, Vittorio Emanuele at least shared their view that his country was unfairly treated by the peace-makers in Paris. He differed from them in saying that he had no imperialist aims. He was even happy to concede a parliamentary constitution to the Arab populations of Tripoli and Cyrenaica: indeed, he approved of 'giving real powers to the native parliaments and not of according only a semblance of power which the government could override'. He was sorry that Italy failed to obtain a foothold in Asia Minor but, after some initial enthusiasm for sending a military force to the Black Sea coast of Russia, was glad when that contingent was withdrawn, since 'the sooner Russia was left entirely to herself, the sooner we should see the end of Lenin, who appeared to be nearing the end of his tether'.[34] He would still have liked a token presence in Dalmatia and was now sure that Italians would never be reconciled to not obtaining Fiume. Yet in private he also admitted that a policy of friendliness towards the southern Slavs was the best road to making Italy the dominant power in the Balkans, and regretted that ordinary Italians might be too unsophisticated to realise this.[35]

His cousin, the Duke of Aosta, had very different ambitions. Nitti was not alone in thinking that the duke still toyed with the idea of seizing the throne with support from dissident generals for whom nationalist ambitions came before their oath of loyalty.[36] Mutinous sentiments were further encouraged by D'Annunzio who advised the king to get rid of parliament altogether, receiving the reply that the constitution was an inviolable guarantee of popular liberties 'to be interpreted if necessary against myself'.[37] So D'Annunzio turned instead to General Caviglia, the minister of war, with another suggestion for organising a military coup to overturn parliament.[38] When this failed to win acceptance, in September he copied Garibaldi by leading a private army of rebellious soldiers to capture Fiume. There he set up an independent 'regency' which, though he claimed to rule in the king's name, was in direct defiance of the authority of the Italian state.

In the previous fifty years there had been no comparable challenge to the monarchy. Vittorio Emanuele hastily summoned a crown council of the main party leaders, only socialists and republicans refusing to come. This council opposed using force against the rebellion and advised waiting to see how other countries reacted. Nitti still hoped to win Fiume by negotiation and was frustrated to find his plans foiled by an armed revolution that he lacked the courage to put down. But he decided to exploit what had happened. First he explained, whether truthfully or not, that he did not dare to use the army against D'Annunzio because his orders would not be obeyed. Then he suggested with some naïveté that the peace conference in Paris might let him annex Fiume in order to stop the revolution spreading.[39] Meanwhile, he appeased the nationalists by sending money and food to D'Annunzio's revolutionaries. Like Albertini of the *Corriere della Sera*, while deploring the example of a successful mutiny, he was ready to give it covert support so long as D'Annunzio could be used as a threat or a bargaining counter at Paris.[40] Sonnino followed suit by encouraging D'Annunzio not to give way, and even the more moderate Orlando felt obliged to call the capture of Fiume 'a holy act of patriotism'.[41]

The king put on a brave face to give an impression of confidence. He admired D'Annunzio's courage but otherwise thought poorly of him as a vain exhibitionist, and probably knew that the poet talked of a 'march on Rome' to set up a military dictatorship.[42] He told Rodd 'that there were not more than a few hundred people really supporting D'Annunzio, and that the latter had realised the mistakes he had made and would be very glad to get out of it, did he know how to'.[43] There was anger at the palace when the Duchess of Aosta immediately went to see the poet in Fiume, and even more indignation when her husband offered his services to replace Nitti and set up a reactionary regime; to which the answer came that, if such a regime was ever required, the duke was hardly the man for it.[44] Most of all, the king was frightened by senior generals and admirals who publicly backed this revolution, especially since some of them were convinced that the government, playing a double game, would eventually support whichever side won. He felt humiliated when foreign statesmen spoke of his army as being disloyal and of his ministers as secretly conniving with a revolution that they merely pretended to deplore.[45]

Another shock towards the end of 1919 was the result of the first general election since 1913, and it showed how greatly the country had changed as a result of the war. Two thirds of those elected had never sat in parliament before. The king had anticipated, correctly, that the Catholic *popolari* would win about one fifth of the chamber, but wrongly assumed that the socialists would do poorly and 'the new chamber would not be more "red" but rather perhaps more conservative'.[46] Instead, the socialists trebled their numbers and emerged with over 150 deputies, the largest party in politics, indeed the first large organised party in Italian history. Far from being willing to collaborate, when the king arrived to open parliament in December they walked out in a noisy protest crying 'long live the socialist republic'.

Under attack from both political extremes, he was resigned to the likelihood that monarchies were doomed to disappear before long, and already the forty-two reigning families of 1914 were reduced to only sixteen.[47] He was seen to be more than usually withdrawn and diffident. As he told Lord Northcliffe, one reason why he disliked making official visits to foreign countries was that he was not much good 'at the representative business' and preferred to avoid public appearances whenever possible.[48] Most people in Rome, so reported the new British ambassador, deplored

> that the King of Italy, who has such great natural gifts and so great a grasp of current problems, should play a very effaced rôle in Italian affairs. His Majesty seems scarcely ever to appear in public and then only with reluctance, while his court plays little if any part in the social life of the capital.[49]

Vittorio Emanuele subsequently recollected how, after having recently enjoyed what he called a much more natural existence at the front with his soldiers, his first year back in Rome was about the most unpleasant he had experienced. Other people noted that a mixture of shyness, scepticism, and fear kept him from asserting himself. Nevertheless, he always took pains to show an outward calm which he thought was the chief duty of a sovereign,[50] despite accusations from the Right that by remaining impassive he failed to act as a real king. Even in the traditionally royalist areas of southern Italy an official enquiry revealed 'that monarchist sentiment had almost disappeared, and the old mystique of monarchy had disappeared completely'.[51]

Nitti now found him much less easy to get on with than before the war, especially as he rarely spoke his mind and seemed to assume that others were always trying to deceive him. The monarch in turn, though he admired Nitti's intelligence, was contemptuous of the premier's conceit, cynicism, and utter lack of courage when confronted by opposition. If the king allowed this government to continue in office for a full year, it was without much enthusiasm and mainly to avoid people's blaming him for what he saw as its inevitable collapse.[52]

One proposal that he gladly accepted was to give up many royal palaces that were an increasing financial burden on himself but that could be used as public museums. These included some with famous historical names: the Doge's palace in Venice, Capodimonte and Caserta near Naples, the Sforza castle and Monza in Lombardy, Moncalieri and Stupinigi in Piedmont, the Pitti palace and Boboli gardens in Florence, the royal palace and La Favorita in Palermo. In return for being relieved of the enormous costs of their upkeep, he agreed that the civil list paid to him could be reduced by a quarter. In deciding this settlement, some details were at last given of the king's private income, though incomplete as later became clear. He claimed credit for sacrificing what he called 'almost a third of his fortune' and hoped other property-owners would follow his example; but almost certainly the crown did not lose financially by the exchange.[53]

In June 1920 Giolitti became prime minister once again, albeit with a much less assured majority than ever before. More realistic than Nitti, he succeeded in persuading the king that heroic measures would be needed to prevent national bankruptcy as well as to confront alarming signs of disobedience on Right and Left. Giolitti shamed Nitti by the ease with which the army, when given firm orders, forced D'Annunzio's followers out of Fiume. He further defied the nationalists by withdrawing Italian troops from Albania; he proposed higher and progressive taxes, the confiscation of excessive war profits, as well as stringent laws to stop large-scale tax evasion by the rich which he recognised as a principal cause of Italy's annual deficit. All this, together with his unwillingness to use the army to put down strikes, made him highly unpopular with the Right, just as his reduction of broad subsidies annoyed the Left.

Another courageous proposal was aimed at curtailing the king's statutory right to make war and sign treaties without parliamentary consent. This proposal was an indirect criticism of the decision by the crown in May 1915. That decision had brought Italy into the war at the wrong moment, for what seemed the wrong reasons, with inadequate military preparation, and by yielding to mob violence. Giolitti was sure that if only there had existed a standing parliamentary committee for foreign affairs, the inadequacies of the Treaty of London might have been foreseen and analysed before any irreversible commitment was made. The prime minister was not long enough in office to effect this limitation on the royal prerogative, but the challenge and the implied criticism were much resented at the palace.

Giolitti and Nitti were not on speaking terms with each other, but both accepted, as indeed did the king, that the best hope of obtaining a workable parliamentary majority would be if Turati and the moderate socialists could be persuaded to ally with the liberals in the centre and support or even join a 'bourgeois' government. Other apparent irreconcilables had been similarly disarmed in the past – including Garibaldi, Crispi, Carducci, Fortis, and Bissolati, all of whom had at one time been critics of the monarchy. But Turati refused to break ranks with his more extreme companions and continued talking of revolution and republicanism, though without any serious intention of translating words into action. So doing he terrified the conservatives into counter-revolutionary violence at the same time as he deprived himself of any useful political function in defending the liberal state against fascism.

4   Fascism and the march on Rome

In a brave but unwise attempt to teach the socialists a lesson, Giolitti moved some way towards another would-be revolutionary who had the superficial advantage of being more of an opportunist, someone who since June 1919 had been ready to desert the extreme Left by giving his followers what he called 'a violent shove towards the Right'.[1] Mussolini, according to the British ambassador, had already by June 1919 'transferred his activities from socialist to nationalist and chauvinistic objects'; he was 'an unscrupulous politician...ready to adopt any policy which would pay'.[2] The king had briefly met him during the war and used to read his newspaper. Here was someone whose political opinions were unimpressive, who had only a small if devoted following, but who had an instinctive understanding of power politics and would clearly have to be taken into account.[3]

Mussolini in the course of 1920–1 revealed himself to be a man of violence who, with tacit connivance on the part of successive governments, employed a new technique of gang warfare to intimidate his former socialist companions. He had picked up almost no votes at all in earlier elections when standing as a socialist, but in June 1921 he and thirty-four members of a new fascist movement entered parliament; and a key factor was positive electoral support by Giolitti who mistakenly had been led to believe that they would back his government and become a force for law and order. Giolitti did not long survive in office after this uncharacteristic error of judgement. His successor, Bonomi, made the same tactical mistake of continuing to tolerate fascist violence. Bonomi, too, struggled in vain to construct a reliable parliamentary majority, and his failure left the king under the unwelcome threat of having to resume a more direct personal responsibility for resolving a political impasse.

Vittorio Emanuele disapproved of Mussolini's criminality but appreciated that the fascists claimed to be good patriots, and was reported as saying to General Giardino, perhaps in jest, that he would not have been sorry if their irregular blackshirt militia had acted forcibly against the 'reds' who sometimes staged noisy demonstrations outside the Quirinal palace.[4] Mussolini continued to speak in favour of republicanism[5] and in 1920 discussed a plan with D'Annunzio for an anti-monarchist revolution,[6] but remained open to offers from the opposite side. Moreover, other prominent fascists, notably General De Bono and Cesare De Vecchi, were dedicated supporters of monarchy and sometimes hinted at turning against their leader if he held to his republican opinions.[7]

Mussolini, as a party leader, was summoned to give his views at the Quirinal when Giolitti resigned in June 1921. He was summoned again for half an hour when Bonomi gave way to Luigi Facta in February 1922, and it was noted with surprise that this ostentatiously plebeian outsider procured a top hat for the occasion in deference to official protocol.[8] Yet another surprise was that this ex-socialist went straight from the palace to a long meeting with the strongly monarchist nationalist party and some of the right-wing liberals; and the object of this meeting was to discuss formulating a common policy. Possibly some such coalition was what the king had mentioned to him, because the lack of agreement between small parties was the reason why three successive prime ministers had failed to form a stable majority in parliament. A few days later the fascist leader was summoned to the palace for another longer meeting about which, once again, we can only speculate.[9]

So confident was Mussolini that early in 1922 he spoke of himself and the king as being the only two serious forces in Italian politics.[10] Parliament was to his mind almost irrelevant, and he rarely bothered to attend its sessions. Nor did he conceal that he was 'resolutely anti-democratic'.[11] Winning power was his aim, and already before seeing him the king would have known of his published desire for a military dictatorship. Mussolini let it be known that he would support the monarchy if no action was taken against the fascist movement, but hinting that otherwise anything could happen.[12] To gain power he would join anyone, whether the socialists and *popolari*, or the nationalists on the extreme Right whom he clearly preferred. If necessary he would join Nitti, who provocatively said that he preferred Mussolini to Giolitti; or else would join any of the other liberal factions led by Orlando, Giolitti, and Salandra who found it so hard to agree with each other.[13]

If the completely ineffective and colourless Facta lasted as prime minister from February to October 1922, this was only because the other parliamentary leaders could not work together and were too distrustful of each other to take the responsibility of government without some prospect of a working majority. Facta lacked not only the authority but the intelligence and political skill needed to deal with an opportunist such as Mussolini, nor had he the courage to counter the tactics of terrorism, reprisals, and squad violence by which local fascist groups proceeded to destroy the hold of socialism over town councils and provincial administrations.

Since the government remained passive, many people among the middle classes were delighted when, early in August, the fascist squads took to the streets and foiled a badly timed socialist attempt to organise a general strike. Even some cabinet ministers were pleased at this, while those among their colleagues who demanded martial law against fascist violence were outvoted in cabinet when they argued that the police merely required clear orders to control both strikers and strike-breakers. The king was still ready to invite the moderate socialists to join the government if that would help restore law and order, but Turati again refused,[14] while the more extreme socialists and the small communist party persisted in thinking liberals and social democrats to be a greater enemy of the proletariat than a disorganised movement such as fascism.[15]

Mussolini was astonished and contemptuous at finding that not a single liberal leader would accept the king's invitation to replace Facta as premier. He was equally and justifiably contemptuous of those who let him organise a private army and terrorise opponents without hindrance from prefects or police. Early in August he began to talk of a possible 'march on Rome', while making it clear that he would still take power by peaceable means if given the chance. His major fear was of the army, because even those generals who sym- pathised with fascism were almost certainly more royalist than fascist, whereas other generals were anti-fascist, and all or almost all of them would obey any royal order to support the government. Likewise, the armed squads of the nationalist party would back the king against any fascist revolution.[16] To neutralise any opposition from the conservatives, Mussolini therefore played on the theme of patriotic sentiment, advocating an imperialist policy for the annexation of Dalmatia. He even talked of fighting to destroy the British empire and convert the Mediterranean into an Italian lake.[17] Realising that his fascist supporters were turning away from republicanism,[18] he decided to move in the same direction after calculating that this would make him acceptable to the conservative establishment; and no decision in his life was more timely.

The king is said to have been in touch with some fascist sympathisers earlier in 1922, and this is not improbable.[19] Facta remembered discussing with him in early autumn whether fascism could ever be trusted as a participant in government.[20] In mid September, Mussolini declared in a public speech that the monarchy might have a positive role to play as an element of continuity with Italy's past. He went on to argue that the crown had no interest in opposing fascism; on the contrary, the survival of the monarchy might depend on accepting the fascist belief that the parliamentary regime had failed and should be replaced. When at the end of his speech Mussolini's audience raised a shout of 'long live the king', De Vecchi in vain asked him to join in this loyal salute.[21] His remarks were intended as a threat. He still had to avoid alienating the republicans in his movement.

During the fatal autumn of 1922, Vittorio Emanuele kept away from the capital in the hope that this crisis would resolve itself without his active participation. During a brief visit to Belgium he reassured people that Giolitti would eventually return to power and put things to rights.[22] He then spent ten days at his holiday home in Tuscany. Meanwhile, the various liberal leaders, jealous and suspicious of each other, entered into separate and secret negotiations with the fascists in the expectation of scotching Giolitti's chances, and also hoped to get credit for themselves by 'constitutionalising' this new and dangerous force in Italian politics. Mussolini let Facta, Nitti, and Salandra severally imagine that they could rely on his support against each other. Orlando was another liberal who had lost confidence in the normal functioning of parliamentary politics. Orlando had, perhaps regretfully, come round to wanting the fascists represented in government; so had the distinguished economist Luigi Einaudi; so had Albertini, whose newspaper had so far been surprisingly subdued in its condemnation of the brutalities and illegalities of fascism or its manifest contempt for parliament.

Almost equally ambiguous was Giolitti himself, who was in Mussolini's opinion the person chiefly to be feared, the man who having successfully used a show of force against D'Annunzio in Fiume might order the army to march against fascism if allowed back into power.[23] Giolitti waited at home in the vain expectation of an invitation from the king and no doubt remembered his disastrous clash with the palace at another moment of crisis in May 1915. He was in any case an old man whose eightieth birthday fell on 27 October. Recent experiences left him dubious about forming a coalition that included socialists and *popolari*, both of whom had shown reluctance to join a bourgeois anti-fascist alliance. Instead, he too believed that the fascists might have to be brought into government, where they would probably do less damage than the socialists and would hardly last long.[24]

The king kept his thoughts very much to himself, though he cannot have been uninfluenced by the opinions of these recognised leaders of liberal Italy. Facta's coalition was hopelessly divided and Facta himself became increasingly indecisive. Despite what the socialists claimed, fascism was surely not much to the king's liking, but neither did he greatly like the machine politics of Giolitti nor the latter's proclaimed policy of reducing the royal prerogative. Vittorio Emanuele disapproved of political violence and was much happier when a vote in parliament gave a clear indication on policy, but ten times already in his reign an extra-parliamentary crisis had compelled him to enter the arena when important decisions had to be taken, and now once more he feared being forced into an arbitral position that he would have preferred to avoid.

The fascists numbered barely six per cent of the deputies in parliament. At court, however, there existed a group of pro-fascists, which included not only the Duke of Aosta whom the king cordially hated, but also the queen mother who was enchanted by Mussolini and had no scruples about encouraging fascist violence.[25] The chief royal aide-de-camp, General Cittadini, was thought to sympathise with fascism, and similarly Count Mattioli Pasqualini who administered the royal household. This helps to explain why, to the puzzlement of some foreigners, the monarch remained so passive; but his tragedy, and no doubt his fault, was to have preferred the company of soldiers and courtiers to politicians, especially the kind of soldiers whom General Caviglia called lap-dogs rather than watch-dogs.[26] Giolitti and other politicians outside the cabinet were never allowed to give him their views except at moments of crisis; sometimes not even then.

No comment was therefore forthcoming from the king's holiday home when Mussolini on 24 October, after reviewing thousands of his armed blackshirts in the streets of Naples, announced that he was about to march on Rome to 'take by the throat our miserable ruling class'. Nor could the cabinet agree on how to react to this astonishing threat. Instead, ministers meekly put their portfolios at Facta's disposal so that if necessary he could bring some fascists into a new cabinet, and the king agreed that this evident surrender to violence might be the only way of avoiding revolution.[27] Even now he did not return to Rome, despite the fact that he envisaged the possibility of revolution, civil war, and perhaps abdication.[28] He admitted that martial law might have to be imposed as a last resort,[29] but otherwise his only advice was for Facta to establish secret contact with the rebels. The senior generals, even those close to fascism, agreed that the army would obey if instructed to put down any rebellion, and the government was sure of it. General Badoglio was confident that the threat of a march on Rome would disappear at once if such an order were given and a dozen rebels were arrested; but no such order came.[30]

Only at midnight on 26/27 October, when more news arrived of mobilisation by the fascist militia, did the government at last send a telegram begging the king to return from his Tuscan retreat. Not only was this delay inexplicable, but eight more valuable hours passed between receipt of the telegram and the king's departure from San Rossore, and his unbelievable explanation was that no one told him the matter was urgent.[31] On arrival at Rome on the evening of the 27th, after hearing of more outrages throughout northern and central Italy, he seemed angry and dejected, but 'resolutely' ordered Facta to defend Rome at whatever cost from the blackshirt squads.[32] He confirmed this order later that night; and did so once again at another meeting at about 2 a.m. on 28 October, from which meeting the prime minister emerged with instructions to draw up a decree proclaiming martial law.[33]

General Pugliese commanding the army in Rome was at this point given full powers and promised Facta that he had ample strength to restore order.[34] Ministers were summoned for an emergency session of the cabinet several hours later, and there they heard in person from the king's representative, General Cittadini, that martial law was necessary; indeed, without it the king might abdicate.[35] After Cittadini returned to the royal residence with the news that the cabinet had unanimously agreed, the required decree was signed by ministers and posted on the walls of Rome. Facta waited for a telephone call summoning him for the formality of the royal signature. But no call arrived, and by 9 a.m. it became known that the king had unaccountably changed his mind.

To overrule a unanimous cabinet, especially on such an important issue, was without precedent in his reign and all the more remarkable since ministers were merely agreeing to what he had repeatedly urged them to do. His motives must be guessed. No doubt he wanted to avoid bloodshed, but in that case it is incredible that he did not consult General Pugliese who was confident that the insurrection would collapse with perhaps no bloodshed at all.[36] Probably he had decided to get rid of the feeble Facta, relying on his knowledge that Salandra had already agreed to form a new government that included Mussolini and excluded Giolitti.[37] Almost certainly the king wanted to avoid appointing Giolitti, and this is of great importance since Giolitti was the politician most feared by the fascists as well as being the one liberal leader who could with least difficulty have formed a viable coalition.[38] The king is also known to have feared that, unless he gave way, the fascists were intending to dethrone him and put Aosta in his place.[39]

Though he insisted that the decision to reject martial law was taken personally by himself,[40] he was certainly influenced by mysterious visitors or telephone conversations in the early hours of the 28th, and these convinced him (or gave him the excuse to believe) that he ought to surrender to what Mussolini now called an ultimatum. The officers on duty at the palace would certainly have influenced his decision, and, though the fact was denied, Diaz apparently sent him advice that the army might be unreliable. The army, it was said once again, would of course obey an order to disarm the fascists, but better not to put this to the test.[41]

Whatever the king's reasons, one explanation he gave rings false, which was that the defences of Rome were inadequate. He later explained that Pugliese had only eight thousand soldiers to resist a fascist army of over a hundred thousand.[42] But putting the blame on the army was quite as unfair as Cadorna's blaming his soldiers for the defeat at Caporetto or Baratieri for that at Adowa. In fact the king must have known, and certainly ought to have known, that Pugliese had 30,000 men and these (as Mussolini later admitted) outnumbered the fascists; moreover, the soldiers had armoured cars, machine guns, and artillery, with orders to use them, whereas the fascists were mostly a stage army with little more than cudgels and daggers. So little were the rebels to be feared that soon after 8 a.m. on the 28th, when Pugliese ordered the railway lines into Rome to be cut fifty kilometres from the city, four hundred policemen were enough to bring this so-called march on Rome to a complete halt for the next two days.

Another relevant fact is that the nationalists and the large veterans' organisation were ready to help put down any revolution. The nationalists mobilised four thousand of their blueshirt militiamen and cavalry in Rome with arms provided by the army, and were notoriously better disciplined than the blackshirts.[43] Also important is the strange fact that De Vecchi, one of the four 'quadrumvirs' in command of the fascist march, was at the Quirinal for much of 28 October; and, even stranger, De Vecchi let it be known that he and his fascist friends would never disobey whichever way the king decided. De Vecchi later agreed with Pugliese and the minister of war (the two people best able to judge) that the revolution was already fizzling out when the palace decided to succumb.[44]

Vittorio Emanuele took on his shoulders a huge responsibility by ignoring these facts and rejecting his ministers' unanimous advice. The fascists were challenging the authority of the state by mobilising an irregular army with the avowed intention of replacing what Mussolini called the 'ruling class'. Ministers had at last decided to act against this revolution as their predecessors had acted against D'Annunzio. But by his uncharacteristic intervention the king stopped them, thus attracting to himself much of the responsibility for the collapse of liberal Italy.

Mussolini watched the unfolding of this drama from his editorial chair in Milan – near a possible escape route into Switzerland, as the critics pointed out. At the first hint of martial law being applied, the fascist movement in Milan seemed to collapse in minutes, but a few hours later the contrary news arrived and was recognised as signifying capitulation by the state. An order to arrest Mussolini was even disobeyed by the prefect, who no doubt read the signs of the times and preferred to ingratiate himself with the victorious party. This act of disobedience was another crucial fact in the débâcle.[45]

The king might at this point have taken soundings with the parliamentary leaders as was normal before appointing a new prime minister, but chose not to because he had already made up his mind. The only one he consulted was the conservative Salandra who, instead of advising him to suppress the revolt, advised the opposite and confirmed that the refusal to proclaim martial law was correct. Salandra suggested the immediate formation of a new government before Giolitti had time to arrive in Rome.[46] Comforted by this advice, the king invited Salandra to take office who, almost certainly with the king's approval or at his request, immediately turned for help not to the other liberal leaders, but to the fascists De Vecchi and Dino Grandi, informing them with astonishing naïveté that he would accept the royal mandate only if Mussolini agreed to join his cabinet.

Mussolini realised from this final capitulation that the fascists could name their own terms, and replied to an invitation from the palace by refusing any subordinate position, requiring nothing less than the premiership for himself. No one had ever treated the sovereign in such an unceremonious and threatening manner. Mussolini's demand was further supported by Albertini and a group of leading Milanese industrialists who sent an urgent telegram to Rome advising acceptance, no doubt fearing that the only alternative was a return to power of Giolitti with his programme of unacceptable social reforms. Early on the 29th Mussolini was invited to form a government, and Salandra declared himself overjoyed at such a happy ending to the crisis.[47]

In appointing Mussolini, the king was surrendering to the leader of a private army who not only boasted of committing terrorist outrages but, after several recent defections from his party, had only 32 fascists out of over 500 deputies in parliament. Vittorio Emanuele later invented the excuse that he had been deserted by all the parliamentary leaders – whom in fact, most unusually, he had not so much as consulted. He pretended, quite falsely, that for two whole days he had been compelled to govern in person by issuing his own orders to army and police.[48] To other observers these events, much like those of May 1915, looked more like a royal *coup d'état* in collusion with a few generals, a few conservative politicians, and prominent spokesmen of the industrialist and agrarian classes.[49] By insisting that the decision was his own and not one covered by ministerial responsibility, he was inevitably criticised for identifying the monarchy with fascism. By yielding to an ultimatum, he had forfeited almost all control over events – a fact he possibly did not realise until too late.

At least the crisis was over. Rome during the days 28–30 October was *en fête*, with crowds cheering the king now that they knew in which direction he was moving.[50] There was some violence. Shops and houses were looted, embassies invaded, and one of Mussolini's first actions was to order the 'scientific' destruction of the offices of the main socialist and liberal newspapers. In later years he wondered if he should not have immediately deposed the king and executed the opposition leaders.[51] But there was no need, because his victory was complete, and there was a familiar stampede by members of parliament to ingratiate themselves with the new premier. He himself reached Rome on 30 October by sleeping car and arrived at the palace wearing the black shirt of fascism. When he returned soon afterwards to present a list of ministers, he had changed into an ill-fitting morning dress and accessories borrowed from various colleagues. Only the socialists did not join his cabinet. Liberals, radicals, and the *popolari* accepted. Even if they had some private reservations, not one of those he invited refused. None even asked for a serious preliminary discussion of policy. Never had a government been formed so quickly and easily.

The king welcomed this as fully justifying his decision. He was no doubt relieved at Mussolini's timely demonstration of a desire for consensus and moderation, as he must have been delighted when the liberal leaders, Salandra, Giolitti, Orlando, and Einaudi, all made public declarations of approval.[52] The editor of the *Corriere della Sera*, while objecting that the cabinet included representatives of the moderate Left, praised fascism for saving Italy from the socialist menace.[53] The socialists, as Mussolini admitted, might possibly have frustrated his triumph if they had proclaimed a general strike, but Pietro Nenni declared that the collapse of the liberal state was regarded by the extreme Left with indifference.[54] Fascism, they thought, would merely clear away obstacles in the way of their own more serious revolution.

The next day, when Facta went to the palace to take his leave and countersign Mussolini's appointment, an embarrassed sovereign spoke of nothing except the weather.[55] He then stood patiently for four hours on the balcony of the Quirinal while a motley black-shirt parade marched past. Mussolini said there were a hundred thousand marchers and sometimes claimed three times as many, but smilingly agreed with a foreign journalist who counted about twenty thousand.[56] By order of the new minister of war, General Diaz, soldiers from the Rome garrison joined this desultory parade to make it look more impressive, and generals in incongruous black shirts ostentatiously mounted guard outside the palace gate.[57]

Mussolini's intention was to create the illusion that he had imposed himself by force on king and parliament. With the same purpose a few days later he harangued the legislature with a fiercely Cromwellian speech in which, to great applause from the Right, he boasted of carrying out an illegal conquest of power, and even threatened to sent troops into parliament if anyone challenged him. But none of the newly appointed non-fascist ministers, whether liberals, radicals, or Christian democrats, resigned after this contemptuous speech, and Giolitti surprised some people by saying that the deputies deserved no better after their complete failure to support any liberal govenment.[58] Huge majorities in both houses granted plenary powers to dispense with parliament for the next year, and the senate actually gave Mussolini a standing ovation. Salandra, Orlando, Bonomi, Facta, Alcide De Gasperi all joined with Giolitti in voting this grant of full powers; only socialists and most of the republicans voted against. Some on the extreme Left gave part of their game away by applauding Mussolini when he talked of governing without parliament.[59] Nitti was among the few who walked out of the chamber rather than vote one way or the other, but most representatives of Italy's ruling class showed that they had lost any confidence in the operation of parliamentary government.

As the king's son, Umberto, later recalled, these convincing votes of approval, especially in a parliament where fascists were a tiny minority, convinced the king that in taking a justifiable risk he had acted correctly.[60] Even Gaetano Salvemini and other social democrats were for the moment prepared to accept Mussolini as just one more in a long line of parliamentary dictators, as no worse than Depretis, Crispi, or Giolitti, as someone who was not so much a negation of the past as the natural product and 'sublimation' of a fundamentally flawed political system. Fascism, according to Salvemini, was in one sense an improvement on leaders such as Orlando, Bonomi, and Facta. Mussolini might at least provoke a healthy reaction that would teach a new generation of younger Italians to appreciate the value of liberty and remove 'the old pseudo-democratic oligarchies' that for so long had monopolised and misused political power.[61]

5 *The fascist dictatorship*

Vittorio Emanuele cannot have much liked hearing himself applauded as 'the fascist king'.[1] At first he gave the impression that Mussolini's accession to power was not particularly irregular, and perhaps hardly realised that he was riding on the back of a revolution. As a self-confessed fatalist, he admitted only an indirect responsibility, because he had learnt from history that political events 'were much more automatic than a result of individual action and influence'.[2] Mussolini's appointment, he said, was not strictly unconstitutional, and probably the new cabinet would last no longer than previous administrations.[3] In the meantime he welcomed the restoration of order and authority under the new regime. He appreciated Mussolini's patriotism and outward deference to the monarchy, just as he greatly preferred a minister who knew his own mind and made political decisions seem easy. Above all, he welcomed the relief from political crises which everyone expected the crown to resolve.

A number of people soon learnt of his admiration for Mussolini's industry, judgement, and quick understanding of political problems;[4] and almost certainly his appreciation was genuine. He did not readily award praise, but bestowed more on the duce than on any other of the seventeen prime ministers of his reign, and his sense of relief was immediate. Never before had the royal family accepted invitations from a political party, but their presence at the Palazzo Venezia in October 1923 must have seemed a special kind of royal investiture, and ordinary citizens must have been encouraged by it to think that fascism was particularly acceptable at court.[5]

Far from reciprocating this admiration, Mussolini sometimes referred to his sovereign as a useless and boring person, 'too diminutive for an Italy destined to greatness'. In Mussolini's entourage there was much anger at popular demonstrations of monarchist loyalty which were taken as indirect criticisms of fascism. The crown was nevertheless useful in attracting the loyalty of conservatives and the army to the new regime, for which the prime minister was genuinely grateful, and he therefore continued to observe the formalities, regularly going to the palace twice a week in morning suit and spats like any normal bourgeois minister.

Whether there was much serious discussion of policy on these occasions cannot be known, and Mussolini let it be thought that he slightly resented them as a chore because his republican instincts were not entirely dead. One day, he warned, a more serious fascist revolution would take place and this time 'without contraceptives'. In the meantime he would diminish the royal prerogatives piecemeal, 'plucking the chicken feather by feather to lessen its squawking'. He wanted the appearance of royal support but also the appearance of not needing it. Though invariably respectful in private, in public he aimed at showing a scruple of indifference, and could turn up at a state banquet having not shaved for several days, or could arrive to take his seat next to the king when the meal was half over.[6]

Some prominent fascists, for instance Italo Balbo, remained strongly republican even after October 1922. Mussolini's slightly ambiguous attitude on this point may explain why Colajanni and Chiesa, two leaders of the small republican party, briefly supported fascism, and why other members seceded in December 1922 to form a fascist republican federation. Most republicans, however, remained firmly loyal to their democratic and international ideals, convinced that Italians were too sensible and freedom-loving to allow such a vulgar dictatorship to last for long.[7]

To allay suspicion, Mussolini's first cabinet included only a minority of paid-up fascists. But one early step towards dictatorship was a royal decree of January 1923 instituting an armed fascist militia 'for the defence of the revolution', and unlike the regular armed forces the militiamen were at first exempted from taking an oath of loyalty to the king – in clear breach of the constitution. Another change was the institution of a Grand Council of fascism parallel with the cabinet, and this weakened ministers of the crown who thereby lost most of their say in the formulation of policy: the king in fact demurred for several days before giving his consent. A third move was to fuse the nationalist and fascist parties, so raising the number of Mussolini's disciplined supporters to nearly ten per cent of the chamber. The nationalists were strongly monarchist, and to persuade them to accept this union the Grand Council declared that there would be no further diminution in the royal prerogatives,[8] not for the moment at least. Further plucking of the chicken was better postponed, or at least unpublicised.

Most radical of all was the proposal for a drastically changed electoral law by which any party winning a quarter of the popular vote would be guaranteed two thirds of the seats in parliament; and against this revolutionary suggestion the king put up more resistance than his liberal ex-prime ministers dared to voice when it was debated in parliament. Before it became law he refused a request to allow the government to hold new elections. He also refused Mussolini's further request to alter the electoral law by means of a simple royal decree.

But thereafter his resistance crumbled and he had to accept this radical change in the system when in July 1923 the lower house of parliament gave a convincing vote by over two-to-one in its favour: its supporters included Giolitti, Salandra, and Orlando, who all thought that the greater danger still lay on the Left. Approval in the senate was by four-to-one. The socialists and *popolari* between them had over 250 deputies in the chamber, yet no more than 139 votes were registered against a measure that effectively guaranteed that Mussolini would never have to fear opposition in any future parliament. The presence of armed fascists at the doors and in the galleries of the parliament building were an argument that was perhaps hard for some members to resist.

When parliament's grant of full powers expired in December 1923, Mussolini persuaded the palace to let him hold his first election. He said that this would be the last time he intended to indulge in such ridiculous 'paper games' because 'half a million rifles outweigh five million votes'. But he first needed to create a fascist majority in parliament so as to give the outside world the illusion that he had overwhelming popular support. For home consumption he shamelessly explained that even if the election went against him he would remain in office; but of course Italian governments never lost elections.

Some twenty rival lists of candidates were presented to the electorate in April 1924. Mussolini made doubly sure of success by bringing into his own *listone* a great number of non-fascists, relying on the fact that many liberals needed government endorsement so as to defeat their socialist and *popolari* opponents. Patronage and intimidation were freely employed in the weeks before the election. Opposition candidates were wounded, some even killed. Individual fascists were apparently allowed to vote fifty times for the same candidate,[9] but the tactics of terrorism were his main weapon. The *listone* was easily successful, securing the return of over 350 deputies, of which almost half were not members of the fascist party, and the inclusion of Salandra, Orlando, and other liberals on the official ticket must have been an important ingredient in this overwhelming electoral victory. After such a success, so he said, only an armed revolution could deprive him of power.[10]

The king aroused the pity of some observers as he opened the next parliament in May 1924 with a badly read speech written for him by Mussolini. He cannot have known that non-fascist deputies arriving in the customary formal dress ran the risk of having it torn off them by party officials waiting at the doors. His speech showed clearly that the monarchy was already a prisoner of the regime. It included praise for the fascist militia and for the party emblem of the Roman *fasces*. It declared that a new epoch had begun for Italy by the electoral legitimisation of the fascist revolution. Without a plurality of effective competing parties in parliament the monarch now found himself without his former discretionary ability to select a prime minister or play off individual groups against each other. But already during twenty previous years as a constitutional sovereign he had let his residual powers fall into disuse except at critical moments such as May 1915 and October 1922. As he opened this parliament the diminutive monarch seemed puny and defenceless beside the uniformed squad-leaders on the government benches.[11]

Mussolini confidently demanded from his disciplined majority the immediate validation of three thousand royal decrees issued since the last session of the previous legislature. He further demanded that it should refuse to investigate thousands of protests officially registered against the murderous assaults that attended the elections. But he was immediately thrown off course by a speech of outright condemnation from the social-democrat Giacomo Matteotti. This man had been repeatedly assaulted and tortured by the fascist squads, and his speech denouncing fascist violence and financial corruption marked him out as a dangerous man and the leader of a now much reduced opposition.

Matteotti had recently evaded an order forbidding him to travel, and in England and Belgium had presented in detail a terrible indictment of the way the elections had been conducted.[12] Such a public exposure of Mussolini's methods had to be stopped, and orders were therefore issued from fascist party headquarters that this dangerous critic must be made to disappear 'definitively' if he could not be intimidated into silence.[13] During an angry parliamentary debate, which had to be toned down before the record was published, Mussolini threatened opposition leaders with death if they continued to criticise the government in public.[14]

Three days later, on 10 June, his threat was fulfilled when this leader of the parliamentary opposition was murdered after abduction in broad daylight on a Roman street, and the assassins were clumsy enough to leave a clue that identified them as acolytes in daily contact with the duce. Such was the outcry that Mussolini feared his government might fall. Never in the next twenty years did he come so close to defeat. At once a number of fascists, blaming their leader for bringing their movement into discredit, began to distance themselves from someone who might soon be in gaol.[15] Mussolini forced his three chief assistants to resign as scapegoats, namely the chief of police and two of the four directors of the fascist party. By his own admission the fascist movement was on the point of collapse.[16]

But nothing happened, partly because Salandra's friends saw the alternative prospect of a shift to the left as being much more frightening than what they optimistically hoped might now become a less violent and corrupt version of fascism. Giolitti partially supported Salandra and refused to join a hundred socialist and other deputies who decided in protest to boycott the proceedings of parliament. On 13 June, to defuse this boycott, sittings of the chamber were suspended by royal decree. There was no call by the socialists for a general strike. There was no intervention by the king, though the resignation of four ministers provided a perfectly good enough pretext. There were no popular demonstrations or armed insurrection such as Mussolini had been fearing. Towards the end of the month, when the immediate shock had subsided, two of Salandra's followers were even persuaded to join the cabinet. Despite Matteotti's death and despite detailed and published allegations of criminal behaviour, members of the senate, very few of whom had joined the fascist party, gave the government another resounding ten-to-one majority in a vote of confidence. Albertini was one conservative liberal who now joined the opposition. But among the pro-fascist majority was Benedetto Croce, a distinguished liberal and the most prominent figure in Italian culture, who later put all the blame on Vittorio Emanuele for keeping the fascists in power.[17] Croce at the time issued a public statement to say that Mussolini had done much good and despite everything should still be supported.[18]

A number of responsible politicans disagreed and thought that the king should have brought fascism to an end by immediately appointing a new government. There was a conviction even among some fascists that he could have done so by 'merely lifting a finger', and opposition leaders, including some who had accepted his decision in October 1922, came to the palace to say that it was his constitutional right and indeed his duty to dismiss Mussolini at once.[19] Although he must have seen the irony in receiving such a demand from people who had previously criticised his exercise of the royal prerogative, apparently he agreed that the liquidation of fascism would not have been difficult; but he thought that while the chamber remained shut he ought not to act on his own, especially when a large majority of liberal senators publicly supported the government.[20] There were inauspicious precedents in 1900, 1915, and 1922 which suggested that the greatest caution was needed before acting without clear support from the legislature. Eventually, in 1943, he would exercise his prerogative and dismiss Mussolini without any parliamentary sanction, but in 1924 he took a surely considered decision not to do so.

Three weeks after the opposition leader had been assassinated, the British ambassador reported that 'His Majesty once told me that he had never had a premier with whom he found it so satisfactory to deal as with Signor Mussolini, and I know from private sources that recent events have not changed his opinion.'[21] One relevant fact was that the only alternative would have been another unstable minority coalition. There was no chance at all of permanent agreement between the followers of Giolitti, Salandra, Orlando, Nitti, and Luzzatti. A viable coalition would certainly have had to include representatives of the Left who, especially since the events of October 1922, had little further use for the House of Savoy.

Vittorio Emanuele may possibly have wavered but had no serious doubts. Another royal decree on 10 July 1924 allowed Mussolini to exercise stringent controls over the press, and this decree blocked the publication of opposition views at a moment when fascist newspapers sold only a tenth as many copies as their rivals. It was of course condemned by anti-fascists as a further violation of the constitution and of the king's coronation oath. Fascist newspapers continued without censorship to publish demands for the assassination of their opponents, and did so without the intervention of the police or the courts, while opposition papers could not so much as question this perversion of justice.

Since the press was curbed and the chamber remained shut for five months, three former cabinet ministers, Carlo Sforza, Giovanni Amendola, and Ivanoe Bonomi, went to the king with detailed evidence of Mussolini's complicity in murderous attacks on Matteotti and other deputies. But he merely glanced at the documentation and refused to read it on the grounds that this was a matter not for him but for parliament and the courts. To another deputation of protest from the veterans' organisation his only reply was to change the subject and remark inconsequentially that 'my daughter killed two quails today'. Bonomi, a former prime minister, warned him that he was assuming a responsibility that he might one day regret, to which he replied that he had fully considered the matter and would not change his attitude even if it cost him the throne.[22]

When parliament reassembled in November a hundred deputies still refused to attend. Mussolini was heard to admit that if only Giolitti had joined this boycott the government might have collapsed.[23] Alternatively it was said that, without the boycott, Mussolini might have been placed in a parliamentary minority, or at least might have had only a small majority, in which case the king was apparently ready to demand the government's resignation.[24] It is possible that the hundred deputies would have been joined by a hundred or more of those liberals who had been elected on Mussolini's *listone*. They would have been supported by some fascists who were unhappy with their growing unpopularity and who would have backed a new government under Federzoni or Tittoni if they knew that this was the king's wish.

Some people at least hoped that an alternative was now possible, but their calculation left out of account the familiar unwillingness of deputies to turn against any government that might be in charge of the next election. Mussolini had vast patronage in his gift and could intimidate the electorate by means of his murder squads and the fascist militia. Moreover, few politicians were keen to risk changing their allegiance so long as the king remained silent and the opposition was divided and leaderless. The result was that in November the government, because of abstentions, won another overwhelming vote in the chamber by 314 to 6, and in the senate by 206 to 54. Orlando was by this time doubtful enough to abstain. Salandra still voted for the government but reluctantly, terrified that a hostile vote would bring awkward facts to light and expose Italy to the outside world as governed by a gang of criminals.[25] But Giolitti at last sided with the opposition: as well as protesting that violent fascist outrages were becoming more numerous, he condemned the decree against press freedom as an illegality without precedent.[26]

Public opinion, as always, cannot be reliably assessed. But one indicator is that fascist newspapers continued to sell very badly indeed. Another is that a congress of journalists during October voted almost unanimously against fascism, and similar condemnation was registered by a congress of lawyers in Turin.[27] The British ambassador considered that Mussolini was personally strong but fascism 'is more unpopular every day', and the Vatican thought of fascism as 'a spent force'.[28] Public demonstrations organised by the government were falling very flat and sometimes seemed to be applauding the king rather than his ministers. In Reggio Calabria, when a false rumour spread that Mussolini had resigned, cheerful crowds poured into the streets for an all-night celebration in which even the fascist authorities happily participated.[29]

Opposition newspapers in December must have greatly exaggerated when they wrote that Mussolini was entirely without popular support, but Giolitti was sure that this was quite true in Piedmont and Sicily.[30] Other politicians asserted that no one apart from the *squadristi* of the militia wanted the regime to continue, and Orlando assured the king that a word from him would be enough to topple an unpopular government.[31] The most authoritative newspaper in the country, the *Corriere della Sera*, thought that fascism, being supported by only a small minority, would never survive a free election, and its continued illegalities were now so blatant that the king had a duty to intervene.[32]

Mussolini knew that he was in serious trouble and could with difficulty survive if the palace turned against him. He announced in public that he would humbly obey if the king asked for his resignation, but warned that this would be in defiance of a clear majority in parliament.[33] Towards the end of December a suggestion was made for a new national government to include all the ex-premiers, and a meeting was convened by one member of the nationalist party at which forty fascist deputies supported this proposal. A number of prominent generals also made opposition speeches in the senate. Three senior members of the royal household, not only General Brusati but Mattioli Pasqualini and Senator di Campello, were also directly or indirectly involved in such criticisms, and this could hardly have been without the king's knowledge and permission.[34]

But any serious chance of compromise collapsed when, on 29 December, further damning evidence of Mussolini's involvement in torture and murder was published and presented to the king. Sixty commanders of the fascist militia at once forced their way into the prime minister's office and threatened to depose him unless he prevented the judiciary from taking cognisance of these incriminating allegations. For them, as for their leader, the simple alternative was either their own imprisonment, or else a frank admission that Italy must submit to a full dictatorship where the rule of law no longer applied.

During three days of acute crisis, newspapers all over Italy were sequestered and more fascist brutalities took place. The liberal leader Giovanni Amendola optimistically took this as a further indication that the regime was bound to collapse.[35] At the customary palace reception for the new year, Mussolini looked isolated and was ostentatiously cut by Salandra, Giolitti, and Bonomi.[36] The next day he returned in some trepidation for a private audience at the Quirinal, and this marked another turning-point in his career, because he was greeted with surprising cordiality and a reassurance that the king disbelieved the accusations of misbehaviour and illegality.[37]

Shortly after receiving this encouragement, Mussolini sent to ask for powers to dissolve parliament, but his messenger was told that the king could agree only if the prime minister came personally to explain his reasons. No one knows what they then said to each other, but on 3 January, without warning the palace, Mussolini felt confident enough to make a public statement accepting full personal responsibility for not only Matteotti's murder but for all the assaults and murders committed by fascism in its conquest of power. He then challenged the opposition to use their constitutional right to use this admission as evidence for his impeachment; but no one took up the challenge, either from fear, or else assuming that the king would do all that was necessary by emerging from his cover and taking positive action as he had done in 1915 and 1922.

This, in Mussolini's opinion, was the moment when the palace lost its last chance to rescue what remained of parliamentary government.[38] The resignation of three non-fascist ministers on 5 January provided the king with a pretext and the two military ministers would certainly have resigned had it been the royal wish; which would have compelled him to appoint a new cabinet. But the monarch, who was at first angry and astonished by Mussolini's confession of guilt, let the chance slip and had another affable meeting with his chief minister. He let it be known that he disapproved of repressive measures against the press, but added 'that he did not think there was any alternative statesman who could cope with the actual situation', and protested that the calumnies of the opposition newspapers had gone much too far.[39]

Any signs of dissent were consequently disregarded. One foreign newspaper correspondent reported that the king's popularity slumped at once after his failure to take this opportunity to dismiss a self-confessed assassin and restore the rule of law; he had missed several chances to intervene, but 'if he lets it slip through his fingers and leaves it to others to bring about the fall of fascism, then, as one of the opposition leaders said to me, "the monarchy may fall with it".'[40] When he appeared in Florence, the streets suddenly emptied in silent protest, a fact that had to be concealed by the censorship. When the editors of twenty-five newspapers complained collectively to the king that he was in breach of his coronation oath, their letter was ignored and simply handed to Mussolini for a reply. Neither did Nitti receive an answer when he wrote to remonstrate that the king had often said he would abdicate rather than violate his oath to defend the liberties enshrined in the constitution. Nitti had until now kept quiet so as not to expose the monarchy for its collusion with fascism, but felt he could no longer remain silent: he accused the king of underwriting a government that had little following inside Italy while being entirely discredited abroad.[41]

From now onwards the king was almost inextricably identified with Mussolini. Fascist newspapers warned him to break off all contact with any other politicians. He never spoke to Giolitti again. Nor until 1943 did he speak to Orlando, Bonomi, or Nitti who as ex-prime ministers could without impropriety have been called upon for advice. Salandra abandoned active politics in disgust, though accepted appointment to the senate and did little to dissuade his followers from joining Mussolini. Other members of the liberal political élite quickly shifted to support the new regime. These included Boselli and Luzzatti, while Tittoni, another one-time royal favourite, became suddenly eager to confess his 'invincible repugnance' for parliamentary government.[42]

One of the former ministers who refused to surrender was Amendola. In June 1925 and again in November this staunch liberal sent protests to the palace against the continual violations of the constitution, but finally had to accept that there was no hope for Italy unless the monarchy was discarded. Repeatedly assaulted by fascist militiamen, Amendola died in 1926 of his injuries. On his death-bed he blamed the king for ruining Italy out of cowardice.[43] But only abroad could such criticisms be made in public, as they were, for example, in the United States' senate – to be met by an immediate diplomatic protest from Rome.[44]

Throughout 1925–6, Vittorio Emanuele signed a series of laws that suspended every guarantee of personal liberty. No longer would there be a right to free speech, free assembly, or a free press; no longer would citizens be equal before the law. Although in 1922 he had rejected his ministers' demand to outlaw fascism, he now approved a law suppressing all parties except fascism. The fact that he accepted from Mussolini what he had denied to prevous liberal governments was bound to seem a deliberate party-political commitment on his part. He must by now have realised that the monarchy had little chance of survival if the regime collapsed, so his choice was almost automatic.

Another law signed by the king allowed the dismissal of any civil servants 'whose views were incompatible with government policy', and this included judges. Yet another prescribed that journalists needed official approval to exercise their profession. Neither did he see any impropriety in signing an amnesty designed to release from prison prominent fascists accused of Matteotti's murder. Many years later he was criticised by the nationalist leader, Luigi Federzoni, for helping to create a fascist state and allowing his regal prerogatives to be whittled away. But Federzoni, as one of Mussolini's ministers, signed many of these very same decrees and did his best at the time to persuade foreigners 'that most Italians were sick of the claims made in the name of liberty'.[45]

Most radical of all was a law of December 1925 which with Federzoni's full approval granted almost plenary powers to Mussolini, fusing the legislature and executive in his own person, and it received the royal assent without discussion in the chamber. From now onwards no legislation could be presented to parliament without the consent of the prime minister, who was therefore able to avoid any vote of no-confidence. Henceforward cabinet ministers would by law be responsible to him rather than to parliament, and be only indirectly responsible to the crown. The chief remaining power of the monarch was to appoint a prime minister and dismiss him,[46] but for eighteen years there is no suggestion that the palace even considered using this power.

The king claimed that he had not been first consulted over most of these fundamental changes and at one point took advice from a constitutional lawyer, but was then heard to call them necessary reforms which might bring additional strength to the monarchy.[47] Less and less were his views taken into consideration. Less and less were his opinions even known by anyone outside his household. Ronald Graham, the British ambassador, commented that 'the king is generally supposed to dislike his responsibilities, and is known to shun publicity and display to an extent that must be considered unfortunate'.[48] Even the annual receptions at the palace were discontinued as he cut himself off from all nonconformists in the prefascist political class. 'The king has been immersed in a fascist bath', wrote one minister: 'I do not know how far it has washed him clean, but certainly he has been impressed by the experience'.[49]

In January 1926 some of the deputies who had boycotted parliament since Matteotti's murder made a belated attempt to return and make their voices heard, but Mussolini called this a 'provocation' against what he now called 'the fascist chamber', and the intruders were physically assaulted even inside the parliament building. The elected legislature, Mussolini explained, was no longer a place for discussion, and anyone voting against his 'fascist laws' would in future be guilty of indiscipline.[50] As a further inducement for members of parliament to conform he doubled their salaries. He also took powers to issue ministerial decrees with the full force of law. Towards the end of 1926, the hundred deputies of the irreconcilable opposition – socialists, communists, *popolari* and republicans – were simply declared to have forfeited their seats. Many years later the king said he had disapproved of this arbitrary measure, but by refusing to intervene he failed in his elementary duty,[51] and many people must have wondered if the monarchy had any purpose except as a rubber stamp upon fascist legislation.

At the end of 1926 Mussolini appointed himself minister of the interior in addition to the other six ministries he personally directed, so that he held half the posts in the cabinet. He also broke another article of the constitution by instituting a special tribunal for 'political crimes'. Its judicial bench would consist of generals, admirals and consuls of the fascist militia, all chosen by himself as minister of war: from its decisions there could be no appeal except to royal clemency, which was not forthcoming. This law bore the royal signature. So did another that introduced the death penalty, in particular for attempts on the life of either prime minister or king – a juxtaposition that underlined the existence of a diarchy in which head of government and head of state were on the same level. A further royal decree declared that the *fasces* were no longer merely an emblem of the fascist party but 'by long custom' had become a symbol of the state. Monarchist pressure, however, prevented the *fasces* from being added to the national flag.[52]

The Grand Council of the fascist leadership was also promoted into an organ of the state itself, taking precedence over the cabinet of ministers and replacing parliament as 'the constitutional organ for giving advice to the sovereign'.[53] In future the opinion of this council had to be sought on all constitutional matters, and Mussolini decreed that it should draw up a list from which the crown would eventually choose his successor. This was a further infringement of the king's power of choice. Another minor infringement was that the Grand Council had to be consulted on all future treaties with foreign governments – something that parliament had never been allowed. It was also given a role in deciding which prerogatives were retained by the crown; and most provocative of all was the statement that this directorate of the fascist party could intervene in determining who would succeed if the throne became vacant.

This last clause was more threat than reality because it was imprecisely drafted and Mussolini was obliged to admit that the king's son Umberto had an indefeasible right to the succession.[54] Nor was the Grand Council in practice ever asked to draw up any list of possible prime ministers for the future, and even fascist jurists continued to believe that the crown remained unfettered in its choice.[55] But for a few days the king held back from giving his approval to this particular law until he had consulted his legal advisers.[56] This brought him closer than he ever came again to halting the 'fascistisation' of the country, and his doubts were over regalian and dynastic rights, not over wider constitutional principles where the liberties of the subject were involved.

In 1929 Mussolini decided to consolidate his parliamentary majority by a plebiscite to sanction the existence of a *de facto* dictatorship. Elections, he said once again, were mere paper games, because any other party than his own was now illegal and he personally was in effect nine tenths of the legislature. The democratic process, he explained, wasted political energy. Fascism, on the contrary, believed in politicians being not elected but selected by those in authority, while he himself was one of those 'supermen' who elected themselves.[57] During the previous legislature, five thousand royal decrees had been presented to parliament for confirmation, of which fewer than one per cent had actually been debated, and this practice was now said to be an essentially fascist procedure since 'the chamber of deputies presupposses a world that we have demolished'.[58] For the new plebiscite there would be only one list of candidates, all hand-picked by the fascist Grand Council, and voters would be asked to accept them *en bloc*. The king instructed doubtful monarchists to vote in favour of this revolutionary electoral law since for some reason he thought that it did not damage the interests of the crown,[59] and both houses gave their approval with overwhelming majorities, even the senate, where the blackshirts were still a small minority.

Among forty senators in active opposition was Albertini who was brave enough to say that no one who had sworn an oath to uphold the constitution could approve what was tantamount to the ending of parliamentary government. Hitherto a devoted monarchist, Albertini followed Amendola in condemning the king as a traitor to his trust who would one day suffer the consequences and be called to account.[60] Giolitti registered a contrary vote a few months before his death. The king did not wish or dare to attend Giolitti's funeral, following the example of his grandfather who had avoided that of Cavour. Other fascist politicians after their demise were shown more respect and gratitude than the most distinguished prime minister of his reign.

The plebiscite by a 98.4 per cent majority returned a chamber that was 100 per cent fascist, and the king simultaneously agreed to the upper house's being packed with 130 new senators. He opened parliament with a speech praising the discipline that had caused outmoded political practices to be superseded by an original and typically Italian system of government. What he quite frankly called 'fascist Italy' was said to be ahead of every nation in social policy and in preparing a profound renewal of the country's cultural life. When he added that the chief remaining task was to increase still further the power of the state he was much applauded by parliament.[61] Mussolini, too, received applause when he told the senate that 'the Holy Sepulchre is empty; the constitution of 1848 no longer exists'. As the king privately admitted, this fraudulent plebiscite was no indication of real popular wishes. Yet paradoxically he was anxious for people to believe that, if parliament had no further function, this was not a royal decision but was the wish of the electorate. Italians, he said, had in 1848 wanted a parliamentary constitution, but now preferred authoritarianism, and his duty was to obey their wishes.[62]

Mussolini's other triumph of 1929 was to persuade the Vatican at long last to recognise the existence of Italy as a united state. Earlier in his reign the king had advocated negotiating a settlement with the Church,[63] but the pro-Austrian conduct of the Vatican during the first world war changed his mind, and in 1919 he had made one of his many threats of abdication to prevent Orlando ending this festering disagreement.[64] Still strongly anti-clerical, he used to make cynical comments about the venality of senior ecclesiastics.[65] In private conversation he showed little interest in religion, though stoutly championed the authenticity of the sacred shroud of Turin which was a relic in his family's possession.[66] In 1926 he allowed Mussolini what he had refused Orlando, to open negotiations with Cardinal Gasparri for a concordat – he liked to recall that Gasparri's brother was a shepherd on one of the royal estates.[67] In 1929 he welcomed with moderate enthusiasm the treaty and concordat with the Vatican that were one of Mussolini's most notable achievements.

6   The 'diarchy'

By 1930 Vittorio Emanuele had been edged almost entirely out of public affairs and gave little sign of being displeased. More than ever he liked to avoid ceremonial occasions because gaudy fascist festivals and uniforms were not to his taste, and anyway his presence was not much appreciated. One former minister described him as having abdicated in all but name. According to another his one remaining political concern was the survival of the dynasty. Lack of self-confidence and lack of skill at the 'representative business' were characteristics that he freely admitted.[1] Not only did he never try to meet opponents of fascism, but he no longer talked freely with ambassadors of foreign countries after they had presented their credentials: perhaps he feared that he might be trapped into indiscreet comments on the regime. Without the information provided for posterity by ambassadorial reports it now becomes even harder than before to penetrate his taciturnity and know his opinion on current events.

His isolation was all the greater because social life at court was reduced to almost nothing. Disgusted by the petty gossip of 'so-called elegant society' he had no difficulty in withdrawing to the solitude of family life; and against the frivolity of the Roman aris-tocracy he quoted Leninist dogma, that 'if a man does not work, neither shall he eat'. Hating city life, ill at ease in general conver-sation, he preferred the unsociable pleasures of fishing or reading history. He had plenty of time to indulge his passion for shooting animals, though complained that game was becoming scarce and his daily bag was down from 350 to fewer than 200 head. He tried to introduce Mussolini to the delights of the hunt, but without success.[2]

The regular meetings between these two men were, according to Mussolini, 'cordial but never friendly'.[3] The fear persisted among some monarchists that the duce might never have entirely renounced his earlier republicanism. In 1926–7 there were persistent rumours that extremist fascists were plotting another republican coup and in 1928 an attempt to assassinate the king was ascribed to such dis-sidents in the party.[4] But powerful factions inside fascism remained champions of monarchy, and Mussolini was sensible enough to value the goodwill and loyalty derived from the king's outward support; as one foreign diplomat observed, 'manifestations of de-votion to the sovereign and respect for the Church are both excel-lent political moves'.[5] Another diplomat reported in November 1927 that ministers were satisfied 'at present' with the docile self-effacement of the palace.[6] Whereas Mussolini's activities were, by order, fully treated each day on the front page of every newspaper, the king's were usually buried in the inner pages or ignored alto-gether. On some public occasions, when both men had to be present, the dictator was clearly embarrassed at having to take second place.

Some people were surprised at how Vittorio Emanuele endured the empty rhetoric, the parades, and the amateurish militarism that fascism affected. Still more were they surprised that he did not re-act against the corruption that the regime tolerated and that the British ambassador reported as pervading 'every stratum of the pub-lic administration'. Rumours about corruption, said the king, were greatly exaggerated;[7] but at least the rumours must have reached him. Though he occasionally allowed himself very private criticisms of the duce's ignorance, credulity and superficiality, outside obser-vers until the late 1930s could discern little if any of the tension between monarch and dictator that could be found in Spain.[8]

On the contrary, his basic feelings seem to have been gratitude and even admiration; or at least that is what he let people think. As Graham wrote,

His Majesty has a strong personal feeling for Mussolini. He considered him a wonderful foreign minister and declared that his minutes and the telegrams he personally drafted were far the best in His Majesty's experience since the days of San Giuliano.[9]

And the same sentiment of esteem, whether genuine or pretended, was noted by other foreign observers.[10] To General Silvio Scaroni, a trusted aide-de-camp, he spoke of Mussolini's profound honesty, generosity, lucidity of mind, and political sense;[11] but he must have known that Scaroni had once been Mussolini's personal pilot and would report these flattering comments. Another palace official described the king as 'infatuated' with a prime minister who spared him the strikes, the political in-fighting, and the frequent changes in government of previous years: on the whole, so the king explained, the country had emerged 'pretty well' out of the turbulent years of 1919–22 'when we were at the mercy of the priests and the socialists'.[12]

Another relevant indication is that, though in earlier years he had often talked of abdicating rather than act against his conscience, no such threat seems to have been made during the first fifteen years of fascism. Some people, as he knew, expected him to use this threat and thought it might have been effective in preventing erosion of the constitution. But in the fascist period he found it convenient to say that abdication would be an act of weakness and a dereliction of duty.[13]

Mussolini claimed that fascism received more than merely passive collaboration from the palace.[14] The king could speak of 'our fascist fatherland' when he might easily have avoided the adjective. He agreed to a law that made his signature necessary for the appointment of the general secretary of the fascist party, just as though this official was a state functionary. In return he regularly received the party's *foglio d'ordini*. Another very strange fact was that on at least one occasion he persuaded Starace, who was party secretary, to stage a monarchist demonstration outside the Quirinal.[15] He personally lit a votive lamp in memory of those fascist 'martyrs' who died during Mussolini's conquest of power,[16] and no other party in his reign could claim anything like that degree of acquiescence. Nor did he flinch when professors were compelled by royal decree to swear an oath of obedience not just to himself but to the fascist regime. In private conversation he sometimes revealed a positive predilection for authoritarianism and press censorship or for decisions being taken by a single person instead of wasting time in discussion and debate.[17]

Most of all he sympathised with the military pretensions of fascism. Bored by talk about art, literature and philosophy, his favourite topic of conversation continued to be military matters, and soldiers of the royal household continued to receive his closest confidences. Military traditions were for him, as for Mussolini, the most important of all in the history of any country. More than once he was quoted as saying that war and hunting were the two activities proper to a real man; and this was more than half-way towards Mussolini's belief that every nation needed to make war every twenty-five years.[18] A soldier by upbringing and predilection, he preferred to wear military uniform when his ministers brought laws for the formality of his signature.[19] He disliked the ceremonial sword that fascist regulations encouraged him to carry, because it made such a small person look awkward when mounting a horse or emerging from his automobile, but usually was pedantically punctilious about uniforms. His only recorded criticism of films – and he was proud of having possessed his own personal cinematograph as early as 1909[20] – was to list anachronistic mistakes over medals or the details of cavalry harness.

The sovereign remained nominally commander-in-chief of the armed forces, but this was another point on which fascism was determined to make inroads upon his prerogative, and decrees of June 1925 and February 1927 put the chief of general staff directly under the duce's orders. In foreign policy, too, the regal right to declare war and make peace was said by the minister of justice to have in practice lapsed,[21] another failure of theory and practice to coincide. Diplomatic documents continued to be sent in copy to the palace,[22] but this became less regular during the 1930s and was never more than a formality. It was more than symbolic when Mussolini moved the headquarters of the foreign office away from the Consulta palace adjacent to the Quirinal. Its new seat in the Palazzo Chigi gave the minister a greater sense of autonomy, and its balcony overlooked the Piazza Colonna where he could address the fascist masses with less restriction or inhibition.

There is little evidence that the king directly influenced fascist foreign policy, though he did not always like it. Sometimes he was consulted, sometimes only informed. From casual remarks we know that he approved of Mussolini's attack on Corfu in 1923;[23] and he agreed with Mussolini that the League of Nations was not only an absurd anomaly but was dangerous by reason of its domination by France and Britain who were potential enemies.[24] In February 1934 he was enthusiastic when a pro-fascist government in Austria used artillery against the socialist workers in Vienna. Indeed he called this the most important fact in fifteen years of international politics.[25] He criticised the working of democracy in France and rejoiced that fascist Italy by comparison enjoyed a more stable regime.[26] One day, so he hoped, Nice might be annexed by Italy, and so might Malta and the Italian-speaking cantons of Switzerland.[27] Almost certainly he knew from army officers of Mussolini's occasional remarks about his intention of one day making war on France and Britain,[28] and in private meetings would have advised caution. At least he wanted to postpone such a war as long as possible and was more worried than his chief minister about the extent of Italy's military unreadiness.

His government's intention to conquer Ethiopia and give him an imperial crown were hardly a secret[29] and must have been known at court. He visited Eritrea and Somalia when preparations for this war were in train. By January 1935, when he gave an assurance to the Ethiopians that Italy had no aggressive intentions,[30] he knew that plans for an aggressive war were well advanced. At first he was fearful that fighting in East Africa would be too costly and would leave Italy's Alpine frontier unguarded.[31] But later in 1935, at a time when some senior generals were becoming strongly pacifist, he accepted the inevitable 'with lively satisfaction' and encouraged Mussolini to defy a collective protest by the League of Nations.[32]

The Ethiopian war was a great success for the regime, at least in its effect on public opinion. Its initial commander, the incompetent De Bono, tried to make it a special triumph for the fascist militia, but after a few weeks had to be hurriedly replaced by officers of the regular army whose loyalty was primarily to the king. Though Prince Umberto was not allowed to take an active command, four dukes of the royal family were drafted to Ethiopia, and Umberto had no doubt that it was a legitimate war that even a Giolitti would have accepted.[33] When economic sanctions were introduced against Italy by the League, the king and queen gave their wedding rings to set a patriotic example in helping to meet the serious deficiency of foreign exchange. He contributed nine kilograms of gold to the government, and Queen Elena was seen to make the fascist salute as she publicly made her own oblation;[34] though he decided not to surrender the nest-egg savings secretly held by Hambro's bank in London.

After Marshal Badoglio entered Addis Ababa in triumph, the king in May 1936 gratefully received another crown as Emperor of Ethiopia. He even called Mussolini a military genius who had won the greatest colonial war of all time on behalf of 'our fascist fatherland'. The duce must have been pleased by this tribute though could not conceal his anger at having to share the popular applause with Badoglio and the sovereign. Subsequently Mussolini wondered once again if he should not have exploited this moment of success to depose the king and take the imperial crown for himself.[35]

In July 1936 the government could not resist the temptation to intervene in the Spanish civil war, miscalculating that this would enable General Franco to win in a matter of weeks. Vittorio Emanuele gave his approval; but not with much enthusiasm, because he feared that Italy would lose her freedom of action if she further antagonised the western democracies and was forced into a subordinate position allied with nazi Germany. His own preference was for the traditional policy of the House of Savoy, that of a makeweight in the balance of power, bartering Italy's support and playing rival groups in Europe against each other.[36] But Mussolini, as he became less in touch with reality, refused to appreciate this danger and in any case was sure that his own superior intelligence would make him the senior partner in an Italo-German alliance.

Another minor disagreement was over Mussolini's strange conviction that Franco could be persuaded to accept Duke Amedeo of Aosta as nominal sovereign of Spain.[37]Sixty years earlier the king's uncle had lasted as King of Spain for only a few months and the humiliation still rankled. When this new project failed, Amedeo was consoled by appointment as viceroy in Ethiopia and later, with some difficulty, was elevated by the propagandists into a national hero. But the king had little respect for his various cousins whom the regime sometimes tried to exploit. He had no great opinion of Amedeo. He positively disliked the Count of Turin who had the good sense to be alarmed by the invasion of Ethiopia. The Duke of Bergamo, who publicly lectured the School of Fascist Mysticism about Mussolini's being 'a man sent by divine providence', was referred to by the king as an imbecile; and the same word was used of the Duke of Pistoia who in 1937 wrote a pro-fascist article for Mussolini's personal newspaper. Nor can the palace have approved when the Duke of Genoa sent an unreservedly pro-nazi statement for publication by the journal of Dr Goebbels in Berlin.[38]

Neither did Umberto, the crown prince, enjoy the consideration at court that might have been expected. In accordance with another constant tradition of the dynasty, the heir to the throne was allowed none of the experience in public affairs that a future sovereign would need; 'in the House of Savoy we reign one at time,' said his father. Umberto was expected to conform as a disciplined soldier, just as he had to show an exaggerated deference to his father, bowing when spoken to and standing to attention, even kissing the king's hand in public.[39] Sometimes Umberto was unguarded in privately criticising the more ridiculous failings of fascism, and this was bound to annoy ministers when it became a topic of gossip.[40] At other times he could speak uncritically in the opposite sense, and after Mussolini's death protested that he had not been against fascism but merely kept the strictly impartial attitude that characterised the best tradition of constitutional monarchy.[41]

Vittorio Emanuele had a similar notion of constitutional impartiality, which he interpreted as meaning the endorsement of all government proposals while refusing to listen to any critics. Mussolini occasionally continued to express gratitude for the crown's loyalty and encouragement of fascism. At the same time he resented a potentially rival authority that he could never completely disregard or override, and he knew that a monarch who had played false to one government in 1922 might as easily betray another. He also resented that history books had been 'manipulated by the monarchists'. History would have to be re-written round a more virile and invigorating theme.[42]

Twenty years, however, was not long enough a period for change in the mentality of a whole people. In form if not substance, Italy was governed by a 'diarchy' in which loyalties were sometimes divided, even though one of the two rulers was immensely stronger than the other. Set against the Quirinal palace was the Palazzo Venezia; against the royal guard of cuirassiers were the ceremonial 'musketeers of the duce; alongside the regular army were the blackshirt brigades. The military salute favoured by the king was paralleled by the new 'Roman salute' of fascism which even army officers were often obliged to use. A new regulation also required that on public occasions the royalist national anthem had to be coupled with the fascist 'giovinezza' – after an absurd attempt to conflate the two had come to grief. The *carabinieri* or military police, owing obedience to the king, continued to co-exist with the fascist militiamen who had a quite different structure and function, and whose oath bound them to be ready to die in defence of the duce.

This division of loyalties rarely showed any sign of becoming open conflict. But the existence of underlying tension became apparent with the king's preliminary doubts about military participation in Ethiopia and Spain. After October 1936, when he was caught by surprise to learn that an 'axis' had been forged with Hitler, he let it be known in Paris that he was greatly alarmed to see Europe divided into two hostile camps – though he took care to add that the fascist government still enjoyed his full confidence.[43] Even if he lacked contact with liberals in opposition, he cannot have failed to know about renewed signs of discontent among prominent fascists with the personal dictatorship of a wilful and irresponsible leader. Though the Ethiopian war became very popular, that in Spain was much less so, and any enthusiasm was known to have been artificially amplified by official propaganda in order to prepare people for a belligerent alliance with Germany.[44] No accurate or even approximate estimate of public opinion can be made, especially as the national press could never hint at dissent, but one Canadian visitor saw women lying down on the railway tracks to prevent the movement of troops to Africa – just as Mussolini had encouraged them to do when he opposed the African war of 1911.[45] The Canadian's comments did not get past the censor, but without doubt there was much more dissent than the newspaper-reading public was allowed to know about.

Other differences of opinion between monarch and minister were the subject of current rumour, for instance about how the king had blocked Mussolini's intention to abolish the royal *carabinieri*; or how he had rejected a proposal to fuse the fascist militia with the regular army. In January 1938 these rumours were referred to by Blondel, the French chargé d'affaires, who commented that although effective power lay with the government, this might change dramatically in the event of a military defeat or a serious economic crisis. Blondel also reported that the monarchy might regain more room for manoeuvre now that there were some signs of popular disaffection against the regime.[46] Mussolini must have thought the same. In March he informed the fascist Grand Council that he would soon introduce major changes in the constitution,[47] and to his son-in-law, Count Ciano, made further angry remarks deprecating the king as a person and hinting that 'as soon as possible' he intended turning Italy into a republic.[48]

One immediate step was to establish that the effective military commander in wartime would be himself, not the king, nor the chief of staff, Marshal Badoglio. A plan to introduce this provocative constitutional novelty was prepared in 1936 and formally announced in a speech of March 1938. The same speech made a number of assertions that were most alarming since the king must have known them to be far removed from reality. One was that the wars in Ethiopia and Spain had not diminished but rather increased military potential. A second was that Italy could now mobilise over nine million men, in other words twice as many as in fact could be mobilised during the whole emergency of 1939–43. A third was that the duce spent most of each day preparing the armed forces for war.[49]

The next stage was for Mussolini to give himself a top military rank, and in order to place himself above Badoglio he invented for himself a new title as First Marshal of the Empire. The king objected that this curtailed his prerogative as commander-in-chief, apart from the fact that it was without prior consultation; indeed, he said he would have abdicated had he not feared to precipitate a political crisis.[50] A splendidly comic scene was then staged when the disciplined fascist deputies, after marching through the streets of Rome singing 'giovinezza', burst into the senate house, stealing its ornaments, ransacking its tobacco kiosk, forcing the senators to reconvene so that the new title could be approved by acclamation.[51] As a final insult, the same rank was conferred on the king himself so as to underline that the two men were virtually equal in status. No other act of fascism caused so much offence at court, except possibly the abortive attempt ten years earlier to interfere in the royal succession. The king's one threat to abdicate was over another attack on his own status, not over successive attacks against individual constitutional rights and liberties.

7 *Alliance with Germany*

Vittorio Emanuele was quoted as saying that, while fascist domestic policy might be acceptable, its foreign policy was increasingly amateurish,[1] and what chiefly worried him was the gradual drift into another alliance with Germany. Mussolini in September 1937 unexpectedly announced his 'unshakable' support of Hitler in marching together towards the fascist domination of Europe.[2] To soften the blow he sent a note to tell the king that these fierce words should not be taken too seriously. But the palace was informed in this same note that the government supported the Japanese conquest of China, and equally frightening was its simple-minded statement that fascist Italy had little or nothing to learn from Germany about rearmament and preparation for war.[3] That such nonsense could be believed by the duce was seriously alarming. Seen from the Quirinal, the Germans were not only well ahead in the arms race, but were a dangerous threat to Italy, as well as thoroughly untrustworthy. The king's anxious hope was that rearmament in Britain would accelerate so that a balance of power would be restored and any idea of fascist domination would remain an illusion.[4]

So eager was Mussolini to impress Hitler, that six months were spent earnestly embellishing the city of Rome in preparation for a state visit by the Führer to put the seal on their 'axis'. Though the king had already met Goebbels and created a good impression,[5] this would be his first and last meeting with Hitler, and was not a success. A visiting head of state had to be the guest not of Mussolini but of the Quirinal. The royal palace was therefore sumptuously redecorated at government expense just as forty years earlier for a visit by the German emperor. But on his arrival in May 1938 Hitler was indignant at having to submit to the unbearable formalities of court ceremonial,[6] and his own neurotic fetishes and supposed drug addiction were equally distasteful to his host.[7] In proposing Hitler's health at a court banquet, the king bravely referred to the firm and intimate ties that bound their countries in friendship. But in private this distinguished guest was already urging Mussolini to get rid of the monarchy as a useless drag on the regime, and some tactless remarks were overheard by members of the royal household who understood German.[8]

Cut off from the mainstream of political discussion, the king depended more than ever on a rough-and-ready system of private informers, and he also received regular reports from the *carabinieri*.[9] Perhaps what he now heard may have frightened him into an excessively subservient behaviour during the next few months. On 8 June he accompanied his queen on a visit of homage to the country cottage where Mussolini was born, and they placed flowers on the tombs of the duce's parents at Predappio: no previous minister, as newspapers noted, had ever been awarded such a tribute.[10] A few weeks later the monarch signed a series of savage racialist laws, which were then approved by acclamation in the chamber of deputies without a single dissenting voice. Mussolini was empowered by these laws to decide who were or were not Jews, and no appeal was allowed against his decision. Those designated as such lost their civil and political rights, and in addition they could be deprived of their property above a certain minimum, their children were expelled from state schools, and they were prohibited from marrying members of the 'aryan race' – whatever that might be.

The king had earlier warned Mussolini against introducing racialist legislation and until this change in policy had encouraged the government to admit foreign Jewish refugees into Italy. He was personally convinced that Italian Jews 'were entirely assimilated and were very loyal and patriotic'; they had contributed much more to national life than their small numbers suggested, and he gave precise figures showing that he knew how many Jews were generals in the army and how many had served fascism with loyalty and distinction. But on second thoughts he told Mussolini he agreed with using severity against Jewish immigrants.[11] Even though he intervened on behalf of a few individuals to mitigate the application of the racial laws, he put up less opposition than rulers of some other axis satellites.

No doubt he thought it prudent to indulge the dictator's whims while there was still some chance to avoid another world war. At the end of September he shared the general sense of relief when the two dictators met in Munich and were reported to have saved the peace of Europe at the price of sacrificing Czechoslovakia. He told Mussolini that Hitler was not as strong as people imagined and, indeed, possessed less personal authority than the duce wielded in Italy. But the Germans in his view were nevertheless dangerous bandits, worse than the British who at least could usually be trusted to keep their word. Once again he repeated that Italy needed to avoid any close alliance so that she could throw her weight on either side of any international dispute.[12] Foreign ambassadors at the end of 1938 reported that people were again turning towards the monarchy 'as a stabilising element in time of trouble' and its prestige was once more rising as that of the duce declined.[13] One ambassador noted the reaction of an audience to a newsreel of Mussolini's return from Munich; in the obscurity of a cinema there was no applause for the returning hero, but 'when the little figure of the king was then seen waiting to greet the duce at Florence railway station, the whole theatre clapped loudly'.[14]

Apart from the general public, inside the fascist movement there were some individuals, perhaps many, who hoped for a return to 'monarchist normality' and were ready to support the king if he refused to surrender his residual powers.[15] Even among those uninfected by this heresy, there was a novel sensation by the end of 1938 that fascism was becoming isolated in an indifferent or potentially hostile country. One fascist minister was ready to confess that the king, the Church, and most younger people no longer took the regime seriously; and more than one member of the fascist Grand Council was sufficiently disloyal to inform the king privately about their secret debates.[16]

How deeply this disaffection went is impossible to say, but without doubt the imminent threat of war caused a shift in opinion during the years 1938–40. The foreign minister, Galeazzo Ciano, who had no very high opinion of the monarch, was at least more of a royalist than his father-in-law, while Marshal Balbo had long since renounced republicanism and hoped that the palace would somehow assert itself against an increasingly irresponsible duce.[17] De Vecchi, another permanent member of the Grand Council, remained unshakable in his devotion to the crown.[18] Balbo, De Vecchi, Grandi, General De Bono[19] – in other words the surviving commanders of the 'march on Rome' of 1922 – all were hoping that the king would save the country by taking an initiative that they did not dare to organise themselves. 'The royal family is both popular and respected', wrote Lord Perth the British ambassador, and was widely seen as 'a more enduring element of stability than even the most gifted of dictators'.[20]

The duce strongly resented such symptoms of disloyalty or

divided loyalty. But he could not arrest or dismiss his chief colleagues because that would have impugned his wisdom and judgement in having ever appointed such men – especially since his
authority rested on the legend, 'Mussolini is always right'. He himself, when referring to the king, more than ever used contemptuous
and coarse language. He was tapping the telephones in the royal
palace, and he continued to say that both monarch and pope would
be dethroned when the time was ripe;[21] but evidently feared defeat if
he put this threat into practice too soon. His constitutional position
in relation to the crown was left vague because too much precision
might have been embarrassing. Fascist constitutional lawyers had to
accept that the king retained his right to dismiss Mussolini and was
even free to choose a non-fascist as a replacement.[22] At the same time
they agreed that constitutional monarchy had ceased to exist in May
1915,[23] yet they also agreed that the two offices, duce of fascism and
head of government (in that order), were fused by law into a single
entity; which presumably meant that the king would choose not only
the next prime minister but simultaneously the next head of the fascist party.[24] This was an unwelcome prospect to the more zealous
fascists who feared for their future.

In January 1939 another radical change was made in the constitution of 1848 by the formal abrogation of the chamber of deputies: it
would be replaced by a 'chamber of *fasci* and corporations' whose
members would be designated, not elected. This 'abolition' of parliament, as Mussolini inaccurately called it,[25] was not only accepted
by the king but unaccountably welcomed by him as a return to 'constitutional normality', and he advised senators to vote for it, once
more on the strange assumption that the prerogatives of the crown
were not involved.[26] He simultaneously agreed to pack the traditionally monarchist senate with another batch of obedient newcomers.
In March the newspapers reported 25 generals being appointed to
the senate in a bunch, and the unprecedented number of 211 new
senators were created during the course of the year, representing
almost half the total number. Fewer than forty senators remained
who were not members of the fascist party.[27]

When the new chamber of *fasci* assembled in March, its members,
no longer deputies but 'councillors', were under strict orders to wear
fascist uniform, but Balbo rebelliously defied the order and ostentatiously wore his royalist decorations, advising others to follow
suit. Councilors still had to swear an oath to be faithful to the by-
now attenuated constitution of 1848 which Mussolini had claimed to
be defunct. They also took the customary oath to the king, but
ominously omitting the normal phrase about loyalty to 'his successors'. That done, they joined in collectively singing the hymns of

the fascist revolution. Newspapers reported, whether truthfully or not, that both king and queen were sufficiently carried away on this occasion to raise their outstretched arms in the fascist salute. In his inaugural speech, written as usual by Mussolini, Vittorio Emanuele praised the government for its racial laws and for withdrawing from the 'useless' League of Nations. Immense applause greeted the passage where he stated that the armed forces of fascist Italy would soon become as strong in number and quality as those of any other nation on earth[28] – a remark that he must have known to be false.

There was little enthusiasm at court when, in April, Mussolini compensated for Hitler's occupation of Prague by moving troops into Albania. Vittorio Emanuele thought Albania an unprofitable conquest yet agreed to accept its crown for himself, displacing King Zog who had once impertinently asked for a princess of the House of Savoy in marriage. He did not much like the German move into Czechoslovakia, though admitted that in Hitler's shoes he might have acted similarly, and he now hinted that Italy ought to have her own plans for expansion.[29] She should at least be ready to annex Corsica when the right moment came. He also expressed 'an intense interest' when Mussolini told him of plans to recruit a large Ethiopian army that would help Italy to win in Africa an outlet on either the Atlantic or Indian ocean.[30] But, frightened by the mounting cost, he tried and failed to persuade Mussolini to withdraw Italian troops from Spain, later, however, acknowledging his mistake when he welcomed Franco's victory as 'a triumph of civilisation and justice'.[31]

In May Mussolini signed a formal alliance with Hitler, and a few weeks later informed the Germans that they could rely one hundred per cent on Italy's readiness to fight whenever the Führer decided that the time had come for war against the west.[32] The king was given a copy of this astonishingly irresponsible message. He later said untruthfully that the Pact of Steel was made without consulting or even informing him.[33] Certainly it was never formally ratified by the monarch, a fact that rendered it legally invalid;[34] nevertheless, he had to send a telegram to tell Hitler that he sincerely welcomed the alliance as a sign of the 'profound community of interests' between their two countries.[35] Treaties, as he had once remarked, were only worthless bits of paper.

His genuine thoughts must be guessed rather than known with any certainty. Some people were informed that he still secretly detested the Germans. Yet he was perhaps equally sincere in letting it be thought that he despised as well as detested the French – though he sent a private and almost desperate plea to Paris for help in preventing Italy from being sucked into total dependence on Berlin.[36]

One of his English fishing companions had recently been warned not to rely on France which was on the verge of a social revolution.[37] But English politicians were also criticised at court as being 'pigs' for having short-sightedly left him in the lurch by not rearming fast enough and by not agreeing to appease Mussolini with territorial concessions while there was yet time.[38]

Outwardly conformist towards the regime, inwardly the king was sufficiently alarmed by the threat of war to take a few tentative steps towards recovering some of his independence, and with this in mind appointed a more active and younger person as minister in charge of the royal household. His choice was Count Pietro Acquarone, a rich man of affairs who, as well as looking after the royal finances, tried to win for the Quirinal a more autonomous political role.[39] Acquarone was a member of the fascist party, but his public adulation of the duce as a great military genius[40] was overlaid by a devotion to the crown, and as an economist he knew that fascism was pushing the country close to bankruptcy.

Dino Grandi was another dedicated but partially disillusioned fascist who moved nearer to the palace in the hope of avoiding an irretrievable international catastrophe. As minister of justice from 1939 to 1943, Grandi had to countersign royal decrees, and his anomalously concurrent job as Speaker of the chamber of *fasci* placed him very close to the centre of power. Some people even thought that he hoped one day to displace Mussolini as leader of a more benevolent and less totalitarian version of fascism. In June 1939 Grandi was warned by the king that there were storms ahead and he should use his central position to work towards a restoration of the old balance in the constitution; if possible he should use his legal expertise to ensure that future legislation was not quite what the duce intended. Mussolini prided himself on keeping up a regular average of fifty decisions an hour and notoriously used to sign documents without reading them, which meant that he was very easily disobeyed and deceived.[41] Grandi was told to remain closely in touch with the Quirinal and keep the crown informed of how, if necessary, it could act.[42] In reply, at least according to his own unreliable memoirs, Grandi told the king that Italians were unanimous in disliking the fascist dictatorship, and he added – most remarkable of all – that even among the hand-picked members of the lower house of parliament a majority was eagerly waiting for 'an act of force' by the king to block Mussolini's war policy.[43]

As Speaker of the *camera*, Grandi was in the best position to know this crucial fact and, if true, it provided the necessary pretext for reasserting royal authority. Vittorio Emanuele had in 1922 supported a fascist revolution against his ministers by claiming that a majority of Italians backed Mussolini. If the majority now thought differently he had a chance to show if that explanation had been sincere or a mere pretence. But the expectant majority waited in vain for any action. From watching the recent summer manoeuvres, and from more than thirty inspections that he had personally made, he knew that Mussolini's much-vaunted army was in a 'pitiful' state and quite unable to engage in a serious war; but he preferred to stay well out of the way where no one could ask him to intervene.

Late in August, a few days before the Germans precipitated a European war by invading Poland, William Phillips, the ambassador of the United States, travelled urgently to one of the royal hunting lodges in the Alps. He there delivered a personal message from President Roosevelt begging the Italian head of state to use his influence for peace, only to be told in reply that a constitutional sovereign had no power to overrule his ministers; and the conversation was immediately changed to the subject of seven hundred trout that the royal couple had just caught.[44] The king cannot have forgotten that in October 1922 he had overruled a unanimous cabinet of ministers, but evidently had no wish to repeat the experiment.

On the contrary, he was observed to be greatly annoyed by Roosevelt's attempt to involve him personally,[45] even though he frankly admitted to agreeing with Grandi that 'not a single person in Italy wanted war' – and he repeated the words 'not one person'.[46] Foreign correspondents in Rome who reported that he was thought to favour neutrality had their despatches stopped or 'adjusted' by another American who had recently taken Italian citizenship and worked in the fascist censorship.[47] Phillips returned to Rome reflecting that the king was 'a mere puppet, and not even a decorative one at that'; this brief and frustrating conversation was

> an admission of his own feeble character and the helpless position he occupied under fascism. It was tragic to find Italy's sovereign so completely, and so contentedly, isolated in his mountain retreat when events were rushing to their dreadful climax.[48]

Some people thought that the outbreak of hostilities came just in time to prevent Mussolini from turning Italy into a republic.[49] His war policy had been pure bluff, and now that this bluff was called he dared not add to his acute embarrassment by either joining the war or breaking with the monarchy.[50] If the democracies refused to fight, he would of course be glad to support Germany and obtain some 'booty', but if serious war began, he intended to break free 'honourably' from the axis, perhaps on the plea that the Pact of Steel had never been ratified. He wrote to spell out this alternative to the king.[51] Perhaps if his letter had arrived a few days earlier the interview with Phillips might have had a different result. Mussolini knew by now that members of the Grand Council, in other words the collective wisdom of the fascist party, were almost unanimous in demanding neutrality. Equally pacific, according to the chief of police as well as Grandi and the king himself, was public opinion. Paris and London both received information that not only the royal court, but Ciano, Badoglio, Balbo, and Grandi were all strongly for peace, and 'many people state openly that their only hope of salvation lies in the certainty that the king will not allow them to be butchered for the benefit of the Germans'.[52]

The monarchy was still recognised by fascist constitutional lawyers as possessing more than merely formal powers as the supreme organ in the constitution, and at no time since Matteotti's murder could it have more easily used these powers to dismiss Mussolini. Never since 1924–5 had the regime looked so vulnerable, if not moribund.[53] Whether from cowardice, insensibility, or simply lack of self-confidence, or because he trusted Mussolini (that 'very great man' as he described him to Sumner Welles), or merely from love of a quiet life and dislike of taking responsibility, the king refused to consider what even some fascist leaders accepted, namely that their regime was crumbling and his intervention might have been decisive, perhaps easy.[54] Even abdication, which he had so often threatened in the past, would have had a tremendous effect at this moment. By his own confession he was not much attached to the throne, and his brother sovereign, Edward VIII, had abdicated for much less. But the rumour that he was about to step down was quickly denied,[55] and most of those who were looking to him for leadership assumed that he must have good reasons for doing nothing at all; hence they had better follow his example of conformism.

Germany invaded Poland early in September 1939, just before his seventieth birthday. When Britain and France declared war he was greatly relieved that Italy remained neutral, though embarrassed to imagine that, as in 1914–15, he was assumed to be waiting only to join whichever of the two belligerent groups would win.[56] According to the British ambassador, he would rather abandon the throne than declare war against the western democracies, especially after Hitler's recent pact with Stalin: 'the mass of the population is sick of the regime', wrote Loraine, and 'would not care two straws about a "betrayal" of Germany; on the contrary it would welcome it with a deep sigh of relief'.[57] After a few weeks, however, the king accepted that Hitler would probably be victorious, which would mean the disappearance of Poland and Belgium, and he agreed with Mussolini that there was no room for small nations in an axis-dominated Europe.[58]

One personal initiative was to repair some broken fences with that other great neutral power, the Vatican. On 21 December he sufficiently overcame his anti-clerical feelings to pay a state visit to the pope, the first such visit for many years, and insisted that royal prestige would demand a return visit to eliminate any suspicion of deference or subordination on his part. There was some anxiety in the Vatican that he might omit to make the sign of the cross or kneel at the proper moment, but he behaved with perfect decorum and merely asked that there should be a handshake instead of any undignified kissing of the papal ring.[59]

The return visit was even more momentous because Pius XII would have to be received at the Quirinal, a former papal palace which had been seized by force and secularised in 1870. Appearances were saved once again and the ecclesiastical press reported that the king made as if to kiss the sacred ring but Pius by a gracious gesture restrained him. Another concession was that the pontiff was then placed between the royal couple on a throne which at least appeared higher than theirs.[60] Mussolini was not present on either occasion; nor can he have been much pleased by this demonstration of independence and neutrality, especially when the pope took the opportunity to speak against German aggression.

5
The End of the Monarchy

1 Italy drifts into war

Italy remained neutral or, rather, non-belligerent for eight months until June 1940, during which critical period the king was his usual reticent and enigmatic self except with a chosen few. A senior general received the impression that he was anti-German, anti-British, anti-French, even anti-Italian, but was clinging to a desperate belief in Mussolini as an expert politician who would find the correct course of action.[1] Of his opposition to Germany he made no concealment in conversation with the foreign minister, Count Ciano, who fully shared his distrust and hostility. Queen Elena, when talking to her Spanish friends, spoke more in favour of Germany, but Umberto supported his father in fearing that the axis alliance might be leading Italy to destruction.[2] In London there was a continuing belief or hope that the House of Savoy would somehow succeed in remaining neutral.[3]

By mid-March 1940 the king could no longer doubt that his government meant to join the Germans as soon as their victory seemed certain, and at last he told one other person that he would intervene 'energetically' to stop this happening.[4] But he reiterated his demand to be covered by some plausible constitutional excuse. In the absence of a free parliament he therefore sent Acquarone to meet Ciano at their golf club in order to ask for another discussion and vote by the fascist Grand Council. That, evidently, would be enough to justify using his veto, because this council was 'a constitutional organ of the state' as well as 'the supreme collegial organ of the fascist party'.[5] Almost certainly he already knew that at a recent meeting of the grand councillors there had been royalist and anti-war interventions by Balbo, De Bono, and De Vecchi, the three most senior members after Mussolini himself, and Acquarone after taking soundings confirmed once again that in a free vote there would be a clear majority against Mussolini – precisely what happened three years later when it was too late to save Italy from catastrophe.[6]

By law the council could assemble only at the duce's request and with an agenda composed by himself. But the king possessed one trump card: his formal approval was necessary for any declaration of war, and he had every right to ask that the Grand Council should first give its advice. For some reason he backed away from his initial decision to take this elementary precaution, only to lay the blame subsequently on members of the Grand Council for failing to insist on a meeting.[7]

No doubt they like himself lost their nerve when a succession of great German victories produced a general sense of triumph or at least resignation. Ciano continued to believe that the king had a duty to take the initiative, and let the Vatican know that he agreed with the chief of police about the likelihood of popular revolution if war was declared.[8] But the duce relied on the presumption, as Loraine reported, that the blackshirt militia would fight in obedience to whatever decision he took, and 'the immense army of bureaucrats created by the regime have every reason to dread its fall'.[9] On 31 March Mussolini informed the palace that the western powers might soon surrender, in which case Italy would gladly take her booty without having to fight; otherwise it was best to wait until hostilities were virtually over and then declare war so as to obtain Corsica, Malta, Tunisia, Gibraltar, and Suez. The generals were told that the king entirely agreed with this policy.[10] A few days later, to confirm his full confidence in the duce, Vittorio Emanuele paid a much publicised visit to the office in Milan where Mussolini had planned the fascist conquest of power. Newspapers saw this as another spontaneous act of devotion and pilgrimage, and no doubt it helped to persuade some of the waverers to renew their allegiance to the regime at this crucial moment.[11]

Four years later the king protested that he himself at no point wavered in his objection to entering the war,[12] and it must be agreed that he never had much active enthusiasm for fighting. Yet in June 1940 he gave his consent to a declaration of war after being convinced that a quick victory was assured. Nor was this a casual decision on his part, because we know that he acted only after very carefully considering the alternatives and possible consequences.[13] He knew that, as well as the Grand Council, the senior military authorities – Marshals Balbo, Caviglia, Badoglio, and De Bono – were against fighting. So was the foreign minister, Ciano. The Viceroy of Ethiopia, Amedeo of Aosta, personally told him that war would be suicidal because it could not be won, and this was also the opinion of the chief of general staff who must have known better than anyone.[14] Nitti, Sforza, and Prince Doria wrote to warn him of the terrible consequences of fighting, and Cardinal Schuster took him a personal plea from the pope – all the more significant since both these clerics strongly supported much of fascist domestic policy.[15]

His own explanation of why he refused this advice is unconvincing. It suited him to argue that a constitutional sovereign was powerless, despite the fact that in the past he had been glad to take credit for overruling ministers when he thought this was in the national

interest. According to his family and friends he justified his momentous decisions of May 1915, October 1922, and June 1940 by claiming
that in each case he was carrying out the wishes of public opinion;[16]
in May 1940 he once again admitted that the 'overwhelming majority of Italians' was against war, despite which his chief concern at
that moment was not so much whether but when to fight.[17] Public
opinion can of course only be guessed at, but reputable authorities
have concluded that at this point the king could have got rid of
Mussolini and Italians would have accepted this almost unanimously
with delight.[18]

Whether or not this is correct, other alleged explanations of his
conduct are equally unpersuasive. One was that Hitler would invade
Italy if she refused to fight. But Hitler would have had nothing to
gain from an invasion and already had enough on his plate without
occupying another country of forty million people. Many Germans
in any case calculated that Italy could help them much more as a
neutral than as a partner in fighting,[19] apart from which they cannot
have wanted at this critical stage in the war to make an enemy of
their most useful ally in Europe. Nor is there much force in the
king's claim that he gave way in order to preserve the monarchy as a
counter-weight to fascism, because he must have known that the
throne would not survive a nazi-fascist victory. Nor is he likely to
have acted merely in the hope of making territorial acquisitions,
because by the end of May the western powers offered to discuss the
cession of territory without any need for Italy to fight.

Whatever his reasons, by his own later admission he miscalculated,
so contributing to the collapse of the monarchy and much else
besides. Mussolini wanted war above everything, even if it meant
the 'destruction of all civilised values';[20] he wanted war for its own
sake, because he held the strange belief that 'nothing else conferred
true nobility on a nation'. Such statements had so often been quoted
that it was hard for the duce to back down with dignity once
the Germans showed every sign of having soundly defeated the
other armies of Europe. In supporting him the king became an
unenthusiastic but necessary and ultimately willing accomplice.

Their joint responsibility is all the more grave in that the Italian
armed forces were unready; indeed, General Spigo who headed the
Supreme Defence Committee said they were more unready than at
the beginning of World War I, and the king knew this since it was
one aspect of policy in which he directly interested himself by means
of frequent inspections. But he could not agree that the general
public had any right to know such vital facts, not even about
mistakes made in long-past campaigns where the royal prerogative
as supreme military commander might be exposed to question. The

government relied on deceit rather than publicity; it needed to deceive the outside world into thinking that Italy had ten or even twelve million soldiers fully equipped to fight. And this piece of implausible bluff had tragic results, especially since Mussolini was deluding himself rather than anyone else. The king was therefore consciously gambling when he agreed to fight. He better than anyone must have known that his chief minister was basing policy on either deliberate deceit or unpardonable ignorance.

Perhaps it was both. He had been told by Mussolini himself that the partial mobilisation carried out in September 1938 and September 1939 revealed an astonishing lack of discipline and organisation. The British, French, and German intelligence services were aware that, just as in 1915, the Italian artillery was grossly insufficient, yet Mussolini confessed ignorance of this fact despite having been for ten years the minister responsible for all three armed forces. He proudly boasted that his air force was the strongest and most modern in the world, though in practice he almost never visited his ministerial office at the air ministry: he had to be told by the king that, as foreign governments knew and so did his own air force staff, this was another empty boast. Mussolini also relied on his own amateurish intuition to claim that the Italian navy was in a perfect state of readiness and could exclude the British navy from the Mediterranean, but neither the naval staff nor the king shared his confidence, and British experts with no doubt excessive optimism reported that 'the Italian navy was in a deplorable condition both from the point of view of material and personnel'.[21]

Few people at the time or subsequently have challenged the assumption that army and navy rated loyalty to the throne above loyalty to fascism,[22] and this assumption must have entered into the king's calculations. Mussolini admitted having tried to 'fascistise' the army, and also admitted having failed as a result of resistance by the palace.[23] The royal *carabinieri* continued to retain a degree of independence and the fascists never succeeded in fusing the army with the blackshirt militia. Where they partially succeeded was in promoting many senior army officers for political rather than military reasons, though Mussolini eventually accepted that this not only weakened the army's efficiency but contributed towards creating disaffection among the more proficient and professional commanders. By taking the rank of marshal he caused considerable offence among regular officers who had known him as a corporal and sergeant in the first world war, and one result was a growing lack of enthusiasm among the generals after 1938.[24]

Marshal Badoglio in fifteen years as chief of general staff was allowed to do very little to make preparations for war, and his advice was rarely even sought. This was the man who three years later was chosen by the king to succeed Mussolini. In 1940 Badoglio knew as well as anyone that the army had no offensive capability, but never seriously considered resigning when war was declared. Unfortunately for Italy he was a dedicated careerist who lacked initiative or backbone. He notoriously enjoyed the largest salary of any of Mussolini's colleagues and ingratiated himself with the duce by inaccurately and irresponsibly stating that the Italian armaments' industry was 'in every field more advanced than the German'.[25] Mussolini had learnt to despise Badoglio, as he seems to have despised most of the other generals, and was determined that neither they nor the king should claim credit for the easy military victory that he now expected. He intended to take the supreme military command into his own hand, and even expected people to believe that this additional job on top of his many other responsibilities would require no more than the help of a single secretary.[26] Once again he was unwilling to confront his sovereign face to face with such a revolutionary proposal, so sent a subordinate with a request that the king might take the initiative of suggesting this radical diminution of the royal prerogative.

Only once, when Mussolini appointed himself a marshal, had the king ever been so angry with his minister, and his anger was not over joining the war so much as over diminishing the authority of the crown. He held out for two weeks, finally and reluctantly agreeing on a compromise by which he would delegate enough of his powers for Mussolini to command the troops 'in combat', but refusing to register this limited concession in a formal decree. Here was another issue where some people objected that he failed in his duty and should have threatened to abandon the throne rather than give way.[27] Mussolini also objected, but for the very different reason that other ministers could now see from this partial and tardy royal consent that the fascist dictatorship was less than total. Though he did not dare to challenge the king's decision at this critical moment, he reacted in private by repeating that the monarchy was 'an absurd anachronism' which would soon be removed.[28]

War against France and Britain was declared on 10 June and Mussolini was able to say that the king, if he had truly disapproved, would have been in duty bound to refuse his assent.[29] Prince Umberto dared to hint at using the royal veto, for which he incurred a stonily silent rebuff from the sovereign; and Umberto in retrospect made the illuminating comment that his father was too much under Mussolini's spell to realise that public opinion was more royalist than fascist.[30] The king explained his own decision by saying that France and Britain had by how been defeated, which left Italy no option if she wanted a share of the spoils. Nor would he need to make more than a merely token military demonstration. Any further delay would permit the British to sign a compromise peace with Hitler and inherit parts of the French empire that by rights should fall to Italy.[31]

On 10 June a well-rehearsed crowd gathered outside the Palazzo Venezia, whence it moved to the Quirinal to greet the king as he appeared on the balcony in marshal's uniform surrounded by his family. In a patriotic proclamation to the troops he spoke as supreme head of the armed forces who had entrusted Mussolini with practical direction of the war. The following day he moved to the north-western frontier where Umberto, at the king's request, commanded the army group that would spearhead the attack on an already defeated France. But immediately they were embarrassed by Mussolini's extraordinary and contradictory orders. The instructions were to remain strictly on the defensive so as to avoid any chance of a military reverse, because Mussolini needed to keep Italian forces intact while Hitler completed his victory. Yet they must not let it appear that they were waiting to attack a defeated enemy, because such an attack would be entirely alien to the fascist sense of fair play.[32] Only on 20 June, too late for any military success and several days after the French had requested an armistice, did Mussolini realise his mistake in timing and decide to risk a full offensive.

Vittorio Emanuele briefly set foot on French soil, but Umberto's forces were ill-equipped and caught unprepared by this sudden change of plan, so that they made almost no headway before the French capitulated. Mussolini met Hitler on 18 June and was offered Nice, Corsica, Jibuti, Tunisia, and the right to occupy much of southern France, but turned these offers down in a quixotic gesture that he later regretted. The king was merely informed of this strange refusal without his views being solicited, and was inaccurately told that the Germans were to blame for it. He himself would have preferred to occupy at least the Rhône valley; he was against actually annexing Savoy, but wanted Nice and Corsica, and realised unlike Mussolini that the Tunisian port of Biserta should have been occupied as an absolutely essential key to supremacy in the Mediterranean.[33]

Whereas this nominal victory over the French gave him real pleasure, he reacted to the imminent defeat of Britain with mixed feelings which included both surprise and compassion.[34] He was even suspected by cynical fascists of secretly hoping for a British victory since he distrusted the Germans and much of his 'immense wealth' was on deposit in London.[35] But in fact as a patriotic Italian he looked forward to a speedy occupation of Egypt and a successful invasion of England.[36] At a meeting of the Italian Academy, having listened to a lecture describing the epic beauty of British cities engulfed by fire after bombing by Italian planes, he leapt to his feet to lead the audience in a standing ovation.[37] Certainly, he had more sense than to share the euphoria of his chief minister who absurdly claimed that the longer the war continued the better for Italy, since her booty would be the greater. Mussolini now confessed in triumph to Umberto's wife that 'war alone makes life worth living', but such remarks were greeted with some derision in the royal palace.[38]

Since the fascists were planning to abolish the monarchy when the war was over, they were eager to prevent the royal family sharing the laurels of victory. Umberto was detailed to command an attack on Jugoslavia in the summer of 1940,[39] but the project was cancelled, and thereafter, perhaps fortunately but to his own displeasure, he was given little to do. Newspapers were ordered to drop even their minimal reporting of the king's activities.[40] No publicity was given to his fortnightly meetings with the chief of staff and the undersecretary for war.[41] Ministers continued to bring or send laws for the royal signature, but to the general public he was more than ever King Log, and though Mussolini must have kept him informed in their private meetings, no documentary evidence suggests that his views on strategy or major appointments were sought, still less acted upon.

Another moment when he might have reasserted himself came at the end of 1940 when a series of catastrophic mistakes was made over the invasion of Greece and a hundred thousand troops were forced to surrender in North Africa. Nothing hitherto had so shown up the fraudulence and incapacity of the regime and its leader. Some senior fascists and military commanders realised from the incredible reverse at the hand of the small Greek army that the duce was incompetent to direct a continuance of the war, while most Italian families must at last have learnt from soldiers at the front that fascist propaganda had no correspondence with the truth. Among German generals there was a growing conviction that the regime was on the edge of collapse. There was talk of a possible coup by officers in the army, and the king received further information to suggest that he would receive overwhelming support if as commander-in-chief he now revoked his delegation of military authority.[42]

But there is no indication that he gave the matter much thought, and perhaps he assumed that he was well out of it. He, too, had earlier been deluded into thinking that the Greeks would collapse immediately before the might of fascist Italy; after which he had hoped that his army would proceed to invade Switzerland, which was another of those small nations that would be anachronistic in a fascist Europe.[43] He keenly felt the humiliation of defeat by the soldiers of such a small country as Greece, and refused to support Badoglio when the latter was punished by demotion from his post as chief of staff. Instead he expressed confidence that Mussolini would weather this storm as he had weathered others in the past.[44] Yet he must have known that some people believed the war to have been unpopular from the beginning.[45] Alternatively it may have been only this defeat that started to make it generally unpopular. By January 1941 he began to think that the Germans would lose the war and it would be wise to bring his own armies back home to withstand a possible British invasion.[46] He admitted to General Puntoni that Mussolini's prestige had been greatly damaged, but there was no obvious replacement, and any false move by the crown might leave the way open to a republican faction that had powerful supporters inside the fascist party as well as among the anti-fascist opposition.[47]

2   *The regime disintegrates*

In the spring of 1941, after the Germans moved unwillingly into the Balkans to restore Italy's position, the king was permitted to visit his soldiers at the front, once in Jugoslavia, once in Albania where he survived another assassination attempt.[1] He was dismayed by what he saw of his government's brutal imperialism in Dalmatia, Slovenia, and Montenegro, because he had the sense to recognise that this would impose impossible burdens on Italy and gratuitously create new enemies. Before long a quarter of the Italian army was needed to quell a popular insurrection in this huge area at a time when there was a desperate need to concentrate all available resources against the British in North Africa. He resisted the suggestion that he should replace his father-in-law and become king of Montenegro.[2] But in May he had to allow his much-despised cousin, Aimone, to receive a newly invented crown of Croatia as King Tamislav II; the unfortunate prince, whom Mussolini called a mental defective, never visited his Balkan kingdom. In the same month Aimone's elder brother, Amedeo, duke of Aosta, surrendered what was left of the Italian empire in East Africa.

The shock produced by these events was considerable. Marshal De Bono spoke again of a possible monarchist coup against the regime[3] and other members of the fascist Grand Council shared his distress.[4] The venerable Marshal Caviglia went so far as to say that nearly all Italians were not only reconciled to losing the war but would welcome the prospect.[5] Grandi, the minister of justice, was additionally upset by Mussolini's 'anti-bourgeois' campaign against 'our class': fascism, said Grandi, was dying by its own hand and its leader ought to be removed before more damage was done.[6] What particularly offended Grandi was that he and other senior cabinet ministers were suddenly drafted to military duties in Albania, because Mussolini spitefully invoked an earlier fascist law which prescribed that all members of parliament 'of whatever age or physical disability' would be compelled to enjoy the 'privilege' of fighting with the front-line troops.[7] The duce had no need of ministerial colleagues in Rome.

No doubt the critics exaggerated, but a foreign newspaper correspondent in Rome confirmed that Mussolini after his defeat in Greece could count on the loyalty 'of scarcely more than a few hundred Italians'.[8] Such criticisms must have been known to the king, especially as Caviglia and Grandi were among the few people outside his immediate household who had any chance to talk with him. Information arrived regularly from the *carabinieri* – his private police force as the fascists called them[9] – and from a few senators, industrialists, and churchmen who also had occasional right of access. Even some members of the fascist party let him know that public opinion looked to him for a lead.[10]

Seldom had his aides seen him so worried. Yet it was not in his nature to lead, or work actively to mitigate the damage. Though he could accept in theory the need for making indirect contact with the enemy in case a compromise peace was possible, he made another of the great mistakes of his reign by refusing his chance when an emissary arrived from Roosevelt to set up such a contact in the Vatican.[11] Meanwhile, as the king knew, the Germans were gradually infiltrating Italy. They even had a contingency plan to seize the sovereign, that 'acid and untrustworthy little man' as Hitler called him, whose monarchist 'gang' was thought in Berlin to be under-mining fascism and the war effort.[12] Vittorio Emanuele had no confidence in the capacity of General Cavallero, especially when this new chief of staff could not even persuade the three armed services to drop their mutual jealousies and work together. He also feared that over-ambitious generals were trying to win promotion by persuading a credulous and impulsive Mussolini to disperse limited military resources over an ever-widening field of action.[13] He must have been appalled to hear Mussolini's glib and presumably unserious remark that the war, which had been expected to last only weeks, might continue for six years or more. The duce, he sadly commented, 'looks on events as a journalist, not as a military leader'.[14]

The truth of this judgement was confirmed in June 1941 when Mussolini extended his commitments still further by declaring war on Russia and warning that he soon expected to be fighting the

United States as well. The king was merely informed and was in time only to advise against sending more than a token force to eastern Europe[15] – advice that was not taken. A few weeks later a senior general of the *carabinieri* sent word to the palace that the military police were waiting for a royal order to act against fascism; also that the ordinary civilian police under their chief, Carmelo Senise, could be relied on to support such action. In September, however, when the foreign minister Count Ciano gave his opinion to the king that fascism was doomed, the latter was merely disgusted by what he called disloyalty and unwarrantable defeatism.[16]

Vittorio Emanuele had hoped and expected that America would not enter the war, but in December the Japanese attack on Pearl Harbour was greeted by him without evident displeasure. On the contrary, he hoped that hostilities would thereby be diverted towards the Far East, so relieving some of the pressure on Italy.[17] None of his earlier scruples seems to have surfaced when on 11 December he agreed to a declaration of war against the United States. According to one journalist he was so much under Mussolini's influence as to be entirely identified with the regime and was therefore earning the contempt of many of his subjects. His feebleness, wrote Marshal Caviglia, was shocking, even criminal; unwilling to abdicate, unwilling to raise a finger to save his country, his chief priority appeared to be saving his throne.[18]

Throughout 1942, while the fortunes of war went this way and that, everyone waited either for Mussolini to regain charge of military events and behave more realistically, or else for someone to take the lead in displacing him. The longest-serving cabinet minister, Giuseppe Bottai, joined those who spoke very strongly against Mussolini in private. The chief of police meanwhile kept in touch with court officials and with some of the more realistic elements in the army in case it might be possible or necessary to give a new direction to affairs.[19] Grandi, too, by his own account begged Vittorio Emanuele once again to end the dictatorship and withdraw from the war, only to be greeted by such anodyne remarks as 'trust your king', and 'stop speaking like a mere journalist'. Grandi told Ciano that the sovereign must be crazy or senile if he remained so passive while the country was drifting towards its ruin, whereas Bottai, more honestly, blamed himself and his ministerial colleagues for not having resigned in June 1940.[20]

What seemed to confound the pessimists and justify the king were the victories of Rommel's Afrika Korps in the summer of 1942. But in November came two major defeats in Egypt and Stalingrad, followed by the landing of a large enemy force in Morocco and Algeria. After a comparable set-back in 1917 the king had not hesitated to dismiss Cadorna, but he now turned a deaf ear when further direct appeals to intervene arrived from Admiral Baistrocchi and General Scuero who was Mussolini's junior minister at the war office.[21]

The Italian armed services were by long tradition averse from political intervention, but the duce was so ill and incapacitated that the chief of general staff, who was no anti-fascist, made private preparations late in 1942 to dislodge him and restore royal authority. To which the king's reaction once again was to suggest that not Mussolini but the evidently disloyal generals should be replaced.[22] At the much the same time, Marshals Badoglio and Caviglia, both of them retired from active service, sent word to London via Switzerland that they might support a military coup and make peace.[23] Badoglio told his friends that he was ready to take Mussolini's place if ordered to do so by the king. Other possible candidates were said to be Caviglia, Grandi, Ciano, and Federzoni; and once again there were rumours of either a voluntary or forced abdication.[24]

The king, however, let it be known that he still trusted Mussolini. Clearly he was too prudent to emerge from his cover and take more than tentative steps to find any alternative answer. His immediate reaction to bad news, as always, was to appear optimistic and let the critics talk while giving no indication of his own mind.[25] He knew by now that he had been deceived by the rhetoric of a regime that was far more inefficient, corrupt, and divisive that he had imagined. But he continued to keep up appearances as though he himself remained firmly loyal to fascism[26] and was evidently pleased when his army proceeded in November to the 'liberation' of Corsica from French rule: without Corsica and Nice, he said, 'Italy would remain incomplete'.[27] No longer after mid-1942[28] did he repeat his wish to annex part of Switzerland. He strongly criticised the British for what he called their barbarous naval bombardment of Genoa, perhaps forgetting his own air raids on Britain. As well as expressing esteem for Marshal Pétain, who was his opposite number in German-occupied France, he continued to say, possibly without much inner conviction, that Italy would eventually win the war with the help of secret weapons; and he persuaded himself that the Vatican was bound to support the axis powers in their fight against Jews, bol-sheviks, and protestants.[29]

During the last months of 1942, Mussolini was too ill to take any constructive initiative and had to cancel most of his customary meetings with the king. The latter was ready to say that Italy must somehow 'make peace with honour', but in practice could do little more than advise bringing back Italian troops from Russia and seeking some kind of contact with Washington and London.[30] On

Ciano's instructions the Italian ambassador in Lisbon tried to discover from British intelligence services what terms might be on offer; his instructions were to use the argument that allied bombing attacks on Italy might lead to a left-wing revolution which in turn might result in deposition of the monarchy, and the western allies should help to avert such a disaster.[31]

Another move, with the knowledge of Umberto and so presumably of the king, was taken by the feckless Aimone of Aosta who sent a message through the Italian consulate at Geneva to ask London if the western allies would guarantee a continuance of the monarchy in return for Italy's making peace.[32] In October Umberto was promoted to the rank of marshal, and Mussolini reassured the Germans that both the prince and his father were loyal to fascism and the German alliance.[33] The new marshal had earlier been disappointed at the rejection of his father's request that he be appointed to command Italian troops in Russia. Instead he had been given an army group in southern Italy that included a force being trained for the invasion of Malta.[34] But the defeats of Stalingrad and El Alamein forced him, for the first time and very tentatively, into partisan politics.

His wife, the Princess Marie José of Belgium, was the only member of the royal family who, even before these battles, kept some contact with the anti-fascist opposition inside Italy. She was in touch with communists as well as conservatives, and already in September had sought to make contact on her own initiative with Americans and British through the Vatican.[35] The king strongly resented any intervention in public affairs by his son or daughter-in-law. As an anticlerical he also could not bring himself to accept the Vatican as an intermediary. Above all, he was a dogmatic anti-feminist who believed that women lacked men's intelligence and should be completely excluded from matters of state.[36] Unfortunately for Italy and the monarchy, he was too cynical and narrow-minded to realise that Marie José showed far more intelligence and political realism than he did himself, and her courageous initiative was blocked by a royal veto.

In January 1943, after Italian forces were driven out of Libya, Mussolini as usual disclaimed any personal responsibility for this major set-back and reverted to the traditional excuse of previous wars by blaming the army's lack of fighting spirit. Others knew better. In Rome there was further expectation that the king would be compelled by the defeat to appoint an alternative military government.[37] According to the minister of the royal household, who knew his master's mind as well as anyone, there was no insuperable difficulty in effecting such a palace revolution. But the king kept putting it off.[38] Subsequently he said that he decided in January 1943 to get rid of Mussolini, but this lacks any corroboration whatsoever.[39] At the time he continued to insist that as a constitutional sovereign he could not override his ministers. Nor would he personally take the responsibility of suing for peace; indeed, he still apparently supported Mussolini's view that Italy had nothing to gain from a compromise peace and ought to keep the war going as long as possible.[40]

Whether he meant this, or possibly was trying to evade responsibility and postpone a decision, cannot be known. What he could legitimately claim was that by doing nothing he at least remained on the throne and so kept alive the possibility of a non-revolutionary end to fascism in the future. Yet by refusing to speak out he paralysed (or provided another alibi for) those generals and loyal monarchists who might have led a rebellion, and for this he has been frequently blamed.[41] Acquarone rather blamed everyone else for lacking the courage and independence of mind to create a constitutional excuse for royal intervention;[42] but what kind of excuse is hard to identify.

Since the Grand Council and the *camera dei fasci* remained shut, Acquarone took soundings among individual senators and found a large majority in favour of some royal initiative. At least six senators, perhaps at his prompting, visited the king and asked him to assert his royal authority, but were simply told that the time was not ripe and the wise course was to remain loyal to the German alliance.[43] One of these senators, Thaon di Revel, who for eight years had been a fascist minister and was close to the court, thought that Mussolini was blackmailing the palace into subservience by threatening to reveal unsavoury facts about the private life of one member of the royal family.[44]

Another visitor to the Quirinal, Admiral Baistrocchi, warned in March that other monarchies had been swept away by revolution when they put their own interest before that of their people. He added that the sovereign had once been applauded by cinema audiences who greeted Mussolini's appearance in silence, but now was himself greeted with cries of sarcasm and derision for protecting a corrupt and defeated fascist government. Baistrocchi quoted Crispi's remark in 1892 that a monarch, even if 'constitutionally irresponsible', could not escape a moral responsibility for what was done in his name.[45] How these forthright words were received is not known.

One difficulty was a division of opinion among those leading fascists who wanted to end the war, one group thinking that Mussolini must be removed to make this possible, while most of them believed that he alone could persuade the Germans to let Italy out of the war without reprisals. The palace lent towards the latter view, despite the objection that the western allies would not negotiate while

Mussolini remained in charge. Ciano, who was foreign minister until early in 1943, knew that negotiations must at any cost be opened before the enemy, after landing on Italian soil, could demand unconditional surrender. Ciano lamented that the king, as well as being inscrutable, could be told nothing in confidence without his at once informing Mussolini. Another regret was that Umberto refused to do anything or even state his views until his father gave permission. The foreign minister was desperate at hearing Mussolini say that, even if the country could not be defended, the war must continue 'until the last Italian was killed'. Speaking to cabinet ministers on 19 June, Mussolini continued to repeat mindlessly that he was confident in victory and would reject any compromise peace; he intended to 'burn his boats behind him' and would not let them discuss the matter.[46]

Having a leader who could make such disconcerting and contradictory remarks was Italy's tragedy. Almost as tragic was that fascism had created a ruling class that was incapable of taking any practical initiative until far too late. The first serious sign of rebellion was by factory workers who had the courage to strike in March 1943, and the strikers were joined by soldiers singing communist songs as well as by rank-and-file members of the fascist party.[47] Another problem for the government was passive resistance by civil servants who very generally refused to obey orders, or else merely pretended to obey and knew that Mussolini had no means of discovering their deceit.[48] In February Ciano's successor at the foreign office, Giuseppe Bastianini, was instructed to refrain from making any contact with the enemy, but within two weeks was disobeying this order. Evidently the regime was on the point of collapse.

3   Mussolini is dismissed

Other senior officials who were appointed in the spring of 1943 were equally unreliable and disobedient, because no one with the requisite ability for office could fail to see the need for change. General Chierici, an eminent fascist, was chosen to succeed Senise as chief of police, only to turn against his master almost at once. The new commander of the *carabinieri*, General Hazon, had long since distanced himself from the regime and began to make plans in the expectation that the king might at some point order Mussolini's arrest. The successor to Cavallero as chief of general staff was General Ambrosio, no anti-fascist but a loyal monarchist and professional soldier who understood that the war was lost and Mussolini would have to give way or be removed. All three of these senior officers realised by May, when the axis forces abandoned their last foothold in North Africa, that the king had the opportunity and the authority to stave off the final shame of an allied invasion on the mainland of Italy.

But their trust was misplaced. Always his instincts were against clear decisions and any exercise of personal initiative, all the more so when he realised that others were trying to saddle him with the responsibility for accepting military defeat and a peace settlement that was bound to be unfavourable. He complained, no doubt correctly, that those who urged him to act might cynically leave him in the lurch when the crunch came.[1] With equal cynicism he listened to their advice and then warned Mussolini of their disloyalty.[2] Almost never did he reveal his own feelings and thoughts, apparently not even to his family, nor to his chief aide, General Puntoni, nor to others even when he engaged in long talks about the political situation.[3] He defended his inaction by saying that the duce's continued popularity was indicated by public applause, though he knew as well as anyone that applause in the Piazza Venezia was pure artifice and no test of public opinion.[4] Every day brought death to many more of his subjects, yet he waited for 'the right moment' when 'either a clear demonstration of public opinion or a revolution inside fascism' would allow him to intervene.[5]

Princess Marie José, though living in the Quirinal, was never allowed any personal contact with her father-in-law, but she let him know through his chief confidant Acquarone that an anti-fascist front was in process of formation and needed to know his intentions. On the left there was readiness to compromise and drop any unqualified republicanism; while on the right, the elderly pre-fascist liberals whom she sometimes met were threatening to desert the monarchy unless it showed some sign of leadership. In April the princess had meetings with Grandi and Einaudi; in May with Bonomi, Ambrosio, and the future Pope Montini; in June with Badoglio and Ambrosio again.[6] The critics were growing in number, but were not keen on meeting the king because they knew his practice of immediately telling Mussolini what they said. Nevertheless, they wanted him to know that the royal prerogative, if it could be used in 1940 to declare war without parliamentary sanction, could certainly be used to dismiss an unpopular minister who was leading the nation to destruction.[7]

Vittorio Emanuele must have realised long ago that by permitting the suppression of parliament he had left himself constitutionally vulnerable. He was afraid that the British might suddenly ask him to negotiate for a separate peace, in which case he said that as a constitutional monarch he would be obliged to consult Mussolini – whose exceptional intelligence he mentioned once more.[8] He nevertheless had to admit that the duce had recently changed 'for the worse', a circumstance that he ascribed to the excessive demands of 'that woman', Clara Petacci.[9] He can hardly have failed to note, what ministers knew well, that Mussolini was close to mental collapse as well as often in almost unbearable pain, sometimes hardly aware of what was happening around him, or talking incoherently of how the war was on the point of turning in Italy's favour.

On 15 May a written note from the palace at last suggested to Mussolini that Italy ought to consider resuming her neutrality before the imminent collapse of nazi Germany. But Grandi, when he saw the king on 4 June, recommended a more drastic change, since the only way to get an advantageous peace was to join the western allies and end the war on the winning side. Grandi repeated that the royal prerogative had been used in 1915 and 1922 to override parliamentary wishes and should now be used again, this time with overwhelming support in the country and with at least majority support in the Grand Council and *camera dei fasci*. On hearing this the king admitted being in theory ready to act, but not yet, especially as he doubted whether the allies could successfully invade Italy. He repeated that at the right moment he could be relied on, and he hoped that Grandi would prepare the ground among other fascist leaders. Meanwhile, as he told Grandi, not even his closest advisers Acquarone or Puntoni should be informed of what he had just said.[10]

In the same week, at the prompting of Marie José through Acquarone, he agreed to see his former prime minister, Bonomi, with whom he had had no contact for almost twenty years. The advice given by what he scornfully called a 'ghost from the past' was to arrest Mussolini, withdraw from the war, and appoint either Badoglio or Caviglia to form a government. This advice was received in a silence that was baffling and impenetrable, which merely confirmed the view of many liberals that there was little point in further collaboration with the palace.[11] Another one-sided interview took place on 8 June with Marcello Soleri, a former minister and once an associate of Giolitti. Acquarone begged Soleri to speak more vehemently than Bonomi about how the crown itself and not only Italy was in grave danger; but once again the king gave nothing away except to admit that the war was probably lost. He gave the impression that he had no enthusiasm for anti-fascist Italians and still less for the Anglo-Americans.[12]

On this latter theme he was more straightforward when speaking to the papal nuncio. Firstly, he did not trust the United States, a country that knew little about Europe; secondly, Britain was unimaginably corrupt, indeed 'rotten to the core'; thirdly, the Russian army was in poor shape; finally, the eagerness of the Anglo–Americans for peace was one more sign of an unsuspected weakness, and it told in Italy's favour.[13]

The Vatican cannot have been much impressed with such absurdly unrealistic talk, but wanted to help and had special reasons for fearing a reaction towards communism once people realised how they had been deceived by fascism.[14] The Vatican authorities blamed the king for not seeing earlier that he could avert this danger and purchase a satisfactory peace in return for ditching Mussolini.[15] Naturally they were eager to gain credit for the pope as the saviour of Italy from invasion. They also needed to correct the unfortunate impression that the papacy had unduly favoured fascism. Equally, however, they did not want to offend the Germans prematurely before the sovereign had committed himself by some active initiative, nor would they risk offering mediation before being fairly sure that their offer would succeed. One handicap for them as for others was the inability to say anything to the king without his at once telling the fascist leader. Since he was 'weak, indecisive, and excessively devoted to Mussolini', they had better wait for him to commit himself before they gave more practical assistance.[16]

One helpful fact was that the pope, after being asked by the Americans for advice about what kind of government ought to replace fascism, replied that monarchy would suit Italy better than a republic. The pope furthermore advised Washington, in a note that he asked should be destroyed, that the best transition government might be a coalition between liberals and moderate fascists, and names mentioned included Caviglia, Orlando, and Federzoni. On receipt of a reply from America, the Vatican was able to inform the king on 14 June that the allies would support his dynasty if he made peace, though he could expect no consideration if the war continued.[17]

One excuse for his slowness to respond was his strangely confident belief that the allies would invade other countries but not Italy, and he agreed with Mussolini that any landing in Sicily would be a grave strategic mistake on their part.[18] Umberto had taken the trouble to make a personal inspection and knew that his father had been deceived by fascist propaganda about the defences of Sicily.[19] When a massive invasion of that island took place on the night of 9/10 July, its immediate success destroyed any remaining hope that political decisions could be further postponed. The king commented that Mussolini would never go to investigate the situation in Sicily 'since he never exposes himself to serious danger'. An even more cynical afterthought was that the duce might resolve an intolerable predicament by going there and being captured by the enemy.[20]

By this time the machinery of government was in complete disarray and the one doubt was who would give the final push – whether Grandi and other dissident fascists, or the armed forces, or possibly the anti-fascists, or the king himself. General Ambrosio and the army staff already had a contingency plan for Mussolini's arrest and replacement by either Badoglio or Caviglia.[21] The king had allowed them to devise this plan, but made quite clear that he did not envisage a wholesale removal of the fascist regime, only of what he called its 'deleterious aspects'. This made him less than keen to choose Marshal Caviglia, the one military leader who had not compromised with the regime, and who had the 'disadvantage' of excessive sympathy with the Anglo-Americans.[22]

The alternative was Marshal Badoglio, Duke of Addis Abeba, whose character the king heartily despised. Badoglio had support in the army, but he was known to have committed fearful atrocities in Ethiopia. He had also zealously and obsequiously served fascism until dismissed for incompetence in 1940. He was not quite as old as Caviglia, but strongly resented Mussolini for the humiliation of his dismissal, and being notoriously avaricious was eager to win power. Badoglio had been telling his friends that a rebellion would succeed easily in forty-eight hours; he might even be ready, if the palace remained silent, to get rid of both government and monarch simultaneously.[23] On 15 July this elderly general was secretly authorised by the king to think of possible names for an alternative government, but was told to exclude Bonomi, Orlando, or any other 'ghosts' from the liberal anti-fascist opposition.[24]

Ten days after the Sicilian invasion began, and perhaps as important in its psychological effect, was an allied bombing raid on Rome, the first in three years of war. The king personally visited the damaged areas, and the angry hostility he encountered was seen to affect him greatly.[25] On the same day, 19 July, Mussolini had a disastrous meeting with Hitler in which he was almost speechless, and his failure to put Italy's case convinced even the more extreme fascists that he was a broken man, resourceless, perhaps inwardly reconciled to defeat. He had promised them that he would persuade Hitler to let Italy withdraw from the war, but in the event had not dared so much as to mention this vital issue. On 22 July, after receiving the advice of other leading fascists, the king at last told Mussolini that his resignation was the only solution, and when the latter was too bewildered to understand or react, an order was issued for the army and *carabinieri* to make preparations for his arrest.[26]

This order was known to Mussolini through his telephone-tapping system,[27] and no doubt the knowledge hastened his acceptance of Grandi's alternative project to reconvene the Grand Council. Although this body had not met since 1939, Grandi as minister of justice advised the palace that its decisions should carry the same weight as those of parliament.[28] The minister's hope was to pre-empt or forestall what he called a South-American *pronunciamento* by the army. While curtailing Mussolini's powers, the Council could advise the king to accept a less authoritarian version of fascism and resume his constitutional rights as supreme military commander. Many leading fascists saw this as an imaginative and courageous proposal which might preserve something from the wreck of a discredited regime.

When the Grand Council met during the night of 24/25 July, Grandi's proposal was supported by a large majority of its members, and these were men hand-picked by Mussolini for their loyalty to himself. No demand was made for withdrawing from the war or replacing the duce as national leader; only for restoring some of the royal prerogatives and diluting dictatorship by a more collegiate form of government. Mussolini put up a feeble defence, blaming the army for Italy's defeat, and told the meeting that he had in any case been intending to give up his powers as military commander. He insisted that the monarchy firmly supported him. He claimed that he had always shown deference to the crown and had never acted to diminish its prestige or without its full co-operation.[29] After the meeting he repeated that he was confident about remaining in power; he meant to punish his rebellious colleagues and drew up a list of replacements for the monarch's approval.[30] Only in retrospect could he admit that his confidence was misplaced and ingenuous.[31]

It has been argued that the vote of the Grand Council in the early hours of 25 July was the immediate cause of Mussolini's arrest.[32] But members of the Council, including Grandi and Bottai, were strongly opposed to this arrest and discovered too late that they had been the unwitting cat's-paw of the army who already had royal authority for a more radical course of action. The king was glad to have the support of the Council's vote, but was equally determined not to let it thwart what he had already settled upon with Ambrosio and Acquarone; and that included getting rid of Mussolini, which was necessary 'if the dynasty was to survive'.[33] Later the same morning Badoglio was appointed head of government by a royal decree which, in a novel constitutional procedure, had to be countersigned by Badoglio himself. The king then gave a personal order for Mussolini's 'protective custody', and after a brief meeting the ex-duce was arrested as he left the royal residence.

At this final encounter, Puntoni was listening behind the door in case of trouble, but it was undramatic and outwardly respectful on both sides. Mussolini acknowledged that he had become the most hated man in Italy, and had bitter words for his fellow countrymen who had deserted him, but knew that they were fickle and would quickly change back again. However, his request to be confirmed in office was politely refused. He could not deny that the head of state had a constitutional right to dismiss him as head of government – and also as duce of fascism since the two offices were now constitutionally combined. The king explained that, since the war was lost, it was important to prevent further casualties and seek some accommodation with the enemy. Mussolini gave the impression of being completely listless and mainly concerned with his own personal safety, so a pledge was given that no harm would come to him.[34]

Seldom in the history of any country has the news of a politician's fall been immediately greeted with more overwhelming scenes of public delight, and some people were bound to see this as proof that the king should have acted earlier, perhaps much earlier. But in speaking to his new ministers he was cynical about such popular demonstrations and had no intention of being influenced by public opinion in his choice of policy.[35] Four million members of the fascist party, including the heavily armed fascist militia, put up no resistance at all despite their oath to die in Mussolini's defence, and were no doubt mostly thankful to see him go. A hundred battalions of the blackshirt militia had already deserted before 23 July.[36] Those who were disappointed included Grandi and his associates in the Grand Council who were caught unprepared by a royalist and military takeover. But a vast majority in the country was overjoyed to think, over-optimistically, that the collapse of dictatorship meant the war was over.

4   *The armistice*

With the disappearance of Mussolini the king was truly in command for the first time in his reign. He rejected his new prime minister's request that the cabinet be given emergency powers to legislate on its own, and once again vetoed the appointment of Bonomi, Soleri, Einaudi, and other spectres from the distant liberal past.[1] He wanted no politicians, especially not those who might call the monarchy into question. Instead he insisted on choosing ministers from among non-political 'technicians' who had served in the fascist bureaucracy, some of whom were impenitent about their previous association with Mussolini. Dozens of senior fascists, including Ciano and (though he tried to deny the fact) Grandi, immediately laid claim to consideration by sending to Badoglio obsequious letters of perhaps not very sincere congratulation and solidarity.[2] Mussolini himself, writing from police custody in a friendly note that he later had difficulty justifying, promised the new government 'every possible collaboration'.[3]

One encouraging sign for some of the die-hards, was an important pronouncement which, without the king's asking for the cabinet's advice, pledged his own and the country's honour to continue the war in alliance with Germany. This was an extraordinary and insufficiently thought-out decision that pleased almost no one except the more extreme fascists, and if the intention was to deceive the Germans, it failed. The king would have liked to end the fighting, but only if this could be done honourably, without provoking a German reaction, and without the indignity of having to surrender to the western allies. Somehow he hoped to pacify Hitler, at the same time as he hoped to persuade the allies to stop their raids and halt their plans for an invasion of the Italian mainland. But in practice, by associating his own name with what many thought of as Mussolini's war, his pronouncement further damaged the monarchy as well as ensuring that he lost his best chance to obtain a favourable peace by resuming neutrality or joining the victors.

No one can say what would have happened if he had immediately proclaimed Italian neutrality, but some of the authorities in Berlin would have been more than ready to accept it.[4] If only he had consulted his senior generals he might have learnt that there were good arguments in favour of an immediate peace, or even for a declaration of war against Germany whose troops in Italy were heavily outnumbered. Among those who inclined to one or other of these possibilities were the chief of general staff, Ambrosio, and his two chief assistants, Generals Rossi and Castellano.[5] The chiefs of army staff, Roatta, Zanussi, and Utili, saw that Italy's best chance might be to break with the Germans at once, and so did General Carboni who was soon given joint command of the intelligence services and an army corps defending Rome.[6] The same advice was given to the king by Grandi;[7] also by a newly composed national liberation committee representing liberals, catholics, socialists, and communists;[8] and was supported inside Badoglio's cabinet – except that ministers were, by the king's command, not allowed any voice in major policy.[9]

After declaring that the war would continue, four valuable days passed while he waited to see if or how the Germans would react. He

then decided that some contact should be made with the enemy, but
discussions were also opened with the Germans to discover whether
they or the western alliance presented the greater immediate danger.
The king chiefly feared the Germans and made preparations to
abandon Rome in case they tried to capture him.[10] The Americans
and British on the other hand, while distrustful of Vittorio Emanuele
because of his pro-fascist past, and while they had no intention of
underwriting the future of the monarchy,[11] were more than ready to
accept his collaboration, so long as he kept the loyalty of his army
and would accept an honourable surrender.

The western allies had long since publicly stated that surrender
must come first and must be unconditional because there was no
time for protracted negotiations. More importantly they feared that
anti-nazi resistance movements in Europe might collapse if favourable conditions were offered to an Italian enemy that had invaded
and was still occupying large areas in France and the Balkans. Nor can
the king have been surprised by this demand, since his own government had demanded the unconditional surrender of Italy's enemies
in Africa and the Balkans. But he resolutely refused to accept such
humiliation when applied to himself, especially since unconditional
surrender would in his opinion imply, what he now meant to deny,
that he shared Mussolini's responsibility for the war. On the contrary, he gambled on the possibility that the allies could be pushed
into paying a high price for Italian neutrality, and above all that
they would guarantee a continuance of the monarchy. Meanwhile it
would be prudent to avoid prejudicing his parallel negotiations with
Hitler.[12]

These latter negotiations took place in two meetings with the
German general staff during the first half of August. The king
already knew that his own generals would have liked to raise with
Hitler the possibility of letting Italy withdraw from the war. But he
rejected their advice because he feared German reprisals and possible
civil war.[13] Whether or not this was a justifiable fear, he instructed
them to restrict negotiation to details of future military collaboration
with the nazis. He himself thought it wise to tell the German ambassador that Mussolini remained his friend. The new Italian foreign
minister, Raffaele Guariglia, also pledged his word of honour to
Ribbentrop on 6 August that the government had no contact with
the western allies[14] – though both men knew this to be untrue.

During the first week of August, five separate attempts were made
to establish contact with the west: in Berne and Begazi that brought
no result, then in Algiers and Lisbon it partially succeeded. The
messages sent were, first, that the request for unconditional surrender was, as the king put it, dishonourable and 'truly monstrous';

second, Italy was merely pretending to support Hitler and badly needed allied help to get out of the war with as little damage as possible; third, the allies should stop their air raids and their anti-monarchist propaganda, because if the king was dethroned there would be chaos, a blood bath, and perhaps a communist revolution. What was required of the west was a guarantee of the monarchy's survival, as well as a guarantee of existing national frontiers and the restoration of Italy's colonial empire in Libya, Somalia, and Eritrea. Equally important, the allies should renounce any idea of a military campaign in Italy, and instead invade France or the Balkans, so compelling German troops to withdraw from the peninsula and leave the Italians in peace.[15]

There was a desperate lack of realism about these demands. Far from wanting a German withdrawal from Italy, the allies were hoping to draw as many German divisions as possible into the peninsula, away from the main fronts in Russia and Normandy where the war would be won or lost.[16] And Hitler made what he later admitted was the mistake of overruling good advice by falling into this trap.[17] As for the survival of the dynasty, that in the opinion of London and Washington was a matter for Italians to decide. Also, if revolution was feared, the best way of avoiding it was for the king to make peace at once. 'Our attitude to the House of Savoy is opportunist', wrote Anthony Eden, since it 'has become so dis-credited in Italy as to have lost its old appeal to the Italian people'.[18]

If Vittorio Emanuele was unrealistic in his demands on the western alliance, he was equally unrealistic in domestic policy by not seeing that his continued coquetting with survivors of the previous regime might deprive him of credibility at home and abroad. He allowed Badoglio to abolish the fascist party and the Grand Council, but an attempt to intern the fascist leadership met with an angry royal veto. Many anti-fascists remained in prison. Others were arrested. The racial laws were not rescinded and the formation of anti-fascist parties was forbidden. Control of radio and the press was left in the hands of people who had exercised that same function under the dictatorship. To some people this seemed like 'fascism without Mussolini', and one minister even complained that 'the new regime is even more fascist than the old'.[19] The king was warned by the liberals that this was bound to damage the monarchy, but preferred to listen to the fascist ex-minister Bastianini who told him the opposite, namely that the old fascists were the only sincere monarchists in Italy and any attempt to prosecute fascism would surely expose details of royal involvement with the previous regime.[20]

During July and August, despite continued censorship, there was the first chance in twenty years for public opinion to register its views, and there were signs that the king was not popular. He had tolerated Mussolini for too long and was now continuing to support a war in which the casualties were no longer soldiers so much as the civilian population.[21] Some people thought that his immediate abdication in favour of Umberto would be best for both Italy and the survival of the dynasty.[22] Badoglio believed this and said so to Acquarone, who recommended that the prime minister keep such opinions to himself since the monarch believed that his son lacked the qualities needed in a reigning sovereign.[23] Dozens of times in the past the king had hinted at his readiness to return to private life, but if he had been serious he would have given Umberto some training and experience as the heir presumptive. In mid-August he tentatively mentioned the possibility of abdication, but was easily argued out of it by conservative ex-fascists who saw him as their safest barrier against radical social change.[24]

Although Badoglio was considered by many to be too pro-fascist, in the king's opinion he was not sufficiently so. This one-time dedicated servant of fascism was now accused by the crown of leading Italy to perdition by making too many concessions to the Left,[25] and his failure to stop anti-monarchist propaganda might, in the king's strange words, 'result in the absurdity of people thinking to judge the actions of the sovereign himself'.[26] The king demanded a government of non-political bureaucrats who would run day-to-day administration but leave political matters to the head of state. At one point word was sent from the palace to Grandi and Carboni that either of them might be appointed to replace Badoglio, and the king was improbably reported as saying that Mussolini himself might before long return to power.[27] In practice, however, he needed to avoid any ministerial crisis while an invasion might be imminent, and decided to retain Badoglio as an obedient general who would enforce any direct royal order.

During most of August the king's over-optimistic expectation was that Italy could make peace with the consent of both contestants, and perhaps this was worth a try, though it needed more tact and energy than he possessed. What strains credulity is, first, the lack of urgency in seeking talks with the western allies, and then his complete failure to prepare the army for any conflict with Germany that an armistice might provoke. He knew from Washington by the middle of June that his only hope of an honourable settlement was if he ended the war at once. But a month went by before Mussolini's arrest. Then he let another week pass before sending envoys to Algiers and Lisbon, and all they could discover was that the allied offer of an honourable peace still stood, though time was running out. Yet another week of indecision then followed before General Castellano was sent to meet Eisenhower's representatives in Lisbon, but this man left Rome without first seeing either Badoglio or the king, without the credentials of an official envoy, without any permission to negotiate an armistice, indeed without any orders at all except to discover the allied plan of campaign; and the Italian foreign office innocently confessed that this was deliberate in case Castellano gave too much away and his mission might have to be repudiated.[28] Instead of travelling on one of the regular air flights from Rome to Lisbon, Castellano was instructed to take his time and wasted five more days before reaching Portugal.

These successive delays suggest a lack of seriousness if not deliberate prevarication, and so does the fact that Castellano was neither given a radio for communication with Rome, nor informed that the Italian army and naval intelligence services both had radios and ciphers at Lisbon that he could have used; nor even did he think of sending home any urgent message by air.[29] Travelling back to Italy, again by the slow land route, he could not report to Rome until 27 August that the allied offer remained precisely the same and was not negotiable. His mission had taken two weeks, with nothing to show for it.

By that time a second officer, General Zanussi, had been sent to Lisbon, this time on a direct flight but again with no credentials, and he aroused great suspicion in Portugal when it was found that he represented a rival and possibly pro-German faction in the army command. The allies began to suspect that the king was not in full control of events in Rome or else, more likely, was confusing the issue and playing for time in the hope of avoiding the risks involved in commitment to either side. Zanussi repeated the request that there should be no invasion of the Italian mainland. He hardly helped by telling Eisenhower's representatives that the monarch and Badoglio were both 'worn-out men' who were unreliable and tainted by twenty years of collaboration with fascism.[30] On the same flight as Zanussi, unknown to his fellow passengers, travelled yet another envoy, Dino Grandi, who represented not the army but (according to his own testimony) the king personally. Grandi had a quite separate and mysterious mission to the British which only added to the confusion, especially as he unwarrantably assumed that they trusted him as an old friend.[31]

Hitler learnt that these talks with the enemy were proceeding, for which he blamed the king personally, and accordingly transferred a specialised parachute unit to Italy with another plan to capture the royal family.[32] The Führer cynically remarked that Vittorio Emanuele was interested only in seeking a guarantee of personal safety; and he added, with even more justified cynicism, that the dynasty of Savoy had always been able to find venal journalists and historians to falsify the record and save successive monarchs from an accountability before history.[33]

The allies were not much less cynical in analysing the king's motives. They were surprised and unimpressed when, instead of negotiations for an armistice, Badoglio seemed more interested in asking for special consideration to be shown to the royal family.[34] Castellano's apparent delaying tactics were hard for them to interpret, because he did not seem greatly worried by the prospect of unconditional surrender, and rather gave the impression that he was chiefly intending to discover their invasion plans before Italy chose which side to support. Apparently the king was not much interested in defeating Hitler, but far more in his own salvation and avoiding any damage to Italy. He showed little interest in opposing fascism or nazism. The furthest he might go was to undertake the bare minimum of fighting needed to claim a place among the victors, changing sides only after or if the allies proved by a successful landing that they could win.[35]

The allied commander calculated that, compared with his own five divisions ready to invade, 'the Italians had sixteen divisions, who might jump either way'.[36] The first landing was to be a minor diversion timed to take place on 3 September in Calabria. This would be barely a week after Castellano's return to Rome, during which critical period a succession of further deadlines went by without Italy's accepting an armistice; and all the time the casualties of war continued to mount. Confronted by such a momentous issue the king retreated behind his constitutional irresponsibility and, when called upon by Badoglio to take a decision, avoided expressing an opinion one way or the other. His advisers were divided, but a meeting on 28 August showed a majority for repudiating Castellano and refusing to surrender. Guariglia, the foreign minister, was supported by General Carboni in arguing that to change sides and join the allies would be a 'catastrophe'.[37]

Ambrosio and Castellano thought on the other hand that an honourable surrender was their best hope, but when the king refused to decide, three more days were lost in further inconclusive discussions. From one direction there was pressure on the palace to continue fighting alongside Germany,[38] but once again it was thought best to continue playing for time, and Castellano on 31 August was sent back to Eisenhower in Sicily with a deliberately ambiguous message that was neither acceptance nor a refusal.[39]

The next day this general returned to Rome after being told by the allied commanders that the invasion was not far off and the monarchy would be in serious danger if by then the Italians were still fighting on the German side.[40] The king therefore decided to placate the allies by sending them a telegram accepting an armistice in principle, but without going so far as to sign any binding document, and his principal adviser Acquarone agreed that this was another piece of legitimate deceit which would allow them to back down at the last moment if the invasion ran into difficulties.[41] Castellano was sent to Sicily once more, again with no credentials empowering him to sign any formal commitment. Eisenhower, however, continued to insist on no deal without a signature, and after two more days of desperate vacillation a meeting at the Quirinal on 3 September accepted the inevitable. The same day Castellano signed an unconditional armistice. The fact was kept strictly secret for the next five days while the Anglo-American command made preparations for the main landing due to take place at Salerno on the 8th.

How closely the king was involved in these six weeks of dithering is not easy to say, but he had insisted on retaining extraordinary powers in his own hand and knew what was happening without registering any protest. No doubt, like Acquarone as well as Badoglio and Guariglia, he believed deceit to be justified in the national interest, and during the five days following the armistice he once again promised the Germans that he would fight to the end as a loyal ally of Hitler.[42] But deception lacked the justification that success might have brought. Prevarication won time, but with no other advantage, and in fact lost a great deal by merely cloaking an inability to decide. It had the practical disadvantage of forfeiting any claim to respect or consideration from either side, and by positively hindering the chances of a successful invasion it was a major contributory cause of the immense losses suffered by Italians and the invading forces in eighteen more months of destructive war.

Signing the armistice was part of the deceit. Badoglio had not only done his best for six weeks to avoid committing himself, but continued even after 3 September to regard its signature as in no way binding.[43] Nor was he a man who would take such a view if he thought that the king disapproved. Even during the first five critical days after the initial landing in Calabria, no serious preparation was made to help the invasion succeed or to resist the Germans when inevitably the news of the armistice leaked out.[44] Evidently the government had no intention of actively assisting the western allies, despite what Castellano and Zanussi had promised and despite specific clauses in the armistice. The ministers in charge of the armed forces, according to their own testimony, were before 8 September given only vague instructions about the armistice and the imminent prospect of an allied landing; and though senior staff officers knew more, an order of 6 September prescribed that divisional commanders responsible for protecting airfields and seaports should be left without any instructions except to use their own judgement.[45]

Possibly the king was not directly involved in this aberrant defeatism, but he did not demur, and he must take direct responsibility for appointing and supporting the men who made this week one of the most disastrous in Italian history. Marshal Badoglio, the prime minister; Guariglia, the foreign minister; General Ambrosio, chief of general staff; General Roatta, chief of army staff; and General Carboni who commanded the forces round Rome – these were the officials immediately responsible. Ambrosio, for example, even after learning (or because he learnt) on 5 September that a large allied convoy was at sea moving northwards from Sicily,[46] left his post of command, and did so after first informing people that the allies might invade any day after the 7th, in which case any German attack on Rome had to be resisted.[46] But he himself went to Turin 'for private reasons'. He also travelled there by rail when he could have easily used his personal plane and returned the same day if he had wanted to. He even refused an emergency request to return to Rome by air. Nor is there much doubt that his motive was to avoid meeting two senior American officers who he knew were due to arrive in Rome to discuss joint action against the German forces.

One of these officers was General Taylor who commanded the only air-borne division available for the allied landing at Salerno on the 8th. His division was at the last moment diverted from Salerno to prepare for an air-drop in support of General Carboni at Rome. This was an immensely complex and dangerous change of plan and was made only in response to urgent requests by Castellano and Zanussi independently, in addition to a promise of Carboni's full and active co-operation.[47] Yet when Taylor arrived in Rome late on the 7th he found no one ready to discuss details of their agreed plan. Ambrosio's deputy refused to see him. Ambrosio himself was still in Turin. Only after vital hours had elapsed did General Carboni reluctantly appear, and now said that he could give no support to the air-drop so that it must be cancelled; and he added that if the allies persisted in their invasion they might find the Italian army and navy actively supporting the Germans against them. Carboni privately admitted, and took credit for the fact, that he had purposely deceived the allies into thinking that there were no chances of successful resistance at Rome.[48] His refusal to co-operate with Taylor was immediately confirmed by Badoglio and later by Ambrosio on his return from Turin. The fact that the higher command during the previous week had made no military preparations for this air-borne attack is another indication that they must have planned in advance to leave the allies in the lurch.

Eisenhower was only just in time to stop Taylor's division as the planes were starting their flight to Rome. He was not in time to divert it back to help the hazardous Salerno landing, which had to continue without its support. Suddenly he realised that the king's government, far from helping the allies, was ready to put the invasion at risk rather than give the assistance that had been promised. In the late afternoon of 8 September he therefore called their bluff by informing the world in a radio communication that Vittorio Emanuele had signed an armistice five days earlier and would be expected to honour his signature or take the consequences.

Hurriedly and in obvious distress the king had by this time summoned a crown council at the Quirinal. His purpose, even now, was not to discuss urgent matters of national defence but only whether promises made in the armistice could at this last minute be denounced without danger. Six hours earlier he had again told Hitler's ambassador that Italy would remain faithful to the German alliance – and this was five days after signing an armistice with the enemy. In the crown council a majority, which included Carboni, Acquarone, and Guariglia, supported this view and favoured repudiating their pledge to the western allies.[49] But as the decision was being drafted, a junior officer presumed to suggest that, since signing the armistice had been filmed, any disavowal would irretrievably dishonour the monarchy and provoke terrible reprisals; after which only Carboni persisted in his opinion. The king contributed nothing to the discussion. When the meeting ended, he was once more advised that he could still repudiate the armistice by pretending that it had been concluded without his knowledge, to which he replied that after Eisenhower's broadcast this would not be believed.[50]

There was no microphone available, so Badoglio was sent to announce the armistice from the Rome radio station, but still with so little sense of urgency that he waited in the studio for most of another hour until the end of a programme of light music. In the meantime nothing was done to warn the army that the Germans were a likely enemy against whom immediate plans should be made. Instead, divisional and corps commanders were left to take decisions that the general staff lacked the courage to take. The only order issued was that any attack by anyone, whether Germans or the western allies, should be resisted – as though such resistance would not have been automatic. As the allied invasion took place, Badoglio and the king continued to assume that the Anglo-American forces would do any fighting that was required. Allied troop-carriers off Salerno were even attacked by Italian planes and the Italian battle fleet was prevented with only minutes to spare from doing likewise. The newspapers on 9 September, after the invading force had landed, continued to carry reports of successful action against the Anglo-American 'enemy'.[51]

5   *The flight from Rome*

In the early hours of 9 September, since General Taylor's attack had been cancelled, Vittorio Emanuele hurriedly withdrew from Rome. Yet again he left only verbal orders that were so ambiguous as to be unintelligible, appointing no one with clear authority to act in his stead. A large army of a million men was thus abandoned to choose between desertion or captivity. His prisoner Mussolini was also left behind to be liberated by German troops who took control over most of Italy. The two German divisions near Rome had until the very last minute been expecting to withdraw to the north,[1] but quickly changed when they found that the Italian forces, despite superior numbers, were too demoralised to put up more than a disorganised fight. If given clear orders and good leadership they could have greatly hastened the liberation of their country. At the very least they could have done more to hinder German reinforcements from reaching the critical area of Salerno where one of the decisive battles of the war was being fought.[2]

Eisenhower had to accept after recent events that the royal government would not be a trustworthy ally. He had been promised that Mussolini was in safe custody. He had also been led by Castellano to expect help from a popular resistance movement – including sabotage and the cutting off of roads and railways, as was proving so effective in Jugoslavia; but the generals and the conservatives in government had political reasons for discouraging guerrilla action by 'Garibaldian' irregulars who were bound to have political and probably anti-monarchist views of their own.[3] Especially disillusioning was Badoglio's last-minute cancellation of the American attack near Rome, an attack that the Italians had themselves requested. Even if unsuccessful this air-borne operation would have gained valuable time for the landing at Salerno. At best it would have shortened the war by months. The risks had been carefully weighed and its sudden cancellation was greatly regretted by some Italian commanders[4] as well as by the allied planning staff in Algiers and Sicily.[5]

Almost as damaging was a suspicion that the request for the air-drop might have been a deceptive ruse to hinder the invasion.

General Carboni, who was in charge of the defence of Rome, cannot have intended to give the air-drop any assistance or else he would have made quite different preparations before 8 September. To stop it he waited until the eleventh hour before inventing a series of inaccurate arguments that there was no time to investigate or refute. He alleged for instance, what as head of the intelligence services he knew to be untrue, that the airfields round Rome were under German occupation. After reporting earlier that his motorised corps was in full readiness, he suddenly claimed in the early hours of 8 September that he lacked the fuel and ammunition to give any help to a direct allied attack on Rome – though he must have known that abundant stores were available, and these were left to be captured by the Germans for their own use.

Other excuses were invented by Badoglio to disguise the fact that he meant to avoid active support of the invasion. To blame the allies he pretended that they had promised him two weeks' warning before the Salerno landing and had given a positive undertaking that it would not take place before 12 September; but no such undertakings had been given at any stage, nor had there been mention of any date, and Ambrosio assumed that the invasion might happen any day after the 7th. Badoglio and the king repeatedly claimed that Eisenhower deceived them by advancing the date, and this fabrication has ever since been taken to explain and excuse their refusal to co-operate.

Vittorio Emanuele, though he pretended the opposite, had for some weeks talked about abandoning Rome if events turned out badly, but went on hoping to be left undisturbed by both contestants. The night of 8/9 September he spent with Badoglio and Ambrosio at the war ministry, where he discovered that, while the Germans had detailed alternative plans for whatever might happen, his own government had none at all except to remain neutral as long as possible. Despite numerous appeals by subordinate commanders, Badoglio's one positive order was for no initiative to be taken against the Germans, and newspapers were ordered to print nothing that might offend their former ally.[6] Not until very early on the 9th, when reports arrived of minor clashes, was it apparent that procrastination had failed and serious fighting could no longer be avoided. But still no orders were given for organised resistance. Instead, hurried preparations were made to abandon the capital to its fate. A desperate appeal from Eisenhower 'to issue immediately a clarion call to all patriotic Italians' and 'seize every German by the throat' met no response because none was intended.[7]

The king remained calm as always, but Badoglio was in a state of panic about his personal safety and quite unable to take rational decisions. Before leaving Rome he forgot, or perhaps deliberately omitted, to telephone other ministers with the news of his departure, or where he was going, or of whether they should leave Rome, or how otherwise government should be carried on. If Rome was indefensible he could at least have prepared for this possibility and organised an orderly retreat that would have kept the bulk of the army in being. But to the disgust of some operational commanders, only an entirely vague and contradictory order (in pencil and unsigned)[8] was left about how the soldiers remaining in Rome should act, with the result that a far from disadvantageous military position was thrown away. Almost it seems that this may have been intended, because the king six weeks earlier had made preparations to leave Rome and there had been plenty of time to make contingency plans. Nor is it clear why he as commander-in-chief did not satisfy himself before leaving on the 9th that generals and ministers had issued clear instructions about what to do. On 25 July he had asserted his right to override ministers and speak in the national interest, but on this occasion gave no indication that he thought similar action was required.

While civilian ministers and operational commanders were abandoned to defeat and imprisonment, all the officers of the general staff simply disappeared from Rome, most of them in civilian clothes to avoid detection. The Germans were delighted to see them go and no attempt was made to halt the royal convoy of limousines at checkpoints along the road to Pescara. At the small port of Ortona on the Adriatic there was an unseemly scramble as two hundred generals and colonels unexpectedly appeared on the quay, where they struggled, vainly for the most part, to board a small corvette waiting to transport the royal party to southern Italy. During their sea passage the king on the 10th sent a telegraphic message appointing the 81-year-old Marshal Caviglia to co-ordinate a defensive battle round Rome, but the message never arrived, and anyway was sent as a casual afterthought and much too late. Some units of the Italian army fought courageously and effectively, but most of them without orders or leadership simply disintegrated. By contrast the bulk of the navy at once joined the allies when Admiral De Courten took responsibility for issuing a clear order to this effect.

The king's son-in-law, Calvi di Bergolo, and the minister of war, Antonio Sorice, were the only generals who disobeyed a royal instruction to abandon their troops and join this precipitate flight.[9] The Crown Prince Umberto, for perhaps the first time in his life, was heard to criticise an order from his father, but obediently if reluctantly left his post of command. It is an interesting commentary on the secretiveness of this uncommunicative monarch that Umberto, now nearing his 39th birthday, had not been consulted about such a dramatic decision, nor even so much as informed during the previous six weeks about negotiations for an armistice. Like his forbears, Vittorio Emanuele was jealous of his heir and unwilling to prepare him for the arduous task of the succession,[10] with unhappy results for the survival of the dynasty.

Another controversial decision was to leave Mussolini where he could be recaptured by the Germans on 12 September. The king mentioned the possibility of this recapture as he was moving out of Rome, so it can hardly have been unforeseen, and it permitted the ex-duce to set up a fascist republican government in northern Italy which led to the additional horrors of a terrible civil war for the next eighteen months. The king perhaps felt bound by his promise to guarantee the personal safety of his former minister, whom he continued to speak of with sympathy.[11] The fascist leader, on the contrary, had only harsh and contemptuous words for the man he called Vittorio Savoia and a 'diminutive delinquent'. Despite his initial offer to co-operate with Badoglio's regime, Mussolini once he was free referred to the king as the greatest traitor in history who, following a dynastic tradition, had defected to his country's enemies by inviting into Italy an army of 'Hottentots, Sudanese, mercenary Indians, American negroes and other zoological specimens'.[12]

After arriving at Brindisi in southern Italy, the king issued a statement to justify his change of front and explain the flight from Rome as having been necessary to keep a free government in being. Far from running away from danger, he insisted that he was ready to die if necessary in his country's service. Another proclamation admitted, despite what Eisenhower had been told, that in signing the armistice there had been no intention of proceeding further to the point of co-operating against Germany; only the unexpected Germany hostility at Rome forced him, evidently with reluctance and not until a full month after leaving Rome, to declare war as a member of the western alliance.[13]

His ministers were of course chiefly responsible for the casta-strophic blunders of September 1943. He even complained that they had never shown him the armistice terms, but here he was being untruthful or unbelievably incompetent. In the next few months he developed an even stronger dislike of Badoglio to whom he showed none of the conventional courtesies.[14] Somewhat unfairly he above all criticised his chief minister for insufficient zeal in defending the interests of the crown;[15] whereas in practice the latter obeyed orders by excluding opponents of the monarchy from junior as well as senior posts in the administration at Brindisi. Badoglio loyally did his best to convince the allies that the Italian population, being unsuited to a republican form of government, should be allowed no say in altering the existing constitution once the war was over;[16] but this gratuitous and partisan advice fell on deaf and uncomprehending ears in Washington and London.

Eisenhower appointed the British General Mason-Macfarlane to direct the Allied Control Commission at Brindisi, assisted by two civilian ministers, the American Robert Murphy and the English Harold Macmillan. To these men the king again stressed the danger of allowing the Italian people any opportunity to vote for a republic.[17] Murphy later remembered the king as 'a far more clever political operator than most people gave him credit for, and he overlooked no device to defer his fate'. The two Englishmen were somewhat less impressed: they found him to be a sad, plaintive, obstinate old man who cynically put the interests of his dynasty before those of Italy. Macmillian wrote of him as

> physically infirm, nervous, shaky, but courteous, with a certain modesty and simplicity of character which is attractive. He takes an objective, even humorously disinterested view of mankind and their follies. 'Things are not difficult', he said, 'only men'. I do not think he would be capable of initiating any policy except under extreme pressure.

On another occasion the king spoke to them of his pessimism about Italian public life: in Italy 'politics were very difficult and people would never agree. Everything was very difficult. Life was very difficult.'[18]

Characteristically he reacted to defeat by putting on an outward aspect of bravado and punctilio. He at first continued to style himself Emperor of Ethiopia and King of Albania, arguing somewhat pedantically that in a constitutional monarchy only parliament could change his title. He was genuinely shocked, like many subsequent Italian historians, that Mason-Macfarlane presumed to enter the royal presence in shirt sleeves and shorts, a practice that his brother sovereign of Great Britain never seemed to mind or even notice. No doubt he was touchily sensitive that leaving Rome would injure his reputation by appearing like desertion of his soldiers in the face of the enemy, and he must have been alarmed when Bonomi's Committee of National Liberation unanimously condemned his disastrous failure to leave any orders for resistance as he hurried to safety. Another critic, Arturo Toscanini, categorically refused ever again to speak to a 'cowardly and degenerate king' who had treacherously handed over half of the country to civil war and a more vicious form of fascism.[19]

The king preferred to shift the blame on to the allied commanders. As well as repeating the legend that they had promised not to invade until 12 September, he invented a new story (later accepted by some gullible historians) that they had left him defenceless by foolishly cancelling their promised air-drop at Rome[20] – a cancellation that his own ministers had so brusquely demanded. He furthermore tried to pretend that Mussolini had until 1939 enjoyed more support abroad than in Italy.[21] Writing to the British king and President Roosevelt on 23 September, he also tried to bury the past by boasting of his firm attachment to the practice of parliamentary government, and expressed the hope that the allies would make it possible for him to return to Rome as soon as possible. In private he made self-righteous (and in the circumstances, tasteless) remarks about the lack of courage and poor fighting qualities of the Anglo-American forces, especially since the slower their progress the greater the threat to his throne.[22] Never did he imagine that their assignment was to treat the Italian campaign as merely a holding operation to attract as many German divisions as possible away from the Normandy beaches.

His private comments squared oddly with his own delay in declaring war against Hitler. To justify this delay he repeated the typically legalistic excuse that a declaration of war would be unconstitutional unless sanctioned by parliament – though this had never worried him in successive declarations of war against Ethiopia, Albania, France, Britain, Greece, Russia, and the United States. His true reason may have been that, after repeatedly pledging his support for Hitler up to and including the morning of 8 September, he was sensitive about appearing once again as a perfidious turncoat. Under pressure he declared war against Germany on 13 October, but querulously blamed Badoglio for not using this 'concession' to Washington as a bargaining counter so as to obtain from the Control Commission something in return.[23]

Equally tactless and impercipient was his determined attempt in Brindisi to appoint Dino Grandi as foreign minister, with no apprehension of how this might remind people of his own pro-fascist past. Incredibly he tried to make Eisenhower believe that Grandi was nothing less than 'a symbol of the anti-fascist movement', his appointment being 'a matter of urgent necessity'.[24] The American in reply pointed out that the allies were fighting against all that Grandi had stood for in the past twenty years; their sympathy for Italy would rather depend upon whether the king showed a change of heart by bringing genuinely anti-fascist elements into the administration. For six months the hint was not taken: at first because he categorically refused to take it, and subsequently because his refusal made the anti-fascists, whether conservative or radical, unwilling to join a discredited monarchist regime.

The government in Washington was unhappy collaborating with Vittorio Emanuele and Badoglio in view of their past history, and thought that they commanded little popular respect or support. But

Eisenhower backed Churchill's alternative argument that there was no immediately obvious alternative round whom Italians would agree to rally: instead of imposing a solution that might be resented as outside interference, there were good reasons for leaving Italians to make their own choice when the war was over and a free vote was possible. 'Victor Emanuel is nothing to us', wrote Churchill. Despite the fact that British public opinion would probably prefer him to be deposed, foreign pressure to make him go might well be counter-productive in its effect on Italian opinion, and any political crisis at the moment would divert attention from the war effort. 'The king may well have to go in due time', but was useful 'for the moment': the deposing of Mussolini had, after all, been due to the crown, not to the anti-fascists.[25]

Many devoted monarchists in Italy had been hoping that Vittorio Emanuele would at once abdicate and so help to recapture credibility for the dynasty. Among the older generation, many were turning towards republicanism, especially those who recalled the events of October 1922 and June 1924. The newly emerging anti-fascist parties, whether Christian democrats, republicans, socialists, or the new Party of Action, had not participated in the events that over-threw Mussolini in July, and partly for that reason joined the com-munists in regarding the crown as a convenient scapegoat for much of what had gone wrong. All of them were suspicious that the court might be rebuilding an entrenched group of pseudo-fascist interests to protect the royal family and the throne.

Such was the view of the philosopher and historian Benedetto Croce. This conservative elder statesman was a dedicated monarchist who even managed to convince himself that, of all monarchies in European history, the House of Savoy was 'perhaps the finest and most noble'.[26] But the person of Vittorio Emanuele, wrote Croce, was 'hopelessly discredited' by his long support for Mussolini, and his continued presence was an obstacle in the way of rallying Italians behind the allies: indeed he was more guilty than the ex-duce, having far more intelligence and having been educated in a system of liberal government that he had irresponsibly betrayed. The monarch had latterly changed back to a genuine or simulated liberalism but only when military defeat imperilled his dynasty.[27]

No doubt there was some tincture of hypocrisy about making the king into a unique scapegoat to assuage a collective sense of guilt. But Croce's criticisms were fully shared by Bonomi's committee in Rome, and even more strongly by Carlo Sforza, formerly Giolitti's foreign minister, who arrived at Naples in mid-October after long years in exile. Sforza told the British that he too remained a mon-archist in principle and thought that 'the Italians were not fitted for republican government'. But he condemned the king personally as a 'despicable weakling' and Umberto as 'a pathological case', neither being capable of giving a lead to the Italian people, and their desperate clinging to power could only encourage the growth of communism.[28] The last hope for the monarchy, said Sforza, would be if both of them gave way to Umberto's six-year-old son, possibly with Badoglio as regent.

This was the proposal that Badoglio put to the king on 24 October after explaining that, though his personal allegiance was not in doubt, only such a change would make it possible for the leading anti-fascist politicians to join a broad-based administration. The king, highly indignant, refused categorically. He first summoned a group of leading military commanders, not for advice, but only to ask them provocatively if he could rely on support from the army in case of trouble ahead. Then he sent Acquarone to Naples in search of a replacement for Badoglio; but no one would accept. As Murphy commented, the king was unable to appreciate that he himself was the chief obstacle in the way of a return to representative government.[29]

So removed was he from realistic considerations that he invited Sforza to become prime minister – clumsily hoping to repeat Giolitti's practice of appeasing the opposition with the hope of high office – only to be rebuffed with the demand that abdication was indispensable. Sforza explained to Churchill that

> it is impossible to unite Italy with a king who through his long complicity with fascism has brought upon Italy the most terrible disaster of her history. Of the fatal meaning of this disaster he seems utterly unconscious. He thinks only of his house and not of Italy.[30]

The monarch, wrote Sforza to Eden, was making no serious effort to rouse the nation against Germany. On the contrary, he had 'become the symbol and the alibi of all those fascists and neo-fascists who go on shouting that they are now in your favour while secretly they hate you':

> what is happening in Italy today is an attempt to create a new Vichy. The Pétain of Italy is not Marshal Badoglio, but the king with a gang of corrupt generals.[31]

6   *The monarchy under attack*

By general consent, if sometimes tacit or grudging, the 'institutional question' was postponed in the expectation that the Germans would soon be driven out of Rome, when a more representative government could be formed. But in January 1944, since this deliverance still seemed far off, an earlier decision was demanded by the six antifascist parties whose existence was now permitted. There seems to have been little popular enthusiasm for the king personally, something that for some reason he blamed partly on British hostility.[1] On right and left he was said to be 'utterly discredited' by his support of Mussolini until July 1943. Since then he had given the impression of trying to revive a 'fascism without Mussolini' and deliberately hindering a return to democratic government. He also carried much of the responsibility for the surrender of his army at Rome.[2] Nevertheless, his critics disagreed with each other over how, when, and by whom he could be replaced.

Macmillan reported on 13 January that 'the representatives of the parties struck me as an unimpressive lot of typical small-town politicians. Nearly all were lawyers. There must be serious doubt as to how much they really represent.'[3] Almost their only point of agreement was that the Allied Control Commission should take responsibility for making the king renounce his authority. One argument employed was that his controversial presence weakened the war effort. Another was that by recruiting ex-fascists into the armed services he meant to defend his position by armed force. At a meeting held at Bari the six parties issued a joint statement that 'by unanimous wish of the Italian people' he should withdraw and so 'wash away the shame of the past'.

Washington and London disliked having their attention diverted from a bitterly fought war to such matters of domestic Italian politics. The British in particular wanted to postpone any change, especially as the royal government was 'tame and completely in our hands; it will obey our direction far more than any other that we may laboriously constitute'. Nevertheless, as Churchill had already explained, 'our policy is to broaden the base and increase the leftward emphasis of the Italian government'.[4] The main difficulty was that while the Party of Action wanted the allies to use their power to put an end at once to the monarchy as an institution, others wanted Umberto to succeed, others preferred Umberto's son with Badoglio as a caretaker regent, and others, the creation of a temporary 'lieutenancy of the realm' until the whole population was free to vote on the issue.

General Maitland Wilson, who took Eisenhower's place in December 1943, agreed with Mason-Macfarlane and Cordell Hull that the allies ought probably to accept the responsibility of forcing an abdication, but Roosevelt, and much more strongly Churchill, still thought that so long as Vittorio Emanuele held the loyalty of the armed forces, better avoid the distraction of further controversy and make no change until Rome was overrun.[5] One further difficulty was that politicians in Bari could not speak for northern Italy. Nor could the underground Committee of National Liberation in German-occupied Rome be prevented from sooner or later introducing an altogether more radical component into politics, and its views could not be ignored. The king sent to warn Bonomi in Rome against allowing this committee to indulge in anti-monarchist controversy, but his warning was ill-received.[6]

An acceptable compromise would no doubt have been found had the crown prince been more obviously fitted for the succession. More attractive and outgoing than his father, he was even more a soldier at heart, and completely inexperienced as a politician. Croce spoke of Umberto's character as 'entirely insignificant' and tainted by scandal. Anthony Eden thought him the 'poorest of creatures'. More favourable was Sam Reber, an American official in Naples who had known the prince in earlier years and found him 'greatly improved. The Balkan playboy period was over. But he has a weak face and, to judge by first meeting, has not, I should say, the personality to inspire confidence and devotion in others'.[7]

Umberto caused alarm among anti-fascists by tactlessly speaking of the Italian army as the only sound part of the nation and the surest defence of the monarchy. Though he claimed to be 'sincerely democratic', he was seen to be 'always surrounded by generals'. He even asked the allies to exert their authority to prevent criticism of the crown and spoke of using the lawcourts to prosecute anyone who cast discredit on the king or the armed forces.[8] According to Sforza, such views indicated a lack of comprehension and finesse and should bar him from the succession: he was, wrote Sforza, a 'stupid' young man who knew nothing of the real Italy: 'he had been as closely associated with fascism as his father. In addition he was weak and dissipated, with a degenerate and even oriental disposition inherited from his Balkan mother'.[9] Even more damaging was the verdict of the sovereign himself who was so anxious to continue in power that he maladroitly let it be known that he thought his son incapable of governing or of being acceptable to the country.[10]

In February the king moved the seat of government from Brindisi to Salerno and his personal residence to nearby Ravello; and here on 19–20 February he made his first major concession to the critics. After studying books on constitutional law borrowed from the university library at Naples, he discussed the various possibilities with Enrico De Nicola, a distinguished Neapolitan lawyer. This man had in 1920–4 been close to the king as Speaker of the lower house of parliament, since when they had had no contact because of the complete severance between the court and the elder statesmen of pre-fascist Italy. De Nicola had told the king three months earlier that he and his son should withdraw altogether from politics.[11] Now he suggested a compromise: they should wait until Rome was liberated and then arrange for Umberto to take the post of 'lieutenant general' or viceroy, leaving his father as a merely titular monarch.

This proposal was discussed for many hours at Ravello. Vittorio Emanuele was very reluctant and hinted that his own preference was for a new militarist government based on support from the army,[12] but gave ground on discovering that even the more conservative liberals would absolutely refuse to collaborate unless he disappeared from the political scene. On 21 February he complained to Mason-Macfarlane that the allies had improperly allowed him 'to be openly discredited and attacked', but said he would consider De Nicola's suggestion, though only 'as a great personal sacrifice in the interests of his country'. He tried to make it a condition that there should be no more attacks on him by the radio or the press. In a surprising afterthought he revealed that his motives were more selfish than dynastic, because, if pressed to go further he would forbid his son or grandson to accept the succession, 'and the House of Savoy would come to an end'.[13]

Fortunately this last remark was made in private. And meanwhile his public statement of intent went some way towards reaching a compromise settlement. Some of the politicians in Washinton were nevertheless worried by a forthcoming presidential election in America and, with an eye to the Italian–American vote, expressed a preference for the king to withdraw at once. What decided the issue was the arrival during March of Palmiro Togliatti, the Italian communist leader who had been for many years an exile in Russia. Togliatti introduced a note of realism into the rhetoric of party-political squabbles by announcing, to general surprise, that the communists would disregard the 'manifesto of Bari'. He, too, would ideally have preferred the king to abdicate at once because he was clearly unfitted to rule over a democratic state and was partly responsible for Italy's humiliating defeat.[14] But since this obvious solution had been rejected, Togliatti was ready to put the 'institutional question' on one side and join the royal government in order to concentrate on winning the war.

Once the communists had entered Badoglio's cabinet, the other parties were obliged to drop their own objections in order to balance the extreme Left inside the government. This was, said Sforza, far from an ideal solution. He feared that Togliatti was acting under orders from Moscow 'and in the long run would destroy the basis of democratic government in Italy by prolonging the neo-fascist rule of the king'.[15] Sforza and Croce would still have preferred abdication so as to remove an unpopular ruler and thereby save the institution of monarchy. Togliatti on the other hand thought that the best chance of Italy's becoming a republic was if the electorate were given enough time to observe the king and his son in action.[16]

The immediate crisis was resolved on 10 April when Murphy and Macmillan met the king at Ravello to ask for a formal public pronouncement, either for abdication as Washington would have preferred, or at the very least for a post-dated retirement as he had agreed in principle on 21 February. Their argument was simple – that his continued presence was an obstacle to any coalition of liberal forces as well as damaging to the war effort. At first he affected astonishment that the allies were backing the politicians against him. Public opinion, he was sure, still supported him. He had no responsibility for fascism, he said, nor for the hundreds of thousands of allied casualties caused by Mussolini's war; his contrary argument was that he had signed the declaration of war under duress and had constantly sought an opportunity to overturn that 'misguided' regime.[17]

His tearful and sometimes excited reaction was described in a report to Washington. When resisting allied demands

> he spoke with pride of the thousand-year history of the House of Savoy. He said mournfully: 'a republican form of government is not suited to the Italian people. They are not prepared for it either temperamentally or historically. In a republic every Italian would insist upon being president and the result would be chaos. The only people who would profit would be the communists'.[18]

Macmillan commented that 'old age has not deprived this monarch of any of his subtlety in negotiation and ingenuity of mind'. Two whole days passed in discussion of the alternatives. At last it was agreed to make no change until Rome fell. Umberto would then take over, not with the title of 'lieutenant of the king' as Vittorio Emanuele would have preferred, but the more non-committal 'lieutenant of the kingdom'. Only at the last moment was Macmillan able to insert that this surrender of royal authority would be 'final and irrevocable'.[19]

Another week went by during which Badoglio with some difficulty persuaded socialists, communists, liberals, and Christian democrats to join him in a broader and more representative government. When they came to Ravello to take their seals of office, even the more conservative ministers were silent and embarrassed, while the king himself could barely greet them civilly but merely complained of the traffic.[20] In private he was 'disgusted' at the way that Badoglio and others were giving credibility to the communist party; but, as Murphy explained, their appointment had become possible only because the communists were trying to help; and Badoglio confessed 'that without the support of Togliatti he could never have formed a new government. Togliatti had rendered him great assistance throughout and he had a very high opinion of his intelligence'.[21]

The prime minister would ideally have preferred a straight abdication and was doubtful if the monarchy could be saved by anything less, though he dutifully tried to conceal his alarm over the king's obstinacy.[22] The fiercest criticism came from Dino Grandi, now in exile, who saw the new government as a victory for an anti-fascist oligarchy imposing itself on public opinion in a more dictatorial manner than anything seen in a century of national history.[23] At the opposite extreme, the strongly republican Party of Action accepted this turn of events with equal reluctance. Sforza joined the cabinet but only 'as an unpleasant duty'; frightened by what seemed to him an undoubted victory by the communists, he now tried to persuade himself that, in comparison to his father, Umberto 'after all is not such a bad fellow'.[24]

The crown prince meanwhile tried hard to improve his reputation by showing a new sense of responsibility and statesmanship. In an interview with the *Daily Express*, he said he hoped that Italy could work her passage into the western alliance by using her fleet in the war against Japan and contributing troops for the invasion of Germany. His own ideal government, he explained enigmatically, was 'patterned on the British monarchy, and at the same time incorporating as much of America's political framework as possible'.[25]

But his choice of advisers continued to arouse disquiet in London,[26] and so did another tactless interview on 19 April, this time to *The Times*. Among his remarks was one advocating control of the press to stop anti-monarchist articles, and he criticised the exaggerated liberalism of the Allied Control Commission, which wrongly 'seemed to expect the Italian people to run before they could walk'. If he himself had formerly felt obliged to obey Mussolini, that was because otherwise he would have been cut out of the succession to the throne. It was sad but true, he added, that Mussolini 'at first had the full support of the nation'. Even in 1940, when his father agreed to declare war, this was only because 'there was no sign that the nation wanted it otherwise. No single voice was raised in protest. No demand was made for summoning parliament.'[27]

Possibly this last remark about parliament was a slip of the tongue. If not, Umberto must have been astonishingly ignorant about the realities of Mussolini's Italy. Only with difficulty was the cabinet restrained from resigning when news of such a highly compromising interview reached Salerno, and Sforza could think only that Umberto had been put up to it by the king himself, that 'little monster' who might have been intending to discredit his son.[28] Others claimed that the prince had been misquoted, but the author of the interview, who was no anti-monarchist, could not agree.[29] Croce was outraged, because in his view 'the whole war guilt falls on Mussolini and through him on the king'. The philosopher forgot his own earlier support for fascism and now contrived to believe that the whole responsibility for putting Mussolini in power lay on foreigners and the royal court:

> The king has been trying to shelter himself behind the fact that the chamber and senate nominally existed, and behind the argument that the fascist party militia and Grand Council were constitutional organs. I have no desire to use strong language, but I must call this hypocrisy. The Prince of Piedmont for twenty-two years has never shown any sign of acting independently of his father. Now he is simply repeating his father's arguments. He chooses to do this at the very moment when, having been designated lieutenant of the kingdom, he ought to be overcoming doubt and distrust as I personally hoped he would succeed in doing. To me it seems unworthy to try to unload the blame and errors of royalty on the people. I, an old monarchist, am therefore specially grieved when I see the monarchs themselves working to discredit the monarchy.[30]

Events were moving rapidly towards the occupation of Rome, which took place at the beginning of June 1944. The intention had been for Badoglio to resign at this point so as to bring into government some of the more radical Rome politicians who had experienced the German occupation. But during May the marshal arranged with the king and Umberto that his own mandate should be extended. His hope was to form a right-wing administration to include both liberals and Christian democrats,[31] and for some reason he assumed that the Committee of Liberation in Rome would not object. He agreed with the allies that Vittorio Emanuele should not be allowed back in Rome, since his appearance might make harder the task of forming a government. To prevent anti-royalist demonstrations in Rome he also wanted Umberto to remain in the south for a few days longer. Umberto, however, insisted on moving to Rome at once, and the citizens of the Italian capital, after nine months of hardship and persecution under nazi rule, gave him a warm welcome; to perhaps most people he was a symbol of liberation and a return to something like normality.

By a decree of 5 June, Vittorio Emanuele established the lieutenancy and surrendered effective power. What he gained by continuing to avoid formal abdication is hard to say, unless he had some hope that his 'irrevocable' surrender of authority might eventually be overturned by popular demand. Possibly this was the last moment when he could have saved the dynasty from its collapse two years later, just as his great-grandfather had saved the House of Savoy by abdicating after the military defeats of 1849. He merely said he was ready to abdicate whenever this was requested by the new head of state,[32] and probably relied on no such request being made. In Rome the welcoming crowds 'did not seem to notice his absence'.[33]

At a final meeting with the British authorities the monarch blamed them and Badoglio for 'leaving it to the Russians and the communists to initiate and get the credit for the coalition now in office'. He promised that he would disappear from politics and in future would be only an 'onlooker'.

> He spoke for some time on the subject of the communist menace to Italy. He felt very strongly about this and was most disquieted at the way in which Badoglio and most of his cabinet and many of the senior generals were currying favour with the communist party and following their lead.

A note appended to Mason-Macfarlane's report commented that 'the king seems to have tried to make mischief to the end'.[34] The British foreign office did not appear particularly worried 'even if the Italian people should eventually embark upon the experiment of a communist dictatorship', because Italian communism would 'for commerical as well as sentimental reasons' probably remain closer to the west than to Russia.[35]

7   Umberto II

Umberto was head of state for barely two years, first with the title of *luogotenente* or lieutenant, then for thirty-four days as king in name and deed. During this short time he had little chance to make his mark. In personality less astute and intelligent than his father, much less strong a character but also less obstinate, he was far more open, affable and ready to learn. Like all his predecessors his mind and tastes had been conditioned by an essentially military education which hardly equipped him for his new position. Under constitutional monarchy, people have to be convinced rather than dragooned; discretion and consensus are far more important than obedience and protocol.

Umberto's political views were flat and conventional but not reactionary. He told a foreign journalist that he hoped to change his country and make it genuinely democratic by carrying out 'the vastest education programme Italy has ever seen'.[1] In retrospect he could admit that his father had made mistakes,[2] and in particular complained that as a prince he had never been permitted views of his own or any political initiative.[3] After a few months in office he convinced some doubters that the experience of government was making him into a more responsible politician than his past reputation might have suggested.[4] If only his father had abdicated sooner, or even if Umberto had been earlier brought more into consultation and given some administrative responsibility, the vote that in June 1946 narrowly defeated the monarchy might possibly have gone a different way.

·The advice he received from Croce was to make a complete change by choosing advisers from the democratic parties, and he went part of the way by appointing Falcone Lucifero as Minister of the Royal House. This man was a lawyer who was thought to support the social democratic party once led by Matteotti, and at first this appointment caused some alarm among republicans who feared a more liberal monarchy. Lucifero tried to diminish the number of generals and aristocrats and Piedmontese who had predominated at court, replacing them with at least some professional and academic personalities; but met serious and usually successful resistance from the army officers with whom Umberto felt most at home.[5]

Before leaving southern Italy on 6 June 1944, Umberto charged Badoglio with forming another government to include representatives of the Committee of National Liberation,[6] and Badoglio told the Control Commission that he did not anticipate much difficulty. On arriving in Rome, the prince went at once to the Quirinal palace, while the leading politicians from Naples and Rome met at the Grand Hotel to formulate a common policy. Members of the Rome committee were unanimous in opposing Badoglio because of his fascist past. By general agreement the new prime minister ought in their view to be Bonomi who had held that position in 1921 and was an ideal consensus candidate. So Badoglio accompanied Mason-Macfarlane to the Quirinal and together they recommended Bonomi's appointment. Umberto could possibly have held out for his original choice since Churchill, Stalin, even at first Togliatti, favoured Badoglio, but wisely he gave way.

He also permitted a novel procedure by which, in order not to prejudge the 'institutional question' of republic versus monarchy, the new ministers would not swear the normal oath of fealty. Bonomi alone did so. Badoglio was offered a post but declined.[7]

Churchill accepted the new government with great reluctance, even annoyance; in his view, not only was it 'without the slightest popular mandate', but any resurgence of civilian politics could distract attention from the reconquest of northern Italy. In his opinion, military considerations should have priority, and he thought that Umberto was allowing himself, consciously or not, to be manipulated by 'a group of aged and hungry politicians' who were 'trying to intrigue themselves into an undue share of power'.[8]

The authority of the Allied Control Commission had gradually been surrendered as the German armies were pushed northwards, but its continued presence remained an anomalous restriction on Italian domestic politics now that Italy was a co-belligerent in the war against Germany. The commission had always refused to exert any pressure either for or against the monarchy. Churchill, while admitting that he 'did not care for the Italian king', agreed that a popular vote on the institutional question was the only way of insuring against civil strife. After the war Italians should choose whatever constitution suited them best, though he hoped that they would vote to remain a united country with a democratic form of government.[9]

On 25 June Bonomi issued a decree stating that after the final liberation of northern Italy a vote by universal suffrage would choose a constituent assembly to decide the matter. In the meantime ministers undertook to abstain from saying anything that would prejudge this issue. Bonomi himself hoped for a continuation of the monarchy.[10] The Christian democrat leader, Alcide De Gasperi, rather thought that an immediate vote would overwhelmingly demand a republic,[11] and information from the Vatican estimated that only twenty-five per cent of Italians were firmly monarchist. Opinion in the Vatican was known to favour Umberto who unlike his father was a devoutly practising Christian. The crown was also seen by many conservative Catholics as a valuable symbol of stability, though 'it was difficult to answer the argument that the monarchy had done little to serve the interests of the country or people during the past thirty years'.[12]

There was some disagreement over whether a popular vote by universal suffrage might be preferable to leaving the decision to an elected assembly. Roosevelt inclined towards a plebiscite of the whole nation. Umberto, too, despite signing the decree for an assembly, gave another perhaps indiscreet interview to the *New York Times* at the end of October in which he suggested that a plebiscite would better reflect public opinion. This statement caused resentment as an intrusion into partisan politics, and though Bonomi in private agreed with what he said, the parties on the Left had some reason to fear that a popular plebiscite might be manipulated to favour the monarchy. The other ministers therefore reaffirmed their original call for a constituent assembly.

Umberto's interview contained other revealing remarks, some of which he cut out of the published version. He thought that monarchies everywhere should and would move further to the left. He was against forming an actual monarchist party since he said he wished to remain above party conflicts. He had spoken a number of times with the communist Togliatti, 'finding him clever, agreeable, and easy to discuss problems with'. One phrase he censored was about an Italian republic possibly leading to a presidential dictatorship. He also indicated that a monarchy would best ensure that the move to the left took place 'in an ordered, liberal way'. He 'fully realises that the weight of the past is the monarchy's greatest handicap', and therefore intended to work for a 'radical revision' of the old constitution of 1848.[13]

Only very imperfectly was it possible to assess the likely degree of popular support behind the many parties that prepared for an appeal to the electorate. The pre-fascist liberals seemed to have little backing and once again disagreed with each other over fine points of principle or practice. Orlando, Nitti, Bonomi, Croce, and Soleri were out of touch with the public and sometimes out of sympathy with each other; they were survivors from a distant period before the organised mass parties – whether fascism, communism, or Christian democracy – came into existence. Another minority group, the doctrinaire Party of Action, included people of great intelligence who had far better anti-fascist credentials than the liberals, but was held together only by its unequivocal republicanism. Popular support and party discipline were most in evidence among Togliatti's communists and Pietro Nenni's socialists; and to a lesser degree among De Gasperi's Christian democrats whose centre of gravity lay in the Centre or perhaps on the Centre-Right.

The chief danger to the throne came from the Left. De Gasperi warned the British that the socialist Nenni was a potential revolutionary, but one who fortunately feared the triumph of communism; whereas the communist Togliatti 'was far more reasonable' than the socialists, as had been shown by his joining Badoglio's government, and he might well break with Moscow if Stalin's intrusion into Italian politics became too assertive.[14] Stalin had confessed to Churchill that although the Russians might not be able to control the Italian communists, Togliatti was 'a wise man, not an extremist, and would not start an adventure in Italy'. And this corresponded with Croce's expectation or hope that Italian communism would eventually become more independent, more progressive, more 'moral' than the Russian variety.[15]

Umberto remarked on other occasions that, while he would have preferred a government that included a stronger right-wing component, he found Togliatti 'to be a very congenial companion whose intelligence he respected, but was afraid that he suited his conversation according to his company'.[16] Togliatti for his part explained to a member of the British parliament that the Italian crown was not above parties like that in Britain: 'the House of Savoy had never hesitated to use the reactionary elements in the country to suppress any democratic movement from the Left'.[17]

Almost certainly Umberto supported or instigated an approach made to the allies in September when Badoglio suggested that Italy should become a fully independent member of the western alliance; in which case Badoglio, together with Orlando and Bonomi, would be able to form an anti-communist government. Badoglio explained that the army would support this change, and he would then replace the prefects who were 'agents of Togliatti and Nenni', appointing instead more trustworthy officials who would ensure a reliable result from the elections. His hope was that this prospect would please the allies and persuade them to accept Italy as a full partner. He also hoped that Umberto's hand would in that way be greatly strengthened against claims made against Italy by Jugoslavia, Greece, and France, who had old scores to settle and had preceded Italians in joining the anti-fascist front in Europe. But this intention was all too obvious and the proposal was rejected.[18]

The allies also counselled Umberto against accepting a decision by Bonomi's cabinet to institute an investigation into the failure to defend Rome in September 1943. This investigation, it was hoped by some people, would exculpate Badoglio and Vittorio Emanuele by blaming the army commanders. But the Control Commission, while insisting that only Italians could decide such a matter, pointed out that the king would surely be strongly criticised by any enquiry, and it would prematurely raise the institutional question at a time when divisive political issues were best avoided.[19]

There were further matters on which Umberto disagreed with the occupying forces. One was over the negotiations that ultimately led to the peace treaty in 1947. Umberto later recalled that he would 'most probably' have refused to sign this treaty, as he was optimistic enough to think that the allies could have been made to give Italy back her old colonies and a better frontier with Jugoslavia.[20] Another difference was over the purge of ex-fascists that had been confirmed by a royal decree of 27 July 1944, but which was carried out slowly and very partially despite repeated urging from the Control Commission. Umberto, even though he signed the decree, was strongly against what he called this 'iniquitous' purge,[21] because too many people would have suffered from it. Here was a highly delicate matter, since not only had Umberto and his father supported fascism for twenty years, but half a dozen members of Bonomi's cabinet had helped to justify Mussolini's dictatorship by once voting for him in parliament.

Disagreements over such issues led to some loss of cohesion inside the Committee of National Liberation which had effectively appointed Bonomi in June 1944. When in November he resigned, this committee failed to agree over the succession, and Umberto used the impasse to regain some of the crown's powers of intervention. He furthermore tried to persuade the allies to help his cause by allowing the publication of more monarchist newspapers, and an unlikely appeal was sent to ask Churchill for a public statement in support of the crown. But the allies were determined to remain neutral and advised the *luogotenente* to respect the political truce by avoiding partisan politics.[22]

Appeals for allied intervention in domestic politics came from every direction, so many indeed that Admiral Stone, the American who now headed the Control Commission, refused to receive any more.[23] The communists and socialists, alarmed at signs of Umberto's increasing popularity, wondered once again if Stone could help to remove him and appoint instead a council of regency for his young son. Another appeal came from Bonomi who asked the Control Commission for permission to modify the law about electing a constituent assembly. He was supported by monarchists and right-wing liberals in preferring the alternative of a direct popular referendum on the 'institutional question', believing that this would favour the monarchy, and he hoped that the occupying forces would take responsibility (and incur the odium) for imposing this change in the law.

But the allies, though inclined to agree that a referendum would be the fairer method, again refused to intervene.[24] Eden explained that, whether or not an assembly was more likely than a plebiscite to support a republic, this was no concern of other countries; for the British, the monarchist question was secondary to the main issue of whether Italy would become a parliamentary democracy or a communist totalitarian state. Eden's personal opinion was that the monarchy, after being discredited by its association with fascism, would probably be a source of weakness rather than strength for Italy.[25]

Vittorio Emanuele had meanwhile kept his promise to remain a mere onlooker of events. Lucifero, Umberto's personal minister, would have preferred the king to leave Italy altogether so as to make his son's task easier.[26] Instead the retired sovereign moved to the Villa Maria Pia at Posillipo which some years before the war had been presented to the Italian government by Lord Rosebery. There, according to his own diary, he seems to have been visited by his son only three times in two years.[27] For a few days in August 1944 he was the next-door neighbour of King George. The British sovereign, visiting allied troops, first stayed at the Palace of Caserta which he found far grander than royal palaces in Britain – Umberto had once been shocked at Buckingham Palace by having to share a communal bathroom at the end of a long corridor.[28] Protocol excluded any meeting between two warring heads of state who had not yet signed a peace agreement, but Vittorio Emanuele refused a request to leave Posillipo. Perhaps he was hoping for a casual encounter, and at one point he and his queen were arrested by a British naval patrol when fishing before breakfast outside King George's bedroom window.[29]

As the time drew closer for a vote on the monarchy, politicians found it harder to observe the political truce, and a broad division became clearer between the Right, who mostly saw the crown as their best hope of avoiding radical social change, and the Left, who feared that it might be an important obstacle to change. Feelings ran so high that Sandro Pertini, the socialist and future president of the Italian republic, threatened Umberto that if he dared to visit Milan he would be lynched.[30] Others hostile to the monarchy were found among adherents of Mussolini's puppet republic in the north who revived the theme of how successive kings had perverted the course of the risorgimento by imposing an over-centralised and reactionary regime on the Italian people.[31]

North Italy continued to be the scene of bitter partisan warfare, which ended only in April 1945 when the partisans executed Mussolini and the Germans finally surrendered. Some of the anti-fascist military units had been strongly monarchist in sympathy; most were the very opposite. No prince of the House of Savoy joined their ranks, although Umberto once claimed, whether genuinely or not, that only the duties of high office prevented him. Ferruccio Parri, the most prominent partisan leader, was in June 1945 appointed prime minister in the first government of liberated Italy. Parri belonged to the republican Party of Action, but undertook to observe the political truce and instructed the prefects to remain neutral when preparations for the election began.[32]

There were two main issues in this election, separate but related, one being whether the monarchy should continue, the other being whether the first free elections for twenty-five years would lean to

the right or the left. For many and probably most leading politicians
the second question was the more vital. Some eighty different parties
had come into existence to fill the void left by fascism, many of
whom were reluctant to commit themselves too openly on the first
issue because a firm commitment might have alienated some supporters whose votes they needed for the second. Many politicians
preferred to hedge their bets on the institutional question, fearing to
find themselves on the defeated side in what looked increasingly like
a close vote.

This was true of De Gasperi who was the most skilful politician
in Parri's government and who in December succeeded to the premiership. Unlike the Vatican which saw the crown as a welcome
bulwark against communism, De Gasperi's Christian democrats
wanted to avoid attracting too right-wing a label: not only were
many of them convinced republicans, but their leaders calculated
that communism would be most effectively beaten if their own party
emerged from elections with at least a relative majority, and this
meant appealing to a wide electorate which might vote either way on
the monarchy. De Gasperi's personal views on this latter issue were
never clearly stated.

Umberto found that few reputable politicians would declare openly
for his cause while they waited to gauge which way public opinion
was moving.[33] This also left him without good enough advice at a
critical moment. Early in 1946 some of the liberals again tried to
persuade him to hand over power to a regency for his young son in
the hope of rallying more support, but he refused what may have
seemed to him an electoral gimmick or a counsel of despair.[34] His
chief problem was that the minister in charge of running the elections
was Giuseppe Romita, a socialist and committed republican. Romita
carefully arranged that local-government elections were first held in
selected areas where there was a large pro-republican majority, and
the result of this local vote then persuaded some of the fence-sitters
that a bandwagon was beginning to roll.[35]

The date for the main national election was fixed for 2–3 June.
The original intention had been to elect a constituent assembly that
would take all the necessary decisions, but De Gasperi realised that
such a body would be composed of political activists who might well
choose either Nenni or Togliatti as its president, and he therefore
continued to hope that Washington and London would insist on the
alternative method of voting by a direct plebiscite.[36] Once again the
allies refused, so the cabinet took responsibility for stipulating that
there should be two simultaneous votes, one of them a popular
referendum to choose between monarchy and republic, the other for
electing a constituent assembly to put that choice into practice.

The agreed procedure prescribed that, if the vote went against Umberto, the prime minister would become provisional head of state until a president could be chosen. If on the other hand the monarchy won, Umberto would continue as *de facto* ruler while the assembly drew up a new constitution to replace the old *statuto* of 1848. Both elections would be by universal suffrage, with women voting for the first time. One clause that went almost unnoticed laid down that the referendum would be decided by a majority not of valid votes, but of all electors who cast a vote; and this eventually allowed the lawyers to indulge in unseemly quibbles that came close to impugning the final tally.

On 9 May, three weeks before the referendum, Vittorio Emanuele surprised everyone by at last formally abdicating. He tried to make out that he took this decision under pressure from the Control Commission, though actually the allies disapproved.[37] In fact, it was a move that he had long considered as a means of winning popularity for a younger man less tainted by a fascist past. Why he waited so long is hard to say, and he left it much too late. After taking formal and unemotional leave to his son, he was conducted by an Italian cruiser to Egypt travelling as the 'Count of Pollenzo'. He departed with no word of thanks to his servants, timid, taciturn, impenetrable as ever; and, equally in character, he took with him dozens of crates containing family documents and state papers.[38] Nor did he let fall any word of regret for the past. Occasionally in Egypt he admitted that Mussolini's foreign policy might have been a disaster, but of all his prime ministers the duce was still remembered with something close to a grudging admiration.[39]

The timing of this abdication was ill-received on the extreme Left where it was rightly seen as an electoral trick to win votes. The same accusation was levelled at an unsuccessful attempt by the new King Umberto II to introduce a wide amnesty for prisoners, and at his profligate grant of royalist titles to many thousand aspirants.[40] After some initial doubt, the cabinet found itself legally obliged to accept his accession as a legitimate king, though they refused to allow the customary but prejudicial appellation 'by grace of God and will of people'.[41]

From now onwards the political truce was very generally broken on both sides. The unabashed process of electioneering might have seemed undignified in a crowned head, but Umberto made a hurried visit through the principal cities of Italy to be seen by as many as possible of his subjects, and met with a usually favourable reception especially in the south. His supporters produced some unpersuasive arguments in their election campaign, for instance that the monarchy alone could check regional separatism and recover Italy's great power status; also that a republic was bound to be anti-clerical. The Vatican therefore backed him, and the British minister to the Holy See reported that 'all the pains of hell are predicted for those who vote for democratic parties of the Left'.[42] His opponents based their anti-monarchist campaign on the past record of the dynasty. Somewhat unfairly the British and Americans, apart from Admiral Stone who was thought to back Umberto, were blamed at court for giving partisan support to the republicans and the Left.[43]

The election took place with a large turn-out of voters, and foreign observers as well as most Italians were impressed with the good order, good humour, and correct observance of the regulations. By 6 June, as the count proceeded, an informed forecast estimated that the republicans were likely to win by about twelve millions to ten, and Umberto made preparations to leave the country. At this point some of the more extreme monarchists pointed out that the law demanded a majority not of 'valid votes' but of all votes. No one had foreseen that this might include blank, defaced, or otherwise invalid voting slips, and these would take another ten days to count before an unambiguous result could be proclaimed.

Neither Romita nor De Gasperi had calculated on the uncertainty of such a prolonged and dangerous interregnum. The cabinet reacted by deciding on 10 June, with one dissentient, that Umberto should not wait for the final count but ought to leave the country at once. When he made difficulties, there was disturbing talk on both sides about resorting to force. The government was clearly at fault in not having foreseen and provided for such an impasse. But Umberto also acted with apparent impropriety when he revived unfortunate memories of the past by breaking constitutional practice and refusing to accept his ministers' advice.[44] By so doing he gave the impression of seeking a captious pretext to justify his retention of power. Some supporters vainly appealed yet again for the Allied Control Commission to intervene on his side.[45] Others were ready for armed rebellion, and some southerners suggested setting up a separatist monarchical regime in Naples and Sicily.[46]

Common sense and patriotism saved Umberto from accepting such counsel. To those who urged him to use his undoubted powers and dismiss the government he replied that such an action might lead to civil war and was unthinkable. Lucifero warned him that Vittorio Emanuele had used the same excuse of avoiding bloodshed as a reason for appointing Mussolini in 1922, with tragic results. To which the obvious reply was that the tragedy of 1922 had been brought about by the king defying his own ministers, and the same mistake should not lightly be made again.[47]

For three days Umberto held out indecisively and the country was

poised on the edge of self-destruction. Only on 13 June did he submit
and leave the country for Lisbon, five days before a pronouncement
by the court of appeal declared that 12,700,000 Italians had voted for
a republic, 10,700,000 for the monarchy, and the non-valid votes had
been only 1,500,000. He publicly protested at his expulsion from the
Quirinal as an 'outrageous illegality', though it was far less so than
his predecessor's forcible expulsion of the pope from the same palace
in 1870; nor did it compare unfavourably with his father's treatment
of King Zog of Albania and Haile Selassie of Ethiopia. On his
departure he issued a defiant proclamation against what he called a
coup d'état by ministers who were acting illegally and as revolutionaries. He therefore refused to recognise the legality of the republic,
and in so doing ensured that the change of regime took place in the
worst possible way with bitterness and recriminations on both sides.
De Gasperi issued a counter-statement referring with sadness but
also anger to an 'unworthy page of history' which brought the
monarchy to an end:

> We must strive to understand the tragedy of someone who, after
> inheriting a military defeat and a disastrous complicity with dicta-
> torship, tried hard in recent months to work with patience and
> good will towards a better future. But now this final act of the
> thousand-year-old House of Savoy must be seen as part of our
> national catastrophe; it is an expiation, an expiation forced upon all
> of us, even those who have not shared directly in the guilt of the
> dynasty.[48]

The adverse vote came as no great surprise to Vittorio Emanuele
who had anticipated that his son would lose;[49] but Umberto had
hoped to win by a small majority[50] and in that case had been ready to
corroborate or overturn the result by holding a second confirmatory
referendum when the country was more settled under peace-time
conditions. His queen, who was described by one British diplomat
as 'the only member of the royal family with political instinct and
some popular following', had at one point been afraid that the
monarchy might obtain less than one fifth of the vote.[51]

The fact that such varying estimates were posible is an indication
of the incalculability and volatility of popular wishes. By showing
that nearly half the population supported the king, the result gave a
shaky start to the republic. And another divisive fact was that the
monarchy had a majority in almost all southern provinces but was
outvoted almost everywhere in the north. The north-south divide
was already dangerous enough without this further divergence.

Umberto in Portugal continued to style himself King of Italy and
refused to admit the legitimacy of the republic. This made impos-

sible his return from exile as an ordinary citizen, especially when he confirmed that he was ready to resume his royal prerogatives if ever the Italian electorate changed its mind.[52] Many of his loyal followers clung to the belief that the results of the referendum had been deliberately falsified to ensure their defeat.[53] But this was a familiar argument from losing parties in Italian elections, and one can assume that there may have been some irregularities on the part of both vanquished and victors. One fact beyond doubt is that the referendum of June 1946 was a good deal fairer and less irregular than the plebiscites of 1859–60 upon which four kings based their title to the Italian throne.

Equally revealing was the simultaneous election of a constituent assembly when, for the first time ever, the political allegiance of ordinary Italians could be assessed by universal male and female suffrage. The most dramatic result was that the old ruling class which emerged out of the risorgimento found little support, being widely blamed for connivance with Mussolini or at least an almost incomprehensible failure to resist him. Few votes went to the various liberal factions and even fewer to the neo-fascists. Only three parties had any substantial following out of the fifty that finally presented themselves for election: these were the Christian democrats with 32.5 per cent of the vote, the socialists with 20.7 per cent and the communists with 18.9 per cent. Between them these three won 426 seats out of 556 in the assembly, and their victory seemed to mark the eclipse of that small élite of liberal monarchists who claimed lineal descent from Cavour, Crispi, and Giolitti.

On 1 January 1948 a new republican constitution came into force which banned the ex-king and his male descendants from returning to Italy. By its terms their property would also have been forfeited to the state had not Vittorio Emanuele escaped this law by dying three days earlier in his Egyptian exile. Sometimes he had complained of his poverty, but this complaint rather reflected an extreme close-fistedness and in fact he had continued to enjoy a considerable income.[54] Ironically his large investments in London had been placed in British war loan by the Custodian of Enemy Property, but at least they remained intact, and the British courts after 1948 rejected three attempts to have them confiscated on behalf of the Italian republic.[55] As a former head of state his death would normally have been commemorated in the Italian legislature, but this custom, though allowed for Joseph Stalin, was in his case forbidden by the communist who presided over the constituent assembly. The ex-king was buried in Egypt.

Like the British in 1688 and the French in 1789, Italians had thus carried out their own constitutional revolution. But politically the events of 1946 in Italy were less revolutionary than those of 1922, and socially they left the underlying structure of the country remarkably unchanged. Umberto lived for thirty-five years in exile. During this time he periodically sent messages to a dwindling number of loyalist supporters. In these pronouncements he tried to maintain that monarchy stood ideally for liberty and progress, whereas republicanism was foreign to Italian traditions; and he made quite clear that he would return at any time if summoned by popular wish. When he died in 1983, no member of the Italian government appeared at his funeral at Hautecombe in Savoy, though some republican politicians thought their absence unnecessary and perhaps a mistake.[56] Long before this the minuscule monarchist party had split into two bickering factions, and a further split after Umberto's death found some die-hards hailing his son as Vittorio Emanuele IV, while others backed the young Duke of Aosta as a more suitable and attractive pretender. The oldest surviving dynasty in Europe had run its course. After eighty-five years, during which it presided over national unification and enjoyed many triumphs as well as failures, the end came in tragedy and anticlimax.

Abbreviations used in the notes

Alexander Papers	Public Record Office, London
Asquith Papers	Bodleian Library, Oxford
Avon Papers	Public Record Office, London
Balfour Papers	Public Record Office, London
Bertie Papers	Public Record Office, London
Brusati Papers	Archivio di Stato, Rome
CAB	Cabinet Office records, Public Record Office, London
Cavan Papers	Churchill College, University of Cambridge
Chamberlain Papers	Birmingham University Library
Clarendon Papers	Bodleian Library, Oxford
Crispi Papers	Archivio di Stato, Rome, but partly consulted at their former location in Palermo
Curzon Papers	India Office, London
DBFP	*Documents on British Foreign Policy*, ed. E.L. Woodward and R. Butler, London, 1947–
DDI	*Documenti Diplomatici Italiani 1870–1939*, Ministero degli Esteri, Rome, 1952–
Delmé-Radcliffe Papers	In possession of the family
FO	Foreign Office Papers, Public Record Office, London
FRUS	*Papers Relating to the Foreign Relations of the United States 1935–1961*, Department of State, Washington, D.C.
Lloyd George Papers	House of Lords Library, London
Mason-Macfarlane Papers	War Museum, London
PREM	Prime Minister's office, Public Record Office, London
PRO	Public Record Office, London
Robertson Papers	Liddell Hart Archives, King's College, University of London
Rodd Papers	Bodleian Library, Oxford
Royal Archives	Windsor Castle
Russell Papers	Public Record Office, London

St Antony's Documents	Mussolini's archive, photocopies held by St Antony's College, University of Oxford
Salisbury Papers	Hatfield House, Hertfordshire
Smuts Papers	Microfilm in Cambridge University Library
Sonnino microfilm	University of Michigan, Ann Arbor
Staatsarchiv, Vienna	Haus, Hof, und Staatsarchiv
Stillman Papers	Union College, Schenectady, N.Y.
Templewood Papers	Cambridge University Library
Vatican Archives	Rome
Vittoriano Documents	Istituto per la storia del Risorgimento, Rome
War Museum Library	London
Washington Archives	Partly in microfilm
WO	War Office papers, Public Record Office, London
Wilson Papers	War Museum, London

I am grateful to the owners and curators of the documentary sources listed above. In particular I acknowledge the gracious permission of Her Majesty the Queen to use material in the Royal Archives; also the Public Record Office at Kew; the Earl of Clarendon; the families of Lord Rennell of Rodd and General Delmé-Radcliffe; the curators of the Bodleian Library, Oxford; the syndics of the Cambridge University Library; the War Museum in London; the Archivio di Stato and the Museo del Risorgimento in Rome; St Antony's College, Oxford; the House of Lords library; the University of Birmingham library; the India Office; Lord Bonham Carter; the Liddell Hart Centre at King's College, London; and the Archives Centre at Churchill College, Cambridge.

Notes

Vittorio Emanuele II

1 The king and the constitution, 1861

1. P. Matter, *Cavour et l'unité italienne*, Parıs, 1922, ı, 351.
2. Royal Archives, diary of Queen Victoria (1 Dec. 1855).
3. F. Crispolti, *Corone e porpore: ricordi personali*, Milan, 1937, 13; *Carteggi e documenti diplomatici inediti di E. d'Azeglio*, ed. A. Colombo, Turin, 1920, ıı, 306.
4. Russell Papers, 30/22/68 (10 Aug. 1861).

2 An abortive march on Rome, 1862

1. *DDI*, ser. 1, ıı, 112–13 (ed. R. Moscati); *L'unificazione italiana vista dai diplomatici statunitensi*, ed. H. R. Marraro, Rome, 1971, ıv, 69.
2. E. Della Rocca, *Autobiografia di un veterano: ricordi storici*, Bologna, 1897, ıı, 94; M. Rosi, *Il risorgimento italiano e l'azione d'un patriota*, Rome, 1906, 427; Russell Papers, 30/22/68 (24 May 1861, Hudson).
3. *Rassegna Storica del Risorgimento*, Rome, 1984, 292, 300–1.
4. Denis Mack Smith, *Vittorio Emanuele II*, Bari, 1972, 361, 365, 368; *Die Auswärtige Politik Preussens*, ed. R. Ibbeken, Oldenburg, 1935, ıı, tome 2, 162; Frances Cobbe, *Italics*, London 1864, 179.
5. Russell Papers, 30/22/69 (26 Jan. 1862).
6. L. Thouvenel, *Pages de l'histoire du second empire*, Paris, 1903, 343–4; L. Thouvenel, *Le secret de l'empereur*, Paris, 1889, ıı, 232.
7. A. Luzio, *Aspromonte e Mentana: documenti inediti*, Florence, 1935, 132; Russell Papers, 30/22/69 (30 Nov. 1862, Hudson).
8. *Carteggi di Alfonso Lamarmora*, ed. A. Colombo, Turin, 1928, 107, 139–40, 145; *Atti Parlamentari: Camera dei deputati, discussioni*, Rome, 27 Nov. 1862, 4579.
9. *Carteggi di E. d'Azeglio*, ıı, 306; *Carteggi di Lamarmora*, 142–5; *DDI*, ser. 1, ıı,

110, 123; *Lettere e documenti del Barone Bettino Ricasoli*, ed. M. Tabarrini and A. Gotti, Florence, vı, 314–15.
10. *Carteggio politico di Michelangelo Castelli*, ed. Luigi Chiala, Turin, 1890, ı, 549; Domenico Farini, *Diario di fine secolo*, ed. E. Morelli, Rome, 1962, ıı, 1006; *Il problema Veneto e l'Europa*, ed. N. Blakiston, Venice, 1967, ıı, 556–8.
11. L. Lipparini, *Minghetti*, Bologna, 1947, ıı, 283; Mme Rattazzi, *Rattazzi et son temps: documents inédits*, Paris, 1881, ı, 615.
12. *DDI*, ser. 1, ıı, 435; *Camera, discussioni*, 20 July 1862, 3457.
13. *Camera, discussioni*, 22 July 1862, 3462; Giuseppe Garibaldi, *Scritti politici e militari*, ed. D. Ciàmpoli, Rome, 1907, ı, 268; G. Durando, *Episodi diplomatici del risorgimento italiano dal 1856 al 1863*, Turin, 1901, 273–4; M. Puccioni, *L'unità d'Italia nel pensiero e nell'azione del Barone Bettino Ricasoli*, Florence, 1932, 346.
14. Russell papers, 30/22/69 (10 Aug. 1862).

3 From Turin to Florence

1. *DDI*, ser. 1, ııı, 135; *Auswärtige Politik*, ıı, tome 2, 749; C.G. Bapst, *Le Maréchal Canrobert*, Paris, 1898, ııı, 233; Russell Papers, 30/22/69 (30 Nov. and 2 Dec. 1862, Hudson).
2. *DDI*, ser. 1, ııı, 205; Rosi, *Il risorgimento*, 439; *Camera, discussioni*, 30 Nov. 1862, 4654–5 (Pettinengo).
3. Federigo Sclopis, *Diario segreto (1859–1878)*, ed. P. Pietro Pirri, Turin, 1959, 352.
4. Russell Papers, 30/22/69 (2 Dec. and 13 Dec. 1862); *DDI*, ser. 1, ııı, 224; Luzio, *Aspromonte e Mentana*, 154; *Il Principe Napoleone nel risorgimento italiano*, ed. A. Comandini, Milan, 1922, 233.
5. Sclopis, *Diario*, 351–2.
6. *Ibid.*, 354; *Auswärtige Politik*, ııı, 433; *DDI*, ser. 1, ııı, 366.

7. *Carteggi di Bettino Ricasoli*, ed. S. Camerani and G. Arfè, Rome, 1962, XVII, 459–60; G. E. Curàtulo, *Garibaldi, Vittorio Emanuele, Cavour, nei fasti della patria: documenti inediti*, Bologna, 1911, 363; *Carteggi politici inediti di Francesco Crispi (1860–1900)*, ed. T. Palamenghi-Crispi, Rome, 1912, 182; *Discorsi parlamentari di Francesco Crispi*, Rome, 1915, I, 75; Russell Papers, 30/22/69 (30 Nov. 1862).

8. *Ibid.*, 30/22/70 (17 Sept. 1864, Elliot); Denis Mack Smith, *Victor Emanuel, Cavour and the risorgimento*, London, 1971, 276.

9. G. Rothan, *Souvenirs diplomatiques: l'Allemagne et l'Italie*, Paris, 1885, II, 412–13, 418; C. Grün, *L'Italie en 1861*, Brussels, 1862, II, 279; Russell Papers (23 Nov. 1863, Elliot).

10. Alberto Mario, *L'Italia libera*, Rome, 1925, 198.

11. William James Stillman, *The union of Italy*, London, 1909, 392.

12. *Scritti editi ed inediti di Giuseppe Mazzini*, ed. M. Meneghini, Imola, 1938–40, LXXIX, 255, LXXXIII, 119; *Roma e Venezia: ricordi storici d'un romano*, Rome, 1895, 220–1; *Politica segreta Italiana 1863–1870*, Turin, 1891, 44–9.

13. Russell Papers, 30/22/70 (22 July 1864, Elliot).

14. *Benedeks Nachgelassene Papiere*, ed. H. Friedjung, Dresden, 1904, 329–31.

15. *Il problema Veneto*, II, 654, 700, III, 425–6; FO, 45/56 (1 Jan. and 7 Jan. 1864, Elliot).

16. *DDI*, ser. 1, IV, 415, 439.

17. Russell Papers, 30/22/110 (27 Dec. 1863 and 2 May 1864).

18. *Ricordi di Michelangelo Castelli (1847–1875)*, ed. Luigi Chiala, Turin, 1888, 166; *Carteggio di Castelli*, II, 6–7, 310; *Rassegna Storica del Risorgimento*, Jan. 1927, 145, 155 (I. Bellini).

19. Marco Minghetti, *La convenzione di settembre*, Bologna, 1899, 29, 200–1; Della Rocca, *Autobiografia*, II, 385–6; *DDI*, ser. 1, V, 248; *Le lettere di Vittorio Emanuele II*, ed. F. Cognasso, Turin, 1966, II, 805.

20. Sclopis, *Diario*, 367, 375–6, 379; Mme Rattazzi, *Rattazzi*, I, 669.

21. Russell Papers, 30/22/70 (23 Sept. 1864 and 20 Jan. 1865).

22. *Ibid.*, (18 Feb. 1865); G. Di Revel, *Sette mesi al ministero: ricordi ministeriali*, Milan, 1895, 2–3; Minghetti, *La convenzione*, 73.

4 The war for Venice

1. *Epistolario di Carlo Cattaneo*, ed. R. Caddeo, Florence, 1954–6, III, 518, IV, 30.

2. *Camera, discussioni*, 25 Feb. 1863, 5328 (Mordini); *Discorsi parlamentari di Marco Minghetti*, Rome, 1888, II, 83–4.

3. *Carteggi di Ricasoli*, XXVI, 38.

4. Mme Rattazzi, *Rattazzi*, I, 642–3, II, 10–11; Russell Papers, 30/22/70 (22 July 1864); *Carteggi di Lamarmora*, 138; *Le carte di Alfonso della Marmora*, Turin, 1979, 37; *Discorsi parlamentari di Agostino Depretis*, Rome, 1891, VI, 570.

5. Friedrich Vitzthum von Eckstadt, *London, Gastein und Sadowa 1864–1866*, Stuttgart, 1889, 109.

6. *Le carte di Giovanni Lanza*, Turin, 1936, III, 441; *Il Principe Napoleone*, 228; *Auswärtige Politik*, V, 189; *Carteggio di Castelli*, II, 127; Cristoforo Negri, *La grandezza italiana: studi, confronti e desiderii*, Turin, 1864, 445.

7. *Auswärtige Politik*, II, tome 2, 721, VI, 311, 563; *Aus dem Leben Teodor von Bernhardis*, Leipzig, 1897, VII, 37; Luigi Chiala, *Ancora un po' più di luce sugli eventi politici e militari dell'anno 1866*, Florence, 1902, 229, 244, 286; *Il problema Veneto*, II, 941.

8. Chiala *Ancora un po' più*, 627–8.

9. Mack Smith, *Victor Emanuel, Cavour and the risorgimento*, 104, 309; Paolo Paulucci, *Alla corte di Re Umberto: diario segreto*, ed. G. Calcagno, Milan, 1986, 53 (Gen. Pallavicini).

10. Della Rocca, *Autobiografia*, II, 244; Chiala, *Ancora un po' più*, 560–70; *Deutsche Revue*, Stuttgart, March 1900, 318 (Türr).

11. *Carteggi di Ricasoli*, XXII, 85; Chiala, *Ancora un po' più*, 628; *Aus dem Leben Bernhardis*, VII, 178.

12. *Bismarck: die gesammelten Werke*, ed. F. Thimme, Berlin, 1928, VI, 34, 50; *Aus dem Leben Bernhardis*, VII, 164, 172–4; *Il problema Veneto*, I, 869.

13. *Revue des Deux Mondes*, Paris, May 1925, 96–100 (E. d'Hauterive).

14. *DDI*, ser. 1, VII, 110; *Carteggi di Ricasoli*, XXII, 336.

15. *Ibid.*, XXII, 397–9; *Aus dem Leben Bernhardis*, VII, 223.

16. *Ricordi di Castelli*, 373; Chiala, *Ancora un po' più*, 350, 628, 642.

17. *Les origines diplomatiques de la guerre de 1870–1871*, Paris, 1926, XII, 127; *Carteggi di Ricasoli*, XXIII, 99.

5 Court politics, 1866–7

1. Pietro Ellero, *La tirannide borghese*, Bologna, 1879 (2nd edn.), 550–60.
2. *Discorsi parlamentari di Crispi*, I, 717; Alessandro Guiccioli, *Quintino Sella*, Rovigo, 1887, I, 137.
3. Stefano Jacini, *Due anni di politica italiana*, Milan, 1868, 106; *Epistolario di Quintino Sella*, ed. G. and M. Quazza, Rome, 1984, II, 204; *Carteggi di Ricasoli*, XXII, 55, XXIV, 281–3; Giuseppe Garibaldi, *Scritti e discorsi politici e militari*, Bologna, 1935, IV, 335–7.
4. *Carteggio di Castelli*, II, 154–7.
5. *Le lettere di Vittorio Emanuele*, II, 1094; *La campagna del 1866 nei documenti militari austriaci*, ed. A. Filipuzzi, Padova, 1966, 395.
6. *Rassegna Storica del Risorgimento*, 1963, 94–5; *Nuova Antologia*, Florence, May 1961, 23; *Revue des Deux Mondes*, May 1925, 118–19; *Les origines diplomatiques de la guerre*, XII, 299, XIII, 39; *Carteggio di Castelli*, II, 157.
7. Cesare Cantù, *Della indipendenza italiana: cronistoria*, Turin, 1877, III, 659, 821; *Revue des Deux Mondes*, 15 Apr. 1886, 766 (Rothan); *Carteggi di Ricasoli*, XXIII, 441; *Epistolario di Sella*, II, 89; P. Silva, *Il sessantasei: studi storici*, Milan, 1917, 311.
8. *Alfonso La Marmora: commemorazione, 5 Jan. 1879*, Florence, 117; Alfonso Lamarmora, *Quattro discorsi sulle condizioni dell'esercito italiano*, Florence, 1871, 8, 80; A. D'Ancona, *Ricordi storici del risorgimento italiano*, Florence, 1913, 525; *Complemento alla storia della campagna del 1866 in Italia*, Rome, 1919 (premessa, ed. A. Cavaciocchi).
9. *The Evening Post*, New York, 7 July 1904; *Le Opere e i Giorni*, Rome, May 1937, 9.
10. *Carteggi di Ricasoli*, XXII, 73; Mack Smith, *Victor Emanuel, Cavour and the risorgimento*, 333.
11. *L'Italie*, Florence, 1 Jan. 1867; *Carteggio di Castelli*, II, 199; *Le lettere di Vittorio Emanuele*, II, 1168.
12. Staatsarchiv, Vienna (8 Feb. 1867, Kübeck); *Auswärtige Politik*, VIII, 252, 365 (ed. H. Michaelis); *Rassegna Storica del Risorgimento*, 1963, 94–5 (Gen. Möhring).
13. FO, 45/90 (17 Nov. 1866); *Le lettere di Vittorio Emanuele*, II, 1034; *Carteggi di Ricasoli*, XXIV, 81.
14. *Ibid.*, XXV, 212–13; *Carteggio di Castelli*,

II, 215; Sclopis, *Diario*, 404–6, 412; R. Mori, *Il tramonto del potere temporale, 1866–1870*, Rome, 1967, 110–11.
15. *Le carte di Lanza*, IV, 123; Niccola Nisco, *Storia civile del regno d'Italia*, Naples, 1892, VI, 60–1; *Carteggi di Ricasoli*, XXV, 519–20.
16. *Carteggio di Castelli*, II, 225.
17. Di Revel, *Sette mesi*, 76; Staatsarchiv, Vienna (15 Apr. 1867, Kübeck).
18. *Carteggi di Ricasoli*, XXV, 525, XXVI, 13, 140; *Camera, discussioni*, 15 June 1867, 484.
19. M.P. Trauth, *Italo-American diplomatic relations*, Washington, 1958, 165; *Carteggi di E. d'Azeglio*, II, 416; *Carteggio di Castelli*, II, 244; Mori, *Il tramonto*, 105–6.

6 A failed revolution, 1867

1. FO, 45/105 (11 May 1867, Elliot); *ibid.*, 45/106 (8 Aug. 1967, Edward Herries); *Auswärtige Politik*, IX, 94.
2. *Le lettere di Vittorio Emanuele*, II, 857.
3. *Mattia Montecchi nel risorgimento italiano*, ed. E. Montecchi, Rome, 1932, 189; *Carteggi di Ricasoli*, XXIV, 461; *Carteggio di Castelli*, II, 184, 187.
4. *Discorsi parlamentari di Urbano Rattazzi*, ed. G. Scovazzi, Rome, 1880, VII, 109 (22 July 1867).
5. Gaspare Finali, *Memorie*, ed. G. Maioli, Faenza, 1955, 294–5; *Les origines diplomatiques de la guerre*, XIX, 82; Russell Papers, 30/29/249 (25 Oct. 1867, Paget); *Carteggi politici di Crispi*, 263; *Politica segreta italiana (1863–1870)*, Turin, 1891, 330; Vincenzo Riccio, *Francesco Crispi: profilo ed appunti*, Turin, 1887, 55; *Nuova Antologia*, 1 Nov. 1913, 50 (Cadolini).
6. Di Revel, *Sette mesi*, 184, 194; *Carteggi di Ricasoli*, XXIV, 125, 128.
7. *Journal of Modern History*, Chicago, 1944, XVI, 119 (ed. H.R. Marraro); Luzio, *Aspromonte e Mentana*, 364–5; Jessie White Mario, *Agostino Bertani e i suoi tempi*, Florence, 1888, II, 342; Ferdinand Gregorovius, *Roman Journals*, London, 1907, 295.
8. Angelo Bargoni, *Risorgimento italiano: memorie*, Milan, 1911, 249; T. Sandinnini, *In memoria di Enrico Cialdini*, Modena, 1911, 99; Mme Rattazzi, *Rattazzi*, I, 185; M. Mari, *L'arresto di Garibaldi e il ministero Menabrea, con documenti inediti*, Florence, 1913, 3–5.
9. *Le carte di Alfonso della Marmora*, 175; *Carteggi di Ricasoli*, XXVI, 133, 145.

10. Mme Rattazzi, *Rattazzi*, II, 189; *Carteggi di Ricasoli*, XXVI, 135.
11. *Les origines diplomatiques de la guerre*, XIX, 380, XXIX, 469; Hermann Oncken, *Die Rheinpolitik Kaiser Napoleons III, von 1863 bis 1870 und der Ursprung des Krieges von 1870–1871*, Leipzig, 1926, III, 195–6, 496; Mori, *Il tramonto*, 144; *Auswärtige Politik*, X, 6–7.
12. *Discorsi parlamentari di Urbano Rattazzi*, VII, 197, 215, 225–6; Di Revel, *Sette mesi*, 233–5; Luzio, *Aspromonte e Mentana*, 407.
13. Sclopis, *Diario*, 420; Di Revel, *Sette mesi*, 229; *Camera, discussioni*, 22 Dec. 1867, 3358 (Menabrea); *Le lettere di Vittorio Emanuele*, II, 1251; *Carteggi di Ricasoli*, XXVI, 139; *Carteggi politici di Crispi*, 312.
14. FO, 45/109 (31 Dec. 1867, Paget).
15. Clarendon Papers, Dep. c 555 (23 Dec. 1867); Mack Smith, *Victor Emanuel, Cavour and the risorgimento*, 349, 352.

7 Personal rule

1. Russell Papers, 30/22/16E (1 Jan. 1868); Mori, *Il tramonto*, 567 (31 Dec. 1867, Kübeck).
2. Clarendon Papers, Dep. c 555 (23 Dec. 1867); *ibid.*, Dep. c 488/100 (27 May 1869); Staatsarchiv, Vienna (15 Apr. 1867 and 2 Jan. 1868, Kübeck to Beust).
3. Trauth, *Italo-American diplomatic relations*, 165 (10 Apr. 1867, George Marsh); *Carteggi di Ricasoli*, XXV, 525.
4. Oncken, *Die Rheinpolitik*, II, 489; Luigi Federico Menabrea, *Memorie*, ed. L. Brigaglio and L. Bulferetti, Florence, 1971, 176–7.
5. *Die Auswärtige Politik*, IX, 653–4, 771–4.
6. *Ibid.*, X, 6, 79–80, 185–7; Otto von Bismarck, *Reflections and reminiscences*, London, 1899, II, 112.
7. *Les origines diplomatiques de la guerre*, XIX, 382; Mori, *Il tramonto*, 567–8; Oncken, *Die Rheinpolitik*, III, 497.
8. Clarendon Papers, Dep. c 488/41 (13 Mar. 1869).
9. Staatsarchiv, Vienna (8 Nov. 1867, Kübeck); Clarendon Papers, Dep. c 488/43–4 (13 Mar. 1869, Paget).
10. *L'opera di Stefano Türr nel risorgimento italiano (1849–1870)*, Florence, 1928, I, 165, 172; Mme Rattazzi, *Rattazzi*, II, 213.
11. *Das Ende des Kirchenstaates*, ed. N. Miko, Vienna, 1964, 1, 566–7; Oncken,

Die Rheinpolitik, III, 194–5, 198, 224–5, 251.
12. Petruccelli della Gattina, *Storia d'Italia dal 1866 al 1880*, Naples, 1882, 46, 55–6; *Le lettere di Vittorio Emanuele*, II, 1422; Mme Rattazzi, *Rattazzi*, I, 587, 642–3, II, 283–4, 293.
13. *Pio IX e Vittorio Emanuele II dal loro carteggio privato*, ed. P. Pietro Pirri, Rome, 1961, III, tome 2, 213–18; *Carteggio di Castelli*, II, 423; *DDI*, ser. 3, II, 170–1.
14. *Carteggi di Ricasoli*, XXVI, 468.
15. *Le carte di Lanza*, IV, 322.
16. Vittorio Bersezio, *Il regno di Vittorio Emanuele II*, Turin, 1895, VIII, 340–1.
17. Clarendon Papers, Dep. c 488 (23 Dec. 1869, Paget).

8 The conquest of Rome

1. Oncken, *Die Rheinpolitik*, III, 273–4, 387–8.
2. S. William Halperin, *Diplomat under stress: Visconti-Venosta and the crisis of July 1870*, Chicago, 1963, 159 (16 July 1870).
3. Oncken, *Die Rheinpolitik*, III, 496–8.
4. *DDI*, ser. 1, XIII, 261, 286; *Les origines diplomatiques de la guerre*, XXIX, 438; *La vita e i tempi di Giovanni Lanza: memorie ricavate da suoi scritti*, ed. E. Tavallini, Turin, 1887, I, 510; Bersezio, *Il regno di Vittorio Emanuele*, VIII, 361.
5. *Le carte di Lanza*, VI, 40, 420; Minghetti, *La convenzione*, 214.
6. *La vita di Lanza*, II, 34; S. Castagnola, *Da Firenze a Roma: diario storico-politico del 1870–1871*, Turin, 1896, 9–12, 26; *Il Secolo*, Milan, 19 Mar. 1891.
7. Francesco Crispi, *I doveri del gabinetto del 25 Marzo*, Rome, 1876, 65; Mme Rattazzi, *Rattazzi*, II, 349–51; White Mario, *Bertani*, II, 353–4; *Camera, discussioni*, 15 Mar. 1884, 7019 (Mancini).
8. Guiccioli, *Sella*, I, 316.
9. Castagnola, *Da Firenze a Roma*, 32–3; *Le carte di Lanza*, VI, 73; *La vita di Lanza*, II, 40–1.
10. *DDI*, ser. 1, XIII, 484.
11. *Ibid.*, 491; Guiccioli, *Sella*, I, 304; *Le lettere di Vittorio Emanuele*, II, 1495.
12. Alessandro Guiccioli, *Diario di un conservatore*, Rome, 1973, 188; *Le carte di Lanza*, VI, 65, 80–1.
13. Federico Chabod, *Storia della politica estera italiana dal 1870 al 1896*, Bari, 1951, 678.

9 The Left in power

1. Garibaldi, *Scritti e discorsi*, III, 423; G.E. Curàtulo, *Il dissidio tra Mazzini e Garibaldi*, Milan, 1928, 326.
2. Chabod, *Storia della politica estera*, 328; *Carteggio di Castelli*, II, 511; A. Ghisleri, *Lo statuto del 1848*, Rome, 1923, 25–7.
3. Mazzini, *Scritti*, XCIII, 186–9.
4. Stefano Jacini, *Sulle condizioni della cosa pubblica in Italia dopo il 1866*, Florence, 1870, 81; Sidney Sonnino, *Del governo rappresentativo in Italia*, Rome, 1872, 3–4.
5. Luigi Chiala, *Giacomo Dina e l'opera sua nelle vicende del risorgimento italiano*, Turin, 1903, III, 374; *La vita di Lanza*, II, 112–13.
6. *Carteggi di Ricasoli*, XXVIII, 183; Curio Chiaraviglio, *Giovanni Giolitti nei ricordi di un nipote*, Turin, 1981, 48; Guiccioli, *Sella*, II, 70.
7. Sclopis, *Diario*, 481, 487; *Carteggio di Castelli*, II 573; Mack Smith, *Victor Emanuel, Cavour and the risorgimento*, 238; G. Barbèra, *Memorie di un editore*, Florence, 1930, 342–3.
8. Mme Rattazzi, *Rattazzi*, II, 408.
9. *Discorsi parlamentari di Urbano Rattazzi*, VIII, 342–4; P.S. Mancini, *Discorsi parlamentari*, Rome, 1894, III, 367, 377; Petruccelli della Gattina, *Storia d'Italia dal 1866*, 121–4.
10. *Le carte di Lanza*, X, 121.
11. Marco Minghetti, *Copialettere 1863–1876*, ed. M.P. Cuccoli, Rome, 1978, II 863, 870; E. de Laveleye, *Nouvelles lettres d'Italie*, Brussels, 1884, 99.
12. *Déposition de Monsieur Thiers sur le dix-huit mars: documents sur les événements de 1870–71*, Paris, 1872, 12; G. Rothan, *Souvenirs: l'Allemagne et l'Italie*, Paris, 1885, II, 143; Mme Rattazzi, *Rattazzi*, II, 493.
13. *Le lettere di Vittorio Emanuele*, II, 1533.
14. *Pio IX e Vittorio Emanuele*, III, tome 2, 333.
15. *DDI*, ser. 2, V, 110–11 (ed. F. Valsecchi and R. Mori); FO, 64/775 (27 Sept. 1873, Adams); *ibid.*, 64/776 (4 Oct. 1873).
16. *Carteggi di Ricasoli*, XXVIII, 381, 396; Minghetti, *Copialettere*, II, 819; Guiccioli, *Diario*, 15; Guiccioli, *Sella*, II, 70; *Carteggio di Castelli*, II, 580–2.
17. Guiccioli, *Diario*, 14.
18. FO, 45/310 (1 Jan. 1877, Paget); *Corriere della Sera*, Milan, 3 July 1901 (Gadda);

Chabod, *Storia della politica estera*, 668.
19. *Discorsi parlamentari di Agostino Depretis*, VI, 258–60.

10 Death, and retrospect

1. FO, 45/284 (2 Jan. and 8 Jan. 1876, Paget); Ferdinando Martini, *Confessioni e ricordi 1859–1892*, Milan, 1929, 153.
2. FO, 45/286 (5 May 1876); *Camera, discussioni*, 2 Dec. 1908, 24,213 (De Marinis).
3. Salisbury Papers (30 Nov. 1876, Salisbury to Derby).
4. FO, 45/315/378 (7 Nov. 1876, Paget); *DDI*, ser. 2, VIII, 652.
5. Guiccioli, *Sella*, I, 241–2.
6. Mme Rattazzi, *Rattazzi*, II, 407; Francesco Crispi, *Scritti e discorsi politici 1849–1890*, Rome, 1890, 661.
7. R. Lill, *Die Deutsch-Italienischen Beziehungen 1869–1876 (Quellen und Forschungen aus Italienischen Archiven)*, Tübingen, 1966, XLVI, 435; *Memoirs of Prince Hohenlohe*, London, 1907, II, 139; Nello Rosselli, *Saggi sul risorgimento e altri scritti*, Turin, 1946, 241; Mme Rattazzi, *Rattazzi*, II, 326; *DDI*, ser. 1, XIII, 386.
8. *Ibid.*, ser. 2, VII, 357–8; *ibid.*, ser. 2, VIII, 652.
9. *Ibid.*, 115, 136.
10. Chabod, *Storia della politica estera*, 665, 676–7.
11. Francesco Crispi, *Politica estera: memorie e documenti*, ed. T. Palamenghi-Crispi, Milan, 1929, 9; Luigi Chiala, *Pagine di storia contemporanea*, Turin, 1892, II, iii.
12. *Documents diplomatiques français (1871–1914)*, ed. Ministère des Affaires Etrangères, Paris, 1930, ser. 1, II, 207–8.
13. Crispi, *Politica estera*, 23–8, 45–6.
14. *Nuova Antologia*, 16 Dec. 1911, 702; Crispi, *Politica estera*, 62–3.
15. FO, 170/251/328 (5 Oct. 1877, Derby to Paget); Crispi, *Politica estera*, 59.
16. FO, 45/315/366 (16 Oct. 1877, Paget).
17. *Nuova Antologia*, 16 Dec. 1911, 704.
18. *Atti Parlamentari: Senato, discussioni*, Rome, 16 Jan. 1878, 2298; *The Times*, London, 5 Jan. 1878; Chabod, *Storia della politica estera*, 684; P. Turiello, *Governo e governati in Italia*, Bologna, 1889, II, 235; Francesco Crispi, *Discorsi di politica estera, Aprile 1887 – Gennaio 1891*, Rome, 1892, 16.
19. *Journal of Modern History*, 1941, 51 (28

Aug. 1870, Marsh); E. A. Vizetelly, *In seven lands*, London, 1916, 357–9; A. Gallenga, *The pope and the king*, London, 1879, II, 30–2, 216–17.

20. *Pio IX e Vittorio Emanuele*, III, tome 2, 436–45.
21. Mme Rattazzi, *Rattazzi*, II, 426–30.
22. *Pio IX e Vittorio Emanuele*, I, 4–5 (10 Oct. 1847).
23. *Le lettere di Vittorio Emanuele*, II, 856–7, 1264, 1668.
24. *Ricordi di Castelli*, 270; General P.H. Sheridan, *Personal memoirs*, London, 1888, II, 440–2.
25. *Discorsi parlamentari di Agostino Bertani*, Rome, 1913, 358–61; *Discorsi parlamentari di Depretis*, VI, 570–2.
26. *Le carte di Lanza*, VIII, 126, 286; Minghetti, *Copialettere*, I, 50–1.
27. Nello Quilici, *Banca Romana: fine di secolo*, Milan, 1935, 143–5, 601; *Carteggi di Ricasoli*, XXIX, 10; *Scritti e discorsi di Agostino Bertani*, ed. Jessie White Mario, Florence, 1890, 227–8; Napoleone Colajanni, *Banche e parlamento*, Milan, 1893, 236; Henry A. d'Ideville, *Victor-Emmanuel II: sa vie, sa mort, souvenirs personnels*, Paris, 1878, 86.
28. D. Zanichelli, *Politica e storia*, Bologna, 1903, 85, 96.
29. *Carteggi di Ricasoli*, XXVI, 212, XXIX, 300; *Le carte di Lanza*, X, 23; A. Comandini, *Il Principe Napoleone nel risorgimento*, XI; W.R. Thayer, *Italica: studies in life and literature*, Boston, 1908, 236, 240.
30. Barbèra, *Memorie di un editore*, 342–3; Bapst, *Canrobert*, II, 234–5.
31. Alfredo Oriani, *La rivolta ideale*, Bologna, 1912, 68, 77, 113, 257; Alfredo Oriani, *La lotta politica in Italia*, Bologna, 1941 (5th edn.), III, 109, 116, 340, 351–2.
32. *Nuova Antologia*, 15 Jan. 1879, 26.
33. Marco Minghetti, *Scritti vari*, Bologna, 1896, 333–5; Arangio Ruiz, *Storia costituzionale del regno d'Italia*, Florence, 1898, 321; *Corriere della Sera*, 1 Jan. 1879.
34. Crispolti, *Corone e porpore*, 14.
35. Giuseppe Massari, *La vita ed il regno di Vittorio Emanuele II di Savoia*, Milan, 1878, II, 479; *Carteggi di Ricasoli*, XXV, 520; *Nuova Antologia*, 16 July 1935, 214 (Guiccioli).
36. Finali, *Memorie*, 352, 539; Chiala, *Giacomo Dina*, III, 502; Chiala, *Ancora un po' più*, 627–8.

Umberto I

1   The new reign

1. Royal Archives, diary of Queen Victoria (12 July 1875); Sidney Lee, *King Edward VIII*, London, 1925, I, 59.
2. Paolo Paulucci, *Alla corte di Re Umberto: diario segreto*, ed. G. Calcagno, Milan, 1986, 127; Francesco Saverio Nitti, *Scritti politici*, ed. G. De Rosa, Bari, 1961, VII, 533; Silvio Spaventa, *Lettere politiche (1861–1893)*, ed. G. Castellano, Bari, 1926, 55.
3. Federigo Sclopis, *Diario segreto (1859–1878)*, ed. P. Pietro Pirri, Turin, 1959, 495; F. Crispolti, *Corone e porpore: ricordi personali*, Milan, 1937, 7; Henry d'Ideville, *Journal d'un diplomate en Italie*, Paris, 1872, I, 63–4.
4. Domenico Bartoli, *La fine della monarchia*, Milan, 1947, 23; Royal Archives, diary of Queen Victoria (18 Apr. 1879).
5. Alessandro Guiccioli, *Diario di un conservatore*, Rome, 1973, 131.
6. *Discorsi parlamentari di Felice Cavallotti*, Rome, 1914, I, 263; Petruccelli della Gattina, *Storia d'Italia dal 1866 al 1880*, Naples, 1882, 307.
7. Royal Archives, J. 41/18 (21 Nov. 1878, Paget to Queen Victoria).
8. FO, 45/335/42 (15 Jan. 1878, Paget); M.P. Trauth, *Italo-American diplomatic relations*, Washington, 1958, 166 (4 Mar. 1878, Marsh to Evarts); Charles Louis Moüy, *Souvenirs et causeries d'un diplomate*, Paris, 1909, 226.
9. *Corriere della Sera*, Milan, 4 Feb. 1880 and 3 June 1881.
10. Federico Chabod, *Storia della politica estera italiana dal 1870 al 1896*, Bari, 1951, 646, 667; Paolo Romano (Paolo Alatri), *Silvio Spaventa: biografia politica*, Bari, 1942, 249–52.
11. Alfonso Lamarmora, *I segreti di stato nel governo costituzionale*, Florence, 1877, 173; Pasquale Turiello, *Governo e governati in Italia*, Bologna, 1889, 180, 182, 231; Pietro Ellero, *La tirannide borghese*, Bologna, 1879 (2nd edn.), 181–2, 548–9; Pietro Sbarbaro, *Re travicello o re costituzionale?*, Rome, 1884, 57, 91.
12. Sidney Sonnino, *Scritti e discorsi extraparlamentari 1870–1902*, ed. Benjamin Brown, Bari, 1972, I, 223, 347–8, 356–8.
13. *Crispi: lettere dall'esilio (1850–1860)*, ed. T. Palamenghi-Crispi, Rome, 1918, 99, 103; Francesco Crispi, *Politica interna:*

diario e documenti, ed. T. Palamenghi-Crispi, Milan, 1924, 156.

14. *Discorsi parlamentari di Francesco Crispi*, Rome, 1915, I, 395; Francesco Crispi, *I doveri del gabinetto del 25 Marzo*, Rome, 1876, 44.

15. Gaspare Finali, *Memorie*, ed. G. Maioli, Faenza, 1955, 409–10.

2   The Triple Alliance

1. FO, 45/335/77 (29 Jan. 1878, Capt. Ardagh).
2. Luigi Campo Fregoso, *Del primato italiano sul Mediterraneo*, Turin, 1872, 187; Chabod, *Storia della politica estera*, 562 (Gen. Cialdini); Salisbury Papers, XI, 13 (2 Nov. 1878, Paget); *DDI*, ser. 2, VII, 284.
3. FO, 45/336/154 (19 Feb. 1878, Paget).
4. *DDI*, ser. 2, X, 462.
5. FO, 45/335/77 (29 Jan. 1878, Paget); Luigi Chiala, *Pagine di storia contemporanea*, Turin, 1892, II, 31–4.
6. *DDI*, ser. 2, X, 31, 336; FO, 45/337/240 (29 Mar. 1878, Paget).
7. *DDI*, ser. 2, X, 270.
8. *Ibid.*, 391, 444.
9. Salisbury Papers, XI, 11 (10 Aug. 1878, MacDonell).
10. FO, 45/457/419 (25 Nov. 1882, Paget).
11. Trauth, *Italo-American relations*, 162 (17 Feb. 1880, Marsh); Stefano Jacini, *I conservatori e l'evoluzione naturale dei partiti politici in Italia*, Milan, 1879, 29.
12. Guiccioli, *Diario*, 40, 92.
13. *Discorsi parlamentari di Crispi*, II, 380; Francesco Crispi, *Politica estera: memorie e documenti*, ed. T. Palamenghi-Crispi, Milan, 1929, 69.
14. *DDI*, ser. 2, VIII, 652; Finali, *Memorie*, 318.
15. *DDI*, ser. 2, VI, 651; *ibid.*, ser. 2, VII, 507; *Carteggio politico di Michelangelo Castelli*, ed. Luigi Chiala, Turin, 1890, II, 228; *Atti Parlamentari: Camera dei deputati, discussioni*, Rome, 31 Jan. 1879, 3797 (Adamoli).
16. *Le carte di Giovanni Lanza*, Turin, 1936, VI, 387–8, 395; FO, 45/402/10–13 (7–9 Jan. 1880, Paget).
17. *Carteggi e bibliografia di Costantino Nigra*, ed. A. Colombo and E. Passamonti, Turin, 1931, 111.
18. *Documents diplomatiques français (1871–1914)*, ed. Ministère des Affaires Etrangères, Paris, 1930, ser. 1, II, 392–3.
19. *Documents français*, ser. 1, III, 300–2; *La*

vita e i tempi di Giovanni Lanza: memorie ricavate da suoi scritti, ed. E. Tavallini, Turin, 1887, II, 199–200.

20. Stefano Jacini, *Sulle condizioni della cosa pubblica in Italia dopo il 1866*, Florence, 1870, 14, 36; Carlo Tivaroni, *L'Italia durante il dominio austriaco*, Turin, 1894, III, 469, 495; *Camera, discussioni*, 20 June 1881, 6326 (Mameli); Cesare Cantù, *Gli ultimi trent'anni*, Turin, 1880, 194.
21. Stefano Jacini, *Pensieri sulla politica italiana*, Florence, 1889, 64–7; *Nuova Antologia*, 15 July 1882, 335; *Camera, discussioni*, 17 Mar. 1885, 12,936 (Toscanelli).
22. FO, 45/455/284 (15 July 1882); *ibid.*, 45/456/388 (27 Oct. 1882); Edmund G.P. Fitzmaurice, *Life of George Granville*, London, 1905, II, 270–1; P.S. Mancini, *Discorsi parlamentari*, Rome, 1894, VII, 269.
23. *Lettere fra la Regina Margherita e Marco Minghetti, (1882–6)*, ed. L. Lipparini, Milan, 1947, 189; *Camera, discussioni*, 17 Apr. 1882, 9907 (Perazzi).
24. *Discorsi parlamentari di Crispi*, I, 717 (8 May 1866); Rocco De Zerbi, *Diffendetevi!*, Naples, 1882, 49; Turiello, *Governo e governati*, 52, 234–5; *Camera, discussioni*, 15 May 1883, 3101 (Bonghi).
25. *Documents français*, ser. 1, II, 413–14; *ibid.*, ser. 1, III, 276–7.
26. FO, 45/456/325 (2 Aug. 1882, Paget quoting Depretis).
27. Julius Moritz Busch, *Bismarck: some secrets of his history*, II, 2/418–19; *Documents français*, ser. 1, II, 524; *ibid.*, ser. 1, III, 277; *German diplomatic documents 1817–1914*, ed. E.T. Dugdale, London, 1928, I, 112; Alfred Francis Pribram, *The secret treaties of Austria-Hungary, 1879–1914*, Cambridge, 1921, II, 45.
28. *The Saburow Memoirs*, ed. J.Y. Simpson, Cambridge, 1929, 119; FO, 45/431/391 (19 Oct. 1881, Paget); *Die grosse Politik der europäischen Kabinette, 1870–1914*, ed. J. Lepsius, A. Mendelssohn Bartholdy, and F. Thimme, III, 541.
29. *Camera, discussioni*, 24 Jan. 1882, 8441 (Ricotti); *ibid.*, 10 Mar. 1883, 1844–5 (Sonnino)
30. *Camera, discussioni*, 24 Jan. 1882, 8445 (Mancini); Alfonso Lamarmora, *Quattro discorsi sulle condizioni dell'esercito italiano*, Florence, 1871, 176; *Nuova Antologia*, Florence, 1 Nov. 1937, 59 (Guiccioli).
31. Finali, *Memorie*, 407, 689; Pribram, *The secret treaties*, II, 12–13, 20; Luigi Chiala,

La triplice e la duplice alleanza, Turin, 1898, 319; Arturo Labriola, *Storia di dieci anni 1899–1909*, Milan, 1910, 149.

32. *Camera, discussioni*, 29 Mar. 1909, 57 (Brunialti).

33. *Die grosse Politik*, III, 207–8.

3 Depretis and the transformation of parties

1. *Camera, discussioni*, 2 Apr. 1879, 5497, 5529; *ibid.*, 18 Dec. 1882, 265.

2. *Il Secolo*, Milan, 30 Dec. 1875; Napoleone Colajanni, *I partiti politici in Italia*, Rome, 1912, 28–9; *Camera, discussioni*, 10 Dec. 1878, 3176 (Bertani).

3. Alberto Mario, *L'italia libera: scritti politici e sociali*, Rome, 1925, 182, 185–6, 222–3.

4. *Discorsi parlamentari di Cavallotti*, I, 12–13; Alessandro Galante Garrone, *Felice Cavallotti*, Turin, 1976, 145–6, 217–19.

5. Giuseppe Garibaldi, *Scritti e discorsi politici e militari*, Bologna, 1937, VI, 281–2, 303–4, 520.

6. E. Garlanda, *La terza Italia: lettere di un Yankee*, Rome, 1911, 313–18; Giuseppe Maranini, *Storia del potere in Italia 1848–1967*, Florence, 1967, 235.

7. Ruggero Bonghi, *Programmi politici e partiti*, ed. G. Gentile, Florence, 1933, 166, 221; Alfredo Baccarini, *Discorsi politici 1876–1890,* Bologna, 1907, 142; *Discorsi parlamentari di Silvio Spaventa*, Rome, 1913, 551; Marco Minghetti, *I partiti politici*, Rome, 1945, 19–20.

8. *Camera, discussioni*, 20 Dec. 1882, 323 (Depretis); Silvio Spaventa, *La politica della destra*, Bari, 1910, 474 (1862); Francesco Crispi, *Scritti e discorsi politici, 1849–1890,* Rome, 1890, 578; Giovanni Giolitti, *Discorsi extraparlamentari*, ed. N. Valeri, Turin, 1952, 101–2.

9. Domenico Zanichelli, *Studi di storia costituzionale e politica del risorgimento italiano*, Bologna, 1900, 107; *Nuova Antologia*, 16 July 1935, 229; *La vita di Lanza*, II, 118; Colajanni, *I partiti politici in Italia*, 10.

10. *Nuova Antologia*, 15 July 1882, 332; W.T. Thornton, 'Parliament without parties', *Macmillan's Magazine*, London, Jan. 1880, 259; Moüy, *Souvenirs*, 227.

11. FO, 45/457/419 (25 Nov. 1882, Paget).

12. *Documents français*, ser. 1, IV, 181; *Il Secolo*, 10 Aug. 1887.

13. *Pio IX e Vittorio Emauele II dal loro carteggio privato*, ed. P. Pietro Pirri, Rome, 1961, III, tome 2, 225–6; Sonnino, *Scritti e discorsi*, I, 369.

14. Sonnino, *Scritti e discorsi*, I, 4, 302; *Discorsi parlamentari di Sidney Sonnino*, Rome, 1925, I, 22, 40–1.

15. *Corriere della Sera*, 17 Mar. 1906.

16. *Il Secolo*, 30 July 1887; *Nuova Antologia*, 16 Aug. 1935, 594; *ibid.*, 16 Aug. 1936, 442; *ibid.*, 1 Sept. 1937, 26, 30; *Discorsi parlamentari di Marco Minghetti*, Rome, 1890, 500.

17. FO, 45/432/466 (22 Dec. 1881, Paget).

18. Bonghi, *Programmi*, 309.

19. *Camera, discussioni*, 15 June 1886, 66; *ibid.*, 8 Mar. 1890, 1626–7.

20. FO, 45/404/155 (7 Apr. 1880, Paget); *ibid.*, 45/404/167 (21 Apr. 1880); *ibid.*, 45/429/252 (15 June 1881, Paget quoting Blanc).

21. *Camera, discussioni*, 30 June 1887, 4298 (Mancini); Carlo Zaghi, *P.S. Mancini, l'Africa e il problema del Mediterraneo 1884–5*, Rome, 1955, 9; E. Bellavita, *Adua*, Genoa, 1931, 17; *Nuova Antologia*, 16 Nov. 1935, 132–3; A. Giani, *Italia e Inghilterra alle porte del Sudan*, Pisa, 1940, 77.

22. FO, 45/546/9 (11 Jan. 1886, Lumley); Earl of Cromer, *Modern Egypt*, London, 1908, II, 56–7; A. Ramm, 'Great Britain and the planting of Italian power in the Red Sea', *English Historical Review*, 1944, 236; Rodd Papers, box 38 (diary entry for 1 May 1897).

23. Egidio Osio, *Il generale Osio*, Milan, 1909, 375; Guiccioli, *Diario*, 126–7; Garibaldi, *Scritti e discorsi*, III, 283.

24. Crispi, *Scritti e discorsi*, 544; *Discorsi parlamentari di Crispi*, II, 696; *Camera, discussioni*, 15 Jan. 1885, 10,621 (Brunialti).

25. Zaghi, *Mancini*, 55–6; Roberto Battaglia, *La prima guerra d'Africa*, Turin, 1958, 192–3; Angelo Del Boca, *Gli italiani in Africa orientale: dall'unità alla marcia su Rome*, Bari, 1976, 184; *Rivista di Politica e Scienze Sociali*, Rome, 30 Mar. 1896, 274; Vico Mantegazza, *La guerra in Africa*, Florence, 1896, 4–5.

26. *Camera, discussioni*, 26 May 1899, 3694 (Crispi); *Nuova Antologia*, 1 Aug. 1905, 530 (Tittoni); Zaghi, *Mancini*, 173.

27. Ferdinando Martini, *L'Eritrea economica*, Novara, 1913, 2–3; Tancredi Saletta, ed. Stato maggiore dell'esercito, Rome, 1935, 8.

28. *Camera, discussioni*, 17 Mar. 1885, 12,943 (Mancini); *ibid.*, 5 Dec. 1885, 15,488 (Depretis).

29. Carlo Giglio, *L'impresa di Massaua 1884 –5*, Rome, 1955, 171–2.

30. *Discorsi parlamentari di Crispi*, II, 735–6, 741–3.

31. *Discorsi parlamentari di Giovanni Giolitti*, Rome, 1953, I, 35, 106; A. Plebano, *Storia della finanza italiana*, Turin, 1900, II, 388–9, 492; L. Chiala, *La spedizione di Massaua*, Turin, 1888, v–vi, 337–8.

32. *Camera, discussioni*, 17 Mar. 1885, 12,943–4 (Mancini); *Atti Parlamentari: Senato, discussioni*, Rome, 23 Mar. 1885, 3195.

33. *Ibid.*, 21 Mar. 1885, 3170 (Caracciolo).

34. *Camera, discussioni*, 15 June 1886, 68–9.

35. *Senato, discussioni*, 7 July 1887, 1538; Charles Lacaita, *An Italian Englishman, Sir James Lacaita*, London, 1933, 266–7; Chabod, *Storia della politica estera*, 631; *Senato, discussioni*, 11 Apr. 1883, 706–7 (Mancini).

36. *Camera, discussioni*, 2 June 1887, 3155 (Ferdinando Martini); Joseph Grabinski, *La triple alliance d'après de nouveaux documents*, Lyon, 1904, 598–600.

37. *Camera, discussioni*, 30 June 1887, 4303.

38. Guiccioli, *Diario*, 142.

39. *Discorsi parlamentari di Crispi*, II, 811, III, 65.

40. Baccarini, *Discorsi politici*, 105–7.

41. *Nuova Antologia*, 16 Mar. 1887, 324.

42. *Documents français*, ser. 1, VI bis, 79; *Il Secolo*, 19 and 23 Feb. 1887.

43. *Camera, discussioni*, 3 Feb. 1887, 2002–4 (Mussi), 2004–5 (Di Robilant), 2026–8 (Odescalchi).

44. *Ibid.*, 3 June 1887, 3199 (Di Rudinì); *Senato, discussioni*, 7 July 1887, 1540 (Di Robilant).

45. *Il Secolo*, 10 Feb. 1887.

4 Crispi, 1887–1891

1. *Discorsi parlamentari di Crispi*, II, 817; Francesco Crispi, *Pensieri e profezie*, ed. T. Palamenghi-Crispi, Rome, 1920, 112; *Il Secolo*, 22 Nov. 1890 (Crispi quoted by Cavallotti); Ferdinando Martini, *Confessioni e ricordi 1859–1892*, Milan, 1929, 151; Giovanni Bovio, *Scritti filosofici e politici*, Naples, 1883, 71.

2. *DDI*, ser. 2, XXI, 21; *Discorsi parlamentari di Crispi*, II, 891, III, 292.

3. Salisbury Papers, LXVI, 20 (12 and 22 Jan. 1888, Kennedy); *The Holstein Papers*, ed. N. Rich and M.H. Fisher, Cambridge, 1963, III, 244; William Stillman, *The autobiography of a journalist*, London, 1901, II, 253 (Lumley).

4. *Camera, discussioni*, 5 Mar. 1890, 1524 (Luigi Ferrari).

5. FO, 45/603/239 (15 Sept. 1888, Kennedy).

6. *Il Secolo*, 9 Mar. 1890; *Camera, discussioni*, 10 Mar. 1890, 1644; *ibid.*, 17 Nov. 1888, 5297; *Discorsi parlamentari di Crispi*, III, 359–60.

7. Francesco Crispi, *Discorsi elettorali 1865–1886*, Rome, 1887, 235–6; *Discorsi parlamentari di Crispi*, II, 870, III, 499–500.

8. Salisbury Papers, LXVII, 9 (11 Apr. 1890, Dufferin); FO, 45/646/24 (8 Feb. 1890).

9. *The Nation*, New York, 25 Dec. 1890, 499 (Stillman); Sidney Sonnino, *Diario 1866–1912*, ed. P. Pastorelli, Bari, 1972, I, 131; FO, 45/601/16 (22 Jan. 1888, Kennedy); Salisbury Papers, LXVII, 14–15 (9 and 13 June 1890, Dufferin).

10. *Discorsi parlamentari di Crispi*, III, 289.

11. *Ibid.*, III, 75, 91; Crispi, *Pensieri*, 20; Francesco Geraci, *Crispi intimo: rivelazioni, intuizioni, pensieri*, Piacenza, 1923, 39–40.

12. Crispi, *Pensieri*, 182.

13. Crispi, *Politica estera*, 281.

14. *Il Secolo*, 7 Oct. 1890 (Cavallotti).

15. *Rassegna Toscana*, Florence, Jan. 1970, 102–4 (Renato Mori); Renato Mori, *La politica estera di Francesco Crispi (1887–1891)*, Rome, 1973, 91, 122–3; *DDI*, ser. 2, XXI, 518; *The memoirs of Francesco Crispi*, London, 1912, II, 394–5.

16. FO, 45/601/41 (21 Feb. 1888, Kennedy); *The Holstein Papers*, III, 253 (Solms, quoting Crispi).

17. Salisbury Papers, LXVI, 58 (23 July 1889, Henry Dering); Gaetano Natale, *Giolitti e gli italiani*, Cernusco, 1949, 155.

18. FO, 45/499/1 (4 Jan. 1884, Lumley).

19. *Ibid.*, 45/429/227 (1 June 1881, Paget); *ibid.*, 45/575/151 (23 May 1887, Kennedy).

20. Gwendolin Cecil, *The Life of Robert, Marquis of Salisbury*, London, 1932, IV, 20–3; *German diplomatic documents 1871–1914*, ed. E.T. Dugdale, London, 1928, I, 123.

21. *Le Figaro*, Paris, 3 and 9 June 1891; C.J. Lowe, *Salisbury and the Mediterranean*, London, 1965, 36–40; Mori, *La politica estera di Crispi*, 174–5.

22. PRO, 30/29/182 (7 June 1880, Paget); FO, 45/576/215 (4 Aug. 1887, Kennedy); Salisbury Papers, LXVI, 32 (16 Oct. 1888, Kennedy).
23. Salisbury Papers, LXVIII, 78 (28 Dec. 1888, Salisbury to Dufferin); *Documents français*, ser. 1, VII, 259 (10 Oct. 1888, Jusserand quoting Salisbury).
24. Lacaita, *An Italian Englishman*, 265 (10 Feb. 1889, quoting Gladstone); *Contemporary Review*, London, Apr. 1891, 494–5.
25. *Crispi Papers*, Palermo, 193/iv (copies of British despatches for Oct. 1890).
26. *Carteggi politici inediti di Francesco Crispi (1860–1900)*, ed. T. Palamenghi-Crispi, Rome, 1912, 424.
27. Guiccioli, *Diario*, 157.
28. Pribram, *The secret treaties*, II, 81.
29. *Die grosse Politik* IX, 54; *The Holstein Papers*, IV, 103.
30. *Discorsi parlamentari di Matteo Renato Imbriani-Poerio*, Rome, 1923, 1–3.
31. *Nuova Antologia*, 16 Nov. 1939, 110; Salisbury Papers, LXVII, 8 (3 Apr. 1890, Dufferin).
32. *Documents français*, ser. 1, VII, 287; *ibid.*, ser. 1, VIII, 47.
33. Domenico Farini, *Diario di fine secolo*, ed. Emilia Morelli, Rome, 1962, II, 1533; Crispi, *Politica interna*, 191–2; Francesco Crispi, *Questioni internazionali: diario e documenti*, ed. T. Palamenghi-Crispi, Milan, 1913, 9, 12.
34. Gian Francesco Guerrazzi, *Ricordi di irredentismo: i primordi della 'Dante Allighieri' (1881–1894)*, Bologna, 1922, 347–57.
35. *Bismarck and Europe*, ed. W. N. Medlicott and Dorothy Coveney, London, 1971, 165 (quoting Brück, 15 Oct. 1887); Crispi, *Questioni internazionali*, 130.
36. Finali, *Memorie*, 409; Crispi, *Questioni internazionali*, 135–6; *Discorsi parlamentari di Crispi*, II, 408.
37. *Il Secolo*, 4 Jan. 1889; Osio, *Il generale Osio*, 458.
38. FO, 45/601/16 (31 Jan. 1888, Kennedy); *ibid.*, 45/603/326 (12 Dec. 1888, quoting Brin); *ibid.*, 45/603/338 (24 Dec. 1888, Kennedy).
39. Geraci, *Crispi intimo*, 36–9, 48; Francesco Crispi, *Discorsi di politica estera*, Rome, 1892, 16, 99.
40. Francesco Crispi, *La prima guerra d'Africa*, ed. T. Palamenghi-Crispi, Milan, 1914, 28; *Discorsi parlamentari di Crispi*, II, 840.
41. *Senato, discussioni*, 7 July 1887, 1542 (Di Robilant); *ibid.*, 1545 (Corte); *DDI*, ser. 2, XXI, 405 (3 Jan. 1888, Salisbury); *ibid.*, 527–8 (Bismarck).
42. Crispi, *La prima guerra d'Africa*, 37; *Discorsi parlamentari di Crispi*, III, 19, 77, 224–5.
43. *Ibid.*, III, 359; Crispi, *Discorsi di politica estera*, 373; *Camera, discussioni*, 10 May 1888, 2476, 2479; *ibid.*, 11 May 1888, 2506 (Toscanelli).
44. *Camera, discussioni*, 19 May 1885, 13,834–5.
45. *Il Secolo*, 11 May 1888; *Camera, discussioni*, 10 May 1888, 2457 (Musso); *ibid.*, 8 May 1889, 1351 (Nicotera).
46. Stefano Jacini, *Pensieri sulla politica Italiana*, Florence, 1889, 85–7; Ferdinando Martini, *Cose Africane*, 57; Giovanni Giolitti, *Memorie della mia vita*, Milan, 1922, I, 48; Crispi, *La prima guerra d'Africa*, 128–9 (Saracco); *Nuova Antologia*, 1 July 1891, 55 (Antonelli)
47. *Discorsi parlamentari di Crispi*, III, 226, 332, 359.
48. *Ibid.*, III, 8, 566; Enrico Serra, *La diplomazia in Italia*, Milan 1984, 135–6.
49. *Il Secolo*, 7 Jan., 29 Apr., 1 May 1888; *Corriere della Sera*, 13 Mar. 1888; *ibid.*, 6 Mar. 1890.
50. *Discorsi parlamentari di Crispi*, III, 470; *Camera, discussioni*, 29 July 1895, 2155.
51. *Camera, discussioni*, 8 May 1889, 1341; *ibid.*, 6 Mar. 1890, 1563; E. Crosa, *La monarchia nel diritto pubblico italiano*, Turin, 1922, 216–18.
52. Crispi, *La prima guerra d'Africa*, 134, 152–3; T. Palamenghi-Crispi, *L'Italia coloniale e Francesco Crispi*, Milan, 1928, 125–6.
53. Crispi, *Scritti e discorsi*, 736–7; Finali, *Memorie*, 411, 588, 644–5; *Nuova Antologia*, 1 July 1909, 163 (Tittoni).
54. Crispi Papers, Palermo, fasc. 2138 (7 Aug. and 27 Sept. 1889, Umberto to Crispi); Crispi, *Politica interna*, 251.
55. *Discorsi parlamentari di Crispi*, III, 470, 509, 527; Crispi, *La prima guerra d'Africa*, 235; Crispi, *Discorsi di politica estera*, 341.

5   Two interim governments

1. Crispi, *Politica interna*, 266; Finali, *Memorie*, 413–15; *The Speaker*, London, 7 Feb, 1891 (Bonghi).
2. *Documents français*, ser. 1, IX, 108, 112; *Nuova Antologia*, 1 Dec. 1939, 242; William James Stillman, *Francesco Crispi: insurgent, exile, revolutionist and statesman*,

London, 1899, 189.

3. Farini, *Diario*, I, 14, 16–17; Crispi, *Pensieri*, 197.

4. *Contemporary Review*, Oct. 1889, 482 (Gladstone); Lowe, *Salisbury*, 77; *The Holstein Papers*, IV, 103–4.

5. *Documents français*, ser. 1, VIII, 402.

6. *Camera, discussioni*, 26 May 1892, 7918 (Villa); Eugenio Chiesa, *La triplice alleanza No!*, Rome, 1913, 21; *Il Secolo*, 29–30 June 1891.

7. Farini, *Diario*, I, 8, 13; Napoleone Colajanni, *Politica coloniale*, Palermo, 1892, 17–18.

8. *Camera, discussioni*, 1 Apr. 1892, 7630; Salisbury Papers, LXVII, 56 (30 Mar. 1891); *ibid.* LXVII, 63 (4 Aug. 1891, Dering quoting Di Rudinì); Farini, *Diario*, I, 77 (Cosenz).

9. *Camera, discussioni*, 11 Mar. 1891, 784 (Di Rudinì), 788–90 (Colajanni); *Illustrazione Italiana*, Milan, 8 Mar. 1896, 146 (Martini quoting Baldissera); *Discorsi parlamentari di Imbriani*, 65, 74, 232–3, 237–8.

10. *Camera, discussioni*, 16 Dec. 1891, 4765.

11. FO, 45/666/159 (14 Oct. 1891, Dering).

12. Farini, *Diario*, I, 67, 77, 86–7.

13. *Camera, discussioni*, 4–5 May 1891, 7802, 7820, 7833.

14. T. Palamenghi-Crispi, *Giovanni Giolitti: saggio storico-biografico*, Rome, 1914, 18–24; Farini, *Diario*, I, 89–90.

15. *Ibid.*, 102–3.

16. *House of Commons debates*, London, 11 Aug. 1892, 338 (Chamberlain).

17. Farini, *Diario*, I, 105–6.

18. *Camera, discussioni*, 25 May 1892, 7868; *ibid.*, 9 June 1892, 8373–5; *Senato, discussioni*, 19 June 1892, 3220 (Vitelleschi); Salvatore Barzilai, *Luci ed ombre del passato: memorie di vita politica*, Milan, 1937, 293.

19. Giolitti, *Discorsi extraparlamentari*, 140.

20. *Discorsi parlamentari di Giolitti*, I, 125, 246.

21. *Ibid.*, I, 500; Giolitti, *Discorsi extraparlamentari*, 127, 156; V. Pareto, *Ecrits épars*, Geneva, 1974, 96.

22. *Il Secolo*, 14 and 17 June 1891.

23. E. Giampietro, *Pensieri politici*, Bari, 1892, 41; V. Pareto, *Le spese militari e i mali d'Italia*, Milan, 1892, 5–7; Cesare Lombroso, 'Le piaghe d'Italia' (1893), in *Il momento attuale*, Milan, 1903, 21; Farini, *Diario*, I, 76 (Gen. Ricotti); *Contemporary Review*, Apr. 1891, 503–4.

24. *Documents français*, ser. 1, X, 95 (Billot, quoting Umberto).

25. Farini, *Diario*, I, 74–5, 87, 100, 107.

26. Giolitti, *Discorsi extraparlamentari*, 135, 158.

27. Ruggero Bonghi, *Come cadde la destra*, ed. F. Piccolo, Milan, 1929, 231–6, 247–52.

28. *Dalle carte di Giovanni Giolitti: quarant'anni di politica italiana*, ed. P. D'Angiolini, Milan, 1962, I, 184.

29. *Il Secolo*, 4 and 20 Nov. 1893.

30. *Senato, discussioni*, 30 June 1891, 1294–7; Costantin Dumba, *Memoirs*, Boston, 1932, 42, 47.

31. Sonnino, *Diario*, I, 145; *The Speaker*, 29 Oct. 1882, 531 (Pareto); Napoleone Colajanni, *Banche e parlamento*, Milan, 1893, 237; Nello Quilici, *Banca Romana, fine di secolo*, Milan, 1935, 143, 601.

32. Stillman, *Autobiography*, II, 277.

33. *Camera, discussioni*, 20 Dec. 1892, 708–12, 718–21; *Documents français*, ser. 1, X, 128; Colajanni, *Banche*, 236–7; Napoleone Colajanni, *Corruzione politica*, Catania, 1888, 92–3.

34. Quilici, *Banca Romana*, 185, 484, 601–2; Eligio Vitale, *La riforma degli istituti di emissione e gli 'scandali bancari' in Italia 1892–1896*, Rome, 1972, I, 104.

35. Farini, *Diario*, I, 190, 197, 575, 620; Arturo Labriola, *Storia di dieci anni 1899–1909*, Milan, 1910, 11.

36. Natale, *Giolitti e gli italiani*, 216; Farini, *Diario*, I, 247.

37. Royal Archives, diary of Queen Victoria (13 Apr. 1893).

38. Farini, *Diario*, I, 340–1.

39. Paulucci, *Alla corte di Re Umberto*, 87, 93; Farini, *Diario*, I, 350–1; *Nuova Antologia*, 16 Jan. 1940, 176 (Guiccioli).

40. Paulucci, *Alla corte di Re Umberto*, 91; *Nuova Antologia*, 15 Dec. 1893, 577–8 (Bonghi); *ibid.*, 16 Oct. 1915, i–viii; Augusto Sandonà, *L'irredentismo nelle lotte politiche*, Bologna, 1938, III, 252.

6 Crispi and the politics of force

1. Luigi Pelloux, *Quelques souvenirs de ma vie*, ed. G. Manacorda, Rome, 1967, 157; Farini, *Diario*, I, 271, 317, 696.

2. FO, 45/700/312 (6 Dec. 1893, Edwardes); Sidney Sonnino, *Carteggio*, ed. P. Pastorelli, Bari, 1974, I, 88; *Il Secolo*, 24 Nov. 1893; G.F. Guerrazzi, *Ricordi di irredentismo*, 156.

3. *Camera, discussioni*, 20 Dec. 1893, 6396–7 (Imbriani); *ibid.*, 22 Dec. 1893,

6457 (Bovio); Vittoriano Documents, 1042/26 (18 Aug. 1894, Di Rudiní); Pareto, *Ecrits épars*, 107; Farini, *Diario*, I, 466 (Rattazzi); *Il Secolo*, 8 and 10 Dec. 1893.

4. *Discorsi parlamentari di Crispi*, III, 691; Farini, *Diario*, I, 389, 407; Stillman, *Autobiography*, II, 253, 279; *Nuova Antologia*, 16 Jan. 1940, 179 (Guiccioli).

5. *Nuova Antologia*, 1 Nov. 1893, 17 (Pasquale Villari); *La Vita Italiana*, Rome, Nov. 1895, 137 (Crispi); *Discorsi parlamentari di Giovanni Bovio*, Rome, 1915, 349; *Il Secolo*, 29 Jan. 1895; *ibid.*, 18 Oct. 1896 (Guglielmo Ferrero).

6. *Ibid.*, 6 Sept. 1888.

7. *Nuova Antologia*, 1 Feb. 1935, 324 (7 Jan. 1894, Crispi); Farini, *Diario*, I, 404, 465.

8. Stefano Jacini, *Pensieri sulla politica italiana*, 59, 62; Giustino Fortunato, *Il mezzogiorno e lo stato italiano*, Florence, 1926, I, 238–9.

9. D. Zanichelli, *Studi politici e storici*, Bologna, 1893, 60, 86; *Documents français*, ser. 1, X, 675.

10. *Ibid.*, ser. 1, XI, 2 and 17 (Jan. 1894); FO, 45/733/7 (7 Jan. 1895, Clare Ford); Farini, *Diario*, I, 540.

11. *Ibid.*, 104; *The Holstein Papers*, IV, 103–4.

12. *Documents français*, ser. 1, VIII, 435–6; *ibid.*, ser. 1, XI, 107.

13. *Illustrazione Italiana*, 15 Apr. 1894, 242; *Il Secolo*, 13 Apr. 1894; Farini, *Diario*, I, 461.

14. *Die grosse Politik*, VIII, 328.

15. *The Holstein Papers*, III, 459.

16. Sandonà, *L'irredentismo*, III, 260–1.

17. Farini, *Diario*, I, 113, 116–18, 256, 594; Paulucci, *Alla corte di Re Umberto*, 81; Labriola, *Dieci anni*, 40.

18. Farini, *Diario*, I, 388.

19. *Il Mattino*, Naples, 20 Nov. 1894; *Il Secolo*, 20 Feb. 1894.

20. *Documents français*, ser. 1, XI, 163; *German diplomatic documents*, II, 157.

21. *Francesco Crispi: Ultimi scritti e discorsi extraparlamentari (1890–1901)*, ed. T. Palamenghi-Crispi, Rome, n.d., 189–90; *Camera, discussioni*, 15 June 1894, 10,177 (Crispi).

22. Farini, *Diario*, I, 468, 471–2, 514, 732; *Il Secolo*, 23 Jan. 1899.

23. *Camera, discussioni*, 20 Dec. 1893, 6396 (Imbriani); Farini, *Diario*, I, 442, 449, 478.

24. Guiccioli, *Diario di un conservatore*, 190; Farini, *Diario*, I, 431, 434, 484.

25. *Ibid.*, I, 442, 454, 465.

26. *La Critica Sociale*, Milan, 16 Nov. 1893, 337.

27. Farini, *Diario*, I, 500, 510, 563.

28. *Documents français*, ser. 1, XI, 401; Farini, *Diario*, I, 403, 415, 518, 536.

29. Stillman, *Autobiography*, II, 249.

30. Chabod, *Storia della politica estera*, 547; *Nuova Antologia*, 1 Jan. 1941, 76–7; Farini, *Diario*, I, 549.

31. *Ibid.*, 462, 465; *Camera, discussioni*, 17 Apr. 1894, 7754; *Carteggi politici inediti di Crispi* , 81.

32. Pareto, *Ecrits épars*, 107; *The Speaker*, 29 Oct. 1892, 631 (Pareto); *Camera, discussioni*, 9 June 1892, 8372; Guiccioli, *Diario*, 186.

33. Farini, *Diario*, I, 437, 457, 459, 492, 509.

34. *Corriere della Sera*, 8 June 1894; *Il Secolo*, 29 July 1894; *Illustrazione Italiana*, 5 Aug. 1894; Guiccioli, *Diario*, 192; Paulucci, *Alla corte di Re Umberto*, 110; *Dalle carte di Giolitti*, I, 213–14; Farini, *Diario*, I, 556.

35. Crispi, *Scritti e discorsi*, 582–3.

36. *Nuova Antologia*, 1 Feb. 1941, 263 (Guiccioli); Farini, *Diario*, I, 594, 597, 612, 677; *Gazzetta Ufficiale*, Rome, 15 Dec, 1894, 6154.

37. Pelloux, *Quelques souvenirs*, liii (Manacorda); *Documents français*, ser. 1, XI, 458; Farini, *Diario*, I, 577.

38. Vittoriano Documents, 1041/40 (29 Dec. 1894, Ferruccio Macola).

39. Paulucci, *Alla corte di Re Umberto*, 123; Farini, *Diario*, I, 649–50.

7 Defeat in Africa

1. *Il Secolo*, 22 July 1894; Farini, *Diario*, I, 553; Crispi, *La prima guerra d'Africa*, 287–8; *Discorsi parlamentari di Crispi*, III, 868.

2. FO, 78/4986 (29 Feb. 1896, Salisbury); *Die grosse Politik*, VIII, 374; *Discorsi parlamentari di Felice Cavallotti*, Rome, 1914, II, 413; *Camera, discussioni*, 15 Dec. 1895, 3166.

3. *Corriere della Sera*, 24 Jan. and 14 Feb. 1895; Finali, *Memorie*, 645; Farini, *Diario*, II, 843; *Il Secolo*, 19 Apr. 1899.

4. Farini, *Diario*, I, 628; *Documents français*, ser. 1, XI, 588.

5. *Almanach de Gotha*, 1896, 1059.

6. *Documenti diplomatici: avvenimenti d'Africa (Libro Verde*, XXIII bis, Rome, 27 Apr. 1896), 36–8, 45.

7. Salisbury Papers, CXXV, 1 (29 July 1895,

Edwardes); *Camera, discussioni*, 25 July 1895, 1873 (Blanc); *ibid.*, 29 July 1895, 2158 (Crispi).

8. *Camera, discussioni*, 29 July 1895, 2155; Farini, *Diario*, I, 736.

9. *Documents français*, ser. 1, XI, 511; V. Pareto, *Cronache italiane*, Brescia, 1965, 342, 398; Guiccioli, *Diario*, 173; Stillman, *Autobiography*, II, 250–1; Crispi Papers, Rome, collection 'Reggio Emilia', IV, 9 (receipts from various journalists).

10. *Il Secolo*, 1, 3, 25 Jan. and 5 Mar. 1895.

11. *Il Secolo*, 9 Feb. 1895; Pareto, *Ecrits épars*, 116; *La Critica Sociale*, 16 May 1895, 145; E. Nathan, *Il dovere presente*, Rome, 1895, 30–3.

12. Farini, *Diario*, I, 697; Crispi, *Politica interna*, 177; *The Nation*, 11 Jan. 1894, 27 (Stillman).

13. Paulucci, *Alla corte di Re Umberto*, 135–7.

14. *Corriere della Sera*, 24 May 1895.

15. *La Vita Italiana*, July 1895, 473, (Bonghi); *ibid.* Aug. 1895, 89 (Bonghi); *Il Secolo*, 20 May 1895 (Di Rudinì); E. d'Orazio, *Fisiologia del parlamentarismo*, Turin, 1911, 430–1.

16. *Rivista di Politica e Scienze Sociali*, Rome, 15 July 1895, 5–6; *The Nation*, 28 May 1896, 413 (Stillman).

17. *Camera, discussioni*, 19 June 1895, 135–6 (Crispi); *ibid.*, 25 Nov. 1895, 2580 (Imbriani); Farini, *Diario*, I, 688.

18. *Camera, discussioni*, 25 June 1895, 242; Paulucci, *Alla corte di Re Umberto*, 133; *Il Secolo*, 20 June 1895; *ibid.*, 21 Nov. 1895; *ibid.*, 17 Jan. 1896.

19. *Libro Verde*, XXIII bis (27 Apr. 1896), 53, 62.

20. *Camera, discussioni*, 10 June 1895, 3; *ibid.*, 18 Dec. 1895, 3343.

21. *Camera, discussioni*, 21 Mar. 1896, 2570 (Pais); *Rassegna Storica del Risorgimento*, Rome, Sept. 1987, 343; Farini, *Diario*, I 770; Crispi Papers, Rome, *carteggi* 889 (21 Feb. 1896, Antonelli); *ibid.*, 1915 (18 Oct. 1897, Sonnino).

22. *Camera, discussioni*, 28 Nov. 1895, 2603 (Blanc); *ibid.*, 3–4 Dec. 1896, 2765, 2768 (Crispi); *ibid.*, 2762 (Brin); *Il Secolo*, 14 Oct. 1895; *Discorsi parlamentari di Imbriani*, 542 (29 Nov. 1895); *Rivista d'Italia*, 15 Apr. 1900, 699 (Adolfo Rossi).

23. *Bologna Incontri*, Bologna, Feb. 1986, 13 (diary of Bassi, 22 Dec. 1895); Crispi, *La prima guerra d'Africa*, 377–8 (Gen.

Arimondi); *Rivista di Politica e Scienze Sociali*, 30 Mar. 1896, 274; *ibid.*, 30 June 1896, 371 (Gen. Mocenni).

24. Sonnino, *Carteggio*, I, 165–7; Crispi, *La prima guerra d'Africa*, 389.

25. *Camera, discussioni*, 15 Dec. 1895, 3170–1; *ibid.*, 18 Dec. 1895, 3344, 3351; *Rivista di Politica e Scienze Sociali*, 15 Nov. 1895, 133–4.

26. *Libro Verde*, XXIII bis, 118–20, 129, 193.

27. Crispi, *Questioni internazionali*, 193, 238–9, 252–3; Sonnino, *Diario*, 212–13, 218; Gabriel Hanotaux, *Les carnets (1907–1925)*, ed. G. Dethan, Paris, 1982, 30; *Knowing one's enemies*, ed. E.R. May, 217 (Gooch).

28. Enrico Serra, *La questione tunisina da Crispi a Rudiní*, Milan, 1967, 358; Crispi, *La prima guerra d'Africa*, 330–1.

29. Crispi, *Questioni internazionali*, 283, 290.

30. Sonnino, *Diario*, 207–8, 212, 256; Farini, *Diario*, II, 854.

31. *Il Secolo*, 6 Feb., 30 Mar., 2 Apr. 1896.

32. *Libro Verde*, XXIII bis, 166, 172.

33. *Il Secolo*, 11 Mar., 4 Sept., 11 Oct. 1896; *La Critica Sociale*, 16 June 1896, 17–18; Giovanni Borelli, *Discorsi: l'idea liberale*, Modena, 1957, 212; *Camera, discussioni*, 22 June 1907, 16,503 (Enrico Ferri).

34. Sonnino, *Diario*, 212–14, 221, 231, 238, 251; Crispi Papers, Rome, *carteggi* 1915 (22 Feb. 1896, Sonnino to Crispi).

35. *Il Secolo*, 2 Mar. 1896.

36. *Libro Verde*, XXIII bis, 218; G.F.H. Berkeley, *The campaign of Adowa and the rise of Menelik*, London, 1902, 256.

37. J.R. Slade, *Eritrea and Abyssinia*, London, 1896, 33–5; *Rivista d'Italia*, Mar. 1902, 426–7 (Mocenni); A. Bizzoni, *L'Eritrea nel passato e nel presente*, 1897, 492; A. Del Boca, *Gli Italiani in Africa Orientale*, Bari, 1976, 694–70; *Carteggi di Bettino Ricasoli*, ed. S. Camerani and G. Arfè, Rome, 1962, XXII, 73; Enrico Ferri, *Battaglie parlamentari*, Milan, 1899, 9–11.

8 Umberto reasserts his authority

1. *Discorsi parlamentari di Crispi*, III, 881; Palamenghi-Crispi, *L'Italia coloniale e Crispi*, 181.

2. *Il Secolo*, 8 Apr. 1896 (from the *New York Herald*).

3. Farini, *Diario*, II, 865, 875, 877; Fausto Fonzi, *Crispi e lo 'Stato di Milano'*, Milan, 1965, 519; *La Vita Italiana*, Mar. 1896, 283 (De Gubernatis); *Il Secolo*, 12 Mar.

1896 (Colajanni); G. Arangio Ruiz, *Storia costituzionale del regno d'Italia,* Florence, 1898, 524.

4. Sonnino, *Diario,* 259, 262–3; Farini, *Diario,* II, 871, 878.

5. Francesco Papafava, *Dieci anni di vita Italiana, 1899–1909,* Bari, 1913, I, 105; *Rivista di Politica e Scienze Sociali,* 10 Mar. 1896, 274; *ibid.,* 15 May 1896, 322; *Il Secolo,* 4 Mar. 1896; *The Nation,* 28 May 1897, 413 (Stillman).

6. *Senato, discussioni,* 25 Mar. 1896, 1435, 1438; *Storia e Politica,* Milan, Apr. 1968, 216 (R. Mori).

7. Sonnino, *Diario,* I, 264; *Camera, discussioni,* 17 Mar. 1896, 3437.

8. *Ibid.,* 6 May 1896, 3933; *ibid.,* 6 June 1896, 5366; *ibid.,* 16 June 1896, 5931–2.

9. Farini, *Diario,* II, 1094; Labriola, *Dieci anni,* 18–19; Fonzi, *Crispi,* 525.

10. Crispi, *La prima guerra d'Africa,* 407–8; Crispi, *Politica estera,* 281; *Storia e Politica,* July 1968, 378–80 (E. Serra); E. Scarfoglio, *Abissinia (1888–1896),* Livorno, 1937, II. 254, 279, 412.

11. Sonnino, *Diario,* I, 272; *Il Secolo,* 23 May and 31 Oct. 1896.

12. Farini, *Diario,* II, 1172, 1179, 1184–5; *Il Secolo,* 9 Jan. 1902.

13. Farini, *Diario,* II, 928, 1064–5; Sonnino, *Diario,* I, 313; Palamenghi-Crispi, *L'Italia coloniale,* 183.

14. Luigi Luzzatti, *Memorie tratte dal carteggio e da altri documenti,* ed. E. de Carli, Bologna, 1933, II, 472; Sonnino, *Diario,* I, 299; Farini, *Diario,* II, 1094, 1211.

15. *Die grosse Politik,* XI, 262; Salisbury Papers, CXXV, 6 (12 Mar. 1896, Ford quoting Sermoneta); FO, 45/750/218 and 227 (4 and 18 Nov. 1896, Ford quoting Di Rudinì).

16. *Camera, discussioni,* 21 May 1896, 4480 (Valli); *La Vita Italiana,* Mar. 1896, 196.

17. Sonnino, *Diario,* I, 297–8.

18. *Camera, discussioni,* 15 June 1896, 5777; *ibid.,* 21 July, 7575; *Senato, discussioni,* 24 July, 2713 (Gen. Ricotti); Stillman, *Autobiography,* II, 293; Pelloux, *Quelques souvenirs,* xxxvi–xxxviii (Manacorda).

19. DDI, ser. 3, I, 24; *Documents français,* ser. 1, XII, 547, 601.

20. *Il Secolo,* 7 June 1896 (first and second editions both confiscated); *ibid.,* 20 June 1896 (Pareto); *Avanti!,* Milan, 16 Jan. 1897 (Ferrero).

21. *Camera, discussioni,* 10 July 1896, 7574; Farini, *Diario,* II, 962–3, 1041, 1049.

22. Guiccioli, *Diario,* 222; *Nuova Antologia,*

16 Mar. 1941, 156; Sonnino, *Diario,* I, 302.

23. *Ibid.,* 313, 323.

24. *British documents on the origins of the war, 1898–1914,* ed. G.P. Gooch and H.W.V. Temperley, London, 1926–38, IX, 309.

25. Farini, *Diario,* II, 905, 924, 1017.

26. *Camera, discussioni,* 25 May 1896, 4707–8 (Imbriani); *Il Secolo,* 4 July and 15 Oct. 1896; Farini, *Diario,* II, 1199.

27. *Camera, discussioni,* 29 June 1896, 6795 (Lucifero); *Discorsi parlamentari di Crispi,* III, 696–7; G. Fortunato, *Il mezzogiorno e lo stato italiano,* Florence, 1973 edn., II, 435.

9   Two turbulent years

1. Pareto, *Ecrits épars,* 74; *Political Science Quarterly,* New York, Dec. 1893, 682–3 (Pareto).

2. *Rivista Popolare di Politica, Lettere e Scienze Sociali,* Milan, 30 July 1897, 25 (Colajanni); Crispi, *Discorsi parlamentari,* II, 208; Crispi, *Scritti e discorsi politici,* 509.

3. *Il Mattino,* Naples, 15 May and 14 Oct. 1896 (Scarfoglio); *Carteggio di Castelli,* II, 510–11.

4. Sonnino, *Scritti e discorsi,* II, 575–7, 591–4.

5. Crispi, *Pensieri,* 97, 102, 113, 120; Fonzi, *Crispi,* 526.

6. Denis Mack Smith, *Storia di cento anni di vita italiana visti attraverso il 'Corriere della Sera',* Milan, 1978, 86.

7. Farini, *Diario,* II, 1185, 1189, 1196.

8. *Camera, discussioni,* 20 May 1897, 862.

9. DDI, ser. 3, I, 293; *ibid.,* ser. 3, II, 120, 133–4.

10. Ferdinando Martini, *Il diario Eritreo,* Florence, 1942, I, 2; Sonnino, *Diario,* I, 348, 354–5; Farini, *Diario,* II, 1158.

11. *Camera, discussioni,* 8 May 1897, 464; *Il Secolo,* 1 Jan. 1898.

12. *Camera, discussioni,* 18 Mar. 1896, 3480; *ibid.,* 4 May 1897, 307; *Nuova Antologia,* 16 Nov. 1899, 258 (Villari); *Discorsi parlamentari di Giolitti,* III, 1537; G. Fortunato, *Politica militare,* Rome, 1901, 91, 97–8, (4 May 1897); Fortunato, *Il mezzogiorno e lo stato italiano,* II, 396 (9 Oct. 1898).

13. Farini, *Diario,* II, 1286.

14. *Camera, discussioni,* 4 May 1897, 306.

15. *Ibid.,* 4 May 1897, 275; *Nuova Antologia,*

15 Sept. 1895, 217 (Codronchi); John Davis, *Conflict and control : law and order in nineteenth century Italy*, London, 1988, 239–41.

16. Farini, *Diario*, ii, 1277.
17. *Corriere della Sera*, 24 Feb. 1902; Giovanni Giolitti, *Memorie della mia vita*, Milan, 1922, i, 139–40; Bolton King and Thomas Okey, *Italy today*, London, 1909 (2nd edn.), 93.
18. *La Perseveranza*, Milan, 7 Nov. 1898; *Il Giornale degli Economisti*, Rome, 1 June 1898 (De Viti de Marco); *The National Review*, London, Aug. 1898, 905.
19. U. Alfassio Grimaldi, *Il re 'buono'*, Milan, 1970, 423; V. Pareto, *Libre échangisme*, Geneva, 1965, 296; *Il Secolo*, 5 July 1899 (Romussi).
20. Farini, *Diario*, ii, 1304, 1321, 1324, 1346.
21. *Ibid.*, ii, 1320, 1336, 1345; *The Speaker*, 25 June 1898, 781.
22. Sonnino, *Diario*, i, 391; U. Levra, *Il colpo di stato della borghesia: la crisi politica di fine secolo in Italia 1896–1900*, Milan, 1975, 236, 261–2.
23. Guiccioli, *Diario*, 238, 240.
24. *Camera, discussioni*, 16 Nov. 1897, iii.
25. *Senato, discussioni*, 23 Nov. 1898, 56; Farini, *Diario*, ii, 1366.
26. *La Educazione Politica*, 30 June 1899, 257–8; Cesare Lombroso, *Il momento attuale*, Milan, 1903, 71.
27. *Il Mattino*, 29 May 1899.

10   The collapse of parliamentary government

1. Guiccioli, *Diario*, 92; *Discorsi parlamentari di Bovio*, 473.
2. *Documents français*, ser. 1, xiii, 217.
3. Farini, *Diario*, ii, 1138, 1140, 1151, 1172; *Il Secolo*, 2 Jan. 1898.
4. *Ibid.*, 9 Sept. 1899 (Ferrero); G. Ferrero, *Il militarismo*, Milan, 1898, 338, 360; Farini, *Diario*, ii, 1251.
5. *Documents français*, ser. 1, xiv, 243, 379.
6. FO, 45/798/48 (18 Jan. 1899, Currie); Luzzatti, *Memorie*, ii, 527; *Nuova Antologia*, 16 May 1941 (Guiccioli).
7. Guiccioli, *Diario*, 251.
8. *Senato, discussioni*, 19 Dec. 1899, 307–8.
9. Martini, *Diario Eritreo*, i, 244, 247, 300; Pelloux, *Quelques souvenirs*, 205, 216; Borelli, *Discorsi*, 204; Ugo Ojetti, *I taccuini 1914–1943*, Florence, 1954, 72–3;

L. Lodi, *Venticinque anni di vita parlamentare*, Florence, 1923, 34.
10. *Il Secolo*, 30 Oct. 1899; Crispi, *Ultimi scritti*, 248; *Camera, discussioni*, 1 May 1899, 3598–9.
11. Salisbury Papers, cxxv, 33 (12 Mar. 1899, Currie); *Documents français*, ser. 1, xv, 291; G. Borsa, *Italia e Cina nel secolo XIX*, Milan, 1961, 181–2; *Dalle carte di Giolitti*, i, 360; *Nuova Antologia*, 1 Jan. 1943, 85.
12. *Senato, discussioni*, 18 Mar. 1899, 844; *Nuova Antologia*, 16 Apr. 1899, 746–7.
13. *DDI*, ser. 3, iii, 111–12, 117 (ed. E.Serra); *Senato, discussioni*, 18 Mar. 1899, 838–9; *La spedizione italiana in Cina 1900–1901*, ed. Stato Maggiore Guerra, Rome, 1925, 25.
14. *Camera, discussioni*, 13 Dec. 1899, 809 (Giolitti).
15. Guiccioli, *Diario*, 258; *Esercito e Nazione*, Rome, July 1928, 664–5.
16. Guiccioli, *Diario*, 247, 255.
17. Giolitti, *Discorsi extraparlamentari*, 208; *Camera, discussioni*, 27 May 1899, 3709; *ibid.*, 30 May 1899, 3803.
18. Sonnino, *Diario*, i, 428, 441–2; *Camera, discussioni*, 16 June 1899, 4532 (Barzilai); *Corriere della Sera*, 3 Sept. 1899.
19. Giolitti, *Discorsi extraparlamentari*, 218.
20. Luzzatti, *Memorie*, ii, 559, 561.
21. *Camera, discussioni*, 16 June 1899, 4534; *Dalle carte di Giolitti*, i, 382.
22. *Discorsi parlamentari di Giuseppe Zanardelli*, Rome, 1905, i, 444; *Il Secolo*, 7 Dec. 1899.
23. *La Educazione Politica*, Milan, 15 Apr. 1899, 150; *Il Secolo*, 14 Nov. 1899; *ibid.* 25 Mar. 1900.
24. *Camera, discussioni*, 17 Mar. 1900, 2730; Saverio Cilibrizzi, *Storia parlamentare politica e diplomatica d'Italia*, Naples, n.d., iii, 120.
25. *Camera, discussioni*, 3 Apr. 1900, 3139–40; Francesco Brancato, *Storia del parlamento italiano*, Palermo, 1973, x, 354.
26. *Discorsi di Zanardelli*, i, 421; Giolitti, *Discorsi extraparlamentari*, 214–15; Barzilai, *Luci ed ombre del passato*, 317.
27. *Corriere della Sera*, 24 Dec. 1905.
28. *Il Secolo*, 11 Apr. 1900; *Discorsi di Bovio*, 473.
29. O. Zuccarini, *Esperienze e soluzioni*, Rome, 1945, 48; Labriola, *Dieci anni*, 162.
30. *Review of Reviews*, London, 15 June 1925 (Wickham Steed).

11   Retrospect

1. Paulucci, *Alla corte di Re Umberto*, 31, 138; *Documents français*, ser. 1, xɪ, 539; Farini, *Diario*, ɪɪ, 968, 1144.
2. FO, 45/817/126 (31 July 1900, Currie); Salisbury Papers, cxxv, 53 (1 Aug. 1900, Currie).
3. Paolo Boselli, *La patria negli scritti e nei discorsi*, Florence, 1917, 333.
4. *Corriere della Sera*, 5 Apr. 1949 (Ruffini); R. Bracalini, *La regina Margherita*, Milan, 1983, 229–30; Guiccioli, *Diario*, 247; Carlo Casalegno, *La regina Margherita*, Turin, 1956, 179; Farini, *Diario*, ɪ, 222, 756–7.
5. Carlo Morini, *La decadenza del sentimento monarchico in Italia*, Florence, 1900, 38.
6. *Documents français*, ser. 1, ɪx, 143.
7. Dario Papa, *Confessioni e battaglie*, Milan, n.d., 42–3.
8. *Il Secolo*, 2 Jan. 1898.
9. Luigi Albertini, *Epistolario, 1911–1926*, ed. O. Barié, Milan, 1968, ɪɪɪ, 1288; *Il Secolo*, 30 Dec. 1893.
10. *Nuova Antologia*, 1 Nov. 1900, 155 (Maggiorino Ferraris); Arturo Labriola, *Spiegazioni a me stesso*, Naples, 1945, 109–11,
11. *L'Aurore*, Paris, 14 Dec. 1897 (quoted by P. Milza, *Français et Italiens à la fin du XIX siècle*, Rome, 1981, ɪ, 391); *Il Secolo*, 29 Aug. 1899 (Ferrero).
12. Alfredo Oriani, *Fuochi di bivacco*, Bari, 1915, 127–8; *Nuova Antologia*, 16 May 1900, 347; *ibid.*, 1 Sept. 1900, 6–7, 10 (Zanichelli); *ibid.*, 16 Dec. 1900, 347 (Boselli).
13. Guiccioli, *Diario*, 255.
14. Francesco Papafava, *Dieci anni di vita italiana 1899–1909*, Bari, 1913, 105 (Sept. 1900); King and Okey, *Italy today*, 7–8; William James Stillman, *Francesco Crispi*, London, 1899, 146; *Nuova Antologia*, Sept. 1900, 42.
15. Morini, *Decadenza del sentimento monarchico*, 103; Mario Missiroli, *La monarchia socialista*, Bari, 1914, 113–14; Lodi, *Venticinque anni di vita parlamentare*, 33–4.
16. Stillman, *Crispi*, 13–14; King and Okey, *Italy today*, 26.
17. *Giornale degli Economisti*, Dec. 1899, 599–600 (Papafava).
18. *Review of Reviews*, Aug. 1900, 122–5.
19. Stillman, *Autobiography*, ɪɪ, 254, 292–3.
20. *North American Review*, Boston, 16 Feb. 1903, 250 (Sidney Brooks).

Vittorio Emanuele III

1   A new direction in politics

1. Antonio Salandra, *Il diario*, ed. G.B. Gifuni, Milan, 1969, 31; Paolo Puntoni, *Parla Vittorio Emanuele III*, Milan, 1958, 221.
2. Angelo Gatti, *Caporetto: dal diario di guerra*, ed. A. Monticone, Bologna, 1965, 392–3; G. Levi Della Vida, *Fantasmi ritrovati*, Venice, 1966, 207; M. Mureddu *Il Quirinale del re*, Milan, 1977, 69.
3. Royal Archives, diary of Queen Victoria (24 July 1891).
4. Earl of Oxford and Asquith, *Memories and reflections*, London, 1928, ɪɪ, 120.
5. Egidio Osio, *Il Generale Osio*, Milan, 1909, 349–56; Silvio Scaroni, *Con Vittorio Emanuele III*, Milan, 1954, 79; *Rivista Italiana di Numismatica*, Milan, 1911, 127–9.
6. Lloyd Griscom, *Diplomatically speaking*, London, 1941, 296; Thomas Morgan, *Spurs on the boot: Italy under her masters*, London, 1942, 110; Luigi Morandi, *Come fu educato Vittorio Emanuele III*, Turin, 1903, 131; Ferdinando Martini, *Diario 1914–1918*, ed. G. De Rosa, Milan, 1966, 1190; Francesco Saverio Nitti, *Edizione nazionale delle opere*, ed. A. Saitta, Bari, 1980, xvɪ, tome 2, 559.
7. Osio, *Generale Osio*, 326, 346, 351.
8. Domenico Farini, *Diario di fine secolo*, ed. E. Morelli, Rome, 1962, ɪɪ, 1050.
9. Salisbury Papers, cxxv, 53 (1 Aug. 1900, Currie); FO, 800/132/11 (20 Nov. 1900).
10. *The letters of William Roscoe Thayer*, ed. C.D. Hazen, Boston, 1926, 125–6.
11. Theodore Roosevelt, *Selections from the correspondence*, ed. H.C. Lodge, New York, 1925, ɪɪ, 129; J.B. Bishop, *Theodore Roosevelt and his time*, London, 1920, ɪɪ, 203.
12. FO, 170/568/191 (29 Nov. 1901, Currie); *FRUS*, 1906, vɪ, 845.
13. Francesco Saverio Nitti, *Il partito radicale e la nuova democrazia industriale: prime linee di un programma del partito radicale*, Turin, 1907, 48–9.
14. *Badminton Magazine*, London, Feb. 1905, 123–8 (Varé).
15. Farini, *Diario*, ɪ, 676, ɪɪ, 1050.
16. Francesco Crispi, *Questioni internazionali*, ed. T. Palamenghi-Crispi, Milan, 1913, 240–1.

17. *North American Review*, Boston, 16 Feb. 1903, 250 (Sidney Brooks); *Fortnightly Review*, London, March 1901, 493 (Zimmern); *Atti Parlamentari: Camera dei deputati, discussioni*, Rome, 2 Dec. 1900, 969 (Ferri); Carlo Morini, *La decadenza del sentimento monarchico*, Florence, 1900, 103; *Nuova Antologia*, Florence, Sept. 1900, 42.

18. *Dalle carte di Giovanni Giolitti: quarant'anni di politica italiana*, ed. G. Carocci, Milan, 1962, ii, 57–9; Osio, *Generale Osio*, 603; *The Holstein Papers*, ed. N. Rich and M.H. Fisher, Cambridge, 1963, iv, 221 (von Wedel); Sidney Sonnino, *Carteggio*, ed. P. Pastorelli, Bari, 1974, i, 269.

19. *Relazioni e proposte della commissione per lo studio delle riforme costituzionali*, Florence, 1932, 28–9; *Il Secolo*, Milan, 11 Sept. 1900.

20. Sonnino, *Carteggio*, i, 269; Alessandro Guiccioli, *Diario di un conservatore*, Rome, 1973, 264.

21. Gaspare Finali, *Memorie*, ed. G. Maioli, Faenza, 1955, 481.

22. Francesco Saverio Nitti, *Rivelazioni: dramatis personae*, Naples, 1948, 587; *Documents diplomatiques français (1871–1914)*, ed. Ministère des Affaires Etrangères, Paris, 1976, ser. 2, x, 664–5.

23. Rodd Papers, box 12 (16 Oct. 1904); Sonnino, *Carteggio*, i, 276.

24. *Nuova Antologia*, 16 Feb. 1942 (Sonnino, 14 Oct, 1900); Guiccioli, *Diario*, 278; Luigi Pelloux, *Quelques souvenirs de ma vie*, Rome, 1967, lxxviii–lxxix (Gastone Manacorda).

25. *Corriere della Sera*, Milan, 17 Aug. 1900; *ibid.*, 1 June 1901.

26. *Nuova Antologia*, 16 June 1900, 729; *ibid.*, 1 July 1900, 168 (Franchetti); Bolton King and Thomas Okey, *Italy today*, London, 1909 (2nd edn.), 19.

27. Pasquale Villari, *Storia, politica e istruzione*, Milan, 1914, 205; *Nuova Antologia*, 1 Jan. 1942, 69 (Guiccioli); Arturo Labriola, *Storia di dieci anni, 1899–1909*, Milan, 1910, 152; *Rassegna Internazionale*, Milan, 20 June 1925, 16 (Ferrero).

28. *Discorsi parlamentari di Matteo Renato Imbriani-Poerio*, Rome, 1923, 591.

29. *La Perseveranza*, Milan, 17 Sept. 1900; *Dalle carte di Giolitti*, i, 106–7; Sidney Sonnino, *Diario*, ed. P. Pastorelli, Bari, 1972, i, 311.

30. *Review of Reviews*, London, Feb. 1907, 150–1 (interview with W.T. Stead);

Giovanni Artieri, *Cronaca del regno d'Italia*, Milan, 1977, i, 804 (9 Sept. 1900, Vittorio Emanuele to Osio).

31. Nitti, *Edizione nazionale*, xvi, tome 2, 561.

32. FO, 45/853 (11 Apr. 1902, Calthorpe); Paolo Paulucci, *Alla corte di Re Umberto: diario segreto*, ed. G. Calcagno, Milan, 1986, 148.

33. *Documents français*, ser. 2, i, 663; *Giornale degli Economisti*, Rome, 1 Mar. 1901, 299 (Papafava).

34. *Corriere della Sera*, 8 and 16 Feb. 1901.

35. FO, 800/132/54 (20 Feb. 1901, Currie).

36. *DDI*, ser. 3, v, 30–1 (Visconti-Venosta).

37. *Camera, discussioni*, 21 June 1901, 5513; Giovanni Giolitti, *Discorsi extraparlamentari*, ed. N. Valeri, Turin, 1952, 247–8.

38. *Ibid.*, 120, 191, 225, 240; *Camera, discussioni*, 21 June 1901, 5500–1.

39. Enrico Caviglia, *Diario*, Rome, 1952, 223; Salandra, *Diario*, 35.

40. *Nuova Antologia*, 16 Aug. 1900, 770; *ibid.*, 16 Sept. 1901, 346; A. d'Atri, *Giovanni Giolitti et les libertés en Italie*, Fontenay, 1908, 14–15.

41. *Discorsi parlamentari di Giovanni Giolitti*, Rome, 1953, ii 1202; Giolitti, *Discorsi extraparlamentari*, 225–7, 246.

42. *Discorsi parlamentari di Giuseppe Zanardelli*, Rome, 1905, ii, 622–5; *Atti Parlamentari: Senato, discussioni*, 20 Feb. 1902, 6; Sonnino *Carteggio*, i, 275.

43. *The Times*, London, 13 July 1900; *The Nation*, New York, 10 Nov. 1892 (Jessie White Mario); *Discorsi parlamentari di Filippo Turati*, Rome, 1950, i, 314–20; *Camera, discussioni*, 12 June 1902, 2780 (Giolitti).

44. *La Critica Sociale*, Milan, 1 Sept. 1902, 261; *ibid.*, 1 Feb. 1904, 68 (Bissolati); Arturo Labriola, *Spiegazioni a me stesso*, Naples, 1945, 111–12; *Camera, discussioni*, 28 Jan. 1905, 640 (Bissolati).

45. *La Educazione Politica*, Milan, 15 Aug. 1900, 346; A. Ghisleri, *Il parlamentarismo e i repubblicani*, Modena, 1912, 66, 80; *I congressi nazionali del partito repubblicano dal 1871 al 1925*, Rome, 1925, 18.

46. FO, 45/872 (26 Feb. 1903, Rodd).

47. *Discorsi parlamentari di Giolitti*, ii, 767–8.

48. W.D. Howells, *Roman holidays and others*, New York, 1908, 190.

49. *La Critica Sociale*, 1 Sept. 1900, 287; *La Educazione Politica*, 31 Dec 1900; *ibid.*, 15 Nov. 1901; *ibid.*, 31 May 1902; *ibid.*, 15 June 1902; *Il Secolo*, 29 Aug. 1904.

50. A. Ghisleri, *Democrazia in azione*, Rome, n.d., 145.

51. Guglielmo Ferrero, *La monarchia e la situazione presente*, Rome, 1905, 93; *Rassegna Contemporanea*, Rome, Mar. 1909, 83–4 (Fovel).

52. *Il Secolo*, 1 July 1901 (Sacchi); *ibid.*, 4 Jan. 1905; King and Okey, *Italy today*, 75; *Nuova Antologia*, 16 Nov. 1901, 334.

53. Denis Mack Smith, *Storia di cento anni di vita italiana visti attraverso il 'Corriere della Sera'*, Milan, 1978, 114.

2 Foreign policy, 1900–4

1. Alfredo Niceforo, *L'italia barbara contemporanea*, Milan, 1898, 247–8; Giuseppe Sergi, *La decadenza delle nazioni latine*, Turin, 1900, 100.

2. *Rivista Politica e Letteraria*, Rome, 15 Aug. 1900, 7; *Il Regno*, Florence, 29 May 1904.

3. *Corriere della Sera*, 18 Oct. 1900; *Il Secolo*, 16 June 1900 (Ferrero); Napoleone Colajanni, *Razze inferiori e razze superiori: latini e anglo-sassoni*, Rome 1903, xiii, 317; G. Fortunato, *Il mezzogiorno e lo stato italiano*, Florence, 1973, ii, 467 (Oct. 1900), 531 (Oct. 1904).

4. Sonnino, *Carteggio*, i, 274, 276.

5. *Documents français*, ser. 1, xvi, 518; *ibid.*, ser. 2, i, 240; Pierre Milza, *Français et italiens à la fin du XIX siècle*, Rome, 1981, 978; Enrico Decleva, *Da Adua a Sarajevo: la politica estera e la Francia, 1896–1914*, Bari, 1971, 151.

6. FO, 45/836/62 (14 Apr. 1901, Currie): *Nuova Antologia*, Dec. 1952, 428–30 (Serra).

7. Artieri, *Cronaca*, i, 806; *Corriere della Sera*, 17 Aug. 1900; *Camera, discussioni*, 28 May 1902, 2174–8.

8. *Camera, discussioni*, 23 Mar. 1901, 2795 (Fortunato); *ibid.*, 26 Mar. 1901, 2891 (Sonnino); FO, 45/800/209 (1 Nov. 1899, Currie quoting Sonnino); *Nuova Antologia*, 1 Nov. 1900, 159 (Maggiorino Ferraris).

9. *Giornale degli Economisti*, Nov. 1900, 533; *Il Domani d'Italia*, 30 Mar. 1901; *Camera, discussioni*, 3 Dec. 1900, 971 (Ferri); *Il Secolo*, 12 Oct. 1901 (Ferrero); Cesare Lombroso, *Il momento attuale*, Milan, 1903, 253; *Gli anarchici ed il regicidio di Monza*, Rome, 1907, 7.

10. FO, 45/836/74 (7 May 1901, Ottley).

11. FO, 45/817/153 (28 Sept. 1900, Currie).

12. Pasquale Villari, *Scritti e discorsi per la 'Dante'*, Rome, 1933, 15–16; *Il Secolo*, 21 Apr. 1903.

13. Vico Mantegazza, *L'altra sponda: Italia ed Austria nell'Adriatico*, Milan, 1906, 26; *Discorsi parlamentari di Giovanni Bovio*, Rome, 1915, 473.

14. Artieri, *Cronaca*, i, 803; Sonnino, *Carteggio*, i, 273–6.

15. *Camera, discussioni*, 2 Dec. 1910, 10,181.

16. FO, 45/853/61 (11 Apr. 1902, Calthorpe).

17. Stillman Papers, 3 Mar. 1897 (Curzon to Stillman); *Nuova Antologia*, 16 Nov. 1903, 325 (Tittoni).

18. FO, 45/853/1 (1 Jan. 1902, Currie).

19. Bertie Papers, 800/173/6 (8 Feb. 1903).

20. Griscom, *Diplomatically speaking*, 281.

21. Ferdinando Martini, *Il diario Eritreo*, Florence, 1943, iii, 86.

22. Raymond Poincaré, *Au service de la France: neuf années de souvenirs*, Paris, 1926–33, ix, 245.

23. Livio Zeno, *Ritratto di Carlo Sforza*, Florence, 1975, 140; *Documents français*, ser. 3, x, 61; FO, 45/826/62 (14 Apr. 1901, Currie).

24. *Documents français*, ser. 1, xvi, 552; Francesco Tommasini, *L'Italia alla vigilia della guerra: politica estera di Tommaso Tittoni*, Bologna, 1943, i, 82.

25. *La Vita Internazionale*, Milan, 20 June 1901, 371 (Pareto); *Il Secolo*, 26 Mar. 1901.

26. *Nuova Antologia*, 1 May 1904, 156 (Tittoni).

27. FO, 45/477/119 (13 Apr. 1883, Paget quoting Mancini); *Die grosse Politik der europäischen Kabinette. 1871–1914*, Berlin, 1924, xviii, tome 2, 522 (Jan. 1902); *ibid*, 731.

28. DDI, ser. 3, v, 423.

29. Tommasini, *Italia alla vigilia*, i, 83.

30. *Documents français*, ser. 2, i, 156, 662.

31. *Die grosse Politik*, xviii, tome 2, 615, 629–30; Enrico Serra, *Camille Barrère e l'intesa italo-francese*, Milan, 1950, 102; DDI, ser. 3, ii, 218; Alfred Francis Pribram, *The secret treaties of Austria-Hungary, 1879–1914*, Cambridge, 1921, ii, 228.

32. *Die grosse Politik*, xviii, tome 2, 683–5.

33. *Ibid.*, 689, 698.

34. *Ibid.*, 703–6; *Il Politico*, Pavia, 1987, i, 128–32 (Ceva); Luigi Albertini, *Le origini della guerra del 1914*, Milan, 1942, i, 135; G. André-Fribourg, *L'Italie et nous*, Paris, 1947, 155.

35. *Il Secolo*, 30 Mar. 1901; *ibid.*, 26 July 1901; *ibid.*, 15 May 1902; *ibid.*, 3 July 1902.
36. *La Educazione Politica*, 15 May 1902, 214; *ibid*, 31 July 1902, 305; *La Critica Sociale*, 1 Jan. 1898, 8 (Arturo Labriola).
37. FO, 45/855/142 (9 July 1902).
38. *The Holstein Papers*. iv, 249; *British documents on the origins of the war 1898–1914*, ed. G.P. Gooch and H.W.V. Temperley, London, 1926–38, i, 292–3; Tommasini, *Italia alla vigilia*, i, 319–20.
39. Rodd Papers, box 20 (17 Oct. 1919).
40. *Die grosse Politik*, xviii, tome 2, 613; *Nuova Antologia*, 16 Jan. 1942, 91 (Guiccioli); Decleva, *Da Adua a Sarajevo*, 251; Alberto Pirelli, *Taccuini 1922–1943*, Bologna, 1984, 187.
41. FO, 800/133/79 (22 Feb. 1904, Col. Lamb); FO, 45/890/187 (29 Nov. 1904, Lister); *Die grosse Politik*, xviii, tome 2, 613–14 (9 May 1903, Von Bülow).
42. *Discorsi parlamentari di Giolitti*, ii, 809.
43. *Nuova Antologia*, 16 Nov. 1903, 323.
44. Frederick Ponsonby, *Recollections of three reigns*, ed. Colin Welch, London, 1951, 168; Charles Hardinge, *Old diplomacy*, London, 1947, 138.
45. Guiccioli, *Diario*, 285.
46. *Die grosse Politik*, xviii, tome 2, 613; *ibid.*, xx, tome 1, 54–5.
47. *Ibid.*, xviii, tome 2, 642; *Documents français*, ser. 2, iv, 131; Tommaso Tittoni, *Nuovi scritti di politica interna ed estera*, Milan, 1930, 219; *Il Secolo*, 10 July 1905 (quoting Giolitti).
48. *Documents français*, ser. 2, v, 280; *Die grosse Politik*, xx, tome 1, 55.
49. *Documents français*, ser. 2, iv, 305, 361.
50. *Die grosse Politik*, xx, tome 1, 40, 45–7; Tommasini, *Italia alla vigilia*, i, 325.
51. *British documents on the origins of the war*, viii, 33; *Documents français*, ser. 2, vi, 448, 490.
52. FO, 800/132/235 (20 May 1904, Bertie quoting Barrére).
53. *British documents on the origins of the war*, iii, 391; *Nuova Antologia*, 1 May 1904, 149 (Tittoni).

3 The beginning of Giolittismo

1. *Die grosse Politik*, xx, tome 1, 54 (25 Apr. 1904, Monts).
2. *Corriere della Sera*, 27 Oct. 1903.
3. FO, 800/133/42 (31 Oct. 1903, Bertie); *Camera, discussioni*, 8 Apr. 1911, 13,741.
4. Bernhard von Bülow, *Memoirs*, London, 1932, ii, 599.
5. *Discorsi parlamentari di Giolitti*, ii, 672, 772; *Die grosse Politik*, xx, tome 1, 84.
6. Griscom, *Diplomatically speaking*, 283; FO, 45/890/155 (5 Oct. 1904, Rodd).
7. Francesco Saverio Nitti, *Napoli e la questione meridionale*, Naples, 1903, 53; Guiccioli, *Diario*, 272; *Camera, discussioni*, 10 Dec. 1901, 6579–80 (De Martino); *Discorsi parlamentari di Giolitti*, ii, 632.
8. *Letters of Thayer*, 126.
9. *Corriere della Sera*, 27 May 1902.
10. *Ibid.*, 20 May 1902; Guiccioli, *Diario*, 272.
11. *Giornale d'Italia*, Rome, 4 Oct. 1910 (Villari); Fortunato, *Il mezzogiorno e lo stato italiano*, ii, 469.
12. Ernesto Nathan, *Vent'anni di vita italiana attraverso all'"Annuario'*, Rome, 1906, 346–7; *Camera, discussioni*, 27 June 1906, 9210, 9216.
13. Francesco Saverio Nitti, *L'Italia all'alba del secolo XX*, Turin, 1901, 120–1; Nitti, *Napoli e la questione meridionale*, 8–12; *Camera, discussioni*, Dec. 1901, 6596 (Lollini).
14. *Dalle carte di Giolitti*, ii, 365 (Giampiero Carocci, quoting Gen. Brusati).
15. Nitti, *Edizione nazionale*, xvi, tome 2, 561–2.
16. Paulucci, *Alla corte di Re Umberto*, 137.
17. *Corriere della Sera*, 1 June 1904.
18. *Osservatore Romano*, Vatican, 19 Aug. 1900; FO, 45/817 (20 Aug. 1900, Currie).
19. FO, 800/133/188 (3 June 1904, Bertie); Farini, *Diario*, i, 45, ii, 1397; *Die grosse Politik*, xx, tome 1, 55.
20. FO, 45/890/155 (5 Oct. 1904, Rodd).
21. Gabriel Hanotaux, *Les carnets (1907–1925)*, ed. G. Dethan, Paris, 1982, 138; *Camera, discussioni*, 23 Mar. 1905, 1645 (Tittoni).
22. FO, 371/82/24050 (11 July 1906, Egerton); *Il Regno*, 23 June 1906 (Corradini).
23. *Corriere della Sera*, 30 May 1906; Luigi Albertini, *Venti anni di vita politica*, Bologna, 1950, i, tome 1, 224; Giovanni Borelli, *Discorsi*, Modena, 1957, 187–8.
24. E. d'Orazio, *Fisiologia del parlamentarismo in Italia*, Turin, 1911, 432.
25. *Documents français*, ser. 2, x, 665.
26. *Il Secolo*, 13 Aug, 1908; *Review of Reviews*, Feb. 1907, 151.
27. A. Marazio, *Del governo parlamentare italiano*, Turin, 1904, 33.

28. Rodd Papers, box 16 (19 Jan. 1914, Rodd to Carey).
29. FO, 371/469/979 (14 Dec. 1907, Delmé-Radcliffe).
30. *Ibid.*, 371/479/6961 (12 Feb. 1908, Delmé-Radcliffe).
31. Salandra, *Diario*, 35.
32. Galeazzo Ciano, *Diario, 1937–1938*, Bologna, 1948, 128; Galeazzo Ciano, *Diario, 1939–1943*, Milan, 1946, II, 245; Scaroni, *Con Vittorio Emanuele III*, 119; Puntoni, *Parla Vittorio Emanuele III*, 7.
33. Federigo Sclopis, *Diario segreto* (1859–1878), ed. P. Pietro Pirri, Turin, 1959, 491; Farini, *Diario*, I, 668; Templewood Papers (4 July 1918).
34. FO, 371/469/6961 (12 Feb. 1908, Delmé-Radcliffe); *La Settimana Incom Illustrata*, Rome, 3 Jan. 1959, 8 (Maurano quoting King Umberto II); Labriola, *Storia di dieci anni*, 224.
35. *Fortnightly Review*, Mar. 1901, 494 (Zimmern); King and Okey, *Italy today*, 15–19.
36. *Il Secolo*, 20 Dec. 1900.
37. *Nuova Antologia*, 16 June 1911, 677–9; *Camera, discussioni*, 31 Mar. 1909, 141 (Giolitti); *ibid.*, 24 Feb. 1910, 5355 (Morgari); FO, 371/683/58 (22 Mar. 1909); Gaetano Salvemini, *Il ministro della mala vita*, Florence, 1910, 199–202.
38. *Camera, discussioni*, 21 May 1909, 1092–6 (Chiesa).
39. Rodd Papers, box 13 (9 Feb. and 22 Mar. 1909, Rodd to Hardinge).
40. Giovanni Artieri, *Il re, i soldati e il generale che vinse*, Rocca S. Casciano, 1951, 15.
41. *Camera, discussioni*, 7 July 1909, 3895–6.
42. *Ibid.*, 4 Dec. 1908, 24,307.
43. *Ibid.*, 9 June 1909, 2162 (Alessio); *Corriere della Sera*, 16 Mar. 1909; *Nuova Antologia*, 1 May 1910, 162; Labriola, *Storia di dieci anni*, 234; Fortunato, *Il mezzogiorno e lo stato italiano*, 529 (Oct. 1904).
44. *Camera, discussioni*, 9 May 1906, 7947; *ibid.*, 30 Mar. 1909, 96 (Chiesa); *ibid.*, 20 Dec. 1909, 4751 (Sonnino); *Giornale degli Economisti*, Apr. 1906, 302.
45. Sidney Sonnino, *Scritti e discorsi extraparlamentari 1903–1920*, Bari, 1972, II, 1386.
46. Giovanni Giolitti, *Memorie della mia vita*, Milan, 1922, II, 319; *Il Secolo*, 19 Apr. 1895.
47. *Camera, discussioni*, 15 Apr. 1916, 10,422; *Nuova Antologia*, 1 Feb. 1918, 235 (Tittoni).
48. *Camera, discussioni*, 28 Jan. 1905, 639; *Nuova Antologia*, 16 Sept. 1911, 305–7; Albertini, *Venti anni*, I, 310–11.
49. Guglielmo Ferrero, *Il fenomeno Crispi e la crisi italiana*, Turin, 1894, 8; *The Century Illustrated Monthly Magazine*, New York, Dec. 1894, 206 (Stillman); Ruggero Bonghi, *Come cadde la destra*, Milan, 1929, 186–7.
50. Nitti. *Il partito radicale*, 3–4.
51. See pp. 81–2 above.
52. Napoleone Colajanni, *I partiti politici in Italia*, Rome, 1912, 6–7; *Nuova Antologia*, 16 July 1909, 324; d'Orazio, *Fisiologia del parlamentarismo*, 450–1.

4 Great-power politics

1. FO, 371/82/20308 (9 June 1906, Egerton); Decleva, *Da Adua a Sarajevo*, 264.
2. Mantegazza, *L'altra sponda*, 54–5; *Camera, discussioni*, 15 Apr. 1916, 10,421; *Il Secolo*, 10 July 1905.
3. *Die grosse Politik*, XX, tome 2, 436–7.
4. *Camera, discussioni*, 15 May 1907, 14,144 (Romussi); *ibid.*, 3 Dec. 1908, 24,252 (Mirabelli and Barzilai).
5. *Ibid.*, 2 Dec. 1908, 24,204 (Sonnino); *Corriere della Sera*, 24 Jan 1909 (Luzzatti).
6. Griscom, *Diplomatically speaking*, 271; *Camera, discussioni*, 15 May 1907, 14,160 (Tittoni).
7. *Documents français*, ser. 2, III, 461; *ibid.*, ser. 2, IV, 227.
8. *Nuova Antologia*, 16 Jan. 1905, 356–7; *ibid.*, Feb. 1905, 270–1; *ibid.*, 16 Mar. 1908, 344.
9. *Ibid.* 15 Feb. 1905, 716–17; *ibid.*, 16 Oct. 1905, 693; *ibid.*, 16 Oct. 1906, 666; *ibid.*, 16 Mar. 1907, 357.
10. *Ibid.*, 1 Mar. 1906, 144; *ibid.*, 16 Mar. 1906, 333–4; *ibid.*, 16 Apr. 1906, 724; Rodd Papers, box 13 (9 Feb. 1909); FO, 800/173/27 (5 Apr. 1910, Bertie); FO, 800/173/126 (5 Nov. 1916, Grahame); Curzon Papers, 112/214a/78 (23 June 1919).
11. FO, 800/133/177 (26 May 1904, Pansa).
12. Royal Archives W. 44/42 (26 Feb. 1904, Bertie to Lord Knollys); *Documents français*, ser. 2, VI, 86–7 (3 Feb. 1905, Luzzatti); *Die grosse Politik*, XVIII, tome 2, 618–19, 625–6 (20 Sept. 1903, von Bülow).
13. *Ibid.*; Sonnino, *Diario*, I, 465.
14. *Die grosse Politik*, XX, tome 2, 296

(3 Apr. 1905, von Bülow); *Documents français*, ser. 2, vi, 282 (2 Apr. 1905, Barrère).

15. FO, 45/906/100 (10 June 1905, Egerton).
16. *Die grosse Politik*, xxi, tome 2, 365; Pribram, *The secret treaties*, ii, 143.
17. *British documents on the origins of the war*, iii, 391 (21 Sept. 1906, Lascelles); *Documents français*, ser. 2, x, 705 (Mar. 1907, Lecomte); *Die grosse Politik*, xx, 75–6 (21 Aug. 1907); Tommasini, *Italia alla vigilia*, ii, 307–8, 314, 325.
18. *Documents français*, ser. 2, xi, 939; *Nuova Antologia*, 16 Feb. 1905, 719.
19. *Documents français*, ser. 2, xii, 241, 509–10.
20. Bertie Papers, 800/173/45 (13 Apr. 1905).
21. *Nuova Antologia*, 1 June 1906, 526.
22. *Camera, discussioni*, 15 May 1907, 14,152–4.
23. *Österreich-Ungarns Aussenpolitik vor der Bosnischen Krise 1908 bis zum Kriegsausbruch 1914*, Vienna, 1930, i, 106, 154, 163, 593.
24. *Documents français*, ser. 2, xi, 985.
25. *American Historical Review*, New York, June 1968, 1414 (9 Dec. 1908, Griscom, quoted by W.A. Renzi).
26. *Documents français*, ser. 2, xi, 942–3 (24 Nov. 1908, Barrère); *Camera, discussioni*, 1 Dec. 1908, 24,239 (Fortis); FO, 371/682/326 (26 Jan. 1909, Rodd); *Il Secolo*, 7 Nov. 1909 (Fortunato).
27. *Camera, discussioni*, 15 May 1907, 14,144 (Romussi); *ibid.*, 9 June 1909, 2177 (Bissolati); *Rassegna Contemporanea*, Mar. 1909, 91–2 (Fovel).
28. FO, 371/469/6961 (12 Feb. 1908, Delmé-Radcliffe); FO, 371/683/11 (19 Feb. 1909, Delmé-Radcliffe).
29. Rodd Papers. box 13 (12 Nov. 1909, Hardinge).
30. *Documents français*, ser. 1, xi, 164; Emile Zola, *Oeuvres complètes*, ed. H. Mitterand, Paris, 1968, vii, 1020 (Billot).
31. FO, 371/82/10469 (21 Mar. 1906, Delmé-Radcliffe); FO, 371/683/10 (19 Feb. 1909, Delmé-Radcliffe).
32. Rodd Papers, box 13 (6 May 1909, Rodd).
33. *Ibid.*, (23 Aug. 1909); *ibid.*, box 14 (14 Jan. 1911).
34. Alexandre Iswolsky, *Au service de la Russie*, Paris, 1937, i, 273–4 (June 1906, Mouravieff).
35. Hanotaux, *Les carnets*, 139 (15 Apr. 1915).

36. FO, 371/82/10469 (21 Mar. 1906).
37. FO, Confidential Print no. 9171 (14 Dec. 1907).
38. C. Scarfoglio, *La memoria di un giornalista*, Rome, 1964, 288; *Camera, discussioni*, 9 June 1909, 2103 (Antoni); *ibid.*, 9 June 1909, 2165 (Alessio); *ibid.*, 17 June 1909, 2548 (Arlotta); Nitti, *Il partito radicale,* 48; *Discorsi parlamentari di Francesco S. Nitti*, Rome, 1973, i, 303; Ferri, *Il nuovo regno*, 45.
39. Brusati Papers, ix, 7 (29 Dec. 1906, Gen. Viganò); *Camera, discussioni*, June 1911, 15,355; Enrico Serra, *La diplomazia in Italia*, Milan, 1984, 86–7.
40. *Knowing one's enemies*, ed. E.R. May, Princeton, 1984, 209 (24 Dec. 1912, Pollio to Brusati); Lucio Ceva, *Le forze armate*, Turin, 1981, 161.
41. *Documents français*, ser. 2, xi, 939; Tommasini, *Italia alla vigilia*, ii, 259–61.
42. *Il Messaggero*, Rome, 31 Dec. 1907; *Corriere della Sera*, 1 Jan. 1908; Luigi Cadorna, *Lettere famigliari*, ed. R. Cadorna, Milan, 1967, 90.
43. Rodd Papers, box 13 (6 May 1909); R.A. Webster, *Industrial imperialism in Italy 1908–1915*, Berkeley, 1975, 186–7.
44. *Camera, discussioni*, 12 June 1909, 2296 (Barzilai); *Senato, discussioni*, 21 Apr. 1905, 710; Eugenio Chiesa, *Discorsi parlamentari*, Milan, 1960, 31–2.
45. *Nuova Antologia*, 1 Mar. 1902, 101–2 (Gen. Biancardi); Sonnino, *Scritti e discorsi*, ii, 1247–8; *Camera, discussioni*, 11 June 1909, 2270 (Guicciardini).
46. *Documents français*, ser. 2, x, 735 (Apr. 1907, Admiral Mirabello).
47. FO, 45/853/61 (15 Apr. 1902, Calthorpe); Nathan, *Vent'anni di vita italiana*, 341.
48. Rodd Papers, box 14 (18 July 1910); *Camera, discussioni*, 15 June 1909, 2427.
49. Paul G. Halpern, *The Mediterranean naval situation 1908–1914*, Cambridge, 1971, 190, 206; Rodd Papers, box 14 (8 Feb. 1910); FO, 371/917/224 (31 July 1910, Rodd); *Corriere della Sera*, 27 and 28 July 1910.
50. A.J. Marder, *From the Dreadnought to Scapa Flow*, London, 1961, i, 171; *Camera, discussioni*, 9 June 1909, 2175–7 (Bissolati).
51. *Ibid.*, 30 Mar. 1909, 94 (Gen. Martinelli); *ibid.*, 8 June 1909, 2092–4 (Gen. Dal Verme); *ibid.*, 12 June 1919, 2312 (Turati).
52. *Corriere della Sera*, 15 May 1905; *ibid.*,

19 May 1908.
53. *Nuova Antologia*, 16 Oct. 1905, 694–5.
54. *Il Secolo*, 7 Jan. 1909; *Rassegna Contemporanea*, Feb. 1909, 12; *Camera, discussioni*, 15–17 June 1909, 2442 (Colajanni), 2488–90 (De Felice), 2500 (Mirabello), 2554 (Arlotta).
55. *Il Secolo*, 11 Jan. 1909 (Colajanni and Ghisleri).
56. FO, 371/682/245 (22 Apr. 1909, Delmé-Radcliffe); *ibid.* (5 May 1909, Rodd); *Nuova Antologia*, 16 Feb. 1909, 695 (Guicciardini).

5   Victory in Libya

1. FO, 371/1135/154 (24 Aug. 1911, Delmé-Radcliffe); Scaroni, *Con Vittorio Emanuele III*, 104–5.
2. FO, 371/1133/396 (24 Jan. 1911, Rodd); d'Orazio, *Fisiologia del parlamentarismo*, 436.
3. *Österreich-Ungarns Aussenpolitik*, II, 833 (26 Apr. 1910, Mérey); *British documents on the origins of the war*, VII, 252 (16 May 1911, Rodd); FO, 371/1135/249 (27 Nov. 1911, Rodd).
4. FO, 371/469/696 (12 Feb. 1908, Delmé-Radcliffe); *ibid.*, 371/1135/153 (24 Aug. 1911, Delmé-Radcliffe).
5. Iswolsky, *Au service de la Russie*, I, 270–1; *La Tribuna*, Rome, 25 Jan. 1905.
6. Bishop, *Theodore Roosevelt*, II, 202, 211.
7. FO, 371/683/62–3 (22 May 1909).
8. Francesco Guicciardini, *Cento giorni alla consulta: diario e ricordi*, Florence, 1943, 35; *Camera, discussioni*, 19 Dec. 1909, 4717 (Ferri); Hartmut Ullrich, *La classe politica nella crisi di partecipazione dell'Italia Giolittiana, 1903–1913*, Rome, 1979, III, 623; Washington Archives, M. 527/19 (21 Mar. 1910, Leishman).
9. Albertini, *Venti anni*, I, tome 2, 35; Gioacchino Volpe, *Saluto a un maestro*, Rome, 1951, 193.
10. Alberto Bergamini, *Il Re Vittorio Emanuele III di fronte alla storia*, Turin, 1950, 24.
11. FO, 371/1134/78 (30 Mar. 1911, Rodd).
12. *Carteggio di Filippo Turati e Anna Kuliscioff*, ed. Alessandro Schiavi and Franco Pedone, Turin, 1977, III, 648–9.
13. FO, 371/469/979 (14 Dec. 1907, Delmé-Radcliffe); FO, 371/1384/22 (1 June 1912, Rodd).
14. F. Barbagallo, *Il 'Mattino' degli Scarfoglio*, Milan, 1979, 76–7 (8 Aug. 1900, Scarfoglio); *Rivista d'Italia*, Sept. 1906,

515–16.
15. FO, 371/469/979 (14 Dec. 1907, Delmé-Radcliffe); Martini, *Diario Eritreo*, II, 299–300; Sonnino, *Carteggio*, I, 269, 274–5.
16. *Österreich-Ungarns Aussenpolitik*, II, 795, 797.
17. *Storia Contemporanea*, Bologna, Dec. 1983, 104 (diary of Dino Grandi); Ciano, *Diario, 1937–1938*, 128; Antonio Salandra, *La neutralità italiana, 1914: ricordi e pensieri*, Milan, 1931, 351.
18. *Camera, discussioni*, 2 Dec. 1910, 10,171–5; *ibid.*, 9 June 1911, 15,449–50.
19. Gioacchino Volpe, *Vittorio Emanuele III*, Milan, 1939, 177–9.
20. *Il Regno*, 13 Dec. 1903; *ibid.*, 31 Mar. 1905; Enrico Corradini, *La guerra lontana*, Milan, 1911, 85; Enrico Corradini, *Discorsi politici (1902–1924)*, Florence, 1925, 105–6; *L'Idea Nazionale*, Rome, 11 May 1911.
21. Alfredo Oriani, *La rivolta ideale*, Bologna, 1912, 258; Enrico Corradini, *Il nazionalismo italiano*, Milan, 1914, 41–2; *Il nazionalismo italiano: atti del congresso di Firenze*, Florence, 1911, 51.
22. Enrico Corradini, *L'ora di Tripoli*, Milan, 1911, xix (17 Sept. 1911); *La Voce: 1908–1916*, ed. G. Ferrata, Rome, 1961, 173; *Il Regno*, 20 Oct. 1905; *Il Giornale d'Italia*, 14 Sept. 1911.
23. *La Stampa*, Turin, 11 June 1911 (Bevione); *Giornale degli Economisti*, Jan. 1912, 95–6 (Pantaleoni); Gualtiero Castellini, *Tunisi e Tripoli*, Turin, 1911, 166, 171, 194; *Camera, discussioni*, 8 June 1911, 15,408 (Foscari).
24. *Ibid.*, 7 June 1911, 15,369 (Caetani); Francesco Saverio Nitti, *Peaceless Europe*, London, 1922, 85; Lombroso, *Il momento attuale*, 247, 252; *Il Secolo*, 19 Jan. 1902 (Ferrero); Gaetano Salvemini, *Come siamo andati in Libia e altri scritti*, ed. A. Torre, Milan, 1963, 469.
25. *Documents français*. ser. 2, XIV, 488, 490; *Österreich-Ungarns Aussenpolitik*, III, 434; Rodd Papers, box 14 (3 Oct. 1911); *Camera, discussioni*, 23 Feb. 1912, 17,151, 17,170; *Corriere della Sera*, 14 Sept. 1911.
26. *Discorsi parlamentari di Giolitti*, III, 1667; Giolitti, *Memorie*, II, 329, 357; David G. Herrmann, 'Italian strategy in the Libyan war 1911–1915', Oxford M. Litt. thesis, 1987, 46, 69; Ullrich, *La classe politica*, II, 985.
27. Royal Archives (3 Oct. 1911, Delmé-

Radcliffe); *Die grosse Politik*, xxx, tome 2, 547–9.

28. Carlo Galli, *Diarii e lettere*, Florence, 1951, 45–7, 59.
29. *Ibid.*, 78.
30. *Dalle carte di Giolitti*, iii, 52–3; *Österreich-Ungarns Aussenpolitik*, iii, 389.
31. Rodd Papers, box 14 (3 Oct. 1911); Francesco Malgeri, *La guerra Libica (1911–1912)*, Rome, 1970, 139, 161.
32. Francesco Saverio Nitti, *La democrazia*, Paris, 1933, ii, 275.
33. Albertini, *Venti anni*, i, tome 2, 123; Giuseppe Bevione, *Come siamo andati a Tripoli*, Turin, 1912, 200; R. Rainero, *Paolo Valera e l'opposizione democratica all'impresa di Tripoli*, Rome, 1983, 18.
34. *Österreich-Ungarns Aussenpolitik*, iii, 480; *Documents français*, ser. 3, ii, 454; Rodd Papers, box 14 (27 Nov. 1911); Tommasini, *Italia alla vigilia*, v, 591; Angelo del Boca, *Gli Italiani in Libia*, Bari, 1986, 76–7; Sergio Romano, *La quarta sponda: la guerra di Libia*, Milan, 1977, 59–62.
35. Roberto Bencivenga, *Saggio critico sulla nostra guerra*, Rome, 1930, i, 338–41.
36. Francis McCullagh, *Italy's war for a desert*, London, 1912, 3–5, 370; G.M. Trevelyan, *English songs for Italian freedom*, London, 1911, xxx–xxxi; William Askew, *Europe and Italy's acquisition of Libya, 1911–12*, Durham, N.C., 1942, 68–72; *Nuova Antologia*, 1 Mar. 1914, 149–50.
37. *Österreich-Ungarns Aussenpolitik*, iii, 513, 520.
38. *Documents français*, ser. 3, i, 383–4; *The Economist*, London, 11 Nov. 1911, 981; FO, 371/1135/274 (27 Nov. 1911, Rodd).
39. *Ibid.*; Malgeri, *La guerra Libica*, 164 (quoting Brusati, the king's chief aide de camp).
40. FO, 371/2006/186 (25 May 1914, Rodd).
41. *Camera, discussioni*, 18 Dec. 1912, 22,515 (San Giuliano).
42. *Österreich-Ungarns Aussenpolitik*, iii, 508; *Die grosse Politik*, xxx, tome 1, 72, 98–9, 115.
43. *Documents français*, ser. 3, ii, 454 (5 Nov. 1911).
44. *Nuova Antologia*, 1 Jan. 1912, 130–1.
45. Luigi Albertini, *Epistolario*, ed. Ottavio Barié, Milan, 1968, i, 25, 84, 111, 118.
46. *Camera, discussioni*, 13 June 1913, 26,860; *Discorsi parlamentari di Giolitti*,

iii, 1693; Salandra, *Diario*, 33, 37; Brusati Papers, xi, 92 (2 March 1915, Spingardi).
47. *Camera, discussioni*, 23 Feb. 1912, 17,177; *ibid.*, 28 Mar. 1912, 18,660.
48. *Ibid.*, 23 Feb. 1912, 17,162–4, 17,169–70.
49. Herrmann, 'Italian strategy in the Libyan war', 101–2.
50. *Documents français*, ser. 3, ii, 451; *Österreich-Ungarns Aussenpolitik*, iv, 77; *Die grosse Politik*, xxx, tome 2, 548–9.
51. *Discorsi parlamentari di Giolitti*, iii, 1668–9; *Camera, discussioni*, 13 June 1913, 26,859–60 (Bertolini).
52. *Pro e contro la guerra di Tripoli*, Naples, 1912, 115 (A.O. Olivetti).
53. *Giornale degli Economisti*, Oct. 1912, 365; *Camera, discussioni*, 22 Feb. 1913, 23,325 (Padulli), 23,328 (Di Saluzzo).
54. Nitti, *Rivelazioni*, 315; Malgeri, *La guerra libica*, 296 (Zoli).
55. *British documents on the origins of the war*, ix, part 1, 436 (27 Oct. 1912, Rodd).
56. Benito Mussolini, *Opera omnia*, ed. E. and D. Susmel, Florence, 1951–61, iv, 203 (1 Sept. 1912).

6 Giolitti in difficulties, 1912–14

1. FO, 371,/1135/274 (27 Nov. 1911, Rodd); Bergamini, *Il Re Vittorio Emanuele*, 26.
2. *Dalle carte di Giolitti*, ii, 307, iii, 61; Albertini, *Epistolario*, i, 7–8.
3. Albertini, *Venti anni*, i, tome 2, 113.
4. *Dalle carte di Giolitti*, ii, 244–5, 423–30; FO, 371/683/61 (22 Mar. 1909, Rodd).
5. *Ibid.*, 371/1383/158 (10 Feb. 1912, Rodd); *Il Regno*, 8 Mar. 1906.
6. *Dalle carte di Giolitti*, iii, 69; *Camera, discussioni*, 23 Feb. 1903, 5772–8, (Ricci); *ibid.*, 1 Mar. 1910, 5505 (Chiesa); FO, 371/2004/61 (17 Feb. 1914, Rodd).
7. *Camera, discussioni*, 25 Feb. 1913, 23,423 (Rava, minister of education during 1906–9).
8. Francesco Crispi, *Pensieri e profezie*, ed. T. Palamenghi-Crispi, Rome, 1920, 183; *Nuova Antologia*, 1 Dec. 1908, 506.
9. *Ibid.*, 1 Nov. 1907, 18; *ibid.*, 1 Mar. 1909, 151 (Tittoni); Villari, *Scritti e discorsi*, 15–16; *Camera, discussioni*, 11 May 1911, 13,846 (Colajanni); *Discorsi parlamentari di Giolitti*, ii, 1187.
10. *Il Secolo*, 19 July 1909.
11. *Senato, discussioni*, 4 June 1912, 8335;

Archivio Storico Italiano, Florence, 1912, 381.

12. *Camera, discussioni*, 13 June 1913, 26,860; *Nuova Antologia*, 1 Jan. 1913, 125.

13. *Documents français*, ser. 3, VIII, 428; *Camera, discussioni*, 25 Feb. 1914, 1722 (Federzoni); Alfredo Rocco, *Che cosa è il nazionalismo*, Padua, 1914, 8–10.

14. *British documents on the origins of the war*, X, part 1, 284 (21 Nov. 1913, Russell from Vienna); *Camera, discussioni*, 16 Dec. 1913, 478.

15. Farini, *Diario*, I, 157, II, 1139.

16. Giolitti, *Discorsi extraparlamentari*, 255.

17. Mussolini, *Opera*, III, 136–9, IV, 165–6.

18. *Discorsi parlamentari di Giolitti*, III, 1540.

19. *Nuova Antologia*, 16 Sept. 1911, 307 (Sonnino).

20. FO, 800/64/857 (29 Jan. 1913, Rodd).

21. *Documents français*, ser. 3, V, 244, 333; *ibid.*, ser. 3, VI, 308 (Tittoni).

22. *British documents on the origins of the war*, IX, part 2, 124–5; *Documents français*, ser. 3, IV, 471.

23. *Österreich-Ungarns Aussenpolitik*, III, 12, 27–8; *ibid.*, IV, 59, 712; *DDI*, ser. 5, II, 651–2; *American Historical Review*, June 1968, 1418 (Meyer, quoted by Renzi); Sonnino microfilm, reel 47 (6 Feb. 1915).

24. Conrad von Hötzendorf, *Aus meiner Dienstzeit*, Vienna, 1922, II, 209–10.

25. Martini, *Diario 1914–1918*, 11; *Corriere della Sera*, 8 Feb. 1915; Albertini, *Venti anni*, II, tome 2, 12.

26. FO, 371/684/75 (2 Nov. 1909, Delmé-Radcliffe); *Die grosse Politik*, XXVI, tome 2, 793; *Rassegna Italiana*, Dec. 1923, 757–8; von Bülow, *Memoirs*, III, 461.

27. *Documents français*, ser. 3, X, 61.

28. FO, 371/1135/152 (24 Aug. 1911, Delmé-Radcliffe).

29. *Österreich-Ungarns Aussenpolitik*, III, 667; Poincaré, *Au service de la France*, IX, 248.

30. Eugenio Chiesa, *La triplice alleanza, No!*, Rome, 1913, 17; *Camera, discussioni*, 23 Feb. 1912, 17,172 (Chiesa); O. Zuccarini, *Il partito repubblicano e la guerra d'Italia*, Rome, 1916, X, 5.

31. *Camera, discussioni*, 20 Nov. 1912, 21,852–3 (Colajanni); *ibid.*, 4 Dec. 1914, 21,953–4 (Treves); *ibid.*, 18 Dec. 1912, 22.504 (Giolitti); *ibid.*, 21 Feb. 1913, 23,264–5 (Incontri); *Critica Sociale*, 1 Mar. 1914, 67 (Graziadei).

32. *British documents on the origins of the war*, VI, 634; *Documents français*, ser. 3, I, 567;

ibid., ser. 3, II, 218; *ibid.*, ser. 3, IV, 558–9; *ibid.*, ser. 3, VIII, 428.

33. *Ibid.*, ser. 3, VII, 583; *Camera, discussioni*, 16 Dec. 1913, 476; *British documents on the origins of the war*, X, 627.

34. *Dalle carte di Giolitti*, III, 95; *Documents français*, ser. 3, IV, 510, (20 Nov. 1912, Poincaré).

35. FO, 371/2005 (memo no. 23,578 by Crowe, 17 May 1914).

36. *Die Kriegsschuldfrage*, Berlin, July, 1929, 643 (29 Jan. 1913, Waldersee); Conrad, *Aus meiner Dienstzeit*, III, 599, 752; *Rassegna Italiana*, Rome, Dec. 1923, 761–2 (Gatti).

37. Gianluca André, *L'Italia e il Mediterraneo alla vigilia della prima guerra mondiale*, Milan, 1967, 169–70; Guicciardini, *Cento giorni alla consulta*, 37.

38. *Documents français*, ser. 3, IX, 418; André, *L'Italia e il Mediterraneo*, 302–3; Mariano Gabriele, *Le convenzioni navali della triplice*, Rome, 1969, 393; Albertini, *Venti anni*, I, tome 2, 463–4; Halpern, *The Mediterranean naval situation*, 232, 237.

39. *Die grosse Politik*, XXXIV, tome 2, 773; *ibid.*, XXXV, 134–5; *Dalle carte di Giolitti*, III, 91.

40. Luigi Capello, *Note di guerra*, Milan, 1920, I, xiv.

41. Brusati Papers, X, 442 (24 Dec. 1912, Pollio).

42. *Die Kriegsschuldfrage*, May 1927, 407 (April 1914, Von Kleist); Albertini, *Origins of the war*, I, 519–20, 561.

43. *Central European History*, Atlanta, Dec. 1979, 359, 371 (M. Palumbo); *Rassegna Italiana*, Dec. 1923, 762, 767.

7   *Salandra, 1914*

1. FO, 800/65/24 (10 Jan. 1914, Rodd).

2. *Camera, discussioni*, 3 Dec. 1913, 65 (Gaudenzi); *ibid.*, 4 Dec. 1913, 95 (Comandini).

3. *Ibid.*, 16 Dec. 1913, 478; *Dalle carte di Giolitti*, III, 96–7.

4. *L'Osservatore Politico–Letterario*, Milan, Aug. 1971, 37 (Salandra diary for 2 Apr. 1910).

5. Albertini, *Epistolario*, I, 213, 216–17 (Palamenghi-Crispi).

6. Rodd Papers, box 15 (19 Jan. 1914).

7. Brusati Papers, XI, 16 (13 Apr. 1914), 18 (29 Apr. 1914); *XII congresso nazionale del partito repubblicano italiano*, Bologna, 1914, 35–6 (Zuccarini).

8. FO, 371/2004/105 (21 Mar. 1914, Rodd).

9. *DDI*. ser. 4, xii, 207; *British documents on the origins of the war*, xi, 63.

10. *DDI*, ser. 4, xii, 271; Albertini, *Origins of the war*, ii, 319.

11. *Documents français*, ser. 3, xi, 131–2; *British documents on the origins of the war*, xi, 141; *DDI*, ser. 4, xii, 301.

12. *Ibid.*, 302, 314–15, 350, 414.

13. Georges Wagnière, *Dix-huit ans à Rome*, Geneva, 1944, 45.

14. Carlo Sforza, *Jugoslavia: storia e ricordi*, Milan, 1948, 101; *DDI*, ser. 4, xii, 160.

15. *Die grosse Politik*, xxxix, 340.

16. Conrad, *Aus meiner Dienstzeit*, iv, 103, 108; Erich von Falkenhayn, *Die oberste Heeresleitung 1914–1916*, Berlin, 1920, 58; Albertini, *Venti anni*, ii, tome 1, 51; J. Andrassy, *Diplomacy and the war*, London, 1921, 126, 134; *Central European History*, Dec. 1979, 358–60.

17. Gianni Rocca, *Cadorna*, Milan, 1985, 12; Gatti *Caporetto*, 393; Albertini, *Epistolario*, i, 257; Nitti, *Edizione nazionale*, xvi, tome 2, 534; S. Bertoldi, *Vittorio Emanuele III*, Turin, 1971, 265–9.

18. *DDI*, ser. 5, i, 29, 52, 500, 538 (ed. A. Torre); Rodd Papers, xxxv, 3 (diary for 12 Oct. 1914); Salandra, *La neutralità*, 350.

19. Zuccarini, *Il partito repubblicano*, 43–5, 56–7, 76, 91.

20. *La stampa nazionalista*, ed. Franco Gaeta, Rocca S. Casciano, 1965, xxiv (Forges), 83–4 (Fauro), 86–7 (Rocco); *Rassegna Storica del Risorgimento*, Rome, Apr. 1972, 200 (Pantaleoni).

21. Sidney Sonnino, *Carteggio*, ed. P. Pastorelli, Bari, 1974, ii, 7; Brunello Vigezzi, *Da Giolitti a Salandra*, Florence, 1969, 38.

22. Angelo Gatti, *Un Italiano a Versailles*, Milan, 1958, 358–9; Bencivenga, *Saggio critico sulla guerra*, i, 48.

23. *Rivista Storica Italiana*, Naples, 1960, iii, 450–1 (Valiani).

24. Olindo Malagodi, *Conversazioni della guerra 1914–1919*, ed. B. Vigezzi, Milan, 1960, i, 16–17.

25. Sonnino, *Diario*, ii, 10, 12; Albertini, *Epistolario*, i, 254.

26. *Die deutschen Dokumente zum Kriegsausbruch*, ed. Karl Kautsky, Charlottenburg, 1919, iii, 145; G. André-Fribourg, *L'Italie et nous*, Paris, 1947, 229 (Chabrié, French Consul at Milan).

27. Malagodi, *Conversazioni*, i, 18.

28. *DDI*, ser. 4, xii, 449; *ibid.*, ser. 5, i, 2; *Die deutschen Dokumente*, iv, 8.

29. Luigi Cadorna, *Altre pagine sulla grande guerra*, Milan, 1925, 18, 26; Angelo Gatti, *La parte dell'italia: rivendicazioni*, Milan, 1926, 45; *Rassegna Italiana*, Dec. 1923, 765–6.

30. *DDI*, ser. 5, i, 4; Malagodi, *Conversazioni;* i, 198–9.

31. *Die deutschen Dokumente*, iv, 12, 23, 77–8.

32. FO, 800/65 (10 Sept. 1914, Rodd).

33. Martini, *Diario 1914–1918*, 104.

34. *DDI*, ser. 5, i, 83–4, 109, 115; G.M. Trevelyan, *Grey of Fallodon*, London, 1937, 292.

35. *DDI*, ser. 5, i, 93, 160, 245; *Nuova Rivista Storica*, Milan, 1961, ii, 331 (ed. Giorgio Rochat).

36. Malagodi, *Conversazioni*, i, 20; Enrico Serra, *Camille Barrère e l'intesa italo-francese*, Milan, 1950, 305; *DDI*, ser. 5, i, 275, 388; *Nuova Rivista Storica*, 1961, 331 (26 Aug. 1914, San Giuliano, quoted by G. Rochat).

37. Brusati Papers, xi, 67 (3 Sept. 1914).

38. *DDI*, ser. 5, i, 293–4, 297, 441, 466.

39. Italo Pietra, *I tre Agnelli*, Milan, 1985, 48.

40. Royal Archives G.V., Q.688/8–9 (27 August and 10 Sept. 1914, Delmé-Radcliffe to Lord Stamfordham).

41. Martini, *Diario 1914–1918*, 104, 214.

42. FO, 800/173/84–5 (19 Sept. 1914)

43. WO, 106/749 (10 Oct. 1914, Col. Granet); Conrad, *Aus meiner Dienstzeit*, iv, 815.

44. Brusati Papers, xi, 120 (12 Sept. 1914); Rocca, *Cadorna*, 57; Luigi Cadorna, *La guerra alla fronte italiana*, Milan, 1921, i, 47.

45. Bencivenga, *Saggio critico*, i, 51, 188–9, 191–2; Falkenhayn, *Die oberste Heeresleitung*, 57–8; Albertini, *Venti anni*, ii, tome 1, 359; *ibid.*, ii, tome 2, 38; Christopher Seton-Watson, *Italy from liberalism to fascism*, London, 1967, 420.

46. WO, 106/749 (14 Sept. 1914, Granet).

47. Von Bülow, *Memoirs*, iv, 219.

48. Malagodi, *Conversazioni*, i, 28 (Giolitti); Albertini, *Epistolario*, i, 270 (G.A. Borgese); Martini, *Diario 1914–1918*, 216; *Nuova Antologia*, 1 Feb. 1923, 217 (Bertolini, quoting Salandra).

49. Salandra, *La neutralità*, 330–1.

50. *DDI*, ser. 5, i, 500; FO, 800/173/88 (28 Oct. 1914, Bertie).

51. Antonio Salandra, *I discorsi della guerra*,

Milan, 1922, 4–8; Francesco Coppola, *La crisi italiana*, Rome, 1916, 20–2; *DDI*, ser. 5, ɪ, 412.

52. Albertini, *Epistolario*, ɪ, 284; *Nuova Antologia*, 1 Feb. 1923, 214–15.

53. *Il carteggio Avarna-Bollati, Luglio 1914 – Maggio 1915*, ed. C.A. di Gualtieri, Naples, 1953, 32; Matthias Erzberger, *Erlebnisse im Weltkrieg*, Stuttgart, 1920, 30; *Nuova Antologia*, 1 Feb. 1923, 215, 217.

54. *Camera, discussioni*, 10 Mar. 1883, 1844–5; *ibid.*, 23 Feb. 1912, 17,145; Sonnino, *Scritti e discorsi*, ɪɪ, 1230–3.

55. *Camera, discussioni*, 5 Dec. 1914, 5641; *Senato, discussioni*, 15 Dec. 1914, 1226–7; Salandra, *La neutralità*, 296; P. Treves, *Come ho veduto la guerra*, Rome, 1921, 7.

56. *Senato, discussioni*, 15 Dec, 1914, 1229; *ibid.*, 18 Dec. 1915, 1320.

57. FO, 800/65/231 (18 Dec. 1914, Rodd).

58. Malagodi, *Conversazioni*, ɪ, 32; Martini, *Diario 1914–1918*, 295.

59. *DDI*, ser. 5, ɪɪ, 5, 377, 426; Galli, *Diarii*, 233.

60. Cadorna, *Altre pagine*, 104–5.

61. Martini, *Diario 1914–1918*, 297, 303; Charles Benoist, *Souvenirs (1883–1933)*, Paris, 1934, ɪɪɪ, 293; *Camera, discussioni*, 4 Dec. 1914, 5576 (Chiesa); *ibid.*, 5 Dec. 1914, 5639 (Altobelli).

62. Mussolini, *Opera*, vɪɪ, 140; Galli, *Diarii*, 245; A. De Grand, *The Italian nationalist association*, Nebraska, 1978, 67.

63. *Lacerba*, Florence, Jan. 1915, 1–3.

8 To fight or not to fight?

1. Royal Archives G.V., Q. 688/11 (4 Mar. 1915, Delmé-Radcliffe); *DDI*, ser. 5, ɪɪ, 601–2.

2. Sonnino, *Carteggio*, ɪɪ, 145–6; Salandra, *La neutralità*, 90.

3. Malagodi, *Conversazioni*, ɪ, 31–2; Martini, *Diario 1914–1918*, 401.

4. Sonnino microfilm, reel 31 (Jan. 1915); Sonnino, *Diario*, ɪɪ, 49, 89.

5. *DDI*, ser. 5, ɪɪ, 530, 562, 574.

6. Sonnino, *Carteggio*, ɪɪ, 25, 58; *DDI*, ser. 5, ɪɪɪ, 138; Antonio Salandra, *L'intervento, 1915*, Milan, 1930, 195–6; *Storia e Politica*, Apr. 1968, 180 (Toscano); Erzberger, *Erlebnisse*, 32.

7. *Camera, discussioni*, 19 Feb. 1915, 6181; Albertini, *Epistolario*, ɪ, 313; Martini, *Diario 1914–1918*, 300, 342.

8. Malagodi, *Conversazioni*, ɪ, 37; Albertini, *Epistolario*, ɪ, 320.

9. FO, 371/2375/83 (14 Mar. 1915, Rodd).

10. Giolitti, *Memorie*, ɪɪ, 533; Malagodi, *Conversazioni*, ɪ, 64.

11. *DDI*, ser. 5, ɪɪ, 689, 748, 759.

12. Nitti, *Rivelazioni*, 487; Malagodi, *Conversazioni*, ɪ, 17; Albertini, *Epistolario*, ɪ, 321; Vigezzi, *Da Giolitti a Salandra*, 94; *Studi Storici*, Rome, 1965, ɪɪ, 229 (Procacci); *Il Ponte*, Florence, Apr. 1952, 422 (Salvemini); J.A. Thayer, *Italy and the Great War*, Madison, 1964, 342–50.

13. Sonnino, *Carteggio*, ɪɪ, 290–1.

14. Salandra, *L'intervento*, 120; Sonnino, *Diario*, ɪɪ, 153, 364–5; Malagodi, *Conversazioni*, ɪ, 51 (Sonnino); Albertini, *Epistolario*, ɪɪ, 434.

15. Martini, *Diario 1914–1918*, 373, 389; Nitti, *La democrazia*, ɪɪ, 275.

16. *Rivista di Studi Politici Internazionale*, Florence, Jan. 1957, 72–8 (Monticone).

17. Eva Amendola Kühn, *Vita con Giovanni Amendola*, Florence, 1960, 388 (Casati); Martini, *Diario 1914–1918*, 382; *Rivista d'Italia*, June 1908, 1006–7.

18. *Camera, discussioni*, 15 Apr. 1916, 10,422; Ugo Ojetti, *I taccuini 1914–1943*, Florence, 1954, 184.

19. Sonnino microfilm, reels 47 and 52.

20. *Ibid.*, 52 (16 Apr. 1915).

21. FO, 800/65 (2 Apr. 1915, Rodd).

22. Martini, *Diario 1914–1918*, 393; Freiherr von Macchio, *Wahrheit! Fürst von Bülow und ich in Rom*, Vienna, 1931, 70, 124.

23. *Rassegna Contemporanea*, 10 Mar. 1915, 325–6; Mussolini, *Opera*, vɪɪ, 311–12, 315–16.

24. Martini, *Diario 1914–1918*, 285, 452–3, 462; Angelo del Boca, *Gli italiani in Libia 1860–1922*, Bari, 1986, 294–5, 305.

25. Cadorna, *Altre pagine*, 48, 52–62, 99; Rocca, *Cadorna*, 64; Albertini, *Epistolario*, ɪɪ, 428.

26. *DDI*, ser. 5, ɪ, 116, 495; Sonnino, *Carteggio*, ɪɪ, 319.

27. Martini, *Diario 1914–1918*, 397; Sonnino, *Diario*, ɪɪɪ, 192.

28. *Ibid.*, 400–1; Vittorio Emanuele Orlando, *Memorie (1915–1919)*, ed. R. Mosca, Milan, 1960, 337.

29. Albertini, *Venti anni*, ɪɪ, tome 1, 486; G. Bruccoleri, *Dal conflitto europeo alla guerra nostra*, Rome, 1915, 217; Col. Charles Repington, *The first world war*, London, 1920, ɪɪ, 492.

30. Martini, *Diario 1914–1918*, 610.

31. Sonnino, *Diario*, ɪɪ, 138–41; Sonnino, *Carteggio*, ɪɪ, 478.

32. Erzberger, *Erlebnisse*, 30, 50.

33. Francesco Margiotta Broglio, *Italia e Santa Sede dalla grande guerra alla conciliazione*, Bari, 1966, 399–400, 405.
34. Salandra, *Diario*, 31.
35. *Ibid.*, 31, 35–6.
36. *Ibid.*, 37–9; Salandro, *L'intervento*, 252–4; B. Vigezzi, *Giolitti e Turati: un incontro mancato*, Naples, 1976, II, 694.
37. Salandra, *Diario*, 40; Malagodi, *Conversazioni*, I, 84; Sonnino microfilm, reel 52 (intercepted note of 11 May 1915); C.J. Lowe and F. Marzari, *Italian foreign policy 1870–1940*, London, 1975, 155–6; Vigezzi, *Da Giolitti*, 133; *Idea Nazionale*, Rome, 14 May 1914 (Brusati).
38. Orlando, *Memorie*, 39; Gatti, *Un Italiano a Versailles*, 43 (Cadorna).
39. *The diary of Gino Speranza: Italy 1915–1919*, ed. Florence Colgate Speranza, New York, 1941, I, 169–70; Benoist, *Souvenirs*, III, 297–8; Zuccarini, *Il partito repubblicano*, 118–21; *Quaderni di Cultura e Storia Sociale*, Livorno, 1952, II, 64 (Barzilai, quoted by Spellanzon).
40. *Lacerba*, 15 May 1915 (Papini); *La civiltà fascista illustrata nella dottrina e nelle opere*, ed. G.L. Pomba, Turin, 1928, 98 (Gentile); Maffeo Pantaleoni, *Note in margine della guerra*, Bari, 1917, 46–7; Mario Missiroli, *Il fascismo e il colpo di stato dell'Ottobre 1922*, Rocca S. Casciano, 1939, 34.
41. *Corriere della Sera*, 14 May 1914; Albertini, *Venti anni*, II, tome 1, 546–7.
42. Mussolini, *Opera*, VII, 386–90; *ibid.*, XXXVIII, 85.
43. *Camera, discussioni*, 20 May 1915, 7915–6; Salandra, *L'intervento*, 310.
44. Hanotaux, *Les carnets*, 138, 143; Poincaré, *Au service de la France*, IX, 238; Scaroni, *Con Vittorio Emanuele*, 58.
45. K. Epstein, *Matthias Erzberger and the dilemma of German democracy*, Princeton, 1959, 139.
46. Severus, *Zehn Monate italienischer Neutralität*, Gotha, 1915, 101.
47. FO, 800/65/454 (26 May 1915, Rodd).
48. FO, 371/2377 (22 May 1915, Rodd).
49. Royal Archives, G.V., Q.688/21 (12 June 1915, Delmé-Radcliffe).

World War I, and the Rise of Fascism

1 Italy at war 1915–17

1. *DDI*, ser. 5, IV, 21.
2. *Ibid.*, ser. 5, I, 412; *ibid.*, ser. 5, II, 136–8; O. Malagodi, *Conversazioni della guerra 1914–1919*, ed. B. Vigezzi, Naples, 1960, I, 32 (Sonnino); Ferdinando Martini, *Diario 1914–1918*, ed. G. De Rosa, Milan, 1966, 488 (Salandra); M. Erzberger, *Erlebnisse im Weltkrieg*, Stuttgart, 1920, 33.
3. *DDI*, ser. 5, IV, 233, 244–5; WO, 106/758/9 (21 June 1915, Delmé-Radcliffe); Sidney Sonnino, *Carteggio*, ed. P. Pastorelli, Bari, 1974, II, 608.
4. FO, 371/2375/75 (6 Mar. 1915, Rodd).
5. Antonio Salandra, *Il diario*, ed. G.B. Gifuni, Milan, 1969, 40; Brusati Papers, XI, 161 (20 July 1915, Salandra).
6. *Nuova Antologia*, Florence, Dec. 1955, 545 (7 May 1915, Zupelli); Martini, *Diario 1914–1918*, 116, 126.
7. L. Aldrovandi-Marescotti, *Nuovi ricordi*, Milan, 1938, 213; Sonnino, *Carteggio*, II, 464.
8. *Lacerba*, Florence, 28 Feb. 1915, 65–6 (Salandra); Martini, *Diario 1914–1918*, 9, 390.
9. FO, 371/267/8449 (10 Mar. 1907, Delmé-Radcliffe); *Nuova Rivista Storica*, Milan, 1961, II, 334 (Rochat).
10. Gabriel Hanotaux, *Les carnets (1907–1925)*, ed. G. Dethan, Paris, 1982, 140; A. Monts, *Erinnerungen und Gedanken des Botschafters Anton Graf Monts*, ed. K.F. Nowak and F. Thimme, Berlin, 1933, 88.
11. Silvio Scaroni, *Con Vittorio Emanuele III*, Milan, 1954, 92.
12. Piero Pieri, *L'Italia nella prima guerra mondiale*, Turin, 1965, 65–6; *Il Risorgimento*, Milan, Feb. 1961, 13–14 (Rochat); Giulio Douhet, *Diario critico di guerra*, Turin, 1921, I, 229–33, 239.
13. Felice de Chaurand, *Come l'esercito italiano entrò in guerra*, Milan, 1929, 272; Douhet, *Diario*, I, 269; Luigi Capello, *Note di guerra*, Milan, 1920, I, 53, 92.
14. FO, 371/1135/251 (27 Nov. 1911, Rodd); *Minerva*, Rome, 16 Nov. 1914, 988; Gen. Guido Liuzzi, *I servizi logistici nella guerra*, Milan, 1934, 99; Douhet, *Diario*, I, 40, 271.
15. Luigi Cadorna, *Pagine polemiche*, Cernusco, 1950, 239; Pieri, *L'Italia nella prima guerra*, 66–8; Giulio Douhet, *Sintesi critica della grande guerra*, Rome, 1925, 46, 49.
16. Hanotaux, *Les carnets*, 141–2; Martini, *Diario 1914–1918*, 292; Angelo Gatti, *Uomini e folle di guerra*, Milan, 1929, 112; Angelo Gatti, *La parte dell'Italia*, Milan, 1926, 107.

17. Luigi Albertini, *Epistolario, 1911–1926,* ed. O. Barié, Milan, 1968, ɪ, 275; Salandra, *Diario,* 35.

18. *Atti Parlamentari: Camera dei deputati, discussioni,* Rome, 26 Feb. 1913, 23,456; Brusati Papers, xɪ, 92 (2 Mar. 1915).

19. *Discorsi parlamentari di Giovanni Giolitti,* Rome, 1953, ɪɪɪ, 1693; Malagodi, *Conversazioni,* 58, 200; Salandra, *Diario,* 37; Martini, *Diario 1914–1918,* 413.

20. *Corriere della Sera,* Milan, 21 Oct. 1919; Angelo Gatti, *Un italiano a Versailles,* Milan, 1958, 440–1.

21. Sidney Sonnino, *Diario,* ed. P. Pastorelli, Bari, 1972, ɪɪ, 50; Charles Benoist, *Souvenirs 1883–1933,* ɪɪɪ, 251; Franceso Saverio Nitti, *Rivelazioni: dramatis personae,* Naples, 1948, 387–8; Angelo Gatti, *Caporetto: dal diario di guerra,* ed. A. Monticone, Bologna, 1964, 221; *Clio,* Rome, Nov. 1965, 483–4; Mario Alberti, *Il tornaconto della nostra guerra,* Milan, 1915, 10; Hanotaux, *Les carnets,* 167.

22. Douhet, *Diario,* ɪ, 410; Nitti, *Rivelazioni,* 183–4; Capello, *Note di guerra,* ɪ, 112–15; *Nuova Antologia,* 1 Feb. 1923, 220; *Nuova Rivista Storica,* 1961, 40 (Cadorna, quoted by G. Rochat).

23. Royal Archives G.V., Q. 688/21 (12 June 1915, Delmé-Radcliffe).

24. FO, 800/65/497 (16 July 1915); *ibid.,* 371/2379/251 (10 Sept. 1915); *The diary of Gino Speranza, Italy 1915–1919,* ed. Florence Colgate Speranza, New York, 1941, ɪ, 13 (Signora De Bossis); H. Vivian, *Italy at war,* London, 1917, 66.

25. *Comitati segreti sulla condotta della guerra, giugno-dicembre 1917,* Rome, 1967, 96 (Gen. Marazzi).

26. Sonnino, *Carteggio,* ɪɪ, 546.

27. *Ibid.,* ɪɪ, 517; Martini, *Diario 1914–1918,* 534, 537.

28. Douhet, *Diario,* ɪ, 115; Martini, *Diario 1914–1918,* 498.

29. Sonnino, *Carteggio,* ɪɪ, 545.

30. Royal Archives G.V., Q. 688/21 (12 June 1915, Delmé-Radcliffe).

31. Roberto Bencivenga, *Saggio critico sulla nostra guerra,* Rome, 1930, ɪ, 241–2; Nino D'Aroma, *Vent' anni insieme: Vittorio Emanuele e Mussolini,* Rocca S. Casciano, 1957, 20; F. Cognasso, *I Savoia,* Varese, 1981, 887.

32. V.E. Orlando, *Memorie,* 293–4; Antonio Salandra, *I retroscena di Versailles,* ed. G.B. Gifuni, Milan, 1971, 114; Gatti, *Un italiano a Versailles,* 424–5.

33. Sonnino, *Carteggio,* ɪɪ, 585–8.

34. Albertini, *Epistolario,* ɪɪ, 517; Martini, *Diario 1914–1918,* 596–7, 604, 613.

35. *Ibid.,* 453, 480–1; Angelo del Boca, *Gli italiani in Libia, 1860–1912,* Bari, 1986, 305.

36. H. Wickham Steed, *Through thirty years, 1892–1922,* London, 1924, ɪɪ, 105; Martini, *Diario 1914–1918,* 619; *Nuova Antologia,* Dec. 1967, 456 (diary of Sforza).

37. Carlo Sforza, *Jugoslavia,* Milan, 1948, 96; Cadorna, *Pagine polemiche,* 147; Bencivenga, *Saggio critico,* ɪ, 337.

38. *DDI,* ser. 5, ɪv, 611.

39. WO, 106/758/67 (10 Sept. 1915, Delmé-Radcliffe).

40. *DDI,* ser. 5, ɪx, 238; Sonnino, *Carteggio,* ɪɪ, 604.

41. Martini, *Diario 1914–1918,* 558, 621; Piero Melograni, *Storia politica della grande guerra 1915–1918,* Bari, 1972, 175–6.

42. Luigi Cadorna, *Lettere famigliari,* Milan, 1967, 137, 142; G. Rocca, *Cadorna,* Milan, 1985, 108–9.

43. Antonino Di Giorgio, *Scritti e discorsi vari (1899–1927),* Milan, 1938, 355; Malagodi, *Conversazioni,* ɪ, 89–90; Cadorna, *Pagine polemiche,* 159.

44. Albertini, *Epistolario,* ɪɪ, 505.

45. Raymond Poincaré, *Au service de la France: neuf années de souvenirs,* Paris, 1926–33, ɪx, 240; Tommaso Tittoni, *Conflitti politici e riforme costituzionali,* Bari, 1919, 54; Rodd Papers, xxxv, 63 (diary for 18 June 1916).

46. *Camera, discussioni,* 15 Apr. 1916, 10,418–23 (Labriola), 10,446–7 (Petrillo); *ibid.,* 16 Apr. 1916, 10,455 (Treves); Gaetano Salvemini, *Dal Patto di Londra alla pace di Roma,* Turin, 1925, 209, 213.

47. Asquith Papers, cxxvɪɪ, 209 (13 June 1916, Delmé-Radcliffe); Martini, *Diario 1914–1918,* 699, 709, 936; *Inchiesta su Caporetto: dall'Isonzo al Piave,* Rome, 1919, ɪ, 11; Cadorna, *Pagine polemiche,* 136.

48. Paolo Paulucci, *Alla corte di Re Umberto: diario segreto,* ed. G. Calcagno, Milan, 1986, 99; Cadorna, *Lettere famigliari,* 158; Asquith Papers, cxxvɪɪ, 209 (13 June 1916).

49. Gatti, *Un italiano a Versailles,* 428–9; Salandra, *Diario,* 62.

50. Domenico Bartoli, *I Savoia: ultimo atto,* Novara, 1986, 9; Martini, *Diario 1914–1918,* 985; *La Stampa,* Turin, 12 Feb. 1982 (Federzoni); *Lezioni sull'anti-*

fascismo, ed. P. Permoli, Bari, 1960, 281 (Carandini); *La Rivoluzione Liberale*, Turin, 10 June 1924, 93–4 (Ansaldo); C. Scarfoglio, *La memoria di un giornalista*, Rome, 1964, 352–3.

51. Scaroni, *Con Vittorio Emanuele*, 111–12.
52. C.A. Repington, *The first world war*, I, 236; Speranza, *Diary of Speranza*, I, 143–4 (Ojetti).
53. Bencivenga, *Saggio critico*, I, 244; F. Charles-Roux, *Souvenirs diplomatiques: Rome-Quirinal*, Paris, 1958, 34, 260; Martini, *Diario 1914–1918*, 849–50.
54. Asquith Papers, CXXVI, 6 (27 Mar. 1916, Asquith), 97 (6 Apr. 1916, Hankey); Lord Hankey, *The supreme command 1914–1918*, London, 1961, II, 485; Albertini, *Epistolario*, II, 566; *DDI*, ser. 5, VIII, 213.
55. WO, 106/768 (6 Jan. 1917, Col. Lamb); Delmé-Radcliffe Papers, (27 Dec. 1916); Balfour Papers, 800/203/31 (16 May 1918, Rodd); Hankey, *The supreme command*, II, 484; G.M. Trevelyan, *Grey of Fallodon*, London, 1937, 299; Martini, *Diario 1914–1918*, 669.
56. Royal Archives (7 Mar. 1916, Delmé-Radcliffe, and 21 Mar. 1916, Stamford-ham).
57. *Ibid.* (3 Dec. 1916, Delmé-Radcliffe).
58. FO, 800/202/139 (19 Jan. 1917, Rodd).
59. Delmé-Radcliffe Papers (25 Dec. 1916); Lloyd George Papers, F/16/1/17 (12 Jan. 1917, Rodd); *ibid.*, no. 26 (24 Mar. 1917, Lloyd George); *Les armées françaises dans la grande guerre*, Paris, 1932, V, part 1, 663; Francesco Saverio Nitti, *Edizione nazionale delle opere*, ed. A. Saitta, Bari, 1980, XVI, tome 2, 745–6; Bencivenga, *Saggio critico*, II, 26; Hankey, *The supreme command*, II, 608; Salandra, *Diario*, 95, 98; Sonnino microfilm, reel 52 (2 Nov. 1916, Boselli).
60. Templewood Papers (14 Aug. 1917).
61. FO, 800/202/139 (19 Jan. 1917, Rodd); Rodd Papers, box 17 (25 Mar. 1917, Rodd to Balfour); Salandra, *Diario*, 120.
62. FO, 371/2946/121 (26 May 1917, Cecil); A. Ribot, *Journal d'Alexandre Ribot*, Paris, 1936, 59; Salandra, *Diario*, 95; Sonnino, *Carteggio*, II, 727–8.
63. G. de Monteyer, *Austria's peace offer*, London, 1921, 59; David Lloyd George, *War memoirs*, London, 1933–6, IV, 2008.
64. *Ibid.*, IV, 2007–8; Nitti, *Edizione nazionale*, XVI, tome 2, 742; Salandra, *Diario*, 184; Malagodi, *Conversazioni*, II, 252 (Orlando); C.J. Lowe and M.L. Dock-

rill, *The mirage of power*, London, 1972, II, 259, 394.
65. *DDI*, ser. 5, VIII, 120; Salandra, *Diario*, 128.
66. *DDI*, ser. 5, XI, 21; Sonnino, *Diario*, III, 190–1.
67. *DDI*, ser. 5, IX, 161–2, 197.

2 Defeat and triumph, 1917–18

1. FO, 800/202/194–5 (30 Mar. 1917, Rodd); *ibid.*, 371/2946/108 (28 Apr. 1917).
2. Ribot, *Journal*, 108–9; Poincaré, *Au service de la France*, IX, 246.
3. Gatti, *Un italiano a Versailles*, 386–7.
4. Gatti, *Caporetto*, 87; *Comitati segreti sulla condotta della guerra*, 143.
5. Cadorna, *Lettere famigliari*, 196.
6. Brusati Papers, XII, 497 (11 Nov. 1917).
7. Paolo Puntoni, *Parla Vittorio Emanuele III*, Milan, 1958, 97; Martini, *Diario 1914–1918*, 979; Gatti, *Caporetto*, 324; Luigi Albertini, *Venti anni di vita politica*, Bologna, 1950, II, tome 3, 53.
8. V. Morello, *L'Adriatico senza pace*, Milan, 1920, 190; A. Valori, *La condotta politica della guerra*, Milan, 1934, 418; Salandra, *Diario*, 148; Martini, *Diario 1914–1918*, 905; Delmé-Radcliffe Papers (8 Oct. 1917, to Lord Derby); *ibid.* (26 Dec. 1916, to Lloyd George); Lloyd George Papers, F/56/1/28 (30 Mar. 1917, Rodd); WO, 106/808 (Trevelyan).
9. R. Monteleone, *Lettere al re, 1914–1918*, Rome, 1973, 36–7, 53; *Verbali delle riunioni tenute dal capo di stato maggiore generale*, Rome, 1983, 58.
10. Sonnino microfilm, reel 48; Templewood Papers, (11 Dec. 1917, Col. Marchetti).
11. *Ibid.* (21 Aug. 1917); *Istituto Storico del Risorgimento, congresso*, Rome, Oct. 1963, xli (De Capraris); E. Forcella and A. Monticone, *Plotone d'esecuzione*, Bari, 1968, xvii.
12. FO, 371/2944/108627 (27 May 1917, Rodd); FO, 371/2944/129317 (28 June 1917, Rodd).
13. Martini, *Diario 1914–1918*, 985, 1003, 1020; *Nuova Antologia*, 16 Dec. 1934, 501 (diary of Aldrovandi).
14. *DDI*, ser. 5, VIII, 551; Melograni, *Storia della guerra*, 395; *Nuova Antologia*, 1 Jan. 1935, 101; Malagodi, *Conversazioni*, I, 212, 214.
15. Delmé-Radcliffe Papers (18 Oct. 1917,

to Lord Derby); Melograni, *Storia della guerra*, 398; Enrico Caviglia, *Diario (Aprile 1925 – Marzo 1945)*, Rome, 1952, 111, 114; St Antony's Documents, 249/067609 (March 1928, Caviglia to Mussolini).

16. Robertson Papers (24 Oct. 1917, Cadorna to Robertson, Chief of General Staff in London).

17. Cadorna, *Lettere famigliari*, 227.

18. Giovanni Artieri, *Cronaca del regno d'Italia*, Milan, 1977, II, 129–30.

19. CAB, 24/31/2594 (6 Nov. 1917); Malagodi, *Conversazioni*, II, 390; Giovanni Artieri, *Il re, i soldati e il generale che vinse*, Rocca S. Casciano, 1951, 96.

20. Scaroni, *Con Vittorio Emanuele*, 134.

21. *Inchiesta su Caporetto*, II, 546; Malagodi, *Conversazioni*, I, 210.

22. *Inchiesta su Caporetto*, II, 548; Cadorna, *Lettere famigliari*, 238; Albertini, *Epistolario*, III, 1410 (Cadorna); CAB, 24/31/2503 (3 Nov. 1917, Delmé quoting Cadorna); Orlando, *Memorie*, 296, 503–4.

23. FO, 438/10/243 (3 Nov. 1917, Rodd); Maréchal Ferdinand Foch, *Memoires à servir à l'histoire de la guerre*, Paris, 1931, II, XXXVII.

24. Sonnino microfilm, reel 47 (6–7 Nov. 1917, British War Cabinet Paper I.C.30); V. Bonham-Carter, *Soldier true: the life and times of Field Marshal Sir William Robertson*, London, 1963, 268.

25. CAB, 23/4/163 (9 Nov. 1917, War Cabinet minutes); Wilson Papers (diary for 8 Nov. 1917).

26. WO, 106/803 (16 Dec. 1917, Gen. Maurice); *DDI*, ser. 5, IX, 287; Gatti, *Caporetto*, 313, 319, 456.

27. *Nuova Antologia*, 16 Jan. 1935, 213 (Aldrovandi).

28. Sonnino microfilm, reel 47 (8 Nov. 1917, British War Cabinet Paper I.C.32); Smuts Papers, 682/44 (24 Nov. 1917); *The Spectator*, London, 3 May 1935, 723 (Smuts); *DDI*, ser. 5, IX, 270–2; CAB, 23/4/170 (15 Nov. 1917, Lloyd George); Lloyd George, *War memoirs*, IV, 2325–9.

29. *ABC*, Rome, 1 Jan. 1958, 17; Gioacchino Volpe, *Il risorgimento dell'Italia*, Rome, 1934, 304; Amedeo Tosti, *La guerra italo-austriaca 1925–1918*, Milan, 1938, 302; Angelo Gatti, *Ancoraggio alle rive del tempo*, Milan, 1938, 305, 311; M. Viana, *La monarchia e il fascismo*, Rome, 1951, 373–4; Ugo D'Andrea, *La fine del regno: grandezza e decadenza di Vittorio Emanuele III*, Turin, 1951, 258; A. Con-

siglio, *Vita di Vittorio Emanuele III*, Milan, 1950, 127.

30. Orlando, *Memorie*, 241–2; Scaroni, *Con Vittorio Emanuele*, 58.

31. Gatti, *Un italiano a Versailles*, 313; Cadorna, *Pagine polemiche*, 167; Malagodi, *Conversazioni*, I, 207–9; Rocca, *Cadorna*, 306–7.

32. WO, 106/808 (2 Jan. 1918).

33. Abel Ferry, *Les carnets secrets (1914–1918)*, Paris, 1957, 213 (30 Dec. 1917).

34. Nitti, *Edizione nazionale*, XVI, tome 2, 549–51.

35. Giuseppe Bottai, *Diario 1935–1944*, ed. G.B. Guerri, Milan, 1982, 118; Scaroni, *Con Vittorio Emanuele*, 139.

36. Orlando, *Memorie*, 504–5; Hankey, *Supreme command*, II, 724; Leonida Bissolati, *Diario di guerra*, Turin, 1935, 96–7.

37. Melograni, *Storia della guerra*, 420–3; Piero Pieri and Giorgio Rochat, *Pietro Badoglio*, Turin, 1974, 319–26; Caviglia, *Diario*, 122; St Antony's Documents, 249/067661 (5 May 1932, Mussolini).

38. *DDI*, ser. 6, IX, 300; *Nuova Antologia*, 16 Jan. 1935, 214.

39. CAB, 24/32/2618 (10 Nov. 1917, Lord Cavan); WO, 106/797/8 (13 Nov. 1917, Delmé-Radcliffe); *ibid.*, 106/796/2 (14 Nov. 1917, Gen. Robertson); Lloyd George Papers, F/55/4/3 (13 Dec. 1917, Rodd).

40. Delmé-Radcliffe Papers (28 June 1918, Gen. Wilson); Albertini, *Epistolario*, II, 1001.

41. Cavan Papers, XII, 24 (undated); Robertson Papers, 1/34/40 (4 Dec. 1917, Gen. Plumer); Wilson Papers, 2/22/20 (17 Sept. 1918, Delmé-Radcliffe).

42. Delmé-Radcliffe Papers (10 July 1918); Cavan Papers, XII, 22.

43. *Il Cardinale Gasparri e la questione romana, con brani delle memorie inediti*, ed. G. Spadolini, Florence, 1972, 215–21; Alberto Monticone, *Nitti e la grande guerra*, Milan, 1961, 258–61; Salandra, *Diario*, 186.

44. Martini, *Diario 1914–1918*, 1087 (Boselli); Orlando, *Memorie*, 517; Melograni, *Storia della guerra*, 471–4.

45. FO, 371/2948/23624 (8 Dec. 1917, Col. Lamb); Templewood Papers (8 Feb. 1918, Col. Marchetti).

46. Lloyd George Papers, F/56/1/61 (16 Dec. 1917).

47. Enrico Caviglia, *La battaglia della Bainsizza*, Milan, 1930, 202–3; Charles-

Roux, *Souvenirs*, 279, 314; A. Lumbro-so, *Fame usurpate: il dramma del comando unico interralleato*, Milan, 1934, 286; Wilson Papers, 2/22/15 (2 Aug. 1918, Delmé-Radcliffe); Monticone, *Nitti*, 273.

48. Lloyd George Papers, F/56/2/5 (27 June 1918, Rodd).

49. Malagodi, *Conversazioni*, II, 382; Martini, *Diario 1914–1918*, 397.

50. Delmé-Radcliffe Papers (7 June 1918, to Lord Stamfordham); Rino Alessi, *Dall'Isonzo al Piave*, Milan, 1966, 219.

51. *DDI*, ser. 5, IX, 558–9; *Camera, discussioni*, 12 Apr. 1897, 160; Carlo Sforza, *Contemporary Italy: its intellectual and moral origins*, New York, 1944, 211.

52. Wilson Papers, 2/22/17–18 (11–12 Sept. 1918, Delmé-Radcliffe); FO, 79/70 (undated memo. by Lord Cavan).

53. *Corriere della Sera*, 27 Oct. 1968 (Rodolfo Mosca); *La Settimana Incom Illustrata*, Rome, 7 Feb. 1959 (King Umberto to Maurano); C. Scarfoglio, *La memoria di un giornalista*, Rome, 1964, 402–5.

54. Nitti, *Edizione nazionale*, XVI, tome 2, 752–4; Malagodi, *Conversazioni*, II, 424; Albertini, *Epistolario*, II, 1000–1; Lloyd George Papers, F/56/2/10 (27 Sept. 1918, Rodd).

55. Gioacchino Volpe, *Vittorio Emanuele III*, Milan, 1939, 196–7; Enrico Caviglia, *Vittorio Veneto*, Milan, 1920, 29; *Testimonianze straniere sulla guerra italiana 1915–1918*, ed. A. Alberti, Rome, 1933, 16–17 (Mussolini); Giovanni Gentile, *Origini e dottrina del fascismo*, Rome, 1929, 26; Rosario Romeo, *L'Italia unita e la prima guerra mondiale*, Bari, 1978, 157; S. Cilibrizzi, *Francesco Nitti e l'avvenire d'Italia*, Naples, 1919, 286.

3   Post-war difficulties

1. Alberto Pirelli, *Taccuini 1922–1943*, ed. D. Barbone, Bologna, 1984, 187; *DBFP*, ser. 1, IV, 186 (15 Nov. 1919, Buchanan); Albertini, *Epistolario*, III, 1191.

2. Balfour Papers, 800/203/195 (18 Nov. 1918, Rodd); Enrico Caviglia, *Il conflitto di Fiume*, Cernusco, 1948, 64–5.

3. *The papers of Woodrow Wilson*, Princeton, 1986, LIII, 439; *Actes et documents du Saint Siège relatifs à la seconde guerre mondiale*, ed. P. Blet, R.A. Graham, A. Martini and B. Schneider, Rome, 1967, VII,

116–17; Pirelli, *Taccuini*, 379–80.

4. Templewood Papers (7 Aug. 1918, Col. Luigi Marchetti); Lloyd George Papers, F/56/1/1 (25 Dec. 1916, Delmé-Radcliffe).

5. R. Albrecht-Carrié, *Italy at the Paris peace conference*, New York, 1938, 83–4 (17 Jan. 1919, diary of Gino Speranza).

6. Sonnino, *Diario*, III, 314.

7. Bissolati, *Diario di guerra*, 137; Sonnino, *Diario*, III, 397–8; *La conferenza della pace 1919–1920*, ed. F. Curato, Milan, 1942, II, 168.

8. Orlando, *Memorie*, 386; Malagodi, *Conversazioni*, II, 378, 407, 667; A.A. Bernardy and V. Falorsi, *La questione Adriatica visto d'oltre Atlantico 1917–1919: ricordi e documenti*, Bologna, 1923, 178–9.

9. *Documents diplomatiques suisses*, Bern, 1981, VI, 808; Malagodi, *Conversazioni*, I, 52, II, 263, 382, 456–7; *Il Cardinale Gasparri e la questione romana*, ed. G. Spadolini, Florence, 1972, 220–4; *Virginia Quarterly Review*, Charlottesville, autumn 1962, 582–3.

10. Malagodi, *Conversazioni*, II, 379, 510, 550; Albertini, *Epistolario*, III, 1171.

11. *DDI*, ser. 6, II, 35, (ed. Rodolfo Mosca), 79, 133, 567, 636, 674; *La politica italiana dal 1914 al 1943*, ed. RAI, Turin, 1963, 65 (Rodolfo Mosca).

12. Rodd Papers, box 20 (6 Feb. 1919, Hardinge).

13. Lloyd George Papers, F/56/2/21 (5 Jan. 1919).

14. S. Crespi, *Alla difesa d'Italia in guerra e a Versailles*, Milan, 1937, 574–5; Malagodi, *Conversazioni*, II 595; FO, 371/3804/418 (17 Jan. 1919, Rodd).

15. FO, 371/2946/221 (23 Mar. 1917, Delmé-Radcliffe); M. Petricioli, *L'occupazione italiana del Caucaso*, Milan, 1972, 38.

16. FO, 371/3808/214 (23 May 1919, Rodd); Malagodi, *Conversazioni*, II, 517, 545, 640; Salandra, *I retroscena di Versailles*, 102.

17. Templewood Papers (1 Jan. 1919).

18. *Il Giornale d'Italia*, Rome, 27 Apr. 1919; Salandra, *I retroscena di Versailles*, 109–10; L. Aldrovandi-Marescotti, *Guerra diplomatica: ricordi e frammenti di diario*, Milan, 1942, 254–6.

19. T. Torella di Romagnano, *Villa Iela*, Cernusco, 1948, 66.

20. *DBFP*, ser. 1, IV, 185–6; Salandra, *Diario*, 249.

21. Wilson Papers, 2/22/25 (13 Feb. 1919,

Delmé-Radcliffe); Georges Wagnière, *Dix-huit ans à Rome*, Geneva, 1944, 46.

22. Lloyd George Papers, F/56/2/35 (18 Aug. 1919, Rodd); Rodd Papers (17 Oct. 1919).

23. *Saluto a un maestro: scritti di Gioacchino Volpe*, Rome, 1951, 144.

24. *Corriere della Sera*, 8 Apr. 1919; Enrico Flores, *Eredità di guerra*, Rome, 1947, 15 (Nitti); *DBFP*, ser. 1, v, 443.

25. *Corriere della Sera*, 20 June 1919; *Il Secolo*, Milan, 25 May 1919.

26. Ottavio Dinale, *Quarant'anni di colloqui con lui*, Milan, 1953, 83–5.

27. Curzon Papers, cxii, 214 (8 June 1919, Rodd to Balfour); *ibid.*, 214a (19 June 1919, Rodd to Curzon); *DBFP*, ser. 1, iv, 8; *Il Secolo*, 12 June 1919; *La Destra*, Rome, Aug. 1972, 7 (Susmel).

28. Roberto Vivarelli, *Il dopoguerra in Italia e l'avvento del fascismo*, Naples, 1967, 460–1; Francesco Margiotta Broglio, *Italia e Santa Sede dalla grande guerra alla conciliazione*, Bari, 1966, 366–7 (Colosimo).

29. Templewood Papers (4 July 1918); Nitti, *Edizione nazionale*, xvi, tome 2, 689–9.

30. Rodd Papers, box 20 (2 July 1919); *DBFP*, ser. 1, v, 289 (22 Aug. 1919, Rodd).

31. *Ibid.*, ser. 1, iv, 212–13; *ibid.*, ser. 1, v, 289–90.

32. Curzon Papers (18 Aug. 1919).

33. *Documents suisses*, vii, 857; Salandra, *Diario*, 225; Caviglia, *Il conflitto di Fiume*, 65; Nitti, *Edizione nazionale*, xvi, tome 2, 564–7, 570.

34. *DDI*, ser. 6, ii, 688; Curzon Papers (18 Aug. 1919, Rodd).

35. FO, 371/3805/406 (15 Nov. 1919, George Buchanan); *Nuova Antologia*, Jan. 1968, 66 (Sforza).

36. Nitti, *Edizione nazionale*, xvi, tome 2, 568; *DBFP*, ser. 1, iv, 80 (Kennard).

37. Giovanni Giuriati, *Con D'Annunzio e Millo in difesa dell'Adriatico*, Florence, 1944, 4–5; Luigi Federzoni, *Italia di ieri per la storia di domani*, Milan, 1967, 38.

38. Caviglia, *Il conflitto di Fiume*, 69–71, 127.

39. *DBFP*, ser. 1, iv, 75, 106, 140–2.

40. Albertini, *Epistolario*, iii, 1318–9, 1324–5; Flores, *Eredità di guerra*, 100–4.

41. Sonnino, *Diario*, iii, 350–1; *Discorsi parlamentari di Vittorio Emanuele Orlando*, Rome, 1965, iv, 1580.

42. Scaroni, *Con Vittorio Emanuele*, 29; Nitti,

Edizione nazionale, xvi, tome 2, 95; *DBFP*, ser. 1, iv, 97; *Movimento di Liberazione in Italia*, Jan. 1965, 62.

43. Curzon Papers, cxii, part 2, 14 (17 Oct. 1919).

44. Nitti, *Rivelazioni*, 458; Ferdinando Gerra, *L'impresa di Fiume*, Milan, 1966, 197–8; WO, 106/853 (6 Nov. 1919, diary of Col. Peck): Paolo Alatri, *Nitti, D'Annunzio e la questione adriatica*, Milan, 1959, 252–5.

45. *DBFP*, ser. 1, iv, 91, 166; Scaroni, *Con Vittorio Emanuele*, 52; Albertini, *Epistolario*, iii, 1311, 1330–1, 1613.

46. Curzon Papers (17 Oct. 1919, Rodd).

47. Wagnière, *Dix-huit ans à Rome*, 46.

48. Wickham Steed, *Through thirty years*, ii, 105; FO, 371/3811/402 (3 Jan. 1920, Buchanan).

49. Royal Archives (2 Jan. 1922, Graham).

50. Ugo Ojetti, *I Taccuini*, Florence, 1954, 73; Artieri, *Cronaca*, ii, 554 (Gatti); L. Zeno, *Ritratto di Carlo Sforza*, Florence, 1975, 139; Scaroni, *Con Vittorio Emanuele*, 52.

51. Francesco Saverio Nitti, *La democrazia*, Paris, 1933, i, 334; Gioacchino Volpe, *Guerra, dopoguerra, fascismo*, Venice, 1928, 271.

52. Puntoni, *Parla Vittorio Emanuele*, 7; Scaroni, *Con Vittorio Emanuele*, 91, 133; D'Aroma, *Vent'anni insieme*, 39.

53. *Nuova Antologia*, 16 July 1919, 412–17; Rodd Papers, box 20 (17 Oct. 1919); G. Ansaldo, 'Il re democratico', in *Le Riviste di Piero Gobetti*, ed. L. Basso and L. Anderlini, Milan, 1961, 592; Flores, *Eredità di guerra*, 100–2; Abertini, *Epistolario*, iii, 1288.

4 Fascism and the march on Rome

1. Benito Mussolini, *Opera omnia*, Florence, 1955, xvi, 401–2.

2. *DBFP*, ser. 1, iv, 7, 132.

3. Nitti, *Edizione nazionale*, xvi, tome 2, 581; D'Aroma, *Vent'anni insieme*, 9.

4. *Ibid.*, 42–3.

5. Mussolini, *Opera*, xii, 54, 326; *ibid.*, xiii, 265; *ibid.*, xiv, 52; *ibid.*, xvi, 364, 403.

6. Giorgio Pini, *Filo diretto con Palazzo Venezia*, Bologna, 1950, 169.

7. Cesare Rossi, *Trentatrè vicende Mussoliniane*, Milan, 1958, 131.

8. Cesare Rossi, *Mussolini com'era*, Rome, 1947, 186.

9. Mussolini, *Opera*, xviii, 498–9, 506.

10. Emil Ludwig, *Leaders of Europe*, London, 1934, 327.
11. Mussolini, *Opera*, xviii, 56; Antonio Salandra, *Memorie politiche*, Milan, 1951, 14.
12. Mussolini, *Opera*, xviii, 46, 138; Attilio Tamaro, *Venti anni di storia 1922–1943*, Rome, 1953, i, 224–5.
13. Mussolini, *Opera*, xviii, 276–7, 321, 327, 528; Nitti, *Edizione nazionale*, xvi, tome 1, 93.
14. Puntoni, *Parla Vittorio Emanuele*, 289; Stefano Jacini, *Il regime fascista*, Cernusco, 1947, 31.
15. A. Tasca, *Nascita e avvento del fascismo*, Florence, 1950, 540; V. Serge, *Memoirs of a revolutionary*, London, 1963, 163.
16. Raffaele Paolucci, *Il mio piccolo mondo perduto*, Bologna, 1947, 232–3.
17. Mussolini, *Opera*, xviii, 411, 439.
18. *La Battaglia*, Rome, 15 June 1922 (Balbino Giuliano).
19. Nino D'Aroma, *Mussolini segreto*, Rocca S. Casciano, 1958, 390.
20. Efrem Ferraris, *La marcia su Roma veduta dal Viminale*, Rome, 1946, 52.
21. Mussolini, *Opera*, xviii, 418–19; *La Settimana Incom Illustrata*, 1 Dec. 1959.
22. Tasca, *Nascita del fascismo*, 420–1; Nino Valeri, *Da Giolitti a Mussolini*, Florence, 1956, 156–7 (Lusignoli).
23. Mussolini, *Opera*, xviii, 581.
24. Arturo Labriola, *Spiegazioni a me stesso*, Naples, 1945, 200; Antonino Répaci, *La marcia su Roma: mito e realtà*, Rome, 1963, ii, 143, 401.
25. *Corriere della Sera*, 5 Apr. 1949 (Croce); *Il Popolo d'Italia*, Milan, 28 Aug. 1923; Rossi, *Trentatrè vicende Mussoliniane*, 133; Italo Balbo, *Diario 1922*, Milan, 1932, 185.
26. Washington Archives, 865.00/1162 (9 Oct. 1922, Child); Caviglia, *Diario*, 565–6; Nitti, *Edizione nazionale*, xvi, tome 2, 591; P. Berardi, *Memorie di un capo di stato maggiore dell'esercito*, Bologna, 1954, 199–200.
27. Répaci, *La marcia su Roma*, ii, 69.
28. Emanuele Pugliese, *Io difendo l'esercito*, Naples, 1946, 147.
29. Michele Terzaghi, *Fascismo e massoneria*, Milan, 1950, 64 (Soleri).
30. G. Alessio, *La crisi dello stato parlamentare e l'avvento del fascismo*, Padua, 1946, 55; Ferraris, *La marcia su Roma*, 92–4; Marcello Soleri, *Memorie*, Turin, 1949, 331, Pugliese, *Io difendo l'esercito*, 26, 126, 154; Nino Bolla, *Il segreto di due re*,

Milan, 1951, 75–6; Giorgio Rochat, *L'esercito italiano da Vittorio Veneto a Mussolini*, Bari, 1967, 403–4; Renzo De Felice, *Mussolini*, Turin, 1966, ii, 324; V. Vailati, *Badoglio racconta*, Turin, 1955, 254–5.
31. Salandra, *Memorie*, 22; Salandra, *Diario*, 271; Répaci, *La marcia su Roma*, i, 457.
32. Soleri, *Memorie*, 150; *La Politica Parlamentare*, Rome, Mar. 1949, 32 (Facta); Alessio, *La crisi*, 57.
33. Répaci, *La marcia su Roma*, i, 507; *ibid.*, ii, 398, 404–5.
34. Ferraris, *La marcia su Roma*, 95–6; Répaci, *La marcia su Roma*, ii, 415.
35. *La Politica Parlamentare*, Mar. 1949, 32; *ibid.*, July 1949, 64; D'Aroma, *Vent'anni insieme*, 124; *Nuova Antologia*, Mar. 1967, 297 (Paratore); Ferraris, *La marcia su Roma*, 107–8; Répaci, *La marcia su Roma*, ii, 388 (Cingolani), 406 (Paratore).
36. Pugliese, *Io difendo l'esercito*, 154.
37. Ferraris, *La marcia su Roma*, 37.
38. Répaci, *La marcia su Roma*, ii, 142 (Soleri), 390 (Cocco-Ortu), 406 (Paratore).
39. Soleri, *Memorie*, 147.
40. *La Gazzetta del Popolo*, Turin, 31 Oct. 1922; G.A. Chiurco, *Storia della rivoluzione fascista 1919–1922*, Florence, 1929, v, 208.
41. Alberto Bergamini, *Il Re Vittorio Emanuele III di fronte alla storia*, Turin, n.d., 11; Ferraris, *La marcia su Roma*, 143–4 (Bencivenga); *Il Ponte*, Florence, Sept. 1951, 1073–4 (De Nicola); Artieri, *Cronaca*, ii, 272.
42. Puntoni, *Parla Vittorio Emanuele*, 288; Salandra, *Diario*, 271.
43. Paulucci, *Il mio piccolo mondo perduto*, 240; Massimo Rocca, *Come il fascismo divenne una dittatura*, Milan, 1952, 82; Eno Mecheri, *Chi ha tradito? Rivelazioni e documentazioni inedite di un vecchio fascista*, Milan, 1947, 102.
44. *La Settimana Incom Illustrata*, 8 Dec. 1959; Salandra, *Memorie*, 23; Répaci, *La marcia su Roma*, ii, 405–6 (Paolucci).
45. Rossi, *Mussolini com'era*, 123–7; St Antony's Documents, 261/072740 (police report); A. Albertini, *Vita di Luigi Albertini*, Milan, 1945, 215; Carmine Senise, *Quando ero capo della polizia 1940–1943*, Rome, 1946, 13; Mario Missiroli, *Il fascismo e il colpo di stato dell'Ottobre 1922*, Rocca S. Casciano, 1969, 37.
46. Salandra, *Memorie*, 22, 24.
47. Salandra, *Diario*, 273; Ferraris, *La marcia*

su Roma, 123, 125.

48. Puntoni, *Parla Vittorio Emanuele*, 40.
49. Missiroli, *Il fascismo*, 224.
50. *New York Times*, 29 Oct. 1922; Ettore Ciccotti, *Il fascismo e le sue fasi*, Milan, 1925, 401–2.
51. Mussolini, *Opera*, xxiv, 154; *ibid.*, xxxiv, 406.
52. *La Stampa*, Turin, 1 and 3 Nov. 1922; Salandra, *Diario*, 274; *Discorsi di Orlando*, ii, 1467; *Atti Parlamentari: Senato, discussioni*, Rome, 28 Nov. 1922, 4280.
53. *Senato, discussioni*, 26 Nov. 1922, 4213–4; Albertini, *Epistolario*, iv, 1642.
54. Rossi, *Mussolini com'era*, 115, 122.
55. Répaci, *La marcia su Roma*, ii, 389 (Cingolani).
56. Charles H. Sherrill, *Bismarck and Mussolini*, Boston, 1931, 207–8; Benito Mussolini, *My autobiography*, London, 1928, 177; Mussolini, *Opera*, xix, 1, 17.
57. Federzoni, *Italia di ieri*, 240; Pugliese, *Io difendo l'esercito*, 108.
58. *Corriere della Sera*, 17 Nov. 1922.
59. Mussolini, *Opera*, xix, 18, 23; *Filippo Turati, Anna Kuliscioff, Carteggio (1919–1922)*, ed. Alessandro Schiavi, Turin, 1953, v, 600.
60. *La Settimana Incom Illustrata*, 3 Jan. 1959 (Maurano).
61. *Dove va il mondo? Inchiesta tra scrittori italiani*, ed. G. Conti, Rome, 1923, 45 (Augusto Monti), 68–9 (Gaetano Salvemini).

5   The fascist dictatorship

1. Orlando Danese, *Vittorio Emanuele III, il re fascista*, Mantua, 1923, 52.
2. Curzon Papers, cxii, 214a (17 Oct. 1919, Rodd).
3. Bolla, *Il segreto di due re*, 37.
4. Rossi, *Trentatrè vicende Mussoliniane*, 578 (Alfieri); Rossi, *Mussolini com'era*, 192 (Frignani); Missiroli, *Il fascismo*, 29 (Albertini); D'Aroma, *Vent'anni insieme*, 140 (Vaucher).
5. Albertini, *Epistolario*, iv, 1761.
6. Federzoni, *Italia di ieri*, 256; Rossi, *Mussolini com'era*, 166, 193–7.
7. *La Critica Politica*, Rome, 25 Nov. 1922, 440 (Zuccarini); *Almanacco Repubblicano*, Rome, 1923, 153: *ibid.*, 1924, 82–3.
8. *L'Idea Nazionale*, Rome, 14 and 16 Jan. 1923.
9. FO, 800/257/39 (8 Jan. 1925, Nitti).
10. Mussolini, *Opera*, xx, 261.
11. *Riviste di Gobetti*, 593–6; Artieri, *Cron-*

aca, ii, 352; Titta Madìa, *Storia terribile del parlamento italiano*, Milan, 1941, 641; Volpe, *Vittorio Emanuele III*, 209–11.
12. *The New Leader*, London, 28 Mar. 1924; *Westminister Gazette*, London, 19 June 1924; *English Life*, London, July 1924, 86–7.
13. *Il Popolo d'Italia*, 1 June 1924; G. Rossini, *Il delitto Matteotti tra il Viminale e l'Aventino*, Bologna, 1966, 979, 989; C. Silvestri, *Matteotti, Mussolini, e il dramma italiano*, Rome, 1947, 201.
14. *Camera, discussioni*, 6 June 1924, 206; *Studi e ricerche su Giacomo Matteotti*, ed. E. Bedeschi, Urbino, 1979, 69–70 (Mack Smith); *Almanacco Repubblicano*, 1925, 64.
15. Yvon De Begnac, *Palazzo Venezia: storia di un regime*, Rome, 1950, 245; Rocca, *Come il fascismo divenne una dittatura*, 220, 238; R. Farinacci, *Un periodo aureo del partito nazionale fascista*, Foligno, 1927, 25; Soleri, *Memorie*, 183.
16. Dinale, *Quarant'anni di colloqui con lui*, 115; Guido Leto, *Ovra, fascismo, antifascismo*, Rocca S. Casciano, 1952, 17; P. Orano, *Mussolini da vicino*, Rome, 1923, 89; Alberto Pirelli, *Dopoguerra 1919–1932: note ed esperienze*, Milan, 1961, 133.
17. Benedetto Croce, *Scritti e discorsi politici (1943–1947)*, Bari, 1963, i, 17; *Corriere della Sera*, 5 Apr. 1949; G. Levi della Vida, *Fantasmi ritrovati*, Venice, 1966, 195.
18. Benedetto Croce, *Pagine sparse*, Naples, 1943, ii, 377–8.
19. *Nuova Antologia*, Dec. 1967, 455 (Sforza); *Dalle carte di Giovanni Giolitti: quarant'anni di politica italiana*, ed. C. Pavone, Milan, 1962, iii, 424–7 (Zaniboni and Senator Conti); Caviglia, *Diario*, 566; D'Andrea, *La fine del regno*, 330; Giovanni Giuriati, *La Parabola di Mussolini nei ricordi di un gerarca*, Bari, 1981, 160; *Corriere della Sera*, 1 June 1946 (Mario Borsa).
20. *Domenica del Corriere*, Milan, 10 July 1966 (King Umberto to Luigi Cavicchioli).
21. FO, 371/9939/361 (4 July 1924, Graham).
22. Ivanoe Bonomi, *Diario di un anno 1943–1944*, Cernusco, 1947, xxvi; Paolo Alatri, *Le origini del fascismo*, Rome, 1956, 122–34; Carlo Silvestri, *Turati l'ha detto*, Milan, 1946, 110–13; G. Andreotti, *Intervista su De Gasperi*, ed.

A. Gambino, Bari, 1977, 38.

23. De Begnac, *Palazzo Venezia*, 357.
24. Silvestri, *Turati*, 116–17; Torella, *Villa Iela*, 74.
25. Salandra, *Diario*, 292–3.
26. *Camera, discussioni*, 15 Nov. 1924, 521–2, 524.
27. *La Critica Politica*, 25 Oct. 1924, 240.
28. FO, 800/256/7 (7 Nov. 1924, Graham); *ibid.*, 800/256/386 (16 Dec. 1924, Graham).
29. *Il Caffé*, Milan, 368–9 (11 Jan. 1925); *La Critica Politica*, 25 Nov. 1924, 480–1; *ibid.*, 25 Jan. 1925, 1; *Corriere della Sera*, 13 May 1925; Albertini, *Epistolario*, IV, 1828–9.
30. FO, 371/9941/353 (27 Nov. 1924, Harvey); *Il Lavoro*, Genoa, 23 and 25 Dec. 1924.
31. *Camera, discussioni*, 12 Nov. 1924, 341 (Repossi); *ibid.*, 20 Nov. 1924, 643 (Soleri); *Discorsi di Orlando*, IV, 1690.
32. *Corriere della Sera*, 21, 27 and 30 Dec. 1924.
33. Mussolini, *Opera*, XXI, 196, 203–4.
34. Paolucci, *Il mio piccolo mondo perduto*, 256–9; St Antony's Documents, 250/068207 (29 Dec. 1924, Acerbo).
35. FO, 371/10783/12 (2 Jan. 1925, Graham).
36. *Turati, Kuliscioff, Carteggio*, VI, 334.
37. Giuriati, *La parabola*, 160–1.
38. Benito Mussolini, *Il tempo del bastone e della carota: storia di un anno*, Milan, 1944, 41; Galeazzo Ciano, *Diario, 1939–1940*, Milan, 1946, 116.
39. FO, 371/10783/38 (9 Jan. 1925, Graham); Puntoni, *Parla Vittorio Emanuele*, 289; Giuriati, *La parabola*, 161–2.
40. *Daily News*, London, 26 Jan. 1925; *ibid.*, 29 Sept. 1925.
41. FO, 800/257/39–40 (8 Jan. 1925); Nitti, *Rivelazioni*, 583–5, 594; *Non Mollare*, Florence, March and May 1925.
42. Tommaso Tittoni, *Nuovi scritti di politica interna ed estera*, Milan, 1930, 201–2; Paolo Boselli, *Discorsi per la 'Dante Alighieri'*, Turin, 1932, 167–9; Luigi Luzzatti, *Memorie tratte dal carteggio e da altri documenti*, Bologna, 1966, III, 625, 750–60; Albertini, *Venti anni* I, tome 2, 37.
43. Raffaello Uboldi, *Il cittadino Sandro Pertini*, Milan, 1982, 51–2 (Cianca); Alatri, *Le origini*, 131–2; Eva Amendola Kühn, *Vita con Amendola*, 606.
44. *United States Congressional Record: Senate*, Washington, 1 Apr. 1926, 6687 (McKellar); Washington Archives, M/527/19 (3 Apr. 1926, Kellogg).
45. FO, 371/11383/112 (22 Jan. 1926, McClure); Federzoni, *Italia di ieri*, 247.
46. A. Rocco, *Scritti e discorsi politici*, Milan, 1938, III, 786; *Rassegna Italiana*, Rome, Dec. 1925, 782 (Rocco); Emilio Crosa, *Diritto costituzionale*, Turin, 1937, 432–5; *Lo Stato*, Rome, Oct. 1937, 552–3; *Dizionario di politica*, ed. PNF, Rome, 1940, I, 391 (Costamagna).
47. Bolla, *Segreto di due re*, 72; D'Aroma, *Vent'anni insieme*, 180.
48. FO, 371/10785/79 (27 Nov. 1925, Graham).
49. St Antony's Documents, 273/079433 (5 Nov. 1925, Suardo).
50. Mussolini, *Opera*, XXI, 425; *ibid.*, XL, 7.
51. Puntoni, *Parla Vittorio Emanuele*, 290; Caviglia, *Diario*, 18.
52. Attilio Tamaro, *Due anni di storia*, Rome, 1948, I, 307–8 (Paolucci); Federzoni, *Italia di ieri*, 229.
53. Mussolini, *Opera*, XXIII, 222; *ibid.*, XXXIV, 409; *Lo Stato*, Rome, July 1930, 382 (Giuriati).
54. Federzoni, *Italia di ieri*, 225; Carlo Scorza, *La notte del Gran Consiglio*, ed. Gianfranco Bianchi, Milan, 1968, 81–2; Dino Grandi, *Il mio paese: ricordi autobiografici*, ed. Renzo De Felice, Bologna, 1985, 471; *Il Tempo*, Rome, Dec. 1959, LII, 29 (De Vecchi).
55. Pietro Chimienti, *Manuale di diritto costituzionale*, Rome, 1934 edn., 187, 396; Crosa, *Diritto costituzionale*, 262, 435; *Archivio Giuridico*, Oct. 1941, 164.
56. D'Aroma, *Vent'anni insieme*, 158; Mussolini, *Il tempo del bastone*, 41.
57. Mussolini, *Opera*, XXII, 286; *ibid.*, XXIII, 144.
58. *Senato, discussioni*, 8 Apr. 1930, 2245; *Lo Stato*, Dec. 1933, 826–7 (Costamagna).
59. Vanna Vailati, *Badoglio risponde*, Milan, 1958, 159, 241.
60. *Corriere della Sera*, 22 Nov. 1946; Luigi Albertini, *In difesa della liberta*, Milan, 1947, 112; Albertini, *Venti anni*, I, tome 2, 280–1.
61. *Senato, discussioni*, 20 Apr. 1929, 1–2; Caviglia, *Diario*, 73.
62. Scaroni, *Con Vittorio Emanuele*, 35; Soleri, *Memorie*, 210.
63. *DDI*, ser. 7, IV, 66 (ed. R. Moscati and G. Carocci).
64. Margiotta Broglio, *Italia e Santa Sede*, 366–7, 537–8.
65. Chamberlain Papers, AC/55/197 (26

Jan. 1927).

66. *Actes du Saint Siège*, VII, 118; Matteo Mureddu, *Il Quirinale del re*, Milan, 1977, 66; Scaroni, *Con Vittorio Emanuele*, 44; Tamaro, *Venti anni di storia*, II, 454 (Giuliano).

67. Earl of Asquith, *Memories and reflections*, London, 1928, II, 121.

6 The 'diarchy'

1. Scaroni, *Con Vittorio Emanuele*, 112; Soleri, *Memorie*, 207–9; Luigi Gasparotto, *Diario di un deputato: cinquant'anni di vita politica italiana*, Milan, 1945, 251; FO, 371/3811 (3 Jan. 1920).

2. Mureddu, *Il Quirinale*, 85; Scaroni, *Con Vittorio Emanuele*, 66, 75.

3. Mussolini, *Il tempo del bastone*, 16.

4. C. Rossi, *Il tribunale speciale*, Milan, 1952, 204–5; De Begnac, *Palazzo Venezia*, 50; C. Camilleri, *Polizia in azione*, Rome, n.d., 226–30; Nino Bolla, *Colloqui con Umberto II*, Rome, 1949, 107; Eugene Young, *Looking behind the censorships*, London, 1938, 225–6; *Le Matin*, Paris, 18 Feb. 1927; Emilio Canevari, *La guerra italiana: retroscena della disfatta*, Rome, 1948, I, 158; De Felice, *Mussolini*, III, 219; Federzoni, *Italia di ieri*, 231.

5. FO, 371/107841/106 (23 July 1925, Graham).

6. Washington Archives, M/527/19 (4 Nov. 1927, Warren Robbins).

7. FO, 371/15977/63 (2 Aug. 1932, Graham); Gasparotto, *Diario*, 247–50.

8. Charles Petrie, *Monarchy in the twentieth century*, London, 1952, 159.

9. *Chamberlain Papers*, AC/54/213 (14 Jan. 1927).

10. *Documents diplomatiques français*, ed. Ministère des Affaires Etrangères, Paris, ser. 2, III, 569 (Chambrun); Thomas Morgan, *Spurs on the boot: Italy under her masters*, London, 1942, 116; G. Nelson Page, *L'Americano di Roma*, Milan, 1950, 156; D'Aroma, *Vent'anni insieme*, 370 (Gentizon).

11. Scaroni, *Con Vittorio Emanuele*, 36, 40, 116, 119, 137.

12. Mureddu, *Il Quirinale*, 78; D'Aroma, *Vent'anni insieme*, 160; Scaroni, *Con Vittorio Emanuele*, 52.

13. *Il Tempo*, 6 Sept. 1965 (Prince Ruprecht); Caviglia, *Diario*, 223.

14. Giuseppe Bastianini, *Uomini, cose, fatti: memorie di un ambasciatore*, Milan, 1959,

108; Mussolini, *Opera*, XXXII, 242; Scorza, *La notte del Gran Consiglio*, 192.

15. *St Antony's Documents*, 131/036412 (13 Feb. 1937, Starace); Alberto Aquarone, *L'organizzazione dello stato totalitario*, Turin, 1965, 520; *Foglio d'Ordini*, Rome, 28 Feb. 1929.

16. Mussolini, *Opera*, XXIII, 253.

17. Scaroni, *Con Vittorio Emanuele*, 56, 61.

18. *Ibid.*, 44, 52, 92, 100; Mureddu, *Il Quirinale,* 61; Baron Aloisi, *Journal (25 juillet 1932 – 14 juin 1936)*, Paris, 1957, 255.

19. Giuseppe Gorla, *L'Italia nella IIᵃ guerra mondiale*, Milan, 1959, 21.

20. Frederick Ponsonby, *Recollections of three reigns,* ed. Colin Welch, London, 1951, 262.

21. Alfredo Rocco, *La trasformazione dello stato: dallo stato liberale allo stato fascista*, Rome, 1927, 139 (26 May 1925).

22. Roberto Cantalupo, *Fu la Spagna: ambasciata presso Franco*, Milan, 1948, 38.

23. *DDI*, ser. 7, II, 137.

24. Wagnière, *Dix-huit ans à Rome*, 46; Scaroni, *Con Vittorio Emanuele*, 42.

25. *Ibid.*, 88.

26. *Ibid.*, 63, 79–80.

27. *Ibid.*, 134.

28. *Corriere di Genova*, 18 Feb. 1950 (D. Soprano, 6 July 1935); Giuriati, *La parabola*, 59.

29. Aloisi, *Journal*, 287; Raffaele Guariglia, *Ricordi 1922–1946*, Naples, 1950, 239.

30. Gaetano Salvemini, *Prelude to World War II*, London, 1953, 178.

31. Angelo Del Boca, *Gli Italiani in Africa Orientale: la conquista dell' impero*, Bari, 1979, 229–31; Caviglia, *Diario*, 128; Ojetti, *I taccuini*, 463–4; Federzoni, *Italia di ieri*, 245; Mussolini, *Il tempo del bastone*, 16.

32. *St Antony's Documents*, 329/112910; *La Settimana Incom Illustrata*, 10 Jan. 1959, 21–2 (King Umberto); D'Aroma, *Vent'anni insieme*, 234, 316.

33. *La Settimana Incom Illustrata*, 31 Jan. 1959 (Umberto).

34. Artieri, *Cronaca*, II, 1048–9.

35. Mussolini, *Opera*, XXXII, 177; Dino Grandi, *25 Luglio: quarant'anni dopo*, ed. Renzo De Felice, Bologna, 1983, 164; Carlo Silvestri, *I responsabili della catastrofe italiana*, Milan, 1946, 202.

36. Scaroni, *Con Vittorio Emanuele*, 108–9.

37. Cantalupo, *Fu la Spagna*, 85 147–8; Tamaro, *Venti anni di storia*, III, 245.

38. *St Antony's Documents*, 329/112630

(11 Sept. 1935); *Documents français*, ser. 2, VII, 770, 863–4; Mureddu, *Il Quirinale,* 70; Adalberto di Savoia-Genova, Duca di Bergamo, *Mistica fascista in Africa orientale*, 35 (5 Feb. 1939).

39. D'Aroma, *Vent'anni insieme*, 231; Ojetti, *I taccuini*, 259; Mureddu, *Il Quirinale*, 68–9; Giovanni Artieri, *Il tempo della regina e appunti per una biografia di Vittorio Emanuele III*, Rome, 1950, 146.

40. FO, 371/10783/57 (2 Feb. 1925, Lampson); *Chamberlain Papers,* AC/55/216 (2 Feb. 1929, Graham); Paolucci, *Il mio picccolo mondo perduto*, 268; Pirelli, *Taccuini*, 127.

41. *La Settimana Incom Illustrata*, 3 Jan. 1959; St Antony's Documents, 132/036876 (9 Jan. 1941, Pescamona); Ciano, *Diario, 1937–1938*, 117, 232–3.

42. Mussolini, *Il tempo del bastone*, 29.

43. *Documents français*, ser. 2, III, 569; J. Blondel, *Au fil de la carrière*, Paris, 1960, 326.

44. Cantalupo, *Fu la Spagna*, 51.

45. Pierre Van Paassen, *Days of our years*, London, 1939, 292.

46. *Documents français*, ser. 2, VII, 861.

47. *Il Gran Consiglio del fascismo nei primi quindici anni dell'era fascista*, Bologna, 1938, 645.

48. Galeazzo Ciano, *Diario, 1937–1938*, Rocca S. Casciano, 1948, 149, 191, 211, 285–6, 300; Galeazzo Ciano, *Diario, 1939–1940*, Milan, 1946, 30, 67, 111, 115, 256.

49. Mussolini, *Opera*, XXIX, 75–7, 82; *Il Tempo*, 8 Mar. 1960, XVIII, 33 (De Vecchi).

50. Mussolini, *Il tempo del bastone*, 42; St Antony's Documents, 166/048944–5 (2 Apr. 1938, Medici); *Domenica del Corriere*, 31 July 1966 (King Umberto to Cavicchioli); *ibid.*, 14 Apr. 1970 (Susmel).

51. Federzoni, *Italia di ieri*, 168–75; Bergamini, *Il Re*, 37–8; Ottavio Zoppi, *Il senato nel 'ventennio'*, Milan, 1948, 32.

7 Alliance with Germany

1. *Domenica del Corriere*, 14 July 1984 (Artieri).

2. Mussolini, *Opera*, XXVIII, 252.

3. Benito Mussolini, *Corrispondenza inedita*, ed. D. Susmel, Milan, 1972, 166.

4. Pirelli, *Taccuini*, 206–7; Ciano, *Diario, 1937–1938*, 93.

5. *Die Tagebücher von Joseph Goebbels*, Munich, 1987, II, 426 (14 June 1933).

6. Friedelind Wagner and Page Cooper, *The royal family of Bayreuth*, London, 1948, 181–2.

7. William Phillips, *Ventures in diplomacy*, London, 1955, 112; Ciano, *Diario, 1937–1938*, 169.

8. *La Settimana Incom Illustrata*, 10 Jan. 1959 (King Umberto to Maurano).

9. Ettore Conti, *Dal taccuino di un borghese*, Cremona, 1946, 464; Cantalupo, *Fu la Spagna*, 85; Caviglia, *Diario,* 135; Gasparotto, *Diario*, 255; Mussolini, *Opera*, XXXIV, 409.

10. *Il Gazzettino*, Venice, 9 June 1938; *Nuova Antologia*, 1 July 1938, 99.

11. Rodd Papers, box 20 (17 Oct. 1919); St Antony's Documents, 263/pt.2/075001 (12 Sept. 1938); D'Aroma *Vent'anni insieme*, 267, 275; Hanotaux, *Les carnets,* 167; Meir Michaelis, *Mussolini and the Jews*, Oxford, 1978, 130; *The Contemporary Review*, London, Dec. 1938, 701.

12. St Antony's Documents, 263/075001 (12 Sept. 1938); Ciano, *Diario, 1937–1938*, 272; D'Aroma, *Vent'anni insieme*, 260.

13. *Documents français*, ser. 2, XIII, 680; DBFP, ser. 3, III, 348.

14. *Ibid.*

15. De Felice, *Mussolini*, IV, 8; *ABC*, 1 Jan. 1959, 14; *Nobiltà Della Stirpe*, Rome, Jan. 1938, 11, 32; T. Cianetti, *Memorie dal carcere di Verona*, ed. Renzo De Felice, Milan, 1983, 68; A. Zanetti, *Il dovere della monarchia*, Paris, 1927, 3–4, 18–20.

16. Bastianini, *Uomini, cose, fatti*, 243; Ciano, *Diario, 1939–1940,* 37.

17. André François-Ponçet, *Au Palais Farnèse: souvenirs d'une ambassade à Rome 1938–40*, Paris, 1961, 116; Ojetti, *I taccuini*, 430–1; Virginia Cowles, *Looking for trouble*, London, 1941, 257.

18. Rossi, *Trentatrè vicende Mussoliniane*, 131; Giuseppe Bottai, *Diario 1935–1944*, ed. G.B. Guerri, Milan, 1982, 133; Caviglia, *Diario*, 299.

19. Gianfranco Bianchi, *Perchè e come cadde il fascismo*, Milan, 1970, 178, 674.

20. FO, 371/22436/1 (13 Jan. 1938).

21. St Antony's Documents, 329/112630 (intercept dated 11 Sept. 1935); Ciano, *Diario, 1939–1940*, 38, 67, 211, 263.

22. *Gerarchia*, Milan, July 1938, 445–8 (Chimienti).

23. *Dizionario di politica*, III, 195 (Costamagna).
24. *Dottrina Fascista*, Milan, Oct. 1939, 411–12; *Manuale della camera dei Fasci*, Rome, 1939, 31–4.
25. Mussolini, *Opera*, XXXII, 241.
26. Grigore Gafencu, *Ultimi giorni dell' Europa: viaggio diplomatico nel 1939*, Milan, 1947, 138–9.
27. Spartaco Cannarsa, *Senato e camera nei loro rapporti e conflitti (1848–1948)*, Rome, n.d., 282; *Corriere della Sera*, 24 Mar. 1939; De Felice, *Mussolini*, IV, 224.
28. *Gazzetta Ufficiale*, Rome, 23 Mar. 1939; *Corriere della Sera*, 24 Mar. 1939; *Storia e Politica Internazionale*, Milan, 31 Mar. 1939, 7–10.
29. Federzoni, *Italia di ieri*, 245; Ciano, *Diario, 1939–1940*, 67; D'Aroma, *Vent'anni insieme*, 280.
30. Ciano, *Diario, 1939–1940*, 98: Gaetano Contini, *La valigia di Mussolini*, Milan, 1982, 95.
31. *Relazioni Internazionali*, Milan, 1 Apr. 1939, 247; D'Aroma, *Vent'anni insieme*, 277.
32. *DDI*, ser. 8, XII, 497–8 (ed. G. Vedovato and G. Rossini); M. Magistrati, *L'Italia a Berlino (1937–1939)*, Milan 1956, 383.
33. St Antony's Documents 274/080001 (11 July 1939, Mussolini to king); Pietro Badoglio, *L'Italia nella seconda guerra mondiale: memorie e documenti*, Milan, 1946, 30; Puntoni, *Parla Vittorio Emanuele*, 100; Ciano, *Diario, 1939–1940*, 16.
34. Crosa, *Diritto constituzionale*, Turin, 1937, 269; Mario Toscano, *Le origini del patto d'acciaio*, Florence, 1948, 199.
35. *American Historical Review*, New York, June 1968, 1414 (ed. Renzi); *Relazioni Internazionali*, 27 May 1939, 408.
36. *DBFP*, ser. 3, V, 130; Ciano, *Diario, 1939–1940*, 62, 105.
37. Avon Papers, 954/13/103 (31 July 1937, Graham).
38. *La Settimana Incom Illustrata*, 24 Jan. 1959 (King Umberto); D'Aroma, *Vent'anni insieme*, 265, 269, 280.
39. D'Aroma, *Mussolini segreto*, 399; Ciano, *Diario, 1937–1938*, 301.
40. *Senato, discussioni*, 28 Mar, 1935, 896.
41. Ludwig, *Leaders of Europe*, 332; De Begnac, *Palazzo Venezia*, 651; Felice Guarneri, *Battaglie economiche tra le due grandi guerre*, Milan, 1953, I, 435; Senise, *Quando ero capo della polizia*, 93–4; Leto, *Ovra*, 145–54.
42. Grandi, *Il mio paese*, 462; Grandi, *25 Luglio*, 181–2; S. Bertoldi, *Vittorio Emanuele III*, Turin, 1971, 388; *Daily Express*, London, 21 Feb. 1945, 21 (Grandi).
43. *Storia Contemporanea*, Bologna, Dec. 1983, 1059 (Grandi's diary).
44. William Phillips, *Ventures in diplomacy*, London, 1955, 128–9.
45. Mureddu, *Il Quirinale del re*, 94.
46. Cordell Hull, *The memoirs of Cordell Hull*, London, 1948, I, 661 (Phillips); Washington Archives, 760 c 62/987 (25 Aug. 1939, Phillips).
47. Richard Massock, *Italy from within*, London, 1943, 157; G. Nelson Page, *L'Americano di Roma*, Milan, 1950, 439, 570, 611.
48. Phillips, *Ventures in diplomacy*, 127–9.
49. Filippo Anfuso, *Roma Berlino, Salò: 1936–1945*, Milan, 1950, 123.
50. *DBFP*, ser. 3, VII, 93.
51. Mussolini, *Opera*, XXXV, 396; Ciano, *Diario, 1939–1940*, 142.
52. *Actes et documents du Saint Siège*, I, 261 (Bocchini); *DBFP*, ser. 3, VII, 136, 220.
53. *Stato e Diritto*, Rome, Nov. 1941, 423; Leto, *Ovra*, 185; St Antony's Documents, 238/036875 (Caviglia); Ciano, *Diario, 1939–1940*, 117; Luigi Salvatorelli and Giovanni Mira, *Storia d'Italia nel periodo fascista*, Turin, 1964, 1029.
54. Washington Archives, 121.840 (16 Mar. 1940, Welles to Sumner); Federzoni, *Italia di ieri*, 244; Grandi, *Mio paese*, 261–3; A. Giannini, *Io spia dell'ovra*, Rome, n.d., II, 37–9; Conti, *Dal taccuino di un borghese*, 673; Luigi Sturzo, *Italy and the new world order*, London, 1944, 133;
55. *DDI*, ser. 8, XIII, 203.
56. D'Aroma, *Vent'anni insieme*, 287.
57. FO, 371/23819 (9 Sept. 1939, Loraine).
58. Bastianini, *Uomini*, 224; D'Aroma, *Vent'anni insieme*, 288.
59. *La Settimana Incom Illustrata*, 2 Feb. 1960 (De Vecchi); Mureddu, *Il Quirinale*, 67.
60. *La Civiltà Cattolica*, Rome, 20 Jan. 1940, 153.

The End of the Monarchy

1 *Italy drifts into war*

1. Giacomo Carboni, *Memorie segrete 1935–1948*, Florence, 1955, 33.
2. FO, 371/24940 (19 Apr. 1940, Charles); Galeazzo Ciano, *Diario, 1939–1940*, Milan, 1946, 200, 232.

3. FO, 371/24939 (28 Mar. 1940).
4. Ciano, *Diario, 1939–1940*, 237.
5. *Dizionario di politica*, ed. PNF, Rome, 1940, III, 391.
6. *Domenica del Corriere*, Milan, 24 July 1966, 24–5 (King Umberto); *Storia Contemporanea*, Bologna, Apr. 1963, 335.
7. Nino Bolla, *Colloqui con Umberto II*, Rome, 1949, 105; *La Settimana Incom Illustrata*, Rome, 31 Jan. 1959, 22 (Umberto).
8. Giuseppe Bottai, *Diario 1935–1944*, ed. G.B. Guerri, Milan, 1982, 190; *Actes et documents du Saint Siège relatifs à la seconde guerre mondiale*, ed. P. Blet, R.A. Graham, A. Martini and B. Schneider, Rome, 1967, I, 417.
9. FO, 434/7/150 (11 Apr. 1940, Charles).
10. *DDI*, ser. 9, III, 576–9 (ed. G. Vedovato and P. Pastorelli); *ibid.*, ser. 9, IV, 495.
11. *Il Popolo d'Italia*, Milan, 7 Apr. 1940; *Corriere della Sera*, Milan, 7 Apr. 1940.
12. Ugo D'Andrea, *La fine del regno: grandezza e decadenza di Vittorio Emanuele III*, Turin, 1951, 318–19 (to Bergamini); Paolo Puntoni, *Parla Vittorio Emanuele III*, Milan, 1958, 290, 315.
13. *Domenica del Corriere*, 14 Aug. 1966.
14. Pietro Badoglio, *L'Italia nella seconda guerra mondiale: memorie e documenti*, Milan, 1946, 37; Puntoni, *Parla Vittorio Emanuele*, 290; *L'Europeo*, Milan, 15 Feb. 1968 (Queen Marie José to Trionfera).
15. *DDI*, ser. 9, III, 468: Aldo Garosci, *Storia dei fuorusciti*, Bari, 1953, 282: Piero Calamandrei, *Diario 1939–1945*, ed. G. Agosti, Florence, 1982, I, 225; Gianfranco Bianchi, *Perchè e come cadde il fascismo*, Milan, 1970, 178.
16. Alberto Bergamini, *Il Re Vittorio Emanuele III di fronte alla storia*, Turin, n.d., 41–2; *The Times*, London, 20 Apr. 1944 (King Umberto).
17. Ciano, *Diario, 1939–1940*, 273; Puntoni, *Parla Vittorio Emanuele*, 14–15.
18. Renzo De Felice, *Mussolini*, Turin, 1981, V, 776, 811; Dino Grandi, *25 Luglio: quarant'anni dopo*, Bologna, 1983, 31; (introduction by Renzo De Felice); Mario Missiroli, *Il fascismo e il colpo di stato*, Rocco S. Casciano, 1969, 39; Luigi Federzoni, *Italia di ieri per la storia di domani*, Milan, 1967, 247; L. Sturzo, *Italy and the new world order*, London, 1944, 133.
19. Enno von Rintelen, *Mussolini als Bundesgenosse: Erinnerungen des deutschen Militärattachés in Rom 1936–1943*, Tübingen, 1951, 82; *The memoirs of Field-Marshal Keitel*, London, 1965, 111; *Le testament politique de Hitler*, Paris, 1959, 101–2; Eugenio Dollmann, *Roma nazista*, Milan, 1951, 125; Mario Donosti, *Mussolini e l'Europa: la politica estera fascista*, Rome, 1945, 234; Leonardo Simoni, *Berlino: ambasciata d'Italia 1939–1943*, Rome, 1946, 85; *Trial of the major German war criminals before the international military tribunal*, Nuremberg, 1947–9, XV, 398 (Gen. Jodl).
20. Benito Mussolini, *Opera omnia*, Florence, 1959, XXIX, 252–3.
21. FO, 434/6/7006 (27 Dec. 1938, Perth); St Antony's Documents, 1/000249, 000264; *ibid.*, 274/080084; *Verbali delle riunioni tenute dal capo di Stato Maggiore Generale*, Rome, 1983, I, 38; Rodolfo Graziani, *Ho difeso la patria*, Cernusco, 1947, 179, 182; Puntoni, *Parla Vittorio Emanuele*, 290; Nino D'Aroma, *Vent' anni insieme: Vittorio Emanuele e Mussolini*, Rocca S. Casciano, 1957, 266, 283; Galeazzo Ciano, *Diario, 1937–1938*, Bologna, 1948, 93.
22. MacGregor Knox, *Mussolini unleashed, 1939–1941: politics and strategy in fascist Italy's last war*, Cambridge, 1982, 10; De Felice, *Mussolini*, V, 19; Giorgio Rochat, *L'esercito italiano da Vittorio Veneto a Mussolini*, Bari 1967, 204; Alberto Aquarone, *L'organizzazione dello stato totalitario*, Turin, 1965, 292; CAB, 21/978 (11 Apr. 1940, Charles); Richard Massock, *Italy from within*, London, 1943, 339.
23. Ciano, *Diario, 1939–1940*, 111.
24. Guido Leto, *Ovra, fascismo, antifascismo*, Rocca S. Casciano, 1952, 143; *Documents français*, ser.2, VII, 861; Cesare Rossi, *Mussolini com'era*, Rome, 1947, 130.
25. Filippo Anfuso, *Roma, Berlino, Salò*, Milan, 1950, 56–7.
26. Quirino Armellini, *La crisi dell'esercito*, Rome, 1945, 98.
27. Dino Grandi, *L'evitabile 'asse': memorie*, ed. Gianfranco Bianchi, Milan, 1984, 145; Enrico Caviglia, *Diario (Aprile 1925–Marzo 1945)*, Rome, 1952, 262, 567; Benedetto Croce, *Scritti e discorsi politici (1943–1947)*, Bari, 1963, I, 17; Federzoni, *Italia di ieri*, 247; Missiroli, *Il fascismo*, 39.
28. Ciano, *Diario, 1939–1940*, 276.

29. Mussolini, *Opera*, xxxii, 244.
30. *Domenica del Corriere*, 31 July 1966; *ibid.*, 21 July 1984.
31. *La Settimana Incom Illustrata*, 31 Jan. 1959, 22 (King Umberto to Maurano); Nino D'Aroma, *Mussolini segreto*, Rocca S. Casciano, 1958, 227; D'Aroma, *Vent'anni insieme*, 304–5; Carlo Sforza, *L'Italia dal 1914 al 1944 quale io la vidi*, Rome, 1945, 159 (Acquarone).
32. *DDI*, ser. 9, iv, 496; Graziani, *Ho difeso la patria*, 200.
33. Giuseppe Gola, *L'Italia nella II^a guerra mondiale*, Milan, 1959, 381; Alberto Pirelli, *Taccuini 1922–1943*, ed. D. Barbone, Bologna, 1984, 379; Puntoni, *Parla Vittorio Emanuele*, 16, 19, 88.
34. Gioacchino Volpe, *L'Italia che fu: come un italiano la vide, sentì, amò*, Milan, 1960, 43–4.
35. Ciano, *Diario, 1939–1940*, 295.
36. St Antony's Documents 2/000867 (23 Aug. 1940, Vittorio Emanuele to Mussolini); Bianchi, *Perchè e come cadde il fascismo*, 185; Puntoni, *Parla Vittorio Emanuele*, 17.
37. *Accademia Reale d'Italia: annuario 1940*, Rome, 143–5, 154 (24 Nov. 1940, Crocco); *Nazione Militare*, Rome, Oct. 1940, 606 (Varanini).
38. Adèle Cambria, *Maria José*, Milan, 1966, 73; Quirino Armellini, *Diario di guerra: nove mesi al comando supremo*, Cernusco, 1946, 91; Ciano, *Diario, 1939–1940*, 294.
39. Giacomo Zanussi, *Guerra e catastrofe d'Italia*, Rome, 1945, i, 24.
40. C. Matteini, *Ordini alla stampa*, Rome, 1945, 114.
41. Washington Archives: microfilm, T.821 /IT/1122a/125/289; Jo Di Benigno, *Occasioni mancate*, Rome, 1945, 62.
42. Anfuso, *Roma, Berlino, Salò*, 170–1; Armellini, *Diario*, 174–7, 183, 239; Puntoni, *Parla Vittorio Emanuele*, 34 (Gen. Amè), 38 (Gen. Hazon); A.S. Monghini, *Dal decennale alla catastrofe*, Milan, 1954, 274–5; Simoni, *Berlino ambasciata*, 190–2.
43. Gorla, *Italia nella guerra*, 94–5.
44. *Ibid.*, 169; Bottai, *Diario 1935–1944*, 239; Puntoni, *Parla Vittorio Emanuele*, 31–2.
45. Carmine Senise, *Quando ero capo della polizia, 1940–1943*, Rome, 1946, 39; Caviglia, *Diario*, 326–7; Marcello Soleri, *Memorie*, Turin, 1949, 332.
46. Ciano, *Diario, 1941–1943*, 13.
47. Puntoni, *Parla Vittorio Emanuele*, 34.

2 The regime disintegrates

1. Silvio Bertoldi, *Vittorio Emanuele III*, Turin, 1971, 414–15.
2. Giuseppe Bastianini, *Uomini, cose, fatti: memorie di un ambasciatore*, Milan, 1959, 217.
3. Armellini, *Diario*, 265–6.
4. Anfuso, *Roma, Berlino, Salò*, 174.
5. Caviglia, *Diario*, 326–7.
6. Dino Grandi, *Il mio paese: ricordi autobiografici*, ed. Renzo De Felice, Bologna, 1985, 609–10; Pirelli, *Taccuini*, 296.
7. *Gazzetta Ufficiale*, Rome, 3 Feb. 1929.
8. *Daily Telegraph*, London, 23 Apr. 1941 (John Whitaker of *Chicago Daily News*).
9. Mussolini, *Opera*, xxiii, 409.
10. Grandi, *L'evitabile 'asse'*, 128; D'Aroma, *Vent'anni insieme*, 314; Pirelli, *Taccuini*, 290; Calamandrei, *Diario* i, 345; Puntoni, *Parla Vittorio Emanuele*, 38, 50.
11. Ennio Di Nolfo, *Vaticano e Stati Uniti 1939–1952: dalle carte di Myron C. Taylor*, Milan, 1978, 53, 208; D'Aroma, *Vent'anni insieme*, 315–16.
12. Simoni, *Berlino ambasciata*, 256; Ciano, *Diario, 1939–1940*, 111; W. Warlimont, *Im Hauptquartier der deutschen Wehrmacht 1939–1945*, Frankfurt, 1962, 323.
13. Anfuso, *Roma, Berlino, Salò*, 171; Galeazzo Ciano, *Diario, 1941–1943*, Milan, 1946, 37; Puntoni, *Parla Vittorio Emanuele*, 74.
14. *Ibid.*, 39; *Verbali . . . Stato Maggiore Generale*, ii, 19.
15. Puntoni, *Parla Vittorio Emanuele*, 61, 65; Ciano, *Diario, 1941–1943*, 72; FO, 371/ 28/10578 (16 Oct. 1941, Stronski).
16. Puntoni, *Parla Vittorio Emanuele*, 73, 77, 84.
17. Gorla, *Italia nella guerra*, 265; Bottai, *Diario 1935–1944*, 295; *Actes du Saint Siège*, iv, 319.
18. Massock, *Italy from within*, 341; Caviglia, *Diario*, 350, 354, 359, 366.
19. Senise, *Quando ero capo della polizia*, 141–3.
20. Giuseppe Bottai, *Diario 1944–1948*, ed. G.B. Guerri, Milan, 1988, 495; Bianchi, *Perchè e come cadde il fascismo*, 349–51; Grandi, *25 Luglio*, 191–2; Ciano, *Diario, 1941–1943*, 122.
21. *La Settimana Incom Illustrata*, 14 Feb. 1959, 20; Puntoni, *Parla Vittorio Emanuele*, 106–7.
22. Enzo Galbiati, *Il 25 Luglio e la M.V.S.N.*, Milan, 1950, 175–7; Ciano, *Diario, 1939–1940*, 221.
23. Avon Papers, 954/13/238 (14 Jan. 1943,

Eden); *FRUS*, 1943, ii, 320–1.

24. *Actes du Saint Siège*, vii, 155–6; Pirelli, *Taccuini*, 374, 381–2: Luigi Gasparotto, *Diario di un deputato: cinquant'anni di vita politica italiana*, Milan, 1945, 308; Calamandrei, *Diario*, ii, 78–9, 90.

25. Bottai, *Diario 1935–1944*, 339; Pirelli, *Taccuini*, 376, 381 (Cini).

26. *Akten zur deutschen auswärtigen Politik 1918–1945*, Göttingen, 1969, E/4/148.

27. Calamandrei, *Diario*, ii, 85; Puntoni, *Parla Vittorio Emanuele*, 88.

28. Gorla, *Italia nella guerra*, 325.

29. *Actes du Saint Siège*, vii, 116–17; Pirelli, *Taccuini*, 379; Matteo Mureddu, *Il Quirinale del re*, Milan, 1977, 91.

30. Bastianini, *Uomini, cose, fatti*, 215; Ciano, *Diario, 1941–1943*, 220; Puntoni, *Parla Vittorio Emanuele*, 103–4.

31. Countess of Listowel, *Crusader in the secret war*, London, 1952, 113–16.

32. *FRUS*, 1943, ii, 315–16; *Clio*, Rome, Apr. 1965, 320 (Toscano).

33. *Akten zur deutschen auswärtigen Politik*, E/4/150; *ibid.*, E/5/210; Bastianini, *Uomini, cose, fatti*, 215.

34. Ugo Cavallero, *Diario 1940–1943*, ed. G. Bucciante, Cassino, 1984, 326–7, 354.

35. *L'Europeo*, 15 Feb. 1969, 16–17 (Queen Marie José to Trionfera); *ibid.*, 22 Feb. 1968, 12–14; Cambria, *Maria José*, 88–9; *Il Politico*, Pavia, Dec. 1979, 677–80 (Donatella Bolech Cecchi, quoting Sir Miles Lampson).

36. Silvio Scaroni, *Con Vittorio Emanuele III*, Milan, 1954, 38; Puntoni, *Parla Vittorio Emanuele*, 59; Mureddu, *Il Quirinale*, 56.

37. Gasparotto, *Diario*, 308; Calamandrei, *Diario*, ii, 107.

38. Pirelli, *Taccuini*, 402 (Acquarone).

39. Guido Leto, *Polizia segreta in Italia*, Naples, 1961, 83; Bianchi, *Perchè e come cadde il fascismo*, 259–60; Puntoni, *Parla Vittorio Emanuele*, 289.

40. Gorla, *Italia nella guerra*, 403; Cavallero, *Diario*, 672; *Akten zur deutschen auswärtigen Politik*, E/4/535–6.

41. Grandi, *25 Luglio*, 315–16; Rintelen, *Mussolini als Bundesgenosse*, 199; Cambria, *Maria José*, 95 (Bergamini); Leto, *Ovra*, 250.

42. Bianchi, *Perchè e come cadde il fascismo*, 778.

43. *Ibid.*, 782; Gorla, *Italia nella guerra*, 397–8; Puntoni, *Parla Vittorio Emanuele*, 121–2, 125; Pirelli, *Taccuini*, 414–15; Caviglia, *Diario*, 402–3; Guido

Cassinelli, *Appunti sul 25 luglio*, Rome, 1944, 16.

44. Caviglia, *Diario*, 414.

45. Vatican Archives, Segretario di Stato, Italia, 1302 s.nr. (3 May 1943, to Cardinal Maglione)

46. St Antony's Documents, 161/046637–8 (24 June 1943, Cini); *Actes du Saint Siège*, vii, 331–5; *Storia Contemporanea*, Dec. 1983, 1079; Mussolini, *Opera*, xxxi, 165; M. Kallay, *Hungarian premier: a personal account*, London, 1954, 158.

47. St Antony's Documents, 53/026454–5 (1 Apr. 1943, Farinacci); Senise, *Quando ero capo della polizia*, 171–2.

48. *Ibid.*, 113–15, 120; Mario Caracciolo di Feroleto, *E poi? La tragedia dell'esercito italiano*, Rome, 1946, 105; Armellini, *Diario*, 103; Bottai, *Diario 1935–1944*, 320; Giannini, *Io spia dell'ovra*, ii, 30; Q. Navarra, *Memorie del cameriere di Mussolini*, ed. Leo Longanesi and Indro Montanelli, Milan, 1946, 134.

3   Mussolini is dismissed

1. Alessandro Lessona, *Memorie: al governo con Mussolini*, Rome, 1963, 403–4 (17 Apr. 1943).

2. *Akten zur deutschen auswärtigen Politik*, E/6/360.

3. *L'Europeo*, 18 Jan. 1948 (Ansaldo).

4. Pirelli, *Taccuini*, 433; Gasparotto, *Diario*, 307.

5. *Ibid.*, 308; *La Settimana Incom Illustrata*, 10 Jan. 1959 (King Umberto to Maurano).

6. *L'Europeo*, 22 Feb. 1968 (Queen Marie José to Trionfera); Cambria, *Maria José*, 100–2.

7. *Nuova Antologia*, Feb. 1956, 187 (Einaudi); Bianchi, *Perchè e come cadde il fascismo*, 752 (Gallarati Scotti); Lessona, *Memorie*, 405.

8. Puntoni, *Parla Vittorio Emanuele*, 77, 132, 135, 352; D'Aroma, *Mussolini segreto*, 402.

9. Puntoni, *Parla Vittorio Emanuele*, 148.

10. Ruggero Zangrandi, *1943: 25 Luglio – 8 Settembre*, Milan, 1964, 900–2; Grandi, *Il mio paese*, 626–8; *Storia Contemporanea*, Dec. 1983, 1059–60.

11. Ivanoe Bonomi, *Diario di un anno*, Cernusco, 1947, 4–7; *Il Mondo*, Milan, 23 Apr. 1949.

12. Soleri, *Memorie*, 231–5, 240; Bonomi, *Diario*, 9; *Actes du Saint Siège*, vii, 422.

13. *Ibid.*, v, 116; *ibid.*, vii, 433–4.
14. *Ibid.*, vii, 318.
15. *Ibid.*, vii, 594; Di Nolfo, *Vaticano e Stati Uniti,* 270 (quoting Tittmann).
16. *Actes du Saint Siège*, vii, 319–20; *ibid.*, vii, 414–15; Pirelli, *Taccuini,* 422.
17. *Actes du Saint Siège*, vii, 222, 362, 365, 416–17; *L'Europeo*, 18 Jan. 1948.
18. Grandi, *L'evitabile 'asse'*, 128; Galbiati, *Il 25 Luglio*, 182; Mussolini, *Opera*, xxxi, 196.
19. *La Settimana Incom Illustrata*, 7 Feb. 1959.
20. Puntoni, *Parla Vittorio Emanuele*, 138–9.
21. Giuseppe Castellano, *Come firmai l'armistizio di Cassibile*, Milan, 1945, 48; Bianchi, *Perchè e come cadde il fascismo*, 777.
22. Puntoni, *Parla Vittorio Emanuele*, 136.
23. Cassinelli, *Appunti*, 23–4, 29; *L'Europeo*, 22 Feb. 1968; Calamandrei, *Diario*, ii, 117.
24. Bonomi, *Diario*, 22; *Trent'anni di storia italiana (1915–1945)*, ed. F. Antonicelli, Turin, 1961, 326 (Leopoldo Piccardi).
25. Puntoni, *Parla Vittorio Emanuele*, 139–40; Galbiati, *Il 25 Luglio*, 214.
26. Senise, *Quando ero capo della polizia*, 196, 199–200; Giacomo Acerbo, *Fra due plotoni di esecuzione*, Rocca S. Casciano, 1968, 497; Luigi Marchesi, *Come siamo arrivati a Brindisi*, Milan, 1969, 40; Giuseppe Castellano, *La guerra continua*, Milan, 1963, 37.
27. Mussolini, *Opera*, xxxi, 204.
28. Grandi, *25 Luglio*, 270.
29. Carlo Scorza, *La notte del Gran Consiglio*, ed. Gianfranco Bianchi, Milan, 1968, 80; Bottai, *Diario 1935–1944*, 418; Galbiati, *Il 25 Luglio*, 241.
30. Mussolini, *Opera*, xxxvii, 164; Scorza, *La notte*, 185, 192.
31. Giovanni Dolfin, *Con Mussolini nella tragedia*, Cernusco, 1949, 80; Graziani, *Ho difeso la patria*, 328–9.
32. *Panorama*, Milan, 5 Dec. 1983, 152 (De Felice).
33. T. Torella di Romagnano, *Villa Iela*, Cernusco, 1948, 75; Mureddu, *Il Quirinale*, 86; CAB, 122/852 (5 Aug. 1983, D'Ajeta).
34. Puntoni, *Parla Vittorio Emanuele*, 144–5, 148; Bolla, *Colloqui con Umberto*, 123–4; *Meridiano d'Italia*, Milan, 6 Apr. 1947.
35. *Trent'anni di storia*, 326–7 (Piccardi).
36. Washington Archives: microfilm, T.821/IT/4531/355/131.

4   The armistice

1. Puntoni, *Parla Vittorio Emanuele*, 148; Badoglio, *L'Italia nella seconda guerra mondiale*, 70–1.
2. St Antony's Documents, 3/001260–002402.
3. Mussolini, *Opera*, xxxiv, 358.
4. Dollmann, *Roma nazista*, 276; F-K. von Plehwe, *The end of an alliance: Rome's defection from the axis in 1943,* London, 1971, 125; W. Hoettl, *The secret front: the story of nazi political espionage*, London, 1954, 232–3; Simoni, *Berlino ambasciata*, 378.
5. Francesco Rossi, *Come arrivammo all' armistizio*, Cernusco, 1946, 293; Marchesi, *Come siamo arrivati a Brindisi*, 49; Harry Butcher, *Three years with Eisenhower*, London, 1946, 4–6.
6. Castellano, *Come firmai*, 78; Zanussi, *Guerra e catastrofe*, ii, 40, 72, 80; Ivan Palermo, *Storia di un armistizio*, Milan, 1967, 436; Giacomo Carboni, *L'armistizio e la difesa di Roma*, Rome, 1945, 23; Giacomo Carboni, *L'Italia tradita dall' armistizio alla pace*, Rome, 1947, 77–8.
7. Grandi, *25 Luglio*, 270, 369.
8. Bonomi, *Diario*, 53–4.
9. *Il Ponte*, Florence, July 1953, 918 (Piccardi).
10. Puntoni, *Parla Vittorio Emanuele*, 147.
11. Avon Papers, 954/13B/268 (24 July 1943); Martin Gilbert, *Winston S. Churchill*, London, 1986, vii, 457.
12. Grandi, *25 Luglio*, 377; Puntoni, *Parla Vittorio Emanuele*, 150.
13. Washington Archives: microfilm, T.821/144/1223 (5 Aug. 1943, diary of Ambrosio); Guariglia, *Ricordi*, 584–5.
14. *Ibid.*, 617, 622; *Akten zur deutschen auswärtigen Politik*, E/6/360; St Antony's Documents, 2/000653.
15. Guariglia, *Ricordi*, 596–7, 606; Vanna Vailati, *L'armistizio e il regno del sud*, Milan, 1969, 132; CAB, 122/852 (5 Aug. 1943, Campbell).
16. *London Gazette*, supplement for 12 June 1950, 2880–1; FO, 898/168 (19 Oct. 1943, Crossman).
17. *Brassey's Naval Annual*, Portsmouth, 1948, 347–8; Hoettl, *The secret front*, 234; C. Amè, *Guerra segreta in Italia 1940–1943*, Rome, 1954, 182–4.
18. Avon Papers, 954/13/268 (25 July 1943).
19. F. Maugeri, *From the ashes of disgrace*, New York, 1948, 165; Soleri, *Memorie*, 255–8.

20. Bastianini, *Uomini, cose, fatti*, 201–6.
21. Mureddu, *Il Quirinale*, 92; Grandi, *25 Luglio*, 315; David Ellwood, *Italy 1943–1945*, Leicester, 1985, 53; Puntoni, *Parla Vittorio Emanuele*, 153, 162.
22. Caviglia, *Diario*, 424; Bottai, *Diario 1935–1944*, 430 (Visconti di Modrone).
23. Badoglio, *Italia nella seconda guerra mondiale*, 74–5.
24. Guariglia, *Ricordi*, 688; Puntoni, *Parla Vittorio Emanuele*, 154.
25. Gorla, *Italia nella guerra*, 433–4; Grandi, *25 Luglio*, 434.
26. Attilio Tamaro, *Due anni di storia, 1943–1945*, Rome, 1948, I, 309–10; Mussolini, *Il tempo del bastone*, 26.
27. D'Aroma, *Vent'anni insieme*, 369 (Gen. Zingales); Carboni, *Memorie*, 240; Grandi, *L'evitabile 'asse'*, 116.
28. Guariglia, *Ricordi*, 645.
29. Maugeri, *From the ashes*, 166–7; Amè, *Guerra segreta*, 188.
30. Avon Papers, 954/13/428 (27 Aug. 1943, Campbell); CAB, 122/856 (31 Aug. 1943, Eisenhower).
31. Avon Papers, 954/13/457 (3 Sept. 1943, Eden); FO, 660/362 (27 Sept. 1943, Grandi); Grandi, *25 Luglio*, 436–8; Graziani, *Ho difeso la patria*, 304 (quoting Grandi); Aldo Castellani, *Tra microbi e re*, Milan, 1961, 156–7; Guariglia, *Ricordi*, 744–5.
32. S. Westphal, *Heer in Fesseln: aus den Papieren des Stabschefs von Rommel, Kesselring und Rundstedt*, Bonn, 1950, 223; Warlimont, *Im Hauptquartier der Wehrmacht*, 361.
33. *Brassey's Naval Annual*, 1948, 356.
34. Castellano, *Come firmai*, 213; Palermo, *Storia di un armistizio*, 114.
35. *London Gazette*, 12 June 1950, 2888–9 (Gen. Alexander); Alfred Wagg and David Brown, *No spaghetti for breakfast*, London, 1943, 7.
36. Robert D. Murphy, *Diplomat among warriors*, London, 1964, 236–7.
37. Rossi, *Come arrivammo all'armistizio*, 126–7; Castellano, *Come firmai*, 125–6; Guariglia, *Ricordi*, 669; Carboni, *Memorie*, 242.
38. E. Canevari, *Graziani mi ha detto*, Rome, 1947, 41.
39. Castellano, *Come firmai*, 128–31; Pirelli, *Taccuini*, 471–2.
40. Palermo, *Storia di un armistizio*, 132.
41. *Ibid.*, 357 (Simonetti), 399 (Ambrosio); Ruggero Zangrandi, *1943: l'8 Settembre*, Milan, 1967, 71.
42. Rudolf Rahn, *Ambasciatore di Hitler a Vichy e a Salò*, Milan, 1950, 265–6; E.F. Moellhausen, *La carta perdente*, Rome, 1948, 55; *Akten zur deutschen auswärtigen Politik*, E/6/472.
43. Palermo, *Storia di un armistizio*, 451 (Badoglio).
44. Zanussi, *Guerra e catastrofe*, II, 134–5; *Studi Storici*, Apr. 1972, 317 (Pinzani); Pieri and Rochat, *Badoglio*, 817; Albert N. Garland, and H.M. Smyth, *The Mediterranean theatre of operations*, Washington, 1965, 513.
45. Palermo, *Storia di un armistizio*, 144 (Zanussi); *Storia Illustrata*, Milan, Sept. 1982, 30 (Gen. Utili); Zangrandi, *1943: l'8 Settembre*, 115 (Gen. Sorice); *L'Italia dei quarantacinque giorni: studio e documenti*, Milan, 1969, 157.
46. *La marina italiana nella seconda guerra mondiale*, ed. G. Fioravanzo, Rome, 1971, XV, 8; Castellano, *La guerra continua*, 159; Palermo, *Storia di un armistizio*, 157, 181, 410; Lussu, *La Difesa di Roma*, 212–13, 319.
47. Alexander Papers, WO 214/5/345 (31 Aug. 1943); Castellani, *Come firmai*, 142; Zanussi, *Guerra e catastrofe*, II, 109; Murphy, *Diplomat*, 236; Bonomi, *Diario*, 78.
48. Carboni, *Memorie*, 274; Rossi, *Come arrivammo all'armistizio*, 243.
49. Carboni, *Memorie*, 283–4; Palermo, *Storia di un armistizio*, 152 (Marchesi), 225–6, 229, 417, 419 (Gen. Pirzio Biroli); Ruggero Zangrandi, *L'Italia tradita, 8 Settembre 1943*, Milan, 1971, 388 (Sandalli).
50. Palermo, *Storia di un armistizio*, 152, 451 (Badoglio); Marchesi, *Come siamo arrivati a Brindisi*, 100–3; Carboni, *Memorie*, 285; Puntoni, *Parla Vittorio Emanuele*, 162.
51. *Otto Settembre 1943: l'armistizio italiano 40 anni dopo*, ed. Ministero della Difesa, Rome, 1985, 147–8 (G. Galuppini); G. Santoro, *L'aeronautica italiana nella seconda guerra mondiale*, Milan, 1957, II, 569; Zangrandi, *1943: 25 luglio*, 379.

5   The flight from Rome

1. B.H. Liddell Hart, *The other side of the hill: Germany's generals 1939–1945*, London, 1948, 362–4 (Gen. Kesselring); Westphal, *Heer in Fesseln*, 149–50; Dollmann, *Roma nazista*, 257 (Gen. Student); Eugenio Dollmann, *The Interpreter*,

London, 1967, 262–4.

2. Castellano, *Come firmai*, 199 (Eisenhower); Caracciolo di Feroleto, *E poi?*, 175–9; Ettore Musco, *La verità sull'8 Settembre*, Milan, 1965, 161; Pieri and Rochat, *Badoglio*, 812–13.

3. Bonomi, *Diario*, 85, 88, 98–9, 104; Vailati, *L'armistizio*, 215–16; Castellano, *Come firmai*, 177.

4. Carlo De Risio, *Generali, servizi segreti e fascismo*, Milan, 1978, 227–30; Castellano, *La guerra continua*, 127, 139; Maugeri, *From the ashes*, 182; Musco, *La verità*, 55, 150; Renzo Trionfera, *Valzer di marescialli: 8 Settembre 1943*, Milan, 1979, 157.

5. Kenneth Strong, *Intelligence at the top*, London, 1968, 117–18; P. Monelli, *Roma 1943*, Milan, 1979, 353 (Taylor), 368–9 (Alexander); Castellano, *Come firmai*, 225–6 (Bedell Smith); Murphy, *Diplomat*, 242; Samuel Eliot Morison, *History of United States naval operations in World War II*, Boston, 1954, IX, 241; David Hunt, *A don at war*, London, 1966, 225; Richard Lamb, *Ghosts of peace, 1935–1945*, London, 1987, 204; *Infantry Journal*, Washington, Aug. 1946, 26 (Gen. Gavin).

6. Zangrandi, *1943: 25 Luglio*, 380.

7. Avon Papers, 954/13/492 (10 Sept. 1943).

8. Raffaele Cadorna, *La riscossa: dal 25 luglio alla liberazione*, Milan, 1948, 52; Rossi, *Come arrivammo all' armistizio*, 414; Musco, *La verità*, 107; Zanussi, *Guerra e catastrofe* (1st ed. 1945), II, 225.

9. Puntoni, *Parla Vittorio Emanuele*, 163.

10. Soleri, *Memorie*, 233; Grandi, *Il mio paese*, 621.

11. Carboni, *L'armistizio*, 93; Soleri, *Memorie*, 273.

12. Mussolini, *Opera*, XXXII, 11, 253; St Antony's Documents, 270/078597-8 (to Ellwangen); G. Zachariae, *Mussolini si confessa*, Cernusco, 1948, 68.

13. CAB, 122/857 (18 Sept. 1943, quoting Badoglio); Tamaro, *Due anni di storia,* I, 453, 587; ibid., II, 107.

14. *FRUS*, 1943, II, 438; D. Soprano, *L' ultimo colloquio con Vittorio Emanuele*, Genoa, 1956, 8; Filippo Caracciolo, *Diario di Napoli '43–'44*, Florence, 1964, 91.

15. Puntoni, *Parla Vittorio Emanuele*, 171–4.

16. Harold Macmillan, *War diaries*, London, 1984, 235; Garland and Smyth, *The Mediterranean theatre*, 549; Croce, *Scritti e discorsi politici*, I, 355.

17. Harry L. Coles and Albert K. Weinberg, *Civil affairs: soldiers become governors*, Washington, 1964, 428.

18. Alexander Papers, WO 214/5/405 (16 Sept. 1943); Murphy, *Diplomat*, 247; Macmillan, *War diaries*, 219–20; FO, 660/381 (1 Nov. 1943).

19. *Arturo Toscanini dal 1915 al 1946: mostra*, ed. Harvey Sachs, Turin, 1987, 107; Bonomi, *Diario*, 106; Soleri, *Memorie*, 309–10.

20. Bolla, *Colloqui*, 20, 135; *Storia Contemporanea*, Sept. 1975, 600 (Mazzetti); Vailati, *L'armistizio*, 226–31; A. Consiglio, *Vita di Vittorio Emanuele III*, Milan, 1950, 243.

21. Nino Bolla, *Il segreto di due re*, Milan, 1951, 37.

22. Puntoni, *Parla Vittorio Emanuele*, 187–8.

23. *Ibid.*, 176–7; CAB, 122/857 (30 Sept. 1943, Badoglio); *Otto Settembre*, 194–5 (Bianchi).

24. FO, 660/362 (28 Sept. 1943, Macmillan).

25. PREM, 3/243/650 (3 Nov. 1943); *ibid.*, 3/242/8 (6 Nov. 1943); FO, 371/43909/6 (22 Dec. 1943, Caccia); Macmillan, *War diaries*, 276, 282, 445; *Storia Contemporanea*, Dec. 1976, 848; *ibid.*, Feb. 1981, 84, 129 (De Leonardis).

26. Benedetto Croce, *Storiografia e idealità morale*, Bari, 1950, 86.

27. Croce, *Scritti e discorsi politici*, I, 17, 19, 25, 28–9, 43–4; FO, 660/381 (31 Oct. 1943, Macmillan).

28. *Ibid*; Avon Papers, 954/13/566 (8 Oct. 1943, Eden); Livio Zeno, *Ritratto di Carlo Sforza*, Florence, 1975, 411.

29. *FRUS*, 1943, II, 415-18; Coles and Weinberg, *Civil affairs*, 431–3; Puntoni, *Parla Vittorio Emanuele*, 180–3; Benigno, *Occasioni mancate*, 218.

30. War Museum Library, MM 22 (undated); FO, 371/43090/761 (23 Feb. 1944).

31. Zeno, *Sforza*, 438 (20 Dec. 1943); *The Times*, London, 1 Dec. 1943.

6 The monarchy under attack

1. FO, 371/43791/50 (25 Jan. 1944, Macfarlane).

2. A. Omodeo, *Per la riconquista della libertà*, Naples, 1944, 46, 55; Croce, *Scritti*, I, 18; Soleri, *Memorie*, 299; Gaime Pintor, *Il sangue d'Europa, (1939–1943)*, ed. V. Gerratana, Turin, 1966, 167.

3. WO, 32/11463 (13 Jan. 1944, Macmillan).

4. PREM, 3/243/8/607 (22 Oct. 1943, Churchill); Avon Papers, 954/14/41 (14

Feb. 1944, Eden).

5. *FRUS*, 1944, III, 1007, 1016, 1020; FO, 371/43090/115–16 (16 Feb. 1944, Churchill).
6. Bonomi, *Diario*, 140–1.
7. Macmillan, *War diaries*, 270 (Croce); Croce, *Scritti*, I, 44; FO, 371/43090/38 (4 Feb. 1944, Eden); *ibid.*, 660/377 (16 Dec. 1943, Caccia quoting Reber).
8. WO, 204/356 (18 Feb. 1944, Macfarlane); FO, 660/381 (23 Jan. 1944, Rospigliosi).
9. *Ibid.*, (31 Oct. 1943, Macmillan); Zeno, *Sforza*, 437.
10. FO, 371/43791/71 (Feb. 1944, Macfarlane); Giulio Andreotti, *Lives*, London, 1988, 3; Croce, *Scritti*, I, 339.
11. FO, 660/399 (22 Nov. 1943, Capt. Manley).
12. Croce, *Scritti*, I, 72, 267.
13. FO, 371/43911/68260 (21 Feb. 1944, Macfarlane); Avon Papers, 954/14/53 (22 Feb. 1944, Macmillan).
14. Palmiro Togliatti, *Opere*, ed. F. Andreucci and P. Spriano, Rome, 1979, IV, part 2, 339–40, 496–8.
15. WO, 204/356 (3 Apr. 1944, Macfarlane).
16. *Trent'anni di storia italiana*, ed. Franco Antonicelli, 370 375 (Togliatti).
17. *FRUS*, 1944, III, 1099.
18. *Ibid.*, 1098–9; Murphy, *Diplomat*, 252; Puntoni, *Parla Vittorio Emanuele*, 218–20.
19. FO, 371/43911 (17 Apr. 1944, Macmillan); Italicus (E. Saini), *Storia segreta di un mese di regno*, Rome, 1947, 31; A. degli Espinosa, *Il regno del sud: 8 Settembre 1943 – 4 Giugno 1944*, Rome, 1946, 334.
20. Maurizio Ferrara, *Conversando con Togliatti*, Rome, 1954, 331.
21. FO, 371/43793/245 (7 June 1944, Charles, quoting the king); WO, 204/356 (22 Apr. 1944, Macfarlane); *FRUS*, 1944, III, 1103.
22. FO, 371/43911 (17 Apr. 1944, Macmillan).
23. Grandi, *25 Luglio*, 481.
24. War Museum Library, MM 22 (22 Apr. 1944, Sforza to Macfarlane); *FRUS*, 1944, III, 1104.
25. *Daily Express*, London, 15 Apr. 1944.
26. FO, 371/43911 (19 Apr. 1944, Charles).
27. *The Times*, 20 Apr. 1944 (C.D. Lumby).
28. WO, 204/356 (12 May 1944, Macfarlane); FO, 371/43945/135 (26 May 1944, PWB).
29. *The Times*, 15 May 1944.

30. FO, 371/43911/20 (30 Apr. 1944, Sprigge); Benedetto Croce, *Due anni di vita politica italiana 1946–1947*, Bari, 1948, 34–5; Benedetto Croce, *Pagine politiche*, Bari, 1945, 91; Croce, *Scritti*, I, 75–6, 81, 324–7.
31. FO, 371/43911/115–20 (6 May 1944, Charles).
32. Torella, *Villa Iela*, 78–9.
33. Murphy, *Diplomat*, 253.
34. FO, 371/43793/165 (6 June 1944, Macfarlane).
35. Avon Papers, 954/14/222 (August 1944, Eden); PREM, 3/242/8 (10 Mar. 1944, Churchill).

7   Umberto II

1. *Daily Express*, 15 Apr. 1944.
2. *Domenica del Corriere*, 3 July 1966.
3. Croce, *Scritti*, I, 319.
4. *Ibid.*, 339; *Corriere della Sera*, 6 Jan. 1960 (Barzini).
5. Franco Garofalo, *Un anno al Quirinale*, Cernusco, 1947, 157; Mureddu, *Il Quirinale*, 210; Macmillan, *War diaries*, 645.
6. FO, 371/43793/245 (7 June 1944, Charles).
7. *Ibid.* (10 June 1944, Charles).
8. FO 371/43815/153, 172, 174 (19 Apr. and 10 June 1944, Churchill); Llewellyn Woodward, *British foreign policy in the second world war*, London, 1971, II, 543.
9. FO, 371/43797/136 (25 Sept. 1944, Charles); Gilbert, *Churchill*, VII, 994.
10. FO, 371/43795 (28 June 1944, Charles).
11. FO, 371/43797/136 (25 Sept. 1944, Charles).
12. Di Nolfo, *Vaticano e Stati Uniti*, 281 (Dec. 1943, Tardini); FO, 371/43913/306 (6 Oct. 1944, Osborne).
13. *New York Times*, 1 Nov. 1944 (Herbert Matthews); M. Vinciguerra, *Il fascismo visto da un solitario*, Florence, 1963, 92; FO, 371/43799/112, 148–50, 155–6.
14. FO, 371/43797 (25 Sept. 1944, Charles).
15. Gilbert, *Churchill*, VII, 994; Croce, *Scritti*, I, 70–1.
16. FO, 371/43797/188 (20 Sept. 1944, Maj. Mott-Radclyffe).
17. *Ibid.* (30 Aug. 1944, Hall).
18. *Ibid.* (24 Sept. 1944, Charles).
19. WO, 204/2765 (2 Sept. 1944, Admiral Stone); *Nuova Rivista Storica*, Milan, May 1960, 410 (Pieri); Vanna Vailati, *La storia nascosta 1943–1944*, Turin, 1986, 412–13.
20. Giovanni Artieri, *Il re: colloqui con Umberto II*, Milan, 1959, 354.

21. *Ibid.*, 237–9.
22. WO, 204/9832 (Nov. 1944, Gen. Infante); *ibid.*, 204/9844 (3 May 1945, Maj. Quayle); FO, 371/49928 (12 Feb. 1945, Osborne, quoting Senator Sant'Elia).
23. FO, 371/60538/336 (24 June 1946, Charles).
24. *Documents on British Policy Overseas*, ed. Rohan Butler and M.E. Pelly, London, 1984, ser. 1, I, 836, 951; WO, 204/8743 (31 Mar. 1945, Stone); *FRUS*, 1945, IV, 964–7.
25. Woodward, *British Foreign Policy*, III, 481–2.
26. Puntoni, *Parla Vittorio Emanuele*, 261.
27. D'Andrea, *La fine del regno*, 429.
28. Castellani, *Tra microbi e re*, 159; Macmillan, *War diaries*, 491.
29. *Ibid.*, 496.
30. Giulio Andreotti, *Concerto a sei voci: storia segreta di una crisi*, Rome, 1945, 50; Raffaello Uboldi, *Il cittadino Sandro Pertini*, Milan, 1982, 157.
31. *Italia e Civiltà*, ed. B. Occhini, Rome, 1971, 69–70 (5 Feb. 1944, Florence).
32. WO, 204/9833 (22 June 1945, Parri); *ibid.*, 204/2164 (23 Nov. 1945, Stone).
33. Garofalo, *Un anno al Quirinale*, 120, 142.
34. *Ibid.*, 131 (Brosio); A. Gambino, *Storia del dopoguerra dalla liberazione al potere DC*, Bari, 1975, 133.
35. Giuseppe Romita, *Dalla monarchia alla repubblica*, Pisa, 1959, 108.
36. *FRUS*, 1945, IV, 985–6; *ibid.*, 1946, V, 875.
37. FO, 371/60537/2097 (17 June 1946, Charles); Puntoni, *Parla Vittorio Emanuele*, 328.
38. *Ibid.*, 333; C. Richelmy, *Cinque re: storia segreta dei Savoia*, Rome, 1952, 243; *Domenica del Corriere*, 10 July 1966 (King Umberto to Cavicchioli).
39. Torella, *Villa Iela*, 70.
40. Mureddu, *Il Quirinale*, 234–5; Garofalo, *Un anno al Quirinale*, 158–9.
41. Domenico Bartoli, *La fine della monarchia*, Milan, 1946, 365–6.
42. FO, 371/60536 (29 May 1946, Osborne); *Corriere della Sera*, 21 May 1946 (Bergamini).
43. *Mercurio*, Rome, Nov. 1946, 102–3 (Luigi Barzini); *Corriere della Sera*, 3 Jan. 1960 (Barzini); Puntoni, *Parla Vittorio Emanuele*, 330; FO, 371/60529 (13 May 1946, Hoyer Millar); Romita, *Dalla monarchia alla repubblica*, 139–40.
44. FO, 317/60537/2097 (17 June 1946, Charles); *La nascita della repubblica: mostra storico-documentaria*, ed. Archivio Centrale dello Stato, Rome, 1988, 390 Togliatti, 399 (De Gasperi).
45. Italicus, *Storia segreta di un mese*, 136–9, 286; Romita, *Dalla monarchia alla repubblica*, 219–20.
46. *Ibid.*, 211–12; Italicus, *Storia segreta di un mese*, 180, 217–19; Bolla, *Il segreto di due re*, 176; Gambino, *Storia del dopoguerra*, 202–3; Bartoli, *La fine della monarchia*, 375–6.
47. *Domenica del Corriere*, 14 Aug. 1966, 22–3.
48. Italicus, *Storia segreta di un mese*, 294–6.
49. Ezio Saini, *Quattro principi in esilio*, Rome, 1952, 30.
50. *Mercurio*, Nov. 1946, 103; Giovanni Artieri, *Umberto II e la crisi della monarchia*, Milan, 1983, 49.
51. FO, 371/43913/306 (6 Oct. 1944, Osborne); Cambria, *Maria José*, 127; *Corriere della Sera*, 5 Jan. 1960 (Barzini); Di Nolfo, *Vaticano e Stati Uniti*, 321 (Taylor).
52. *Messaggi di Umberto II dall'esilio*, ed. Unione Monarchica Italiana, Turin, 1946, 81; Saini, *Quattro principi in esilio*, 38.
53. *Il pensiero e l'azione del Re Umberto II dall'esilio*, ed. Falcone Lucifero, Milan, 1966, 140.
54. Mureddu, *Il Quirinale*, 48; Bertoldi, *Vittorio Emanuele III*, 321.
55. FO, 371/89760 (14 Dec. 1949); Giovanni Artieri, *La pulce nello stivale*, Milan, 1956, 73, 85–7; *Vita Italiana*, Milan, Oct. 1944, 198, 217–228.
56. Andreotti, *Lives*, 15.

Prime Ministers of Italy

Camille de Cavour	January 1860 to June 1861
Bettino Ricasoli	June 1861 to February 1862
Urbano Rattazzi	March 1862 to December 1862
Luigi Carlo Farini	December 1862 to March 1863
Marco Minghetti	March 1863 to September 1864
Alfonso Lamarmora	September 1864 to June 1866
Bettino Ricasoli	June 1866 to April 1867
Urbano Rattazzi	April 1867 to October 1867
Luigi Federico Menabrea	October 1867 to November 1869
Giovanni Lanza	December 1869 to July 1873
Marco Minghetti	July 1873 to March 1876
Agostino Depretis	March 1876 to March 1878
Benedetto Cairoli	March 1878 to December 1878
Agostino Depretis	December 1878 to July 1879
Benedetto Cairoli	July 1879 to May 1881
Agostino Depretis	May 1881 to July 1887
Francesco Crispi	August 1887 to February 1891
Antonio di Rudinì	February 1891 to May 1892
Giovanni Giolitti	May 1892 to November 1893
Francesco Crispi	December 1893 to March 1896
Antonio di Rudinì	March 1896 to June 1898
Luigi Pelloux	June 1898 to June 1900
Giuseppe Saracco	June 1900 to February 1901
Giuseppe Zanardelli	February 1901 to October 1903
Giovanni Giolitti	November 1903 to March 1905
Alessandro Fortis	March 1905 to February 1906
Sidney Sonnino	February 1906 to May 1906
Giovanni Giolitti	May 1906 to December 1909
Sidney Sonnino	December 1909 to March 1910
Luigi Luzzatti	March 1910 to March 1911
Giovanni Giolitti	March 1911 to March 1914
Antonio Salandra	March 1914 to June 1916
Paolo Boselli	June 1916 to October 1917
Vittorio Emanuele Orlando	October 1917 to June 1919
Francesco Nitti	June 1919 to June 1920
Giovanni Giolitti	June 1920 to July 1921
Ivanoe Bonomi	July 1921 to February 1922
Luigi Facta	February 1922 to October 1922

Benito Mussolini	October 1922 to July 1943
Pietro Badoglio	July 1943 to June 1944
Ivanoe Bonomi	June 1944 to June 1945
Ferruccio Parri	June 1945 to December 1945
Alcide de Gasperi	December 1945 to August 1953

Index

393